Contemporary Task-Based Language Teaching in Asia

CONTEMPORARY STUDIES IN LINGUISTICS

Series Editor:
Li Wei, Chair of Applied Linguistics, University College London, UK

The *Contemporary Studies in Linguistics series* presents state-of-the-art accounts of current research in all areas of linguistics. Written by internationally renowned linguists, the volumes provide a selection of the best scholarship in each area. Each of the chapters appears on the basis of its importance to the field, but also with regards to its wider significance either in terms of methodology, practical application or conclusions. The result is a stimulating contemporary snapshot of the field and a vibrant reader for each of the areas covered the in series.

Titles in the Series:

Applying Linguistics in Illness and Healthcare Contexts, edited by Zsófia Demjén

Contemporary Applied Linguistics Volume 1, edited by Li Wei and Vivian Cook

Contemporary Applied Linguistics Volume 2, edited by Li Wei and Vivian Cook

Contemporary Computer-Assisted Language Learning, edited by Michael Thomas, Hayo Reinders and Mark Warschauer

Contemporary Corpus Linguistics, edited by Paul Baker

Contemporary Critical Discourse Studies, edited by Christopher Hart and Piotr Cap

Contemporary Linguistic Parameters, edited by Antonio Fabregas, Jaume Mateu and Michael Putnam

Contemporary Media Stylistics, edited by Helen Ringrow and Stephen Pihlaja

Contemporary Stylistics, edited by Marina Lambrou and Peter Stockwell

Contemporary Task-Based Language Teaching in Asia, edited by Michael Thomas and Hayo Reinders

Contemporary Task-Based Language Teaching in Asia

Edited by Michael Thomas and Hayo Reinders

BLOOMSBURY ACADEMIC
LONDON • NEW YORK • OXFORD • NEW DELHI • SYDNEY

BLOOMSBURY ACADEMIC
Bloomsbury Publishing Plc
50 Bedford Square, London, WC1B 3DP, UK
1385 Broadway, New York, NY 10018, USA

BLOOMSBURY, BLOOMSBURY ACADEMIC and the Diana logo are trademarks
of Bloomsbury Publishing Plc

First published in Great Britain 2015
Paperback edition published 2021

Copyright © Michael Thomas, Hayo Reinders and Contributors 2015, 2021

Michael Thomas and Hayo Reinders have asserted their right under the Copyright, Designs and
Patents Act, 1988, to be identified as Editors of this work.

All rights reserved. No part of this publication may be reproduced or transmitted in any form or by any
means, electronic or mechanical, including photocopying, recording, or any information storage or
retrieval system, without prior permission in writing from the publishers.

Bloomsbury Publishing Plc does not have any control over, or responsibility for, any third-party
websites referred to or in this book. All internet addresses given in this book were correct at the
time of going to press. The author and publisher regret any inconvenience caused if addresses have
changed or sites have ceased to exist, but can accept no responsibility for any such changes.

A catalogue record for this book is available from the British Library.

A catalog record for this book is available from the Library of Congress.

ISBN: HB: 978-1-4725-7221-9
PB: 978-1-3502-0210-8
ePDF: 978-1-4725-7222-6
eBook: 978-1-4725-7223-3

Series: Contemporary Studies in Linguistics

Typeset by RefineCatch Limited, Bungay, Suffolk

To find out more about our authors and books visit www.bloomsbury.com
and sign up for our newsletters.

CONTENTS

List of Figures ix
List of Tables x
List of Abbreviations xii
Foreword xvi
David Nunan
Notes on Contributors xix

1 Introduction 1
   Michael Thomas

PART ONE The South-East Asian context 7

   Introduction 9
   William Littlewood

2 Task-Based Language Teaching in the Asian Context: Where Are We Now and Where Are We Going? 12
   Chun Lai

3 Exploring Ways to Accommodate Task-Based Language Teaching in Chinese Schools 30
   Shaoqian Luo
   Yafu Gong

4 Bridging Communicative Language Teaching and Task-Based Language Teaching in Cambodia: Learners' Reactions to an Integrated Programme in the Non-Formal Education Sector 46
   Nicole Takeda

PART TWO Focusing on the learner 63

Introduction 65
Phil Benson

5 'Old Wine in New Bottles': Two Case Studies of Task-Based Language Teaching in Vietnam 68
Nguyen Gia Viet
Le Van Canh
Roger Barnard

6 Task-Based Language Teaching in the Primary Schools of South China 87
Yuefeng Zhang

7 Significant Task-Based Learning: Empowering Students with Position Search Skills in a University in Singapore 103
Brad Blackstone
Radhika Jaidev

8 Teaching the Teachers: Task-Based Teacher Training in Asia 123
Marilyn Lewis

PART THREE Teachers' perspectives 135

Introduction 137
Jack C. Richards

9 Teachers' Perceived Difficulty in Implementing TBLT in China 139
Shaoqian Luo
Jiaxin Xing

10 Gaining Acceptance of Task-Based Teaching during Malaysian Rural In-Service Teacher Training 156
Stephen J. Hall

11 Preparing for Tasks in Vietnamese EFL High School Classrooms: Teachers in Action 170
Bao Trang Thi Nguyen
Jonathan Newton
David Crabbe

PART FOUR Tasks and technology 189

Introduction 191
Glenn Stockwell

12 Language Learning Performance Using Engineering-Based Tasks via Text Chat 193
Nik Aloesnita Nik Mohd Alwi

13 Employing Online Chat to Resolve Task-Based Activities: Using Online Chat to Promote Cultural Language Exchange between Japanese and Taiwanese Learners 211
Mark R. Freiermuth
Hsin-chou Huang

14 A Digital Shift is Not Enough: Cultural, Pedagogical and Institutional Challenges to Technology-Mediated Task-Based Learning in Japan 228
Michael Thomas

15 A Trade-off in Learning: Mobile Augmented Reality for Language Learning 244
Hayo Reinders
Onuma Lakarnchua
Mark Pegrum

PART FIVE Materials and curriculum design 257

Introduction 259
Nigel Harwood

16 A Needs Analysis for a Korean Middle School EFL General English Curriculum 261
Moonyoung Park

17 Materials Design for TBLT in Thailand: Balancing Process and Content 279
Pornapit Darasawang

18 Designing and Implementing Task-Based Vocational English Materials: Text, Language, Task, and Context in Indonesia 291
Handoyo Puji Widodo

19 The Effects of an Output-based Task on Subsequent Aural Input in a Japanese University Setting   313
Wataru Suzuki
Nobuya Itagaki

20 TBLT Materials and Curricula: From Theory to Practice   328
Brian Tomlinson

PART SIX Assessment and evaluation   341

Introduction   343
Ali Shehadeh

21 Task-Based Assessment for Young Learners: The Role of Teachers in Changing Cultures   348
Yuko Goto Butler

22 Teachers' Adaptations of TBLT: The Hong Kong Story   366
David R. Carless

Epilogue   381
Rod Ellis

Index   385

FIGURES

4.1	Weekly lesson cycle	53
4.2	Bi-semester lesson cycle	54
6.1	Continuum of forms of TBLT (adapted from Tong, 2005)	89
7.1	Fink's taxonomy of significant learning (2003)	108
12.1	Example 1. A sample of text chat	202
12.2	Example 2. LRE on meaning	202
12.3	Example 3. LRE on form	203
12.4	Mean LREs on form	204
13.1	Task prompt	217
15.1	Excerpts from sample experimental group tours in response to the first prompt, 'This is our first site. This is the "Registrar Office". If you are a student, here you can . . .'.	252
15.2	Excerpts from sample control group tours in response to the first prompt, 'This is our first site. This is the "Registrar Office". If you are a student, here you can . . .'.	253
18.1	Classification of English for Specific Purposes (ESP)	294

TABLES

3.1	Example criteria of native-speakerism	32
4.1	Programme Assessment Criteria	55
4.2	Selection of questionnaire results (2012/13 school year)	57
4.3	Selection of questionnaire results (2012/13 school year)	58
6.1	Main factors that affected teachers' implementation of TBLT	96
7.1	Job Identification Worksheet	112
7.2	Overview of tasks in the position search process	115
7.3	Percentage of students finding various tasks useful for learning	119
9.1	Teachers' perceived difficulties in implementing TBLT	144
11.1	Teacher action in the pre-task phase	176
12.1	Learner characteristics	200
12.2	Results	203
15.1	Experimental group pre-test and post-test mean scores	249
15.2	Mann-Whitney U-test for experimental group pre-test and post-test scores	250
15.3	Control group pre-test and post-test mean scores	250
15.4	Mann-Whitney U-test for control group pre-test and post-test scores	250
15.5	Experimental and control group pre-test mean scores	250
15.6	Independent t-test scores for experimental and control group pre-test scores	251
15.7	Experimental and control group post-test mean scores	251
15.8	Independent t-test scores for experimental and control group post-test scores	251
16.1	Teachers' and students' perception of middle school English needs	266
16.2	Teachers' and students' perception of participation style and learning strategy	270
16.3	Teachers' and students' topic preferences	271
16.4	Teachers' and students' preferences for overall class activities	272
16.5	Teachers' and students' preferences of computer-assisted activities	272
19.1	Experimental procedures	317

19.2	Means and standard deviations of the pre-recall scores of word and grammar for three experimental groups	319
19.3	Means and standard deviations of the post-recall scores of word and grammar for three experimental groups	319
19.4	Multiple comparisons among three groups using Bonferoni tests	319

ABBREVIATIONS

ABET	Accreditation Board for Engineering and Technology
ACMC	Asynchronous Computer-Mediated Communication
ALT	Assistant Language Teacher
ANOVA	Analyses of Variance
AR	Augmented Reality
ASEAN	Association of Southeast Asian Nations
BAAL	British Association of Applied Linguistics
BEM	Board of Engineers Malaysia
CALL	Computer-Assisted Language Learning
CAMSET	Cambodian Secondary English Teaching Project
CBI	Content-Based Instruction
CDC	Curriculum Development Centre
CD-ROM	Compact Disc Read-Only Memory
CEE	College Entrance Examination
CEO	Chief Executive Officer
C*f*BT	Centre for British Teachers
CH	Cognition Hypothesis
CLT	Communicative Language Teaching
COLT	Communication-Oriented Language Teaching
CMC	Computer-Mediated Communication
CNECS	Chinese National English Curriculum Standards
CoP	Communities of Practice
CPD	Continuing Professional Development
DVD	Digital Versatile Disc
EAC	Engineering Accreditation Council

EFL	English as a Foreign Language
EGP	English for General Purposes
EIL	English as an International Language
ELCs	English Language Coordinators
ELT	English Language Teaching
ESL	English as a Second Language
ESP	English for Specific Purposes
ETMS	English for Teaching Maths and Science
ETS	Educational Testing Service
EVP	English for Vocational Purposes
FLES	Foreign Language at Elementary School
HARP	Handheld Augmented Reality Project
HR	Human Resources
IA	Individual-Assessment Format
ICT	Information and Communication Technology
IJCALLT	International Journal of Computer-Assisted Language Learning and Teaching
INSETT	In-Service Teacher Training
IRE	Initiate-Response-Evaluation
ISO	International Organization for Standardization
ITEP	Information Technology in Education Project
KBSM	Kurikulum Bersepadu Sekolah Mengengah
KMUTT	King Mongkut's University of Technology Thonburi
KSAT	(Korean) Scholastic Aptitude Test
L2	Second Language
LECS	Language Educational Chat System
LPS	Lesson Planning Sessions
LREs	Language-Related Episodes
MALL	Mobile-Assisted Language Learning
MEXT	Ministry of Education, Culture, Sports, Science and Technology
MOE	Ministry of Education
MOET	Ministry of Education and Training

MOEYS	Ministry of Education, Youth and Sport
NAIT	National Association of Industrial Technology
NECS	National English Curriculum Standards for Compulsory and Senior High Schools
NER-DLPP	National Education Reform and Development of Long-term Planning Programs
NES	Native English Speakers
NGO	Non-Governmental Organization
NNS	Non-Native Speaker
NS	Native Speaker
NSS	New Senior Secondary
NUS	National University of Singapore
PA	Paired-Assessment Format
PETS	Public English Test System
PMR	Penilaian Menengah Rendah
PPP	Presentation-Practice-Production
QSA	Quaker Service Australia
RELC	Regional Language Centre
SALC	Self-Access Learning Centre
SBA	School-Based Assessment
SCMC	Synchronous Computer-Mediated Communication
SHSEE	Senior High School Entrance Examination
SLA	Second Language Acquisition
SPM	Sijil Pelajaran Malaysia
SPSS	Statistical Package for the Social Sciences
STEPSS	Standards for Teachers of English for Primary and Secondary Schools
TBA	Task-Based Approach
TBI	Task-Based Instruction
TBL	Task-Based Learning
TBLA	Task-Based Language Assessment
TBLT	Task-Based Language Teaching
TE	Teacher Educators

TEMTE	Teaching English Mainly Through English
TESOL	Teaching English to Speakers of Other Languages
TL	Target Language
TO	Trade-off
TOC	Target-Oriented Curriculum
TOEFL	Test of English as a Foreign Language
TOEIC	Test of English for International Communication
TPR	Total Physical Response
TSLT	Task-Supported Language Teaching
UNESCAP	United Nations Economic and Social Commission for Asia and Pacific
UNTAC	United Nations Transitional Authority in Cambodia
VE	Vocational Education
VSO	Voluntary Service Overseas

FOREWORD
David Nunan

As language educators, we spend most of our time engaged in small picture thinking. We wrestle with questions such as: What is the place of a focus on form in our curriculum? How can we integrate learner strategy training into our teaching? Why is there a persistent gap between curricular goals and learning outcomes? How can technology support what I do in the classroom?

These are important questions. However, it is a good idea from time to time to pose big picture questions, the biggest of which is probably: What is the purpose of education in the first place? Is it to transmit cultural values from one generation to the next? Is it to turn out skilled workers who can build cars and mend broken bones? Is it to empower individuals and prepare them to deal with the complexities and challenges of living in the twenty-first century? Is it to turn out socially responsible citizens? Essentially, is the purpose to preserve or to transform? Is it for individual liberation or collective good?

Regardless of the purpose or set of purposes to which one subscribes, there is a fundamental challenge for policymakers and curriculum specialists when it comes to selecting content and learning experiences. This challenge is the uncertainty of the future. We don't know what the world will be like next year. How then can we select content and learning experiences that will be appropriate for children born in 2014, who will be graduating from school and entering the world of work or higher education in the 2030s?

When it comes to specific subjects in the school curriculum, the key question (and one that is prior to questions of content or methodology) is: Why should learners be required to study mathematics, literature, or foreign languages? The answer to this question will depend on how one has answered the big picture question above. Cultural preservationists will provide a different answer from liberal educators.

Although not explicitly addressed, the big educational question underpins many of the contributions to *Contemporary Task-Based Language Teaching in Asia*. The collection itself is a richly textured snapshot of an innovation (TBLT) that was imported into second and foreign language education from general education (for example business, psychology, mathematics education) in the 1980s (see Doyle, 1983 for an analysis of 'task' as the fundamental building block in elementary and secondary education). Ideologically, it found fertile ground in the humanistic educational context in Europe. In North America, it provided a rationale for empirical work being carried out in psycholinguistic research.

Conventional wisdom in the curriculum innovation literature has it that it takes around thirty years for a significant innovation to gain traction in the classroom (Stenhouse, 1975). Interestingly, it is thirty years, give or take a few, since TBLT first began attracting attention. The first book-length treatments of the subject appeared in the second half of the 1980s (Candlin & Murphy, 1987; Prabhu, 1987; Nunan, 1989). In the 1990s ministerial curriculum documents began to pay lip service to the notion. In the 1990s the Japanese Ministry of Education, Science and Culture spelled out that:

> [The objectives of ELT are to] develop students' ability to understand and to express themselves in a foreign language; to foster students' positive attitudes towards communicating in a foreign language, and to heighten their interest in language and culture, thus deepening international understanding.
> (Japanese Ministry of Education, Science and Culture cited in Wada, 1994, p. 1)

Later in the decade, in Hong Kong, the Ministry of Education articulated a similar goal for the English language curriculum:

> The task-based approach [upon which the English language curriculum is built] aims at providing opportunities for learners to experiment with and explore both spoken and written language through activities that are designed to engage learners in the authentic, practical and functional use of language for meaningful purposes. Learners are encouraged to activate and use whatever language they already have in the process of completing a task. . . . All in all, the role of task-based language learning is to stimulate a natural desire in learners to improve their language competence by challenging them to complete meaningful tasks.
> (Hong Kong Curriculum Development Council, 1999, p. 41)

Most other countries have made similar pronouncements. However, it is only comparatively recently that these pronouncements are beginning to be contested against the reality of teaching/learning contexts in the region. In 2003, I reported on a survey into the impact of the emergence of English as a global language on educational policies and practice in the Asia-Pacific region. In all countries, developed and developing, post-colonial and independent, there was a gap between ministerial pronouncement and contextual reality (Nunan, 2003). As the contributions to this collection clearly show through their case studies and surveys, policies and precepts, like textbooks, can never be architectural blueprints for pedagogical action, but rather programmatic guidelines and affordances to inform and support teaching and learning along with myriad other contextual supports and constraints. Some of these are identified and articulated in the chapters that follow, and they come as no surprise: teachers' understandings, beliefs, and practices, as well as their competence in English; learner motivation and interpretation/reinterpretation of task procedures and outcomes; materials and other resources; the actual need or future potential to use English beyond the classroom and so on.

This book lives out the reality that there is no such thing as '*the* task-based approach'. Rather, there is a loosely bundled set of principles that share some common ground, but vary in their emphasis and application. The prominence and place of form-focused instruction, embraced in some approaches and rejected in others, is an obvious example, as is the place of learner strategy training, text and task authenticity and so on. The book is an impressive collection of data-based investigations that document the ways in which a significant innovation is currently influencing one of the most politically dynamic and linguistically diverse regions in the world.

References

Candlin, C., & Murphy, D. (Eds) (1987). *Language learning tasks*. Englewood Cliffs NJ: Prentice-Hall.
Doyle, W. (1983). Academic work. *Review of Educational Research, 53*(2), 159–199.
Hong Kong Curriculum Development Council (1999). *Syllabuses for secondary schools: English language secondary 1–5*. Hong Kong: Curriculum Development Council, Ministry of Education.
Nunan, D. (1989). *Designing tasks for the communicative classroom*. Cambridge: Cambridge University Press.
Nunan, D. (2003). The impact of English as a global language on educational policies and practices in the Asia-Pacific region. *TESOL Quarterly, 37*(4), 589–613.
Prabhu, N. S. (1987). *Second language pedagogy*. Oxford: Oxford University Press.
Stenhouse, L. (1975). *An introduction to curriculum research and development*. London: Heinemann.
Wada, M. (Ed.) (1994). *The course of study for senior high school: Foreign languages*. Tokyo: Kairyudo.

NOTES ON CONTRIBUTORS

Nik Aloesnita Nik Mohd Alwi is a Senior Lecturer in the Center for Modern Languages and Human Sciences (CMLHS), Universiti Malaysia Pahang, Malaysia. Her research interests include second language acquisition, task-based language teaching and computer-mediated communication. She is also engaged in consultancy and training projects particularly related to research-based courses, professional communication and programme accreditation.

Roger Barnard has been a Senior Lecturer of Applied Linguistics at the University of Waikato, New Zealand, since 1995. Prior to this he worked in Europe and the Middle East in a number of positions in English Language Teaching. In the past few years, he has occupied Visiting Professorships in Japan, Korea and Vietnam. He publishes frequently, and is currently co-authoring articles and working on two edited volumes of international case studies.

Phil Benson is Professor of Applied Linguistics at Macquarie University. His main research interests are in autonomy and language learning beyond the classroom. He is the author of *Teaching and Researching Autonomy in Language Learning* (2011), co-author of *Second Language Identity in Narratives of Study Abroad* (2012) and *Narrative Inquiry in Language Teaching and Learning Research* (2013), and co-editor of *Beyond the Language Classroom* (2011).

Brad Blackstone has taught at the Centre for English Language Communication (CELC) of the National University of Singapore (NUS) for seven years. Before working in Singapore, he taught in universities in the United States, Portugal, Japan and Malaysia. His research interests include the use of social media for pedagogical purposes, peer learning and learner motivation. He currently serves as the chief editor for *ELT World Online* (ELTWO).

Yuko Goto Butler is an Associate Professor of Language and Literacy in Education at the Graduate School of Education at the University of Pennsylvania, USA. Her research interests are primarily focused on the improvement of second and foreign language education among young learners in both North America and Asia in response to the diverse needs of an increasingly globalizing world.

Le Van Canh is a Senior Lecturer of Applied Linguistics at the University of Languages and International Studies affiliated to Vietnam National University, Hanoi. His recent publications include book chapters in the *Handbook of Asian Education: A Cultural Perspective* published by Routledge and in the *TESOL Classroom Practices* series. His research interests include second language teacher education and context-based pedagogy.

David R. Carless is a Professor in the Faculty of Education, University of Hong Kong. He is particularly interested in how assessment can be reconfigured to stimulate productive student learning. His has published extensively and was the Principal Investigator of the Learning-oriented assessment project (LOAP). Derived from the project is a recent co-authored book entitled *How Assessment Supports Learning: Learning-oriented Assessment in Action*.

David Crabbe works in the field of language curriculum development, with a special interest in learner autonomy. His most recent work has been in defining the quality of learning opportunities and how teachers and learners might describe and manage these opportunities. He has held posts at the Regional Language Centre in Singapore, Lancaster University in England, Bayero University in Kano, Nigeria and as a *lecteur* in Nancy, France.

Pornapit Darasawang is Dean of the School of Liberal Arts, King Mongkut's University of Technology Thonburi (KMUTT) in Thailand and the Director of Studies of the PhD programme in Applied Linguistics. She obtained her PhD in TESOL from the University of Edinburgh. Her areas of interest are learner autonomy, learner training, and motivation in language learning. She has published widely in journals and books in these areas.

Rod Ellis is currently Professor in the Department of Applied Language Studies and Linguistics, University of Auckland. His latest books are *Language Teaching Research and Language Pedagogy* and (with Natsuko Shintani) *Exploring Language Pedagogy* and *Second Language Acquisition Research*. He has held university positions in five different countries and has also conducted numerous consultancies and seminars throughout the world.

Mark R. Freiermuth is Professor of Applied Linguistics in the Department of International Communication at Gunma Prefectural Women's University in Japan. Besides his interests in using computers for task-based language learning, he is also interested in how discourse is affected by computer-mediation and how such discourse compares with more traditional spoken and written discourses. His research is a reflection of these interests.

Yafu Gong is a Senior Research Fellow and Director of the English Education Research Center at the China National Institute for Educational Research and President of the National Association of Foreign Language Education, China Education Society (2000–2015). Gong has over thirty years' experience of teaching English in schools and has been a schoolteacher, textbook writer and researcher in English language teaching.

Stephen J. Hall is Director, Centre for English Language Studies, Sunway University, Malaysia. He was an In-Service Teacher Training (INSETT) nation-wide Project Manager for four years in Malaysia working with the Ministry of Education and trained teachers regionally for Regional Language Centre (RELC). He has published over forty articles and authored several books, including two English for tourism books co-published in China.

Nigel Harwood is a Senior Lecturer in the Department of Language and Linguistics at the University of Essex. He has edited two volumes focusing on materials, *English Language Teaching Materials: Theory and Practice* and *English Language Teaching Textbooks: Content, Consumption, Production* and has published articles in various journals, including *Journal of Second Language Writing, Written Communication* and *Journal of English for Academic Purposes*.

Hsin-chou Huang is Associate Professor of English as a Foreign Language at the Institute of Applied English at National Taiwan Ocean University. Her research focuses on using computer technology for language teaching and learning, second language reading and writing, and teacher education.

Nobuya Itagaki is Professor in the Department of English Education at Miyagi University of Education in Japan. He obtained his PhD from the University of Alberta in Canada. His research interests are in English education, language education pedagogy and psycholinguistics, and he has published widely in these areas.

Radhika Jaidev is a Senior Lecturer at the Centre for English Language Communication (CELC), National University of Singapore (NUS). She has taught language and communication skills for over thirty years in various tertiary institutions in Singapore. Her research is on group learning processes at university with respect to interpersonal and intercultural competence as well as content and language-integrated learning (CLIL) in science communication.

Chun Lai is an Assistant Professor in the Faculty of Education at the University of Hong Kong. Her research interests include how to enhance the effectiveness of TBLT, especially in technology-mediated environments, and how to prepare learners to benefit from TBLT and from the learning experience in technology-mediated environments in general.

Onuma Lakarnchua is a graduate of the English as an International Language programme at Chulalongkorn University in Bangkok, Thailand, as well as an instructor for the Chulalongkorn University Language Institute. She is currently pursuing a doctoral degree in English as an International Language there. Her current research is on the effects of blogs and microblogs on EFL learners' writing process and writing anxiety levels.

Marilyn Lewis has studied and worked in New Zealand, France and Asia. Her qualifications include an MA and Diploma in Teaching (New Zealand), Licence es Lettres (University of Besancon, France) and a Graduate Diploma in Theology (Bryntirion College, Wales). Since retiring from the University of Auckland she continues her interest in language teaching and learning by running workshops in New Zealand and Asia.

William Littlewood worked for several years in secondary schools and teacher education in the UK. He moved to Hong Kong in 1991 to join a project introducing task-based language teaching into primary and secondary schools. He has worked at several tertiary institutions in Hong Kong and served on a number of government committees. His books *Communicative Language Teaching* and *Foreign and Second Language Learning* (CUP) have been used widely in teacher education.

Shaoqian Luo is a Professor in the School of Foreign Languages and Literatures at Beijing Normal University. She is a member of the project team for *Standards for Teachers of English in Primary and Secondary Schools* (STEPSS) in China. Her current research projects include the effectiveness of tasks, EFL teacher education in the Chinese context, and the assessment of primary and secondary students and English majors in teachers' universities.

Jonathan Newton is a Senior Lecturer in the School of Linguistics and Applied Language Studies, Victoria University of Wellington, New Zealand. His research focuses on classroom-based SLA research and intercultural language teaching. His articles have appeared in journals such as *Second Language Research, Language Learning, System, Journal of Pragmatics, Language Teaching Research, Modern English Teacher* and *The Journal of Second Language Writing*.

Bao Trang Thi Nguyen completed his PhD in the School of Linguistics and Applied Language Studies at the University of Wellington, Victoria. His research investigated the use of oral tasks in Vietnamese high school classrooms focusing in particular on revealing patterns vis-à-vis the way teachers use and implement textbook tasks in order to engage students more deeply in using English.

David Nunan is Professor Emeritus, University of Hong Kong, and President Emeritus, Anaheim University, California. He has worked as a teacher, researcher and consultant in Australia, the United Kingdom, Thailand, Japan, Singapore and the United States. His research interests include language curriculum development, classroom research, narrative inquiry and teacher education.

Moonyoung Park holds an MA degree in Second Language Studies from the University of Hawaii at Manoa, and another MA degree in English Interpretation and Translation from the Keimyung University in Korea. He has been teaching at Iowa State University as an instructor and has research interests in computer/mobile-assisted language learning, task-based language teaching, performance assessment, and language programme development and evaluation.

Mark Pegrum is an Associate Professor in the Faculty of Education at The University of Western Australia, where he specializes in mobile learning and, more broadly, e-learning. His recent books include *Brave New Classrooms: Democratic Education and the Internet* (co-edited with Joe Lockard, 2007), *From Blogs to Bombs: The Future of Digital Technologies in Education* (2009), *Digital Literacies* (co-authored with Gavin Dudeney and Nicky Hockly, 2013) and *Mobile Learning: Languages, Literacies and Cultures* (2014).

Hayo Reinders (http://www.innovationinteaching.org) is TESOL Professor and Director of the doctoral programme at Anaheim University in the United States and Head of Education at Unitec in New Zealand. He is also editor-in-chief of *Innovation in Language Learning and Teaching*. His most recent books are on teacher autonomy, teaching methodologies and second language acquisition, and he edits a book series on 'New Language Learning and Teaching Environments' for Palgrave Macmillan.

Jack C. Richards is an applied linguist, teacher educator and textbook author, who has had an active career in the Asia-Pacific region (Singapore, Hong Kong, Indonesia, Hawaii) for many years. He has written over 150 books and articles on language teaching methodology and teacher training, as well as many widely used classroom texts. His most recent books are *Key Issues in Language Teaching* (2014) and *Approaches and Methods in Language Teaching* (2014).

Ali Shehadeh is a Professor in the Department of Linguistics at the UAE University. His research papers have appeared in *Language Learning, TESOL Quarterly, System, Journal of Applied Linguistics*, and *ELT Journal*. Currently he is the co-editor of Brief Reports and Summaries of *TESOL Quarterly* and co-editor of *Asian Journal of English Language Teaching*. His research interests are in SLA and task-based language learning and teaching.

Glenn Stockwell is Professor in the School of Law and the Graduate School of International Cultural and Communication Studies at Waseda University, Tokyo, Japan. He is co-author of *CALL Dimensions: Issues and Options in Computer-Assisted Language Learning* (2006) with Mike Levy, and editor of *Computer-Assisted Language Learning: Diversity in Research and Practice* (2012). He is editor-in-chief of *The JALT CALL Journal* and associate editor of *International Journal of Computer-Assisted Language Learning* and *Language Learning & Technology*.

Wataru Suzuki received his PhD from the Ontario Institute for Studies in Education at the University of Toronto, Canada. He is currently a Lecturer in the Department of English Language Education at Miyagi University of Education, Japan. His main areas of research interests are roles of input, interaction, output, feedback, and languaging in second language learning.

Nicole Takeda is the co-founder and Executive Director of the Bayon English Academy (BEA), an accredited non-government organization (NGO) language school for underprivileged youth in Siem Reap, Cambodia. Her research focuses on the use of English language teaching methods to help address and eliminate poverty complexes among impoverished students. She runs ongoing teacher-training programmes for her staff and students, and is developing task-based writing textbooks for Cambodian teachers.

Michael Thomas is Senior Lecturer at the University of Central Lancashire, UK. He is lead editor of two book series, 'Digital Education and Learning' (Palgrave) and

'Advances in Digital Language Learning and Teaching' (Bloomsbury). Among his books are *Task-Based Language Learning & Teaching with Technology* (2010) and *Contemporary Computer-Assisted Language Learning* (2012). He is currently Principal Investigator of the EU-funded 'CAMELOT Project' with nine European partners (http://www.camelotproject.eu).

Brian Tomlinson has worked as a teacher, teacher trainer, curriculum developer, football coach and university academic in Indonesia, Japan, Nigeria, Oman, Singapore, UK, Vanuatu and Zambia, as well as giving presentations in over seventy countries. He is Founder and President of the international Materials Development Association (MATSDA), a Visiting Professor at Leeds Metropolitan University and a TESOL Professor at Anaheim University. He has published widely on materials development, language through literature and the teaching of reading.

Nguyen Gia Viet has worked as a language teacher and teacher trainer at Ha Tinh University in Vietnam. He is currently pursuing doctoral study at the University of Waikato, New Zealand. His research interests include task-based teaching and teacher cognition, about which he has published articles and presented papers at international conferences. He is currently writing a chapter about his use of narrative frames for a book to be published by Multilingual Matters.

Handoyo Puji Widodo is a research scholar in the Department of Linguistics, University of Adelaide. He has published extensively in the areas of language teaching methodology and language materials design and development. He is also on the editorial board of several refereed international journals including *International Journal of Innovation in ELT and Research, Asian ESP Journal, English Australia* and *TESL-EJ*.

Jiaxin Xing is a Lecturer at Qufu Normal University in China. He received his master's degree from Wuhan University majoring in applied linguistics and was a visiting scholar at Beijing Foreign Studies University (2012–2013). He is currently a PhD candidate at Beijing Normal University and has been teaching English for more than ten years. His research interests include writing feedback, task-based language teaching (TBLT), computer-assisted language learning (CALL), and teacher education.

Yuefeng Zhang is an Assistant Professor in the Department of Curriculum and Instruction and the Associate Director of the Center for Learning Study at the Hong Kong Institute of Education. She also serves as a Council Member of The World Association of Lesson Studies. Her main research interests include curriculum studies, English language teaching and learning, and teacher education.

1

Introduction

Michael Thomas

Over the last decade task-based approaches to language learning and teaching (TBLT) have become the focus of increased amounts of research, leading Carless to argue that it has become a 'well-established field of study' (Carless, 2012, p. 353) in its own right. Governments around the world looking to implement new language teaching policies have turned to TBLT as a potential solution to curricula that are perceived to lack an authentic and meaningful engagement with language learning and that fail to motivate and engage contemporary learners as a result (Ho & Wong, 2004). In the context of globalization, language education policy is no longer a peripheral issue. It has become a matter of strategic national importance as countries attempt to develop their educational infrastructure to produce graduates for the knowledge economy who can effectively communicate and collaborate in the digital age. These socio-economic factors have added more significance and urgency to discussions about what constitutes the most effective approach or combination of approaches for today's language learners (Nunan, 2003). Children leaving school and students graduating from universities need to have a range of employability skills, including intercultural communication, fluency in at least one, if not two or three foreign languages, and digital literacy to promote the mobility and flexibility to enable them to integrate seamlessly into the global economy. Debates about TBLT are therefore part of a much wider debate about the reform of formal education that still owes much in some parts of the world to an industrial model than to one fit for the twenty-first century. Research on TBLT is not marginal to the arts and humanities but central to debates about how important communicative language learning is to individual development in terms of promoting intercultural understanding and tolerance (Bax, 2003; Richards, 2005). As a holistic approach which stresses that language learning is much more than merely learning grammatical structures and vocabulary, TBLT has been advocated as a 'whole-person' developmental approach based on authentic tasks and problem-solving that learners are likely to be involved with and encounter in the real world (Carless, 2003, 2007).

This shift has been particularly evident in the emerging Asian economies where TBLT has steadily been seen as a potential solution to outdated forms of language education that no longer produce confident graduates with effective English language communication skills who are capable of analysis and critical thinking (Littlewood, 2007). Learners are increasingly growing up in a world in which information is placed instantly at their fingertips via a tablet or smartphone and they can network with friends and acquaintances, creating, sharing, publishing and disseminating knowledge in their first or second language in the blink of an eye. Sitting in a classroom listening to an instructor trying to explain a grammar point in abstract terms or ploughing through a commercially available textbook that was not written with their culture in mind might be termed *education* but not qualify as an engaging *learning* experience for these students.

Nevertheless, transitioning to more learner-centred forms of teaching and learning takes a significant effort on a range of levels above and beyond the sphere of influence of individual language instructors and while numerous small- and larger-scale initiatives involving TBLT have been attempted, few however have succeeded. As a consequence, over the last few years there has been a growing interest in the lessons to be learned from research on the implementation of task-based language teaching in specific foreign language contexts, with Japan and China being notable foci in the Asian context (Shehadeh & Coombe, 2012).

The current collection continues this trend and is the first book-length volume that specifically includes chapters focusing only on Asian countries, thus adding to the body of work that acts as a counterbalance to the dominance of Anglo-American research in the field. The twenty-one chapters presented here include previously unpublished research studies and practitioner perspectives on eleven South-East Asian contexts: Cambodia, China, Hong Kong, Indonesia, Japan, Korea, Malaysia, Singapore, Taiwan, Thailand and Vietnam. While China and Japan have generated significant previous interest in this respect, perspectives are also included on contexts in Asia which have been less central and more peripheral to existing debates. These shed new light on a range of factors, from implementation strategies to teacher training initiatives, from research approaches to ethical considerations. In being under-represented in the literature, the book calls for more research on these and other countries to capture the diversity evident in the Asian context.

Reflecting the developing body of work on TBLT in Asia, the book is divided into six main parts that have preoccupied policymakers, teacher trainers, researchers, practitioners and learners over the last two to three decades, each introduced by leading academics with extensive experience of teaching, learning and curriculum design in Asia: the cultural and pedagogical context (Part One, introduced by William Littlewood); the role of the learner in TBLT implementation (Part Two, introduced by Phil Benson); teachers' perspectives (Part Three, introduced by Jack C. Richards); technology-mediated task-based learning (Part Four, introduced by Glenn Stockwell); materials and curriculum design (Part Five, introduced by Nigel Harwood); and assessment and evaluation (Part Six, introduced by Ali Shehadeh). The six introductions preface each part and discuss the synergies between the chapters, locating them in the context of research in their respective fields. The collection is therefore positioned in a way that attempts to aid stakeholders involved in language development, from curriculum reform to materials development, and from programme evaluation to the establishment of assessment standards. The chapters in the book cover a rich variety of language education institutions across

Asia, from schools to tertiary level, from private to public education, as well as innovations at local, regional and national levels.

Arising from the work of Prabhu in India in the late 1970s, TBLT has historical affinities with Asian learners, however it is no longer necessarily regarded as a new innovation. To some extent it continues to be regarded as something of a puzzle or enigma, promising opportunities but often bringing profound challenges to all concerned, and perpetuating a number of rather fundamental ambiguities, from what constitutes a 'task' (Ellis, 2003; Samuda & Bygate, 2008), to how best to balance grammar input with an emphasis on eliciting oral communication. Indeed, previous research in this context has identified a range of potential challenges to the integration of task-based approaches, including those identified with learners, instructors and institutions, as well as the wider macro and strategic context that is decided by educational policy makers (Lee, 2005). Arising from this research and these perspectives, there are a number of positive and challenging conclusions. Central among these is the idea that intended educational reforms are often adapted to fit traditional ways of teaching and learning, thus nullifying the innovation (Adamson & Tong, 2008). Important aspects of TBLT may therefore by lost in the process of implementation (Spillane, Reiser & Reimer, 2002).

Rather than adopting a doctrinaire view that attempts to enforce TBLT as one coherent approach that can be imposed on others regardless of local traditions, more research is needed on effective localization strategies. This would be concerned with how it can be adapted to fit local needs in a more flexible way, inviting acceptance and investment from teachers at the 'chalk face', who are often more concerned with the practicalities of survival rather than the rewards of educational innovation found in the West (Tang, 2004). Accordingly, Littlewood (2007, p. 248) has argued:

> There is now widespread acceptance that no single method or set of procedures will fit all teachers and learners in all contexts. Teachers can draw on the ideas and experiences of others but cannot simply adopt them as ready-made recipes: they need to trust their own voice and develop a pedagogy suited to their own specific situations.

Finally, and perhaps most significantly, Asian countries are often aligned with a focus on high-stakes summative assessments in language education and TBLT needs to convince administrators, instructors, learners and their parents (the latter sometimes overlooked, but even more essential in an Asian context), that it can provide the kind of learning that produces language gains and an accurate assessment of proficiency and skills rather than unfocused discussion. This is an area requiring more research (see Part Six, this volume) and as many of the studies outlined throughout the collection indicate, high-stakes testing is a deeply rooted phenomenon. Transitioning to the more subjective and process-oriented focus evident in task-based approaches and striking an appropriate balance between formative and summative assessments which lead teachers to accept the pedagogical change required by TBLT, remains a priority and a challenge (Carless, 2011; Tong, 2011).

Within a wider educational context, TBLT has of course significant antecedents and is drawn from a tradition of constructivist approaches where tasks and project-based learning were developed to provide learners with authentic learning environments and more holistic ways of learning that avoid memorization and other forms of rote-based instruction (Littlewood, 2004). It seems unnecessary if not unrealistic to argue that TBLT should completely replace what has gone before in terms of language teaching approaches such as Presentation-Practice-Production (PPP). In its place, there has been a broad movement in some Asian contexts toward more communicative forms of language learning, leading to the integration of some features of TBLT alongside traditional foci such as grammatical input in a pre-task phase. This has led to weaker forms of TBLT such as task-supported language teaching (TSLT). In stimulating modes of TBLT that focus on different skills such as reading and writing, rather than exclusively on oral communication, it is important to stress the need to develop hybrid and localized forms of communicative language teaching drawing on a range of traditions in a non-doctrinaire approach that is open to local adaptation.

Above all, as many of the chapters in the volume argue, it is important to interrogate and reassess essentialist assumptions that dominate the debate about TBLT in Asia. Essentialist approaches make overwhelmingly negative assumptions about the impossibility of using tasks in large classes with lower level learners who all seemingly display the same characteristics and stifle all attempts at meaningful collaboration. Such a perspective needs challenging in order to reflect the diversity and complexity of learners and teachers in these countries and to move the field forward.

In the Foreword to this collection, David Nunan argues that it is important to rise above the 'small picture', to consider the larger questions which shape why language policy is the way it is and to ask: Is it the purpose of education to 'preserve or transform'? Task-based learning does not derive from the field of language learning but from reforms in the wider field of education as has been indicated above. It concerns the very purpose of learning. At a time when language learning and the humanities in general are even more under threat in various systems of higher education around the world, now more than ever there is a need to argue for the strategic importance of language learning as central to effective and mutually beneficial globalization. Language learning is central to enhancing cross-cultural understanding, tolerance and promoting interaction with people from different cultures, providing learners with key skills needed for their personal and social development throughout their lives. The collective picture of task-based approaches that emerges from these chapters is that the *revisioning* and *reform* of education is not just a major challenge in Asia but throughout the world, where older industrial models of instructivism still prevail in formal educational contexts. What is needed is a strategy that is attentive to the local and the global in a way that is not overly prescriptive, but includes more focus on the importance of the learner and *learner creativity* (Watkins, 2005).

While TBLT has offered the opportunity to explore authentic language learning environments, then, it also presents a range of challenges on the cultural, pedagogical and institutional level. Some Asian countries have adapted TBLT to deal with local constraints, while others have rejected TBLT and many are still in the process of investigating its implementation in local contexts (Nunan, 1999). By looking at the drivers, stakeholders, obstacles and affordances across the Asian region, it will be possible to gain deeper insights into the ways in which change processes and implementation can occur, as well as the potential range of localized forms TBLT may assume. This book makes an attempt to initiate and contribute to these macro debates, calling for more socioculturally informed designs involving qualitative research of learner and teacher perspectives (Carless, 2004). The book will be of particular interest to those involved in implementing change in the area of language education and to researchers in TBLT seeking a highly nuanced understanding of the cultural, pedagogical and institutional factors influencing its integration and development in the Asian context.

References

Adamson, B., & Tong, S. Y. A. (2008). Leadership and collaboration in implementing curriculum change in Hong Kong secondary schools. *Asia Pacific Education Review*, 9(2), 180–189.
Bax, S. (2003). The end of CLT: A context approach to language teaching. *ELT Journal*, 57(3), 278–287.
Carless, D. (2003). Factors in the implementation of task-based teaching in primary schools. *System*, 31(4), 485–500.
Carless, D. (2004). Issues in teachers' re-interpretation of a task-based innovation in primary schools. *TESOL Quarterly*, 38(4), 639–662.
Carless, D. (2007). The suitability of task-based approaches for secondary schools: Perspectives from Hong Kong. *System*, 35(4), 595–608.
Carless, D. (2011). *From testing to productive student learning: Implementing formative assessment in Confucian-heritage settings*. New York: Routledge.
Carless, D. (2012). TBLT in EFL settings: Looking back and moving forward. In A. Shehadeh & C. Coombe (Eds), *Task-based language teaching in foreign language contexts: Research and implementation* (pp. 345–358). Amsterdam: John Benjamins.
Ellis, R (2003). *Task-based learning and teaching*. Oxford: Oxford University Press.
Ho, W. K., & Wong, R. Y. L. (Eds) (2004). *English language teaching in East Asia today*. Singapore: Eastern Universities Press.
Lee, S.-M. (2005). The pros and cons of task-based instruction in elementary English classes. *English Teaching*, 60(2), 185–205.
Littlewood, W. (2004). The task-based approach: Some questions and suggestions. *ELT Journal*, 58(4), 319–326.
Littlewood, W. (2007). Communicative and task-based language teaching in East Asian classrooms. *Language Teaching*, 40(3), 243–249.
Nunan, D. (1999). *Second language teaching and learning*. Boston, MA: Heinle & Heinle.
Nunan, D. (2003). The impact of English as a global language on educational policies and practices in the Asia-Pacific Region. *TESOL Quarterly*, 37(4), 589–613.
Richards, J. C. (2005). *Communicative language teaching today*. Singapore: RELC
Samuda, V., & Bygate, M. (2008). *Tasks in second language learning*. Basingstoke: Palgrave Macmillan.
Shehadeh, A., & Coombe, C. (2012) (Eds.). *Task-based language teaching in foreign language contexts: Research and implementation*. Amsterdam: John Benjamins.
Spillane, J. P., Reiser, B. R., & Reimer, T. (2002). Policy implementation and cognition: Reframing and refocusing implementation research. *Review of Educational Research*, 72, 387–431.
Tang, E. (2004). Task-based learning in the Asian classroom. *Guidelines*, 26(1), 14–18.
Tong, S. Y. A. (2011). Assessing English language arts in Hong Kong secondary schools. *The Asia-Pacific Education Researcher*, 20(2), 387–394.
Watkins, C. (2005). *Classrooms as learning communities: What's in it for schools?* London: Routledge.

PART ONE

The South-East Asian context

Introduction

William Littlewood

Over the past three decades, increasing levels of globalization and economic development in Asia have led to a corresponding increase in contact between Asian countries and the rest of the world. Since this contact is mediated in major ways by the use of English as an international language, governments in the region have faced what Hu (Hu, 2005, p. 635) terms 'an escalating demand for English proficiency'. However, since the traditional grammar- and transmission-oriented methods are ill suited to satisfying this demand, they have turned to methods developed initially in other contexts. Thus Nunan (2003), in his survey of English language teaching (ELT) policies in seven countries in the Asia-Pacific region, found that they all subscribed to the principles of communicative language teaching (CLT) and several of them promoted 'the latest methodological realization of CLT' (p. 606), namely, task-based language teaching (TBLT). This latter trend has strengthened over the decade since Nunan's survey.

Innovations associated with CLT and TBLT in Asia show how they have stimulated long-needed change. In their 'imported' form, however, they have also raised important questions of principle and posed serious challenges in implementation. In the early years they were often accompanied by what Bax (2003, p. 280) labels 'the CLT attitude': 'assume and insist that CLT is the whole and complete solution to language learning; assume that no other method could be any good; ignore people's own views of who they are and what they want; neglect and ignore all aspects of the local context as being irrelevant.' Gupta (2004) writes of the disorientation and confusion that was caused by such an attempt to suddenly 'transplant' these new ideas and techniques into an Indian university setting which was not ready to receive them. From a similar perspective, Jeon (2009, p. 147) draws this conclusion from her survey of Korean teachers' experiences with CLT: 'different contexts require different methods. It is time for Korean policymakers and practitioners to seek a Korean way to develop communicative competence in English'.

As well as the issue of contextual appropriacy, the innovations have needed to cope with underlying issues of definition. From the start, CLT has existed in 'weak' and 'strong' versions which lead to different conclusions in the domain of classroom methodology (e.g., Allwright & Hanks, 2009; Littlewood, 2011). In other respects, too, CLT 'has always meant a multitude of different things to different people' (Harmer, 2003, p. 289), with the result that 'everyday classroom practices can appear to be quite different when CLT principles are applied in differing social and educational contexts' (Hall, 2011, p. 93). This is confirmed by Ho and Wong's (2004, p. xxxiv) conclusion, from a survey of ELT in fifteen East Asian countries, that CLT has been implemented in various ways 'with the term almost meaning different things to different English teachers'. The move towards TBLT has not resolved this uncertainty. As Richards (2005, p. 27) puts it, 'the notion of task is a somewhat fuzzy one'. There is frequent disagreement about what constitutes a 'task' and what does not, and even more debate about the nature of the overall methodological framework in which tasks play a role (some key issues are mentioned by Ellis in the Epilogue to this volume). It is hardly surprising then that, as with CLT, some surveys have shown teachers to have only a vague understanding of what TBLT means. Carless (2003), for example, provides examples of how teachers in Hong Kong 'had unclear conceptions about task-based teaching and learning, and this hindered its implementation' (this volume). It is sometimes questionable whether the TBLT policymakers themselves, who often work at a far remove from classroom practice, have 'clear conceptions' of what they are asking teachers to do.

Provided we do not present TBLT as a prescribed approach which teachers should (but often do not) 'understand and apply correctly' in their classrooms, this lack of clear definition need not worry us. Indeed, in the present 'postmethod' stage of language pedagogy, such flexibility can be seen as a strength rather than a weakness. It offers TBLT not as a defined, prescriptive methodology but rather as a more general term to describe a pedagogy in which (borrowing the formulation of Hiep, 2007, p. 196, referring to CLT in general) the aim is to teach learners 'to be able to use the language effectively for their communicative needs' through 'classroom practices [which] are made real and meaningful to learners'. A special contribution of the TBLT framework is that this aim cannot now be relegated to a subordinate role (as it sometimes was in Presentation-Practice-Production (PPP), when teachers felt they had no time to carry out the final 'P' because they had to progress further through a structure- or function-based syllabus), since it is now a central guiding principle. But within the framework, teachers can design what Kumaravadivelu (2006) calls their own 'context-sensitive postmethod pedagogy that encompasses location-specific teaching strategies and instructional materials'.

A clear message which emerges from accounts of how CLT and TBLT have been received and implemented in Asia (e.g., Butler, 2011; Littlewood, 2007; Lai, this volume) is that here, perhaps even more than elsewhere, it is essential to seek the 'context-sensitive' and 'location-specific' pedagogy referred to by Kumaravadivelu. The three contributions in this section are vivid illustrations of this search. Chun Lai provides a 'broad brush' and comprehensive survey of the challenges faced by Asian teachers in implementing TBLT. She empathizes, however, that these challenges should lead us not to reject TBLT but to explore its full potential in this complex situation. The paper suggests possible directions to be explored. In the second paper, Shaoqian Luo and Yafu Gong focus on one Asian country (China) but one with huge variation in types of learning context. They describe two major current approaches to introducing TBLT in China, suggest that neither is fully appropriate, and go on to propose ways in which they might be adapted to bring about the desired kinds of change. In the third contribution, Nicole Takeda focuses our attention first on one country (Cambodia) and then on one school within that country. She shows how the school has made efforts to adjust CLT and TBLT to the expectations of local learners and teachers in a programme which also draws on the PPP model.

These contributions may lead some readers to consider, with Beaumont and Chang (2011, p. 291), whether we refer too much to historically-loaded and often ambiguous labels such as CLT, TBLT and 'traditional' when it comes to seeking appropriate strategies for specific contexts. It is more important to define learning activities in terms of their learning outcomes and their 'potential to make a contribution to the general goal of learning a language, i.e., successful communication' (p. 298) in these contexts. Some may also like to join the present writer (Littlewood, 2012) in conceptualizing all these efforts under the more neutral and comprehensive label 'communication-oriented language teaching' (COLT).

References

Allwright, D., & Hanks, J. (2009). *The developing learner: An introduction to exploratory practice.* Basingstoke: Palgrave Macmillan.

Bax, S. (2003). The end of CLT: A context approach to language teaching. *ELT Journal, 57*(3), 278–287.

Beaumont, M., & Chang, K. S. (2011). Challenging the traditional/communicative dichotomy. *ELT Journal, 65*(3), 291–299.

Butler, Y. G. (2011). The implementation of communicative and task-based language teaching in the Asia-Pacific Region. *Annual Review of Applied Linguistics, 31,* 36–57.

Carless, D. (2003). Factors in the implementation of task-based teaching in primary schools. *System, 31*(4), 485–500.

Gupta, D. (2004). CLT in India: Context and methodology come together. *ELT Journal, 58*(3), 266–269.

Hall, G. (2011). *Exploring English language teaching: Language in action.* Abingdon, Oxon: Routledge.

Harmer, J. (2003). Popular culture, methods and context. *ELT Journal, 57*(3), 288–294.

Hiep, P. H. (2007). Communicative language teaching: Unity within diversity. *ELT Journal, 61*(3), 193–201.

Ho, W. K., & Wong, R. Y. L. (Eds.). (2004). *English language teaching in East Asia today.* Singapore: Eastern Universities Press.

Hu, G. W. (2005). Contextual influences on instructional practices: A Chinese case for an ecological approach to ELT. *TESOL Quarterly, 39*(4), 635–660.

Jeon, J. H. (2009). Key issues in applying the communicative approach in Korea: Follow up after 12 years of implementation. *English Teaching, 64*(4), 123–150.

Kumaravadivelu, B. (2006). Dangerous liaison: Globalization, empire and TESOL. In Julian Edge (Ed.), *(Re-) Locating TESOL in an age of empire* (pp. 1–26). Basingstoke: Palgrave Macmillan.

Littlewood, W. (2007). Communicative and task-based language teaching in East Asian classrooms. *Language Teaching* 40(3), 243–249.

Littlewood, W. (2011). Communicative language teaching: An expanding concept for a changing world. In E. Hinkel (Ed.), *Handbook of Research in Second Language Teaching and Learning*, Volume II (pp. 541–547). New York: Routledge.

Littlewood, W. (2012). Communication-oriented language teaching: Where are we now? Where do we go from here? *Language Teaching.* Retrieved http://journals.cambridge.org/action/displayAbstract?fromPage=online&aid=8536155

Nunan, D. (2003). The impact of English as a global language on educational policies and practices in the Asia-Pacific region. *TESOL Quarterly, 37*(4), 589–613.

Richards, J. C. (2005). *Communicative language teaching today.* Singapore: RELC.

2

Task-Based Language Teaching in the Asian Context:

Where Are We Now and Where Are We Going?

Chun Lai

Summary

In the past decade, researchers have been actively examining the implementation of task-based language teaching (TBLT) in the Asian context. Essentialist statements about the Asian context abound in this expanding literature, which is characterized by overwhelmingly negative perceptions about the compatibility between TBLT and the particularities of the Asian context. However, there is an increasing volume of literature that highlights the similarities of learners and teachers in the Asian and non-Asian contexts and the evolving nature of the Confucian-heritage culture and learners. Thus, the essentialist statements about the cultural inappropriateness of TBLT in the Asian context need to be put under scrutiny. Labelling TBLT lopsidedly as inappropriate in this context is misleading. To move this field forward, we may want to focus on exploring the cultural dimensions of task design and sequencing as well as methodological approaches to TBLT, attending to the psychological processes among both students and teachers that are crucial to TBLT implementation, and experimenting with effective implementation models in different contexts.

Introduction

Arising from a professional debate in India on the effectiveness of communicative language teaching, the five-year 'Bangalore Communicational Teaching Project' led by Dr N. S. Prabhu was implemented at eight elementary and secondary schools with eighteen teachers and 390 students in Southern India from 1979 to 1984. This school-based project structured language instruction around a series of problem-solving tasks. Evaluations of this project have been positive overall and have attested to its success in developing students' grammatical competence through a focus on meaning alone (Beretta & Davis, 1985).

Prabhu's success in Asia brought this pedagogical innovation to second language researchers' attention. Since the Bangalore Project, research in this field has been focused on: strengthening the theoretical and methodological basis of tasks and TBLT (Samuda & Bygate, 2008; Ellis, 2013); setting up evidence-informed methodological principles of task difficulty and task sequencing (Ellis, 2003; Robinson, 2011; Skehan & Foster, 2012); putting forward different pedagogical procedures of TBLT (Ellis, 2003; Long, 2000; Skehan, 1998); examining its implementation in different instructional contexts (Shehadeh & Coombe, 2012; Van den Branden, Bygate & Norris, 2009); and exploring the affiliation between TBLT and technology (Lai & Li, 2011; Thomas & Reinders, 2010). However, research on TBLT in Asian contexts has taken a different route. The fact that many Asian governments have progressively advocated and invested heavily in TBLT as a way of reforming the English curriculum has spurred researchers in Asia to focus on evaluating the implementation of TBLT in classroom contexts. In general, research on TBLT in Asia has identified a slow uptake of TBLT in classrooms, and has highlighted areas of incompatibility between TBLT and the particularities of the Asian contexts so far investigated (Carless, 2009; Littlewood, 2007).

Given that TBLT originated in Asia and was acknowledged as quite successful on its début, what has made it inappropriate in this context thirty years later? Among the many challenges that have been highlighted in the expanding literature on TBLT in Asia, how many are unique to the Asian context and how well-justified is the statement regarding the cultural inappropriateness of TBLT when the sociocultural landscape in Asia is constantly changing? With these questions in mind, this chapter first reviews the research findings on TBLT in Asian contexts, and then analyses the current findings with reference to the comparative literature on language learners and teachers in Asian and other cultures, as well as the literature on the implementation of TBLT in other contexts. It ends with a discussion on how we can push the field forward both in terms of the adoption of TBLT in Asian contexts and in terms of how research in Asian contexts can contribute more to the general field of TBLT.

Challenges reported in research studies on TBLT in Asia

The expanding literature on the implementation of TBLT in Asian classrooms is a response to government advocacy of the approach to reform the English language curriculum in several Asian countries, including Hong Kong, China, Taiwan and South Korea, and to the pervasiveness of task-based learning in professional discourse in other Asian countries such as Japan, Turkey, the Philippines, Indonesia, Malaysia and Thailand (Adams & Newton, 2009; Littlewood, 2007). This line of research points out that TBLT has had a limited impact on English language education in these countries.

Citing students' learning styles and preferences, teachers' complaints about the impracticability of TBLT in their classrooms, and analyses on the mismatch between TBLT and the educational ideology and values in Asia, the current literature has generated a multitude of challenges to the implementation of TBLT in Asian contexts.

Learner-related challenges

Learners are placed at the centre of instructional activities in TBLT, and quite a few reported challenges are related to the beliefs and learning habits of the learners. Learners have been found to desire systematic, explicit grammar instruction, expect such instruction to precede language practice and performance, and value accuracy over fluency (Lai, Zhao & Wang, 2011; Lee, 2005; Loewen et al., 2009; Zhang, 2007). As a result, McDonough and Chaikitmongkol (2007) found that the TBLT course they developed for Thai university students was greeted with learner complaints about the lack of rigour in grammar instruction. Learners have also been found to rely heavily on their first language when doing tasks. For instance, Carless (2008) found that Hong Kong secondary school students relied extensively on their first language and avoided the use of the target language in completing the communicative tasks. Burrows (2008) found the same phenomenon with Japanese English as a Foreign Language (EFL) students, even when they are linguistically ready for the tasks in the target language.

Learners have been reported to be uncomfortable with the freedom they are given in the TBLT approach and failed to take the initiative in task performance (Burrows, 2008; Carless, 2004; Lopes, 2004). Burrows (2008) attributed students' lack of initiative to the prevalence of shyness in Asian countries, which leads to students' reluctance to initiate discussions, raise new topics, seek clarifications and volunteer answers when doing tasks. This lack of initiative is also evident when students do not exploit their full language resources during task performance, and only invest the minimal amount of time necessary to get the task done (Carless, 2004; Lee, 2005). Students have reported high levels of anxiety over the freedom they were given in the TBLT approach (Burrows, 2008; Lopes, 2004).

Finally, learners vary in their levels of participation during task performance, which brings about differentiated learning outcomes from TBLT. It has been commonly noted that students of different proficiency levels demonstrated unbalanced involvement and contributions: students with higher language proficiency benefit more from doing tasks (Carless, 2002; Tseng, 2006); and students with lower language proficiency and with shy personalities are frustrated at this 'taxing' approach to learning (Burrows, 2008).

Teacher-related challenges

Teachers' understandings and perceptions of TBLT have also been found to be critical factors. Teachers have been found to subscribe to a synthetic approach to language teaching, as opposed to the analytical approach advocated in TBLT. For instance, studies have shown that Vietnamese EFL teachers stress grammatical accuracy over communication skills (Thien Hiep, 2009). Teachers worry that TBLT does not give sufficient space for grammar teaching (McDonough & Chaikitmongkol, 2007; Xu et al., 2008) and feel that traditional methods are more appropriate

(Iwashita & Li, 2012). They are found to use tasks as a motivator rather than an 'engine' for language learning (Jeon, 2006).

Teachers' limited understanding and acceptance of tasks and TBLT also constrain its adoption (Chacón, 2012; Jeon, 2006). Research studies in various regions such as Hong Kong, South Korea, Taiwan and mainland China have all shown that insufficient training in TBLT renders teachers ill prepared to operationalize TBLT and to face the complexity of TBLT implementation in their classrooms (Deng & Carless, 2009; Jeon & Hahn, 2006; Lin & Wu, 2012; Zhang & Hu, 2010). For instance, teachers find it hard to distinguish tasks from exercises and have no clear idea how to implement the different stages of TBLT in the classroom (Lin & Wu, 2012; Xu et al., 2008). Teachers are not sure about the differences between traditional Presentation-Practice-Production (PPP) and TBLT (Pei, 2008). And teachers, even teacher educators, are puzzled over how to handle focus on form in TBLT (Carless, 2009). Furthermore, teachers tend to overestimate the difficulty of doing tasks and worry too much about students' ability to handle the language demands from the tasks (Carless, 2002; Watson Todd, 2006).

The role teachers are expected to play in TBLT has further challenged teachers' acceptance of TBLT as it requires teachers to shift their teaching role towards a facilitative one in response to students' needs – a shift which might be much more cognitively demanding than the traditional knowledge-transmission role (Samuda & Bygate, 2008). Most Asian teachers perceive their work as essentially delivering knowledge to students (Xu et al., 2008), and have been found to struggle with this demand to change their teaching style and are reluctant to give up control in the classroom (Adams & Newton, 2009; Littlewood, 2007). Other associated challenges include the greater information processing load that teachers face, the demand for group management skills and the ability to support students' learning arising from group or pair interactions (Brandl, 2009). The 'undue psychological burden as a facilitator' makes teachers uneasy about TBLT (Jeon, 2006, p. 198).

Institution and classroom-related challenges

The lack of a supportive school culture is also reported as one of the challenges presented by the implementation of TBLT. Asian schools have a predominantly examination-oriented culture, and test scores are a major determinant of the reputation and attractiveness of schools. Furthermore, the exams are most often characterized by 'norm-referenced, summative, knowledge-based, vocabulary- and grammar focused exams' (Shehadeh, 2012; p. 6), which are incompatible with TBLT and hinder efforts to adopt TBLT in language classrooms (Adams & Newton, 2009; Deng & Carless, 2009). The knowledge-based high stake exams often put teachers under too much stress to experiment with TBLT when they would rather 'teach to the test' (Carless, 2007; Zhang, 2007). Deng and Carless' (2009) study of four EFL teachers from two primary schools in mainland China presents a telling case in this respect. One school was a state-run public school that was heavily examination-oriented and even mandated the amount of time to be allocated for examination preparation in English classes. The other school was a private school with diverse curricula and less examination pressure. The researchers found that the teachers from the private school were more experimental and demonstrated a more communicative-teaching orientation than the teachers from the public school.

The arrangement of instruction time at a school also determines whether its teachers are likely to adopt TBLT in their classrooms. Class time in EFL classrooms is typically restricted to three to four hours per week (Swan, 2005). The limited time that teachers have to cover the tightly-packed curriculum and carry out the examination-targeted teaching and drills at the same time often leads them to resort to explicit instruction, which they deem to be more efficient (Watson Todd, 2006; Zhang & Hu, 2010). A related challenge to the time constraints is the tight curriculum structure in some institutions. For instance, Benson (2010) found that Hong Kong English teachers at some secondary schools are largely constrained by school-based 'schemes of work' that are specified on a weekly basis. Such curricular arrangement does not leave much space and time for teachers to experiment with innovations like TBLT. Similar findings on the restriction of prescribed curricula were reported in studies in the Taiwan area (Lin & Wu, 2012).

Most Asian countries promote TBLT and communicative teaching via a mandated top-down approach. Teachers are most often not given ownership and not involved in the design and dissemination of the new approach (Carless, 2013). Instead, teachers are usually given short-term classroom-independent TBLT training that is found to be inadequate to equip the teachers with the necessary knowledge and skills to deal with the complexity of TBLT in classrooms (Zhang, 2007). Carless (2013) further points out that the pedagogical innovations that originated in the Anglophone world that carry pedagogical values such as 'learner-centered, communicative, or process-oriented approaches' may clash with Asian contexts which emphasize 'whole-class direct instruction, examination preparation, or more product-oriented teaching' (p. 2). Failing to involve teachers and give them ownerships from early on may lead to teachers' resistance to the innovation (Carless, 2013; Hu & McKay, 2012). Without sustained professional development and localized support mechanisms, TBLT, as a curriculum innovation, often does not have much of an effect in the classroom (Adams & Newton, 2009; Carless, 2007).

The challenges at the classroom level have much to do with the large class sizes. The usual class size in Asian countries is somewhere between 40–50 students, and teachers have voiced their concern that such large language classes is not conducive to TBLT (Carless, 2002; Chacón, 2012; Jeon, 2006; Zhang, 2007) due to various logistic barriers (Littlewood, 2007). The large class size makes it hard for teachers to manage group interactions and keep the noise down to a comfortable level (Carless, 2004; Nishino & Watanabe, 2008). The issue is further complicated by the commonality of mixed proficiency classes in Asian contexts (Butler, 2005), which make it hard to design appropriate tasks (Bock, 2000; Chao & Wu, 2008).

Sociocultural-related challenges

Asian countries rooted in Confucian-heritage culture are noted for attaching greater importance to texts, and textbooks play a defining, even confining, role in the process of teaching (Fang & Gopinathan, 2009; Jin & Cortazzi, 2006). Textbooks and the accompanying Teaching Reference Materials have even been found to serve as 'teachers of teachers' for novice teachers (Paine, Fang & Wilson, 2003, p. 54). The textbooks and teaching materials in Asia typically stress the centrality of grammar, adopt a knowledge-transmission model, and value explicit instruction over implicit learning (Tomlinson, 2005). The paucity of genuine TBLT textbooks makes teachers who are accustomed to teaching to the textbook struggle (Carless, 2002; Jeon & Hahn, 2006; Zhang & Hu, 2010). This situation is further exacerbated by the centralized exam systems in most Asian countries. The heavily form-focused, knowledge-centred, and norm-referenced exams dictate the textbooks, and thus constrain what and how teachers teach. Thus, driven by the textbooks dominated by grammar-centred declarative knowledge-heavy syllabi, most teachers resort to the traditional synthetic approach to language teaching (Carless, 2007; Nguyen, 2011).

Another sociocultural constraint to TBLT lies in the conflict between TBLT and the educational values and traditions in Confucian-heritage culture (Littlewood, 2007). Hu (2005) argues that the traditional culture of learning is one where 'education is conceived more as a process of knowledge accumulation than as a process of using knowledge for immediate purposes, and the preferred model of teaching is a mimetic or epistemic one that emphasizes knowledge transmission' (p. 653). This thesis is echoed among researchers in different Asian countries, who reason that the learner-centred experiential-learning underpinnings of TBLT are a mismatch with the traditional culture of learning that is supportive of a teacher-fronted mode of teaching (Carless, 2013; Samimy & Kobayashi, 2004) and inhibitive of students' confidence to take initiative in learning (Jarvis & Atsilarat, 2004).

Researchers have also identified the EFL context as posing an additional layer of challenge to TBLT (Bruton, 2005; Klapper, 2003; Swan, 2005). Nishino and Watanabe (2008) point out that a major obstacle that Japanese teachers face in adopting TBLT is the lack of a communicative environment outside the classrooms. Carless (2009) further argues that the lack of a target language rich environment may make it unfeasible to implement TBLT with school-age beginner-level students, who do not have much linguistic knowledge to build on.

Interplay between various challenges

The literature on the instantiation of language education innovation has suggested that when analysing the influence of contextual factors on the implementation of an innovation, an 'interpretative' perspective needs to be adopted (Kennedy & Kennedy, 1998; Markee, 1997). Namely, individual key players' interpretations and perceptions of the innovation and their selective orientations to contextual features determine the magnitude of the impact from the sociocultural and institutional factors on the implementation of the innovation. The importance of stakeholders' interpretation of the effect of sociocultural and institutional factors on the implementation of TBLT is attested to in the limited washback effects of communication-oriented examinations on classroom teaching. Researchers have found that the initiation of TBLT-aligned exams fail to induce positive changes in teachers' and students' approaches to teaching and learning in Hong Kong (Luke, 2010; Davison, 2007), mainland China (Qi, 2005), Taiwan (Shih, 2009), or South Korea (Butler, 2009). Teachers' differentiated responses to the mandated TBLT syllabus brought Deng (2011) to the conclusion that 'teacher factors, in other words their understandings, beliefs, and perceptions, are found to be the most influential in TBLT implementation' (p. 215).

Are the reported challenges unique to the Asian context?

Since the stakeholders' perceptions and interpretations of an innovation play a determining role in its implementation, it is critical to analyse the discourse on the cultural inappropriateness of TBLT and the imminent failure of transplanting a Western approach into Asian contexts (Carless, 2009; Littlewood, 2007) in consideration of the two stakeholders of language learning in the classroom – students and teachers. In this section, we will analyse whether the challenges reported by the learners and by the teachers are unique to the Asian context so as to shed light on whether TBLT is inherently culturally inappropriate in the Asian context.

How resistant are Asian learners to TBLT?

How different are Asian learners from Western learners?

Asian learners' perceptions of and approaches to learning is affected by their deeply held Confucian values. Researchers suggest that Confucian educational values and traditions are not by nature incompatible with TBLT: the Confucian model for learning is in effect 'a deeply reflective, enquiry-based, experiential way of learning' (Jin & Cortazzi, 2006, p. 13), and shares 'important commonalities with modern views on teaching and learning' (Law et al., 2009). Researchers have also refuted the view that Confucian tradition leads to reticent and passive learners (Gieve & Clark, 2005): Asian students' reticence may not be culturally defined, but rather situation specific in response to their familiarity with the methodology, the types of activities they are engaged in and the availability of language scaffolds during the activities, and so on (Cheng, 2000; Tong, 2010). Thus, the generalization that Asian learners' learning style is incompatible with TBLT is not justified.

Comparative studies on learners across different regions have suggested that the cross-cultural difference in learner perception of language learning is 'subtle rather than polar' (Shi, 2006, p. 125). Littlewood (2001) surveyed students' attitudes towards classroom English learning in eight East Asian and three European countries, and found that the majority of students in all countries preferred active participatory learning and cooperative group work. Littlewood concluded that 'the differences in the means of "whole countries" and "whole cultures" are considerably less than the range of variation between individuals within each country or culture' (p. 22). This finding is supported by Cheng's (2000) and Shi's (2006) study of university and secondary school students in China. The researchers found that both university and secondary school students preferred a student-centred approach and wanted language classrooms to be interactive and collaborative. Tomlinson and Masuhara (2004) compared high school learners of English in Spain and in China and found that 'there is a universal predisposition to learn a foreign language in enjoyable and experiential ways but also a universal belief that you need to learn a foreign language in primarily analytical ways' (p. 141). The preference for systematic, explicit grammar study and error corrections is a recurring finding in studies of foreign language learners in various sociocultural contexts in addition to Asia, such as the US, Brazil and Colombia (Brown, 2009; Loewen et al., 2009; Lopes, 2004; Schulz, 2001).

Are Asian learners responsive to innovative approaches?

Researchers have further pointed out that the Confucian-heritage cultural context is constantly changing (Chan & Rao, 2010), and that the Confucian pedagogy and Asian learners have been evolving over time as well (Law et al., 2009). Researchers have found that when given support, Hong Kong students are very adaptive and can change their learning to fit the new educational demands, and can benefit from new and varied pedagogical approaches as well (Chan, 2009; Watkins & Biggs, 2001). Law and colleagues (2009) found that when encountering new learning experiences, Hong Kong students demonstrated changing epistemologies and views towards learning and teaching: they started to change their expectations on their teachers' role from being the sole provider and authority of knowledge to being the facilitator of their independent learning. Jiang and Smith (2009) compared English language learning beliefs across three generations of learners of Chinese descendants, and found that the third generation learners made less specific mention of grammar learning and believed less in using mother tongue to support English learning. The authors concluded that learners' language learning experiences had a strong impact on their learning beliefs and preferences. Thus, Asian learners' learning beliefs are not stable, but rather malleable in response to learning experience.

Reviewing the volume of literature on TBLT in Asia, Adams and Newton (2009) came to the conclusion that: 'once exposed to task-based teaching, Asian learners can adjust their preferences for learning' (p. 8). Research studies in various regions in Asia, such as mainland China, Taiwan, Japan and Thailand, have shown that, despite initial negative attitudes towards TBLT, students demonstrate acceptance of and preference for TBLT over traditional teaching methods and willingness to use the target language in class later on (Hsu, 2007; McDonough & Chaikitmongkol, 2007; Zhang, 2007). Tomlinson (2005) identified a series of studies in the Asian contexts which showed that teachers successfully introduced seemingly challenging innovative approaches that stretched learners' culture of learning. He concluded that 'it is not cultural appropriateness which is the main factor in determining effective methodology but apparent value' (p. 11).

The aforementioned literature indicates that Asian learners are not inherently resistant to TBLT by culture. They possess great potential in developing favourable attitudes towards TBLT, once they are given a chance to experience a well-designed and supported TBLT programme.

Are Asian teachers alone in their reluctance to embrace TBLT?

The current literature often depicts Asian teachers as holding incompatible epistemological values and perceptions of learning and teaching from TBLT, which is considered as the major challenge to the implementation of TBLT in Asian contexts. However, Asian teachers are not alone in their reluctance to accept TBLT (Andon & Eckerth, 2009; Bateman, 2008; Van den Branden, 2006). Teachers in the non-Asian contexts are found to struggle with similar incompatible epistemological beliefs as their Asian counterparts. For instance, Sparks (2006) found that French teachers in Queensland tended to view language as a system to be learned, held a greater commitment towards achieving accuracy and complexity, preferred to follow a textbook, and complained about the time constraints in carrying out the curriculum. Van den Branden (2006) reported that some Belgian teachers felt uneasy with noisy group work and did not like to relinquish control. Ogilvie and Dunn (2010) found their Canadian pre-service teachers, despite extensive training on TBLT, failed to implement TBLT during teaching practicum at schools, partly due to their belief in students' incapability of learning a language through doing tasks without pre-taught linguistic content and partly due to the cultural norms of the schools that emphasized teacher authority and efficient coverage of learning content. Ogilvie and Dunn concluded that 'cultural norms of the teacher as an expert who controls learning episodes continue to permeate western teaching' (p. 172).

Teachers in non-Asian contexts were also found to modify TBLT and reduce it to the weak form of task-supported language teaching (Leaver & Kaplan, 2004; Van den Branden, 2006). For instance, Brandl (2009) found that the French novice teachers in her study tended to reinterpret task purposes in terms of grammatical points and vocabulary topics, and elected to simplify the process at the expense of the validity of the TBLT syllabus. Plews and Zhao (2010) found their Canadian native speaker (NS) English as a Second Language (ESL) teachers adapted TBLT in ways that violated the principled foundations of TBLT, and turned TBLT into PPP. Andon and Eckerth (2009) came to similar findings with the experienced ESL teachers in the UK, who, despite being well-trained in TBLT, struggled with 'the concept of tasks as knowledge-creating devices' (p. 303). These teachers cited time pressure and student expectations as the reasons behind the modification.

From the above review, it is apparent that learners and teachers in Asian and non-Asian contexts share a lot of similarities. These similarities suggest the fallacy of the essentialist conception of Asia and the West. Edward Saïd, the philosopher who is known for his critique of 'Orientalism', cautioned against a sweeping view of Asia or the West. Researchers are pointing out that within-culture variations far exceed cross-culture differences (Lee et al., 2007; Srite & Karahanna, 2006) and that claims of typical Asian or Western classroom teaching is oversimplified and potentially misleading (Fang & Gopinathan, 2009). Holliday (1996) argues that such a reductionist approach to culture constrains our understanding of social behaviours. All these researchers urge us to take a non-essentialist view of culture and attend to the complexity and dynamic variety of human experience. They advocate a critical view towards the sweeping statements concerning the cultural differences between Asia and the West.

Thus, TBLT may not be a pedagogical challenge unique to the Asian context, but a universal challenge to the predominant culture of language teaching in general. The implementation challenges may vary in specific dimensions and degrees, rather than in nature, in different contexts. Current research has analysed in detail the 'inherent' incompatibility of the 'primary innovation' (Markee, 1997), the pedagogy innovation –TBLT, with the sociocultural contexts. However it has paid less attention to the 'secondary innovation' (Markee, 1997) – the organizational changes in support of the innovation, namely, professional development and support, the particular dissemination model adopted or the particular representation of the innovation. The latter is extremely critical to the implementation of innovation in specific contexts (Carless, 2013; Waters, 2009). Focusing too much on the former may mislead us into adopting an overwhelmingly pessimistic attitude toward TBLT, whereas attention to the latter may lead us into more productive directions: to explore approaches and models that could help reap the benefits of TBLT in the Asian contexts.

Future directions of research on TBLT in Asian contexts

To explore culturally appropriate tasks and TBLT models

There is increasing discourse on adapting TBLT in a culturally appropriate manner. Butler (2011) points out that the adaptation needs to address several major issues: 1) how to enhance the fit between TBLT and the norm-referenced exam culture that focuses on declarative knowledge; 2) how to incorporate form-focused instruction into TBLT; and 3) how to create incentives for and support students' interaction in the target language. To address the exam pressure on declarative knowledge, researchers have argued for the virtue of an eclectic and hybrid approach to TBLT in Asian contexts (Carless, 2009; Littlewood, 2007; East, 2012). The hybridity could be realized at the curriculum level and the pedagogy level. At the curriculum level, Ellis (2013) argues that TBLT syllabi could be used alongside a traditional form-focused syllabus. Ellis (2003) proposes a modular approach which utilizes TBLT syllabi at the beginner level and adds a grammar syllabus at the intermediate level. At the pedagogy level, Carless (2009) proposes that TBLT could alternate with a traditional PPP approach. Class instructions could run primarily through TBLT methodological cycles but be supplemented with a few PPP sessions occasionally that focus on declarative knowledge. Wedell (2003) argues that such an eclectic approach can build 'bridges . . . between the culture of innovation and the traditional expectations of the people with whom [they] work' (p. 446).

To address the form-focused instruction concerns in TBLT, researchers have suggested careful consideration of the TBLT methodological cycles and the tasks used to resolve the issue. Some researchers have proposed adding flexibility to the methodological cycles that allow teacher-input at the pre-task stages and explicit grammar instruction and practice at the post-task stages (East, 2012). Other researchers have proposed adding focus-on-form components into tasks, such as adding guided planning with enhanced input tasks and associated grammar guidance at the pre-task stage (Mochizuki & Ortega, 2008), and letting students repeat the task after form-focused tasks at the post-task stage (Hawkes, 2012). Ellis (2013) proposes three types of TBLT syllabus: a purely task-based syllabus (consisting entirely of unfocused tasks), a grammar-oriented task syllabus (consisting mainly of focused tasks through input enhancement and output enhancement), and a hybrid task syllabus (consisting of both focused tasks and unfocused tasks). The various models proposed by Ellis suggest that given its versatility, TBLT holds great potential to fit into different cultures of teaching and learning with different emphases on and attitudes towards grammar instruction.

To instil in students the incentive and ability for communication in the target language, researchers have proposed using technologies to create authentic needs for communication both inside and outside the classrooms (Butler, 2011; Lai & Li, 2011; Thomas & Reinders, 2010). To get students, especially those with beginner-level proficiency ready for communication in the target language, researchers have suggested employing lengthened pre-task stages with a series of input-providing tasks (Lai, Zhao & Wang, 2011; Shintani, 2011).

Thus, TBLT could be adapted in various ways to enhance its receptivity in the Asian contexts. The most important and urgent issue is to explore potential models that do not violate the theoretical principles of TBLT and at the same time fit instructional expectations in the Asia contexts. More importantly is the need to find the appropriate match between the particular implementation models, types of TBLT syllabus, methodological treatment of attention to form and even tasks and a particular learning context (East, 2012; Van den Branden et al., 2007). Thus, research is needed to empirically test the efficacy of different types of tasks and different variations of TBLT at both the syllabus and the methodological level in different learning contexts, and match the efficacy of different models with the learner, the teacher and the sociocultural environment in different learning contexts. A greater understanding of this issue could help enhance teachers' acceptance of TBLT and enable them select a locally appropriate TBLT model. Furthermore, exploration into appropriate models of technology-enhanced TBLT in different learning contexts in Asia is another promising line of inquiry (Lai & Li, 2011).

To explore ways to turn challenges into affordances

The current literature has suggested that teachers' comfort levels with and knowledge about TBLT and learners' language learning beliefs and learning skills are two major challenges to the adoption and ultimate effectiveness of TBLT. Fortunately, intervention studies have suggested that these two challenges could potentially be turned into affordances.

Song (2009) proposes psychological preparation and strategy training for learners as prerequisites for TBLT in mainland China to achieve optimal student learning outcomes. Similar arguments have been put forward by many other researchers (Burrows, 2008; Lai, Zhao & Wang, 2011; McDonough & Chaititmongkol, 2007). These researchers advocate familiarizing learners with the philosophy, pedagogical approaches and assessment principles of TBLT prior to the course, raising learners' awareness of the rationales behind the design of individual tasks, and alerting learners to specific metacognitive knowledge and cognitive and socio-affective strategies that they could utilize to facilitate task performance. Empirical studies have shown that receiving task-specific training could enhance students' task performance. Praphantateva (2009) found that communicating the learning objectives of tasks to learners helps them to be more autonomous in deciding what to do to achieve the intended outcomes. Fiori (2005) found that students who were trained to focus on both form and meaning during interaction learned grammar better from conversation than those who were trained to focus on meaning alone. Kim (in press) incorporated video modelling that directed students' attention to useful language during task performance prior to the task led to better learning outcomes. Lai and Lin (2012) employed a semester-long TBLT training programme that focused on familiarizing students with the principles and procedures of TBLT and fostering important affective and cognitive strategies for task performance, and found that the training fostered positive attitudes and greater task performance among the students. Examining the efficacy of TBLT learner training and exploring appropriate content and format of training in the Asian contexts could add to our understanding of ways of enhance the effectiveness of TBLT.

Effective teacher training is critical to TBLT, and research has suggested a few important characteristics for successful training programmes. First of all, teachers need to be given ownership. Andon and Eckerth (2009) argue for emphasizing TBLT as 'a set of provisional specifications' (p. 306) and engaging teachers in active task design during training. Tomlinson (2005) found that giving teachers responsibilities and possibilities for taking initiative helped change Indonesian teachers' beliefs toward a more communicative approach. Fuchs (2009) found that a task-based approach to professional development that engaged teachers to design tasks collaboratively was beneficial. Second, the training needs to be institutionalized and contain measures to support teachers in translating the training into classroom practices (Carless, 2013). Waters (2009) suggests supporting initial training with extensive school-based follow-up support for teachers 'in actually USING them within the target teaching context' (p. 450) is critical. Van den Branden (2006) found that school-based practice-oriented coaching by supportive partners at different levels of implementation was successful in promoting Belgian teachers' adoption of TBLT in their classrooms. Third, given the central role of textbooks in teaching and the tradition of peer learning in teacher education in the Asian contexts, providing teachers with task-based teaching materials and opportunities to discuss with colleagues might be an effective way to filter down the ideas to the teachers (Andon & Eckerth, 2009; Fang & Gopinathan, 2009). So far, few empirical studies have explored and tested various propositions on effective TBLT teacher training in the Asian contexts, and this is an area where more research is needed to push the field forward.

To explore effective TBLT dissemination models

Waters (2009) points out that TBLT has been mainly approached through either the 'centre-periphery' model, where the government enforces the adoption of the innovation as in the case of many Asian countries, or the 'research, development and diffusion' model, where the prestige of the innovation is cited to persuade teachers to systematically implement an innovation. He argues that both these two models suffer the consequence of imposing 'an "objective", "one size fits all" view of change' (p. 434), which is almost certain to incite significant resistance from teachers. Waters suggests that the 'Linkage Process' model might be a better alternative to enact large-scale change while circumventing problems associated with the two models that are currently being used in Asia. The Linkage Process model emphasizes identifying problems from the end-user perspective in a local context and bringing in centralized and 'expert' resources to develop provisional solutions for the users' problems. The provisional solutions are then subject to a reiterative design process to gradually develop a suitable innovation for a local context. The Bangalore Project attests to the virtue of this end-user initiated approach as the project started with a few classroom teachers who questioned the then dominant structural approach and were searching for alternative approaches to improve the situation. They tried out TBLT jointly, shared their TBLT experimentation with the later adopters through seminars and open classes, and helped the later adopters internalize TBLT by organizing 'try-outs' and providing feedback for them (Prabhu, 1987). Carless (2013) also recommends fostering small-scale success to generate 'momentum and positive sentiments' and bring a few teachers on board from early on to serve as 'champions' for the innovation (p. 3). Waters (2009) further suggests that early adopters should better be 'leading local academics, teacher trainers, educational administrators, senior teachers, heads of department, principals, advisers and the like' (p. 450) who are viewed positively and have an influence on teachers. He argues that it is equally important to quickly recruit a 'critical mass' of potential adopters through 'whole-school' or 'group-oriented teacher development strategies' (p. 439). That being said, Waters acknowledges that the vast majority of the language innovation literature may be culturally biased towards the English-speaking world and native speaker-led innovation experiences. He calls for more research that investigates these ideas in different cultural contexts. Thus, further research that explores effective implementation models in the Asian context is much needed.

Conclusion

The current literature on TBLT in the Asian context is overwhelmingly filled with evaluation studies on the implementation of TBLT in language classrooms and interview studies on teachers' perceptions of TBLT. This is the product of the top-down TBLT initiatives launched at the government level in Asian countries. This research direction helps us to understand the various constraining factors that impede the implementation of TBLT and is valuable at this particular historical stage of the innovation dissemination. However, essentialist statements about the cultural inappropriateness of TBLT in Asian contexts may not stand and will not help move the field forward. We have now reached the point where we need to focus on exploring culturally appropriate task design and sequencing as well as methodological approaches to TBLT, attending to the psychological processes among both students and teachers that are crucial to TBLT implementation, and experimenting with effective implementation models in different contexts. Such research directions can not only help advance our understanding of ways to maximize the potential of TBLT in the Asian context, but also contribute to the field of TBLT in general.

References

Adams, R., & Newton, J. (2009). TBLT in Asia: Opportunities and constraints. *Asian Journal of English Language Teaching, 19,* 1–17.

Andon, N., & Eckerth, J. (2009). Chacun à son gout? Task-based L2 pedagogy from the teacher's point of view. *International Journal of Applied Linguistics, 19*, 286–310.

Bateman, B. E. (2008). Student teachers' attitudes and beliefs about using the target language in the classroom. *Foreign Language Annals, 41*(1), 11–28.

Benson, P. (2010). Teacher education and teacher autonomy: Creating spaces for experimentation in secondary school English language teaching. *Language Teaching Research, 14*(3), 259–275.

Beretta, A., & Davies, A. (1985). Evaluation of the Bangalore Project. *ELT Journal, 39*, 121–127.

Bock, G. (2000). Difficulties in implementing communicative theory in Vietnam. *Teacher's Edition, 2*, 24–28.

Brandl, K. (2009). Implementational demands in task-based teaching: The teachers' perspective. *Electronic Journal of Foreign Language Teaching, 6*, 117–125.

Brown, A. V. (2009). Students' and teachers' perceptions of effective foreign language teaching: A comparison of ideals. *Modern Language Journal, 93*(1), 46–60.

Bruton, A. (2005). Task-based language teaching for the state secondary FL classroom. *Language Learning Journal, 31*, 55–68.

Burrows, C. (2008). An evaluation of task-based learning (TBL) in the Japanese classroom. *English Today, 24*(4), 11–16.

Butler, Y. G. (2011). The implementation of communicative and task-based language teaching in the Asia-Pacific region. *Annual Review of Applied Linguistics, 31*, 36–57.

Butler, Y. G. (2009). How do teachers observe and evaluate elementary school students' foreign language performance? A case study from South Korea. *TESOL Quarterly, 43*(3), 417–444.

Butler, Y. G. (2005). Comparative perspectives toward communicative activities among elementary school teachers in South Korea, Japan and Taiwan. *Language Teaching Research, 9*, 423–446.

Carless, D. (2013). Innovation in language teaching and learning. In C. A. Chapelle (Ed.), *The encyclopedia of applied linguistics*. Malden, MA: Wiley-Blackwell.

Carless, D. (2009). Revisiting the TBLT versus P-P-P debate: Voices from Hong Kong. *Asian Journal of English Language Teaching, 19*, 49–66.

Carless, D. (2008). Issues in teachers' reinterpretation of a task-based innovation in primary schools. *TESOL Quarterly, 38*, 639–332.

Carless, D. (2007). Learning-oriented assessment: Conceptual basis and practical implications. *Innovations in Education and Teaching International, 44*(1), 57–66.

Carless, D. (2004). Issues in teachers' reinterpretation of a task-based innovation in primary schools. *TESOL Quarterly, 38*, 639–662.

Carless, D. (2002). Implementing task-based learning with young learners. *English Language Teaching Journal, 56*(4), 389–396.

Chacón, C. T. (2012). Task-based language teaching through film-oriented activities in a teacher education program in Venezuela. In A. Shehadeh & C. A. Coombe (Eds) *Task-based language teaching in foreign language contexts* (pp. 241–266). Amsterdam: John Benjamins.

Chan, C. K. K., & Rao, N. (2009). *Revisiting the Chinese learner: Changing contexts, changing education*. Hong Kong: Springer.

Chan, C. K. K. (2009). Classroom innovation for the Chinese learner: Transcending dichotomies and transforming pedagogy. In C. K. K. Chan & N. Rao (Eds). *Revisiting the Chinese learner: Changing contexts, changing education* (pp. 169–210). Hong Kong: Springer.

Chao, J. C., & Wu, A. M. (2008). A study of task-based learning and teaching in a large EFL class. Saarbrüken: Verlag Dr Müller.

Cheng, X. T. (2000). Asian students' reticence revisited. *System, 28,* 435–446.
Davison, C. (2007). Views from the chalkface: English language school-based assessment in Hong Kong. *Language Assessment Quarterly, 4,* 37–68.
Deng, C., & Carless, D. (2009). The communicativeness of activities in a task-based innovation in Guangdong, China. *Asian Journal of English Language Teaching, 19,* 113–134.
Deng, C. R. (2011). 'Communicativeness of activities in EFL primary school classrooms in Guangdong, China: Teachers' interpretations of task-based language teaching.' Unpublished Doctoral thesis, The University of Hong Kong.
East, M. (2012). Taking communication to task – again: What difference does a decade make? *The Language Learning Journal,* 1–14.
Ellis, R. (2013). Task-based language teaching: Responding to the critics. *University of Sydney Papers in TESOL, 8,* 1–27.
Ellis, R. (2003). *Task-Based Language Learning and Teaching.* New York: Oxford University Press.
Fang, Y. P., & Gopinathan, S. (2009). Teachers and teaching in eastern and western schools; a critical review of cross-cultural comparative studies. In L. J. Saha, & A. G. Dworkin (Eds). *International handbook of research on teachers and teaching* (pp. 557–572). New York: Springer.
Fiori, M. (2005). The development of grammatical competence through synchronous computer-mediated communication. *CALICO Journal, 22*(3), 567–602.
Fuchs, C. (2009). Computer-mediated task design: language student teachers' expectations and realizations. *Letras & Letras, Uberlandia, 25,* 37–64.
Gieve, S., & Clark, R. (2005). 'The Chinese approach to learning': Cultural traits or situated response? *System, 33,* 261–276.
Hawkes, M. L. (2012). Using task repetition to direct learner attention and focus on form. *ELT Journal, 66,* 327–336.
Holliday, A. (1996). Large- and small-class cultures in Egyptian university classrooms: A cultural justification for curriculum change. In H. Coleman (Ed.) *Society and the language classroom* (pp. 86–104). Cambridge: Cambridge University Press.
Hsu, Y. J. (2007). 'Elementary school EFL students' learning style preferences and strategy use and their relationship with the students' English learning achievement.' Unpublished Master's thesis, Providence University, Taiwan.
Hu, G. W. (2005). Contextual influences on instructional practices: A Chinese case for an ecological approach to ELT. *TESOL Quarterly, 39,* 635–660.
Hu, G., & McKay, S. L. (2012). English language education in East Asia: some recent developments. *Journal of Multilingual and Multicultural Development, 33,* 345–362.
Iwashita, N., & Li, H. F. (2012). Patterns of corrective feedback in a task-based adult EFL classroom setting in China. In A. Shehadeh & C. A. Coombe (Eds), *Task-based teaching in foreign language contexts: Research and implementation* (pp. 137–161). Amsterdam: John Benjamins.
Jarvis, H., & Atsilarat, S. (2004). Shifting paradigms: From a communicative to a context-based approach. *Asian EFL Journal, 6,* 1–15.
Jeon, In-Jae, & Hahn, J. W. (2006). Exploring EFL teachers' perceptions of task-based language teaching: A case study of Korean secondary school classroom practice. *Asian EFL Journal, 8*(1). Retrieved: http://www.asian-efl-journal.com/March_06_ijj.php
Jeon, I. J. (2006). EFL teachers' perception of task-based language teaching: With a focus on Korean secondary classroom practice. *Asian EFL Journal, 8,* 192–206.
Jiang, X. L., & Smith, R. (2009). Chinese learners' strategy use in historical perspective: A cross-generational interview-based study. *System, 37,* 286–299.

Jin, L. X., & Cortazzi, M. (2006). Changing practices in Chinese cultures of learning. *Language, Culture and Curriculum, 19*(1), 5–20.

Kim, Y. (in press). Effects of pre-task modelling on attention to form and question development. *TESOL Quarterly, 47*, 8–35.

Klapper, J. (2003). Taking communication to task? A critical review of recent trends in language teaching. *Language Learning Journal, 27*, 33–42.

Kennedy, J., & C. Kennedy (1998). Levels, linkages, and networks in cross-cultural innovation. *System, 26*(4), 455–469.

Lai, C., Zhao, Y., & Wang, J. W. (2011). Task-based language teaching in online ab initio Chinese classrooms. *Modern Language Journal, 95*, 81–103.

Lai, C., & Li, G. F. (2011). Technology and task-based language teaching: a critical review. *CALICO Journal, 28*(2), 498–521.

Lai, C., & Lin, X. L. (2012). Strategy training in a task-based language classroom. *Language Learning Journal, 40*(3),

Law, N. W. Y., Yuen, A. H. K., Chan, C. K. K., Yuen, J. K. L., Pan, N. F. C., Lai, M., & Lee V. S. (2009). New experiences, new epistemology, and the pressure of change: The Chinese learner in transition. In C. K. K. Chan & N. Rao (Eds). *Revisiting the Chinese learner: Changing contexts, changing education* (pp. 89–132). Hong Kong: Springer.

Leaver, B. L., & Kaplan, M. A. (2004). Task-based instruction in U.S. government Slavic language programs. In B. L. Leaver & J. R. Willis (Eds), *Task-based instruction in foreign language education. Practices and programs* (pp. 47–66). Washington, DC: Georgetown University Press.

Lee, I. Choi, B., Kim, J., & Hong, S. J. (2007). Culture-technology fit: Effects of cultural characteristics on the post-adoption beliefs of mobile Internet users. *International Journal of Electronic Commerce, 1*(4), 11–51.

Lee, S. M. (2005). The pros and cons of task-based instruction in elementary English classes. *English Teaching, 60*, 185–205.

Lin, T. B., & Wu, C. W. (2012). Teachers' perceptions of task-based language teaching in English classrooms in Taiwanese Junior high schools. *TESOL Journal, 3*(4), 586–609.

Littlewood, W. (2007). Communicative and task-based language teaching in East Asian classrooms. *Language Teaching, 40*, 243–249.

Littlewood, W. (2001). Students' attitudes to classroom English learning: A cross-cultural study. *Language Teaching Research, 5*(3), 3–28.

Loewen, S., Shaofeng, L., Fei, F., Thomson, A., Nakatsukasa, K., Ahn, S., & Chen, X. Q. (2009). Second language learners' beliefs about grammar instruction and error correction. *Modern Language Journal, 93*, 91–104.

Long, M. H. (2000). Focus on form in task-based language teaching. In Lambert, R. D. & Shohamy, E. (Eds), *Language policy and pedagogy. Essays in honor of A. Ronald Walton* (pp. 179–192). Amsterdam.

Lopes, J. (2004). Introducing TBI for teaching English in Brazil: Learning how to leap the hurdles. In B. L. Leaver & J. R. Willis (Eds). *Task-based instruction in foreign language education* (pp. 83–95). Washington, DC: Georgetown University Press.

Luke, J. C. M. (2010). Talking to score: Impression management in L2 oral assessment and the co-construction of a test discourse genre. *Language Assessment Quarterly, 7*(1), 25–53.

Markee, N. (1997). *Managing curricular innovation*. Cambridge: Cambridge University Press.

McDonough, K., & Chaikitmongkol, W. P. (2007). Teachers' and learners' reactions to a task-based EFL course in Thailand. *TESOL Quarterly, 41*, 107–132.

Mochizuki, N., & Ortega, L. (2008). Balancing communication and grammar in beginning-level foreign language classrooms: A study of guided planning and relativization. *Language Teaching Research, 12*, 11–37.

Nishino, T., & Watanabe, M. (2008). Communication-oriented policies versus classroom realities in Japan. *TESOL Quarterly, 42*(1), 133–136.

Nguyen, V. L. (2011). 'Dynamic conceptions of input, output and interaction: Vietnamese EFL lecturers learning second language acquisition theory.' Unpublished Doctoral thesis. University of Waikato.

Ogilvie, G., & Dunn, W. (2010). Taking teacher education to task: Exploring the role of teacher education in promoting the utilization of task-based language teaching. *Language Teaching Research, 14*, 161–181.

Paine, L. W., Fang, Y., & Wilson, S. (2003). Entering a culture of teaching. In T. Britton, L. W. Paine, D. Pimm, & R. Senta (Eds), *Comprehensive teacher induction: Systems for early career learning* (pp. 20–82). The Netherlands: Kluwer.

Pei, C. (2008). Task-based language teaching in classrooms: A study of Chinese EFL practice. *CELEA Journal, 31*, 102–111.

Plews, J. L., & Zhao, K. X. (2010). Tinkering with tasks knows no bounds: ESL teachers' adaptations of task-based language teaching. *TESL Canada Journal, 28*, 41–59.

Prabhu, N. S. (1987). *Second language pedagogy*. Oxford: Oxford University Press.

Praphantateva, B. (2009). 'The effectiveness of implementing classroom tasks: A comparative case study of the effect of informing or not informing mathayom suksa one learners of the objectives of the task.' Unpublished Master's thesis: Mahidol University.

Qi, L. (2005). Stakeholders' conflicting aims undermine the washback function of a high-stakes test. *Language Testing, 22*, 142–173.

Robinson, P. (2011). Task-based language learning: A review of issues. *Language Learning, 61*(1), 1–36.

Samimy, K. K., & Kobayashi, C. (2004). Toward the development of intercultural communicative competence: Theoretical and pedagogical implications for Japanese English teachers. *JALT Journal 26*(2), 245–261.

Samuda, V., & Bygate, M. (2008). *Tasks in second language learning*. New York: Palgrave Macmillan.

Schulz, R. (2001). Cultural differences in student and teacher perceptions concerning the role of grammar instruction and corrective feedback: USA–Colombia. *Modern Language Journal, 85*, 244–258.

Shehadeh, A., & Coombe, C. A. (2012). *Task-based language teaching in foreign language contexts: Research and implementation*. Amsterdam: John Benjamins.

Shehadeh, A. (2012). Introduction: Broadening the perspective of task-based language teaching scholarship: The contribution of research in foreign language contexts. In A. Shehadeh & C. A. Coombe (Eds) *Task-based language teaching in foreign language contexts* (pp. 1–20). Amsterdam: John Benjamins.

Shih, C. M. (2009). How tests change teaching: A model for reference. *English Teaching: Practice and Critique, 8*(2), 188–206.

Shi, L. J. (2006). The successors to Confucianism or a new generation? A questionnaire study on Chinese students' culture of learning English. *Language, Culture and Curriculum, 19*(1), 122–147.

Shintani, N. (2011). A comparative study of the effects of input-based and production-based instruction on vocabulary acquisition by young EFL learners. *Language Teaching Research, 15*, 137–158.

Skehan, P., & Foster, P. (2012). Complexity, accuracy, fluency and lexis in task-based performance. In A. Housen, F. Kuiken & I. Vedder (Eds) *Dimensions of L2 performance and proficiency: Complexity, accuracy and fluency in L2* (pp. 199–220). Amsterdam: John Benjamins.

Skehan, P. (1998). *A cognitive approach to language learning*. Oxford: Oxford University Press.

Song, Y. (2009). How can Chinese English teachers meet the challenge of creating a learner-centered, communicative, intercultural classroom to achieve optimal student learning outcomes? *Canadian Social Science*, 5(6), 81–91.

Sparks, C. (2006). 'Teacher Reaction to and understanding of a task-based embedded syllabus.' Unpublished Master's thesis. Queensland University of Technology.

Srite, M., & Karahanna, E. (2006). The role of espoused national cultural values in technology acceptance. *MIS Quarterly*, 30(3), 679–704.

Swan, M. (2005). Legislation by hypothesis: The case of task-based instruction. *Applied Linguistics*, 26(3), 376–401.

Thien Hiep, C. (2009). Balancing grammar and communication in EFL teaching: A study of teachers' beliefs about grammar instruction and error correction. Paper presented at the Seventh Asian EFL Journal Conference. Pusan, Korea.

Thomas, M., & Reinders, H. (Eds) (2010). *Task-based language learning and teaching with Technology*. New York: Continuum.

Tomlinson, B., & Masuhara, H. (2004). Developing cultural awareness. *Modern English Teacher*, 13(1), 5–11.

Tomlinson, B. (2005). The future of ELT materials in Asia. *Electronic Journal of Foreign Language Teaching*, 2(2), 5–13.

Tong, J. (2010). Some observations of students' reticent and participatory behaviour in Hong Kong English classrooms. *Electronic Journal of Foreign Language Teaching*, 7(2), 239–254.

Tseng, C. Y. (2006). 'A study of the effect of task-based instruction on primary school EFL students.' Unpublished Master's thesis. National Chung Cheng University, Taiwan.

Van den Branden, K., Bygate, M., & Norris, J. M. (Eds). (2009). *Task-based language teaching: A reader*. Amsterdam: John Benjamins.

Van den Branden, K., Van Gorp, K. K., &Verhelst, M. (2007). *Tasks in action: Task-based language education from a classroom-based perspective*. Cambridge: Cambridge Scholars Publishing.

Van den Branden, K. (2006). Training teachers: Task-based as well? In K. Van den Branden (Ed.), *Task-based language education. From theory to practice* (pp. 217–248). Cambridge, UK: Cambridge University Press.

Waters, A. (2009). Managing innovation in English language education, state of art review. *Language Teaching*, 42(4), 421–458.

Watkins, D. A., & Biggs, J. B. (2001). *Teaching the Chinese learner: Psychological and pedagogical perspective*. Hong Kong/Melbourne: Comparative Education Research Centre, The University of Hong Kong/Australian Council for Educational Research.

Watson Todd, R. (2006). Continuing change after the innovation. *System*, 34(1), 1–14.

Wedell, M. (2003). Giving TESOL change a chance: Supporting key players in the curriculum change process. *System*, 31(4), 439–456.

Xu, J., Liu, F., & Jiang, M. (2008). Task-based language teaching: From the practical perspective. *International Conference on Computer Science and Software Engineering 2008* (pp. 1054–1057). Piscataway, NJ: IEEE.

Zhang, E. Y. (2007). TBLT innovation in primary school English language teaching in Mainland China. In K. Van den Branden, K. Van Gorp & M. Verhelst (Eds), *Tasks in action: Task-based language education from a classroom-based perspective* (pp. 68–91). Newcastle, UK: Cambridge Scholars Press.

Zhang, Y. F., & Hu, G. W. (2010). Between intended and enacted curricula: Three teachers and a mandated curricular reform in mainland China. In K. Menken (Ed.). *Negotiating language policies in schools: Educators as policymakers* (pp. 123–140).

3

Exploring Ways to Accommodate Task-Based Language Teaching in Chinese Schools

Shaoqian Luo
Yafu Gong

Summary

Task-based language teaching (TBLT) has been influential in Chinese primary and secondary schools since it was supported in the Chinese National English Curriculum Standards (CNECS) in both experimental version (2001) and revised edition (Ministry of Education, 2011). However, the appropriateness and different interpretations of TBLT in the Chinese context remain controversial among researchers and practitioners alike. In this chapter we discuss the appropriateness and feasibility of current approaches to English language teaching in Chinese schools and argue that instead of the current focus on native-speakerism and content-based instruction, an adapted TBLT approach could be implemented to meet the needs of both teachers and students in Chinese primary and secondary schools. In order to develop this approach and implement it effectively, it is argued that systemic changes in curriculum design, course book development, and language testing and assessment systems will be required.

Introduction

TBLT has been influential in Chinese primary and secondary schools since it was introduced in the Chinese National English Curriculum Standards (CNECS, 2001, 2011.). However, the appropriateness of TBLT in the Chinese context is still a controversial issue among researchers and practitioners. In an Asian context TBLT evokes the famous analogy of five blind men who, each touching the same elephant, all produce a radically different description of the animal. Indeed, *task* has been applied so broadly that it has come to have different meanings for many different researchers (Dubin & Olshtain, 1986). This chapter discusses several different approaches to TBLT in China and attempts to explore some of the underlying challenges, while also advancing some suggestions for solving these problems, by taking the wider reality of China's English as a foreign language (EFL) context into consideration.

Current approaches to communicative and task-based language teaching

The diversity of communicative language teaching (CLT) approaches share a very general common objective, namely, to prepare learners for real-life communication (see Celce-Murcia, Dörnyei & Thurrell, 1997). However, in an English-as-a-school-subject context like China, is this common objective appropriate? In this section, we look at two main approaches to English language teaching (ELT) and CLT/TBLT in China, namely, native-speakerism and content-based instruction (CBI), before going on to discuss the appropriateness of the two approaches in the Chinese context.

Native-speakerism

Native-speakerism (Holliday, 2005) is an approach to ELT that is based on studies in English as a second language (ESL) context, where the purpose of teaching is to help students get access to authentic English use. Most Chinese ELT professionals have been explicitly or inexplicitly following this approach in curriculum design and classroom teaching, in which the thematic content is mainly based on native-speaker cultural norms and daily interpersonal communication. One of the most common interpretations is that TBLT helps learners to perform *real world* tasks in communication and develops communicative competence with reference to native-speakers' cultural norms of knowledge and behaviour (Savignon, 1991; Widdowson, 2007). From the early 1980s, ESL learners' target language competence and proficiency have been understood and measured against native-speakers' language ability (Stern, 1984) and this concept is still the most influential and dominant one among Chinese school English teachers, curriculum designers, teacher trainers, and textbook writers.

Thus, the thematic content of syllabi focuses mainly on interpersonal communication that takes place in an English-speaking environment and 'the content of many of the tasks that figure in both research and language-teaching materials implicitly espouse the cultural values and norms of the western English speaking world' (Ellis, 2003, p. 332). The general assumption underlying the teaching approach is to develop learners' ability in terms of a benchmark of native-speakers' language proficiency and cultural norms. The setting is usually an English-speaking environment and the purpose of the teaching is to help learners assimilate into the main stream of English-speaking countries (Bae, 2004; British Columbia Ministry of Education, 1999; Leung, 2007). Nevertheless, are these goals and conditions of ELT suitable for students in Asian countries such as China? Is the reality of EFL students the same as ESL learners?

Whether the answers are positive or negative, this notion of native-speakers' cultural norms and thematic content is reflected in curricula including the CNECS (2001, 2011). For example, CNECS states that in foreign language teaching, culture refers to the target language countries' history, geography, local conditions and environments, traditional social customs, living habits, ways of life, literature and arts, norms of behaviour, values, and ideology. According to Gong's (2010) survey on the goals of English language education in schools, ninety-five per cent of journals published between 2005 and 2010 on the Chinese mainland for schoolteachers on the teaching of culture referred to intercultural communication as introducing the cultural norms of English-speaking countries. Only one article compared Chinese culture with Western culture, but each comparison concluded with comments on the inappropriateness of Chinese culture (Gong & Holliday, 2013). In terms of language settings, learners are expected to engage in communication with native English speakers in an English-speaking environment. A typical conversation model in school English textbooks involves two or three speakers who share the same values and social customs talking about their common interest. Most of the tasks students perform in classrooms are concerned with tasks such as *asking the way, going shopping* or *ordering food in a fast-food restaurant*. This notion of communicative competence is what Holliday (2005) calls *native-speakerism* (see Table 3.1).

Such goals and criteria shown in Table 3.1 may be appropriate for ESL learners because English is important for them to be part of the society and social integration requires their proficiency in English. As soon as they leave the classroom, they conduct tasks such as taking the subway, eating in fast-food restaurants, and reading a newspaper to find jobs. But it would be problematic if EFL curricula followed this kind of criterion.

Native-speakerism is challenged in light of English as an international language (EIL) from political, cultural, local appropriateness, as well as economical perspectives (Cummins & Davison, 2007; Holliday, 1994; Kumaravadivelu, 2003; Pennycook, 1989; Phillipson, 1992; Rajagopalan, 2004). Increasing globalization and its added dimension of multiculturalism is challenging traditional, regional and local values (Kramsch & Whiteside, 2008). Some recent mainstream second language acquisition research has been criticized as it is unable to capture the complexity of language, the

TABLE 3.1 *Example criteria of native-speakerism*

Goals	Criterion
Pronunciation	Be as accurate as possible in American or British English
Culture	Refers to English-speaking countries' culture norms; understand their way of thinking and value concepts
Assessment	Refers to English native-speakers' communicative competence in their real world context and environment
Teachers	English native-speakers are ideal and the authorities of accurate use of English
Starting age	The earlier the better (so as to achieve native-like pronunciation)

language learner, the processes of language learning, and learners' multiple identities from sociocultural or sociohistorical perspectives (Okazaki, 2005). Others challenge the ideology of native-speakerism as it imposes Western culture and values onto other countries via 'linguistic imperialism' (e.g., Phillipson, 1992). Kumaravadivelu (2003) also points out that the special focus on developing learners' native-speaker ability may result in the marginalization of their individual voice and their cultural identity.

Evidence of this is not difficult to find in our daily life. Outside schools, the reality in major Chinese cities is that Westernization is exerting a profound influence on many areas of business. Brand names are one prominent example. Many Chinese businesses today would think of English names for their products and then transliterate those English names into Chinese so as to sound foreign. Christmas and Valentine's Day are among the most popular holidays in big cities in China.

Considering the issues above and taking China's EFL context into account, we need to ask the following questions. What is the purpose of ELT in China? Are the local contexts and cultural backgrounds the same as those in English-speaking countries or ESL contexts? Once we realize the importance of the current multicultural context for international communication and that English in China is taught as a school subject rather than as a necessary means for communication in our daily life, we will need to reconsider the teaching objectives, content and culture evident in English curricula and textbooks because 'whereas it is possible that target cultural content is motivating to some students, it is also quite possible that such content may be largely irrelevant, uninteresting, or even confusing for students' (McKay, 2003, p. 10).

Take one of the English textbooks in China for example: a task in a textbook asks students to talk about their weekend activities. The model example is that some students plan to go to see a movie/art museum, or learn to play the piano. However, our interview in a countryside school of a central province in China shows that the students there go to pick bamboo shoots and mushrooms or go fishing for food during the weekend. There is no cinema in the town, which is thirty kilometres away from the village. Another task in an English textbook for primary school children is to teach ten-year-old kids to order pizzas in a fast-food restaurant. A teacher reported that some students in their school sometimes do not even have enough food to eat, but the textbooks introduce all kinds of fast food and asks students to choose what they like to eat. This causes some negative effects on the students as they think the society is unfair so they complain to their parents about being poor. This raises the question asked by Ellis (2003, p. 332), 'what are the hidden socio-political messages of task-based teaching?'

We could perhaps now conclude that to do TBLT in China and similar contexts, three issues need to be addressed: political and cultural correctness, the appropriateness of the dual structure of urban and rural areas, and the educational goals of ELT as a general school subject.

First, native-speakerism is challenged within the notion of EIL from political, cultural, local appropriateness, and economic perspectives (Gong & Holliday, 2013). The concept of native-speakerism is not compatible with concepts such as multi-culturalism or cross-cultural communication (Holliday, Hyde & Kullman, 2010) nor is it in line with the benefits of non-English-speaking countries as it is a form of one-sided communication. While what is received concerns the cultural values of English-speaking countries, the cultures of non-English-speaking countries have been submerged, a process which harms students' value systems and approval of their own culture (Alptekin, 1984). The foreignness associated with some English learning materials can make students feel that their own culture is inferior to English culture (Kumaravadivelu, 2003).

Secondly, native-speakerism might be inappropriate for the dual structure of urban and rural areas in China. As we have mentioned earlier, because the content is mostly related to the real world of English-speaking countries and Western culture, it is not suitable and too far removed from the majority of Chinese students' life, especially the life of those from the underdeveloped areas. As a result, in a so called communicative language classroom, some students are not engaged to communicate or express themselves because there is very little related to their real life and real world (e.g., Kumaravadivelu, 2006). They merely spend a large amount of time learning something that they will use infrequently, if at all, and develop an ability that they barely have a chance to practise except in examinations.

Finally, native-speakerism is neither realistic nor in accordance with educational goals of ELT as a general school subject. The current situation of English education is: (1) Chinese students do not have an authentic environment to speak English, so it is difficult to achieve authentic communication; (2) what students have learned cannot be applied to practice; and (3) because it is difficult to learn a foreign language, learners become unconfident and the approval of Western culture does not meet learners' affective needs (Stevick, 1976; Zhang, 2003, 2006). Consequently, native-speakerism puts too much emphasis on communicative competence while neglecting the humanistic aspect of education. The goal of general education is to develop students as human beings and whole persons. In the revised CNEC (forthcoming), English is considered as both instrumental and humanistic (Allwright, 1984; Krashen & Terrell, 1983; Nunan, 1989; Stevick, 1976). In the National Education Reform and Development of Long-term Planning Programmes (NER-DLPP, 2010), it states that the goal of education is to cultivate students' world view, life view, and values; students learn to survive and live, how to be a human being and how to behave in society. However, native-speakerism will make it difficult to achieve the goals stated in NER-DLPP. Many Chinese scholars such as Fu Yonglin, Cheng Xiaotang, Xu Shengheng and Zhao Yanchun have articulated their ideas on various occasions about the goals of foreign language education at a strategic level. Some of them have indicated that the goals are confusing, while others deemed the current approach to foreign language teaching to be too functional and neglectful of humanistic factors.

Content-based/subject-oriented instruction

Considering possible problems in implementing the first approach to TBLT or replicating native-speakers' realities and other alternatives in different situations, Widdowson (1978) suggests that one way of giving language teaching a communicative reality and setting up conditions favourable to authentication might be to combine them into a rhetorical whole whose topic relates to other areas of the learner's studies. This is the second approach, a subject-oriented approach to EFL teaching supported by a group of people in China.

The subject-oriented approach, also called content-based approach, is labelled as the *bilingual education* approach in China. Together with task-based approaches, it reflects the components and parameters of a learner-centred theme 'that engage learners in activities authentic to their communicative, academic and professional interests and goals' (Pica, 2009, p. 75). This approach fits well with teaching English for 'areas of use' and at 'secondary level' as 'general English courses' where English is taught as a foreign language (Widdowson, 1978, p. 15). He points out that it is a common view for language teachers that foreign language teaching should be associated with the 'real world' outside the classroom such as holidays and sports. However, he continues:

> foreign language can be associated with those areas of use which are represented by the other subjects on the school curriculum and that this not only helps to ensure the link with reality and the pupils' own experience but also provides use with the most certain means we have of teaching the language as communication as use, rather than simply as usage.
> (Widdowson, 1978, p. 16)

Obviously, foreign language teaching objectives are integrated with school subjects such as experiments in physics and chemistry, biological processes in plants and animals, map-drawing, descriptions of basic geological features, descriptions of historical events and so on. According to Widdowson (1978, p. 81), the advantages of the content-based approach include: (1) providing students with immediate motivation as it deals with the topics of students' concern; (2) being relevant to students' language use; (3) having the same kind of communicative function as his/her own language; (4) setting up 'conditions favourable to authentication'.

In a similar vein, Wesche and Skehan (2002) propose to integrate TBLT with CBI under the principles of CLT. For Wesche and Skehan, 'CBI refers integration of school or academic content with language-teaching objectives' and they believe that:

> content that is highly relevant to learners' interests and postlanguage needs will be most effective because it is not only more motivating to learners but also more important, because much of what is learned is context specific (e.g., content vocabulary, that includes lexical phrases, usage that respects given discourse communities).
> (Wesche & Skehan, 2002, p. 215)

They have also identified some contextual and pedagogical features shared by different forms of CBI (Wesche & Skehan, 2002).

Wesche and Skehan (2002) believe that there are four areas where CLT could be organized under some consensus principles: (1) instruction that emphasizes cooperative learning such as group and pair work; (2) opportunities for learners to focus on the learning process with the goal of improving their ability to learn language in context; (3) communicative tasks linked to curricular goals as the basic organizing unit for language instruction; and (4) substantive content, often school subject matter from non-language disciplines, that is learned as a vehicle for language development, as well as for its inherent value (p. 208). The four advantages of CBI in their opinion are: (1) the development of both content knowledge and language proficiency; (2) maximizing learners' exposure to the second language; (3) repeated communicative encounters with given topics, functions, language forms and patterns in different contexts; and finally, (4) authentic texts that contain not only content knowledge but also language forms, functions and meanings. Among the possible problems based on previous research findings, the central issue of a CBI programme is the interface of language and content at all levels, 'students struggling to master new concepts and conceptual skills through a language in which they have limited proficiency' (Wesche & Skehan, 2002, p. 220).

Many schools in China are practising CBI, mostly foreign language schools in developed urban areas with few budgetary restrictions. In these schools CBI together with TBLT is considered as a promising approach to ELT and learning. Nevertheless, considering the majority of the schools are in the rural areas with a shortage of qualified teachers, it may not be realistic to practise CBI on a large scale. CBI might encounter similar problems and difficulties perceived by teachers in implementing TBLT (see also Luo and Xing, Chapter 9, this volume): (1) lack of materials and resources; (2) lack of qualified teachers; (3) lack of appropriate language assessment system in the current examination-oriented education; and (4) lack of motivation since learners think it is far easier to learn subjects in their mother tongue.

Taking the above problems into account, we might draw the conclusion that although the CBI approach might not be suitable for most schools in China, the approach provides us with an opportunity to rethink an appropriate approach for China and contexts alike.

From the discussion of native-speakerism and CBI approaches to language learning and teaching, we have argued that neither is appropriate for ELT in China. The former is improper in a non-English-speaking environment and the latter is unrealistic in the Chinese context because CBI is very demanding for the majority of EFL teachers. Despite the problems, we are not suggesting abandoning communicative approaches completely. As Kramsch and Sullivan (1996) state, while communicative approaches in Asian countries might be based on the same principles as in the West, the classroom may be totally different. Consequently, the inappropriateness of native-speakerism and CBI could serve a higher purpose in reminding us to reconsider the goal of English education in China; to make these goals meet local needs; to explore other possibilities in TBLT/CLT in different contexts (see Widdowson, 1978); and to localize TBLT/CLT in similar ways to Western fast-food restaurants, which serve the needs of local communities by adapting their products according to local tastes and traditions.

The study: The reality of TBLT in China

The study aims to explore the extent to which TBLT can be accommodated in Chinese schools. It was based on a multi-site and cross-sectional research design utilizing semi-structured interviews. Randomly selected participants included coordinators, schoolteachers and students (aged 11–18 across primary, junior middle and senior high schools) from twenty schools in eight provinces who took part between 2008 and 2010. There were two types of schools: those in large cities and those in rural areas. Each interview lasted approximately 45 minutes in Chinese and all the interviews were audio-recorded and later transcribed for analysis. The following sections present findings from the study.

The realistic world of coordinators, teachers and students

Coordinators in rural areas: Tests, tests, tests

Coordinators are officially called 'teaching researchers' and they work in local educational bureaus. Their responsibilities include supervision of school subjects in an area, conducting workshops for in-service teachers, writing tests, and organizing all kinds of professional activities for schoolteachers and students. According to the local English coordinators, the learning and teaching goals and objectives in the CNECS (2011) were loosely described, which led to different explanations and interpretations. As a result, the instructions about how to teach and what to teach were largely dependent on the understanding of the individual coordinator who was responsible for a particular area or region. Normally, the local coordinators' conception of the goals and objectives was influenced by traditional tests which usually focused on discrete language items. Although the use of CLT/TBLT was advocated in schools, teachers in general followed the direction of the tests because test results were perceived to be the benchmark of teaching quality in most schools. Interviews with coordinators, to some extent, confirm that the mismatch between the curriculum objectives and the assessment system is the main reason for the inefficiency of CLT/TBLT implementation:

> What is in the content of the test paper is not what the textbooks present every day or what teachers teach in the classrooms. The tests do not lead the teachers towards the direction of the curriculum. At first, teachers were eager to attend the workshops, but gradually, they found that neither the entrance exams of junior high schools to senior high schools nor university entrance exams test the ability to use the language ... the tests were still the 'old way'. Thus, the teachers think that since the tests focus only on knowledge instead of the use of the language, they do not need to develop students' ability to use the language. And they do not care about students' overall development, because to help students pass the exams is far more important. So they teach to the test.
>
> [C1-J-1]

Secondary schools: Burnt-out teachers and miserable students

The interviews with secondary schoolteachers and students give us a general picture of their world from learning interest to textbooks and to test-driven teaching and learning.

(a) Learning interest. Few students in middle schools in the big city really enjoyed learning, but were forced to learn. Eighty-five per cent to ninety per cent of the students were going to tutorial classes after school during the week and at the weekends. The purpose of this kind of school is to teach them with more materials aimed at adults, for example, the Public English Test System (PETS), to prepare the students to take the tests as a proof of their English levels so they could be enrolled in better schools/colleges. As a result, the students were not interested in the school textbooks because they had already acquired the relevant knowledge and skills in tutorial schools.

(b) Teaching content. Both students and teachers commented on the inappropriateness of the textbooks, especially the students in the mountainous areas. They commented that the existing textbooks were not for them. Teachers from both urban and rural areas pointed out that some of the topics such as introducing Western history, literature and historical figures were difficult not only to teach but also for students to learn. What they preferred in materials were topics related to students' daily lives such as healthy eating, personal feelings, school life, hobbies, sports, personal communication skills and learning strategies.

(c) Test-driven teaching and learning. According to the teachers, especially those from mountainous areas, they were confused about the direction of teaching. As a matter of fact, they felt very frustrated because on the one hand, they had to face the challenge of the local exams in which few of their students were able to reach the cut-off score; on the other hand, they had little idea of what content should be covered regarding vocabulary or grammar knowledge. As a result, they tried to cover everything in the course book. Consequently, they not only tired themselves out but also made their students miserable. Both teachers and students felt like they were 'in the abyss of misery'. One teacher said several times during the interview: 'We regret to have chosen to be teachers of English. We ask ourselves why we chose to be an English teacher as our career?!' [MT1-W-2]. Another female teacher complained, 'We do not live like a human being in the last three years and we only want to cry! Can you make our life a bit easier?' [FT-2-W-4]

Primary school pupils in big cities: We want more!

Having observed the above grey areas in Chinese ELT, the interviews with the primary school children in a few big cities provide us with some signs of optimism. The following are some major features summarized from the interviews with the primary pupils regarding English learning: (a) highly motivated; (b) knowing what they need and want; and (c) having a desire to learn. For example, the children articulated that they wanted more authentic materials and more vocabulary even though they had been learning two sets of textbooks at the same time already.

To sum up, the interviews with the teachers and students produced three key issues: (1) although CLT/TBLT is advocated in the CNECS and the principles are embodied in textbooks, the unchanged testing system makes it difficult for teachers to focus on developing students' communicative language ability; (2) the only choice for teachers seems to be to teach for exams, which makes teaching and learning demotivating and thus depressing for both teachers and students; and (3) some topics in the course books are either unfamiliar or improper for either students or teachers.

Discussion

The research results have, to some extent, provided support of what Holliday (2005) terms 'hidden realities':

> [W]hile it is certainly the case that when going into classrooms in many parts of the world, students will *appear* [original emphasis] to be lacking in autonomy, it is false logic to assume that their outward behaviour in these particular institutional settings reflects their internalized perceptions and abilities.
>
> (Holliday, 2005, p. 86)

Such consequences not only expose the hidden problems in current EFL teaching in most schools in China but also give evidence of the problems with native-speakerism as discussed earlier in the chapter.

From our visits to schoolteachers and students, it is obvious that TBLT/CLT is not properly implemented in Chinese schools. It might be easy to put the blame on the unchanged testing system or those who write the tests for this; however, the real cause might be some deep-seated problems with the language testing *system* such as *gaokao* (the college entrance examination, CEE) and *zhongkao* (the senior high school entrance examination, SHSEE), the curriculum implementation mechanism, and course book development.

First, the current language testing system makes it difficult to implement CLT/TBLT. While the CNECS does stress the essentiality of the ability for language use in ELT and provides principles and suggestions for writing tests, there is a lack of an indispensable section on how to assess the ability for use. Competence-based language tests are crucial in an ability-based curriculum. Nevertheless, there is a shortage of professional groups in this area to write large-scale competence-based tests. The fact that coordinators in different regions, who may know little about language testing or competence-based assessments, have to write tests underlines the drawbacks of the language assessment system in China and a need for the systematic training of professional language testers at all levels.

Secondly, the curriculum implementation mechanism is top-down, which means the CNECS is to be executed no matter if a region is ready or not. For example, the CNECS states that English as a school subject must start from Grade Three in primary schools and all the primary schools start English even if only one-third of the teachers are qualified (see Gong & Holliday, 2013 for more of this issue). As a result many teachers from other subjects may be asked to teach English. Apparently, with such a centralized curriculum implementation mechanism, such a shortage of English teachers within the context of the assessment system, puts teachers in an awkward situation to implement CLT/TBLT. On the one hand, as teachers, they care about student learning and welcome new and effective approaches that are beneficial to the students; on the other hand, there is neither professional training for them nor a corresponding assessment system to measure what they teach in class. As a result, teachers are not willing to teach something that seems to have little to do with what is tested in examinations. As long as the test results are the only criterion for measuring the quality of teaching and learning and for selecting students for further study, few teachers will not teach for tests.

Thirdly, course book development is another problem that hinders the implementation of the CLT/TBLT approach. For years, there was one standardized course book for the whole country. The textbook market opened up with the launch of the CNECS (experimental version) in 2001, and more series of textbooks were compiled as a result, either home-made or imported. Accordingly, the appropriateness of course books has become an issue. First, many teachers have not read CNECS, so it is difficult for them to understand the principles and criteria that textbooks need to adhere to. Secondly, the textbooks are mostly imported from English-speaking Western countries and adapted by local Chinese publishers; therefore, the appropriateness of the focus and thematic content in these textbooks is questionable as they may not be authentic to most Chinese students' world (see Gong & Holliday, 2013).

In conclusion, although further research is needed to reveal more about the English teaching situation in primary and secondary schools in China, current research may suggest that due to various factors, the CLT/TBLT curriculum is neither thoroughly nor comprehensively practised in ELT in China.

Reflections on accommodating TBLT in Chinese schools

In view of the problems with the current approaches to ELT in China, the following suggestions are proposed as possible solutions.

Awareness of multiculturalism

While a learner learns a language, s/he inevitably learns the culture of the country in which the language is spoken:

> [T]he fact that as an individual person's experience of language in its cultural contexts expands [s/he] does not keep these language and cultures in strictly separated mental compartment, but rather builds up a communicative competence to which all knowledge and experience of language contributes and in which language interrelated and interact.
>
> (Council of Europe, 2001, p. 4)

As a matter of fact, one of the purposes of foreign language education is to enhance students' understanding of different cultures and their development as multicultural citizens (Nakamura, 2002). To enhance students' cross-cultural awareness is also one of the objectives in the CNECS. As early as the late 1980s, Candlin (1987; see also Cook, 2007) already pointed out that the goal of English education should not be limited to communication with native-speakers in English-speaking countries, but with international English users. Therefore, it is necessary to include more cultures as well as the Chinese culture in the English curriculum.

To embrace a multicultural perspective in ELT, Scollon (1999, p. 127) provided a framework of four major cultural factors in intercultural communication, namely, *Ideology, Socialization, Forms of discourse*, and *Face system*. *Ideology* refers to history and worldview, for example, beliefs, values, and religion. *Socialization* denotes education, enculturation, and acculturation. *Forms of discourse* indicate functions of language and non-verbal communication. *Face system* implies social organization such as the concept of the self, and ingroup–outgroup relationship. Kramsch (2009, p. 244) has also proposed the concept of 'third culture', which signifies the culture that is neither the target culture (C2) nor the native culture (C1), but a new culture (C3) that is constructed in the process of learning a foreign language. In C3, learners need not only know C1 well but also understand C2 and its context. Based on this, learners not only develop their intercultural and communicative competence and learn to interact with others, but also learn to go beyond cultures and critically reflect on their behaviour and identity.

Balance between communication and humanism

ELT in Chinese schools is not limited to the development of language ability for communication since it is not only a language training course but also a concrete form of language education, and a compulsory school subject in primary and secondary schools (see CNECS, 2001, experimental version; 2011, revised version). The English curriculum depends on macro educational goals, future needs, micro-teaching processes and learning content (see Widdowson, 2003). Macro educational goals are related to what kind of citizens we need for the future. We could divide the goals into two categories, external goals and internal goals (see Cook, 1999, 2007). External goals refer to English teaching objectives in schools and internal goals to the actual use of language. The former focuses on how students benefit from language teaching regarding language knowledge and skills; and the latter emphasizes students' overall development as a productive citizen; for example, their personality development, way of thinking, and value concepts. Candlin (1987; see also Cook, 2007) also argues that the goal of English education should not be limited to language goals, but students' overall development as individuals, including sociocultural goals, mental development, thinking and cognition, and learning skills, as well as their personalities, such as cultural awareness, personality, tolerance, self-realization and self-confidence.

Although language skills, knowledge and learning strategies are described in detail and attitude and cognitive skills are also written into the goals in the curriculum, there is no explanation or description of what attitude and cognitive skills are and how they can be developed gradually through the learning process. We thus would like to reconceptualize the goals of ELT from communicative and humanistic perspectives.

Conceptions of the ELT goals revisited

Since EFL is different from ESL, it might be inappropriate to use the criteria of native-speakerism in English teaching in the Chinese context. And since the primary goal of learning English for the majority of Chinese students is as a school subject, which educates students to be quality citizens with creativity and cross-culture competence (NECS, 2011), accordingly, the ELT goals for Chinese primary and secondary schools needs to be reconceptualized. Terms such as communication, learning interest and cognitive skills, course books, and assessment need to be reinterpreted.

First, communication is the activity of conveying information between individuals through the exchange of thoughts, messages, or information, by speech, visuals, signals, writing, or behaviour. In language teaching, communication requires a social context that leads to learning activities for communication, appropriacy, and functional competence. This context requires not only language skills but also discourse and sociolinguistic competence. In this context, teachers are facilitators and students learn to communicate by interaction and negotiation of meaning. Learning activities include information gaps, problem solving, and all types of feedback. The assessment of such learning consists of communicative tasks which focus on both fluency and accuracy. There is no error correction unless errors interfere with communication (see Brown, 1994; Hadley, 1993; Larsen-Freeman, 1986). To be more specific, we expect that students, through English learning, are able to: (1) establish personal relationships, exchange information, ideas and opinions, and express attitudes and emotions not only with English native-speakers but also with speakers of other languages in English; (2) receive information from public resources such as books, magazines, lectures, and intellectual speeches; (3) appreciate literature, drama, poetry, music, movies in different cultures through listening and reading and be able to respond to them; (4) have the desire to be *creative* in language use (see Clark, 1987).

Secondly, in view of the fact that most students are learning English as a school subject, it is important to develop learners' interest and cognitive skills. According to a survey[1] among students as to what subjects they disliked most, English was among the least liked subjects and 'lack of interest' was the key factor that affected English learning. Hence, it is reasonable to say that students' interest in learning English is the priority in English education. To achieve this, language tasks must be both fun and challenging enough so that students are eager to participate in learning. Challenging tasks require competence and thinking. Therefore, to develop learners' cognitive and thinking skills becomes important. Cognition refers to a faculty for the processing of information, applying knowledge, and changing preferences. Bloom's taxonomy is still very helpful in guiding us to design tasks that train students' logical thinking in TBLT textbooks (see Waters, 2004). For example, for ten to eleven year olds, the cognitive skills could include memory, translation, interpretation, application, analysis, synthesis, and evaluation (Adams-Smith, 1981).

Thirdly, to meet the requirements of communicative and cognitive requirements, it is necessary to adapt and write EFL course books based on needs analysis. According to Luo and Xu (2011) and Gong and Holliday (forthcoming), because of the inappropriate topics and tasks, current English textbooks for secondary schools do not attract students either in cities or in rural areas. Hence, course book writers need to take students' reality, especially rural students' real life, into consideration. To have authentic EFL materials, it might be necessary that English textbooks for rural schools be different from those for urban schools.

Last, but not least, as we observed earlier in this chapter, the existing assessment constitutes the biggest obstacle for implementing CLT/TBLT comprehensively. In view of the ultimate goals of ELT for Chinese students and the close relationship between tests and teaching, it is urgent to have systemic change in assessing English teaching and learning. To be in line with what is proposed in the CNECS and to measure students' ability for use, task-based assessment should be part of the assessment system. Test tasks need to be designed to be authentic to students' lives, to the way they are taught and learned, and to prepare them for international communication in English. To make this happen, there needs to be a concerted effort from authorities in the national Ministry of Education, education bureaus at different levels, experts in language testing, teachers, students and communities.

Conclusions

This chapter has reported the current situation of CLT/TBLT in primary and secondary schools in China and identified problems encountered by teachers in practising innovative approaches. Since the mission for us in the field of language education is to improve the quality of English education and to educate a generation from a whole-person point of view with a national and international perspective, multicultural awareness and an ability to communicate in English (CNECS, 2011), it is our responsibility to explore an appropriate way to accommodate TBLT/ELT in the Chinese context to meet local students' learning needs. Such an approach would truly help us to realize the goal of educating our students in line with what is described in the CNECS. It is neither a simple job nor an easy road to follow. Much more research is required in order to fully implement this approach effectively.

Notes

1 Professor G.U. Mingyuan talked about this at the meeting on the evaluation of STEPSS (Standards of Teachers of English for Primary and Secondary Schools) organized by the Ministry of Education in August 2010.

References

Adams-Smith, D. E. (1981). Levels of questioning: Teaching creative thinking through ESP. *Forum*, *19*(1), 15–21.

Allwright, D. (1984). Why don't learners learn what teachers teach? – The interaction hypothesis. In D. Singleton & D. Little (Eds), *Language teaching in formal and informal contexts* (pp. 3–18). Dublin: BAAL/IRAAL.

Alptekin, C. (1984). The question of culture: EFL teaching in non-English-speaking countries. *ELT Journal*, *1*, 14–20.

Bae, G. (2004). Rethinking constructivism in multicultural contexts: Does constructivism in education take the issue of diversity into consideration? Retrieved http://www.usca.edu/essays/vol122004/Bae.pdf

British Columbia Ministry of Education, Special Programs Branch RB 0074. (1999). English as a second language learners: *A guide for classroom teachers*. Retrieved http://www.bced.gov.bc.ca/esl/policy/classroom.pdf

Brown, H. D. (1994). *Teaching by principles: An interactive approach to language pedagogy*. Englewood Cliffs, New Jersey: Prentice-Hall Regents.

Candlin, C. N. (1987). Towards task-based language learning. In C. N. Candlin & D. F. Murphy (Eds). *Language learning tasks* (pp. 16–17). Englewood Cliffs, NJ: Prentice-Hall International (UK) Ltd and Lancaster University.

Celce-Murcia, M., Dörnyei, Z., & Thurrell, S. (1997). Direct approaches in L2 instruction: A turning point in communicative language teaching? *TESOL Quarterly, 1*, 141–153.

Clark, J. L. (1987). *Curriculum renewal in school foreign language learning*. Oxford: Oxford University Press.

Cook, V. (1999). Going beyond the native speaker in language teaching. *TESOL Quarterly, 2*, 185–209.

Cook, V. (2007). The goal of ELT: Reproducing native-speakers or promoting multicompetence among second language users? In J. Cummins & C. Davison (Eds), *International handbook of English language teaching* (pp. 237–248). New York: Springer.

Council of Europe (2001). The *Common European Framework of Reference for Languages*. Cambridge: Cambridge University Press

Cummins, J., & Davison, C. (2007). The global scope and policies of ELT: Critiquing current policies and programmes. In J. Cummins & C. Davison (Eds), *International handbook of English language teaching* (Vol. 1, pp. 237–248). New York: Springer.

Dubin, F., & Olshtain, E. (1986). *Course design*. Cambridge: Cambridge University Press.

Ellis, R. (2003). *Task-based language learning and teaching*. Oxford: Oxford University Press.

Gong, Y. (2010). Reconceptualising the goals of English language education in schools. *Curriculum, Teaching Materials & Teaching Method, 12*, 55–60. (龚亚夫 (2010)。重构基础教育英语教学目标,《课程·教材·教法》, 12, 55–60。)

Gong, Y., & Holliday, A. (2013). Cultures of change. In K. Hyland & L. Wong (Eds), *Innovation and change in English language education* (pp. 44–57). London: Routledge.

Hadley, A. O. (1993). *Teaching language in context*. Boston: Heinle & Heinle.

Holliday, A. (1994). *Appropriate methodology and social context*. New York: Cambridge University Press.

Holliday, A. (2005). *The struggle to teach English as an international language*. Oxford: Oxford University Press.

Holliday, A., Hyde, M., & Kullman, J. (2010). *Intercultural communication: An advanced resource book for students*. New York: Routledge.

Kramsch, C. (2009). Third culture and language education. In V. Cook (Eds), *Volume 1 Language teaching and learning* (pp. 233–254) in *Contemporary applied linguistics* (Edited by Li Wei & V. Cook). London: Continuum.

Kramsch, C., & Sullivan, P. (1996). Appropriate pedagogy. *ELT Journal, 1*, 201.

Kramsch, C., & Whiteside, A. (2008). Language ecology in multilingual settings, towards a theory of symbolic competence. *Applied Linguistics. 29*(4), 645–671.

Krashen, S., & Terrell, T. (1983), *The natural approach*. Hayward, CA: Alemany Press.

Kumaravadivelu, B. (2003). Critical language pedagogy: A postmethod perspective on English language teaching. *World Englishes, 4*, 539–550.

Kumaravadivelu, B. (2006). TESOL methods: Changing tracks, changing trends. *TESOL Quarterly, 1*, 59–81.

Larsen-Freeman, D. (1986). *Techniques and principles in language teaching*. Oxford: Oxford University Press.

Leung, C. (2007). Integrating school-aged ESL learners into the mainstream curriculum. In Cummins, J., & Davison, C. (Eds.), *International handbook of English language teaching* (pp. 249–269). New York: Springer.

Luo, S. (this volume). Teachers' perceived difficulty in implementing TBLT in China. In M. Thomas & H. Reinders (Eds), *Contemporary task-based language teaching in Asia*. London & New York: Bloomsbury.

Luo, S., & Xu, X. (2011). An investigation of task-based English textbook series, *Go for It*, for middle schools. *Curriculum, Teaching Material and* Method, *3*, 69–74. (罗少茜、徐鑫 (2011)。初中任务型英语教材使用情况的调查与分析.《课程·教材·教法》, 3, 69–74。)

McKay, S. L. (2003). Toward an appropriate EIL pedagogy: Re-examining common ELT assumptions. *International Journal of Applied Linguistics*, *1*, 10.

Ministry of Education (2001; 2011). *Chinese National English Curriculum*. Beijing: Beijing Normal University Publication Group. (中华人民共和国教育部 (2001, 2011)。《英语课程标准》。北京：北京师范大学出版集团。)

Nakamura, K. (2002). Developing global literacy through English as an international language (EIL) education in Japan. *International Education Journal* 3(5). WCCES Commission 6 pp.63–74.

Nunan, D. (1989), *The learner-centred curriculum*. Cambridge: Cambridge University Press.

Okazaki, T. (2005). Critical consciousness and critical language teaching. *Second Language Studies*, *23*(2), 174–202.

Pennycook, A. (1989). The concept of method, interested knowledge, and the politics of language teaching. *TESOL Quarterly*, *23*(4), 589–618.

Phillipson, R. (1992). *Linguistic imperialism*. Oxford: Oxford University Press.

Pica, T. (2009). Integrating content-based and task-based approaches for teaching, learning and research. In V. Cook (Ed.), *Contemporary applied linguistics, Vol. 1: Language teaching and learning* (pp. 75–98). London: Continuum.

Rajagopalan, K. (2004). The concept of 'World English' and its implications for ELT. *ELT Journal*, *58*(2), 111–117.

Scollon, R. (1999). Official and unofficial discourses of national identity: Questions raised by the case of contemporary Hong Kong. In R. Wodak, C. Ludwig (Eds), *Challenges in a changing world: Issues in critical discourse analysis* (pp. 21–35). Vienna: Passagen Verlag.

Savignon, S. J. (1991). Communicative language teaching. *TESOL Quarterly*, *2*, 201–265.

Stern, H. H. (1984). Review and discussion. In C. J. Brumfit (Ed.), *General English syllabus design: Curriculum and syllabus design for the general English classroom* (pp. 5–12). Pergamon Press Ltd. and British Council.

Stevick, E. W. (1976). *Memory, meaning, and method*. Rowley, MA: Newbury House.

Waters, A. (2004). *Study tasks in English student's book and teacher's book*. Shanghai: Shanghai Foreign Language Press.

Wesche, M. B., & Skehan, P. (2002). Communicative, task-based, and content-based language instruction. In M. B. Kaplan (Ed.), *The Oxford handbook of applied linguistics* (pp. 207–228). Oxford: Oxford University Press.

Widdowson, H. G. (1978). *Teaching language as communication*. Oxford: Oxford University Press.

Widdowson, H. G. (2003). *Defining issues in English language teaching*. Oxford: Oxford University Press.

Widdowson, H. G. (2007). Un-applied linguistics and communicative language teaching. *International Journal of Applied Linguistics*, *2*, 218.

Zhang, Z. (2003). The content of teaching in China. *Curriculum, Textbooks and Methods*, *5*, 34–39. (张正东 (2003)。我国英语教学的属性和内容.《课程·教材·教法》, 5, 34–39。)

Zhang, Z. (2006). Foreign language is a sword with blades at both sides. *Foreign Language Teaching and Research in Basic Education*, *1*, 19–22. (张正东 (2006)。外语是把双刃剑.《基础教育外语教学研究》, 1, 19–24。)

4

Bridging Communicative Language Teaching and Task-Based Language Teaching in Cambodia:

Learners' Reactions to an Integrated Programme in the Non-Formal Education Sector

Nicole Takeda

Summary

Teaching English as a foreign language (EFL) is particularly challenging in Cambodia since many instructors do not have access to research on teaching methods and have limited, if any, funds for professional development through teacher training. This is especially true in the non-formal education sector, dominated by non-government organizations (NGOs), where the majority of underprivileged Cambodian youth receive their English language instruction in overcrowded and uncomfortable classrooms often with untrained teachers who depend on grammar translation for their lessons. As a way to empower students, teachers and development in language education in Cambodia, an EFL programme using Communicative Language Teaching (CLT) and Task-Based Language Learning (TBLT) was implemented at a Siem Reap government-accredited NGO language school, the Bayon English Academy (BEA), for teenagers living in extreme and moderate poverty in September 2010. This chapter describes the process of incorporating both of these methods into an EFL programme, and adapting them to the cultural expectations of Cambodian teachers and learners while at the same time modifying these expectations away from grammar-focused, teacher-centred instruction. The results of this integrated programme show how these methods complement each other to produce learners with communicative competence and a preference for both CLT and TBLT in one of the most challenging teaching and learning contexts in Southeast Asia.

Introduction

CLT and TBLT have made a few inroads into Cambodian university EFL courses and teacher training programmes, but there is still a very limited understanding of how these methods affect students' attitudes and learning English. This is understandable due to the number of challenges connected with CLT and TBLT in Cambodia, such as misconceptions that CLT and TBLT conflict with local values, limited teacher training and access to resources, and institutional constraints on implementing an integrated programme not only at the university level but also in the public school system. Such hurdles are even higher in the non-formal education sector dominated by NGOs, where the majority of Cambodian youth attend English language lessons. These additional hurdles include the use of grammar translation, high staff turnovers, overcrowded classrooms, substandard facilities and monthly budgets dependent on charitable donations. Despite such challenging teaching and learning environments, this chapter explains how it is possible to introduce an integrated CLT-TBLT EFL programme at a local Cambodian NGO school in Siem Reap for underprivileged youth and adapt methods to reflect the values of Cambodian teachers and learners while moving away from grammar-focused, teacher-centred instruction as a way to move English language education forward in the NGO sector.

Factors leading to the use of English in Cambodia

The economic and political turmoil from the 1970s to the early 1990s left Cambodia as one of the poorest countries in the world. The signing of the 1991 Paris Peace Accord brought stability, but Cambodia still remains in political, economic and social transition to this day. In turn, these transitions have affected the country's foreign language policy – the choice of English as its second language. There were three factors that led to this choice. First, the United Nations Transitional Authority in Cambodia (UNTAC) had over 20,000 international personnel to help in reconstruction from 1992 to 1993 (Widyono, 2008). During the two-year mission, UNTAC employed over 60,000 Cambodians, and most needed English to work with foreign staff (Clayton, 2006). Because of this, English became the dominant second language by the mid-1990s. The next factor was Cambodia's entry into the Association of Southeast Asian Nations (ASEAN) in 1999. Unlike other international organizations that have a myriad official working languages, ASEAN has only English as its official language. As a result, there is pressure on Cambodian representatives to develop their English skills so that they can fully partake in the organization. The last factor is due to Cambodia's status as an aid recipient. With millions of dollars of development assistance flowing into the country every year, international aid agencies have been influential in the spread of English in Cambodia since most of these organizations require Cambodians to use English to perform their duties (Clayton, 2006). In addition, the 1996 decision of the Ministry of Education, Youth and Sport (MOEYS) to start EFL classes from Grade 7 in public schools fortified the dominance of English in Cambodia. Because of these factors, English has made inroads from the national to the local level to become Cambodia's de facto second language.

English language teaching in Cambodia

Cambodia's public school English language programme got its start with help from the Australian NGO Quaker Service Australia (QSA) that trained 300 English language teachers from 1989 to 1993. During the weekends and holidays, Australian volunteers ran twelve-week English language and pedagogy courses for secondary school teachers at the Faculty of Pedagogy in Phnom Penh (Clayton, 2006). The QSA programme was then superseded by the British government-funded Cambodian Secondary English Teaching Project (CAMSET) in 1993, which provided in-service training for Cambodian lower-secondary English teachers at the Faculty of Pedagogy in Phnom Penh and regional training centres. During these full-time, six- to nine-month courses, Cambodian teachers enrolled in English language skills, pedagogy, and classroom management classes under the supervision of teacher trainers from the British government's Voluntary Service Overseas (VSO) organization. To further develop English language teaching in secondary schools, CAMSET developed a series of grammar-based textbooks, *English for Cambodia*, which are still in use today as the nation's compulsory English language course book. By the time the British programme ended in 2001, it had trained over 700 teachers (Clayton, 2006).

Despite early efforts from the Australians and British to secure the future of English language education in secondary school, many public schools, including their English language programmes, are in disarray. This is due largely to a vastly underfunded education sector – only $335 million, or 0.095 per cent, of the $3.52 billion US draft budget will be funnelled into education in 2014 (Zsombor & Hul, 2013). Moreover, salaries are far below a living wage, around US$60–80 per month, and this has led teachers to look for opportunities to supplement their income. This has taken the form of private tutoring in which teachers provide students with course material that they withhold during official teaching hours and offer exam answers (Dawson, 2011). Students who can afford these sessions, about US$15 per month for each subject in secondary school, are guaranteed to pass their exams. Those who cannot, fail and are forced to repeat their grade despite passing their exams. Because of this corruption, students often have no choice but to drop out of secondary school since they cannot afford mounting fees, which can reach as much as $60 per month (Toun, personal communication, 27 July 2012). It is not surprising that secondary school enrolment is only 34 per cent in Cambodia (UNESCAP, 2011). This is where the informal education sector, consisting of NGOs, steps in to provide a basic education in a variety of subjects like foreign languages and technical skills for those not able to remain in school. It is even quite common for public school students to attend NGO schools since many are dissatisfied with the quality of their education (Toun, personal communication, 27 July 2012). However, the majority of Cambodian-run NGO schools are often underfunded, understaffed, and do not have adequate access to resources and training opportunities, but these schools are usually the only available alternative for most youth.

TESOL approaches: Rationale for CLT and TBLT in Cambodia

The use of grammar translation is prevalent in both the public school system and the NGO school sector throughout Cambodia. In secondary school lessons, low teaching salaries have not only resulted in teachers charging students an array of unauthorized fees, but also finding part-time work to supplement their income. As a result, little time, if any, is available for lesson planning and reflection. The choice of grammar translation is partly out of convenience due to time constraints on teachers. At the NGO level, English language programmes often involve overseas volunteers who lack qualifications and experience. They either have their own classes or do team-teaching with Cambodian staff on random topics with no measurable learning outcomes. Although there are private language schools that provide in-service training, most NGOs cannot afford them due to tight monthly budgets. Grammar translation then becomes the only option because of the limited access to training and professional development opportunities.

Whether at the public school or NGO level, the grammar translation method results in 'a tedious experience of memorizing endless lists of unusable grammar rules and vocabulary and attempting to produce perfect translations of stilted or literary prose' (Richards & Rodgers, 2001, p. 6). There is therefore a great need to move away from this model since learners do not develop communicative ability and teachers are not required to develop specialized skills (Brown, 2007). There is also an urgency to move away from this method, especially in the non-formal education sector, since learners want to find better employment opportunities, such as in the tourist sector where there are higher salaries and safer working environments. Without communicative abilities in English, this is not possible. CLT and TBLT are therefore possible options to improve English language education in Cambodia's NGO school sector.

The CLT approach started in the late 1970s and early 1980s, and moved away from focusing mostly on linguistic forms to target the development of communicative competence of English language learners in social interactions (Larsen-Freeman & Anderson, 2000; Richards & Rodgers, 2001). Meaningful communication that is pragmatic, authentic and functional is the means and the goal in CLT – all aspects of learning focus on a communicative purpose. Ideally, instructors provide opportunities for their learners to receive meaningful input to encourage them to use this input in a meaningful way through a variety of interactions (Brown, 2001). For tasks to be considered communicative, Klapper (2003) outlined three requirements: (1) they connect to real-world situations; (2) they have defined goals; and (3) they are flexible and unpredictable. CLT is anchored to both communicative competence and second language learning theories, so this broadness lends itself to a variety of interpretations of either a stronger or weaker application in the classroom. The difference between these versions essentially centres on the role of the teacher in language acquisition. The stronger version designates language acquisition as a natural process that cannot be controlled, so the teacher's role is to facilitate the language learning process rather than explicitly teach linguistic forms. The weaker version has the teacher controlling the process in which linguistic forms are introduced through meaningful communicative activities in a controlled classroom environment. Learners have the opportunity to use these forms gradually and autonomously before moving onto more realistic contexts (Klapper, 2003). The 1980s saw the term *task* replace *communicative activity* (Skehan, 2003), and in this sense, TBLT stems from CLT (Kumaravadivelu, 2006). A language task can be defined as 'an activity in which a person engages in order to attain an objective, and which necessitates the use of language' (Van den Branden, 2006, p. 4). Unlike CLT's focus on forms, TBLT is a meaning-based teaching approach that has the learners in control of choosing their own forms rather than the teacher for classroom tasks (Willis, 1996). Like CLT, there is also a stronger and weaker version of TBLT due to differing interpretations on the use of tasks. The stronger version has tasks as an integral part of a syllabus, while the weaker one uses tasks for communicative practice as part of a grammar- or function-based syllabus (Butler, 2011).

To play a role in helping the informal education sector transition to CLT and TBLT approaches, and to provide English language education to Cambodian youth, the author established her own NGO school in 2010 with a Cambodian teacher she had met during a volunteer placement in August 2007. The purpose of this chapter is therefore to describe this pilot CLT-TBLT integrated programme, and to investigate if there is a receptiveness and readiness for such a programme among Cambodian learners. The following research questions were formulated for this study:

1 What reactions did learners have to an integrated CLT-TBLT EFL programme?
2 What options are there for implementing CLT and TBLT in Cambodia's non-formal education sector?

Institutional context

The EFL programme described in this project is run at the Bayon English Academy (BEA) in Siem Reap, Cambodia. The author's NGO is an accredited educational institution with the status equivalent to a secondary school, and this allows the school to issue its own English language certificates. Unlike the majority of other Cambodian schools, the school has modern facilities. It also uses both CLT and TBLT approaches and limits classroom size to twenty-eight students. The organization focuses on a 'pedagogy of particularity' that is 'sensitive to a particular group of teachers teaching a particular group of learners pursing a particular set of goals within a particular institutional context embedded in a particular social milieu' (Kumaravadivelu, 2006, p. 538). The school's mission is therefore to promote and provide better language teaching and learning through adapting and localizing pedagogy to reflect Cambodian cultural norms.

The school offers four English language courses: Basic (for novice low to novice high learners), Pre-Intermediate (for intermediate low to intermediate mid learners), Intermediate (for intermediate high learners) and Advanced (for advanced low to advanced high learners). Students enrol in one of these one-year courses at the end of August. They study from Monday to Friday for one hour from September to July, which totals approximately 200 hours of classroom instruction.

Teachers

The Cambodian co-founder of the school is the head teacher and managing director. As the head teacher, he is in charge of implementing and running the school's programmes and supervising the school's other full-time teacher and staff. He speaks both Cambodian and English fluently. Although he does not have formal English language teaching qualifications, he has received extensive training in Teaching English to Speakers of Other Languages (TESOL) methods from the author. The students view him as a role model in the community since he was able to break out of poverty through hard work and education. The students trust him as their teacher, and also as a counsellor to help them through personal and family problems. As a teacher, he strives to motivate students through positive reinforcement.

The other full-time teacher is an eighteen-year-old high school student, who completed the author's one-month intensive teacher-training programme in August 2012. For the past year, she has undergone additional training, which has included team-teaching with the head teacher and online lesson planning sessions with the author. Prior to becoming a teacher, she was a student for three years at the school and completed the Pre-Intermediate, Intermediate and Advanced language courses. She now has advanced capabilities in all the four skills. She is extremely competent and dedicated; and has impressive time management skills, especially since she can juggle both her public school studies with a full-time teaching position. She does this to support her family and to save for her university tuition.

Learners

All learners come from families in moderate and extreme poverty, earning US$1 or US$2 per day respectively (Ravallion, Chen & Sangraula, 2009). Almost all students witness and/or suffer from domestic violence on a daily basis. They come from families mostly working in agriculture, such as rice or potato farmers, or working in services, such as market sellers or tuk-tuk drivers. Learners range in age from twelve to twenty-years-old, with seventeen being the median age. A typical day for most of the students starts at the break of dawn with household chores, such as collecting firewood or cooking, or helping their mother run a stall in a village market. They then attend public school from 7:00 a.m. until 11:30 a.m. in classrooms with an average student–teacher ratio of 40:1 (Toun, personal communication, 27 July 2012). They study in a concrete building with open windows and often no electricity to power a single fan. Most learners then attend private tutoring in three to four subjects from their public school teachers in the early afternoon. Afterwards, they come to the author's school for their English language lesson in one of the hour-long time slots from 3:00 p.m. until 7:00 p.m. After their English lesson, students either return home to more housework or to part-time jobs at restaurants or night markets. Essentially, the day revolves around helping their families so that they can all survive until tomorrow.

Integrated CLT and TBLT programme design

Programme goals

Prior to the start of the programme in September 2010, the author spent a year designing the localized programme with help from her Cambodian partner. The first step involved establishing goals that encompassed all four courses, which included:

1. to improve learners' confidence in using English for communication;
2. to improve learners speaking, listening, reading and writing skills; and
3. to help learners become independent through project work.

Since all learners come from impoverished backgrounds, many of them have a 'poverty complex' in which they believe their lower economic status makes them less deserving of success in life. Therefore, building confidence, in language skills and in the students themselves, is the most important goal in the programme. It reinforces to them that if they work hard and finish public school, they can break their families' cycle of poverty. Second, the programme aims to improve the learners' speaking, listening, reading and writing skills; however, there is a strong emphasis on speaking and listening skills in the first semester. The reason is that students want to learn English so that they can get a job in the tourist industry as hotel receptionists, tour guides, or souvenir shop staff. The faster they can learn English, the faster they can get a job to support their families and to pay for their public school studies. Working in tourism is not only more profitable, but a much safer option for teenagers. Finally, most students enter the programme without any friends. This is partly due to their busy workdays at home, in the markets, in the fields, and at public school. Public school teachers also stigmatize those from the lowest economic classes, which often leaves them friendless at school and only reinforces their 'poverty complex'. Project work is therefore one of the programme's goals as a way to help students make friends and gain a sense of community. Since Cambodian families have to work together to survive from day to day, project work reflects their values of cooperation.

Teaching materials

One of the biggest challenges in designing the programme's curriculum was finding an appropriate textbook to help carry out the goals and objectives of the speaking and listening components of the programme. As previously mentioned, there is an emphasis on developing speaking and listening skills so that students can find work in the tourist sector as fast as possible since it is a matter of survival for them and their families. The most common textbooks available are older editions of *British Headway* and *American Cutting Edge*. Both of these texts have a heavy Anglo-Saxon cultural bias, which makes them inappropriate for the needs of Cambodian learners, especially since students will come in contact with tourists from all over the world. In addition, these textbooks have numerous colour photos. Since entire textbooks are copied on old and second-hand copy machines, the photos, and text, are usually not clear. The author therefore chose Pearson Education's *Side by Side International Edition Student*

Books 1, 2, 3 and 4 (Molinsky & Bliss, 2003) for the programme's four courses for three reasons: (1) the units focus on speaking skills, (2) the Presentation-Practice-Production (PPP) stages are easy for teachers to identify, and (3) there is multicultural content in terms of characters and topics. However, the series is not without its drawbacks, which include insufficient practice activities, missing production activities, and no connection to the lives of the school's Cambodian learners.

To compensate for these shortcomings, the author and head teacher rewrote all of the lessons from the textbooks for all the four courses from 2010 to 2012 to include Cambodian content. In this way, learners are exposed to the 'Western content' mostly in the practice activities, but this is balanced with presentation and production activities that reflect Cambodian culture and values. This balance is necessary since learners aim to work in the tourist industry where they will need to have some familiarity with foreign cultures and their own culture as well.

Teaching procedure

The decision to use both CLT and TBLT was not only to help carry out the goals of the programme, but also to give learners consistency and variety in their lessons. To ensure this, the author developed a weekly lesson cycle while planning the teaching schedule. A typical week in any of the courses includes both CLT and TBLT lessons as seen in Figure 4.1. CLT lessons use the PPP model for speaking lessons and the Pre-During-Post (PDP) pattern for listening and reading lessons.

In addition to the weekly lesson cycle, there is also a bi-semester lesson cycle to ensure consistency and variety as seen in Figure 4.2. This cycle starts after a one-week orientation, and is repeated twice during the semester. At the end of the second cycle, there is a three-week writing workshop on paragraph writing using the process method, which falls into the stronger TBLT approach. In total, learners receive between 90 to 100 hours of instruction through CLT and TBLT approaches.

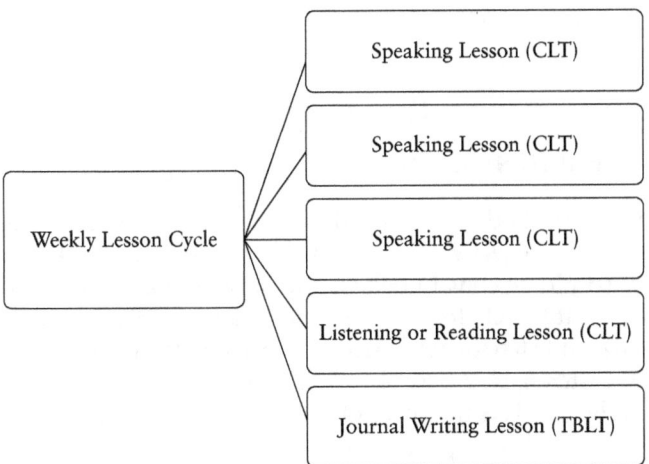

FIGURE 4.1 *Weekly lesson cycle.*

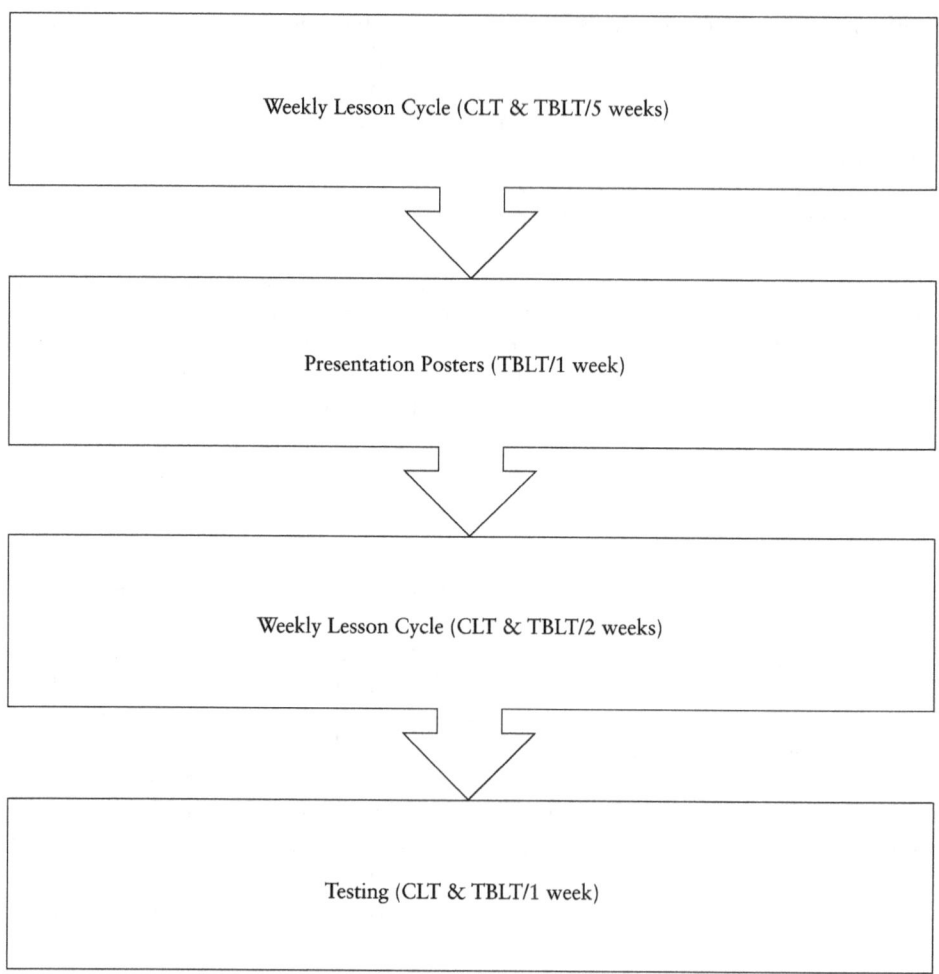

FIGURE 4.2 Bi-semester lesson cycle.

Performance assessment

The programme uses both testing and formal assessment to measure learners' achievement of course objectives. Testing is differentiated from formal assessment in that tests are usually 'time-constrained . . . and draw on a limited sample of behavior' (Brown, 2007, p. 446) while formal assessment can take place over a longer period of time on a range of behaviour. Assessment is broken down into four categories: (1) Speaking and Listening; (2) Reading; (3) Writing; and (4) Attendance and Participation. Table 4.1 lists the types of assessment, their approach and the weight for each one.

The most comprehensive assessment in the programme consists of two tests: one given mid-way through the programme and the other near the end. There are two

TABLE 4.1 *Programme Assessment Criteria*

Skill	Task	Weight
Speaking & Listening	Tests (CLT & TBLT)	30%
	Poster Presentations (TBLT)	20%
Reading	Book Reports (TBLT)	10%
Writing	Journal Writing (TBLT)	20%
	Writing Workshop (TBLT)	10%
Attendance & Participation		10%

components to the criterion-referenced test: a written and a spoken test. The written test is further divided into three sections: vocabulary, grammar and paragraph writing. The test is administered over the course of three days: students complete the vocabulary test on day one, the grammar test on day two and the paragraph-writing task on day three. The spoken test is also carried out during this three-day period: the teacher calls one learner at a time into the office to complete a 5–7 minute real-world task. After each role-play, the teacher assesses the performance on a twenty-point scale rubric and notes down praise and constructive feedback on the assessment form.

In addition to the tests, students also receive a formal assessment on their poster presentations. For these unfocused TBLT tasks, learners receive a group evaluation, which the teacher completes during the preparation and presentation stages of the task. The fifty-point assessment form evaluates learners on six criteria: (1) the content of the poster; (2) the design of the poster; (3) student participation; (4) presentation organization; (5) presentation delivery; and (6) the use of body language. There is also a comment box for the teacher to note down individual feedback for each student.

For the extensive reading component of the programme, students have to read two graded readers and then complete a book report on each one, which is done on their own without instruction. To evaluate these reports, the teacher uses a rubric and then grades the reports on a twenty-point scale.

The journal-writing task is assessed throughout the entire programme on a weekly basis. For this weekly task, students write a three-page entry and then discuss it with their writing partner every Friday. During these discussions, the teacher checks each journal to make sure students have completed their entries. At the end of the programme, the instructor evaluates each journal based on four criteria: (1) organization; (2) focus on topic; (3) content; and (4) participation. Each journal then receives a grade on a twenty-point scale. During the two-week paragraph-writing workshop at the end of the semester, students use the process writing method to write a descriptive and a listing paragraph. A rubric is used to assess these tasks, which consists of five criteria: (1) topic sentence; (2) supporting sentences; (3) concluding sentence; (4) grammar and sentence structure; and (5) mechanics. This rubric is also used to assess the paragraph-writing section of the tests.

Data collection

To gather learners' reactions to an integrated CLT-TBLT programme, fifty-five students completed a 100-question compulsory survey at the end of the school year in July 2013. The survey was completed as a one-hour class lesson: instructors explained the purpose and procedure of the survey in both English and Cambodian, and instructed students to write comments in English. During the lesson, students could ask for additional explanations about the questions in either English or Cambodian. For those students who could not complete the survey during the lesson, they were allowed to complete it for homework and submit it the following day. This survey is carried out annually to not only evaluate the school's programmes, but also the institution's facilities and operations. The questionnaire was divided into seven sections: (1) facilities; (2) materials; (3) programmes; (4) teaching; (5) progress; (6); library programme; (7) certificates; and (8) professionalism and future. Students answered the questions according to a four-point scale (strongly disagree = 1; disagree = 2; agree = 3; strongly agree = 4) and had the option of writing comments in comment boxes throughout the survey.

Results and discussion

The most significant finding is the preference for this integrated programme from an overwhelming majority of the learners (Table 4.2, Section C, statements 23, 33, 40 and 69). This was also evident in students' written comments in the curriculum section of the questionnaire. Communicative features, such as learner-centred lessons, group work and usefulness, all ranked very favourably among students. For learner-centeredness, almost all students responded positively to 'I like the teacher's teaching style' (Table 4.2, Section D, statement 69). One student summarized that 'the way of teaching is very good. We don't have a lot of hours to study, but every minute is spent on the goal of the lesson, and we have a lot of activities to improve our English.' Working in pairs and groups was also embraced enthusiastically with median scores of 3.85 and 3.86 respectively (Table 4.2, Section C, statements 16 and 17). One student noted 'I love to sit in groups with four students at the table because it is easy to have discussions with my partner.' Finally, interesting lesson content and usefulness also received median scores of 3.92 and 3.88 respectively (Table 4.2, Section D, statements 70 and 71). Among several comments on the practicality of lessons, one learner noticed that 'The [school's] lessons aren't the same as in high school. They are better and more useful.' More frankly, another student mentioned 'I was sometimes not interested in the lessons, but I was 95% of the time.' These scores can be attributed to the localized curriculum and materials that emphasized Cambodian cultural and social issues. This falls in line with recommendations from Holliday (1997) and Sullivan (2000) that attention to cultural norms and values can facilitate the implementation of CLT.

These results go against the stream of research that claims approaches with communicative features conflict with Buddhist and Confucian values of learning that strive for the acquisition of knowledge (Cortazzi & Jin, 1996; Hu, 2002; Li,

TABLE 4.2 *Selection of questionnaire results (2012/13 school year)*

No.	Question	M
	Section C (a): Speaking and listening lessons (CLT)	
14.	The goal of each lesson was clear	3.76
15.	I could speak a lot in class.	3.75
16.	I liked working with a partner.	3.85
17.	I liked working with a group.	3.86
19.	When I didn't understand, I asked my teacher for help.	3.59
21.	I have participated in CLT lessons at high school.	1.95
22.	I have participated in CLT lessons at other NGOs	2.13
23.	I liked the CLT lesson style.	3.95
	Section C (b): Writing lessons (TBLT)	
26.	I learned about paragraph writing for the first time at BEA.	3.80
27.	I liked the class activities.	3.85
31.	I understand how to write a paragraph.	3.45
32.	I want to learn more about writing.	3.98
33.	I liked the TBLT lesson style.	3.98
	Section C (c): Presentation lessons (TBLT)	
34.	I learned about task-based projects for the first time at BEA.	3.80
35.	Presentations are a good way to learn English.	3.94
36.	I liked to be the group leader.	3.10
40.	I liked the TBLT lesson style.	3.74
43.	I have more confidence in speaking in front of a group now.	3.86
44.	I want to learn more about presentations.	3.98
	Section C (d): Journal writing exchange (TBLT)	
45.	I wrote a journal in English for the first time at BEA.	3.75
46.	I liked writing in my journal every week.	3.85
48.	I liked my writing partner.	3.67
50.	My partner made enough comments about my writing.	3.52
52.	I can now write more quickly in English.	3.66
	Section D: Teaching	
64.	The teacher is knowledgeable about English.	3.94
68.	The teacher answers my questions.	3.92
69.	I like the teacher's teaching style (as a facilitator)	3.92
70.	The lessons are interesting.	3.92
71.	The lessons are useful.	3.88

1998). In Cambodia, students consider their teachers to be authority figures and enlightened scholars, and teachers view their learners as recipients of their knowledge for literary rather than practical purposes. Teacher-centred lessons are the result of this cultural value towards education. However, this is an overgeneralization that does not take into consideration diversity among students and classrooms (McKay, 2002). Moreover, such oversimplifications stereotype Cambodian students as passive, silent and obedient. These features were not evident among the learners of this study even though they had never participated in English language lessons that used communicative approaches (Table 4.2, Section C, statements 21, 22, 26, 34 and 45). In the TBLT presentations projects, well over half of the students enjoyed leading their groups (Table 4.2, Section C, statement 36). In CLT speaking and listening lessons, students were pro-active when it came to asking their teachers for help when they did not understand (Table 4.2, Section C, statement 19); and believed that they could make substantial contributions during lessons (Table 4.2, Section C, statement 15). Such preferences for student-centred learning can also be found in Chung and Huang's (2009) research on Taiwanese high school students' positive attitudes towards CLT and Hood, Elwood and Falout's (2009) study on preferences for learner-centeredness among Japanese university students towards TBLT. Indeed, this integrated programme was unique to the majority of the study's Cambodian learners, but they were open and eager to the CLT-TBLT approaches, and thrived in a communicative environment that gave them opportunities to practice and use language in a meaningful way.

The other notable finding was that learners believed their skills improved because of this integrated programme. Almost all students reported improvement in the four skills, as well as their confidence in using English (Table 4.3, Section E, statements 72–77). They attributed this progress to the CLT and TBLT lessons styles of the integrated programme (Table 4.3, Section E, statement 78). One student points out how TBLT was especially effective in improving oral communication: 'The programmes include all skills that can improve my English. I can speak English better than before. The [presentation] task-based projects were the best to improve my speaking and they made me more confident to speak in front of a group.' Another student calls attention to the overall changes in her language learning abilities: 'I do love [the school's] programmes and I have changed because of them ... My English has improved a lot, especially my speaking and writing skills. [This programme] has transformed me into a better English learner.'

These learners' claims about the effectiveness of CLT go against Skehan's (1998) belief that CLT's PPP model has become 'out of fashion' (p. 94). DeKeyser (1998) believes that the effectiveness of PPP has not been fully tested and it is premature to dismiss the approach from classrooms. This is especially true in Cambodia's situation

TABLE 4.3 *Selection of questionnaire results (2012/13 school year)*

No.	Question	M
	Section E: Your improvement	
72.	I made progress in my speaking.	3.82
73.	I made progress in my listening.	3.72
74.	I made progress in my reading.	3.76
75.	I made progress in my writing.	3.78
77.	I have more confidence in English.	3.88
78.	The programs and lesson styles helped me to make progress in my English.	3.96

since it is still playing 'catch up' with the rest of Southeast Asia when it comes to teaching approaches, training and resources due to limited government funding for public education and budgetary constraints of local NGO schools. In most cases, this school's students have had English taught through the grammar translation in public schools, and consequently equate language learning with grammar (Toun, personal communication, 27 July 2012). In this integrated programme, PPP allows the teachers to focus on a specific form, which fulfils the students' expectations of learning 'grammar' in their lesson. This grammar component is necessary to launch second language acquisition (Schmidt, 1994). It especially gave the organization's novice learners the 'building blocks' to reach a level of communicative ability to handle TBLT lessons that did not necessarily teach specific forms. In addition, the programme's TBLT 'unfocused' tasks gave students opportunities to use the language in 'general communicatively' (Ellis, 2009, p. 223). The programme embodies Carless's (2009) claim that PPP does not have to be cast aside if it can be combined with TBLT to offset its limitations. Essentially, an integrated programme allows learners opportunities for grammar instruction and meaningful communication.

Challenges and possibilities

Implementing similar programmes in the non-formal education section will prove challenging due to few available training opportunities, especially since few NGO schools have the budget to pay for training from private companies. Instead, training often comes in the form of volunteers on short-term placements, with many not experienced enough to carry out TESOL training or with no teaching credentials at all (Takeda, 2001). One of the reasons for the learners' favourable impressions to the CLT-TBLT programme could be attributed to the capabilities of the two teachers in this programme, and the in-service training they received before the start of their courses, as well as ongoing professional development opportunities from the author. In interviews with the teachers, both believed they were prepared to take on the programme. The head teacher indicated that 'team-teaching and observing other teachers were useful to prepare for teaching CLT and TBLT' (Toun, personal communication, 27 January 2014) while the other instructor emphasized that observing the head teacher and author were the most beneficial because she could 'see' these methods in action and how they can be used to make learning 'interesting' (Sou, personal communication, 27 January 2014). In addition, both teachers considered the programme beneficial for their students. The head teacher exclaimed:

> I freaked out in the beginning because I thought it would be impossible for students to learn with these methods. However, I saw how much the students enjoyed learning and gained from the programme. I myself really enjoyed teaching and learning through this programme.
> (Toun, personal communication, 27 January 2014)

He further asserted that 'all the students get to know each other closer though the programme. They feel comfortable and confident to communicate inside and outside the classroom' (Toun, personal communication, 27 January 2014). This echoes Sano,

Takahashi and Yoneyama's (1984) claim that 'warm-hearted interactions ... among learners themselves is the most essential factor in successful language learning' (p. 171). The other teacher added that '[these approaches] give students more time to speak English rather than just listening to a teacher who keeps talking and talking' (Sou, personal communication, 27 January 2014). Sufficient and ongoing training is therefore essential to make sure non-native English-speaking teachers have the sociocultural and strategic abilities to use both CLT and TBLT.

Despite the funding restraints on most Cambodian NGO schools, there are a few options available to help local English language NGO schools, especially in Siem Reap, with their teaching approaches. One of these options is to develop a 'community of teachers and learners' – a forum for Cambodian NGO teachers to exchange their views on their teaching approaches, challenges in their teaching context, resource development, among a myriad of other sociocultural-economic issues affecting NGO education. The author's school already holds monthly student forums in the form of personal development workshops with its own students. The head teacher and staff organize students in groups of five to discuss designated themes over two hours, and then the leaders of those groups report their conclusions to the entire group. Along these lines, the author's school could host similar workshops for Cambodian teachers working at other organizations once or twice a month. In conjunction with this forum, a website could be set up to allow these teachers to share ideas and resources, as well as to provide them access to EFL sites specifically for non-native English-speaking teachers and learners. Since many NGO teachers have little access to resources, training and professional development this could be a small step towards learning about the circumstances at other schools and working together to bring about more effective English language teaching in the non-formal education sector.

Once there is a 'community of teachers and learners', it would then be possible to gauge how many of these teachers and their respective organizations would be interested in training in CLT and TBLT approaches. These teachers could then join the author's one-month training programme that she offers annually to the students at her organization who are interested in teaching careers. Since the school has accreditation from the MOEYS, the training certificates would be valid – at least in the NGO sector. Moreover, since there are no fees for this programme, it would be a much more affordable option for these teachers who do not have the financial means to pay for training from private companies. However, the crux of professional development will be how to provide ongoing support to transition from teacher-centred, grammar-based lessons to CLT and perhaps later to programmes with TBLT components. Flexibility, ingenuity, and funding, to say the least, will be crucial to deal with such transformations in the non-formal school sector.

Although CLT and TBLT have yet to make inroads into public school classrooms, this study shows that it is possible to combine CLT, specifically PPP, with the stronger version of TBLT and use at a small-sized NGO school, which many Cambodian youths get their English language skills. There is indeed a receptiveness and readiness among Cambodian learners for these approaches. As the school's head teacher observed: 'CLT and TBLT have built such a strong relationship among students, as well as among teachers. After one year, the students not only became better speakers, but confident and independent learners' (Toun, personal communication,

27 January 2014). Despite this success in such a challenging teaching and learning context, implementing CLT and/or TBLT in Cambodia's NGO schools will be like the rural roads surrounding these schools – bumpy, unpredictable and sometimes impassable.

References

Brown, H. D. (2001). *Teaching by principles: An interactive approach to language pedagogy.* Upper Saddle River, NJ: Prentice Hall Regents.

Brown, D. H. (2007). *Teaching by principles: An interactive approach to language pedagogy* (3rd ed.). New York: Pearson Education.

Butler, Y. G. (2011). The implementation of communication and task-based language teaching in the Asia-Pacific region. *Review of Applied Linguistics, 31,* 36–57.

Carless, D. (2009). Revisiting the TBLT versus PPP debate: Voices from Hong Kong. *Asian Journal of English Language Teaching, 19,* 49–66.

Chung, I. F., & Huang, Y. C. (2009). The implementation of communicative language teaching: An investigation of students' viewpoints. *The Asia-Pacific Education Researcher, 18,* 67–78.

Clayton, T. (2006). *Language choice in a nation under transition: English language spread in Cambodia.* New York: Springer.

Cortazzi, M., & Jin, L. (1996). Cultures of learning: Language classrooms in China. In H. Coleman (Ed.), *Society and the language classroom* (pp. 169–206). Cambridge, UK: Cambridge University Press.

Dawson, W. (2011). Supplementary education in Cambodia. *The Newsletter, 56,* 18–19. Retrieved http://www.iias.nl/the-newsletter/article/supplementary- education-cambodia

DeKeyser, R. (1998). Beyond focus on form: Cognitive perspectives on learning and practicing second language grammar. In C. Doughty & J. Williams (Eds), *Focus on form in classroom second language acquisition* (pp. 42–63). Cambridge: Cambridge University Press.

Ellis, R. (2009). Task-based language teaching: Sorting out the misunderstandings. *International Journal of Applied Linguistics, 19*(3), 221–246.

Holliday, A. (1997). The politics of participation in international English language education. *System, 25,* 409–423.

Hood, M., Elwood, J., & Falout, J. (2009). Student attitudes toward task-based language teaching at Japanese universities. *Asian Journal of English Language Teaching, 19,* 49–66.

Hu, G. (2002). Potential cultural resistance to pedagogical imports: The case of communicative language teaching in China. *Language, Culture and Curriculum, 15,* 93–105.

Klapper, J. (2003). Taking communication to task? A critical review of recent trends in language teaching. *Language Learning Journal, 27,* 33–42.

Kumaravadivelu, B. (2006). *Understanding language teaching: From method to post-method.* Mahwah, NJ: Lawrence Erlbaum Associates.

Larsen-Freeman, D. & Anderson, M. (2000). *Techniques & principles in language teaching.* Oxford: Oxford University Press.

Li, D. (1998). It's always more difficult than you planned: Teachers' perceived difficulties in introducing the communicative approach in South Korea. *TESOL Quarterly, 32,* 677–703.

McKay, S. L. (2002). *Teaching English as an international language.* Oxford, UK: Oxford University Press.

Molinsky, S. J., & Bliss, B. (2003). *Side by side international edition, student book 1*. White Plains, NY: Pearson Education.

Ravallion, M., Chen, S., & Sangraula, P. (2009). Dollar a day revisited. *World Bank Economic Review, 23*(2), 163–184.

Richards, J., & Rodgers, T. (2001). *Approaches and methods in language teaching*. Cambridge: Cambridge University Press.

Sano, M., Takahashi, M., & Yoneyama, A. (1984). Communicative language teaching and local needs. *English Language Teaching Journal, 38*(3), 170–177.

Schmidt, R. (1994). Deconstructing consciousness in search of useful definitions for applied linguistics. *AILA Review, 11*, 11–26.

Skehan, P. (1998). *A cognitive approach to language learning*. Oxford: Oxford University Press.

Skehan, P. (2003). Task-based instruction. *Language Teaching, 36*, 1–14.

Sou, S. (2014, Jan. 27). Personal communication.

Sullivan, P. N. (2000). Playfulness as mediation in communicative language teaching in a Vietnamese classroom. In J. P. Lantolf (Ed.), *Sociocultural theory and second language learning* (pp. 115–131). Oxford, UK: Oxford University Press.

Takeda, N. (2012, Feb. 5). Good intentions: Volunteer work in developing countries. *Truman Factor*. Retrieved http://trumanfactor.com/2012/volunteer-work-in-developing-countries-7625.html

Toun, S. (2012, July 27). Personal communication.

Toun, S. (2014, Jan. 27). Personal communication.

United Nations Economic and Social Commission for Asia and Pacific (UNESCAP) (2011). Statistical yearbook for Asia and the Pacific 2011. Retrieved http://www.unescap.org/stat/data/syb2011/I-People/I.27-Primary-secondary-tertiary-education.pdf

Van den Branden, K. (Ed.) (2006). *Task-based language education: From theory to practice*. Cambridge: Cambridge University Press.

Widyono, B. (2008). *Dancing in shadows: Sihanouk, the Khmer Rouge, and the United Nations in Cambodia*. Lanhan, MD: Rowman & Littlefield Publishers.

Willis, J. (1996). *A framework for task-based learning*. Harlow: Addison Wesley Longman.

Zsombor, P., & Hul, R. (2013, Oct. 29). Education to receive 20% boost in 2014 budget. *Cambodia Daily*. Retrieved http://www.cambodiadaily.com/archives/education- to-receive-20-boost-in-2014-budget-46127

PART TWO

Focusing on the learner

Introduction

Phil Benson

Historically, task-based language teaching (TBLT) has its origins among a number of innovative approaches to language teaching and learning that energized the field through the 1970s and 1980s. These include communicative language teaching, the process and negotiated syllabus, collaborative and experiential learning, and various initiatives related to learner-centredness, autonomy and learner development. The title of Tarone and George's (1989) book, *Focus on the language learner*, identified the common factor in these approaches. The book itself argued for an eclectic approach to second language teaching based on identifying and attempting to meet the varied needs and interests of learners. At the time, 'focus on the learner' was a radical idea for a field that had for many years been dominated by the idea that discovering the right 'method' of language teaching, often understood as the right way to sequence and present language content in the classroom, was the key to effective language learning.

It is worth noting at this point in time, however, that there is no necessary connection between TBLT and a focus on the learner in teaching. Tasks may be determined by learners, proposed by teachers on the basis of their assessment of the learners, or simply imposed without regard for the needs and interests of the learners. The connection is, instead, historical, a matter of the connections that were made by researchers and practitioners at a particular moment in time. Nunan (1989), for example, was interested in 'designing tasks for the communicative classroom'. A year earlier, he had outlined a model for curriculum negotiation, that he called 'the learner-centered curriculum' (Nunan, 1988). Breen (1987), similarly, was pursuing his interest in the idea of 'task' in conjunction with interests in communicative teaching, the process syllabus and autonomy. In this context, 'task' had a clear, if disputed, role to play. It described what learners would do in a broadly communicative, learner-centred, negotiated, autonomous curriculum. They would not, at least in the stronger forms of this curriculum, spend their time analysing and memorizing grammar and vocabulary outside any meaningful context of communication. They would, instead, learn the target language by using it and, in an ideal world, by using it to carry out tasks that had real relevance to their needs and interests.

Arguably, TBLT only makes sense in the context of a learner-focused curriculum. Yet because there is no necessary connection between the two, it can and has become divorced from this context. In their discussion of the fate of communicative language teaching, Allwright and Hanks (2009, pp. 46–49) talk about the commercialization of language teaching and the 'packaging' of new ideas as 'methods' enshrined in textbooks. Something similar has clearly happened to TBLT, which began life as the radical new idea of 'task' and has now become an acknowledged method of teaching that is acronymized and embedded in language curricula and textbooks around the world. In Asian English language teaching, moreover, TBLT is viewed, somewhat ambivalently, as an imported method, imposed from the top-down by an alliance of government agencies and overseas experts. There is also a considerable literature that discusses how and why teachers who are supposed to be practising TBLT depart from what TBLT is supposed to be. This literature often targets Asian non-native-speaker teachers, although, as Plews and Zhao (2010, p. 41) have shown, native-speaker teachers are equally capable of 'adapting TBLT in ways that are inconsistent with its principles'.

In this context, however, it is difficult to say exactly what the 'principles' of TBLT are. In the process of its packaging as a method, much that was productively left open in the idea of 'task' has been closed down, such that it now seems possible to judge whether a teacher is implementing TBLT correctly or not. The principles of TBLT are often articulated in lists of criteria that define what a 'task' is and is not, yet such lists can also be misleading if they are interpreted as a set of rules for good teaching. It is in this light, I think, that the idea of 'focus on learner' becomes important. In its historical context, the idea of 'task' signalled a shift in focus in a field that had for many decades equated 'learning' with 'being taught'. What had mattered previously was what and how the learners were taught; what mattered now were the 'tasks' that learners engaged in – what and how they learned. To pay attention to 'task', therefore, is to shift attention away from what the teacher is doing towards what the learners do. Teachers who are unfamiliar with this way of thinking might legitimately ask what and how they should 'teach' when they are engaged in TBLT. A reasonable answer might be that they should teach in the way they feel most comfortable, without worrying to much whether their teaching is consistent with TBLT or not. But as a first step toward TBLT, they might stop and think about their classrooms from the angle of what their students are doing while they are teaching in this way. What tasks are they engaged in and what can they, as teachers, do to make this engagement productive?

In the light of these comments, the four chapters that follow weave fascinating paths through the complex web of Asian TBLT. Viet, Canh and Barnard's contribution is situated in the Vietnamese secondary school system, where TBLT has been implemented through a series of textbooks that are 'claimed to be task-based'. Their case studies indicate that although the teachers have experience of using 'task-based' materials for several years, their beliefs and practices tend to diverge from TBLT principles described in the literature. Zhang's contribution, situated in primary education in China, also refers to TBLT as a 'top-down national English curriculum innovation' and case studies again show that teachers had 'a partial understanding of TBLT'; two of the teachers in this study seldom used tasks while the third teacher 'taught with a medium to strong form of TBLT'.

The question that these chapters raise, of course, is whether the 'problems' of implementing TBLT in Asian school systems lie in TBLT or the teachers, or whether they lie in the top-down nature of the innovation. Interestingly, Viet, Canh and Barnard comment that none of the lessons they observed were 'learner-centred – a key tenet of TBLT'. Yet this is, perhaps, understandable if the teachers are focused, not on the learners, but on the TBLT curriculum as it is articulated in the textbooks. As an alternative to top-down imposition of TBLT, they make the valuable suggestion of school-based professional development in which teachers can see TBLT modelled and experiment with it in a supportive environment.

The third and fourth contributions move out of the school sector into tertiary and teacher education. Blackstone and Jaidev describe a task-based professional English course for second-year undergraduates in Singapore that is based on 'position search'. The students help each other to craft effective resumes and cover letters and participate in role-plays as interviewers and interviewees during mock interviews. Blackstone and Jaidev's account of the course illustrates how an effective task-based approach can be built on tasks that focus on students' real-world needs. Lewis discusses a series of teachers' workshops and her account begins from a distinction between 'teaching by telling' or 'teaching by asking', which to my mind gets to the heart of the question of tasks and focus on the learner. Teaching by asking engages learners in the task of 'discovery' and Lewis describes how discovery tasks were blended with direct teaching in an effective model for the workshop. Returning to the theme of the first two chapters in this section, she also shows how this blend was intended to model what the teachers could do in their own classrooms.

The four chapters that follow, then, raise a number of interesting questions that readers might ponder as they read. How central is the idea of 'focus on the learner' in the various approaches to and interpretations of TBLT that are described? What problems arise when TBLT is imposed from above (as it is in the first two chapters) and how important is it that the TBLT initiative comes from the teachers themselves (as it does in the last two chapters)? Lastly, how important is the context? Are the evident difficulties of the teachers who participated in the first two studies products of the primary and secondary systems that they work in? Are the author/teachers of the last two chapters more able to implement TBLT effectively because they work in systems for adult learners that allow teachers more freedom to design tasks that correspond to their students' needs and interests?

References

Allwright, D., & Hanks, J. (2009). *The developing language learner: An introduction to exploratory practice*. Basingstoke: Palgrave Macmillan.

Breen, M. P. (1987). Learner contributions to task design. In C. Candlin & D. Murphy (Eds), *Language learning tasks*. Englewood Cliffs, NJ: Prentice-Hall.

Nunan, D. (1988). *The learner-centred curriculum: A study in second language teaching*. Cambridge: Cambridge University Press.

Nunan, D. (1989). *Designing tasks for the communicative classroom*. Cambridge: Cambridge University Press.

Plews, J. L., & Zhao, K. (2010). Tinkering with tasks knows no bounds: ESL teachers' adaptations of task-based language-teaching. *TESL Canada Journal, 28*(1), 41–59.

Tarone, E., & George, Y. 1989. *Focus on the language learner: Approaches to identifying and meeting the needs of second language learners*. Oxford: Oxford University Press.

5

'Old Wine in New Bottles':

Two Case Studies of Task-Based Language Teaching in Vietnam

Nguyen Gia Viet
Le Van Canh
Roger Barnard

Summary

This chapter presents findings from two case studies carried out in similar settings in Vietnam, where Task-Based Language Teaching (TBLT) has recently been introduced. Both studies, which employed qualitative multi-methods for data collection, and grounded theory for data analysis, investigated the extent of readiness of a group of Vietnamese teachers for TBLT by exploring their beliefs and practices. The findings indicate that although participant teachers have experienced 'task-based' materials for several years, their beliefs and practices were, to a great extent, divergent from TBLT principles described in the literature. Two major themes are presented in this chapter: *teachers' understanding of tasks*, and *teachers' classroom practices*, which allow discussion of what teachers believe, know and do, in relation to TBLT application in their particular contexts. The chapter concludes with some implications for policymaking and for teachers' professional development in Vietnam and relatable contexts.

Introduction

Although TBLT has emerged as a central feature of curriculum guidelines within the Asia-Pacific region (Carless, 2003; Nunan, 2003), how this approach is actually implemented in the classroom by teachers who are accustomed to a conventional explicitly structure-based syllabus remains under-researched (Carless, 2003; McDonough & Chaikitmongkol, 2007). This chapter reports the results of two separate, but complementary, studies conducted in three Vietnamese high schools regarding teachers' reactions to and use of a recently-introduced textbook series which claims to be based on the principles of TBLT.

Definition of 'task'

Although 'task' has been defined differently in the literature (see Ellis, 2003; Van den Branden, Bygate & Norris, 2009), there seems to be a general agreement that a task is an activity in which:

- meaning is primary
- there is some communication problem to solve
- there is some sort of relationship to comparable real-world activities
- task completion has some priority
- the assessment of the task is in terms of outcome.

(Skehan, 1998)

A fundamental question emerging from the aforementioned definition concerns the treatment of grammar. Advocates of a 'strong' view of TBLT (e.g., Long & Norris, 2000; Long & Robinson, 1998) have argued that a task provides an ideal medium for implementing 'focus on form', by which they mean the transitory treatment of grammatical issues as they arise incidentally within communicative activities. Grammar can also be approached through two types of tasks: *consciousness-raising tasks* and *focused communicative tasks* (Ellis, 2001, p. 21). Tasks of the first type are designed to invite students to make hypotheses about grammar rules from texts containing the target form, while tasks of the second type encourage students to produce the target form during their performance of a given communicative task.

However, other authors argue that an explicit focus on grammar should not necessarily be excluded from TBLT. For example, Skehan (1996) considers a 'weak' version of TBLT to be compatible with the Presentation-Practice-Production model (PPP), where the production phase adopts communicative tasks following an explicit focus on one or more grammatical forms. In Nunan's (2006) view, meaning and form are highly interrelated in TBLT, and grammar exists to enable the language user to express different communicative meanings. In his earlier proposal concerning the sequencing of a staged approach to a TBLT unit of work, the second step is 'to provide students with controlled practice in using the target language vocabulary, structures and functions' (Nunan, 2004, p. 31). In this way, the prior practice of the target language acts as a scaffold for the subsequent task. By contrast, Willis and Willis (2001, p. 25) have 'argued the case against focusing on specific forms before learners engage with a task [but] there are good arguments for studying specified forms at the end of a task sequence'. This theoretical difference motivated the two studies reported in this chapter to focus on where and how forms were addressed in the implementation of a TBLT curriculum in the two Vietnamese contexts.

Implementation of TBLT

In Asia, the implementation of TBLT is considered challenging (Adams & Newton, 2009). Several empirical studies have reported contextual constraints such as: teachers' concerns about their own and their students' English proficiency; students' strong preference for learning grammar; their unwillingness to communicate in the target language; and the backwash effect of standardized examinations (Carless, 2003, 2004; Carless & Gordon, 1997; Deng & Carless, 2009; Ellis, 2003; Tsui, 1996). However, there have been a few success stories (e.g., Finch, 2001; McDonough & Chaikitmongkol, 2007) about institution-initiated projects.

Regrettably, success stories remain rare, thus more classroom-based research is needed to gain further understanding of how teachers handle tasks in the classroom (Bygate, 2005). As an attempt to make a modest contribution to the professional knowledge of how TBLT is implemented, we undertook two separate studies which aimed to answer the following research questions:

1   How do Vietnamese high school teachers understand TBLT?
2   How is such understanding transferred into teachers' classroom practices?

Context of the studies

In an attempt to improve the quality of English language learning and teaching at secondary and high schools, a new English language curriculum has been enacted since 2000. The new curriculum, mandated by the Ministry of Education and Training, is:

> ... based on two popular language teaching approaches in the world: the learner-centred approach and the communicative approach, in which TBLT is the principal methodology. . . . learners are encouraged to engage in pairwork and groupwork, to be willing to carry out the tasks under teachers' support and supervision.
> (Hoang, Hoang, Do, Nguyen & Nguyen, 2006, p. 12)

The curriculum is operationalized through a series of textbooks written by Vietnamese scholars and was institutionalized in 2006 following a five-year-long piloting and subsequent revision. There is one volume for each grade, and each volume consists of sixteen units to be delivered within a period of thirty-five weeks. Every unit comprises five lessons, based on a topic or theme, each of which consists of a number of tasks which are intended to be covered in forty-five minutes. The four skills lessons are – in this order – Reading, Speaking, Listening, and Writing, and these are followed by a lesson called Language Focus, which is intended to allow learners to consolidate the linguistic forms such as language structures, vocabulary and pronunciation covered in the skills lessons. On the surface, this sequence approximates to the task cycle proposed by Willis (1996; Willis & Willis, 2001), rather than to Nunan's (2004) sequence.

The two studies reported in this chapter investigated how teachers understand TBLT, and how such understanding is reflected in their classroom teaching. These two studies are complementary in the sense that the first study concentrates on teachers' understanding and implementation of 'tasks' while the second one focuses on their understanding and practice regarding the role of grammar within the new curriculum using the mandated textbooks. Both studies employed a qualitative multi-method approach to data collection (Denzin & Lincoln, 2000) and grounded analysis procedures (Charmaz, 2006) to facilitate interpretation of the findings.

Eleven teachers (ten female and one male aged 28–36) from two high schools in a suburban area in Central Vietnam participated in the first study. The teachers had Bachelor degrees in English as a Foreign Language (EFL) and all had been using the textbooks for at least three years.

A range of data collection procedures were employed in this first study. Each participant teacher completed a set of three narrative frames (Barkhuizen & Wette, 2008), which elicited their beliefs about teaching and short narratives of recent lessons (Barnard & Nguyen, 2010). Subsequently, two lesson planning sessions (LPS) were audio-recorded of each group of teachers working at the same level in their school, resulting in eight LPS being recorded from four groups of teachers. Following these LPS, two lessons by each teacher were observed, and each lesson was followed by a stimulated recall session. As a result, twenty-two lessons were video-recorded, along with twenty-two stimulated recall sessions. Finally, two school-based focus group sessions were held with five teachers from school A and six teachers from school B participating.

The second study is an intrinsic case study (Stake, 2000), intended to illuminate the beliefs and practices of eight EFL teachers of English working in a high school in a provincial city in the north of Vietnam. Their teaching experience ranged from three years to twenty-three years, with an average of 14.5 years. These teachers were interviewed about their understanding about grammar instruction with reference to TBLT, then each of them was observed teaching three lessons (all of which were video-recorded); each of these was immediately followed by a stimulated recall session.

Findings[1]

Teachers' understandings of tasks

Data from the first study revealed that these teachers had limited understandings of tasks as described in the TBLT literature. Some teachers tried to avoid answering such questions as 'what is your understanding of a task?' and many others were not willing to probe or problematize their understanding of a task. The extract below is from a focus group session:

01	R:	As you see in your textbook, every lesson contains tasks. What is your understanding of a task?
02	Thanh:	Just a name.
03	R:	What do you mean?
04	Thanh:	Like an activity – something students have to do in class.

05	Tho:	Like an activity. Yeah.
06	R:	<turns to Quy> What do you think, Quy?
07	Quy:	<shakes head>
08	R:	Does a task necessarily include grammar learning?
09	Thanh:	No. Tasks are not for grammar. Like, you see, in Language Focus lesson, we don't have tasks – we have exercises. I think tasks are for skills.
10	R:	Uh huh . . .
11	Binh:	But I think grammar is important for tasks. I mean, we need to provide students with grammar to support them in tasks.
12	Linh:	I think so too.

Thanh's understanding that tasks were not purely focused on grammar simply arose because in the textbook all skills components are followed up by 'tasks' while in the *Language Focus* Section, the activities are labelled as 'exercises'. This led to her conception of a 'task' as confined to the skills lessons as opposed to 'exercise' in the grammar lessons. Later in the same focus group, this teacher further exemplified her understanding by referring to a task in the textbook which required the students to read and identify which of the given statements are true and which are false according to the information in the text. Thanh thought it was a good task because 'it forces students to read to find out which statements are wrong. They have to read to find out'. At the same time Binh stated that answering multiple-choice questions was a good reading comprehension task. For her, 'if students can answer these questions, they will understand the text'. Giang, in a stimulated recall session, gave the following rationale for providing students with a matching activity of words occurring in a reading text with Vietnamese translations:

> They would understand the meanings of the words in more depth. Personally I think the most important thing in this type of task [reading] is that students would be able to read, understand and answer the questions without any difficulty; we need to prepare them carefully with any new words. So I think reading should also include students' preparation at home. This activity [matching] can serve as a checking activity, to check whether they had prepared at home or not.

As for the speaking lessons, most of the tasks in the textbook require the students to use particular structures or expressions provided in the textbook to produce similar utterances. In the same focus group session as above, Thanh and Binh stated that if the task did not provide a model, it would be 'difficult', by which, echoing Giang above, they meant tasks which require students to be more responsible for their task performance, and which do not provide students with language support (e.g., structures and vocabulary) prior to performance. My, another teacher, provided a rationale for a model in a stimulated recall session for a speaking task:

> My: I just wanted them [students] to use the model because this would make it easier for them. They could use them because they were there.
>
> R: Was there a requirement to use any specific grammar structures in the lesson?

My: Yes, there was. For example, in Task 2, they had to use 'may'. This was sort of basic requirement, which asked them to use this to agree or to disagree. Just kind of giving opinions. At first, I had intended to get the students to respond to what others say. Like this: one student gives an opinion, another tries to give a counter-argument. This is a bit of a higher level, which they will have in Year Eleven. In this lesson, they were talking about the new kind of zoo, so they didn't have to debate. I had thought about it [debate], but then I realized that it was too much, too difficult for students.

Apparently, these teachers favoured tasks that were more form-focused, scaffolded by models or/and provided with the language structures which are expected to be used during task performance.

Regarding when a focus on forms should occur, all the teachers in the first study believed that grammar and vocabulary should be taught before skills can be developed. Phuong, for example, wrote in her narrative frame that 'students need to memorize grammar rules, because these will help them to speak and write correctly, and even in listening, they need grammar rules to make sense of texts' and 'the most important thing in learning on the part of students is to master the basic of knowledge and then develop the skills'. Lac reported in his narrative frame that his students were unable to 'apply theory [rules] into practice'. For these teachers, language learning should start with basic knowledge of language rules, then communication skills should be built up on that basis. Thanh said in a stimulated recall session:

We must provide them with those [structures]. Even the structures were there in the book, if we don't tell them explicitly, they won't understand. I don't believe that they will be able to use structures that have not been taught to them. If you want students to express their ideas successfully in speaking and writing, they should be provided with relevant structures.

It can be interpreted that the teachers in the first study held strong views of grammar as the prerequisite for tasks to be performed successfully. Also, they believed that an explicit focus on forms should occur before the communicative task, in the sense that the knowledge of forms is fundamental for task completion.

Such an understanding is further justified by how teachers in the second study described their understanding of the form-focused instruction in their interviews. For example, Nhai stated that it was important that the students memorize the explicit knowledge of the taught grammatical structure. She said:

I do believe that the students should know why people use the language the way they do. Without such [explicit] knowledge, they cannot understand what people mean. When I explain the rules explicitly I find that they [the students] understand [the rules].

Regarding the teachers' understandings of the role of grammar, Mai, the head of the English department, stated that:

> Grammar teaching is to form a solid foundation of linguistic knowledge. . . . If today you teach listening, tomorrow, writing, it has nothing to do with grammar, then it is impossible to achieve the goal, which is the use of language for real communication.

Hoa, the most experienced teacher in the department, believed that 'if students are just taught how to speak, to listen, to read and to write without being taught grammar, they cannot achieve accuracy.'

Echoing the importance of grammatical accuracy in task performance, Xuan claimed that:

> My view is conservative but the students first need to have a good knowledge of grammar so that they can apply that knowledge to speaking, listening, reading and writing. This is because supposing you want to make an utterance that you went to Hanoi yesterday, you cannot get the message across if you just know individual words such as 'go', yesterday', 'Hanoi' without knowing what the past tense is.

Lan was quite critical of the new textbook because, in her opinion, it did not provide explicit information about the target grammar, which made the students confused:

> In the old syllabus, grammar was presented in isolation, item by item. When we finished teaching one item, the students applied it to their work. I find it easier. For example, when the students were taught 'to be,' they practised using it immediately. It was easier for them and therefore they used it in their own sentences more accurately. Now, with the new syllabus, which is communicative or something like that, the students are very confused, especially when using verbs. . . . They don't know why something has to be added to make 'to be' negative or why an auxiliary verb should be added to other verbs.

In a similar vein, Cuc complained about the difficulty of providing the students with comprehensible input so that they can internalize the target grammatical structure by working out the form–meaning relationship. She stated that:

> I think it would be more interesting to present the grammar through a text because it provides a situation for the students to understand not only the form, but also meaning and use. But it's really difficult to find such an appropriate text, so I tend to present grammar through isolated sentences.

Regarding the approach to grammar, Nhai described the way she taught grammar as follows:

> Usually, I first present the examples to introduce the grammar point to be taught in the lesson. The students will look at those examples on the board and deduce the rules before I explain and write the rules on board. Then I get the students to practise. Finally, the students are allowed free practise in which they produce their own sentence. At home, the students are requested to write a few sentences so that they can memorize the grammar item.

Mai described the shape of her grammar lesson as being composed of four steps: recognize, analyse, compare, and confirm (which are the original English words she used in the interviews). She clarified this procedure: the students were first provided with the target grammar point in sentences and they recognized the form and use of the grammar point, then they analysed its function(s). In the next step, the students compared the use of the grammar point in different situations. Finally, the teacher confirmed the form, the meaning and the use in order to establish the rules.

Teachers' classroom practices[2]

Observational data from five speaking lessons in the first study show that all the five teachers started the lesson by providing a language model as a pre-task activity. The teachers first wrote the model of conversational exchanges on the chalkboard. Then they asked the students to practise the model before putting them in pairs or groups for practise. This common instructional strategy is illustrated in the following excerpt. Minh was trying to give a model for a task which required students to find out what others in their group felt about a particular kind of film. As can be seen in reproduction of this lesson in Appendix 5.1, the textbook writers (Hoang et al., 2007a) suggested groupwork and an open discussion, and provided a list of kinds of films and relevant adjectives for describing films for students' reference, as well as the following model:

A: What do you think of horror films?
B: Oh, I find them really ***terrifying***.
C: I don't quite agree with you. I find them very ***interesting***.
(English 10, p.135, **bold** words are in the original)

Minh, however, gave a modified model for pairwork:

Excerpt 1

01	T	Task 2. Dialogue <writes on board and reads aloud> A: What kind of film do you like/want to see? B: I like love story films.
02	T	Love story film. *What kind of film is this?*
03	Ss	*Love story.*
04	T	Cartoon film, and so on
05	T	<continues to write> A: What do you think of love story film? B: I find them really interesting/moving ...
06	T	And so on. *That is, what do we think of the film? Is it interesting, exciting, or bad, ok?*

(Book 10, Unit 13)

After presenting the model and getting students to drill the model, Minh explicitly and at length explained the grammatical structure and its function:

Excerpt 2

01	T	*So, to give an opinion ... an opinion about a film or something what structure do you have?* <writes on board> *What do we have? Subject plus what?*
02	Ss	Find
03	T	*Plus somebody or what? Something. Plus what? Adjective. Ok? I find I find plus what? I find them really interesting or terrifying. Are violent, violent, moving and so on.*
04	T	<draws a frame around the structure>

(Book 10, Unit 13)

In the stimulated recall session afterwards, Minh confirmed her intention was to control the language that students were likely to use in her class, saying: 'I wanted them to use the structure "find something or somebody adjective" [find + something/somebody + adjective].'

A similar situation occurred in another speaking lesson in which students were expected to perform an opinion-based task. After presenting the model on the board, My started to elicit ideas from students before putting them in groups. This task first provided students with a short text with information about 'the new kind of zoo', followed by the core task which asked students to discuss the advantages and disadvantages of this zoo. Several cues were also given, including: 'the conditions the animals are in, the money spent on reconstructions of the animals' natural environment, the animals that people can visit, and the dangers that keepers may have' (English 10, p. 107).

Excerpt 3

01	T:	Yes. Er [name]?
02	S1:	Er, I think animals will may er feel happy.
03	T:	*Both 'will' and 'may'? No no no. Er, again.*
04	Ss:	*Again again again.*
05	S1:	I don't think animals will may feel happy.
06	T:	'Will may'? Not 'will may'.
07	Ss:	Will. Will.
08	T:	Will. I think use 'will'.
09	S1:	(xxx) ... feel happy.
10	T:	Again.
11	S2:	I don't think ...
12	S1:	I don't think er animals er will er will feel happy.
13	T:	Ah, yes. I don't think animals will feel happy. Yes.

(Book 10, Unit 10)

It can be seen from the above excerpt that prior to putting students in groups My was focusing her students' attention on the correct form, rather than the meaning. The student's (S1) original meaning (turn 02) was changed completely (turn 12) after several corrective feedback exchanges. At the end, the teacher seemed satisfied with the student producing the correct sentence; at the same time, she did not seem to notice the change in meaning.

Teachers in the second study also placed a strong emphasis on students' explicit knowledge of the target grammar structures. The following excerpt is from an observed Language Focus lesson in one of the mandated textbooks (Hoang et al., 2007b) in which the teacher was trying to help the students revise 'relative clauses' in English (see Appendix 5.2). After Xuan had finished a warm-up activity to begin the lesson, she handed the students a worksheet containing six pairs of simple sentences. She then called upon three students to go to the front and each had to combine two pairs of sentences into one relative clause on the board. Seven minutes later, after the three students had done their work, she called upon one student to stand up to identify the relative clause as well as the function of the relative pronoun in the sentences the students had written on the board.

Excerpt 4

01	T:	<reads aloud> The book which was published last week was written for children.
02	T:	What is the relative clause, Nga? <nominates one female student>
03	S1:	The relative clause is 'which was published last week'
04	T	functions as ...? The relative pronoun functions as ...?
05	S1:	The subject.
06	T:	Is sentence four OK? The sports game ... Does this clause need a comma?
07	Ss:	<in chorus> No.
08	T	A comma is not needed. Is this a proper noun?
09	Ss:	<in chorus> No.
10	T:	which was held ... What is the relative clause? The relative clause functions as ...?
11	Ss:	<in chorus> Object

(Book 11, Unit 11)

The rationale she gave for this kind of grammatical analysis was to refresh the students' knowledge about sentence elements, which she believed could facilitate their doing the exercises that followed.

However, Dao, another teacher, was trying to use a consciousness-raising activity while presenting the target grammar structure.

Excerpt 5

01	T:	So now we do exercise on page 119 [in the textbook]. Open your book page 119 and do exercise one. Complete the following sentences using the correct form of verbs <reads aloud the instruction in the textbook>. And certainly you have to use conditional sentences to complete these sentences. Pay attention to the form of the past participle, use the verb in the past participle. Change the form of the verb into past participle. You have to do this exercise in five minutes, so after five minutes you go to the board and write down your answers.
02	Ss:	<do the exercises silently with few working in pairs>

(Book 10, Unit 11)

In the stimulated recall interview after this lesson, the teacher explained the rationale of her practice as follows:

> The exercises in the textbook are for the students to practise the knowledge they have just been taught.... In my view, all the exercises in the textbook must be done. You cannot say that these exercises are easy and they should be replaced by other exercises. Nothing can guarantee that external exercises are better than those in the textbook.

The teachers also tried to create opportunities for interaction which focus on information exchange. However, this kind of communicative task tended to be very brief before the lesson finished. The following excerpt illustrates the activity Mai used in the last five minutes of her lesson about 'Question forms' after she had spent the preceding forty minutes eliciting and explaining the rules and meanings of some Wh-questions in English:

Excerpt 6

01 T: Now you work in groups. This group you write questions about the university you like to enter, this group you write questions about the place you like to visit. State exactly what university, what place, and this group you write as many questions as possible about the job you want to do. OK? Three minutes. Write down questions.
02 Ss: <Work in groups as they are told. They ask questions in the groups and one writes down the asked questions. Three minutes later, the teacher asks each student to read out their questions and the teacher herself answers the questions>.
03   <The bell goes>
04 T: Thank you very much for working hard.

(Book 12, Unit 9)

In her opinion, which Mai expressed in the stimulated recall session, this 'task' was to integrate skills work into a grammar lesson, and by dividing the students into two groups, she created an information gap for natural communication:

> I wanted to integrate writing skills into this lesson. It was impossible to have 'a serious writing work' in this lesson. This was to create an 'information gap', that is the students write down what they want to ask. This lesson is about question forms, so when the students are able to form a question, the lesson objective has been achieved.

Discussion

Although the two studies reported here were conducted in three different high schools in two locations, the findings were quite similar in that the teachers' understanding of TBLT was somewhat limited. For example, they viewed formal accuracy rather than meaning as the primary focus in language teaching, believing that the students needed an explicit knowledge of relevant grammatical features before they could communicate effectively. Although they emphasized task completion and task outcome, they understood these constructs as being the students' ability to complete manipulated grammar exercises and finishing what was prescribed in the textbook.

Unlike the task cycle proposed by Willis (1996), the teachers in these two studies believed that forms should be taught before communicative tasks are launched. In this respect, their beliefs and practices are inclined towards a synthetic view of language teaching in which forms are believed to accumulate before skills can be developed. As can be seen in the observed lessons, the teachers tried to tightly control how and what students should do in the task phase. However, such scaffolding attempts, unlike Nunan's (2004) proposal, were merely de-contextualized presentation of forms with the expectation that students would use the forms in the 'task' phase. None of the lessons observed in the two studies were learner-centred – a key tenet of TBLT.

As indicated in the findings of these two studies, there was little evidence of genuine classroom communication where students were encouraged to employ their language resources to complete meaning-based tasks, which constitutes an important feature of TBLT. In contrast, while interaction could be observed, especially in skills lessons in the first study, the interaction was interpreted as ample evidence of merely mechanical manipulation of the target language items.

As for grammar instruction, although some of the teachers made an attempt to apply some consciousness-raising techniques, most of the classroom time was devoted to the deductive transmission of sentences containing the target features. The teachers often presented the target grammatical structure explicitly, then asked the students to drill it before they were asked to produce sentences containing that structure. Teaching techniques such as *input flooding, input enhancement, implicit structure-based tasks* and *focused communicative tasks*, which are characteristic of TBLT (Ellis, 2003; Fotos, 2002) were never observed in the classroom.

Results from these studies also support the point raised by McDonough and Chaikitmongkol (2007) that the implementation of TBLT would be challenging where teachers were greatly concerned with the need to cover the prescribed syllabus and required to pay great attention to grammar-based examination requirements.

It can also be interpreted from the findings that the innovation had little impact on the participating teachers' beliefs. In other words, although the teachers had been using the new materials for some years, they still retained their traditional teaching approaches. In this sense, the role of textbooks as agents for change (Hutchinson & Torres, 1994) was not fulfilled.

Conclusion

The findings from these two case studies support what Van den Branden (2006) has elaborated that 'practice-based' and 'research-based' do not always go well together when it comes to implementing educational innovations (p. 16). They also support the point made by Adams and Newton (2009) concerning challenges of TBLT implementation that large-scale top-down innovations are not always realized in actual classroom practice in Asian contexts. It is then crucial to fully take into account contextual constraints and resources, as well as the existing beliefs and practices of the teachers. Given the evidence of successful TBLT implementation in other Asian contexts (e.g., Finch, 2001; McDonough & Chaikitmongkol, 2007), where such innovations were initiated from a bottom-up perspective along with constant support, it is important in Vietnam that similar perspectives should be adopted to allow teachers to explore constraints and potentials of proposed innovations and, with appropriate professional assistance, they will be able to move towards more effective teaching.

The teachers in both of these Vietnamese studies had a broad understanding of the principles of the PPP model of language teaching, and were seen to put into practice the first two of these phases. However, they had little time, or apparently expertise, in implementing the third phase where students should use the target structures in freer production activities. On the basis of building on what teachers already know and can do, it might be suggested that a way forward could be to enable teachers to incorporate the principles and procedures of tasks into the third phase. In this way, a construct of task-*supported* learning might be developed, perhaps as a waystage for a more fully-fledged task-*based* approach, if this is eventually considered appropriate.

Therefore, instead of being issued top-down with a new curriculum, teachers should have opportunities to participate in school-focused professional development programmes. These cyclical programmes would have distinct stages. In the first stage, Orientation, preferably ahead of meeting face-to-face, they could receive input through appropriate print, audio or visual media, in which innovatory ideas – such as potentially useful pedagogical tasks – are explained and exemplified. To facilitate their understanding of these ideas, these inputs should themselves be task-based, i.e., by requiring the teachers to *work with* the input, not merely receive it. The second stage, Activation, would occur when this initial orientation is followed up by school- or local centre-based meetings in which the teachers articulate their new understanding in structured discussions among themselves, facilitated by a local adviser. They would discuss in what ways these innovatory ideas could be incorporated into their current practices, building upon the opportunities that actually exist in their context, and also co-constructing possible solutions to existing constraints. The third stage, Application, would be when these teachers collaborate, perhaps with assistance from the local adviser, in creating tasks or task-like activities, based on adaptations of their textbooks, which could be inserted into the production phase of the PPP model. In the fourth stage, Piloting, they would trial these jointly-created tasks in their own lessons, and afterwards write brief reflective notes as to the extent to which they were able to put the ideas into practice. These notes would then be brought to the next face-to-face meeting, which they could discuss and evaluate with their colleagues. This could be done alongside new input, and so the professional development cycle would continue.

In such a way, teachers could be effectively scaffolded into new ways of teaching to enable them to take ownership of innovatory classroom procedures and materials. Thus empowered, they would feel confident to be knowledge-makers in pedagogical principles and practice, and not merely the consumers of other people's ideas.

Many imposed curricula assume that teachers – the executive decision-makers in the classroom – can easily accommodate their existing beliefs and practices to innovatory ideas. But any attempt to introduce a new curriculum without taking into account these factors is a recipe for what Holliday (1992) called 'tissue rejection'. Indeed, it is necessary for policymakers and curriculum designers to look before they leap.

Finally, by showing that teachers' beliefs and practices were far from the expectations of policymakers and theoretically-oriented researchers, the two studies presented here suggest that classroom-based research (Allwright, 1983) is essential, not only for such a TBLT innovation, but also for other aspects of language teaching. Classroom-based research should be primarily focused on unpacking teachers' understandings and beliefs that guide their implementation of the intended innovation (Borg, 2003, 2006; Karavas-Doukas, 1995; Li, 1998). Empirical information derived from such classroom-based research will help curriculum designers and teacher educators know better what teacher support is needed to facilitate the intended innovation.

Put another way, unless such research fully informs intended curricular reform, and the teachers' beliefs and practices are fully taken into account, the most likely result of actual implementation will be putting old wine in new bottles.

Appendix 5.1

A speaking lesson (English 10)

Unit 13, Speaking lesson, reproduced with permission

B. SPEAKING

Task 1. How much do you like each kind of film? Put a tick (✓) in the right column. Then compare your answer with a partner's.

Kind of film	Very much	Not very much	Not at all
Science fiction			
Cartoon			
Horror			
Detective			
Thriller			

Task 2. *Work in groups.* Find out what your friends feel about each kind of film. Use the words in the table below.

Example:

A: *What do you think of horror films?*
B: *Oh, I find them really **terrifying**.*

C: *I don't quite agree with you. I find them very **interesting**.*

Detective films	Interesting
Science fiction films	Moving
Love story films	Good fun
Cartoon films	Violent
War films	Boring
Thrillers	Exciting
Action films	Terrifying

Task 3. *Work with a partner.* Find out his/her preferences for films. Use the cues below.

Example:

A: Which do you prefer, detective films or science fiction films?

B: Well, it's difficult to say. But I suppose **I prefer science fiction films to detective ones.**

- Thrillers or science fiction films
- Horror films or detective films
- Love story films or cartoon films
- Cartoon films or science fiction films

Task 4. *Work in groups.* Talk about a film you have seen. Use the suggestions below.

1. Where did you see it?
2. What kind of film is it?
3. What is it about?
4. Who is/are the main character(s)?
5. How do you feel about it?
6. Why do you prefer it to other films?

Appendix 5.2

A Language Focus lesson (English 11)

Unit 11, Language Focus lesson, reproduced with permission

E. LANGUAGE FOCUS

- **Pronunciation:** /ʃr/ – /spl/ – /spr/
- **Grammar:** Relative clauses replaced by participles and *to* infinitives (revision)

Pronunciation

- Listen and repeat

/ʃr/	/spl/	/spr/
shred	splash	spring
shrill	split	spray
shrimp	spleen	spread
shrine	splutter	sprightly

- Practise reading aloud these sentences.
  1. They were all shrieking with laughter.
  2. He shrugged (his shoulders), saying he didn't know and didn't care.
  3. My dad hates shrimp paste.
  4. What a splendid spring day!
  5. The stream splits into three smaller streams at this point.
  6. The house has a narrow front, but it splays out at the back.

Grammar

Exercise 1. Rewrite the following sentences, using the present participial phrase.

Example:

The man who spoke to John is my brother.
The man speaking to John is my brother.

1. The boy who is playing the piano is Ben.
2. Do you know the woman who is coming toward us?
3. The people who are waiting for the bus in the rain are getting wet.
4. The scientists who are researching the causes of cancer are making progress.
5. The fence which surrounds our house is made of wood.
6. We have an apartment which overlooks the park.

Exercise 2. Rewrite the following sentences, using a past participial phrases.

Example:

The Sport Games which were held in India in 1951 were the first Asian Games.
The Sport Games held in India in 1951 were the first Asian Games.

1. The ideas which are presented in that book are interesting.
2. I come from a city that is located in the southern part of the country.
3. They live in a house that was built in 1890.
4. The photographs which were published in the newspaper were extraordinary.
5. The experiment which was conducted at the University of Chicago was successful.
6. They work in a hospital which was sponsored by the government.

Exercise 3. Rewrite the following sentences, using an infinitive phrase.

Example:

Yuri Gagarin was the first man who flew into space.
Yuri Gagarin was the first man to fly into space.

1. John was the last man who reached the top of the mountain.
2. The last person who leaves the room must turn off the light.
3. The first person that we must see is Mr. Smith.
4. This is the second person who was killed in that way.
5. The first person who catches the ball will be the winner.

Notes

1 All the data elicited from the participant teachers in both studies (narrative frames, lesson planning sessions, interviews, stimulated recall sessions and focus groups) were originally in Vietnamese. They were then translated into English by the researchers. All the personal names are pseudonyms.

2 In this chapter, the following transcript conventions are used for the classroom data:

01, 02:	speakers' turns
R:	researcher
T:	teacher
Ss:	students [chorus response]
S1, S2:	individual students
Italics:	translation of Vietnamese used in observed lessons
<...>:	observer's comments
(xxx):	inaudible speech

References

Adams, R., & Newton, J. (2009). TBLT in Asia: Constraints and opportunities. *Asian Journal of English Language Teaching, 19*, 1–17.

Allwright, D. (1983). Classroom-centered research on language teaching and learning: A brief historical overview. *TESOL Quarterly, 17*(2), 191–204.

Barkhuizen, G., & Wette, R. (2008). Narrative frames for investigating the experiences of language teachers. *System, 36*(3), 372–387.

Barnard, R., & Nguyen, G. V. (2010). Task-Based Language Teaching (TBLT): A Vietnamese case study using narrative frames to elicit teachers' beliefs. *Language Education in Asia, 1*, 77–86.

Borg, S. (2003). Teacher cognition in language teaching: A review of research on what language teachers think, know, believe, and do. *Language Teaching, 36*(2), 81–109.

Borg, S. (2006). *Teacher cognition and language education: Research and practice*. London, England: Continuum.

Bygate, M. (2005). Some issues in the relationship between teachers' use of tasks and research: The need for a classroom-based approach. Paper presented at the International Conference on Task-based Language Teaching, Leuven, Netherlands.

Carless, D. (2003). Factors in the implementation of task-based teaching in primary schools. *System, 31*(4), 485–500.

Carless, D. (2004). Issues in teachers' reinterpretation of a task-based innovation in primary schools. *TESOL Quarterly, 38*(4), 639–662.

Carless, D. & Gordon, A. (1997). Hong Kong primary teachers' perceptions of the difficulties in implementing task-based language teaching. *Journal of Basic Education, 7*(1), 139–160.

Charmaz, K. (2006). *Constructing grounded theory: A practical guide through qualitative analysis*. London, England: Sage.

Deng, C., & Carless, D. (2009). The communicativeness of activities in a task-based innovation in Guangdong, China. *Asian Journal of English Language Teaching, 19*, 113–134.

Denzin, N., Lincoln, Y. (2000). *Handbook of qualitative research* (2nd ed.). Thousand Oaks, CA: Sage.

Ellis, R. (2001). Investigating form-focused instruction. *Language Learning, 51*(Suppl.1), 1–46.

Ellis, R. (2003). *Task-based language teaching*. Oxford, England: Oxford University Press.

Finch, A. (2001). A formative evaluation of a task-based conversation English program. *The PAC Journal, 1*(1), 125–146.

Fotos, S. (2002). Structured-based interactive tasks for the EFL grammar learner. In E. Hinkel & S. Fotos (Eds), *New perspectives on grammar teaching in second language classrooms* (pp. 135–154). Mahwah, NJ: Erlbaum.

Holliday, A. R. (1992) Tissue rejection and informal orders in ELT projects: Collecting the right information. *Applied Linguistics, 13*(4), 404–424.

Hoang, V., Hoang, H. X., Do, M. T., Nguyen, P. T., & Nguyen, T. Q. (2006). *Tieng Anh 10: Sach giao vien [English 10: Teachers' book]*. Hanoi, Vietnam: Education Publishing House.

Hoang, V., Hoang, H. X., Do, M. T., Nguyen, P. T., & Nguyen, T. Q. (2007a). *Tieng Anh 10 [English 10]*. Hanoi, Vietnam: Education Publishing House.

Hoang, V., Hoang, H. X., Do, M. T., Nguyen, P. T., & Nguyen, T. Q. (2007b). *Tieng Anh 11 [English 11]*. Hanoi, Vietnam: Education Publishing House.

Hutchinson, T., & Torres, E. (1994). The textbook as agent of change. *ELT J, 48*(4), 315–328.

Karavas-Doukas, E. (1995). Teacher identified factors affecting the implementation of an EFL innovation in Greek public secondary schools. *Language, Culture and Curriculum*, 8(1), 53–68.

Li, D. (1998). 'It's always more difficult than you plan and imagine.' Teachers' perceived difficulties in introducing the communicative approach in South Korea. *TESOL Quarterly*, 32(4), 677–697.

Long, M., & Norris, J. (2000). Task-based teaching and assessment. In M. Byram (Ed.), *Encyclopedia of language teaching* (pp. 597–603). London, England: Routledge.

Long, H., & Robinson, P. (1998). Focus on form: Theory, research and practice. In C. Doughty, & J. Williams (Eds), *Focus on form in classroom second language acquisition* (pp. 15–41). Cambridge, England: Cambridge University Press.

McDonough, K., & Chaikitmongkol, W. (2007). Teachers' and learners' reactions to a task-based EFL course. *TESOL Quarterly*, 41(1), 107–132.

Nunan, D. (2003). The impact of English as a global language on educational policies and practices in the Asia-Pacific region. *TESOL Quarterly*, 27(4), 589–613.

Nunan, D. (2004). *Task-based language teaching*. Cambridge, England: Cambridge University Press.

Nunan, D. (2006). Task-based language teaching in the Asia context: Defining 'task'. *Asian EFL Journal*, 8(3), 12–18.

Skehan, P. (1996). A framework for the implementation of task-based instruction. *Applied Linguistics*, 17(1), 38–62.

Skehan, P. (1998). *A cognitive approach to language learning*. Oxford, England: Oxford University Press.

Stake, R. E. (2000). Case studies. In N. Denzin & Y. Lincoln (Eds), *Handbook of qualitative research* (2nd ed.) (pp. 435–454). Thousand Oaks, CA: Sage.

Tsui, A. (1996). Reticence and anxiety in second language learning. In K. Bailey & D. Nunan (Eds), *Voices from the language classroom* (pp. 145–167). Cambridge, England: Cambridge University Press.

Van den Branden, K. (2006). Introduction: Task-based language teaching in nutshell. In K. Van den Branden (Ed.), *Task-based language education: From theory to practice* (pp.1–16). New York, NY: Cambridge University Press.

Van den Branden, K., Bygate, M., & Norris, J. (Eds). (2009). *Task-based language teaching: A reader*. Amsterdam, The Netherlands: John Benjamins.

Willis, D., & Willis, J. (2001). Task-based language learning. In R. Carter & D. Nunan (Eds), *The Cambridge guide to teaching English to speakers of other languages* (pp. 173–179). Cambridge, England: Cambridge University Press.

Willis, J. (1996). *A framework for task-based learning*. Harlow, England: Longman.

6

Task-Based Language Teaching in the Primary Schools of South China

Yuefeng Zhang

Summary

1n 2001, task-based language teaching (TBLT) was adopted as the main pedagogy in the top-down national English curriculum innovation in mainland China to replace the prevailing teacher-dominated, knowledge-transmitting and grammar-based methods. Since then, the pedagogical innovation has been disseminated and implemented in both primary and secondary schools throughout the country. South China has been a gateway to mainland China for exchanges with other countries since ancient times. With rapid development of its economy and trade with other countries since the late 1970s, South China has witnessed a fast spread and ever-increasing prominence of English in society and in schools. It has also maintained a leading role in conducting English language teaching in all sectors, with primary schools being a pioneering area. The promulgation of TBLT has further boosted the development of English language teaching in South China. This chapter reports an in-depth case study about how three primary school English teachers in South China interpreted and implemented TBLT in their classroom teaching. It was found that all three teachers had a partial understanding of TBLT, two seldom used tasks in their teaching, while the third teacher taught with a medium-to-strong form of TBLT. Factors that shaped their enactment of TBLT are then discussed. The findings show that the top-down national pedagogical innovation in China is a complicated process shaped by the interaction of all levels of stakeholders and a variety of complicated contextual factors. The chapter concludes with insights on TBLT practice in China and other contexts where English is taught as a foreign language.

Introduction

Since opening up to the world and launching reforms in the early 1980s, China has experienced rapid economic progress and has been increasingly active in globalization.

In addition, English is having a deeper and more extensive impact on the daily lives and working habits of Chinese people. Grasping English has become crucial for access to higher education inside and outside China as well as well-paid employment, especially in the commercial sector (Adamson, 1998). Citizen mastery of English is making an important contribution to realizing the nation's modernization and promoting its international status (Adamson, 2002; Lam, 2002). The latest English curriculum—*English Language Curriculum Standards (Trial version)*, issued in 2001— stipulates that the English language is to be a compulsory subject taught from at least Grade Three (when children are aged eight or nine) in primary schools throughout mainland China (Ministry of Education, 2001). The official document also began a national top-down English language teaching (ELT) innovation by advocating the TBLT as the main pedagogy for ELT nationwide, in the hope of improving English usage abilities among students.[1] Following its launch in autumn 2001, the *English Language Curriculum Standards* was first tried and implemented in thirty-eight national experimental districts throughout the country. The new curriculum was then implemented in provincial experimental districts in autumn 2002, which reached 10 per cent to 15 per cent of the entire student population. In 2004, its implementation expanded to 2,576 cities and counties to reach 65 per cent to 70 per cent of the students and was supposed to achieve wider implementation throughout the country by 2007 (Liu, 2004, quoted in Zhang & Hu, 2010).

The intended TBLT innovation

In existing research on the subject, 'tasks' are defined in many ways. Some look at tasks in a non-pedagogical sense as 'the hundred and one things people do in everyday life, at work, at play, and in between' (Long, 1985, p. 89) while many others consider a pedagogical task as a classroom activity in which 'the target language is used by the learner for a communicative purpose in order to achieve an outcome' (Willis, 1996, p. 234). Tasks are intended to 'result in language use that bears a resemblance, direct or indirect, to the way language is used in the real world' (Ellis, 2003: 16). Summarizing many definitions put forward in the literature (Breen, 1987; Candlin, 1987; Ellis, 2003; Long, 1985; Nunan, 2004; Prabhu, 1987; Richards et al., 1992; Skehan, 1998; Willis, 1998), Zhang (2005) summarized the main characteristics of tasks as follows: They are communication-oriented; performance involves cognitive processes; contextualized and authentic; primarily meaning-focused; and the completion of a task normally leads to a non-linguistic product with the use of the target language (e.g., a route drawn from a map or a conclusion reached).

A task differs greatly from a purely form-focused activity, also called 'an exercise' or a non-communicative language learning (Cheng, 2004; Ellis, 2003; Littlewood, 2004; Tong, 2005; Tong et al., 2000). Skehan (1998) and Ellis (2003) proposed a strong form and a weak form of TBLT. A strong form of TBLT takes tasks as the only unit of language teaching, in which students acquire the target language by performing tasks in contextualized, meaning-focused communication (Ellis, 2003). A weak form of TBLT considers tasks as an opportunity for learners to practise more freely the language items they have learned in a teacher-controlled way. In this

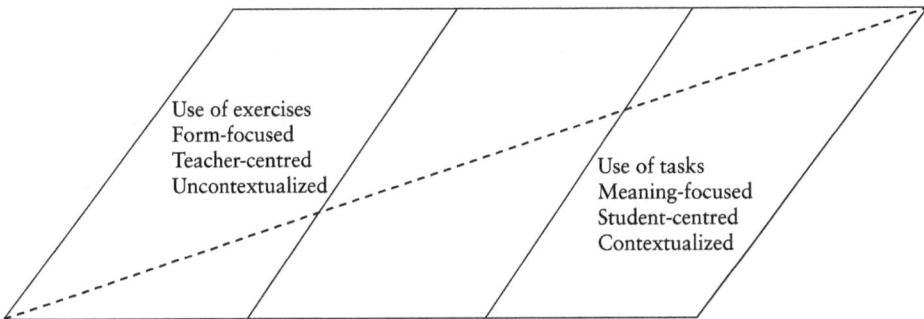

FIGURE 6.1 *Continuum of forms of TBLT (adapted from Tong, 2005)*

weak form, tasks are only supplementary activities before or after the form-focused instruction (Ellis, 2003). After studying the implementation of TBLT by teachers in the Special Administration Region of Hong Kong, Tong et al. (2000) and Tong (2005) identify a medium form of task-based learning that involves tasks as the main activity, supplemented with some form-focused and teacher-controlled activity. This study makes use of the continuum of forms of TBLT (Tong, 2005, see Figure 6.1), as the criteria for explaining the extent to which teachers implement TBLT in classroom teaching.

As TBLT is a Western pedagogy, the Western literature is certainly an important reference for policymakers in China in stating intentions of the task-based innovation in national curriculum documents. The official intention regarding TBLT in China was manifested in *English Language Curriculum Standards*, which was the first national, English language curriculum for all primary and secondary schools in the country.[2] It also marked another breakthrough by espousing a student-centred approach. Though it included very limited introduction of TBLT, the national curriculum document seems to promote a medium form of TBLT.

In *English Language Curriculum Standards*, which was written in Chinese, the term 'tasks' was translated in Chinese as *'renwu,'* and TBLT as *'renwu xing jiaoxuefa'*. Although the term *renwu* appeared twenty times in the text of the document, it was used only ten times to mean tasks. The other ten times, *renwu* was used to refer either to assignments or teaching objectives, which is the most frequently used meaning of the term *renwu* in Chinese. As a result, the official document presents a very ambiguous picture of TBLT to readers. Furthermore, it included no clear definition of tasks or TBLT, not to mention any introduction to the theoretical rationale and pedagogical features of TBLT. The only introduction of TBLT appears in the section titled 'Recommendations on Implementation', which sets six general principles for designing tasks for teachers. These principles typify the characteristics of tasks as purposeful, authentic, real-life-related, holistic, process-oriented, and communication-oriented (Zhang, 2005), which echo some features of tasks as described in the literature, yet these characteristics are not further elaborated upon in the rest of the curriculum. For teachers, there is no specific guidance for implementing TBLT in classroom teaching in the new curriculum document. Given the limited information about TBLT in the centralized curriculum, the official document provided insufficient guidance to other stakeholders (including the teacher trainers, school leaders and teachers) in the top-down national TBLT innovation.

As the previous research indicates, there have been few studies on the practical implementation of task-based approach innovations (Deng, 2008; Wang, 2009; Zhang, 2005; Zhang & Hu, 2010) especially in the context of primary schools in the mainland of the People's Republic of China (Zhang, 2005; Zhang & Hu, 2010). This chapter attempts to address this gap by documenting an in-depth study investigating how TBLT was implemented by three primary school English language teachers in South China and identifying the factors shaping the implementation process.

ELT in the primary schools of South China

The significance of selecting South China as the context of study lies in its leading role in the development of the country especially in terms of economy and English language teaching. ELT in South China has been developed along with the evolving role of English language in the society, which is greatly shaped by South China's economic, political and societal situations and its relations with the rest of the world (Zhang & Wang, 2011). Geographically, South China includes both Guangdong Province and the Guangxi Zhuang Autonomous Region. It has favourable conditions for developing foreign trade as it covers the drainage area of the Pearl River proximate to Hong Kong, Macao and the South China Sea.

Historically, South China has always been a gateway of the country for exchanges with other countries since ancient times. As a result, since 1759, English language teaching was first introduced in Guangzhou (the capital city of Guangdong Province), which was nominated as the sole port for foreign trade by the Chinese government in the Late Qing Dynasty (Hsü, 1990). Then in 1861, the first official organization to offer English language teaching in mainland China, the Tongwen Guan (literally 'School of Combined Learning'), was established by the imperial government. Its Guangzhou branch was opened in 1864, which laid a very solid foundation for further development of ELT in South China. During the Late Qing Dynasty, English courses were only offered in higher senior primary schools with favourable conditions in South China.

During the Republican era (1911–1949), influenced by the political instability in the whole country, the provision of ELT in South China was limited as a selective course in some special primary schools such as the Tangxia Primary school in Tianhe District of Guangzhou (Cai, 2004). In the early years of the People's Republic of China (1949–1976), compared to South China, the other parts of the country only achieved limited development in their ELT due to the Cultural Revolution (1966–1976). Nevertheless, the Cultural Revolution did not seem to interrupt the spread of English language education in Guangdong or other places in China. In 1969, metropolitan areas in South China like Guangzhou started to provide English courses in most primary schools once again to school children (Lu, 2002).

In the late 1970s China's 'open-door policy' encouraged economic and political development in South China. With the shift from a political to an economy-oriented society, South China has become one of the most advanced economic hubs and a major manufacturing centre of the country. With the rapid spread of English in the world and the special strategic position of South China, English has gained even more prominence in Chinese society (Lam, 2002). It was also identified as the main foreign language in secondary education and one of the key subjects in university entrance examinations in 1982. Consequently, there has been an ever-increasing demand for English language education in the whole region, which has hugely stimulated the English language teaching industry.

Due to its geographical location and unique position in international markets, South China education authorities have attached greater importance to primary school English teaching. In the early 1990s, the Guangzhou Education Bureau developed a policy requiring that English teaching in primary school for Grade One should be at least two periods per week, three for Grade Two to Grade Five, and four for Grade Six (Guangzhou Education Bureau, 2007). Shenzhen[3] even outperformed Guangzhou by offering at least four periods of English lessons from Grade One in primary schools. Some Shenzhen schools even offer nine English lessons per week, the same number as their Chinese lessons. Following these developments, many other cities in South China also began to offer English courses from Grade One onwards in the 1990s (Guangzhou Education Bureau, 2008, quoted in Zhang & Wang, 2011), a whole decade before ELT was made compulsory in primary schools nationally in 2001.

Such a quick expansion of ELT to primary schools has attracted many secondary schools' English language teachers from inland China to teach English in primary schools in South China, due to the higher salaries and more favourable working conditions in the region. The promulgation of *English Language Curriculum Standards* and the promotion of TBLT have further boosted the development of ELT in South China, which has maintained its leading role in conducting ELT in all sectors, with primary schools being a pioneering area. The experience of implementing TBLT in the schools of South China will provide insights on TBLT practice in other parts of mainland China and other Asian contexts where English is taught as a foreign language.

Research design

Whether TBLT can be successfully implemented in primary schools in South China is the main focus of the study presented here. The following sections document a study conducted in the early years of TBLT innovation on how three primary school teachers in South China enacted TBLT in their classroom teaching and how various internal and contextual factors shaped their TBLT practices. It attempts to provide answers to the following research questions:

1 How did these three teachers in South China enact TBLT in their teaching?
2 What are the factors shaping the enactment of the innovation by the teachers in South China?

The research methods included document analysis, classroom observations and interviews. It also made use of naturalistic observations to study teacher behaviour in classrooms and the implementation of the curriculum reform inside the schools. By means of purposive sampling, three primary English teachers in Shenzhen who claimed to have used TBLT and were teaching the same grade in different types of schools[4] were selected. At the time of the study, all the teachers taught at least one Grade Three class. Fanny was a novice teacher with two years teaching experience in a city-level school. Gavin was a competent teacher with seven years teaching experience in a district-level school. Helen was an expert teacher with fourteen years teaching experience in a province-level school and she also worked as a student counsellor in her school. Ten lessons of Grade Three taught by each teacher were observed, videotaped and analysed. The types of activities used in teaching were identified and timed. Pre-lesson and post-lesson interviews with teachers were conducted to find out the teachers' understanding of TBLT and the factors shaping their ELT practices.

TBLT implemented in the primary schools of South China

The following reports how the three primary school English teachers enacted TBLT in their classroom practices as well as the factors shaping their implementations.

Fanny's implementation

Fanny graduated from a teacher training college in Guangdong after the launch of the TBLT innovation in 2001. Thinking that she had learned the most advanced and innovative teaching skills from her study of ELT, she believed that she did not need to improve her teaching in the new curriculum reform. However, she had actually experienced a form-focused, knowledge-transmitting approach in her pre-service training and had not learned much about progressive pedagogy, such as the communicative approach or TBLT. She had a copy of *English Language Curriculum Standards* but had not read it. At the time of study, she had limited linguistic knowledge and pedagogical abilities.

There has been no official movement towards adopting TBLT as the main pedagogy for ELT in Fanny's current school. As a relatively inexperienced teacher, Fanny encountered quite a few challenges in teaching English. She lacked the experience needed to deal with a whole set of textbooks, as she was only taught in college how to prepare materials for a single lesson. As she spent too much time marking students' form-focused assignments and tests, she could not find sufficient time to plan her own lessons well. She had difficulty in maintaining discipline and managing students' misbehaviour in her classroom of forty-nine students. Due to the large class size, she believed that classroom management might become more challenging if more communicative activities were used. However, she had to work alone to solve these problems, as there was a lack of support from other teachers in the English department at her school. Although the school had assigned a mentor to support her, Fanny found her mentor using a very strict teacher-dominant way of teaching and did not learn a lot from her mentor about enhancing teaching and learning.

Because of limited exposure to TBLT in both her pre-service and in-service training programmes, Fanny confused tasks with teaching objectives (the most frequently used meaning of its Chinese translation *renwu*). She interpreted TBLT as setting teaching targets or objectives, including teaching forms of English (e.g., words, sentences and grammar). Therefore, she believed she had been using TBLT in every lesson by setting the objectives for instruction related to linguistic items. She aimed her teaching at transmitting as many English words, sentences and grammar points as possible to her students. Thus she often spent most of her class time (four forty-minute periods per week in a class) on students' mechanical practice of linguistic forms, with a careful focus on the accuracy of student pronunciation and speech, as well as teaching a significant amount of grammar in a deductive way. She matched her teaching carefully with the form-focused test papers distributed by the local education bureau. Regarding students as passive learners with limited English ability, she spent much of her time regulating student discipline and took close control of their learning.

Furthermore, she had limited English ability, which prevented her from communicating fluently with her students in authentic and natural English. She used Chinese to translate her speech when students did not understand her English and to give complex instructions. The only types of tasks she used were adapting the surveys included in the textbook, to provide students with freer practice at the end of each unit. For example, one of the tasks in Fanny's textbook is a group survey about the favourite sport of each group. To complete this task, it is suggested that students be divided into groups. In each group, students first collect information about each individual group member's favourite sport. They then find out the favourite sport of their group and report the result to the whole class. Fanny simplified this activity by asking students to find out the favourite sports of ten other students via interview in pairs. Then a few students were asked to report their findings to the whole class. However, Fanny did not know that this activity was actually a type of task. Her teaching was mainly teacher-dominant, form-focused and grammar-based, which displayed many characteristics of a weak form of TBLT.

Gavin's implementation

Similar to Fanny's school, Gavin's school had not officially adopted TBLT as the main pedagogy for ELT either. According to Gavin, the head of his English department was still using traditional, teacher-fronted drill-based instructional methods. His implementation of the TBLT innovation was greatly affected by his limited understanding of TBLT and a school leader's negative attitudes towards it. In his reflection on teaching[5] submitted to the dean in charge of teacher professional development (who was a mathematics teacher) in his school, he explained passionately that he adopted TBLT as his main pedagogy, as recommended by *English Language Curriculum Standards*. Unexpectedly, the dean criticized him for not being creative enough and just copying a method that was already mentioned by others. Gavin totally accepted the dean's interpretation and became unenthusiastic about TBLT from then on. He regarded the goal of curriculum innovation as creating and utilising new teaching methods and activities. Therefore, he tried to find various innovative activities and apply them in his classroom teaching. Following the comments made by the dean, he considered it uncreative to use TBLT, as an educational product borrowed from the West. He even critiqued that the term '*renwu*' (Chinese translation of 'task') was too rigid and thus inappropriate to be used in ELT as it reminded people of the duties soldiers need to carry out in the army. As a result, TBLT did not become the focus of his ELT innovation. Most of the tasks he used were limited to those included in his textbook, which were mainly survey tasks. And he defined TBLT as conducting surveys.

Gavin studied in the discipline of secondary school ELT in a teacher training college in an inland city before he became a primary school teacher in Shenzhen. Although he had seven years of teaching experience, he received limited amounts of pre- and in-service teacher training on teaching primary school children. His current teaching style was mainly shaped by his previous form-focused, memorization-based English learning experience as a student in the primary school. Similar to Fanny, he also regarded his students as passive learners of English due to their weak English ability. He targeted his teaching towards enabling students to read aloud, memorize and write the words in a textbook and found that the limited class time (four forty-minute periods per week in a class) was quite tight for him to cover the whole textbook. Therefore, he mainly followed the arrangements of the textbook. He included mainly form-focused, textbook-centred, teacher-dominated pattern drills, and partial communicative activities such as surveys and riddles. Yet he did not consider riddles to be tasks.

Gavin also matched his teaching with the form-focused test papers mandated by the local education bureau. His limited English proficiency made it difficult for him to engage in natural fluent communication in English with students and to expose them to authentic use of English, which is the basic requirement of TBLT. He taught grammar in a deductive way with form-focused exercises. Believing Chinese was a helpful medium of instruction, he often used Chinese to translate and clarify his points immediately after he spoke English and to give instructions. This also prevented him from communicating smoothly and naturally with his students in English. His teaching was mainly teacher-dominated, form-focused and textbook-centred, which displayed many characteristics of a weak form of TBLT.

Helen's implementation

As a teacher leader in her school, Helen received relatively more opportunities of attending teacher training for the new curriculum reform. She was exposed to the TBLT innovation mainly through her personal communication with the teacher trainer in her district. She understood the focus of the curriculum innovation was to embrace more student-centred, real-life-related education, which happened to be similar to her current ELT practice. Accepting the definition offered by the teacher-trainer in her district, she identified TBLT as problem-based teaching. Meanwhile, she mentioned that there were limited training programmes about the TBLT innovation to teachers in the district. Finding it time-consuming to design tasks, she did not deliberately include tasks in her classroom teaching. However, her teaching practice actually matched the fundamental characteristics of a medium-to-strong form of TBLT. Believing in student-centred, real-life-related and communication-oriented teaching, she targeted her teaching towards stimulating student interest and boosting their confidence in learning and using English. She often allowed students to make decisions about their own learning, which was also facilitated by the relatively smaller class with thirty-nine students and more class time of ELT (seven forty-minute periods per week in a class) than the situation in Fanny's and Gavin's schools. She always paid attention to relating student learning with real-life experiences and situations.

Having a good command of English, she was always able to expose students to natural, meaning-focused English communication in her classroom. Helen's embracing of student-centred education resulted mainly from her experience as a student counsellor, which enhanced her understanding of the needs and characteristics of primary school students. In her mind, each student was a unique person and had great potential to be developed. The role of a teacher was to respect each student's uniqueness and provide a platform for the students to develop their ability, which was quite a progressive approach of looking at the role of students and teachers in education. Her thorough understanding about the students also made her very skilful in managing students' misbehaviour and enabled her to engage her students in classroom activities effectively. Although her textbook did not include any tasks, she did not follow the textbook strictly and designed all the meaning-focused tasks she employed in the classroom. Helen's ELT was mainly student-centred, meaning-focused and communication-oriented and displayed many characteristics of a medium-to-strong form of TBLT, although TBLT was not her deliberate pedagogy.

The findings from Helen's case support Zhu's (2003) point that the development of an understanding of students may act as a key trigger for teacher professional development in other areas, including knowledge of pedagogy, self, subject matter, curriculum, and so on. The above findings indicate that there is a big gap between the intended TBLT innovation and the three teachers' teaching practices, especially in the cases of Fanny and Gavin. Although it is stipulated in the official curriculum document that teachers should adopt TBLT as their main pedagogy, there had been only limited dissemination and promotion of TBLT in schools, and little deliberate enactment by the teachers.

Factors shaping TBLT practices in the primary schools of South China

The above cases also indicate that teacher enactment of the task-based approach was very much shaped by their understanding of TBLT and the curriculum innovation, their professional development process, their experience in learning English, their perceptions of students and the culture of their schools. As shown in Table 6.1, there are more factors inhibiting than facilitating teachers' implementation of TBLT.

To begin with, there was neither sufficient information nor elaboration about TBLT in official documents. Although TBLT was recommended as an intended curriculum in 2001, there was only sporadic dissemination of and limited training of TBLT in resourced curriculum to teacher trainers, school leaders or teachers. For

TABLE 6.1 *Main factors that affected teachers' implementation of TBLT (F = Fanny, G = Gavin, and H = Helen)*

Dimension	Facilitating factors	Inhibiting factors
Attributes of TBLT	TBLT was thought to have positive effect on student learning (H); was compatible with teacher's current teaching style and assessment (H)	TBLT had a confusing Chinese name (F); was time-consuming (H) and tends to foster noise and bad discipline and was incompatible with teacher's current practice (F & G); placed high demands on teachers and clashed with local tests and examinations (F, G & H)
Macro-Context	TBLT was in trend with globalization and the teaching materials included a few tasks (F, G & H)	Confucian values and prevalence of form-focused tests and examinations contradictory to TBLT (F & G); insufficient elaboration in the curriculum, limited dissemination and lack of teaching materials of TBLT (F, G & H)
Micro-Context	Teacher taught a small class and was allowed to use self-designed task-based assessment and there were sufficient periods to accommodate TBLT (H)	Teacher taught a large class and teaching schedule too tight to use TBLT; little support for ELT innovation in school (F & G); no school effort to adopt TBLT; no environment for students to use English (F, G & H)
Teacher factors	Teacher embraced student-centred education, real-life-related, experiential teaching and had good command of English (H)	Teacher had misconception of TBLT innovation, limited English and pedagogic ability; adopted form-focused approach from previous English learning experience; perceived students as passive receivers of knowledge (F & G); teacher had limited teacher training on and limited understanding of TBLT (F, G & H)

example, both the dean of Gavin's school and the teacher trainer in Helen's district had limited or twisted understanding of TBLT. The limited dissemination and support by high-level stakeholders (i.e., policymakers, teacher trainers, textbook writers and school leaders) failed to prepare schools and teachers for a practical implementation of the top-down, task-based approach to innovation.

Given the fact that these leading agents did not mandate the adoption of TBLT by school leaders and teachers, the dissemination of TBLT appeared to have terminated at the school level (i.e., mid-level transactional agent). As a result, although TBLT was adopted in the national syllabus with the hope of further developing English-using skills among students, its successful implementation by teachers at the classroom level was certainly not guaranteed. Without a formal mandate, whether to adopt TBLT as the main pedagogy or not became a personal choice for the frontier teachers. Given that there were so many inhibiting factors from both the top-level change agents and the middle level of school leaders, factors relating to individual teachers played a crucial role in shaping the extent to which TBLT was finally implemented.

Each of the three teachers in this study had only a limited understanding of TBLT due to limited exposure to the new pedagogy. None of them adopted TBLT deliberately as the main English language pedagogy, and their current teaching practices were shaped mainly by processes of their teacher training process, past English learning experience, levels of proficiency in English, perceptions of students and their needs in learning, the working contexts including time constraints and class sizes.

On one hand, Fanny and Gavin experienced an unbalanced, form-focused, knowledge-transmitting teacher training, and possessed limited linguistic and pedagogical abilities. They believed their students were too young and passive to make decisions about their own learning. The lack of ability to speak fluent English also prevented them from communicating naturally and smoothly with students in English. Both of their teaching styles were teacher-dominated, knowledge-transmitting, grammar-based and textbook-centred. Both Fanny's and Gavin's use of tasks was mainly a result of following the activities prescribed in the textbooks. These points echo the findings of Lee (2009) that although teachers were aware of the current English pedagogical innovation, their practices were still teacher-centred and textbook-directed. Fanny's and Gavin's implementation of a weak form of TBLT was also greatly influenced by the form-focused examinations applied by the educational authority to assess student learning outcome.

Conversely, Helen developed a solid understanding of student needs and characteristics from her work experience as a student counsellor. Her high proficiency in English enabled her to communicate more freely with students. She embraced student-centred, communication-oriented, real-life-related teaching, and gave students freedom to make decisions about their own instruction. Even though her textbook did not include any tasks, she took the initiative to design all the tasks for her students to apply the target language in the lessons. It was a medium-to-strong form of TBLT that was implemented in Helen's ELT.

Discussion

The following section describes the current situation of TBLT implemented in the primary schools of South China and explores the future development of TBLT in the coming English curriculum innovation of mainland China.

TBLT in the primary schools of South China

This study investigated how three primary school English teachers in South China, a leading region in ELT in mainland China, implement the TBLT innovation in their classroom practice. On the one hand, part of the findings seemed to disagree with the claim in some studies (e.g., Ellis, 2003) that TBLT might be in conflict with EFL cultural contexts, such as the Confucian culture in China. Helen's case seems to indicate that there has been some change in China's current EFL cultural context, and the use of TBLT need not be inappropriate. Following globalization trends, many foreign cultural values are entering China and seem to coexist with or even integrate into traditional Chinese values that currently dominate the Chinese educational milieu. China's culture is rapidly becoming more pluralistic, and Chinese people are increasingly open-minded and comfortable with the English-speaking world, as well as with progressive ideas. Take Helen as an example: she had a profound understanding of the unique needs of students and embraced student-oriented individualized teaching. Although she did not use tasks deliberately, she identified with real-life-related communicative principles of TBLT and her teaching displayed many features integral to it.

On the other hand, the study has identified many contextual obstacles which need to be overcome before TBLT can be successfully implemented by teachers in the primary schools in South China, even though it is the leading region in conducting ELT in the primary school sector. Such a situation may also be true in the other contexts like China where English is taught as a foreign language. First of all, the existing form-focused tests and examinations in schools, which were in conflict with TBLT, need to be changed. Achieving high scores in examinations remains the best way for students to get access to higher education. Examination results are still the most important criterion for education bureaus and society to evaluate the English teaching quality of a primary school and for schools to appraise English teachers (Zhongxing Primary School, 2007, quoted in Zhang & Wang, 2011). As a result, many teachers tend to stick to exam-oriented, form-focused, and grammar-based teaching instead of doing TBLT.

Second, there needs to be more training to improve the understanding of TBLT by different levels of stakeholders and more support to help teachers to practise TBLT, as is also argued by Deng (2008) and Deng & Carless (2009). Given the unclear explanation of TBLT in the *English Language Curriculum Standards* and the limited exposure to TBLT in the in-service training programmes, many teacher trainers, school leaders and teachers may have a partial or twisted understanding of TBLT. The partial interpretation of TBLT will prevent schools' adoption and teachers' use of TBLT properly, which also supports the findings in Carless (2003; 2004) and Lee (2009). Furthermore, there should be more school-based or even classroom-based support to facilitate teachers' TBLT practices, including designing tasks and relevant task-based materials.

Third, improving teachers' English proficiency was also extremely important to successfully promote TBLT practice, as TBLT has a higher demand on teachers' language knowledge and communicative competence than the traditional form-based approach. Furthermore, TBLT also requires more opportunities for students to use English than many form-focused teaching such grammar-based approach. As many schools have only four periods of English lessons per week (as in the cases of Fanny and Gavin), teachers often find it difficult to squeeze in time for using many tasks besides covering the required syllabus. There may be a need for an English-speaking environment outside traditional classroom study for learners to apply English.

Last but not least, to enable teachers to transform their teacher-dominant approach to a more student-centre approach, improving teachers' mindset and their knowledge about their students is also important. Teachers need to be aware of students' needs and ability of using the target language before they can open up more space in their teaching for students' free use of the language.

Future development of TBLT in mainland China

Similar problems arising from promoting TBLT innovation were also echoed, highlighted and discussed by some renowned ELT experts at a heated academic debate on the current state of China's English curriculum innovation held in Guangzhou on 1 November 2007 (Dong, 2008; Yuan, 2007). For example, there was a lack of a uniform understanding of TBLT among the ELT experts, teacher trainers, school leaders and teachers. Some teachers thought that TBLT was the only pedagogy they could use in ELT and dared not teach grammar and students did not learn effectively in TBLT lessons. Many teachers claimed to use TBLT but their lessons did not include any tasks at all. TBLT produced a high demand on teachers' ability, students' English proficiency and ELT environment and may not be appropriate for students in primary schools and junior secondary schools. Some experts even argued that it was inappropriate for the official document like *English Language Curriculum Standards (Trial Version)* to advocate TBLT as the main pedagogy for ELT in the whole country. However, Professor Cheng Xiaotang, who led the team in writing *English Language Curriculum Standards*, suggested that while he would still recommend TBLT it should not be considered the only pedagogy for teachers. This was later reflected in a revised version of *English Language Curriculum Standards* (Ministry of Education, 2011), as the revised English curriculum document reads,

> The English curriculum Standards set the learning goals of different levels of students in term of 'what students can do in English' and aim to cultivate students' integrated ability of using English. ... Teachers should create all kinds of contexts that are related to real life situations and apply gradually-developed activities for students to practise the target language. The English curriculum Standards advocate the use of language teaching approaches and methods that stress both the language learning process and the final learning outcome, for example, task-based language teaching and so on, to cultivate students' ability to do things in English (author translation, pp. 26–27).

Although the status of TBLT has changed from being advocated as the main pedagogy to becoming one of the recommended pedagogies, the spirit of TBLT seems to have remained and been integrated into the revised English curriculum Standards. The learning goals set in the revised curriculum are more similar to the definitions of tasks set in the above, which are intended to provide opportunities to learners for them to use the target language in a way that 'bears a resemblance, direct or indirect, to the way language is used in the real world' (Ellis, 2003, p. 16). Therefore, to successfully promote and implement the revised curriculum intention, the above insights drawn from the study on TBLT implementation are still of value to the relevant stakeholders and change agents.

Conclusion

This chapter reported the findings from a study on teachers' implementation of TBLT in the South China region and explored the development and future of TBLT in mainland China. Given that there are still significant differences between teachers' TBLT implementation in one of the most developed cities (Shenzhen) in the South China region, the scaling up of TBLT in mainland China in the near future seems to be impossible. Although TBLT was finally advocated as one of the potential ELT pedagogies, its features have been integrated into the revised curriculum to promote students' use of English in their process of learning. The study reported here helps identify teachers' need for further professional development to achieve a more student-centred, real life-related and communication-oriented teaching approach in mainland China and other contexts where English is taught as a foreign language, especially in terms of teachers' language abilities and their knowledge about students and student learning.

Notes

1 TBLT was also adopted as the main pedagogy for English language teaching in the top-down curriculum reform in the Special Administration Region of Hong Kong in 1999.
2 *The English Language Curriculum Standards* issued in 2001 marks the first time that the English language has been recommended as a main subject in Grade Three of primary school education all over the country. All the previous curriculum documents stipulated that English language be taught in all secondary schools and only some primary schools.
3 Shenzhen became China's first Special Economic Zone right after the opening policy was made in 1978. Since 1991, the English language has been taught from Grade One in Shenzhen's primary schools. This has made Shenzhen one of the leading cities in ELT in mainland China.
4 The Ministry of Education ranks the public schools in mainland China into different levels based on their qualities of education and the scales of facilities: province-level, city-level, district-level schools. The province-level schools are the top level of schools, which are meant to offer better education and can get more funding from the government.
5 It is a common practice for the schools in mainland China to request the teachers to write an essay reflecting on his/her teaching and learning at the end of each school year.

References

Adamson, B. (1998). *English in China: The junior secondary school curriculum 1949–94*. University of Hong Kong, Hong Kong.
Adamson, B. (2002). Barbarian as a foreign language: English in China's schools. *World Englishes*, 21(2), 231–243.
Breen, M. (1987). Learner contributions to task design. In C. N. Candlin & D. Murphy (Eds), *Language learning tasks* (Vol. 7, pp. 23–46). Englewood Cliffs, NJ: Prentice-Hall International.

Cai, W. L. (2004). Tangxia Primary School Started to offer English Course in the Republic of China. *Today and Yesterday of Guangzhou, 2004*(1), 60.
Candlin, C. N. (1987). Towards task-based language learning. In C. N. Candlin & D. F. Murphy (Eds), *Language learning tasks* (pp. 5–22). Englewood Cliffs, NJ: Prentice-Hall International.
Carless, D. (2003). Factors in the implementation of task-based teaching in primary schools. *System, 31*(4), 485–500.
Carless, D. (2004). Issues in teachers' re-interpretation of a task-based innovation in primary schools. *TESOL Quarterly, 38*(4), 639–662.
Cheng, X. (2004). *Task-based language teaching*. Beijing: Higher Education Press.
Deng, Chunrao. (2008). Implementation of task-based activities in primary school classrooms in Nanhai Guangdong China – a pilot study. In Mellecker, R. R. et al. (Eds). *Research studies in education: the twelfth and thirteenth Postgraduate Research Conference 2008*, 1–12. Faculty of Education, the University of Hong Kong.
Deng, C. R. & Carless, D. (2009). The communicativeness of activities in a task-based innovation in Guangdong, China. *Asian Journal of English Language teaching, 19*, 113–134.
Dong, J. (2008). Discussion on the hot issues of China's current foreign language teaching. *English Teachers*, (2). Retrieved from http://www.pep.com.cn/xe/jszx/jxyj/lwxz/201008/t20100827_796929.htm
Ellis, R. (2003). *Task-based language learning and teaching*. Oxford, U.K.: Oxford University Press.
Guangzhou Education Bureau. (2007). *Guidelines on Primary English Teaching from Grade 1 to Grade 6 of Compulsory Education New Curriculum Standards in Guangzhou*. Retrieved from http://www.ew.com.cn/jxyj/jxzd/2007/06/2007-06-263282_2.html
Hsü, Immanuel C. Y. (1990). *The Rise of Modern China*. Oxford: Oxford University Press.
Lam, A. (2002). English in education in China: Policy changes and learners' experiences. *World Englishes, 21*(2), 245–256.
Lee, Jackie F. K. (2009). Perceptions of ELT among English language teachers in China. *Education Journal, 37(1–2)*, 137–154.
Littlewood, W. (2004). The task-based approach: some questions and suggestions. *ELT Journal, 58*(4). 319–326.
Long, M. H. (1985). A role for instruction in second language acquisition: Task-based language teaching. In K. Hyltenstam & M. Pienemann (Eds), *Modelling and assessing second language acquisition*. San Diego, Calif.: College-Hill Press.
Lu, Z. G. (2002) *The Final Report of Compiling Guangzhou Junior High School Experimental English Textbook*. Retrieved from http://www.cbe21.com/subject/english/html/050202/2002_12/20021203_2051.html
Ministry of Education. (2001). *English language curriculum standards for full-time compulsory education and senior secondary schools (trial version)*. Beijing: Beijing Normal University Press. (In Chinese)
Ministry of Education. (2011). *English language curriculum standards for full-time compulsory education and senior secondary schools*. Beijing: Beijing Normal University Press. (In Chinese)
Nunan, D. (2004). *Task-based language teaching*. Cambridge: Cambridge University Press.
Prabhu, N. S. (1987). *Second language pedagogy*. Oxford: Oxford University Press.
Richards, J. C., Platt, J., & Platt, H. (1992). *Longman dictionary of language teaching & applied linguistics*. England: Longman Group UK Limited.
Skehan, P. (1998). *A cognitive approach to language learning*. Oxford: Oxford University Press.
Tong, A. S. (2005). Task-based learning in English language in Hong Kong secondary schools. Unpublished PhD dissertation, University of Hong Kong.

Tong, et al. (2000). Tasks in English language and Chinese language. In B. Adamson, T. Kwan & K. Chan. (Eds), *Changing the curriculum: The impact of reform on primary schooling in Hong Kong* (pp.145–174). Hong Kong: Hong Kong University Press.

Wang, Wenfeng (2009). *Exploring teachers' experiences in curriculum implementation in China: case studies of four secondary school English teachers*. Koln, Germany: LAP Lambert Academic Publishing.

Willis, J. (1996). *A framework of task-based learning*. Harlow, Essex: Addison Wesley Longman Limited.

Willis, J. (1998). Task-based learning: What kind of adventure? *TLT Online Editor*. Retrieved http://jalt-publications.org/old_tlt/files/98/jul/willis.html

Yuan, L. (2007). *Discussion on the hot issues of China's current foreign language teaching: A report on an academic debate in Guangzhou on 1 November 2007*. National Basic Foreign Language Teaching Research Centre. Retrieved from http://www.tefl-china.net/Article/ShowArticle.asp?ArticleID=842 (In Chinese)

Zhang, Y. (2005). The implementation of the task-based approach in primary school English language teaching in mainland China. Unpublished PhD thesis, University of Hong Kong.

Zhang, Y. & Hu, G. W. (2010). Between Intended and Enacted Curriculums: Three Teachers and a Mandated Curricular Reform in Mainland China. In Menken, K. & García, O. (Eds). *Conceptualization for Language Policy in Education* (pp.123–142). New York: Routledge, Taylor and Francis.

Zhang, Y., & Wang, J. (2011). Primary school English Language teaching in South China: Past, present and future. In A. Feng (Ed.), *English Language Education across greater China* (pp. 151–168). Buffalo, NY: Multilingal Matters.

Zhu, X. J. (2003). The development of pedagogical content knowledge in novice secondary school teachers of English in the People's Republic of China. Unpublished PhD thesis, University of Hong Kong.

7

Significant Task-Based Learning:

Empowering Students with Position Search Skills in a University in Singapore

Brad Blackstone
Radhika Jaidev

Summary

In a nation state such as Singapore, where competition underscores every aspect of life, nothing empowers university students more than being equipped with the skills to apply for and secure further study opportunities, internships, or full-time employment. To this end the teaching in university of skills associated with the *position search* process is crucial so that students may adopt an informed approach when applying for suitable positions. This chapter describes the teaching of the position search in a segment of a professional communication course at the National University of Singapore (NUS). The position search segment integrates the macro skills needed for a successful position search and the micro skills that include a wide range of sentence structures and discrete grammar units for English language development. To support this integrated approach, the segment is designed and delivered as a multi-modal, task-based learning project that incorporates peer teaching, peer-reviews and role-play, as well as instructional units such as *Discovering Self/Personal Branding/Researching an Organization and a Position, Crafting Effective Résumés and Cover Letters* and *Preparing for and Performing in Interviews*. The authors explain how through this integrated approach, students are exposed to significant learning experiences as they employ a wide range of communication strategies which facilitate their English language development and communicative readiness for work or study positions not just in Singapore or Asia but around the globe.

Introduction

This chapter describes the position search segment of a professional communication course offered as an elective at the NUS. It integrates the macro skills needed for a successful position search and the practice of essential micro skills within the context of a multi-modal, task-based learning project. *Position* in the context of this project refers to full-time and part-time employment positions, internships in companies, overseas university attachment positions (usually for one semester) as well as openings for graduate studies in both NUS and other universities. Thus, this segment of the course aims to equip students, the majority of whom are in their second year and above in their undergraduate programme, with skills needed to research relevant positions, apply for them and prepare for the selection interviews.

It is important to note at this juncture that only students who have been exempted from or who have completed the basic academic English courses are eligible to take this course. Despite this, the proficiency levels of students in this course tend to vary widely, a situation made more complex by the fact that the course is also open to exchange students from a wide range of overseas universities. The latter, a majority of whom apply for this course because they are graduating soon with the view to either entering the workforce or pursuing graduate studies and who would like to hone their professional communication skills, are accepted in the course based on their English grades in their university transcripts. However, it is difficult to gauge their real language and communication abilities until they join the course. Regardless, the course is designed taking into consideration these factors to ensure that students' opportunities to practise and showcase their language and communication skills are still optimal. A task-based pedagogical approach has been adopted to facilitate students' hands-on learning of various topics and skill areas within the different course segments. Among these segments is the position search segment, which will be explained in the ensuing paragraphs.

The position search segment

The position search segment is designed in such a way that it begins with students working in small teams of two to four members researching and gathering data on the various components of the search process: discovering oneself, crafting résumés and application letters, preparing for and participating in position search interviews. The teams then share the content with their classmates in a series of peer teaching sessions. Simultaneously, individual students initiate a position search of their choice, first, by engaging in a process of *self-discovery* through completion of a number of reflective inventories, including one each for values, personality traits, job skills, and transferable skills, and then, by researching an organization and/or a position of interest, be that for an internship, an overseas university attachment programme, a post-graduate study programme or a job. The process of self-discovery enables students to identify their own strengths and weaknesses and to chart their short-term career or study progression, which, in turn, helps them to prepare their own portfolio of application materials. Following that, students work in the company of yet another small team – a mock human resources team – and peer review the portfolios created by the members of a peer team. The position search process culminates when these same teams conduct a final in-class review of their peer team members' materials, and then call the members of the peer team, one by one, up for an interview.

An important skill that students may incidentally acquire through working with two different teams at the same time is the ability to manage different team dynamics and individual personalities within those teams as they complete each required task. This is something that students can eventually list in their résumés and talk about in their actual future interviews as a strength and that will also serve them in good stead when they go out to work.

This chapter also intends to demonstrate how teachers of the course facilitate significant learning of the various sub-sets of skills by managing the instructional process and related task-based project while introducing the relevant instructional units: 1) *Discovering Self/Personal Branding/Researching an Organization and a Position*; 2) *Crafting Effective Résumés and Cover Letters*; and 3) *Preparing for and Performing in Interviews*.

Equipping the global employee

In today's increasingly globalized world, the prevalent 'enterprise culture' requires job search candidates to demonstrate skills and communicative strategies that Wee (2008) describes as 'interactional efficacy' (p. 258). Within such a context, a curricular focus on the authentic task-based activities and project work described herein has great relevance for university students because it aims to provide them with the opportunity to learn and practise not just the vital sub-sets of skills needed for a position search but also the essential language needed to express themselves orally and in writing through this process. Completing a series of integrated, position search-focused tasks allows them to practise both the skills and the language needed to support those skills in a relatively stress-free classroom environment, whether they are acting as peer teachers or learners, as résumé writers or reviewers, as mock interviewers or interviewees. The various position search tasks require students to speak and write in English both in the classroom and outside of it (in the form of homework, preparation and performance), and in so doing they not only 'make learners pay more attention to grammar, thus enabling them to produce more accurate language' but they also 'provide them with the opportunity to try out newly learned grammatical points' (Renandya, 2013, p. 25).

Additionally, while practising language items through these tasks, students also employ a wide range of interpersonal and organizational skills or 'procedural strategies' (Kramsch, 2007, p. 61) that will potentially enhance their communicative readiness for work or further study. In this way, the integrated, position-search focused process and associated tasks provide students with a 'significant learning experience' (Fink, 2003, p. 7) regardless of their national origin, language background, and specific study discipline.

Significant learning experiences in university

In order for learning in higher education to be significant, its applicability in real-world contexts has to be palpable to the student. Fink (2003) states that in higher education a 'significant learning experience' must have 'both a process and an outcome dimension' (p. 7), which motivate students toward acquiring valuable transferable knowledge and skills that not only enrich their personal lives but also enable them to play varied, active roles in society while also preparing them for their professional work lives. Gardiner (1994) asserted that business, government and industry captains expect 'critical competencies' from employees (p. 7). These include qualities such as responsibility and reliability, ethics, spoken and written communication, people skills, problem-solving skills, intercultural competence, the adaptability to change and a thirst for lifelong learning (Gardiner, 1994). In keeping with this move away from a conventional concept of what comprises significant learning, Fink (2003) has constructed a taxonomy of significant learning that stresses both the process as well as the outcome of learning.

Contrary to the conventional hierarchical arrangement of kinds of learning ranging from the highest, 'evaluation,' to the lowest, 'knowledge or recall of information' (Bloom, 1956, p. 3), Fink's taxonomy of learning suggests a cyclical arrangement which includes recall of knowledge and application as well as other elements that are more in keeping with the current demands on students exiting university and entering the workforce. These elements include 'integration of ideas, people and realms of life'; the 'human dimension', which requires students to know themselves and others; the 'caring' element, which refers to students developing new interests over time; and finally, 'learning how to learn', the ability for students to understand, map and direct their own learning so that they may continue to do so long after they have left the university (Fink, 2003, p. 30). The rationale for the cyclical arrangement is that there is and would be considerable overlap of the different kinds of learning at different junctures in students' lives. In a sense, Fink's taxonomy of learning provides outcome-specific goals for students in higher education that are immediately applicable to the demands of both university and working life. The pedagogy that teachers could employ to best enable students to achieve these outcomes would be a task-based pedagogy.

Deep versus surface learning in higher education

In a quantitative study by Trigwell, Ellis and Han (2012) conducted with first-year university students' self-reports, it was found that there was a correlation between 'positive emotions and the adoption of a deeper approach to learning,' which, in turn, resulted in 'higher achievement scores' (p. 811). Prior to this, Pintrich (2004) suggested a guiding framework for improving students' learning in higher education that linked students' learning with pedagogy, students' understanding of learning contexts and the outcomes of their learning. Although Pintrich's research is largely in self-regulated learning and how this is influenced by several factors in the learning environment, he asserts that the careful planning of tasks that not only have specific objectives but also require students to recall and apply previous knowledge actually raises their awareness of their own progress towards achieving the set goals (Pintrich, 2000, 2004). It was also found that carefully planned tasks enable students to drive their own learning and make the required changes to their learning approaches when they encounter problems (Bransford, Brown & Cocking, 1999; Pintrich, 2000). Thus, it seems imperative that the tasks used and pedagogy employed in higher education should not just create opportunities for students to ask questions in relation to specific tasks at hand, but rather, also enable them to see the bigger picture in terms of the overall value of the task within a larger scheme of things in real life. When students are able to see the direct relevance and applicability of what they are doing in class to the world outside of it, they are likely to adopt a positive attitude towards the tasks, and this, in turn, is likely to give rise to deeper learning, which is more likely to correlate with better learning outcomes (Biggs, 1979; Entwistle & Ramsden, 1983; Lindblom-Ylanne, 1999; Trigwell & Prosser, 1991).

Task-based teaching and learning

Ellis (2000) summarizes task-based teaching and learning in second language and communication teaching and learning in two broad categories, one that is based on a psycholinguistic model (Lantolf, 1996; Long, 1983; Skehan, 1996; Yule, 1997), and another based on sociocultural theory (Lantolf, 2000; Lantolf & Appel, 1994), which essentially draws from the work of Vygotsky (1978). While the first perspective assumes that students' output and learning is predetermined by the design of the task, the latter suggests that when students work together on a given task, they bring to bear upon the task their previous individual knowledge and sociocultural exposure. This makes it difficult to predict each individual's learning outcome. Be that as it may, Ellis (2000) supports Van Lier's (1991) earlier claim that the two models are useful in that the psycholinguistic model aids in the planning and design of tasks for teaching and learning while the sociocultural model emphasizes the importance of adaptation and innovation on the part of teachers when delivering task-based lessons in the classroom (Ellis, 2000).

Task-based learning underpins the scope of the entire professional communication module, which integrates sections covering non-verbal communication, interpersonal communication, intercultural communication, project-based communication, and position search communication, with emphasis added to areas of oral and written communication. There have been several definitions of a *task* as opposed to an *exercise* (Bygate, Skehan & Swain, 2000; Pica, Kanagy & Falodun, 1993; Skehan, 1998a, 1998b; Widdowson, 1998). However, for the purpose of this course and specifically the position search segment, the tasks that have been incorporated draw from Fink's taxonomy of significant learning, illustrated in Figure 7.1. In the context of the position search segment described in this chapter, a task is a hands-on activity that incorporates one or more types of learning from the six categories, namely, 'foundational knowledge', 'application', 'integration', 'human dimension', 'caring', and/or 'learning how to learn' (Fink, 2003, p. 35). The tasks are designed in such a way that they lead students into experiencing the 'relational and even interactive' nature of the different types of learning (p. 37).

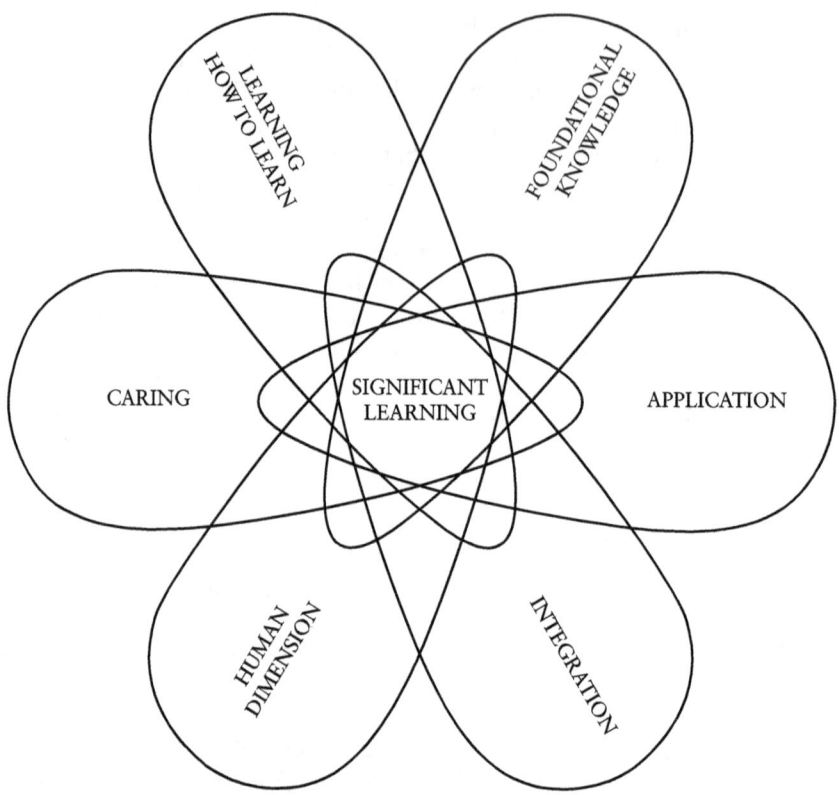

FIGURE 7.1 *Fink's taxonomy of significant learning (2003)*

The position search segment

The position search segment of the module – the focus of this chapter – is comprised of four main parts, offered in the course as instructional units: *Discovering Self/Personal Branding/Researching an Organization and a Position, Crafting Effective Résumés and Cover Letters* and *Preparing for and Performing in Interviews*.

Fink (2003) states that when initially designing a course, a teacher needs to first consider 'situational factors' in order to 'build strong primary components – the learning goals, feedback and assessment measures and teaching and learning activities' (p. 67). The most relevant situational factors for the course under discussion are that it was: 1) created initially for upper-division students (second, third and fourth year) from the NUS Faculty of Engineering, but currently also made available to students from the Faculty of Science, the Faculty of Arts and Social Sciences, the School of Nursing and the School of Pharmacy; 2) conceptualized as a credit-bearing, elective Professional Communication module with its main goal being to assist interested students in developing soft skills relevant to securing professional positions and then performing effectively in the workplace; 3) offered in a 1.5 hour long seminar-style session twice a week for twelve weeks; and 4) focused on practical experiences rather than on theory.

Four factors

These four factors, each fundamental to course design, merit further discussion. With reference to the first factor above, student profile, students enrolling in the course come from various faculties and schools within the university, and so they have a variety of study and career interests. They also represent different cohorts, with some being second-year students soon to be applying for work-related internships or overseas university attachment positions, and others third- or fourth-year students about to graduate and in search of a graduate studies programme or a full-time job, either in Singapore, Asia or elsewhere in the world.

Just as importantly, the students' English language background, including whether the language is spoken in their home and how proficient they are, varies. This is because, while many of these NUS undergraduates come from secondary school systems in which English is the primary language (i.e., Singaporeans and Indians), many do not (i.e., Malaysians, Chinese, Vietnamese, Indonesians, Thais, Koreans, Swedes and Germans). Even among Singaporean students, a noticeable number come from homes where English is used as a second or third language. Added to this mix of English language abilities is the smaller but just as important group of international exchange students who are in NUS for the Asian experience and exposure for one or two semesters and who choose to take this course based on the course description and a desire to hone their professional communication skills. As a result, within the Singapore context this factor necessitates that course planners and teachers provide opportunities for all students to gain further awareness and practice in the use of relevant language forms and communication skills.

The second factor, the course concept, is relevant on multiple levels. One is that the primary focus is professional communication, based on the exigencies of the workplace. Another is that the course is an elective, one that students are not required to take. When these factors are combined with the immediate real-world performance needs of the students, many of whom are about to graduate and enter the working world, student motivation levels tend to be high. This informs not just the particular curricular elements of the course but also any potential learning outcomes.

The third factor, the seminar-style format of the course, has particular merit when considering curricular design because the small size of the class – with an upper limit at eighteen students – readily allows for the implementation of interactive tasks that might emulate real-world communication activities. This fully connects with the fourth factor, which positions the course design as more akin to a practicum, or workshop, rather than as a theory-focused, lecture-based educational offering.

Fink (2003) also suggests that when a learning-centred approach is taken for a course, its design should be initiated with questions about what students should ultimately take away from the experience. Developing such questions for a course involving a position search segment would have to focus on a number of key functional areas. Within the framework of Fink's taxonomy, such questions might include (but not be limited to) the following:

1. Foundational knowledge

    - What should students understand about their own values, interests, personality, qualifications, skills training and talents as these pertain to preparing for a future career?
    - What knowledge might be important for students when they investigate a particular study or job field, a specific position, or a company/organization?
    - What key information and principles would be important for students regarding their crafting of résumés, writing of application letters, and then preparing for and performing during search interviews?
    - What should students understand about the way that all of the issues mentioned in the points above are related?

2. Application

    - What sort of tasks might help students internalize the relevant knowledge and practise the various skills required in preparing an effective portfolio while making an application for a graduate studies programme, company internship, overseas attachment or full-time job?
    - Which non-verbal cues should students take into account for communicating effectively during a peer teaching session or for performing effectively during an interview?
    - Which written language skills are required for students to most effectively produce an effective résumé and application letter?
    - Which oral language skills are required for students to perform most effectively during a selection interview?
    - Which Internet-based search skills might help students gain important knowledge about potential graduate studies programs, company internships, overseas attachments or job positions?
    - What sort of projects would help students develop and practise the skills required for each of the above?

3. Integration

    - What connections exist between peer teaching, discovering self/researching an organization and a suitable position, crafting the résumé and application letter, and preparing for and performing at job interviews?
    - What part do these topics play currently in the students' own personal, social and work life?

4 Human dimension
- What can or should students learn about themselves during this course segment?
- What can or should the students learn about working with and interacting with others through this course segment?

5 Caring
- What changes might occur amongst students — upon reflection in the context of course discussions – related to their values, interests, study habits, personal branding and career choices?

6 Learning how to learn
- How might the peer teaching impact students' self-directed learning?
- To what degree might discussions of crafting the résumé and application letter encourage the students to enhance their own future study and internship choices?
- How might discussions about students' future planning choices impact their becoming more diligent learners?

The answers derived in response to these questions, whether the student's position search is for an overseas attachment, a company internship, a graduate study programme, or a full-time job, should be provided through a mix of relevant tasks and suitable projects.

The central project and key tasks that comprise the position search segment

The following is a detailed explanation of the tasks that make up the position search segment of this professional communication module.

Task 1: Peer teaching (Oral)

In this assignment, each student plays two roles, as peer teacher and learner. For the process, teams of two to four students are created and assigned one course content topic to research and present to their classmates in a thirty-minute peer teaching session. Two of the topics included are relevant to the position search segment: *Crafting Effective Résumés and Cover Letters* and *Preparing for and Performing in Interviews*. Students organize what they learn from library, Web-based or career centre sources in the form of a content lesson, focusing upon an explanation of the content and activities that might help their classmates understand and practise relevant skills and strategies. They develop mini-lectures and tasks suitable to the topic chosen. Finally, in their respective teams, they present what they have learnt to their peers in sessions that are sequenced at time-relevant intervals. When watching their peers teach, other students are given the opportunity to practise active listening, questioning and note-taking.

Task 2: Discovering self/Personal branding/Searching for an appropriate position (Introspective)

In this assignment, based on the instructional unit entitled *Discovering Self/Personal Branding/Researching an Organization and a Position*, each student starts by reading about discovering self and personal branding, then reviewing a group of reflective inventories that serve as guidelines for personal assessment. These guidelines include one each for values, personality traits, job skills, and transferable skills such as people management, numeracy skills, digital literacy, intercultural communication, teamwork, leadership skills, etc. Typically, the assignment requires each student to survey the respective inventories and identify the items that seem to best align with their own background profile and experience. Pairs of students then might share their findings in order to gain peer feedback.

The final step would require the individual student to complete a job identification worksheet aimed at helping him match his values, skills and experience with an appropriate position (see Table 7.1).

Throughout this process, students are encouraged to identify their own strengths and weaknesses, and to chart their short-term career or study progression.

Next, with their goals and profile in mind, the student then acts as a researcher, sourcing for an appropriate position via print-based, web-based or career centre advertisements. As stated earlier, position descriptions need not be solely for jobs but can include those of local, regional or multinational company internships, overseas study attachments and graduate studies programs. Once the student has found one that is most appropriate, the application writing process can begin.

TABLE 7.1 *Job Identification Worksheet*

Job Identification Worksheet

Follow the instructions in each of the subheadings to identify your job/job areas.

Job Goal:

Write the job title representing the kind of job you plan to pursue right now. If you have more than one distinct job goal, complete this exercise for each one.

Required Values:

Review the values (see Values Checklist) that you identified as important to your job goals. Which conditions do you require in a new job opportunity?

Desired Values:

Which conditions do you desire from the Values Checklist?

Reality Check:

Are these expectations reasonable and attainable?

Yes/No

If you answered **no or are unsure**, re-examine your values.

Task 3: Crafting an effective application letter and résumé (Written)/Peer review of résumé and application letter (Oral)

In this assignment, each student plays multiple roles: as document writer and peer reviewer. With the advertised position description in hand, he prepares a one- or two-page résumé and a one-page application letter. A rubric is provided to students as a guiding framework for a quality letter and résumé. Sample letters and résumé are also provided and discussed in class. After the first draft of each document is written, it is submitted during class, where it is reviewed by a peer review team made up of three or four classmates.

While each student serves on the peer review team as an evaluator of classmates' materials, he can reference criteria for the résumé and letter found in document rubrics provided by the teacher. The student should also be able to acknowledge what has been learnt earlier during the peer teaching lesson and from classroom discussions. In his capacity as peer reviewer, the student is encouraged to give constructive feedback that will help classmates improve their letter and résumé. During this step, peer reviewers also have an opportunity to see a range of résumé and letters, which potentially further informs their own crafting of the second draft.

At the end of the peer review session, a general debriefing is held, giving students the chance to reflect on the experience and the teacher an opportunity to highlight key points or needs revealed by the review process. After receiving feedback, each student has an opportunity to rewrite the letter and résumé for submission to the teacher. Once the teacher has provided additional individual feedback, the student needs to prepare yet another draft of the application letter and résumé for use during the mock interview session that follows.

Task 4: Appearing for a mock job/position interview (Oral)

In this assignment, each student again plays multiple roles, first as a member of a mock human resources (HR) team that will conduct yet another review of the application materials of a group of classmates and at the same time as an interviewee who is interviewed by the peer team. For this task, mock HR teams of three or four students are created. Each HR team member reads and, in consultation with teammates, evaluates the application materials prepared by another team's individual members. After the evaluating team reads the materials of all the peer team's members, it then ranks those individuals based on the quality of the portfolio in relation to the specific job, internship, graduate studies programme or overseas attachment being applied for. After all materials have been read and application portfolios ranked, the interview process begins.

The interview process entails setting up the classroom (and perhaps even an adjacent room or some common space outside the classroom) in office-like quadrants, with each of the various HR teams situated in a designated area behind a desk or table. (In this situation, movable whiteboards or office dividers are ideal.) In their respective stations, each team then creates its first set of interview questions for the peer they had ranked first based on an evaluation of the materials presented. In order to do this, HR teams can reference a list of sample interview questions provided by the teacher, but they need to be advised to stylize each interview according to the position being applied for.

After the question preparation process is completed, each team then loses one of its members as the person who is ranked by the peer team as having the best set of materials is called for an interview. This top-ranked person from each of the teams is directed into the corridor, there to wait with other top-rated candidates until being called upon by a peer team for an interview of approximately 15-20 minutes. In a class of sixteen to twenty students, when each HR team includes three or four members, it is still possible for the respective team to conduct the interview even when one member has stepped aside to be interviewed by a different team as the remaining members of the team will be sufficient in number to act as interviewers.

There are several considerations that a teacher might convey to students when organizing position search interview sessions in order to make such a task as authentic as possible. For one, the students who are on the HR teams need to be prepped with regard to the types of questions that are typically presented. In addition, they should be asked to *get into character*, treating the job of interviewer seriously and being advised to act as if they had never met the interviewee before, possibly even playing dramatic roles when conducting the interviews. One of this paper's authors typically prepares specific role assignments for every HR team member – the passive interviewer (not forthcoming with questions), the disengaged interviewer (constantly on the handphone), the sympathetic interviewer, and the aggressive interviewer 'from hell' – roles that were only revealed immediately prior to the interviews on the day of the sessions. Interviewees also need to be encouraged to apply themselves to the task as they would for any interview. In this way, the skills practised might approximate those required in authentic interview sessions.

Following the interview sessions (which might occupy several days' lessons), during which every class member would ideally have an opportunity to serve as an interviewee and as an interviewer, to act on the HR unit during several interviews, a final debriefing session can be held. It is during this review that students can be asked to reflect openly not just on what occurred during their interviews in the various roles but also on their learning from the experience. This is an opportunity for members of the class to discuss their peers' and their own competencies, the strengths and weaknesses demonstrated during the sessions, and for them to further focus on how language has been used during various stages of the entire task.

The information in Table 7.2 illustrates how the key tasks of the position search segment are interconnected and the degree to which they provide students with a significant learning experience.

Student feedback regarding the position search segment

Students in the professional communication course where the position search segment was implemented have reacted very favourably to this task in feedback they have provided after finishing the course. The method of data collection was an online survey questionnaire that students could voluntarily access and respond to

TABLE 7.2 *Overview of tasks in the position search process*

Task 1: Peer Teaching (Oral)

Group work task	Significant learning (Fink's taxonomy)	Skills practised	Language practised
Résumé and application letter writing	1. Foundational knowledge 2. Learning about learning 3. Application	(1i) Knowing the topic, concepts, relationships well (2i) Developing an agenda based on how one would learn and then using this plan to impart to peers (3i) Coordinating and sequencing information and tasks effectively to impart to peers	1. Question types 2. Sequencing words 3. Coordinators and subordinators 4. Adjectives 5. Tenses 6. Formal vs. informal language
Job/position interview	1. Foundational knowledge 2. Learning how to learn 3. Application 4. Human dimension	(1i) Knowing the topic, concepts, relationships well (2i) Developing an agenda based on how one would learn and then using this plan to impart to peers (3i) Coordinating and sequencing information and tasks effectively to impart to peers (4i) Imparting the importance of reflecting on one's own personal and social competence (social skills) in peer teaching	1. Question types 2. Sequencing words 3. Coordinators and subordinators 4. Adjectives 5. Time adverbials

(*Continued*)

TABLE 7.2 *(Continued)*

Task 2: Self-discovery/Searching for a Suitable Position (Introspective)

Individual task	Significant learning (Fink's taxonomy)	Skills practised	Language practised
Self-discovery	1. Human dimension 2. Caring	(1i) Learning about oneself (1ii) Journeying toward self-authorship (1iii) Learning about others (1iv) Developing a broader concept of others/Learning about self and others (2i) Developing new interests	Present tense; adjectives
Looking for a suitable position	1. Foundational knowledge 2. Integration 3. Application 4. Human dimension	(1i) Understanding and remembering information and ideas (2i) Connecting people and realms of life (3i) Practical thinking (4i) Recognizing the value of personal competence (self-awareness/motivation)	1. Job/position advertisement language 2. Understanding the language of company culture 3. Understanding the nature of a workplace through the language of an advertisement/workplace website/feedback from employees

Task 3: Crafting the Résumé and Application Letter (Written)

Individual task	Significant learning (Fink's taxonomy)	Skills practised	Language practised
Crafting résumé	1. Integration 2. Caring 3. Application	(1i) Understanding basic concepts of persuasive written communication and personal branding (2i) Finding out more about what employers are looking for in prospective candidates	1. Tenses, e.g., past and present 2. Active, dynamic verbs 3. Adjectives and other words to describe themselves 4. Time adverbials to express chronology of events or acquisition of skills

		(3i) Putting to work information from the above in the way they write their résumés and application letters	
Crafting application letter	1. Integration 2. Caring 3. Application 4. Human dimension	(1i) Understanding basic concepts of persuasive written communication and personal branding (2i) Finding out more about what employers are looking for in prospective candidates (3i) Putting to work information from the above in the way they write their résumés and application letters (4i) Developing social competence (and awareness of audience/others' feelings and concerns)	1. Tenses – Present, past and future; 2. Modals, e.g., can, will, would 2. Concession-refutation structures to talk about shortcomings 3. Coordinators and subordinators for text cohesion 4. Paragraphing

Task 4: Peer Review of Résumé and Application Letter (Oral)

Pair work task	Significant learning (Fink's taxonomy)	Skills practised	Language practised
Peer review	1. Foundational knowledge 2. Learning how to learn 3. Application 4. Human dimension	(1i) Understanding and remembering information and ideas (2i) Becoming a better student and a self-directed learner (3i) Refining oral communication, interpersonal and intercultural skills (4i) Developing social competence (in producing feedback/critiques)	1. Concession-refutation structures 2. Pronouns 3. Modals, e.g. should, could

(*Continued*)

TABLE 7.2 *(Continued)*

Task 5: Appearing for a Mock Job/Position Interview (Oral)

Pair work task	Significant learning (Fink's taxonomy)	Skills practised	Language practised
Mock job/position interview	1. Application 2. Human dimension	(1i) Understanding how to read job advertisements and matching their own strengths to communicate the fit; understanding basic concepts of persuasive oral communication, interview question types and possible responses in job/position interviews; knowing how to express strengths and weaknesses to their best advantage (2i) Understanding EQ preparing and grooming oneself to become a good interview candidate (3i) Applying above-mentioned knowledge to critically assess interviewers and interview context (e.g. reading body language of interviewers) to help themselves give creative responses; apply oral communication, interpersonal and intercultural skills to present their best selves (4i) Connecting self-knowledge of strengths and weaknesses and the company as well as the job requirements for the interviewer so that the latter can see the fit (5i) Knowing how to convince the interviewer as to why they are better than other candidates even when all things remain equal (6i) Expressing their passion for what they would be doing if employed in this position	1. Use of descriptive language that accurately describes their own abilities; use of comparatives and superlatives 2. Use of modals to express ability, willingness, etc. 3. Use of conditionals when talking about scenarios 4. Use of hedging expressions 5. Use of expressions for social grace, 'may I?', 'thank-you', etc. 6. Use of different question types

TABLE 7.3 *Percentage of students finding various tasks useful for learning (n=149)*

Activity/Views on its usefulness for learning	Useful	Not useful	Not applicable
Preparing a résumé	99.3%	0.7%	0
Preparing an application letter	97.3%	2.7%	0
Conducting an interview	90.6%	7.3%	2.1%
Being interviewed	89.9%	6.0%	4.1%

anonymously. For the two-year period inclusive of four semesters during academic years 2011/12 and 2012/13, a total of 149 students responded, comprising approximately 33.8 per cent of the total number of 441 students who took the course. On the survey instrument, respondents were asked to consider and rate statements on a Likert Scale for the degree to which they found a particular item useful for their learning. Table 7.3 shows how students assessed the usefulness of four of the component activities of the position search.

It is clear from information in the table that nearly all students found value in preparing the résumé and application letter. This is consistent with the expectation that students who elect to enrol in this course anticipate a real-world need for such learning. Since many of them are about to graduate, and a large percentage are ready to embark on overseas attachments or internships, classroom experiences that better prepare them for the immediate future tend to be viewed positively.

For the activities related to the mock interview stage of the process, the responses were favourable though not equally so. Those few students who viewed the experience as not useful might not have taken the opportunity to engage in the tasks seriously, or they might have participated in interviews that were not wholly satisfying. As was mentioned earlier, for successful implementation of the mock interview part of the search process task it is vital that all participants take part in the role-play seriously.

Qualitative feedback on the position search segment was equally impressive. For an item requesting students to explain what area of course content they liked most, the comments of a number of students indicated, as this student has, that the position search segment was highly valued:

> I enjoyed the component on position search the most. I learnt how to craft a good cover letter and résumé, and I am grateful that there was an opportunity for peer review of my work. The mock interview was also a humbling process and helped me to realize that my interview performance has much room for improvement!

Another student wrote as follows:

> I loved the interview aspect of this module. It was highly relevant and thus made me more motivated to excel!

Conclusion

In this chapter we have described the position search segment of a professional communication course offered as an elective at the NUS, a leading university in Asia. The course integrates the development and practice of macro skills needed for a successful position search with the essential supporting language and communication micro skills, all within the context of a multi-modal, task-based learning project. The segment aims to provide students with a *close-to-real-life experience* while helping them discover their own strengths, identify their weaknesses, and reflect on what they value most.

The self-discovery part of the position search process, for example, encourages students to reflect on their experience, skills and talents, life goals and values, and to understand the value of creating a personal brand which they can then match with suitable positions that they might want to apply for, be those full-time jobs, company internships, overseas attachments or openings for further studies. Students also learn to concretize claims about their skills and abilities with examples of what they have done in the past that exemplify these claims. Incidental language acquisition in this stage of the segment includes descriptive language and verb tense forms. This process makes students accountable for their résumés and application letters and helps them become more aware of the importance of building trust in their potential workplace through honesty.

While developing peer lessons on relevant content, crafting multiple drafts of résumés and application letters, and preparing for and participating in position selection interviews, students become providers of the course content. When they participate in peer-taught lessons, conduct reviews of their classmates' application portfolios, and develop interview questions and conduct interviews, they respond to the aforementioned content and provide invaluable guided feedback to their peers. While honing their interpersonal and intercultural communication skills in this part of the process, students also practise question types, imperatives and a variety of tenses. Sessions at each stage of this process are facilitated and debriefed by the teacher.

By taking students through a step-by-step, hands-on process, the position search segment engages students in a task-based process that offers significant learning experiences likely to equip them with the skills to achieve positive outcomes. The process requires students to practise and hone their grammar, speaking, writing and interpersonal communication skills. Also, the fact that students are participating in tasks that are closely related to real-life position searches increases their engagement and sense of accountability, thereby enabling deep learning to take place in a relatively low-risk classroom environment. The concrete takeaways from such a learning experience extend to students' development of a useable portfolio and transferrable macro skills required when applying for a position, securing an interview and then performing in that interview with confidence. The net effect is that students are empowered with a refined position search tool set, and that there is an increase in the likelihood that they will gain a position of their choice once they have embarked on the application process in an authentic setting in the near future.

References

Biggs, J. (1979). Individual differences in study processes and the quality of learning outcomes. *Higher Education, 8*, 381–394.

Bloom, B. S. (Ed.). (1956). Taxonomy of educational objectives. *The classification of educational goals. Handbook 1: Cognitive Domain.* New York: McKay.

Bransford, J. D., Brown, A., & Cocking, R. (1999). *How people learn: Brain, mind, experience, and school.* Washington, DC: National Academy Press.

Bygate, M., Skehan, P., & Swain, M. (Eds). (2000). Introduction. In *Researching pedagogic tasks: Second language learning, teaching and testing.* Harlow, Essex: Longman.

Ellis, R., (2000). Task-based research and language pedagogy. *Language Teaching Research, 4*(3), 193–220.

Entwistle, N. J., & Ramsden, P. (1983). *Understanding student learning.* London: Croom Helm.

Fink, D. L. (2003). *Creating significant learning experiences: An integrated approach to designing college courses.* San Francisco: Jossey-Bass.

Gardiner, L. (1994). Redesigning higher education: Producing dramatic gains in student learning. *ASHE-ERIC Higher Education Report, 7.* Washington, DC: George Washington University.

Kramsch, C. (2007). The uses of communicative competence in a global world. In J. Liu (Ed.), *English language teaching in China: New approaches, perspectives and standards* (pp. 56–74). London: Continuum International.

Lantolf, J., & Appel, G. (Eds). (1994). *Vygotskian approaches to second language research.* Norwood, NJ: Ablex.

Lantolf, J. (1996). Second language acquisition theory-building: 'Letting all the flowers bloom!' *Language Learning, 46*, 713–749.

Lantolf, J. (2000). *Sociocultural theory and second language learning.* Oxford: Oxford University Press.

Lindblom-Ylanne, S. (1999). *Studying in a traditional medical curriculum: Study success, orientations to studying and problems that arise.* Helsinki: The University of Helsinki, Faculty of Medicine.

Long, M. (1983). Native speaker/non-native speaker conversation in the second language classroom. In M. Clarke & J. Handscombe, (Eds), *On TESOL '82: Pacific perspectives on language and teaching.* Washington, DC: TESOL.

Pica, T., Kanagy, R., & Falodun, J. (1993). Choosing and using communication tasks for second language instruction. In G. Crookes & S. Gass (Eds), *Tasks and language learning: Integrating theory and practice.*

Pintrich, P. R. (2000). Multiple goals, multiple pathways: The role of goal orientation in learning and achievement. *Journal of Educational Psychology, 92*(3), 544–555.

Pintrich, P. R. (2004). A conceptual framework for assessing motivation and self-regulated learning in college students. *Educational Psychology Review, 16*, 385–407.

Renandya, W. (2013). Essential factors affecting EFL learning outcomes. *English Teaching, 68*(4), 23–41.

Skehan, P. (1996). Second language acquisition research and task-based instruction. In J. Willis & D. Willis (Eds), *Challenge and change in language teaching.* Oxford: Heinemann.

Skehan, P. (1998a). Task-based instruction. *Annual Review of Applied Linguistics, 18*, 268–286.

Skehan, P. (1998b). *A cognitive approach to language learning.* Oxford: Oxford University Press.

Trigwell, K., Ellis, R. A., & Han, F. (2012). Relations between students' approaches to learning, experienced emotions and outcomes of learning. *Studies in Higher Education, 37*(7), 811–824.

Trigwell, K., & Prosser, M. (1991). Relating approaches to study and quality of learning outcomes at the course level. *British Journal of Educational Psychology, 61,* 265–275.

Van Lier, L. (1991). Inside the classroom: Learning processes and teaching procedures. *Applied Language Learning, 2,* 29–69.

Vygotsky, L. (1978). *Mind and society: The development of higher psychological processes.* Cambridge, MA: Harvard University Press.

Wee, L. (2008). The technologization of discourse and authenticity in English language teaching. *International Journal of Applied Linguistics, 18*(3), 256–273.

Widdowson, H. (1998). Skills, abilities, and contexts of reality. *Annual Review of Applied Linguistics, 18,* 323–333.

Yule, G. (1997). *Referential communication tasks.* Mahwah, NJ: Lawrence Erlbaum.

8

Teaching the Teachers: Task-Based Teacher Training in Asia

Marilyn Lewis

Summary

The following chapter reports on a workshop for tertiary teachers in a minority group state in a country in Asia. Although it would be interesting to name the country, changing circumstances there mean that for the time being the place must remain anonymous. There were two purposes for the workshop: to introduce fresh teaching ideas in a context where lecturing and reading are the traditional sources of input for students, and at the same time to update the teachers' classroom English, which is their third language. Tasks were an important part of the workshop delivery, but there were also small sessions of direct teaching. This bringing together of direct teaching and discovery learning was intended to model what the teachers could do later in their own classrooms.

Theories of learning and teaching

A broad distinction between two approaches to teaching around the world and through the centuries is summarized by Petty (2004, p. 296) as 'teaching by telling' or 'teaching by asking'. People wanting to explore the latter, sometimes referred to as discovery learning, have plenty of advice. Scrivener (2011) provides guidelines for wording questions that encourage guided discovery, such as 'ask questions that encourage learners to reflect on and articulate reasons for their choices' and 'build on earlier questions' (p. 167). His advice is supported by a lesson transcript and a number of other examples. The title of Muller et al.'s (2012) *Innovating EFL teaching in Asia*, shows how regionally specific the advice is becoming for teachers wanting to explore new ideas. Using examples from Indonesia, South Korea, China and other Asian countries contributors to this edited collection explore many concepts including learner autonomy and empowerment. Specifically they describe programmes that introduce students to strategies for language learning, to peer feedback and to tasks.

In our own advice to tertiary teachers (Reinders, Lewis & Kirkness, 2010), as well as giving suggestions for group work, we included ideas for some of the more traditional forms of teaching, such as lecturing, setting writing tasks, and encouraging critical reading. In relation to setting clear writing tasks we quoted some questions asked by students (p. 59), which illustrate how difficult it can be for them to decode teachers' questions and feedback: What exactly does this question mean?; What does the written feedback from the lecturer really mean?; Is it praise or criticism?

Then there is advice to teacher trainers. In this context Farrell (2013) discusses reflective practice which, as he makes clear, 'has still not been reduced to a method' (p. 27). He returns to the thoughts of Dewey in the 1930s for 'five main phases of reflective thought' (p. 29). Some of these phases suggest ideas for the teacher trainer/educator who is planning workshops. For instance, the solving of perceived problems can be encouraged through case studies. Reasoning comes into play as participants cooperate to suggest solutions. Hypotheses about what works or does not work have to wait until ideas are put into action after the workshop. Farrell's term 'evidence-based reflective practice' (p. 31) is a good starting point for planning tasks for in-service workshops.

One way of promoting Farrell's 'reflective practice' and the 'teaching by asking' explained by Petty (2004) is through the use of tasks. Tasks are 'generally considered to be a subset of class activities [and] require holistic language use' since they 'require learners to independently make use of their language resources in order to achieve a specific goal' (Philp et al., 2014, p. 123). From time to time efforts are made to classify what must be thousands of tasks published for language classrooms. However, Ellis (2003, p. 216) believes that not only is there 'no accepted single typology of tasks' but that experts cannot even agree on an 'organising principle for constructing such a typology'. There is, however, agreement on a basic definition for a task.

As explained by Ellis and Shintani (2014, pp. 135–136) a task must fulfil four criteria. First its main focus must be on the meaning (rather than the form) of the language. Next there must be 'a need to convey information, to express an opinion or to infer meaning.' Thirdly, learners are not taught language forms ready to complete the task, and finally the outcome must go beyond using language, which is the means not the end. Ellis and Shintani respond to the criticism that task-based language teaching (TBLT) does not allow for enough input, by pointing out that new language can be learned 'through the input that the performance of tasks provides' (p. 153). Philp et al. (2014) address a number of questions of interest to language teachers. How exactly do tasks influence interaction? What range of cognitive demands do they place on learners? What part is played by the resources provided by the teacher? How can teachers influence the interaction?

The concept of basing a teacher training programme on tasks was well-developed twenty years ago by Parrott (1993) with his carefully organized materials for trainers. Amongst his target users were non-native speakers of the target language. Answers to Philp et al.s' (2014) and others' questions suggest that tasks serve a triple purpose during teacher training workshops. They let teachers consider real-life examples, they model a way of teaching and learning which teachers can use in their own classes, and thirdly they give participants a chance to practise their own English. In their work on language teacher development Richards and Farrell (2005) include the following elements: self-monitoring, peer observation, analysing critical incidents and case analysis, all of which can be incorporated into workshops.

In his most recent work Farrell (2013) classifies suggestions for reflective practice for English as a Foreign Language (EFL) teachers according to the medium and the focus of teachers' reflections. The medium can be oral or written, and the focus can be on the teachers' beliefs, on their roles and on critical incidents. Oral reflection, in the case of participants who are also wanting to improve their own English, comes through peer interaction, a part of language development also explored by Philp et al. (2014.) They point out that this interaction can come about through writing, via computers and, most commonly, orally within a classroom.

Published work on the subject of tertiary teaching in general is important when workshop participants are teaching English for Specific Purposes (ESP) rather than general English. Our own experience of teacher education (Reinders, Lewis & Kirkness, 2010) showed that lecturing, or direct teaching, is an important part of many classes and needs to be addressed in a workshop for teachers. Our advice included suggestions as to what makes for a clear explanation, and the important part played by a range of examples in helping students understand difficult new concepts.

For teachers' workshops in the area ESP, there is even more specific published research. Ruiz-Garrido et al. (2010) address the topic of English for professional and academic purposes, including a five-chapter section 'devoted to teaching perspectives' (p. 6). In the same volume, Bocanegra-Valle's interest is in the evaluation and design of materials. Many of the questions she poses are pertinent to trainers preparing a course where they themselves may not be experts in the topics taught by the workshop attenders. In a word, 'What do I, as an ESP practitioner, know about the carrier content?' (p. 143) Authenticity is an important part of her advice to people looking for materials.

Once the workshop has concluded, the question of evaluation arises. How might the worth of the sessions to participants be evaluated? Graves (1996, p. 32) addressed the question of how to assess the effectiveness of lengthier courses. She included observation during class time, informal talks with participants, time for oral or written input by participants and the teacher's (or in the case of a workshop the trainer's) own reflection. The written evaluation of a course by participants is almost standard now in courses for teachers and Muller et al. (2012, p. 140) mentions the value of frequently updating these, his example being towards 'a user-friendlier format'.

In summary, the theoretical underpinning of this study includes the areas of TBLT, tertiary teaching, teacher education, and teaching language and content.

Planning the workshop

Our workshop was held in a remote part of one Asian country which, for various reasons, is not being named. The participants were teachers of theology. Two trainers ran workshops on more than one occasion, but this report concentrates only on the part taught by the author of this chapter at one of the workshops. The use of English by presenters and participants was not an issue because the teachers use English to deliver their own classes. The reasons for this are complex but include the availability of subject textbooks in English only and the fact that their students, coming from a range of tribal groups, might have different first languages or dialects. As pointed out by Sowden (2012, p. 89), during post-colonial periods 'English had proved an effective means of communication between different ethnic and linguistic groups'. Participants were, however, encouraged to use any common languages as they discussed the course content.

In planning the workshop we had in mind the advice of researchers as summarized above. For instance, a belief in the importance of authenticity in materials meant searching for published sources which could serve a double purpose. The materials we were able to collect beforehand provided us with language samples as the basis for tasks as well as pointing the workshop participants to new sources for their own teaching. As one example, we found a textbook for students of theological English by Pierson, Dickerson and Scott (2010), which included a pair of books, one for students and one for the teacher.

The five areas covered in this part of the workshop were determined after discussions with participants in earlier visits to the town and to similar programmes in another part of the country. The topics were:

1. Ways of reading
2. Doing research
3. Organising tutorials
4. Planning and delivering lectures
5. Setting and marking assignments.

Tasks for participants

Our tasks were designed for the three purposes mentioned above: to give practise in the language of teaching their subject; to show new ideas for teaching; and, in some cases, to provide ready-to-go tasks for their own classes. In reporting on some of the tasks set for the teachers during the workshop, we use as a starting point three of Farrell's (2013) headings: reflecting on teachers' beliefs, on teachers' roles and on critical incidents. We have also added two other categories: reflecting on personal experiences, and reflecting on written academic language, as found in the articles and textbooks they would be encouraging their students to read. As the samples show, some of the tasks focused on language production, while others included the Ellis and Shintani (2014) criterion of providing the opportunity to meet new language in context as a starting point.

Reflecting on teachers' beliefs

One fairly new role required of the teachers was to do research. During the workshop they were supplied with current research-based articles as a starting point to preparing them for this role.

> TASK: Analyse research questions
>
> The following task encouraged them, using their own beliefs as a starting point, to examine questions posed in articles published in their field. They were asked for their opinions on research questions.
>
> *What similarities/differences do you see between the questions* [provided] *from published research?*
> *Which do you predict would be harder to investigate? Why?*
> *What do you think could be the advantages and disadvantages of having sub-questions?*

Reflecting on teachers' roles

The following four tasks focus on a teacher's role in giving written feedback, in teaching strategies for reading and for wording test questions.

> TASK: Share problems
>
> Case studies were used as a starting point for discussing teachers' roles, including some which were solicited from the participants, as in this prompt.
>
> *What difficult situations do you face when writing feedback?*
>
> Their suggestions were summarized on the board, some suggested responses were discussed generally and then people were asked to recommend the best option, with reasons.

> TASK: Compare feedback comments
>
> Here is a comment about teachers' feedback on students' writing of reports and essays:
>   'Experienced teachers can criticize a student's work in a way that sounds like advice.' (Petty 2004, p. 65)
>   Now compare these two comments quoted by Petty. Suggest how students might respond to each.
>
> *'That's great. Your graph has well-chosen scales. Use a pencil, though, then you can rub out any mistakes. All the points look correctly plotted. Well done!'*
>
> *'Don't use a pen to do graphs.'*

TASK: Evaluate your own marking practice

Harkness (2008, pp. 193–194) suggests six strategies for marking essays. How easy would each of these be for you? Note one of these responses.

I do that already.
That would be difficult for me.
I could do that if I tried.

1. Where possible use criteria-referenced (or outcomes-based) rather than norm-referenced strategies.
2. Start with encouraging comments, then give helpful criticism.
3. Return marked assignments within a reasonable time while students still remember what they have written.
4. Comment on the ideas more than on language and formatting mistakes.
5. Keep results confidential by returning assignments directly to the student.
6. Avoid 'school teacher' actions such as marking with red pens. For many mature students this brings back bad memories.

TASK: Collect ideas for working out word meanings

In this task teachers were encouraged to try for themselves some strategies which they could later introduce to their students. The task was based on a reading passage they had already looked at.

Try out some of the following strategies with the words you listed from pp. 33–35.
Analyse the word parts
Find words made up of familiar word parts. e.g., timeless [time + less]
Replace the word with a simpler word that would make sense
Draw lines to match up the words in the left-hand column and the more everyday words in the right-hand column.

Summarize	Very small
Consider	Find that
Investigate	Put together
Establish	Talk about
Describe	Find out
Minute	Think about

Now think of simpler words for some of the new terms you noted earlier.
  e.g., It is difficult . . . to *distinguish* between these two men.
    It is difficult . . . to see the difference *between these two men.*

TASK: Word written questions clearly

Another role of the tertiary teacher is to set questions for assignments and tests. The following task was designed to show that the language of questions need not be complex. The message was that when the goal of a test question is for students to write ideas rather than decode difficult worded questions then the simpler the language the better.

Here are examples of difficult questions. Below the table they are reworded in simpler language. Copy each simpler question into the correct box.

ACTUAL QUESTION	SIMPLE ORAL QUESTIONS
Discuss, with reference to specific examples, the role of X in Y.	
Give an account of the debate	
Discuss the ways in which X derived influence from Y?	
What, according to X, is the relationship between Y and Z?	
Examine the significance of X	

<u>The simpler questions</u>

What does X say about the link between Y and Z?

Why is X important?

What did X do?

What did X and Y say about Z? What was different about their two views?

How did Y lead to X?

Reflecting on critical incidents

TASK: Examine negative experiences

Critical incidents were used to illustrate what can go wrong with tutorials, including:
    Students do not see the purpose of the tutorial.
    Students are too shy to talk.
    Nobody has taught the students how to join in discussions.

That led to a task in which participants exchanged ideas in answer to the question: What's the point of tutorials?

Here are some reasons why tutorials are said to be a good idea. In your opinion, which are the most important? Mark each suggestion as:

A. *very important*
B. *quite important*
C. *not so important*

___ The lecture topics can be discussed.
___ Students can ask questions about assignments.
___ Talking about new ideas is a good way to understand them.
___ Students learn from one another as well as from the teacher
___ The new language of the subject can be practised orally before students need to use it in assignments.

Reflecting on personal experiences

TASK: Interviews

As a starting point to the topic of teaching reading in a second language, teachers were asked to reflect on their own reading practices by interviewing one another.

How do you read in your first language?

Work in pairs to interview someone about the way they read in their first language.

1. What do you do when you are reading and you meet a word you don't know?
2. Do you usually read word for word or in word groups? (Ask someone to watch your eye movements as you read silently.)
3. Can you remember any strategies your teachers taught you for reading your own language when you were a child?
4. Which of these strategies do you still use and which have you changed?

Reflecting on academic English

TASK: Analyse the language

This task could be given to students in this form or adapted to a different reading passage. The purpose was to distinguish between the language of:

a. Chronological order
b. Cause and effect

Here is the part relating to chronological order.

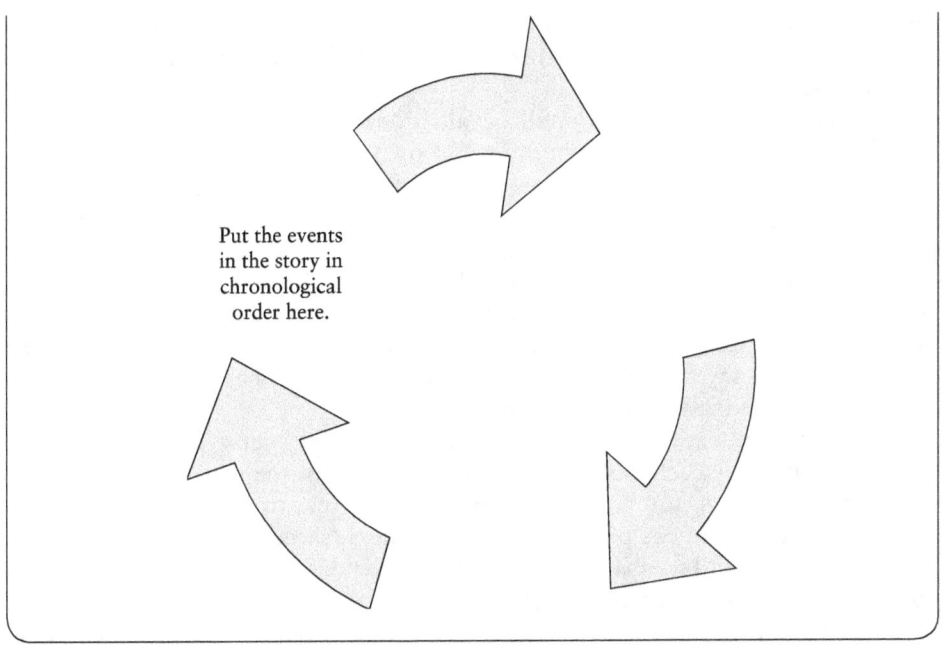

The course was not entirely task-based. Just as the teachers would, back in their classrooms, be giving some lectures, so we did not shy away from some up-front teaching. In particular we took this approach when it would save time and, we hoped, model ways of lecturing that went beyond simply reading, or even dictating, notes. As one example, we taught directly three skill levels for in-depth reading (followed by a task):

Level 1: Finding the details
Level 2: Simple inferencing
Level 3: Complex inferencing

Course outcomes

The ongoing results of a workshop such as this would best be evaluated long term, but the geographical distance between the teachers and trainers mean that we cannot comment on post-workshop outcomes. Of the suggestions by Graves (1996, p. 32) for evaluating a course, we used the following. Our observation of participants while they were doing the tasks included moving from one pair or group to the next, sometimes joining in the activity, sometimes answering questions, and sometimes making suggestions. In addition there were informal talks with the whole group at the end of each task, when the trainer sat down and encouraged discussion of each task in terms of how realistic it might be for their own classes. On occasions the participants spoke of their enthusiasm for trying out a new idea but at other times they were realistic about barriers. For example, anything that took time to prepare would have to compete with the number of hours available to them in between their main work and other employment they had to take to support their families.

Then there is Graves' suggestion that evaluation can happen through the teacher's (or in the case of a workshop the trainer's) own reflection. This happened when notes were taken at the end of each day as the trainer looked back at the programme and made suggestions for improvements, and noted interesting examples from participants. These notes were useful in writing this chapter.

The final written evaluation of a course by participants is almost standard now in courses for teachers. During earlier visits to the country we found that this method did not yield critical data, but rather turned into letters of thanks. People seemed very reluctant to say anything negative about trainers who had come from afar in their own time and at their own expense.

More formally, an evaluation of the success of the course came via a short oral presentation by each participant towards the end of the workshop. They each spoke, in interactive lecture form, on a topic on which they usually lectured. The idea was to include as many as possible of the new ideas learned during the workshop. Notes were taken and feedback given orally at the end, first by the 'audience' (other course members) and then by the trainer. Here is a summary of the categories for which positive comments were made by the trainer. They are grouped according to points made during the workshops, with the feedback comments paraphrased and italicized.

> **Introduce topics with:**
> some links to known information
> > *Used 2nd person to remind them*
> > *Reminded them of a book available in the library*
> > *Pointed at board as a reminder of point already made*
>
> an overview
> > *Spelled out three parts to the lecture*
> > *Gave the title twice*
> > *Explained why the topic was important*
>
> **Explain new concepts through:**
> familiar examples
> > *Used local and international examples*
> > *Chose familiar metaphors*
>
> negative as well as positive examples
> > *'That's not the same as . . .'*
>
> simpler language for definition
> > *Clearly explained*
>
> checking understanding
> > *Asked a question to elicit local example*

visuals
> *Drew quick board sketches*

repetition of key terms
> *Repeated and explained title*

While you are speaking:

vary your voice in tone, volume, speed
> *Sounded enthusiastic*

make only moderate reference to notes
> *Made eye contact with individuals while speaking*

use natural eye contact and gestures
> *Stood to the side so as not to block view of board*

Conclusion

This brief account by no means quantifies the results of our workshop. It is intended as a reflection on one short in-service course with a small group of teachers who were regular in attendance, enthusiastic in their participation and determined to put into action as best they could some new ways of learning. As we know from the literature, change does not come quickly in any educational setting. Furthermore, trainers who fly in and then out of a country may include ideas which are simply not realistic locally. Advice to any people hoping to launch into similar projects would be to aim for more than one visit, to be good listeners and observers as well as speakers and to be grateful for the warm welcome which is so often given in remote areas.

References

Bocanegra-Valle, A. (2010). Evaluating and designing materials for the ESP classroom. In M. Ruiz-Garrido, J. Palmer-Silveira & I. Fortanet-Gomez (Eds) (2010). *English for professional and academic purposes* (pp. 141–165). Amsterdam & New York: Rodopi.

Ellis, R. (2003). *Task based language learning and teaching.* Oxford: Oxford University Press.

Ellis, R., & Shintani, N. (2014). *Exploring language pedagogy through second language acquisition research.* Basingstoke: Palgrave Macmillan.

Farrell, T. S. C. (2013). *Reflective practice in ESL teacher development groups: From practices to principles.* Basingstoke: Palgrave Macmillan.

Graves, K. (Ed). (1996). *Teachers as course developers.* Cambridge: Cambridge University Press.

Harkness, A. (2008). Assessment in theological education: Do our theological values matter?' in *The Journal of Asian Theological Education.* 5(2), 183–201.

Muller, T., Herder, S., Adamson, J., & Shigeo Brown, P. (2012). *Innovating EFL teaching in Asia.* Basingstoke: Palgrave Macmillan.

Parrott, M. (1993). *Tasks for language teachers.* Cambridge: Cambridge University Press.

Petty, G. (2004). *Teaching today*. Cheltenham, UK: Nelson Thornes Ltd.
Philp, J., Adams, R., & Iwashita, N. (2014). *Peer interaction and second language learning*. New York & London: Routledge.
Pierson, C. L., Dickerson, L. J., & Florence R. Scott (2010). *Exploring theological English*. Carlisle, UK: Piquant. [Student and teacher's book].
Richards, J. C., & Farrell, T. S. C. (2005). *Professional development for language teachers: Strategies for teacher learning*. Cambridge: Cambridge University Press.
Reinders, H., Lewis, M., & Kirkness, A. (2010 edition). *Good teacher, better teacher*. Nagoya: Perceptia Press.
Ruiz-Garrido, M., Palmer-Silveira, J., & Fortanet- Gomez, I. (Eds) (2010). *English for professional and academic purposes*. Amsterdam & New York: Rodopi.
Scrivener, J. (2011). *Learning teaching*. Oxford: Macmillan.
Sowden, C. (2012) EFL on a mushroom: The overnight growth in English as a Lingua Franca. *ELT Journal*, 66(1), pp. 89–96.

PART THREE

Teachers' perspectives

Introduction

Jack C. Richards

Attempts to implement task-based language teaching (TBLT) prompt a reminder of the history of communicative language teaching (CLT) in non-European settings in the 1980s and 1990s – experiences that led educators to recognize the impact culturally-based assumptions about teaching and learning can have on curriculum innovation and change (Kramsch, 1993; Richards 1985). One important lesson from the experience with CLT was that conceptions of good teaching are situated and differ from culture to culture. Assumptions about the roles of teachers and learners, the nature of second language learning, the importance of grammar, practice, and the use of the mother-tongue may all be influenced by the culture of learning that shapes teaching practices in a school. Hence successful innovations from one context may not work when attempts are made to repeat them in a different context. In some cultures, a good teacher is one who controls and directs learners and who maintains a respectful distance between the teacher and the learners. Learners are the more or less passive recipients of the teacher's expertise. Teaching is viewed as a teacher-controlled and directed process. In other cultures the teacher may be viewed more as a facilitator. The ability to form close interpersonal relations with students is highly valued and there is a strong emphasis on individual learner creativity and independent learning. These views of teaching and learning are implicit in both CLT and TBLT (Carless, 2004).

Some of these issues are illustrated in the chapters in this section. Shaoqian Luo's paper clarifies obstacles that limit the applicability of standard TBLT methodology in China. These include the teacher's limited English language proficiency and communicative competence, the lack of suitable materials, teachers' assumptions about grammar-based teaching, the pressure of examinations, lack of training opportunities for teachers, class size, and learners' reluctance to communicate in the public setting of a classroom – in short, the same factors that accounted for the limited uptake of CLT and which were generally attributed to 'the Chinese context' and the need for an eclectic approach which drew on a traditional grammar-based methodology.

In the second paper, Stephen J. Hall suggests how some of the issues, described by Luo, can be addressed. Hall describes an approach to an in-service training course for rural teachers in Malaysia. This made use of a Loop Input approach – one in which participating teachers and trainers are engaged in reflective investigation and reflection on classroom practices and where new practices are monitored and revised through a process of critical reflection.

In the final paper in this section, Nguyen, Newton and Crabbe focus on one stage in the task-cycle essential to TBLT – the pre-task phase. Since preparation and support given at the pre-task stage play a crucial role on the effective use of many tasks, teachers' views of the nature of the pre-task phase and how best to implement it provides important insights into the classroom practices associated with TBLT, in this instance with a case study of the practices of teachers in Vietnam.

References

Carless, D. (2004). Issues in teachers' interpretation of a task-based innovation in primary schools. *TESOL Quarterly, 38*(4), 639–662.

Kramsch, C. (1993). *Context and culture in language teaching*. Oxford: Oxford University Press.

Richards, J. (1985). *The context of language teaching*. Cambridge: Cambridge University Press.

9

Teachers' Perceived Difficulty in Implementing TBLT in China

Shaoqian Luo
Jiaxin Xing

Summary

Since the late 1990s, task-based language teaching (TBLT) has been adopted or adapted by a number of Asian governments. Principles associated with TBLT have been advocated in a range of curriculum initiatives. However, since curriculum innovation is affected by multiple and interrelated factors at different stages and at different levels (Shamin, 1996), many accounts have shown that Asian countries still face many difficulties and challenges in implementing TBLT. This chapter presents findings arising from a study of teachers' perceived difficulties in implementing TBLT in China. In order to obtain teachers' perceptions, questionnaires and follow-up interviews were conducted among secondary school English teachers. Teachers' perceptions of difficulties fell into four categories: those caused by the teacher; the students; the educational system; and TBLT itself. Teachers reported that they lacked training in TBLT. Students were not competent or confident enough to participate in tasks. The grammar-translation method and examinations at all levels also constrained implementation. External conditions such as large classes and over-worked teachers were also significant obstacles. The research suggests that numerous stakeholders need to work together to improve the present situation if TBLT is to be effectively implemented.

Introduction

TBLT in second language (L2) education is currently attracting much attention. The literature on this topic includes task needs analysis, task syllabus, task design, task choice, task sequence, task implementation and task-based assessments in English as a Second Language

(ESL) and English as a Foreign Language (EFL) contexts. TBLT encourages syllabi and methodologies driven by learners' needs; learner training and the use of problem-solving pedagogical tasks; cooperative learning and collaborative small groups work; and focuses on both meaning and form (Long, 1995). Consequently, syllabus design and implementation are demanding for teachers of English who play a key role in integrating TBLT in the classroom, particularly in Asian contexts where teachers are traditionally respected as the authority and provider of knowledge. The institutional, classroom and teacher constraints identified above may therefore limit innovations in L2 education and the implementation of TBLT in Asian English language teaching (Adams & Newton, 2009).

A survey in Vietnam shows that large classes and traditional grammar examinations block the implementation of new methodologies (Li, 1998, 2001). Many researchers in Hong Kong, Korea and other Asian countries or regions have investigated these difficulties in implementing TBLT. Attempts to integrate TBLT approaches in Mainland China have also drawn much attention from researchers, teachers and learners and heated discussions and debates have arisen as a consequence (Luo & Yi, 2013). Many advocates in China (e.g., Cheng, 2004; Luo & Gong, 2007) have investigated specific cases of TBLT in some developed areas in China such as Beijing, Guangdong, Jiangsu and Zhejiang. Other Chinese educators suggest that the TBLT model does not work with Chinese classrooms and indicate that Chinese teachers find it difficult to use Communicative Language Teaching (CLT) approaches in the classroom because of traditional attitudes towards course planning, teaching methods and resources (Cheng, 2004). Moreover, limitations involving classroom equipment and teachers' low proficiency of English oral skills and general English abilities are all challenges that need to be addressed (see also Burnaby & Sun, 1989; Hu, 2005).

Is TBLT appropriate for the Chinese context? What are the differences between developed and undeveloped areas in implementing TBLT? Is the traditional teaching method not suitable for learning English? In order to answer these and related questions and determine the success or failure of TBLT in Chinese classrooms, teachers' perceptions of TBLT and their perceived difficulties in implementing TBLT are indispensable. For this reason and based on research in the Asian context, this study investigates Chinese secondary school English teachers' understanding of the uptake of TBLT. As many Asian countries are now encountering the same challenges, this study aims to help stakeholders obtain a better understanding of EFL in the Asian contexts.

Background: TBLT in China

In the late 1990s, some Chinese scholars (e.g., Xia & Hung, 1998) first introduced the theories of TBLT to China, drawing much attention from English teachers and researchers. Since then, the Chinese government has placed English learning and teaching high on its agenda to ensure that China plays an active and important role in politics and the global economy. In 2001 and 2011 the experimental and final version of the National English Curriculum Standards[1] (NECS) were enacted by the Chinese Ministry of Education.

The NECS states that the aim of classroom teaching is to cultivate students' interest to learn English and develop their communicative competence in English. As for the teaching methodology, the NECS emphasizes learner-centredness, language practise and the ability for language use through approaches that focus both on meaning and form. NECS also calls attention to learning strategies, autonomous learning and intercultural awareness and cross-culture communication. Teachers are encouraged to adapt materials to suit learners' needs and interests, to make use of educational resources and organize after-school activities to promote students' learning.

Since 2001 a series of new textbooks have been published in accordance with NECS. Over five sets of English textbooks are now available to secondary schools in Beijing. Education bureaus of different districts are free to choose any set provided that the whole district adopts it. Compared to previous textbooks, there are more communicative materials and related activities, such as listening and speaking tasks, and they are topic-oriented with more authentic activities.

Language teaching methods

In line with the new curriculum and textbooks, TBLT has become popular among teachers and teacher trainers. In order to make this new approach work, teachers and teacher educators and researchers are integrating it into their classrooms and doing research. However, there are many problems to be solved. First of all, the definition of tasks needs to be clarified and understood. Currently, one of the most used definitions is that of Long's (1985):

> A task is a piece of work undertaken for oneself or for others, freely or for some reward. Thus, examples of tasks include painting a fence, dressing a child, filling out a form, buying a pair of shoes, making an airline reservation, borrowing a library book, taking a driving test, typing a letter, weighing a patient, sorting letters, taking a hotel reservation, writing a cheque, finding a street destination and helping someone across a road. In other words, by 'task' is meant the hundred and one things people do in everyday life, at work, at play, and in between.
> (Long, 1985, p. 89)

From this definition it is clear that a task is quite similar to everyday activities such as buying a pair of shoes, borrowing a library book and making an airline reservation. These are simple, practical things in daily life and the goal of using tasks is communication. It is hoped that students learn to use the target language by doing such real-life tasks in the classroom. However, problems occur with this definition as Chinese students are learners of EFL and there are rarely enough authentic contexts in which to practise. Therefore, it is important that teachers create real-life situations and provide learners with opportunities to practise new language and enable their language ability to develop.

Take the example of speaking. In learning speaking, we usually consider six aspects including the learning goal, input from the teacher, learning techniques, the role of the teacher, the role of the learner and evaluation (e.g., Ellis, 2003). Teachers provide a large number of materials on diverse topics and use various techniques such as choral repetition, drilling in the first stage and role-play, interview, discussion and debate in the more advanced stage. Teachers participate in the activities with learners and discuss with them. In a class, the students' involvement is crucial in determining the success or failure of a task. Besides, learners should learn to use the language by doing a task rather than merely learning grammar. Teachers are not the only ones that make the evaluation. The content of evaluation is not only limited to the *product* of the interaction but also the learning *process*.

Nevertheless, this kind of teaching and learning is very demanding for both teachers and learners. Moreover, since most Chinese teachers of English have not been abroad, it is quite difficult for them to imagine contexts and practise the authentic tasks included in the textbooks. Consequently, the goals of learning English need to be reconsidered because English is merely a school subject for the majority of the students in China instead of a means of communicating in the wider society. Given these challenges, is it necessary for EFL learners to learn in English-speaking countries, like ESL learners?

TBLT has been adopted by several Asian governments (e.g., Korea and Japan; see Butler, 2011) and principles associated with task-based teaching have been advocated in a range of curriculum initiatives. By the 1990s, many scholars have investigated the implementation of TBLT in the EFL countries and found that 'large scale top-down curricular revisions may not directly impact actual language teaching practice' (Adams & Newton, 2009, p. 1). They have also discovered that the systematic use of TBLT cannot meet social needs in these countries. Some reports have emphasized how the local needs and the particular English teaching conditions in Asian countries support traditional language teaching methods (Adams & Newton, 2009). While others have strongly advocated the adoption of TBLT in Asian countries, many accounts have shown that Asian countries still face many difficulties and challenges in implementing TBLT effectively (Deng, 2011; Littlewood, 2007; Zhang, 2007).

Zhang's (2007) research finds it difficult to adopt TBLT because there is little commitment to creating a supportive environment for teachers to experiment with new means of classroom practice in China. Adamson and Davison (2003) describe that teachers are struggling to adopt TBLT in their classes and trying hard to put it into practice, but eventually returning to traditional methods of teaching. Adams and Newton (2009) also reveal doubts expressed by students about the effectiveness of curricular innovations in Hong Kong, which may have been influenced by the prevailing conservative view of education. Hu (2002) has indicated that grammar and vocabulary knowledge-focused national examinations are the most influential factors that prevent teaching innovations in China. In a similar vein Littlewood (2007) points out that the large number of multiple-choice testing formats in examinations limits the implementation of TBLT and leads administrators and teachers to teach to tests. Large class size in Korea is another barrier to implementing CLT (Li, 1998) because students must communicate in groups, a factor which raises challenges associated with classroom management. The same situation occurs in Chinese mainland schools.

TBLT requires teachers to understand the nature of tasks and to use them effectively based on students' needs. In many contexts, however, teachers have not had opportunities to gain sufficient understanding of tasks and task-based teaching in terms of the depth required (Adams & Newton, 2009, p. 9). Following previous research of TBLT implementation in Asian countries, this study explores teachers' perceptions of implementing TBLT in Chinese schools, identifying a range of challenges to successful integration.

The present study

Research questions

The research questions in the present study are:

1 To what extent are Chinese teachers prepared to practice TBLT in the classroom?
2 What are the teachers' perceived difficulties in using TBLT?

Participants

The participants included forty-seven middle school English teachers including thirty-five from four schools in the North and twelve from two schools in Central China. Their ages ranged from twenty-six to fifty-four years with the majority in their thirties. Their teaching experience varied from three to thirty-three years. At the time of the study, all the participants were teaching in middle schools. Twenty-two of the participants were teaching in urban middle schools and twenty-five in rural settings.

Research method

The study consists of a written questionnaire and interviews. The questionnaire was based on Li's (1998) research on introducing the communicative approach in Korea. In order to develop a reliable survey, a pilot survey involving five English teachers was conducted. The final questionnaire (see Appendix 9.1) included both open-ended and multiple-choice questions generated from the data collected in the pilot study. It consisted of three parts with the first focusing on the participants' personal information; the second examined teachers' views such as the teaching methods they use in their classrooms and their general views on TBLT in EFL; and the third of twelve investigated difficulties that English teachers may encounter in implementing TBLT in the EFL classroom. Moreover, there were three open-ended questions that collected detailed information on TBLT implementation.

The questionnaire was distributed to teachers from seven secondary schools in Beijing and Hubei. Forty-seven of the questionnaires were returned. Based on the questionnaire results, five teachers were selected and interviewed to explore further the reasons behind the difficulties stated.

Teachers' perceived difficulties in practicing TBLT

The difficulties reported are categorized into four main themes: those caused by the teacher; the students; the educational system; and TBLT itself (see Table 9.1). Among the twelve factors, *Deficiency in spoken English, Deficiency in strategic and sociolinguistic competence, Little time to prepare communicative materials* are related to teachers; *Lack of authentic teaching materials, Grammar-based examinations, Traditional grammar-based language teaching,* and *Large classes* are related to the government and the educational system; *Low English proficiency* and *Resistance to class participation* are factors stemming from the role of learners; and *Lack of training in TBLT, Lack of retraining in TBLT,* and *Insufficient funding, resources and equipment*[2] are related to TBLT knowledge and understanding.

As shown in Table 9.1, *Lack of training in TBLT* (96 per cent), *Lack of authentic teaching materials* (92 per cent), and *Few opportunities for retraining in TBLT* (89 per cent) are ranked as the top three perceived difficulties. When the regions are taken into consideration, Table 9.1 also demonstrates that there is a gap between the two groups of teachers in *TBLT training* and that both groups have a high percentage on the items about training and retraining (83 per cent to 97 per cent). However, a wide gap exists between the two groups in the category of teacher factors (*Little time to prepare communicative materials, Deficiency in strategic and sociolinguistic competence,* and *Deficiency in spoken English*). As for the factors related to the educational system, the two groups also show a relatively big discrepancy (74 per cent versus 92 per cent in *Grammar-based examinations* and 71 per cent versus 92 per cent in *Traditional grammar-based language teaching*). Another point to be noted is that an even bigger difference can be observed between the two groups on student factors (77 per cent versus 100 per cent in *Low English proficiency* and 49 per cent versus 83 per cent in *Resistance to class participation*).

TABLE 9.1 *Teachers' perceived difficulties in implementing TBLT*

Difficulties	Number/Percentage (Beijing: 35 in total)	Number/Percentage (Hubei: 12 in total)	Percentage (47 in total)
Lack of training in TBLT	34 (97%)	11 (92%)	96%
Lack of authentic teaching materials	33 (94%)	10 (83%)	92%
Few opportunities for retraining in TBLT	32 (91%)	10 (83%)	89%
Low English proficiency	27 (77%)	12 (100%)	83%
Grammar-based examinations	26 (74%)	11 (92%)	79%
Traditional grammar-based language teaching	25 (71%)	11 (92%)	77%
Large classes	25 (71%)	9 (75%)	72%
Insufficient funding, resources and equipment	21 (60%)	10 (83%)	66%
Little time to prepare communicative materials	20 (57%)	10 (83%)	64%
Deficiency in strategic and sociolinguistic competence	16 (46%)	11/92%)	57%
Resistance to class participation	17 (49%)	10 (83%)	57%
Deficiency in spoken English	12 (34%)	11 (92%)	49%

Discussion

Question 1: *To what extent are Chinese teachers prepared to practice TBLT in the classroom?*

Based on the data collected in the questionnaire and the interview, it is apparent that teachers are very interested in innovative teaching methods. All of the forty-seven participants reported that they are very much concerned about the effectiveness of their teaching and they try to use different approaches, such as TBLT, CLT and grammar-translation, according to the purpose of the class. Most of them consider TBLT to be a useful and effective method because it not only arouses learning interest, but also engages learners in meaningful communication. Moreover, it provides learners with opportunities to use the target language (italics added):

> It's useful to *arouse the students' interest* and it's easy to make the students understand the key points.
>
> (BJUS1-80-T4)

> It's easy to *arouse the learners' interest* and improve the learners' real capacity. The meaningful input and comprehensible output will help the learners be a good learner. Just as Nunan once said, the important thing is that while doing the tasks, learners are meaning what they say, and focusing on meaning. They are *using language* to exchange meanings for a real purpose. They are free to use whatever language forms they want. The games they play, the problem they solve, the experiences they share may or may not be things that they will do in real life, but their use of language, because it is *purposeful and real*, will replicate features of language use outside the classroom.
>
> (BJUS2-BJGYFZ-T5)

> Because it is *effective* and good for the development of students' abilities. It is very *useful*.
>
> (BJRS1- SQ-T1)

> I think, compared with other methods, it's easier for the students to learn *to use the language* and it's easier for the teacher *to involve the students* in the teaching activity.
>
> (BJRS2-ZGLYFZ-T2)

> The task-based approach aims at *providing opportunities* for the learners to experiment with and explore both spoken and written language through learning activities which are designed *to engage learners* in the authentic, practical and functional *use of language* for *meaningful purposes*.
>
> (HB-HSZX-T1)

From the above comments, it seems that teachers hold a positive attitude toward the TBLT approach and they are willing to practice it. Teacher agency is one of the key factors to successfully implement TBLT. If teachers are neither willing to accept the new teaching approach nor attempt to practise it, the successful implementation of TBLT is not likely to happen. What then is in the way of such an innovative practice? What are the challenges encountered by the teachers in their attempts to utilize tasks effectively? These questions will be explored in the following sections with reference to Table 9.1.

Question 2: *What are the teachers' perceived difficulties in using TBLT?*

To answer this question, four categories summarized above are examined in detail.

1. *TBLT knowledge and training*

Three items are included in this category: *TBLT training and retraining, insufficient funding, resources and equipment*. Forty-five participants chose *lack of training* as one of the main constraints. According to the five teachers interviewed, they had never had any systematic training in TBLT, even though they had a strong desire to receive it. This lack of systematic training led to a fragmented understanding of TBLT and made it difficult for the teachers 'to leave the security of the traditional methods and take the risk of trying new unfamiliar methods' (Li, 2001, p. 155). Consequently, a dilemma arises between teachers' willingness to be innovative and their fear of doing it incorrectly.

Forty-two participants reported that they had few opportunities to be retrained in TBLT. Though the government launched the National English Curriculum in 2001, few teacher education programs provide training, especially for those in the undeveloped areas. This challenge becomes even bigger for China in view of the enormous numbers of teachers and sites involved. Carless (2011) suggested that 'lesson study' or 'research lesson' through which a team of colleagues analyse a taught lesson and seek ways to improve it could be a contextually grounded source of professional development in China. Retraining in TBLT is a good way to help teachers understand tasks better in order to integrate TBLT more effectively in their classroom.

Thirty-one teachers highlighted *insufficient funding, resources and equipment* as a barrier to implementing TBLT. Because of their misconception of TBLT, teachers think that there must be certain equipment such as TV sets, computers, projectors and photocopiers to copy materials for students. As a result, extra funding must be in place. In their opinion, without the support of *funding, resources and equipment*, implementing TBLT becomes much more challenging. This point is in accordance with the other two items, indicating that these teachers do not have sufficient knowledge of the approach.

2. *Educational system*

To a large degree, teachers believe that the shortage of authentic materials seriously constrains the implementation of TBLT (e.g., 94 per cent for Beijing and 83 per cent for Hubei). In all, forty-three teachers reported that lack of authentic materials restricted them from applying TBLT. Because many of them have not been in an English-speaking country, they rely heavily on authentic materials from which they refer to and design tasks.

> I tried to use it [TBLT] in every class. I'd like to design some tasks. But most of them are pedagogical tasks. I find it really hard for me to think of real-world tasks.
>
> (BJUS-BJGYFZ-T5)

> It [TBLT] can be applied to almost all types of English teaching including listening, speaking, reading, writing and grammar. There does exist some problems when I try design tasks in my class.
>
> (BJRS2-ZGLYFZ-T2)

As for the items *Grammar-based examinations* and *Traditional grammar-based language teaching*, a comparatively big discrepancy between the two groups of teachers from Beijing and Hubei can be observed. To some extent, this reflects the different situations of English teaching between developed and undeveloped areas in China. Students in Beijing face less pressure at the National College Entrance Examination. According to the Beijing Municipal Commission of Education (2010), the college entrance rate is 59 per cent whereas the national college entrance rate is about 23.3 per cent[3]. Obviously both students and teachers in the undeveloped areas confront more competition and pressure. The teachers find the traditional teaching methods more controllable and helpful in taking the grammar-based examinations. Under the pressure of examinations, teachers choose the traditional grammar-translation method to help students pass examinations in which speaking is not tested.

Both groups share a similar percentage regarding *large classes* (e.g., 71 per cent for Beijing and 75 per cent for Hubei). Thirty-four teachers stated that the size of their class was so large that they could not conduct the class in an effective way when TBLT was used. In China, it is common to have over fifty or even seventy students of different levels in a class. Therefore, it is difficult for both students and teachers to accomplish communicative activities. When everyone starts to talk, the class may become chaotic. At this time, classroom management is even more important than the teaching approach. This issue has also been pointed out by some previous studies (e.g., Ng & Tang, 1997; Li, 2003). Once there are tasks to be completed, teachers reported that it was difficult for them to manage and control the class (BJRS3-17-T4).

3. Learner factors

The items *Low English proficiency* and *Resistance to class participation* fall into the category of learner factors in the present study. Thirty-nine teachers thought that one big obstacle preventing them from using TBLT was their students' low English proficiency. Four of the five teachers[4] interviewed also expressed the same opinion. Still, teachers in both areas reported that students' vocabulary and English structure were indispensable knowledge and skills to complete some more complicated communicative tasks. A teacher from a rural middle school stated that they dared not adapt to TBLT because they worried that students were not competent enough and it took much time to explain English grammar (BJRS1-SQ-T1). Another teacher commented that students' low proficiency was her concern about doing TBLT (BJRS2-ZGLYFZ-T2).

Among the thirty-nine teachers, twenty-seven (77 per cent) were from Beijing and twelve (100 per cent) from Hubei. This indicates that teachers in Hubei are more concerned about students' proficiency. Students in Beijing usually have an advantage of better oral English over those in undeveloped areas because of the resources and external conditions such as teachers, books, videos, training schools and overall environment. Those students from the rural areas do not learn English until they enter Grade 7, which brings even more difficulties for teachers to design tasks for a class of different proficiency levels.

There is a significant difference in the percentages about the item *resistance to class participation* between the two groups of teachers (e.g., 49 per cent for Beijing and 83 per cent for Hubei). While this situation is better in urban areas with more advanced students' active participation in class, it is less optimistic in the undeveloped area in which the students have become 'accustomed to the traditional classroom structure, in which they sit motionless, take notes while the teacher lectures, and speak only when they are spoken to' (Li, 2001, p. 157). Li (2001) also points out the students rely on the teacher to give them information directly.

As discussed earlier in this chapter, students are at the centre of a task-based approach. If they do not participate, the teachers may give up trying this approach and return to traditional teaching methods. Therefore, learner factors (no matter low English proficiency or resistance to participation) increase the difficulty of implementing TBLT.

4. Teacher factors

Table 9.1 also shows that there is a significant difference in the percentages of the three items related to teacher factors. Thirty teachers reported that they had little time to prepare communicative materials. Though the new textbooks provided many materials for teaching, the teachers still had to write their own teaching plans and design their own activities if they wanted to apply TBLT in their class:

> I try TBLT, but not always. There is so much in the textbook that we have to finish it in time. Teachers are so busy checking homework, designing test papers and so on.
> (HB-HSZX-T2)

Regarding strategic and sociolinguistic competence, twenty-seven of the participants reported that their low strategic and sociolinguistic competence in English constrains their use of TBLT, especially those in the undeveloped areas (eleven out of twelve teachers). As one teacher indicated:

> It [TBLT] can be applied to almost all types of English teaching including listening, speaking, reading, writing and grammar. There do exist some barriers when I adopt TBLT in my teaching.
> (BJRS2-ZGLYFZ-T2)

As for this aspect, there may be some issues directly related to the role of the teacher in the Chinese tradition in which the teacher is the authority figure. In a TBLT class, any questions related to the task or topic, linguistic or non-linguistic, may occur and students may raise problems that are quite challenging. Teachers thus should be prepared for this kind of situation in which they are both teachers and learners.

Within the factor of deficiency in speaking, there is a huge difference between the developed area and undeveloped area as has been mentioned in the last section. Only 34 per cent of the teachers in Beijing claimed low proficiency in spoken English, while the percentage of teachers from Hubei amounted to 92 per cent. The reasons for this could be both external (such as resources and opportunities), and internal in that teachers in undeveloped areas lack confidence. For instance, the schools in Beijing usually require a higher qualification, and the teachers in Beijing have more chances to practise their spoken English.

Implications of the study

Much of what the Chinese teachers say about TBLT in their classroom and the difficulties they have encountered are common in Asian countries. Some of the factors are in line with the problems that other researchers and educators have previously associated with task-based instruction (e.g., Swan, 2005). In responding to the problems, Ellis (2006) has provided corresponding solutions, for example, to devise activities that develop ability gradually when students lack language proficiency; to use small group work and allow planning time plus learner training when students are unwilling to speak. He also suggests that the philosophy of education be reviewed, more new communicative tests be developed, and small group work and tasks suited to large classes be used.

When it comes to the specific pedagogic contexts such as China and other Asian countries, Confucius' teachings offer possible solutions to some of these problems too (see Luo, 2009). For example, Confucius' teachings *To teach to individual differences* plus *Improvization* (因材施教), *To learn without thinking is labour in vain* (學而不思則罔), and *Exploring the old and deducing the new* plus *Cumulative progress* (溫故而知新) can challenge the problems perceived by teachers and raised by Swan regarding the on-line hypothesis, the noticing hypothesis, and the teachability hypothesis respectively.

Having argued theoretically and contextually in response to the problems posed by TBLT, it is clear that the government, schools, teachers and students ought to work together to improve the present situation. First of all, the government is the policy maker for education and plays an important role in making educational reforms. The current grammar-based language examination is the crucial factor in evaluating learners' language competence and even determining their future. Thus, a systemic change in education is needed in China and other Asian countries to reform the examination system (see Adams & Newton, 2009; Ellis, 2003; Littlewood 2007). Nevertheless, such a fundamental change takes time.

Secondly, TBLT training and retraining is essential in implementing TBLT which requires teachers to understand the nature of a 'task' and use it effectively based on students' needs. However, as Adams and Newton (2009) have also noted in many contexts, teachers have not had opportunities to gain sufficient understanding of tasks and task-based teaching. Since teachers play a role of director and facilitator in TBLT practice, there must be a more flexible educational system and innovative curriculum that encourage teachers to support students and offer opportunities for every student in their language learning and task completion.

To have teachers achieve the above, schools need to take charge of education policies and act as a bridge between the government and teachers. They must ensure that they fully understand education policies and curriculum before giving instructions to teachers. Moreover, it is the responsibility of the school to provide sufficient equipment and enough funding to create a supportive environment for both students and teachers to experiment with new means of classroom practice in China (see Adams & Newton, 2009; Zhang, 2007).

Last but not the least, learners' unwillingness to participate and their doubts about the effectiveness of curricular innovations are caused by the grammar and vocabulary knowledge-focused national examinations (see Adams & Newton, 2009; Hu, 2002; Li, 1998, 2001). To have students improve their own language competence and be willing to communicate and learn in a more efficient way, there must be opportunities for them to participate with teachers and become actively involved in processing and completing language tasks (see Ellis, 2003).

Conclusion

This chapter has explored Chinese teachers' perceptions of the challenges faced by teachers and learners in implementing TBLT. Generally speaking, teachers in the present study hold a positive attitude toward TBLT. Their perceived difficulties fall into four categories: those caused by the teacher; the students; the educational system; and TBLT itself. Teachers report that they lack training in TBLT. Students are not competent or confident enough to participate in tasks. The grammar-translation method and examinations at all levels also constrain the implementation of TBLT. Moreover, external conditions such as large classes and over-worked teachers are obstacles for doing TBLT. With the aim of making curriculum innovations happen, we recommend that the government, schools, teachers and students work together to improve the present situation.

Although the study presented was small-scale, the difficulties perceived by the teachers show that either curriculum reform or methodology innovation is 'a socially situated activity, its success is affected by ethical and systemic constraints, the personal characteristics of potential adopters, the attributes of innovations and the strategies that are used to manage change in particular contexts' (Markee, 1997, p. 41). The feasibility of TBLT involves multiple and interrelated factors that may influence it at different stages and at different levels (Shamin, 1996, cited in Li, 1998, p. 698). In fact, there are many challenges for implementing TBLT despite what is stated in government documents. China as a particular context has her own characteristics that need to be taken into consideration when a new approach is introduced, for example, the educational traditions, regional differences, and ways of learning. We need to ask questions such as is it *appropriate* to implement TBLT in China? If TBLT is to be implemented in Chinese schools, what kind of training do teachers need? All in all, how to localize and contextualize the TBLT approach so that it accommodates teachers and benefits students' learning is worthy of more research.

The survey presented in this chapter also has major implications for the contributions that Chinese researchers and teachers of English can make with regard to research and practice involving new approaches. It confirms that we need to engage more closely with teachers and localize or prepare new frameworks for L2 instruction in the Chinese context, with greater attention to preparing teachers to support language education development across China. In the case of TBLT, what we could do is to refine *pedagogic tasks* in the Chinese context, making them accessible to the classroom teachers; design and select tasks that demand fully grammaticalized language or are less demanding in terms of authentic language use; find a balance between focus on meaning and focus on form (language); use small group work; develop tasks well-suited to large classes; and develop more communicative exams to reduce teachers' anxieties about knowledge-based exams.

For further research in this field, a bigger sample is necessary and more in-depth interviews could also be very helpful in identifying key factors that affect TBLT implementation in Chinese schools. The research question regarding learners was answered from the perspective of the teachers and not from that of the learners. Future research with learners' perspectives via surveys and interviews would be valuable in presenting a more holistic understanding.

In summary, on the one hand, the perceived difficulties present significant challenges for educators and teachers in English teaching; on the other hand, these challenges provide teachers with space and opportunities to develop themselves to make changes in English education in China. Tasks provide an interesting basis for exploring language teaching, as Skehan (2006) suggests, and researchers need to understand how to design them effectively using innovative research approaches.

Appendix 9.1

Questionnaire: Teachers' perceived difficulty in implementing TBLT in China

Part I Personal information

1. Age _____
2. Sex _____
3. How many years have you been a teacher of English? _____
4. Are you teaching in a middle school or high school? _____
   A. Middle school   B. High school
5. Which grade (s) are you teaching? _____
6. Are you teaching in an urban or rural middle/school? _____
   A. Urban   B. rural

Part II Views about English teaching

7. Are you concerned about the methods you use in teaching English?   Yes / No
8. What methods are you using now?
9. Have you tried Task-based Language Teaching (TBLT)?   Yes / No

10. Why did you or why didn't you try TBLT?
11. How did you like using TBLT in your classroom?

Part III Perceived difficulties in doing TBLT

12. The following are some difficulties that other EFL teachers had in doing TBLT. Did you come across these difficulties or do you think they might be difficulties for you in doing TBLT in China?

    (1) Teachers' deficiency in spoken English?   Yes / No
    (2) Teachers' deficiency in strategic and sociolinguistic competence in English?   Yes / No
    (3) Teachers' having little time to prepare communicative materials?   Yes / No
    (4) Teachers' lack of training in TBLT?   Yes / No
    (5) Teachers' few opportunities for retraining in TBLT?   Yes / No
    (6) Students' low English proficiency?   Yes / No
    (7) Students' resistance to class participation?   Yes / No
    (8) Lack of authentic teaching materials?   Yes / No
    (9) Grammar-based examinations?   Yes / No
    (10) Large classes?   Yes / No
    (11) Traditional grammar-based language teaching?   Yes / No
    (12) Insufficient funding, resources and equipment?   Yes / No

                                                                              (Adapted from Li, 1998)

Appendix 9.2

Sample of interview transcriptions (in Chinese)

Urban school 1 (80, BJ)

T3: 我们学校的外教曾布置学生去外国人开的餐厅进行实地采访，学生很喜欢这些真实的任务，完成这些任务给了他们一种成就感。因此，他们也要求英语老师多给他们创造这种机会。可实际上，这些实际的任务，对于英语教师来说，操控难度太大。

[The foreign teachers in our school used to have students go to interview foreigners who run restaurants here. Students loved such authentic tasks and felt a sense of achievement once they accomplished such tasks. So they ask their English teachers to provide them with such opportunities. However, such authentic tasks are not feasible for the teachers.]

Rural school 1 (SQ, BJ)

T1: 有时根本不敢采取任务型教学法，因为同样的一个知识点，采用任务型教学法往往比传统的教学法会花费更多的时间去讲解，担心学生的水平达不到这种能力。

[Sometimes we cannot afford to do TBLT, because it costs more time than the traditional method in explaining a language point. We also worry about students' proficiency level.]

Rural school 2 (ZGLYFZ, BJ)

T2: 学生水平过低让我总是犹豫是否要采取任务型教学法，担心过于流于形式，学生不能真正理解知识点，把握知识点不牢导致无法满足考试要求。

[Students' low English proficiency makes me hesitate in doing TBLT. My concern is that we pay too much attention to the method we use and neglect students' understanding of knowledge. If students do not have solid mastery of knowledge, they cannot meet the requirements of the examinations.]

Rural school 3 (17, BJ)

T4: 除此之外，87.2% 的调查对象认为大班授课也限制了任务型教学法的实施。受访的五位老师所任教的班级，最少的人数也在 42人。40-50人的课堂，一旦进行任务活动，操控起来相当困难。

[... Besides, 87.2 per cent of the teachers consider large class size as the constraint of TBLT implementation. The teachers interviewed teach classes of minimum number of forty-two students. It's very difficult to discipline a forty to fifty class once they start doing tasks. (It would be quite chaotic to manage.)]

Notes

1 The NECS (Ministry of Education, 2001, 2011) is for the nine years of compulsory education (Grade 1 through Grade 9), so all the primary schools and secondary schools in China must follow the standards it establishes.
2 This item is categorized into *TBLT knowledge and training* because it relates to the participants' misunderstanding about TBLT.
3 This number is planned to increase to 40 per cent in 2020 (see, The Long-term Planning Framework for the Reform of National Educational Reform and Development (2010–2020)).
4 The other teacher was from a key school in which more advanced students are selected.

References

Adams, R., & Newton, J. (2009). TBLT in Asia: Constraints and opportunities. *Asian Journal of English Language Teaching, 19*, 1–17.
Adamson, B., & Davison, C. (2003). Innovation in English language teaching in Hong Kong primary schools: One step forward, two steps sideways? *Prospect, 18*(1), 27–41.
Beijing Municipal Commission of Education (2010). Retrieved http://www.bjedu.gov.cn/publish/portal27/tab1645/

Burnaby, B., & Sun, Y. (1989). Chinese teachers' views of western language teaching: Context informs paradigm. *TESOL Quarterly, 23*(2), 219–238.

Butler, Y. G. (2011). The implementation of communicative and task-based language teaching in the Asia-Pacific Region. *Annual review of applied linguistics, 31*, 36–57.

Carless, D. (2011). *From testing to productive student learning: Implementing formative assessment in Confucian-heritage settings.* New York, NY: Routledge.

Cheng, X. (2004). *Task-based language teaching.* Beijing: Higher Education Press.

Deng, C. R. (2011). *Communicativeness of activities in EFL primary school classrooms in Guangdong, China: Teachers' interpretations of task-based language teaching.* Unpublished doctoral dissertation, University of Hong Kong.

Ellis, R. (2003). *Task-based language learning and teaching.* Oxford: Oxford University Press.

Ellis, R. (2006, April). *Task-based teaching.* Plenary speech presented at the 2005 Asian EFL Journal Conference on Task-based Language Teaching. A Superior Teaching Approach or Temporary Trend? Pusan, Korea (April 29, 2006).

Hu, G. (2002). Recent important developments in secondary English-language teaching in the People's Republic of China. *Language, Culture and Curriculum, 15*, 30–49.

Hu, G. (2005). CLT is best for China: An untenable absolutist claim. *ELT Journal, 59*(1), 65–68.

Li, C. (2003). A study of in-service teachers' beliefs, difficulties and problems in current teacher development programs. *HKBU Papers in Applied Language Studies, 7*, 64–85.

Li, D. F. (1998). It's always more difficult than you plan and imagine. Teachers' perceived difficulties in introducing the communicative approach in South Korea. *TESOL Quarterly, 32*, 677–703.

Li, D. F. (2001). Teachers' perceived difficulties in introducing the communicative approach in South Korea. In D. R. Hall & A. Hewings (Eds), *Innovation in English language teaching* (pp. 149–166). London & New York: Macquarie University and The Open University.

Littlewood, W. (2007). Communicative and task-based language teaching in East Asian classrooms. *Language Teaching, 40*, 243–249.

Long, M. H. (1985). A role for instruction in second language acquisition: Task-based language teaching. In K. Hyltenstam & M. Pienemann (Eds), *Modeling and assessing second language acquisition* (pp. 77–99). Clevedon: Multilingual Matters.

Luo, S. (2009). *Re-examining factors that affect task difficulty in TBLA.* Shanghai: Shanghai Foreign Language Education Press. (《任务型语言测试中的任务难度研究》。上海：上海外语教育出版社。 2009 年 12 月)

Luo, S., & Gong, Y. (2007). *Task-based language teaching.* Singapore: Thomson Learning.

Luo, S., & Yi, B. (2013). TBLT in China (2001–2011): The current situation, predicament and the future. *Indonesian Journal of Applied Linguistics, 2*(2), 147–156.

Markee, N. (1997). *Managing curricular innovation.* Cambridge, England: Cambridge University Press.

Ministry of Education. (2001, 2011). *National English curriculum standards.* Beijing: Beijing Normal University Press.

Ng, C., & Tang, E. (1997). Teachers' needs in the process of EFL reform in China: A report from Shanghai. *Perspective, 9*, 63–85.

Shamin, F. (1996). Learner resistance to innovation in classroom methodology. In H. Coleman (Ed.), *Society and the Language Classroom* (pp. 105–121). Cambridge: Cambridge University Press.

Skehan, P. (2006). *Using tasks in foreign language instruction: current work and future challenges* ENG 5530 Second Language Acquisition (2005–2006). The Department of English, The Chinese University of Hong Kong.

Swan, M. (2005). Legislation by hypothesis: The case of task-based instruction. *Applied Linguistics, 26*(3), 376–401. Oxford: Oxford University Press.

Xia, J., & Hung, J. (1998). Theoretical basis for problem-based language teaching and task-based language teaching. *Foreign Languages, 4,* 34–40. (夏纪梅、孔宪辉,"难题教学法"与"任务教学法"的理论依据及其模式比较。《外国语》, 1998, 4, 34–40.)

Zhang, Y. (2007). TBLT innovation in primary school English language teaching in mainland China. In K. Van den Branden, K. Van Gorp & M. Verhelst (Eds), *Tasks in action: Task-based language education from a classroom-based perspective* (pp. 68–91). Newcastle: Cambridge Scholars Press.

10

Gaining Acceptance of Task-Based Teaching during Malaysian Rural In-Service Teacher Training

Stephen J. Hall

Summary

The limited adoption of task-based teaching in Malaysia can be attributed to constraints common to other settings in which English is but one of the many language choices. Challenges include teacher-fronted teaching and little community support for English, particularly in rural environments. Adoption of task-based approaches is rarely effective when prescribed by the syllabus, as once the teacher closes the classroom door she will do what she is comfortable with. This is especially so when numerous curriculum changes are centrally implanted (Kabilan, 2007). In some cases teachers adopt new approaches to classroom tasks. It is therefore useful to describe a case study in which there was acceptance of tasks as primary and secondary teachers experienced the loop input approach (Woodward, 2003) during teacher education courses. This chapter will therefore draw on data from the early interaction of in-service courses to suggest approaches to building positive responses to tasks for rural classrooms. Data and participant reflections suggest that deconstructing transmission teaching can occur when tasks are productive and relevant. It is suggested that task-based approaches may need to work with the realities which Canagarajah (2011) and others describe as 'plurilingual' classrooms. This chapter argues that transferable tasks and an awareness of methodologies beyond monolingualism may build acceptance of change.

Introduction

Task-based language teaching (TBLT) has had a multiplicity of propagators and interpretations while the practicality of implementing TBLT and learning has had a number of challenges. The challenges within an in-service project to develop many of the classroom features central to TBLT will be described. The Malaysian Schools English Language Project (henceforth called the Project) was within the Malaysian primary and secondary public education system in which the use of more than one language is an everyday occurrence (Azirah, 2012; Pillay, 1998). Specifically, this description will be drawn from research into teacher and teacher educator interaction during in-service education courses. The challenges of introducing some of the core features of TBLT will be linked to the needs analysis and the early phases of in-service teacher education interaction. The chapter will begin by defining key aspects of task-based approaches before describing the background of early task-based teaching initiatives within Malaysia and related pedagogic challenges.

Task-based features: Communication versus form

A broadly defined dichotomy that informs much of the debate about defining and implementing task-based teaching is that of communication and meaning based tasks versus form-based pedagogy. In widely known work, Skehan (1998) describes the characteristics of a task as learning in which meaning is the primary concern with a relationship to real-world activities. The assessment of tasks is, in his view, in terms of an outcome rather than strictly in terms of reproduction of pre-determined forms. Malaysia reacted to international changes away from form-focused syllabuses in the 1980s and 1990s with a skills-based, communicative syllabus. This syllabus introduced many TBLT features with Ministry directives which supported communicative and meaningful tasks (Kementerian Pendidikan Malaysia, 1989). There were over fifteen years of communicative language teaching advocacy with an emphasis on tasks, especially through the Secondary Schools Curriculum or Kurikulum Bersepadu Sekolah Mengengah (KBSM) (Kementerian Pendidikan Malaysia, 1989). This process was driven through a highly prescriptive centralized national system and reactions towards it inform much of the present day positioning of pedagogy. Firstly, we turn to definitions of task based pedagogy which align to defining features of the earlier syllabus, parts of which remain in contemporary syllabuses. These influences will then be linked to aspects of the case study which follows. Definitions of TBLT can be very broad including interaction in which 'the target language is used by the learner for a communicative purpose (goal) in order to achieve an outcome' (Willis, 1996, p. 234). This definition has been elaborated on as:

> ... a piece of classroom work that involves learners in comprehending, manipulating, producing or interacting in the target language while their attention is focused on mobilizing their grammatical knowledge in order to express meaning, and in which the intention is to convey meaning rather than to manipulate form.
> (Nunan, 2006, p. 14)

Further definitions have been outlined throughout this volume and this terminology of TBLT can be found in the English language syllabuses of Malaysia. Such terms informed nearly fifteen years of syllabus use, although research suggests that 'chalk and talk' grammar transition methods still held a dominant position as implementing features of the task-based approach has had many challenges (Ambigathy, 2002; Musa et al., 2012). These will be outlined and linked to the case study.

Background to in-service research

Much effort and finance has been spent over decades for teacher training as a tool of Malaysian national development and this includes task-based approaches (Rajaretnam & Nalliah, 1998). A summary of contemporary ambitions and directions can be seen in the recent Malaysia Education Blueprint (2013). Yet there are many concerns regarding how effective English language teacher training is when transferred to classrooms with varied models of skills transfer (Hayes, 2000; Johnson, 2006; O'Sullivan, 2002).

Malaysia has also undergone frequent national syllabus changes and as at this time of writing, during 2014, is undergoing another round of text, teaching and resource alignment; the ninth since Independence in 1957. Experienced English language teachers have therefore seen many English language approaches delivered through textbook and multi-media provision, mass training sessions and examination specifications (Selvaraj, 2010). As described by Pandian (2004) all the trends have impacted to varying degrees through centrally driven syllabuses and prescribed national textbooks with changes from situational/structural approaches, communicative task-based approaches, hybridized functionalism to reading literacy-based specifications.

It is possible that teachers working in large class primary and secondary level classrooms may be resistant to what is often delivered as another syllabus change from a centralized agency. The question therefore remains as to how much teachers adapt to changes in a particular setting such as an in-service project which aimed to foster meaningful tasks. It may be useful to see whether pedagogic change occurs with teacher education projects or whether teachers choose to remain entrenched with reproducing the ways in which they themselves were taught.

Analysing the early phases of in-service interaction

Although recent studies have begun to focus on specific settings and models of teacher education in developing nations, there has been little work on linking the introductory phases in pedagogic approaches of teacher education with critically evaluating the acceptance of pedagogic changes during teacher training (Singh & Richards, 2006). One can set up a pedagogic model incorporating good practice based on regionally specific experience and research, but as Malachi (2011) observes many questions still remain as to what happens when Malaysian teacher educators and teachers interact with text, tasks and varied topics. Primacy Theory (Hogg & Vaughan, 1998) would suggest that the links between tasks, interaction in teacher development and acceptance of the process are especially evident in the 'early phases' of courses. The 'early phases' in this research are the beginning of courses in which a teacher educator is introducing the teacher development process with in-service teachers in classrooms.

Whether in the early or later phases, research has shown that much of the work on teacher development projects in rural settings is riddled with problems related to transference of expertise (O'Sullivan, 2002). Visiting expertise is also extremely limited in effectiveness and the area of cross-cultural acceptance is problematic as described elsewhere (Hall, 2007; Holliday, 2006). This research was with teacher educators living in the communities where the teachers lived within rural districts and focuses on tasks, techniques and talk during teacher educator and teacher interaction. Four teacher educators who were so called 'native speakers' and sixteen Malaysian rural classroom teachers at four diverse sites were part of a wider project with thirty rural sites. The interaction was within the Malaysian Schools English Language Project which will now be outlined. The Centre for British Teachers (CfBT), an international non-profit educational trust with its headquarters in Reading, United Kingdom and its Malaysian arm were asked by the Curriculum Development Centre (CDC) of the Malaysian Ministry of Education to provide English Language Coordinators (ELCs) or teacher educators for selected districts throughout Malaysia. CfBT Education Services Malaysia Sdn. Bhd. has been in Malaysia since the early 1970s. The organization took up the contract in May 2002 at the same time that the Prime Minister announced the start of changes in the medium of instruction for mathematics and science from Bahasa Malaysia (Malay) to English. Significantly, the Project came at a time of quantum changes in the country's English language policy, since reversed in a highly contentious change (Goh, 2013).

The aim of the Project was to raise the standards of English in the country, particularly in rural areas, through in-service English language teacher training and to foster teaching which was providing for learners' use of English language. The Project began in June 2002 with a needs analysis which informed the context for the research, namely the courses, workshops and supportive observations for teacher development. This needs analysis, while not the most recent, remains relevant given the unusual access provided to a wide range of primary and secondary teachers. Recent press reports (New Straits Times, 2013) and the Ministry's 2013 Education Blueprint suggest continuity of the challenges and describe the bilingual or multilingual nature of many English language classrooms.

A needs analysis and the context of teacher education

The purpose of the Project needs analysis was to describe teacher needs in a non-urban Malaysian District, the kind of districts in which the ELCs, henceforth called teacher educators worked. The needs analysis, comprising a written form and interviews, provided a basis for focusing collaboration with teachers in Education Districts and provided information for CfBT's partner, the CDC of the Ministry of Education (Hall & Dodson, 2004). It informed the subsequent five years of teacher education. Numerous instances of anecdotal evidence and small-scale research (Costelloe, 2006) confirm the validity of the needs analysis findings during the Project and it has been suggested to this author by numerous parties that little has changed in subsequent teacher education initiatives. The following sections describe the needs analysis findings which underpin the teacher education Project, aspects of which are part of the study and which impact on the implementation of TBLT approaches.

The needs analysis for the Project was co-authored and implemented by this author with the cooperation of the Ministry of Education. This involved 168 primary and secondary teachers from one district, an 86 per cent sample and this was augmented by bilingual interviews with fifty teachers. It remains one of the few Malaysian surveys undertaken which addressed classroom teachers' perceptions of their needs. Along with a smaller localized analysis, the data formed the basis for the principles of course design which was later applied to thirty of eighty-seven Education Districts throughout Malaysia. The data from the pilot district needs analysis is derived from a written interview conducted en masse and fifty bilingual individual oral interviews. The use of two modes provided a means of verifying information as questions contained built-in contradictions. The aim of the analysis was to gather data of the perceptions, approaches, techniques and needs of English language teachers in rural Malaysia. The survey therefore examined second order perspectives of needs, in that it asked the teachers about their perceptions of classroom tasks and training needs. As such, the survey describes teachers' perspectives, views of their own practices and perceived needs.

This needs analysis then informed the situation in which later research was conducted; namely the in-service work of teacher educators living and educating within rural multicultural Malaysia. It was also used to frame the anticipated role of the teacher educators. The teacher educators were asked to devise strategies to improve English teaching and learning and motivation. In order for such activities to be successful it was necessary to see what expectations and needs teachers would bring into the process, especially as the client, the Ministry of Education, was very specific in wanting a collaborative co-constructed process in which learners were led to the productive use of English in tasks relevant to their lives. The use of meaningful communicative English language tasks was advocated. This posed challenges within 'plurilingual situations' (Piccardo, 2013) in which English is one of many languages. The client asked for an English-only approach to learning and target tasks and this was subsequently supported by a Ministry directive. The situation is however one in which English is as much a foreign language as a second or third language and so there were challenges in the objective which was to minimize form based, transmission mode teaching in rural Malaysia. Teachers are often given tasks in syllabuses for which there are no community situations in which to use the English and this has been proven to be demotivating (Mohamed et al., 2006). Classroom interaction is often one of code switching and this aspect is a dynamic which influences how teachers and learners approach tasks (Costelloe, 2006). The Ministry then brought experienced native speaker teacher educators into this situation, a controversial process that continues with more recent initiatives (New Straits Times, 2013).

Many of the teacher educators employed to work in the Project interactive classrooms were 'native speaker' teacher educators with a background in communicative language teaching and in many cases task-based approaches. Most of them had extensive teaching or teacher training experience and so were familiar with the wave of task-based approaches popularized during the 1990s. These facilitators worked directly with Malaysian teachers, the more senior of whom had been trained in communicative language teaching methodology and its related national syllabus and examination structures. This syllabus and the approach shared many task types and techniques with those espoused by task-based proponents such as those which were influential in Hong Kong during the 1990s (see Lin, 2013 for a summary of this and bilingual issues). This was therefore a situation in which teacher educators with a background in communicative methodology and/or task approaches worked with teachers many of whom had been exposed to the rhetoric and task types of TBLT. The Project therefore aimed to deconstruct the large amount of still form-focused methods with participants familiar with TBLT and may therefore provide insights into the challenges of TBLT implementation at the classroom level. We will begin with Malaysian teachers and a description of their needs, before turning to insights from the data which describes acceptance of pedagogic change.

Contextualizing pedagogic change in Malaysian rural teachers' needs

Needs analysis often reveals a gap between what teachers say they do, the syllabus and actual practice as Waters and Vilches (2008) have pointed out. The needs analysis to prepare for the in-service teacher education revealed that teachers stated that they are aware of important pedagogical principles such as using pair work or group activities and creating meaningful language use. These were techniques that the client wished to see develop further through techniques often linked to TBLT, such as negotiating meaning and linking to real-life needs (Skehan, 1998). The more experienced Malaysian teachers would have attended many workshops on these approaches due to the earlier communicative syllabus implementation (Pandian, 2004). However item discrimination questions in the needs analysis about practice revealed discrepancies between what was said to be done and actual practice. Such findings are supported by more recent research in which the gap between espoused methods such as discovery learning and communicative tasks contrasted with teachers verbally describing themselves as providing rote learning and input to be copied from the board. Mohamed et al. (2006) quote classroom teachers who say that the most important consideration that influenced their choice of approach was the pupils' level of proficiency:

> TA: Discovery learning? Baah ... forget it ... they don't have the vocabulary.
> TB: As usual, teachers deliver ... pupils do ... some would do ... some would copy ... some were not interested at all ... a lot not interested.
> (Mohamed et al., 2006, p. 57)

Within the classrooms as researched by the needs analysis, the dynamics of learning were closely tied to the use of the first language, Malaysian English and students' levels of English language proficiency. The written data and interviews both revealed the frequent and widespread usage of the national language to the extent that Bahasa Malaysia was the norm and at times the dominant mode of instruction. Tasks then often were accomplished with what has come to be called 'codemeshing' in a 'translingual setting' (Canagarajah, 2011). We shall return to this central point as much of TBLT has been developed in English as a Second Language settings rather than in a situation where 'codemeshing' or code switching, sometimes within one sentence, is the norm. Many within the Malaysian community, such as this writer, actively code switch in a plurilingual setting, a linguistic hybridity shared with Singapore (Silver & Bokhorst-Heng, 2013). This linguistic hybridity is often ignored by language planners and syllabus designers in both Singapore and Malaysia and in other contexts (Lin, 2013). TBLT has yet to fully address this complexity and to move beyond a monolingual approach to learning environments in which monolingualism is rare. To add to the complexity, the use of English is often driven not by teacher task facilitation, but by the high stakes demanded by national examinations and educational administrators.

The role of national examinations and choosing tasks

In Malaysian classrooms, an important choice in classroom text, task and interactional choices is product-based success in the gatekeeping national examinations: Penilaian Menengah Rendah (commonly abbreviated as PMR); the Lower Secondary Assessment and the Sijil Pelajaran Malaysia (SPM), or the Malaysian Certificate of Education, a national examination taken by all fifth-year secondary school students. The emphasis on these high stake examinations leads to classroom practice in which teachers organize learning so that students get high scores, which are more easily attained in closed tasks such as multiple-choice questions or cloze passages (Ambigathy, 2002).

The dominance of examinations which Koo (2008, p. 56) terms 'the discourse of privileging examination' was reported on numerous occasions during the Project as teachers would choose tasks on the basis of how successful students could be in reproducing discrete point accurate answers (Costelloe, 2006). One could hypothesize that task choices may be driven by staffroom examination displays in which the school pass rates in all subjects feature prominently in graphs comparing school with local, state and national result percentages. This quantitative drive informs much of educational rhetoric and management but the links between this highly centralized and empowered dynamic and teachers' task choices remains under-researched for a number of reasons.

The data in the needs analysis and later research suggests a predominance of translation and the wide use of copying coupled with the need to produce an accurate product: a practice which is still continuing (Hughes, 2014 personal correspondence). This dependence of translation and form-based reproduction may translate into frequent use of closed structured tasks and blackboard copying. In the needs analysis and research questions of the study, teachers also rated a quiet classroom based on textbook input as a frequent norm while reading comprehension tasks, copying from the board and answering worksheets were widely used. The data showed that classroom practices are based on teachers' claims to acknowledge important aspects of language learning such as encouraging English in and outside the classroom, but this rarely happened according to counter indicative questions on actual practice. The needs analysis also revealed a need for training in general methodology, motivational approaches, grammar tools and reading and writing skills development. Both secondary and primary teachers agreed that there were training needs for pedagogy and that there were also needs related to teachers' own language. The needs analysis then informed the Project design with teacher suggestions for their own skills development. According to the more articulate teachers, only by developing skills and use of varied techniques could there be alternatives to grammar translation and examination-based rote learning.

Change through experiencing transferable tasks

The teachers spoke and wrote of wanting to know and use alternative learning arrangements other than a teacher-centred delivery of content. There was therefore a need for both teacher development and teacher training, namely for teachers to develop their own awareness and confidence through professional development and also a training need to gain practical methods and techniques. There were several expressions of the opinion that there was a need to 'do what we could do in our classrooms and learn in that same way' (Participant 26, Hall and Dodson, 2004). This needs analysis finding was supported by the later research project in which teachers reported that their main concern was to acquire transferable tasks which could be applied in classrooms in a 'plug and play' manner.

The Project was therefore based on experiential learning with pedagogy driving content and task choice. This choice of a teacher education approach then followed from data, as described above, as well as client requests for teachers to experience the kinds of tasks that the students would themselves experience. The approach was therefore one of learning by doing or experiential learning with a loop input approach (Woodward, 2003). The context for the research and the data that follows in this chapter is therefore a setting for a conscious attempt to create a 'culture of learning' (Cortazzi, 2000) in which the Project team and the client wanted to incorporate transferable experiences for classroom use. As the pedagogic director of the Project, this writer was then tasked with seeing that Project materials were task-based with learning of direct relevance to rural classrooms in a loop input approach. This meant that teachers would go through a process of learning which they could then apply to their own teaching. The client made it very clear that they had assessed earlier cascade models of training and did not see the returns in classroom change. As such there would be challenges, as much of the other training which teachers may have experienced before was teacher-fronted and less interactive than the loop input approach. The Project then had set itself the task of working with the teaching and learning culture in order to develop more effective English language learning and teaching in rural Malaysia.

Researching the acceptance of novel classroom techniques

The focus of the research study was on early phases of teacher educator teacher interaction during in-service teacher development courses. Through lesson transcripts, field notes, semi-structured interviews over two time frames and teacher education reflective interviews, description was built up and analysed for the early phases of introducing an in-service course. The study of four out of thirty teacher educators in four rural sites in the early phases of nation-wide in-service courses used qualitative methods.

Two main groups of participants are involved: teacher educators, known locally as ELCs, and Malaysian school teachers. I will first describe the teacher educator participants and then the teachers. The project involved thirty teacher educators working with teachers in thirty rural sites or districts of which there are eighty-seven in the nation. The teacher educators lived and worked in rural Malaysian districts in which English language teaching methodology was and still is seen as an area in need of development. All the teacher educators were post-graduate English language specialists with teaching and teacher education experience. Of the sixteen teacher participants, twelve are primary teachers and four are secondary teachers. This reflects the Project direction which the client requested with a two-thirds emphasis on primary teacher development. Including secondary teachers added breadth and depth to the data as graduate secondary teachers have greater English language proficiency and content knowledge (Hall & Dodson, 2004). If one is to look at the experience level of teachers the range was from two to twenty-eight years.

Data included discourse analysis with field notes of the first hour of opening a long course, teacher and teacher educator questionnaires, pre- and post-interviews as well as reflective notes. The data was also used to gain teacher educator reflection. The in-service setting was one in which teacher educators were tasked to foster a new 'culture of learning' (Cortazzi, 2000) with greater learner-to-learner interaction and less dependence on grammar translation and teacher-fronted interaction. The following sections will describe some of the approaches which teachers reported as effective and approaches which teacher educators described as useful for fostering classroom change. What was clear from teacher responses was that they saw their learning as related to how students could learn.

Accepting tasks by doing: The loop input approach

There were many comments about the teacher educators' modelling pedagogy with tasks which could be applied to classroom practice. After commenting that she had not experienced an interactive approach in earlier training, one teacher noted that the start was very different, 'a good approach. I think and we can use it to show our students in our class, different approach' (T 10 1 L 23-24). This difference between past teacher training experiences and the methods described in this study was elaborated on in that teachers experienced and applied techniques they could use. When describing the experiential nature of the courses, a young primary teacher spoke of the links to classrooms through tasks which paralleled children's learning:

> ... very *interesting* because all of us sing the song, it's very *fun*, because the *children* like songs, usually children *like* songs. It's the *first* time to, we all to be *interest* in course. The main things, the song is *fun*, then normally children like the music ... so the *trainer* make *us* like a child, so they *very*, interesting. The *song* is very nice and it's *good* for us and it is fun.
>
> (T 11 1 L 16-20)

In teacher educator reflective interviews, during a later part of the study, teacher educators described how they moved rapidly into tasks which required teachers to interact with either the teacher educator or most frequently with each other – a productive use of language central to TBLT. When the teacher educators were asked by me if this transitioning after their initial introduction into teacher–teacher interaction was in response to Project frameworks, they all said that it was because the activity based approach worked and teachers responded positively to it. One of the difficulties in teacher education is matching teacher educators' perceptions of what was successful with the teachers' perception of what was workable, accepted and useful for plurilingual classrooms. The teacher educators' rationale was that positive response could be measured through continued attendance, the teachers' responses to activities, their use of techniques and lastly, teachers' feedback which was often given informally one to one – the latter is especially difficult to verify. All stated however that the early phase of the course should focus on pair or group interaction; for example 'You want to get them working right away. They have been working all morning ... You get them into lively action as soon as you can. They, like the kids, learn by doing' (TE A Ref Prac 28 02 mins). This was also stated as methodology which teachers applied and saw as effective, namely that transferable tasks or techniques build acceptance of learning.

Task-based language teaching and Malaysian plurilingualism

TBLT has often been described within second language contexts with community support for related real-life links and meaning making. However, many classrooms in rural Malaysia have a complex language ecosystem as they are not in a Teaching English to Speakers of Other Languages (TESOL) setting, even if officially described as such (Ambigathy, 2002). Malaysia is a complex range of contexts (see Lee, 2003 and Puah & Ting, 2013 for case studies of this). There are 139 active languages and a dominant four in use, often in one conversation. Across the country, the national language plays an important social acceptance role and in reality a strong classroom interactional role (Musa et al., 2012).

It is useful to consider a term which may apply to Malaysian classrooms' cultural complexity by drawing on current terminology which is finding acceptance within some Asian contexts (Lin 2013), namely 'plurilingualism'. Moore and Gajo (2009) describe a plurilingual speaker as a speaker with a repertoire of varied linguistic and cultural resources which meet communication needs or enable interaction with people from other backgrounds and contexts. As defined by the Council of Europe (2012) plurilingual competence refers to the repertoire of resources which individual learners acquire in all the languages they know or have learnt, and which also relate to the cultures associated with those languages.

The plurilingual setting comes into conflict with an English-only approach and this reality impacted on the in-service Project aiming to implement task-based approaches. The use of Bahasa Malaysia or other languages such as Tamil or Chinese in vernacular schools was an issue of considerable debate amongst the national Project team, many of the teacher educators had experience in second language rather than 'plurilingual' settings such as those described by Canagarajah (2006). Some of them saw the frequent use of grammar translation as a method which needed challenging in that the frequent use of the national language took over from task completion in English. Some Project team members, mostly in the more urban areas where there is greater English exposure, argued that an immersion approach of English-only would maximize learning, especially as weekly allocation of time for English can be as little as five hours. Others in really rural contexts such as within the linguistic complexity of East Malaysia or Tamil-speaking plantation areas argued that, 'The learners do not have the vocab or the outside environment. It is not TESOL task territory here . . . so we have to use local languages to scaffold meaningful tasks for them. No vocab no action' (TE A. Ref 32).

One of the first C*f*BT in-house courses had been termed 'Teaching English Through English' and after one pilot it was realistically renamed 'Teaching English Mainly Through English' (TEMTE). The addition of the qualifier and additional sections on comparative bilingual teaching techniques in the TEMTE course reflected the rural reality where English is in practice a foreign language. The client, namely the Ministry of Education, was a strong advocate for English only in the classroom in an argument which Lin describes from within the Hong Kong setting as 'the hegemony of linguistic purism and the monolingual principle' (Lin, 2013, p. 526). It is useful to recall that this Project was at the same time as English for Teaching Maths and Science (ETMS) was being advocated, a move since controversially reversed. The issues of the ETMS Project were described as implementation, suggesting that there were real challenges which could relate to not using scaffolding through the use of the national language or other languages.

On the wider scale, a representative of the Ministry has spoken of a memo which it had sent out at the Minister of Education's request for only English to be used in schools (Personal communication, May 2005). The Minister of that time was effectively bilingual and had experienced elite bilingual schooling. I encountered many worried teachers after this Ministerial action during 2003 and teachers in 2013 still recalled this edict from the urban centralized structure. The instruction has not been contradicted since being issued. Yet mine and other research points to the use of other than English in English language teaching classrooms. Acceptance of pedagogy which aimed to create greater interaction in classrooms also developed when teacher educators worked with the realities of varied languages and cultural identities (Lee, 2003) at work in the classroom.

When presenting tasks, teacher educators employed varied amounts of the national language. Task-based teaching may benefit by incorporating greater awareness of the positive effects which teachers perceive from an approach which was not English only. Teachers and teacher educators all spoke of the pedagogic benefits of select usage and the social solidarity building that comes from using the language of the community in which one lives. All the teacher educators were working and usually living *in situ* with the teachers' communities, except for one of the four sites of research. In Site 1 teachers were very responsive to the teacher educator's use of humour in Bahasa Malaysia. Here the most fluent teacher educator Malay speaker at Site 1 raised the pedagogic issues of the use of Malay both in the actual lesson and in the teacher educator follow-up interview. He consciously uses Malay as do all the others, albeit to the greatest extent reflecting his observable fluency. A sociolinguistic viewpoint underpins his view which was, 'As I said in the first interview, the use of Malay shows social convergence so that it's we are not the *orang putih* (Europeans) from far away, delivering lectures and moving out' (TE A Ref Prac 17 mins). Teacher educator A who is fluent in Malay also commented that it made more sense to use the vernacular when you could not show a vocabulary item visually or you were talking of abstract qualities. When he espoused the use of Malay the response was positive and audible, especially from early primary teachers. I heard audible sighs and exclamations of delight when observing the interaction.

In another site the teacher educator was working with secondary school teachers. Teacher educator B said she had begun her earlier days of Malaysian teacher education by asking teachers for Malay translations so that she would use these for comparative grammar. For her, the main use of Malay was social as with teacher educator D. Teacher educator C would use his beginner's level Malay as occasional input to liven up interaction. This range of reported and observed usage links to the notion that one's greater advocacy of bilingualism or plurilingualism in learning may reflect confidence in using both languages, while at the same time modelling the use of more than English as acceptable pedagogy. Although there was varied usage of Bahasa Malaysia in the early phases for each teacher educator, all the teacher educators shared a common approach to linking teacher education to the rural classrooms in which tasks are accomplished in a codemeshing situation (Canagarajah, 2006, 2011). Acceptance of greater learner interactivity, more negotiated tasks, pair work and group work was therefore linked to acceptance of classroom and community language complexity.

Implications learnt from teacher education techniques which foster acceptance

Teacher educators gained acceptance by providing transferable tasks and by using some local language according to the teachers' statements. It may benefit all to acknowledge that explanation of abstract terms in the local language may be a better use of time than an insistence on English only, more so when English in rural Malaysia is often closer to English as a foreign language than English as a second language.

I suggest that an orientation time in international teacher education projects is critical with time focused on classroom needs, rather than national syllabuses or urban statements of the ideal. Adapting to the plurilingual nature of learning was seen as important in acceptance of the teacher educators' approaches to sharing techniques. Teacher educators were involved in communication accommodation as they learnt to build social convergence and acceptance. Teacher educators need to approach development education as a learning process in which local knowledge is as valued as any pedagogic expertise. Techniques can then be accepted into the local learning situation. There is also a need to highlight the importance of open-minded listening and observation before transferring techniques and pedagogy.

When building acceptance of some of the features of TBLT one needs to consider the strong influence of the national language or Bahasa Malaysia over the learning of English in classrooms, as well as the complexity of classrooms which are even more linguistically complex. There is much to be done to move teaching away from rote learning dominated by the nationally prescribed examinations in which discrete point accuracy dominates. This remains a challenge which may be addressed if the National Education Blueprint (2013) is implemented with care. Learning by doing with experiential tasks and acknowledging plurilingualism may be an effective route to greater uptake of innovation as was seen in acceptance of change by teachers' in-service experience with the project described here. There is much to be done to address the pressing needs of English language teaching and learning in Malaysia.

References

Ambigathy, P. (2002). English language teaching in Malaysia today. *Asia Pacific Journal of Education*, 22(2), 35–52.

Azirah, H. (2012). Pragmatics of maintaining English in Malaysia's education system. In E. L. L. & A. Hashim (Eds), *English in Southeast Asia: Features, policy and language in use* (pp. 155–176). Amsterdam/Philadelphia: John Benjamins.

Canagarajah, S. (2006). The place of world Englishes in composition: Pluralization continued. *College Composition and Communication*, 7(5), 86–619.

Canagarajah, S. (2011). Codemeshing in academic writing: Identifying teachable strategies of translanguaging. *Modern Language Journal*, 95, 401–417.

Cortazzi, M. (2000). Languages, cultures and cultures of learning in the global classroom. In H. W. Kum & C. Ward (Eds), *Language in the global context* (pp. 75–103). Singapore: SEAMEO Regional Language Centre.

Costelloe, P. (2006). Exploratory practice: A teacher development programme for trained and untrained primary school teachers in a rural district in Malaysia. Unpublished masters dissertation, University of Leicester, UK.

Council of Europe (2012). Guide for the development and implementation of curricula for plurilingual and intercultural education. Retrieved http://www.coe.int/t/dg4/linguistic/Guide_curricula_EN.asp

Goh, L. (2013). Spelling the blues over English ruling. *Sunday Star*, 6 September, p. 25.

Hall, S. J., & Dodson, A. (2004). *Surveying progressive English language teaching*. Paper presented at RELC International Seminar, Singapore, April 2004.

Hall, S. J. (2007). In-service or in servitude of native speaker myths: Dilemmas of internationalizing pedagogy. *Regional Language Centre Anthology Series 48*, 250–264.

Hayes, D. (2000). Cascade training and teachers' professional development. *ELT Journal*, 54(2), 135–145.

Hogg, M. A., & Vaughan, G. M. (1998). *Social psychology*. Harlow: Prentice Hall.

Holliday, A. (2006). *The struggle to teach English as an international language*. Oxford: Oxford University Press.

Johnson, K. E. (2006). The sociocultural turn and its challenges for second language teacher education, *TESOL Quarterly*, 40(1), 235–257.

Kabilan, M. K. (2007). English language teachers reflecting on reflections: A Malaysian experience. *TESOL Quarterly* 41(4), 681–699.

Kementerian Pendidikan Malaysia (1989). *Kurikulum Bersepadu Sekolah Mengengah (KBSM)*. Kuala Lumpur: Ministry of Education.

Koo, Y. L. (2008). *Language, culture and literacy: Meaning making in global contexts*. Bangi: Penerbit Universiti Kebaagasaan Malaysia.

Lee, S. K. (2003). Multiple identities in a multicultural world: A Malaysian perspective. *Journal of Language, Identity and Education*, 2, 137–158.

Lin A. (2013). Toward paradigmatic change in TESOL methodologies: Building plurilingual pedagogies from the ground up. *TESOL Quarterly, 47*(3), 521– 545.

Malachi, E. V. (2011). Teacher education in Malaysia: Preparing and training of English language educators. *The Journal of Asia TEFL, 8*(4), 85–108.

Mohamed, A. R., Morad, S., Ismail, S.M.M., Omar, H., & Rahman, W.R.E.A. (2006). Reluctant teachers, rustic students and the remoteness of English. *Jurnal Pendik dan Pendidikan, 21*, 47–60.

Moore, D., & Gajo, L. (2009). French voices on plurilingualism and pluriculturalism: Theory, significance and perspectives. *International Journal of Multilingualism, 6*, 137–153.

Musa, C. N., Koo, Y. L., & Azman, H. (2012). Exploring English language learning and teaching in Malaysia. *GEMA Online Journal of Language Studies 12*(1).

New Straits Times (2013). *Stick to education blueprint.* 8 December. Retrieved http://www.nst.com.my

Nunan, D. (2006). Task-based teaching in the Asia context: Defining task. *Asian EFL Journal, 18*(3), 12–18.

O'Sullivan, M. (2002). Action research and the transfer of reflective approaches to in-service education and training (INSET) for unqualified and underqualified primary teachers in Namibia. *Teaching and Teacher Education, 18*, 523–539.

Pandian, A. (2004). English language teaching in Malaysia Today. In H. W. Kam & R. Wong (Eds), *English language teaching in East Asia today* (pp. 272–293). Singapore: Marshall Cavendish.

Piccardo, E. (2013). Plurilingualism and curriculum design: towards a synergic vision. *TESOL Quarterly, 47*(3), 600–613.

Pillay, H. (1998). Issues in the teaching of English in Malaysia. *The Language Teacher, 22*(11), 41–43.

Puah, Y. Y., & Ting, S. H. (2013). *Home ground nations influencing Foochow and Hokkien speakers' language use in Kuching, Sarawak.* Paper presented at Konferensi Antara Universiti Se Borneo-Kalimantan Ke 7, Universiti Malysia Sarawak (UNIMAS) 19–21 November 2013, Kuching Sarawak, Malaysia.

Rajaretnam, T., & Nalliah, M. (1999). *The history of English language teaching in Malaysia.* Shah Alam, Malaysia: Biroteks Institut Teknologi Mara.

Selvaraj, B. (2010). English language teaching (ELT) curriculum reforms in Malaysia. *Voice of Academia, 5*(1), 51–59.

Silver, R. E., & Bokhorst-Heng, W. D. (2013). Neither 'mono' nor 'multi': Plurilingualism and hybrid competence. *TESOL Quarterly, 47*(3), 614–619.

Singh, G., & Richards, J. C. (2006). Teaching and learning in the language teacher education course room; a critical sociocultural perspective. *RELC Journal, 37*(2), 149–175.

Skehan, P. (1998). *A cognitive approach to language learning.* Oxford: Oxford University Press.

Waters, A., & Vilches, M. L. C. (2008). Factors affecting ELT reforms: The case of the Philippines basic curriculum. *RELC Journal, 39*(5), 5–24.

Willis, J. (1996) *A framework for task-based learning.* Harlow: Longman.

Woodward, T. (2003). Loop Input. *ELT Journal, 57*(3), 301–304.

11

Preparing for Tasks in Vietnamese EFL High School Classrooms:

Teachers in Action

Bao Trang Thi Nguyen
Jonathan Newton
David Crabbe

Summary

In the context of a new task-based English curriculum for high school students in Vietnam, this chapter describes the approach taken to pre-task classroom work by nine teachers in a Vietnamese English as a Foreign Language (EFL) high school and the beliefs that influence their pedagogic choices. How a teacher prepares learners to perform communication tasks can be especially revealing of their views of language learning and the function of tasks. While most of the nine teachers used the pre-task phase to focus on meaning and performance, the extent to which they also included guided, explicit language practice or form-focused instruction varied considerably. This varied practice reflected the contrasting beliefs that the teachers held about language learning through tasks, beliefs that aligned with either weak or strong versions of task-based teaching. The students also held a variety of views on how to best prepare for a task. Notably, a number of them saw pre-task language work as constraining; they valued creativity in performance, and therefore appreciated the 'space' to find resources themselves rather than being primed or given language to practise. Taken together, the actions and beliefs of the teachers and students call into question the stereotypes of the 'passive' Asian student and the 'authoritarian' Asian teacher. This points to the need for further classroom research to addresses task-based pedagogy in the Asian context and beyond.

Introduction

In recent years, task-based language teaching (TBLT) has been widely adopted in Asian countries as reported in a number of studies (Barnard & Nguyen, 2010; Carless, 2004, 2007, 2009; Deng & Carless, 2009; Le & Barnard, 2009; McDonough & Chaikitmongkol, 2007; Zhang, 2007). These studies typically show TBLT in Asia moving from 'adoption to adaptation' (Butler, 2011, p. 43) with the adaption being towards a weak version of TBLT or 'task-supported' language teaching (Ellis, 2003; see also Adams & Newton, 2009; Butler, 2011, Littlewood, 2007 for recent reviews). As Carless (2004) points out, '[t]eachers mould innovations to their own abilities, beliefs, and experiences; the immediate school context; and the wider sociocultural environment' (p. 659).

In this chapter we report on the ways in which teachers implemented task-based lessons in a Vietnamese high school. Our particular focus is on how they implemented the pre-task phase, and their beliefs and those of their students as to what constitutes effective pedagogy for this task phase in this particular cultural context. More broadly, this focus offers insights into the uptake of TBLT by teachers and learners in a setting in which traditional cultural values are argued to have a pervasive influence on teaching and learning behaviours (Kramsch & Sullivan, 1996; Sullivan, 2000). In Vietnam, as in other Asian countries, local cultural norms, especially those concerning teacher and learner roles, have been claimed to constrain uptake of communicative approaches to language teaching (e.g., Anderson, 1993; G. Ellis, 1996; Holliday, 1997; Sullivan, 2000). But stereotypes of the passive Asian student and the authoritarian Asian teacher (e.g., Flowerdew & Miller, 1995; Cortazzi & Jin, 1996; Pennycook, 1998) are not without their critics (Butler, 2011; Kennedy, 2002; Littlewood, 2000; Phan, 2004) and are clearly at odds with the classroom data we discuss in this chapter.

TBLT is based on the premise that 'true interlanguage development (i.e., the process of acquiring new linguistic knowledge and restructuring existing knowledge) can only take place when acquisition happens incidentally as a product of the effort to communicate' (Ellis, 2010, pp. 38–39). Thus, TBLT reflects natural processes of language acquisition as captured in the terms 'ecological rationale' (Lynch & Maclean, 2000), 'real world resemblance' (Ellis, 2003; Skehan, 2003) and 'holistic' language use (Samuda & Bygate, 2008). This emphasis on putting language to use to achieve a task outcome rather than on focusing on language forms for their own sake is a distinguishing feature of TBLT. Task proponents such as Van den Branden (2006) generally view a brief *pre-task* focus on form as a valid way to encourage noticing of linguistic forms during task performance. However, too much pre-teaching of language forms can lead to actual 'de-tasking' (Van den Branden, Bygate & Norris, 2009). The pedagogic choices teachers make in the pre-task phase in real classrooms are likely to represent a set of beliefs about the process of learning form-meaning associations and therefore merit detailed investigation in the context of curriculum innovation.

Investigating pre-task work in TBLT

The rationale for building a pre-task phase into TBLT is that because learners have limited processing capacity they will benefit from pre-task activities that reduce the cognitive load of the main task (Skehan, 1996, 1998; see Robinson, 2001 for a contrary view). As Ellis (2003) states, 'the purpose of the pre-task stage is to prepare students to perform the task in ways that will promote acquisition' (p. 244). Most research to date has focused on pre-task-planning (providing time for learners to plan what and how they are going to say) to track the effects of different strategic planning conditions on task performance, measured in terms of accuracy, complexity and fluency (e.g., Ellis, 2005, 2009b; Foster & Skehan, 1996, 1999; Mochizuki & Ortega, 2008; Park, 2010). Other types of pre-task activities such as modelling task-based interaction (Kim & McDonough, 2008; Leeser, 2004; Swain, 1998; Swain & Lapkin, 1998, 2001) have also been addressed (although modelling was not their research focus). Other researchers have investigated whether pre-task modelling, sharing ideas and carrying out collaborative work leads to more learning opportunities via language-related episodes (LREs) (Kim & McDonough, 2011; La Pierre, 1994, cited in Swain, 1998). These studies have consistently found more learning opportunities resulted from pre-task modelling than from tasks performed without modelling. Seeding pre-task input has also been explored (Boston, 2008, 2009; Samuda, 2001). While these studies provide a wider repertoire of pre-task options, they involved the use of discrete tasks designed or elected by the researchers and typically investigated through quasi-experimental studies.

From a more practical classroom perspective, Ellis (2003), Willis (1996) and Willis and Willis (2007) report different activities that the teachers can use to prepare students for tasks. These activities mainly range from attending to input, focusing on the task topic and topic language, vocabulary activities, performing a similar task, and modelling. However, few studies deal with the choices teachers actually make to prepare students for tasks in their daily teaching and why they make these choices, although several mention cases where the teacher used brainstorming as preparation for the main task (Berben, Van den Branden & Van Gorp, 2007; Luk, 2009). In this chapter we describe a study that addresses the lack of research into pre-task work by closely analysing the classroom practice of nine teachers in a Vietnamese high school working with a task-based curriculum. The EFL high school setting also addresses a gap in that the majority of TBLT research has been conducted in English as a Second Language (ESL) contexts and in tertiary programmes. The study also seeks to document students' perceptions of the teachers' pre-task pedagogy. To our knowledge, no research has explicitly looked at how students perceive the pre-task work that the teacher provides and what their preferences are for the task preparation phase. The study addresses, then, the following research questions:

1 What did the teachers do in the pre-task phase to prepare learners for oral communicative task performances?
2 What were the teachers' rationales for and perceptions of their pre-task pedagogic actions?
3 How did students perceive the learning opportunities provided by the teachers in the pre-task phase?

In answering these questions we have sought to identify the extent to which teachers' choices in the pre-task phase opened up space for creative task performance or led to 'de-tasking' (Ellis, 2006).

Pre-task work at a Vietnamese high school

The teacher and student participants

The research took place in the EFL classrooms of a prestigious high school in Vietnam. Nine teachers of English (out of a staff of fourteen English teachers) and nine of their classes volunteered as participants (three teachers and three classes at each grade level for grades 10, 11, and 12). The teachers were all qualified EFL teachers with a minimum of a Bachelor's degree in English. They all had between eleven to twenty-three years' teaching experience except three new teachers with from only two months to three years' experience. The teachers were between twenty-two and forty-seven years of age. Most of them had been trained in how to use the new textbooks via workshops held by the Ministry of Education and Training (MOET) or the local Department of Education and Training. Student participants were aged between fifteen and eighteen and had been studying English as a compulsory subject since they were eleven years old (Grade 6). In Vietnam English is officially a compulsory subject from Grade 6.

The curriculum and the textbooks

In Vietnam, a new high school English curriculum was officially approved and institutionalized in 2006 (Le & Barnard, 2009; MOET, 2010). The curriculum and textbooks designed for it reflect a communicative approach, learner-centeredness and task-based teaching (Hoang, H. Hoang, Vu, Dao, Do & Nguyen, 2006, 2007). This curriculum is by now well embedded in high school English language teaching in Vietnam.

The textbooks used for three grade levels (grades 10, 11 and 12) were *Tieng Anh 10* (English 10), *Tieng Anh 11* (English 11) and *Tieng Anh 12* (English 12) (MOET, 2010). Each textbook contains sixteen units, centred around six main themes, namely *Personal information, You and me, Education, Community, Nature, Recreation*, and *People & places* (MOET, 2010, p. 13). Every unit is composed of five parts (*Reading, Listening, Speaking, Writing* and *Language Focus*), each of which is expected to fill a 45-minute lesson. This structure is the same in all units. The textbook authors (Hoang et al., 2007, p. 6) emphasize the importance of task-based learning for developing learners' communicative competence and state that learners should be proactive and creative agents in the learning process. They describe the teacher's role as including organizer, monitor, mediator, consultant, participant, and knowledge provider.

The data

The research adopted a *multiple case study* approach (Stake, 2005) in which the teaching practices of each of the nine teachers were investigated in depth. According to Stake, 'illustration of how a phenomenon occurs in the circumstances of several exemplars can provide valued and trustworthy knowledge' (pp. 458–459).

Data were collected over a two and a half month period through multiple data sources. These included classroom observations (audio, video and field notes from direct observation), document and materials analysis, stimulated recall and in-depth interviews. Each of the nine teachers and their classes were observed across the five lessons that make up a textbook unit. In total, data was collected from forty-five lessons. All oral task lessons were fully transcribed. Although the focus of the research was only on the oral tasks in each unit, the complete unit was observed to obtain a fuller picture of task-based teaching in these classes. As Samuda and Bygate (2008) argue:

> The interrelationships between a task, its position in a teaching sequence, the pedagogic role it plays within that sequence, and the purpose motivating its use are complex, and from a pedagogic perspective it is necessary to focus on understanding tasks in light of those relationships.
>
> (p. 218)

The teachers were informed that the research focused on how they carried out TBLT but to avoid the danger that they would teach towards the data the precise focus of the research was not specified.

Video recordings of the observed lessons were used in subsequent stimulated recall sessions with the teachers and students (cf. Gass & Mackey, 2000). The recall sessions provide points of departure or contexts for the teachers to spell out the rationale for specific instances in their practice. The teachers were also interviewed as soon as possible after the observed lessons and in separate sessions from the stimulated recall sessions. All interviews were within four days of the class. The Vietnamese language was used in all these sessions to establish rapport and prevent misunderstanding. The first author transcribed all interviews in their entirety and then translated them into English. Care was taken to maintain 'accuracy and subtlety in translation' (Marshall & Rossman, 2006, p. 112). The transcripts and translations were checked and double-checked by another Vietnamese EFL teacher.

One concern raised by Borg (2006) is that teachers might articulate post-hoc rationales that might not be true of themselves. To avoid relying on one source of data, teachers were asked to confirm and elaborate on what they said through the 'multiple session format' interviews (Dörnyei, 2007, p. 135). In addition, the study also looks at students' perceptions of the pedagogical actions the teachers took via stimulated recall in-depth focus group interviews. The approach to student interviews followed the same procedures as that taken in the teacher interviews. Overall, the multiple data sources provided a rich basis for triangulation to enhance consistency and accuracy of the findings.

The data was inductively analysed following approaches to qualitative data analysis proposed by Creswell (2009) and Ellis and Barkhuizen (2005). Data was categorized through an iterative process of analysis of transcripts and observation notes, and where available, from the teachers' stated purposes for their pedagogic choices. Categories were not predetermined but emerged through the analysis.

The emerging picture of pre-task work

There were oral tasks in other components of the units for which the teachers were found to prepare students minimally. Here we report only on the data from the lessons based on the speaking components of the textbook units. There was considerable variation in the way the nine teachers prepared students for the tasks in these speaking components but before we look at the detail of that variation, let us look at the overall shape of the task-based lesson in the nine classrooms in order to establish a wider pedagogic context.

An overview of the shape of the whole task-based lesson

All nine teachers sequenced the lesson in four distinct phases. The first and last were, predictably, the pre-task and post-task phases. Sandwiched between these bookend phases were what we have called the *rehearsal* and *performance* phases. The first of these involved students doing the task in pairs/groups. This phase lasted from between four and nine minutes across the classes. The second involved a public performance of the task by selected pairs/groups of students in front of the class. We have chosen the terms '*rehearsal*' and '*performance*' to describe these phases because these terms capture the orientation and intent of teachers and students as observed in the lessons and described in the interviews. These phases might ostensibly look like a version of present-practise-perform (PPP). This is not the case however. Unlike PPP, the rehearsal and performance phases were both fully communicative, meaning-focused and oriented to task objectives. Teachers and students were also committed to bringing the task through to public performance. Indeed, students often expressed disappointment if they were not chosen to perform the task in front of the class. To our knowledge, the repetition of the task first as a form of rehearsal and second as a public display has received little attention in the TBLT literature despite, we suspect, being quite a common practice in language classrooms but reporting on the rehearsal and performance phases of the lessons is beyond the scope of this particular chapter. We now turn to the data on the pre-task work and address each of the research questions that we started with.

What did the teachers provide for pre-task work?

As described in the methodology section, teacher talk and classroom interaction in the pre-task phase of the nine target lessons was observed, recorded, analysed and categorized. Eight categories of teacher action emerged. These were further classified as focussing either on meaning and performance, or on language practice. Table 11.1 presents the eight categories and indicates whether each category was present or absent in the observed lessons by the nine teachers.[1] Data on the time taken for the pre-task phase by each teacher is also provided. The length of the pre-task phase varied tremendously across the lessons, from four minutes in lesson 611F to twenty-four minutes in 912I. Not surprisingly, the lessons with the shortest pre-task phases (411D, 611F and 712G) contained the fewest distinct teacher actions while the classes with the longest phases (110B and 912I) contained the most.

Within this variety of practices there was however a common core: almost all teachers initiated the pre-task phase by introducing the task topic via a short game (a) followed by a brainstorming activity in which the teacher elicited ideas from the class (b). Three teachers also set up pair/group structured communication

TABLE 11.1 *Teacher action in the pre-task phase*

Note. The tick (✓) here indicates that the teacher took this action and the dash (–) that they did not.

Teacher action	Teacher								
	110	210	310	411	511	611	712	812	912
	A	B	C	D	E	F	G	H	I
Pre-task focus on meaning and performance									
a. Teacher introduces the task topic with a game	✓	✓	✓	–	✓	✓	✓	✓	✓
b. Teacher leads brainstorming of ideas for the main task	✓	✓	✓	✓	✓	✓	✓	✓	✓
c. Teacher gives task instructions and checks student understanding	✓	✓	✓	✓	✓	✓	✓	✓	✓
d. Teacher briefly provides suggestions for how to do the task	✓	✓	✓	–	✓	–	✓	✓	✓
e. Teacher sets up pair/group structured communication activities to prepare for the main task	–	✓	–	–	–	–	–	✓	✓
Pre-task focus on language practice									
f. Teacher introduces language for the task	✓	✓	✓	–	–	–	–	✓	✓
g. Teacher provides controlled language practice	–	✓	–	–	–	–	–	–	✓
h. Teacher models a sample dialogue with a student	✓	✓	✓	–	✓	–	–	–	✓
Time spent (minutes)	19	23	18	5	7	4	16[2]	20	24

activities as task preparation (e). It is interesting that this emphasis on task content and ideas rather than on language forms/controlled language practice was the single unifying feature of the data.[3] In contrast, some kind of focus on language practice was absent in lessons by three teachers (411D, 611F and 712G) and, where present in the lessons by the other six teachers, was approached in a variety of ways. Five of these six teachers introduced some language through teacher talk (f) although only two provided subsequent controlled language practice (g). Four of the five who provided language for the task also followed up by modelling a sample dialogue with a student (h).

What were the teachers' rationales for and perceptions of pre-task work?

We now examine teachers' beliefs and explanations for the pedagogic choices they made in the pre-task phase of the observed lessons. We will focus on the language practice actions (f, g & h) since the teachers varied so much on these, and the students also had clearly articulated positions on the value of such activities. Why did some of the teachers avoid any kind of focus on language form while others included it? It became clear in the interviews that this was not a random phenomenon, nor was it a question of time constraints or lack of relevant expertise. Rather, the teachers all had well thought out positions that underpinned their classroom practices.

Some of the teachers avoided a focus on language form. Here are comments from two of these teachers:

> I don't usually provide useful language before a speaking task because it's not necessary. Students' ideas are varied and rich; they will ask me or friends with some language expressions to convey what they want to, if they feel they need to.
> (411D)

> Students help each other when they do the task within their group; students learn from each other in terms of linguistic items and general knowledge. So I just let students do the task in their group first, and correct errors if any later.
> (611F)

These two teachers show awareness of the need for an open 'pedagogical space' (Samuda, 2007) in task-based learning. The other two teachers who did not introduce language also explicitly stated that the students needed freedom to carry out the task. Excerpt 1 provides one such example. The main tasks involved students talking about their future jobs and then debating about job choices. Prior to the main task, the teacher had students play a miming game (job guesses). He then briefly elicited students' ideas and then quickly noted down each contributed idea onto the board.

Excerpt 1 (712G-SL)

```
01   T: What do you think about 'doctor'? For example, a very amusing job,
     I think so, that's my idea. What do you think of 'nurse'? What do you
     think of 'nurse'? Who, please?
02   S: Boring.
03   T: Hah?
04   S: Boring.
05   T: Boring. Thank you. How about teacher? M, please.
06   S: Intelligent.
07   T: Yep. How about farmer? Do you want to be a farmer?
08   S: Strong.
09   T: Strong. Good. How about businessmen and [business] women? How
     about businessmen and [business] women?
10   S: Rich.
11   T: Rich. And the last one, politician?
```

12	S:	Challenging.
13	T:	Huh?
14	S:	Challenging.
15	T:	Challenging. OK. Don't worry about your opinions, no right or wrong answers, don't worry. Now good points, what about teachers?
16	S:	Take care of children.
17	T:	Take care of children? What about doctor?
18	S:	Help sick people.
19	T:	Help sick people, good. A nurse?
20	S:	Take care of patients.
21	T:	Take care of patients, and doctors?
		(Laugh from the class)
22	T:	Farmer?
23	S:	Erm, erm, produce foods.
24	T:	Produce foods. Businessmen and [business] women? Please, raise your hands. H, please.
25	S:	Develop the economy.
26	T:	Develop the economy.
27	S:	Control the country.
28	T:	Control the country?
29	T:	You can use the jobs and the ideas on the blackboard, or you can use the jobs not on the blackboard, any jobs that you want to do in the future. For example, I want to be a designer, I want to be a model, I want to be a singer, I want to be an engineer or an architect, etc. Discuss with your friend what do you feel about that job, good points and bad points of that job. OK? Clear? Now you have five minutes to talk to the person next to you first.

In this interaction, the teacher did not specify any language to use. Instead, students themselves, by expressing their opinions, produced adjectives describing jobs (boring, intelligent, strong, rich, challenging – lines 2, 6, 8, 10, 12) and collocations (take care of children, help sick people, take care of patients, produce foods, develop the economy – lines 16, 18, 20, 23, and 25). The teacher also encouraged talk by saying there are no 'right' or 'wrong' answers (line 15) and made it explicit that students could talk about any job that they wanted (line 29). Talking about his pedagogic moves, the teacher commented:

> Guiding should be in a way so that students actively come up with input. That's part of my viewpoint on learner-centeredness!
>
> (712G)

The other teacher similarly stated:

> Teacher guidance towards the task is very important. I often give students some hints to go about the task, but I don't ever force them to follow my suggestions. Before students do the task, I make explicit what flexibility students can have, you can't force students to follow teachers; I let them add what they feel relevant so

that they will be more responsible – as long as they use English and talk a lot – this is my teaching experience which has been built up for many years.

(611F)

The flexible and non-prescriptive approach articulated by these teachers echoes the views of the case study teachers in Andon and Eckerth (2009) who sought to give students 'the freedom to say what they want and, to some extent, to decide what language they use' (p. 294).

In contrast, those teachers who introduced pre-task language (and controlled practice) worked from a different set of beliefs. Excerpt 2 provides an example. The teacher elicited and presented phases for asking for and giving opinions, before putting students into groups to do the task which was to decide on the best seats on a boat trip for a group of people.

Excerpt 2 (210B-SL)

01   T: If you want to ask for one's opinion. What do you say? N, please.
02   S: What about you?
03   T: Right. Another way?
04   S: What do you think?
05   T: What do you think? Or, What do you think of? What do you think of something? Right? Or what's your . . .? May be what's your idea, right? If you want to give an opinion, how do you say? H, please.
06   S: I think.
07   T: Very good, I think . . . Another way? M, please.
08   S: I think we should.
09   T: Right. Very good. I think we should . . . I think you . . . should, etc. Do you think we shouldn't?
10   S: No.
11   T: Yeah, we say I don't think we should. Any other way?
12   S: In my opinion.
13   T: Yeah, any other? You can say 'to my mind', or you can say 'as I see it'. If you agree with somebody's opinion, what do you say? How about the others? Come on! N, please.
14   S: I agree with you.
15   T: I agree with you. Very good. Any other? L, please.
16   S: I think so, you're right.
17   T: Good.

During this activity the teacher wrote the elicited language items on the board and then had students do a sorting activity in which they listed expressions for giving opinions or advice in two separate columns. Her beliefs about the importance of a pre-task focus on language are consistent with her pedagogy:

Pre-task language input is very necessary. Without it, students will find it hard to express themselves in English. Without input, it's like in a vast sea, they don't know which way to go and they struggle.

(210B)

The other teachers who provided pre-task language made similar comments.

Continuing the focus on pre-task language input, five of the teachers modelled a sample dialogue orally with one student in the class (four of them also introduced pre-task language). Explaining this action they said:

> I think a model facilitates student task performance. From my teaching experience, I have noticed that some weak students adhered to the model, using some of the structures in the model. While good students might have their own ways of doing the task, weaker ones should have something to rely on.
>
> (310C)

> Directions are better, the core things [a model and some language input] should be provided so that students can expand language use in their own way based on this; for some students they really need those bases. If not properly guided, students are not able to carry out the tasks efficiently. If students don't have [input] directions to go, they won't be able to do the task well.
>
> (912I)

As seen from these last two comments, the teachers emphasized the value of pre-task modelling for weaker students and as the 'core' for students to expand language production. To illustrate, before putting students into groups discussing their future jobs, one teacher (who provided the last comment above) displayed the following sample dialogue on the whiteboard:

> Lan: What would you like to be in the future?
> Nam: I would like to be (a) **a doctor**.
> Lan: Why do you want to be a doctor?
> Nam: Working as a doctor would be (b) **a humane and rewarding job**. I would have a chance to (c) **take care of sick people** and **help save people's lives**.

She then asked one student to act out the model with her. She commented:

> I want students to replace these ideas [in bold in the model above] with their ideas for the jobs given and make a conversation. In this way, students will get to know the core thing.
>
> (912I)

In contrast, one teacher who did not provide modelling made the following comment:

> If I give a model or a sample of any kind, it's my own way. Forty-five students have forty-five ways to go about the task, so no need to [model]. Besides, students usually have better, more interesting ideas to say, I'm sure.
>
> (411D)

Once again, beliefs informed action.

So while all the teachers embraced a task-based methodology, they varied on the crucial issue of whether to focus on language form in the pre-task phase. Furthermore they were all able to articulate a position on this question that was entirely congruent with their classroom practices. This highlights the role of teacher cognition in the implementation of task-based instruction in this context (cf. Borg, 2006, 2009; Woods, 1996). The question of whether to include a pre-task focus on language to TBLT is a controversial issue (cf. Bygate, Skehan & Swain, 2001; Ellis, 2009a). In the words of Kumaravadivelu (2007):

> A central issue in the implementation of task-based instruction is when and how to promote a principled focus on form. To a large extent, one's stand on this issue will shape the nature of task design, syllabus construction and instructional strategies.
> (p. 19)

A danger of pre-teaching linguistic items might prompt students to see the subsequent task as an opportunity to practice the target items and thus compromise the 'taskness' of the task (Ellis, 2003; Willis & Willis, 2007). However, there is a continuum on focus on form and on meaning. As Skehan (1998, p. 96) notes, 'avoidance of specific structures and engagement of worthwhile meanings, are matters of degree, rather than being categorical'. One way to address this question of whether a pre-task linguistic focus de-values the task is to investigate the experience of learners. This is the focus of the next section.

How did the students perceive the learning opportunities offered in the pre-task work?

This third research question looks at student perspectives on the ways the teachers ran the pre-task phase. Like the teachers, the students were able to articulate clear opinions on the value of a pre-task focus on language forms. Indeed, students had strong, internally consistent but contrasting opinions about all three forms of language practice in Table 11.1 (rows f, g & h).

Two-thirds (36/54) of the students expressed a preference for doing the task in their own way without any model, language input or structured communication activities. Interestingly, the students who viewed pre-task language practice as constraining, facilitating or neutral, tended to hold the same attitudes towards modelling (and structured communication activities). The students who held the 'constraining' view valued creativity in task performance as we see in the comments below (student identity code in brackets).

> With vocabulary or structures provided, psychologically we tend to use these words, or think in ways that can use these words, so our thinking is constrained. Without them, we can think further with diverse creative ideas.
> (TQB-12H)

> For me, it is not good to teach vocabulary or structures before I do the task; it should not be too early. It should be done after I have done the task. From my own experience, if I am corrected certain errors after I have used them in my talk, I will remember them better. So, I prefer to do the task freely, and later the teacher can correct the words that students used incorrectly.
> (LVT-10C)

It was surprising that the students were able to articulate such well thought through positions on how they preferred to carry out communicative tasks. Interestingly, also contrary to some reports that learners might not see much relevance in oral communicative tasks in EFL contexts (McDonough, 2004; Pham, 2007), the students here appeared to be well aware of the value of these tasks and how to make the best use of them for language learning.

With regards to pre-task modelling, the majority group of students saw it as constraining and inhibiting:

> In my opinion, there should not be a model of task performance, because students tend to rely on it, thus affecting their ability to be creative in language use. For the teenagers' age, creativity is quite big; the only problem that we face is limited vocabulary to express all that we want to mean. However, this problem is not hard to solve. We can always ask peers and the teacher.
>
> (BDH-12G)

> Without a model, students will have to think in more positive and broader directions. A given model inhibits students from thinking further, and this is very likely to lead to moulding, everybody will do the task in the same way. The imagination of each individual is different, so I believe, without a model we will have a variety of talks, and this is motivating and fun.
>
> (LBN-11E)

Students' opinions here contrast with the positive value placed on pre-task language modelling by students in quasi-experimental studies (e.g., Kim & McDonough, 2011). This suggests that greater attention be given to students' perceptions in the TBLT literature.

Littlewood (2004, 2007) argues that structured communication activities offer teachers in Asian contexts a way to gradually introduce TBLT. However, such general advice addressed to teachers to solve a teaching problem was not universally supported by the perception of this group of Asian learners of effective learning. Indeed, most students in the current study held an opposing view. For example:

> Why not give us this final task right away, no need to do those activities; it's too framing, it's like a predetermined path to follow. It's constraining and boring.
>
> (NTLC-12H)

> In those early activities, there's nothing to talk about, just matching ideas and these are not the jobs we want to do, how can we talk about it?
>
> (NHAV-12I)

> I think just let students do the main task and not do this activity. No need to form questions and answers like this before doing the final communicative activity. It's boring.
>
> (LMT-10C)

In contrast to the students discussed above, a minority of students (12/54) expressed a need for pre-task modelling and language (and structured communication activities) as in the following comments:

I need the basic thing, [like a model of task performance] from which to expand my talk. In this way, I speak better.'

(LHT-10B)

My vocabulary is limited, so with some words or structures given, I can use them when needed. So it's easier.

(LAD-12H)

A smaller number (6/54) expressed a neutral position:

With some vocabulary or a model provided, those who want to be creative, they can at their own wish; and those who cannot create something new nor want to take risks can use what provided to help them move on with the task. In my case, I always think of new ideas and thus I rarely use the vocabulary or model provided. It is like the teacher gives you a pen, whether you use it or not is up to you; as long as you still write something in the end.

(DTT-10A)

Modelling is just a suggestion. We still have the right to be creative and do the task in our own way. The teacher does not force us to follow the model.

(QTHG-12I)

These comments from students reflect the value they place on creativity and on the learning space they need to maximize the benefits from task-based learning. What some teachers did and believed was facilitative of student task performance, was in fact viewed as constraining by many students. This is consistent with Allwright's point that how learning opportunities are viewed is 'more a matter of how those present affectively interpret them' (Allwright, 2005, p. 22). In this study it is students voicing what they experienced as inhibiting or facilitating in task-based teaching that alerts us to the ways pre-task pedagogic actions can thwart or enhance their engagement and learning.

Conclusion

The case studies reveal a number of interesting points. The lessons of all nine teachers fall into a four-part structure: pre-task, task rehearsal, task performance, and post-task where the main focus is on that final task performance. In the pre-task work, the focus of this chapter, all teachers maintained an initial focus on preparing students for the final task performance. The notion of public performance was highly salient in the culture of all these classrooms and all teachers provided preparation for that publicly performed task in the form of generating ideas and preparatory communicative performance.

However there was also considerable variation in the realization of the pre-task phase across the teachers and the classes both in terms of the length of time allocated to it and in the extent to which teachers included a focus on language forms. These varied practices reflect the contrasting beliefs that the teachers hold about language learning and, therefore, the types of learning opportunity to be offered by a teacher.

Just over one-half of the teachers (5/9) included some kind of opportunities for a focus on language in the pre-task phase. These practice opportunities included providing language considered useful for the task, (with or without practice of that language) and modelling a sample dialogue. Their stated beliefs about pre-task language support were consistent with their actions. Similarly, the four teachers who did not provide controlled practice activities articulated beliefs consistent with their action, saying that the resources for the task performance needed to come from the students themselves. These two approaches align with weak and strong versions of task-based teaching (Ellis, 2003).

Just as the teachers had varying views on pre-task work, so did the learners, although in a roughly inverse proportion. The majority of learners expressed an explicit preference for fewer language-focused activities. Thus, in the life of a task we have a dynamic in the classroom in which different beliefs about the value of pre-task work are operating. It would be reasonable to assume that these beliefs, in the case of the students, would have an influence on the way in which they take up the opportunity and really use the pre-task work to some advantage.

While it would also be reasonable to assume that such divergences would appear in most classrooms, it is probable that the actual nature of the beliefs is influenced by the nature of the school (in this case an elite school) and the motivation and experience of the students and the professional experience of the teachers. It is also important to look at the life of a task in its entirety. In this paper we have only reported on the pre-task phase; full understanding can only be gained by looking at how that pre-task phase led into the pair/group rehearsal phase and then into the final public performance.

This chapter supports the view that we cannot rely solely on predictions from Second Language Acquisition (SLA) experiments to inform classroom implementation. The teachers in this study were influenced by other factors that arose from their own teaching experience, leading them to reshape their teaching to better motivate and engage students. However, as we have seen, there was still some mismatch between the pre-task preparations made by some teachers and students' desire for freedom to carry out the task in their own way with their own resources. Interestingly, the student voice in the current study challenges earlier views of Vietnamese cultural values such as the notion of 'classroom as family', in which students responded as a whole group to teacher questions (Kramsch & Sullivan, 1996; Sullivan, 2000). In fact, the student voice in this study supported the challenge that Phan (2004) made against the notion that cultural values (e.g., Confucianism) constrain the implementation of communicative tasks in Vietnamese university contexts. The data also undermines stereotypical views of Asian students as passive receivers of knowledge (e.g., Cortazzi & Jin, 1996; Flowerdew & Miller, 1995; Pennycook, 1998). Indeed, the students, as we have seen, voiced their desire to have space to take an active role in seeking knowledge for themselves and were therefore similar to the students from eight Asian countries in Littlewood (2000). The students also held positive attitudes towards communicative tasks. This finding is in line with recent studies in other Asian countries such as Japan (Hood, Elwood & Falout; 2009), Thailand (McDonough & Chaikitmongkol, 2007) and Taiwan (Chung & Hang, 2009; Savignon & Wang, 2003). As Butler (2011) argues, '[i]t is thus potentially misleading to overemphasize the role of traditional cultural values (such as Confucian values) in shaping Asian classroom practices at all grade levels across Asia' (p. 40).

The findings of the study show teachers and learners embracing a communicative methodology in an Asian setting in which the relevance of communicative tasks has been questioned (Carless, 2007; McDonough, 2004; Pham, 2007). Indeed, contrary to the idea that a weak version of TBLT (i.e., task-*supported* teaching) is both appropriate and typical in some Asian settings (see Adams & Newton, 2009; Littlewood, 2007), the practices of many of the teachers in the current study aligned with a strong version of TBLT (i.e., task-*based* teaching) (Ellis, 2003).

Once again, this broader view underscores the need in classroom research for a balance between research focused on SLA and motivation (Gardner, 2010), on understanding of social and psychological student factors (Block, 2003), and on teacher cognition (Borg, 2006, 2009). This balance would take account of the difference between task as work-plan and task as process (Breen, 2009; Coughlan & Duff, 1994). In the words of Bygate (1999), 'We cannot take for granted the relation between task and language without looking at what learners actually do' (p.34). We could add to that, what *teachers* and learners actually do.

Notes

1 The table does not strictly reflect sequence. The actual sequence for all lessons was as follows: a–b–f–g–e–c–d–h, with the only difference being omission of various actions by different teachers.
2 In this lesson, ten minutes was spent on a group game, and this inflates the overall time.
3 It is important to note here that although the teachers all taught from the same textbook, they did not plan the lessons together and nor were they following any kind of written guide that stipulated this kind of approach.

References

Adams, R., & Newton, J. (2009). TBLT in Asia: Constraints and opportunities. *Asian Journal of English Language Teaching*, 9, 1–17.

Allwright, D. (2005). From teaching points to learning opportunities and beyond. *TESOL Quarterly*, 39(1), 9–31.

Anderson, J. (1993). Is a communicative approach practical for teaching English in China? Pros and cons. *System*, 21(4), 471–480.

Andon, N., & Eckerth, J. (2009). Chacun à son gout? Task-based L2 pedagogy from the teacher's point of view. *International Journal of Applied Linguistics*, 19(3), 286–310.

Barnard, R., & Nguyen, G. V. (2010). Task-based language teaching (TBLT): A Vietnamese case study using narrative frames to elicit teachers' beliefs. *Language Education in Asia*, 1, 77–86.

Berben, M., Van den Branden, K., & Van Gorp, K. (2007). "We'll see what happens": Tasks on paper and tasks in a multilingual classroom. In Van den Branden, K. Van Gorp & M. Verhelst (Eds), *Tasks in action: Task-based language education from a classroom-based perspective* (pp. 32–67). Newcastle: Cambridge Scholars Publishing.

Block, D. (2003). *The social turn in second language acquisition*. Edinburgh: Edinburgh University Press.

Borg, S. (2006). *Teacher cognition and language education: Research and practice*. London: Continuum.

Borg, S. (2009). Language teacher cognition. In A. Burns & J. C. Richards (Eds), *The Cambridge guide to second language teacher education* (pp. 163–171). Cambridge: Cambridge University Press.

Boston, J. S. (2008). Learner mining of pre-task and task input. *ELT Journal*, 62(1), 66–76.
Boston, J. S. (2009). Pre-task syntactic priming and focused task design. *ELT Journal*, 64(2), 165–174.
Breen, M. P. (2009). Learners contributions to task design. In K. Van den Branden, M. Bygate & J. Norris (Eds), *Task-based language teaching: A reader*. Amsterdam: John Benjamins.
Butler, Y. G. (2011). The implementation of communicative and task-based language teaching in the Asia-Pacific region. *Annual Review of Applied Linguistics*, 31(1), 36–57.
Bygate, M. (1999). Task as context for the framing, reframing and un-framing of language. *System*, 7(1), 33–48.
Bygate, M., Skehan, P., & Swain, M. (Eds). (2001). *Researching pedagogic tasks: Second language learning, teaching and testing*. Harlow: Addison Wesley Longman.
Carless, D. (2004). Issues in teachers' reinterpretation of a task-based innovation in primary schools. *TESOL Quarterly*, 3(4), 639–662.
Carless, D. (2007). The suitability of task-based approaches for secondary schools: Perspectives from Hong Kong. *System*, 35(4), 595–608.
Carless, D. (2009). Revisiting the TBLT versus P-P-P. *Asian Journal of English Language Teaching*, 19, 49–66.
Chung, I.-F., & Huang, Y.-C. (2009). The implementation of communicative language teaching: An investigation of students' viewpoints. *The Asia-Pacific Education Researcher*, 18(1), 67–78.
Cortazzi, M., & Jin, L. (1996). Cultures of learning: Language classrooms in China. In H. Coleman (Ed.), *Society and the language classroom* (pp. 169–206). Cambridge: Cambridge University Press.
Coughlan, P., & Duff, P. (1994). Same task, different activities: Analysis of SLA task from an activity theory perspective. In J. P. Lantolf & G. Appel (Eds), *Vygotskian approaches to second language research* (pp. 173–193). Westport: ABLEX Publishing.
Creswell, J. W. (2009). *Research design: Qualitative, quantitative, and mixed methods approaches*. Los Angeles: SAGE.
Deng, C., & Carless, D. (2009). The communicativeness of activities in a task-based innovation in Guangdong, China. *Asian Journal of English Language Teaching*, 19, 113–134.
Dörnyei, Z. (2007). *Research methods in applied linguistics*. Oxford: Oxford University Press.
Ellis, G. (1996). How culturally appropriate is the communicative approach? *ELT Journal*, 50(3), 213–218.
Ellis, R. (2003). *Task-based language learning and teaching*. Oxford: Oxford University Press.
Ellis, R. (2005). Planning and task-based performance: Theory and research. In R. Ellis (Ed.), *Planning and task performance in a second language* (pp. 3–34). Amsterdam: John Benjamins.
Ellis, R. (2006). The methodology of task-based teaching. *Asian EFL Journal*, 8(3), 19–45.
Ellis, R. (2009a). Task-based language teaching: Sorting out the misunderstandings. *International Journal of Applied Linguistics*, 19(3), 221–246.
Ellis, R. (2009b). The differential effects of three types of task planning on the fluency, complexity and accuracy in L2 oral production. *Applied Linguistics*, 30(4), 474–509.
Ellis, R. (2010). Second language acquisition research and language-teaching materials. In N. Harwood (Ed.), *English language teaching materials: Theory and practice* (pp. 33–57). New York: Cambridge University Press.
Ellis, R., & Barkhuizen, G. (2005). Coding data qualitatively. In R. Ellis & G. Barkhuizen (Eds), *Analysing learner language* (pp. 253–276). Oxford: Oxford University Press.
Flowerdew, J., & Miller, L. (1995). On the notion of culture in L2 lectures. *TESOL Quarterly*, 29(2), 345–373.

Foster, P., & Skehan, P. (1996). The influence of planning on performance in task-based learning. *Studies in Second Language Acquisition*, *18*(3), 299–324.

Foster, P., & Skehan, P. (1999). The influence of planning and task type on task-based performance. *Language Teaching Research*, *3*(3), 215–247.

Gardner, R. C. (2010). *Motivation and second language acquisition*. New York: Peter Lang.

Gass, S., & Mackey, A. (2000). *Stimulate recall methodology in second language research*. New Jersey: Lawrence Erlbaum Associates.

Hoang, V. V., H. Hoang, T. X. H., Vu, T. L., Dao, N. L., Do, T. M., & Nguyen, Q. T. (2006). *English 11: Teacher's book*. Hanoi: Education Publishing House.

Hoang, V. V., H. Hoang, T. X. H., Vu, T. L., Dao, N. L., Do, T. M., & Nguyen, Q. T. (2007). *English 12: Teacher's book*. Hanoi: Education Publishing House.

Holliday, A. (1997). The politics of participation in international English language education. *System*, *25*(3), 409–423.

Hood, M., Elwood, J., & Falout, J. (2009). Student attitudes toward task-based language teaching at Japanese universities. *Asian Journal of English Language Teaching*, *19*, 19–47.

Kennedy, P. (2002). Learning cultures and learning styles: myth-understandings about adult (Hong Kong) Chinese learners. *International Journal of Lifelong Education*, *21*(5), 430–445.

Kim, Y., & McDonough, K. (2008). The effect of interlocutor proficiency on the collaborative dialogue between Korean as a second language learners. *Language Teaching Research*, *12*(2), 211–234.

Kim, Y., & McDonough, K. (2011). Using pre-task modelling to encourage collaborative learning opportunities. *Language Teaching Research*, *15*(2), 183–199.

Kramsch, C., & Sullivan, P. (1996). Appropriate pedagogy. *ELT Journal*, *50*(3), 199–212.

Kumaravadivelu, B. (2007). Learner perception of learning tasks. In K. Van den Branden, K. Van Gorp & M. Verhelst (Eds), *Tasks in action: Task-based language education from a classroom-based perspective*. Newcastle: Cambridge Scholars Publishing.

Le, V. C., & Barnard, R. (2009). Curricular innovation behind closed classroom doors: A Vietnamese case study. *Prospect*, *24*(2), 20–33.

Leeser, M. J. (2004). Learner proficiency and focus on form in collaborative dialogue. *Language Teaching Research*, *8*(1), 55–81.

Littlewood, W. (2000). Do Asian students really want to listen and obey? *ELT Journal*, *54*(1), 31–36.

Littlewood, W. (2004). The task-based approach: Some questions and suggestions. *ELT Journal*, *58*(4), 319–326.

Littlewood, W. (2007). Communicative and task-based language teaching in East Asian classrooms. *Language Teaching*, *40*(3), 243–249.

Luk, J. (2009). Preparing EFL students for communicative task performance: The nature and role of language knowledge. *Asian Journal of English Language Teaching*, *19*, 67–90.

Lynch, T., & Maclean, J. (2000). Exploring the benefits of task repetition and recycling for classroom language learning. *Language Teaching Research*, *4*(3), 221–250.

Marshall, C., & Rossman, G. B. (2006). *Designing qualitative research*. Thousand Oaks, CA: SAGE.

McDonough, K. (2004). Learner-learner interaction during pair and small group activities in a Thai EFL context. *System*, *32*(2), 207–224.

McDonough, K., & Chaikitmongkol, W. (2007). Teachers' and learners' reactions to a task-based EFL course in Thailand. *TESOL Quarterly*, *41*(1), 107–132.

Mochizuki, N., & Ortega, L. (2008). Balancing communication and grammar in beginning-level foreign language classrooms: A study of guided planning and relativization. *Language Teaching Research*, *12*(1), 11–37.

MOET (2010). *Guide to implementation of standardized knowledge and skills: The English language subject for Vietnamese high school level*. Hanoi: Education Publishing House.

Pennycook, A. (1998). *English and the discourses of colonialism*. London: Routledge.
Pham, H. H. (2007). Communicative language teaching: unity within diversity. *ELT Journal*, 61(3), 193–201.
Phan, L. H. (2004). University classrooms in Vietnam: Contesting the stereotypes. *ELT Journal*, 58(1), 50–57.
Park, S. (2010). The influence of pre-task instructions and pre-task planning on focus on form during Korean EFL task-based interaction *Language Teaching Research*, 14(1), 9–26.
Robinson, P. (2001). Task complexity, task difficulty, and task production: Exploring interactions in a componential framework. *Applied Linguistics*, 22(1), 27–57.
Samuda, V. (2001). Guiding the relationships between form and meaning during task performance: The role of the teacher. In M. Bygate, P. Skehan & M. Swain (Eds), *Researching pedagogic tasks: Second language learning, teaching and testing* (pp. 119–140). Harlow: Pearson Education Limited.
Samuda, V. (2007). Tasks, design, and the architecture of pedagogic spaces. Paper presented at the TBLT Conference 2007, University of Hawaii. Retrieved http://www.hawaii.edu/tblt2007/PP/presentations.htm
Samuda, V., & Bygate, M. (2008). *Tasks in second language learning*. Hampshire: Palgrave Macmillan.
Savignon, S. J., & Wang, C. (2003). Communicative language teaching in EFL contexts: Learner attitudes and perceptions. *IRAL*, 41, 223–249.
Skehan, P. (1996). A framework for the implementation of task-based instruction. *Applied Linguistics*, 17(1), 38–62.
Skehan, P. (1998). *A cognitive approach to language learning*. Oxford: Oxford University Press.
Skehan, P. (2003). Task-based instruction. *Language Teaching*, 36, 1–14.
Stake, R. E. (2005). Qualitative case studies. In N. K. Denzin & Y. S. Lincoln (Eds), *The Sage handbook of qualitative research* (pp. 443–446). Thousand Oaks, CA: SAGE.
Sullivan, P. N. (2000). Playfulness as mediation in communicative language teaching in a Vietnamese classroom. In J. P. Lantolf (Ed.), *Sociocultural theory and second language learning* (pp. 115–131). Oxford: Oxford University Press.
Swain, M. (1998). Focus on form through conscious reflection. In C. Doughty & J. Williams (Eds), *Focus on form in classroom second language acquisition* (pp. 64–81). Cambridge: Cambridge University Press.
Swain, M., & Lapkin, S. (1998). Interaction and second language learning: Two adolescent French immersion students working together. *The Modern Language Journal*, 82(3), 320–337.
Swain, M., & Lapkin, S. (2001). Focus on form through collaborative dialogue: Exploring task effects In M. Bygate, P. Skehan & M. Swain (Eds), *Researching pedagogic tasks: Second language learning, teaching and testing* (pp. 99–118). Harlow: Longman.
Van den Branden, K. (Ed.). (2006). *Task-based language education*. Cambridge: Cambridge University Press.
Van den Branden, K., Bygate, M., & Norris, J. (2009). Task-based language teaching: Introducing the reader. In K. Van den Branden, M. Bygate & J. Norris (Eds), *Task-based language teaching: A reader* (pp. 1–19). Amsterdam: John Benjamins.
Willis, J. (1996). *A framework for task-based learning*. Essex: Longman.
Willis, D., & Willis, J. (2007). *Doing task-based teaching*. Oxford: Oxford University Press.
Woods, D. (1996). *Teacher cognition in language teaching: Beliefs, decision-making and classroom practice*. Cambridge: Cambridge University Press.
Zhang, E. Y. (2007). TBLT-Innovation in primary school English language teaching in Mainland China. In K. Van den Branden, K. Van Gorp & M. Verhelst (Eds), *Tasks in action: Task-based language education from a classroom-based perspective* (pp. 68–91). Newcastle: Cambridge Scholars Publishing.

PART FOUR

Tasks and technology

Introduction

Glenn Stockwell

There can be no disputing the impact that technology has had on education on a global scale, and it is natural that this is also evident in language teaching and learning situations as well. Some of the effects technology has on education are more salient, and are the result of efforts on the part of teachers and organizations to see a modernization and diversification of the teaching and learning process. In contrast, other effects are a natural result of developments in technology at both global and local levels, and are less noticeable in that they have implications that spread across almost all aspects of society. The ways in which technologies are ultimately used in learning situations will be a result of the interplay between both the efforts of teachers and the ongoing development of technologies and their availability to teachers and learners.

Different technologies have gained acceptance at different rates in different parts of the world, and this acceptance depends not only on the technologies that are available in the individual context, but also on local preferences. Internet-based social networking tools such as Facebook are accessible from essentially anywhere in the world, but it was not initially embraced in many Asian countries such as Japan, South Korea and China as it was in the United States, with locally developed tools such as *Mixi, Cyworld*, and *RenRen* being preferred by users in these regions respectively (see Stockwell, 2012, for a discussion). Indeed, the way in which tools are viewed for non-learning purposes will also naturally have an impact on the way in which they are viewed and accepted for learning purposes as well (Levy, 1997), and there has been evidence of differing preferences for the same tool (i.e., Facebook) for learning purposes within different contexts in Asia, both positively (e.g., Mok, 2012) and negatively (e.g., Liu, 2013). This variation means that the teacher needs to be aware of learner preferences with regard to both technology use and language learning styles, but also to be willing to encourage learners to use technologies that might take them out of their individual comfort zones in order to achieve language learning objectives.

The four chapters that are included in this part provide examples of how teachers have adopted innovative uses of technology in their individual language learning contexts. There is great variation in the learning contexts themselves reflecting the variation in technology use and the idiosyncrasies associated with each of the learning environments being described. The chapters by Alwi, and Friermuth and Huang look at the use of text chat to achieve differing learning objectives, specifically English for Specific Purposes (ESP) for Malaysian learners of English, and cultural awareness for Japanese and Taiwanese learners. From the range of tools available, the text function of Skype and an educational chat site called 'Language Educational Chat System' (LECS) were selected as the means through which to achieve their respective learning goals. In contrast, Thomas provides a discussion of the pedagogical, institutional and technological challenges to integrating technology-mediated task-based learning in Japan, while Reinders, Lakarnchua and Pegrum use mobile devices to develop English discourse markers in Thai learners. These four examples provide insights into the complexities of achieving specific learning goals using the range of technologies available to them, and how these have been adapted to the specific characteristics of the local environment.

References

Levy, M. (1997). *Computer-assisted language learning: Context and conceptualization*. Clarendon Press: Oxford.

Liu, J. Y. (2013, May). *Using Facebook for learning writing: EFL students' perceptions and challenges*. Paper presented at the 30th International Conference on English Teaching and Learning, Tainan, Taiwan, May 18–19, 2013.

Mok, J. C. H. (2012). Facebook and learning: Students' perspectives on a course. *Journal of the NUS Teaching Academy*, 2(3), 131–143. Retrieved http://www.nus.edu.sg/teachingacademy/article/lorem-ipsum-dolor-2/

Stockwell, G. (2012). Conclusion. In G. Stockwell (Ed.), *Computer-assisted language learning: Diversity in research and practice* (pp.164–173). New York: Cambridge University Press.

12

Language Learning Performance Using Engineering-Based Tasks via Text Chat

Nik Aloesnita Nik Mohd Alwi

Summary

While previous research into the area of task-based language teaching and learning (TBLT) focuses on cognitive theories concerning face-to-face settings (Robinson, 2005; Skehan, 2009), relatively little research has evaluated the potential and challenges of employing the task-based approach in digital settings, for example in text chat. Research has shown that learner–learner interaction during task-based text chat increases learner participations, reduces anxiety levels and promotes learner attention to language form while communicating meaning (Smith & Sauro, 2009). Therefore, language learners should be given the opportunities to communicate with each other and to work collaboratively using appropriate materials in the online text chat setting (Chapelle, 2009). To date, rrelatively little research in the context of engineering, technical or science students doing language courses (e.g., Nik, Adams & Newton, 2012) has investigated how engineering-based tasks used in text chat may influence language learning opportunities during task performance. This is particularly important because engineering jobs increasingly require electronic communication (Lee & Yeap, 2005). The current study investigates the role of task complexity on second language (L2) production of engineering degree students in a synchronous computer-mediated communication (SCMC)-based pedagogical task. Following input from the engineering lecturers and professionals, the task was designed to reflect the communication demands engineers are likely to encounter in the multinational workplace. Engineering students (n=48) at a technical university in Malaysia engaged in a 45-minute group SCMC decision-making task. The data gathered from the text chat transcripts provide evidence that task-based text chat interactions to a certain extent may promote attention to language expression and provide language learning opportunities.

Introduction

TBLT has been established for some time now as one of the main approaches to language learning and teaching worldwide (Ellis, 2003; Nunan, 2004). During the last few years, TBLT has become more integrated with research on second language acquisition (SLA) (Samuda & Bygate, 2008). A large body of SLA research based on the Interactionist Approach (Mackey & Gass, 2006) and Cognitive approaches to TBLT (Robinson, 2001a, 2003a, 2005; Skehan, 1998, 2009) have suggested the role of task complexity in influencing L2 production which ultimately affects L2 acquisition, learning and development. Most of these studies, however, were conducted in a face-to-face setting (e.g., Gilabert, 2007; Kim, 2009; Robinson, 2007a; Tavakoli & Foster, 2008). Because the use of technology, particularly SCMC, is growing more pervasive in academic and professional communication in the Asian context (Nik & Adams, 2009), it is timely for empirical research into tasks to be conducted in this setting (Lee, 2008). It is also worthwhile to examine the language learning opportunities that may occur without the presence of the traditional, authoritative nature of Asian teachers (Richards, 2004).

Additionally, very little research has explored the use of text chat in the field of English for Specific Purposes (ESP) (Vetter & Chanier, 2006). For participants in the current study, the ability to communicate meaningfully via one of the technologically-mediated communication tools is as equally important to them as learning English (Endean, et al. 2008). With the demand to be proficient in English which is the language used by many international businesses, becoming proficient in English during e-communication is one of the value added skills for the participants in the current study for use in their future workplace. Additionally, these future engineers must also demonstrate skills such as handling and solving engineering tasks typical of engineering jobs in a real-world context (Brophy, Klein, Portsmore & Rogers, 2008; Fouger, Almgren, Gopalakrishnan & Mailhot, 2008; Redish & Smith, 2008). As such, grasping good communication and professional skills are among the mandatory requirements to become successful engineers worldwide. Due to limited research in this area, the current study aims to bridge this gap.

The Performance Task and TBLT

Engineering degree accreditation at higher learning institutions in Malaysia is managed by the Engineering Accreditation Council (EAC) Malaysia, which is currently a member of one of the international engineering accreditation bodies,[1] i.e., Washington Accord. Governed by Board of Engineers Malaysia (BEM), EAC Malaysia has outlined several criteria as critical success factors for engineering education that mainly focus on outcomes in the preparation of graduates to compete effectively in their engineering professional careers and growth. The following are the engineering graduate criteria required by EAC Malaysia (BEM, 2007, p. 3):

i. Ability to acquire and apply knowledge of science and engineering fundamentals;
ii. Acquired in-depth technical competence in a specific engineering discipline;
iii. Ability to undertake problem identification, formulation and solution;
iv. Ability to utilize systems approach to design and evaluate operational performance;
v. Understanding of the principles of design for sustainable development;
vi. Understanding of professional and ethical responsibilities and commitment to them;
vii. Ability to communicate effectively, not only with engineers but also with the community at large;
viii. Ability to function effectively as an individual and in a group with the capacity to be a leader or manager;
ix. Understanding of the social, cultural, global and environmental responsibilities of a professional engineer; and
x. Recognizing the need to undertake life-long learning, and possessing/ acquiring the capacity to do so.

To assist graduates in fulfilling the above criteria, engineering degree programmes at universities in Malaysia, including the university in which the current study took place, made use of learning tasks that encompass as many as possible of the above measures in the courses offered. Various terms related to the learning tasks have been coined and one is termed Performance Task. According to Scarborough (2011), the Performance Task:

i. is based on the ABET or NAIT standards;
ii. describes a 'real-life' scenario that is authentic and requires active performance;
iii. requires students to collect and process information, using it for an authentic purpose;
iv. incorporates 'Habits of Mind';
v. requires student collaboration and cooperation;
vi. incorporates 'individual' and 'group' learning and performance accountability;
vii. results in a tangible product and/or communication activity.

Based on the above, the teaching and learning of language to the engineering degree learners in higher learning institutions in Malaysia should focus learners' attention to specific terminology and communication skills required in their professional fields. In line with the definition of the Performance Task described above, task-based approaches to language learning and teaching may work as a catalyst to bridge the engineering degree courses and language learning courses for the benefit of the learners. Tasks have been defined by Ellis (2003, pp. 9–10) as:

i. a workplan;
ii. involves primary focus on meaning;
iii. involves real-world processes of language use;

iv. can involve any of the four language skills;
v. engages cognitive processes;
vi. has a clearly defined communicative outcome.

As defined by Ellis (2003), a task is a goal-oriented activity involving a meaningful, real-world process of language use, which engages language skills and cognitive processes. Therefore, the primary focus of a task is meaning where L2 proficiency is developed through communicating, rather than learning specific linguistic items. This emphasizes the notion that TBLT may have potential in teaching language courses to the engineering learners. In addition, studies have demonstrated that meaningful context and interaction are beneficial in assisting SLA (Hsu, 2012).

Tasks can be manipulated for pedagogic and research purposes (Van den Branden, 2006). As learner performance varies according to task characteristics, researchers looking at language tasks have been concerned with identifying which task characteristics to manipulate to promote L2 learning. Various approaches, which may affect the interactional design, intrinsic structure or conditions under which tasks are performed, have been proposed regarding task manipulation to test and measure their effect on L2 learning and development. The following section describes the agendas that have inspired research into task manipulation (although see Platt & Brooks, 2002, for an alternative view).

Learner interaction during tasks performance

Research has explored the potential effects of task types and conditions on interaction (Gass & Varonis, 1985; Pica & Doughty, 1985). During learner–learner interaction while performing collaborative tasks, it is claimed that learners can be encouraged to attend to form (Adams, 2007). Observable instances of attention to form have been labelled by Swain and Lapkin (2001, p. 104) as language-related episodes (LREs) which have been defined as 'any part of a dialogue where students talk about language they are producing, question their language use, or other- or self-correct their language production'. As such, a crucial aspect of LREs is that they are a product of the learner attention directed towards their own L2 output.

A number of studies have reported frequent instances of LREs during learner–learner interactions (Kim, 2009; Watanabe & Swain, 2007). Poole (2005) investigated learner–learner interaction during group discussions on given topics prior to writing individually. Learners were found to reach out to their peers comfortably while attending to their language use and expression as reflected in high occurrences of LREs. In a study by Storch (2007) examining the extent to which performing collaborative tasks pushed learners to reflect on their language use, the findings found frequent occurrences of LREs in learner–learner discourse. Interestingly, most LREs were resolved interactively.

Task complexity in L2 learning

TBLT researchers are developing task design principles to increase the meaningfulness of language use and the amount of communicative interaction learner experience

(Yuan & Ellis, 2003). This is in line with the proposal by Samuda and Bygate (2008) for more research to be conducted to understand the relationship between task design and learner language production. In this regard, task design may be evaluated in terms of its complexity. Skehan (1998) and Skehan and Foster (2001) view L2 learning in terms of the Limited Attentional Capacity Model (Levelt, 1989, 1993), and therefore, a trade-off (TO) between attentional resources will be evident when learners are confronted with complex tasks. In this model an increase in task complexity will put pressure on cognitive processing capacity. In a competing model, Robinson (2005) presents his Cognition Hypothesis (CH), based on Givón's (1985) work on diachrony and Perdue's (1993) untutored SLA research. Task complexity defined by Robinson (2007b) deals with the intrinsic, cognitive complexity of task features. In the CH view, the two complexity dimensions are *resource-directing* that makes increased conceptual demands and *resource-dispersing* that makes increased procedural demands on learners' attentional and memory resources. Robinson (2007a) adds that for monologic as well as interactive tasks, more negotiations will be found in the complex rather than simple versions when manipulated along *resource-dispersing* dimensions. Robinson (2005) emphasizes that 'more cognitively complex oral interactive tasks simply lead to greater quantities of interaction and modified repetitions' (p. 11).

It should be noted that Samuda and Bygate (2008), however, state that the CH model is incomplete in a number of respects, for instance, the different factors (e.g., planning time or the number of elements) hypothesized to contribute to task complexity have not been specified in terms of their importance and/or equality. Therefore, the CH task complexity model 'has to be read as a preliminary hypothesis, and hence is open to modification and refinement' (Samuda & Bygate, 2008:106). Nevertheless, Ellis (2009:492) asserts that 'task complexity is clearly a key variable affecting L2 performance and for this reason alone is attracting considerable attention in its own right'. As such, the current study was designed to examine the effects of one of the task complexity *resource-dispersing* variables, i.e., prior knowledge on learner language production during task-based text chat.

Based on Robinson's (2001a, 2001b) prediction, increasing the complexity of interactive tasks will lead to the production of more interactional modifications and negotiations evident such as in LREs. Most TBLT studies which draw on the concepts of TO or CH, however, have examined learner language production with regard to its complexity, accuracy and fluency. Very few studies have investigated the effects of task complexity on LREs, for example in studies by Hardy and Moore (2004) and Kim (2009). Hardy and Moore (2004) examined the effect of task complexity in oral interactive tasks on learner–learner interaction produced by twenty-eight intermediate low-level learners of German. Each pair was randomly assigned a different task condition based on structural task support and content familiarity (*resource-dispersing* variables). The findings revealed that the more complex the task was, the more the use of questions codes and interactional codes were evident. However, no significant effect of content familiarity on learner–learner interaction could be detected. The researchers attributed this to the benefits of pre-task activity which reduced the need to engage in meaning negotiation. As suggested, part of the findings from Hardy and Moore's study offer support for Robinson's (2001a, 2001b) prediction that more complex tasks will lead to greater quantities of conversational negotiation.

Kim (2009) examined the effects of task complexity on the occurrence of LREs in dyadic interactive tasks among low and high proficiency learners. Unlike Hardy and Moore's (2004) study, task complexity in Kim's study was manipulated along two *resource-directing* variables, i.e., ± reasoning demands and ± few elements, instead of *resource-dispersing* variables. The results illustrated the occurrence of more LREs during the interaction by low proficiency learners in the simple picture narration task as opposed to the complex picture narration task. On the other hand, more LREs were evident in the complex picture narration task than the simple picture narration task among the high proficiency learners. With regard to the picture difference tasks, the low proficiency learners produced a higher number of LREs during the complex task than the simple task. However, no significant difference was evident in the high proficient learners. The findings demonstrate that the production of LREs and task complexity differed according both to task type and to learner proficiency. Nevertheless, this provides proof that task complexity does influence the occurrences of LREs during learner–learner task-based interaction.

The research cited above shows that both *resource-directing* and *resource-dispersing* variables that alter the complexity of a task can influence the occurrence of interactional modifications. Robinson (2001b) has suggested that more studies be conducted to investigate the effects of interactive tasks along *resource-dispersing* (e.g., ± planning time, ± prior knowledge) variables on learner language production. The role of these variables in tasks carried out in text chat may be even more important because the text chat setting lacks paralinguistic features that aid communication in face-to-face settings (Smith, 2003a). More research on task complexity carried out in such settings is needed to understand more and maximize the potential of this medium in language learning and teaching. As such, the current study aims to uncover the extent to which task-based text chat interaction may facilitate language learning.

Tasks performance in text chat

The use of one SCMC mode, in particular text chat, in language learning and teaching has become increasingly prominent (Ortega, 2009; Sauro, 2011) particularly because the simultaneous use of the three SCMC modes may intensify technical constraints (Hampel, 2010). Research indicates that when learners work collaboratively during text chat, they are likely to create opportunities for language learning (AbuSeileek & Qatawneh, 2013). Among the potential benefits of text chat in language learning are the willingness of learners to communicate, reduction of communication apprehension (Satar & Özdener, 2008), and development of autonomous learning (Kessler, 2013). Additionally, learner attention may be directed to their language production particularly when the language output can be viewed on the screen prior to and after the posting (Smith, 2008). Smith and Sauro (2009) found learner engagement in self-repair using deletion and the editing of text chat which confirms the claim by Meskill (2005, p. 48) that 'computer screens can serve to anchor attention to forms'. This may indicate that noticing is likely to occur in text chat because its written modality allows learners the opportunity to re-read information by scrolling the messages backward and forward (Sauro, 2009). Payne and Whitney (2002, p. 14) assert that such activity enables the interlocutors to continually 'refresh memory traces' allowing them to focus and reflect on their output. As such, this visual saliency of language forms offers more opportunities for deeper processing of language forms, especially problematic forms by the learners.

Previous studies by L2 teaching practitioners and researchers found benefits of task-based text chat on L2 learning and development chat (for reviews see Peterson, 2010). Prior research has shown that tasks can be designed to elicit language output in ways that promote L2 learning and development (Stockwell, 2010), for example the occurrences of negotiated interaction and evidences of interlanguage development (Smith, 2003a). Smith (2004) found that the retention of unknown lexical items negotiated through task-based text chat was significantly higher compared to learners who only received pre-emptive input. During learner–learner interaction in task-based text chat, learners are found to engage in self-repairs, an evidence of noticing or focus on forms. This is illustrated in a research by Smith (2008). Smith used four jigsaw tasks and two sequential ordering tasks and found occurrences of error correction episodes in the learner–learner interaction, an evidence of learner engagement in self-repairs during task-based text chat. The notion that the written modality of text chat may anchor noticing is further investigated by Shekary and Tahririan (2006). The researchers investigated sixteen English as a Foreign Language (EFL) Persian learners in dyads engaged in an online text chat using the dictogloss, jigsaw and free discussion tasks. The findings show occurrences of LREs as the evidence for noticing which consequently lead to subsequent learning of forms.

A study by Lee (2008) examined the potential of performing different types of tasks, i.e., jigsaw, spot-the-difference and open-ended question tasks, via text chat on L2 learning. Although the findings contradict the others on the superiority of jigsaw tasks (Morris, 2005), they indicate that task type is not the only variable that could influence learner language production. As described in an earlier section of this paper, the complexity of the task used by Lee could be a contributing factor that affects learner language production.

Taken together, these studies provide insights into text chat as a valuable medium for language learners in their quest for language learning. Nevertheless, Sanders (2006) argues that although text chat enables learner–learner interaction to be extended beyond face-to-face class space and hour, the mixed findings reported in Lin, Huang and Liou (2013) have urged the need for ongoing research into the effectiveness of text chat as a medium for language practice. This challenge is undertaken by the current study which aims to answer this question: Does prior knowledge affect the occurrences of LREs during task-based text chat?

Research approach

The participants and research setting

Forty-eight second year engineering students from a technical university in Malaysia participated in this study. Their ages range from twenty to twenty-four years. They were in their fourth semester of engineering degree studies and were randomly selected from a compulsory English language course. Their prior English education was very uniform. They had three English language courses in the past three semesters

TABLE 12.1 *Learner characteristics*

Characteristics		Group +PK	Group −PK
Gender	Male	20	16
	Female	4	8
Age	Mean	21.9 years	21.6 years
	Range	20–24 years	20–24 years
L1 background	Malay	21	19
	Chinese	2	4
	Tamil	0	0
	Others	1	1

at the university and had learnt English language as a compulsory subject in primary and secondary school as part of the national English curriculum. Based on their English grades from the national examination, their English language proficiency was at an intermediate level. Most obtained a grade of 4–6 on a nine-point scale for the English exam in which '1' represents advanced proficiency, '5' intermediate proficiency, and '9' very low proficiency. For most of them Bahasa Melayu was their native language. Note that although the English language courses at the university are not primarily task-based, the activities were mostly designed in such a way, fulfilling the descriptions of tasks defined by Ellis (2003). This is also to support the goal of EAC in producing the graduates who fulfil the attributes outlined earlier. The English language classes are generally conducted in computer language learning laboratories. All participants were experienced users of computer-mediated communication (CMC). Table 12.1 summarizes the characteristics of the learners.

Half of the learners (n=24) were studying electrical engineering while the rest (n=24) were studying mechanical engineering. The task administered focuses on an electrical engineering topic. As such, the electrical engineering learners formed a +prior knowledge (+PK) group and the mechanical engineering learners formed a − prior knowledge group (−PK). Within these two groups, learners were randomly divided into teams of four for the task performance.

The task

The task required learners to engage in a 45-minute interactive problem-solving task. Learners had to role-play engineers in a multinational company meeting online to decide what type of electrical engineering software the company should adopt. Each learner was provided with the software information to promote to the team members. During the discussion, they were required to discuss the different types of software comparing and contrasting advantages and disadvantages, and to reach consensus on the best software to be purchased based on a set of criteria. In addition, they were allowed to browse the internet for additional and valid sources for the software to support their discussion. The opportunities for the learners to work in groups, engage in issues presented, formulate reasons and identify solutions, and look for more information that may foster lifelong learning attributes are among the graduates criteria described by EAC as outlined earlier. It should be noted that there were no right or wrong options as to the best choice of the software. The task was designed so as to induce debate among the team members. By the end of the task each learner was expected to have completed a sheet with group recommendations on the ranking of the software which was to be sent to the company's CEO.

Prior to the task, instructions and detailed software descriptions were given to each learner. Five minutes were allocated to the learners for reading the information and clarifying the task. The learners were seated far apart from their team members and used pseudonyms to ensure that the task took place in the text chat, not orally. They were connected to each other via Skype. The preference to utilize Skype in the current study is to make it easier for the findings and pedagogical recommendations to be applied to a wider audience. In addition, using Skype is straightforward and the users do not need to purchase the expensive, commercially available software packages from the market. Similar to other text chat systems widely available on the internet, for example Yahoo Messenger and GTalk, learners could type messages, and exchange them when they hit the ENTER key. New and subsequent chat messages are added at the bottom of a scrolling screen, allowing the interlocutors to view messages as they are delivered. Apart from a reminder by their respective lecturer, since the data collection was carried out during normal English class hours, the learners were aware of the expectation that they had to use the English language to complete the task. The instructor and the researcher monitored and captured each learner's screen from the main terminal using the classroom management systems, i.e., Renet system.

Data collection

Data were collected from task-based text chat sessions which took place on-site and during normal classroom hours. Following each chat session, the chat exchanges were saved in log files. The transcript data in log files are naturally divided by an individual's turn as illustrated in Figure 12.1[2] (all examples are from the data set). This type of data is referred to by Chapelle (2009, p. 98) as 'process data' which served as the primary data source for this study. In order to seek for more understanding of the transcript as well as to obtain information on learners' perception of the task performance and the value of task-based text chat for language learning, face-to-face interviews with six teams, i.e., three teams from each of the condition, were carried out. The interviews were semi-structured and the learners were allowed to use Malay and/or English language. During each team's interview their chat transcript was used as a stimulus. While reviewing the transcript there were several occasions where learners themselves chose to discuss the chat exchanges they found to be interesting. Learners also responded to forum postings (asynchronous) after the text chat session.

Line	Learner	Chat exchange
1	Chu	but orcad perfectly handless- dos,unic and max file format..
2	Chu	features- graphic editor, symbol editor, waveform editor, text editor, compiler, simulator and timing analyzer
3	Tara	UNIC environment? what's that?
4	Chu	the fees-RM8000 per year
5	Ayu	wahhhhhhh!
6	Tara	wahhhh ffor what: ayu?
7	Hana	Some kind of file format i think.. right chu?
8	Hana	i mean: unix

FIGURE 12.1 *Example 1. A sample of text chat*

Coding

Swain and Lapkin (2001) define an LRE as any part of a dialogue where learners talk about, question, or correct the language produced. Following their definition, LREs in the current study were defined and coded into two categories:

1 LREs on meaning – Discourse in which learners talk or ask or question implicitly or explicitly their own or others use about meaning, content or lexical items.

2 LREs on form – Discourse in which learners talk or ask or question implicitly or explicitly their own or others use about linguistics or grammatical items.

Following Gass, Mackey and Ross-Feldman (2005), the occurrences of LREs in the current study was also extended to instances of students asking for glosses of individual words or phrases. Figures 12.2 and 12.3 illustrate LREs on meaning and form.

Line	Learner	Chat exchange
1	Tan	mine: works in linux
2	Rex	Wiat! wats linux? → **LRE initiation**
3	Feris	also works in windows?
4	Syira	u don knoe linux? oh man!
5	Tan	linux = operating system. Same like winsows → **LRE response**

FIGURE 12.2 *Example 2. LRE on meaning*

Line	Learner	Chat exchange
1	Ain	hw about de matlab??
2	Nas	can u describe some part of it??
3	Devi	I've hear about MATLAB... → **LRE initiation**
4	Asilah	well, MATLAB is not only a tool for doing nuerical computations with matrices and vectors (which we had used during our time in university),
5	Asilah	it can display information graphically
6	Nas	I've hear = I've heard. cek gramar guyz! → **LRE response**

FIGURE 12.3 *Example 3. LRE on form*

Intrarater and interrater reliability

Intrarater and interrater measures were calculated based on simple agreement between raters. Intrarater reliability (on 25 per cent of the data) reached 96 per cent. Interrater reliability (on 25 per cent of the data) reached 90 per cent. Based on this, it was determined that the researcher could independently code the rest of the data.

Task complexity and L2 learning opportunities

Independent samples t-test analysis was used to analyse the effect of prior knowledge on LREs on meaning (LREs M) and LREs on form (LREs F) during task-based text chat performance. Because LREs are collaborative, analysis was based on LREs per team. The results are displayed in Table 12.2.

As indicated in Table 12.2, there is no significant difference between PK groups with regards to the LREs on meaning. On the other hand, there was a significant effect on the groups with regards to the LREs on form, in which the +PK group produced significantly higher occurrences of LREs ($M = 2.17$) than the −PK group ($M = 0.50$). This is illustrated in Figure 12.4.

Overall, there were sixteen instances of LREs on form in the data. In the +PK condition, thirteen instances of LREs on form were evident while three instances of

TABLE 12.2 *Results*

	Group	N	mean	s.d.	p
LREs M	+PK	6	1.50	.548	1.000
	−PK	6	1.50	.837	
LREs F	+PK	6	2.17	.753	0.005
	−PK	6	0.50	.837	

Note: PK = Prior Knowledge; $p < .05$

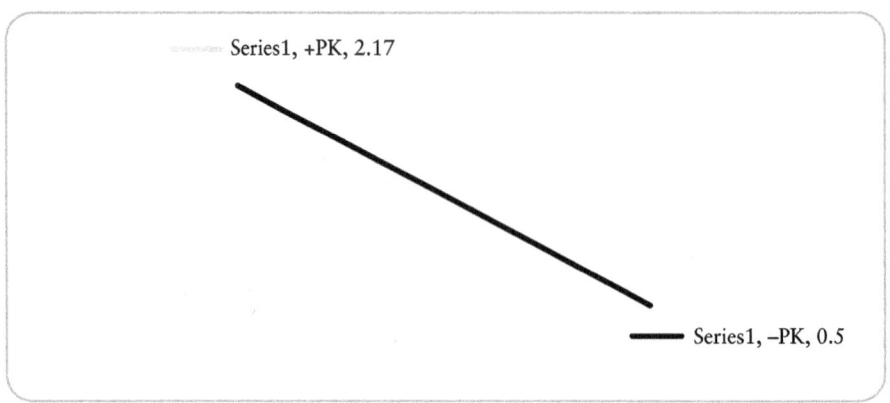

FIGURE 12.4 *Mean LREs on form*

LREs on form were evident in the –PK condition. Looking closely at the results, in the +PK condition, all teams were found to produce LREs on form while in the –PK condition, one LRE on form was evident in three teams respectively while the other three teams did not produce any LREs on form.

As predicted by Robinson (2001a, 2001b), the interactive complex task encouraged more negotiation or interactional modifications as reflected in the high occurrences of LREs. The result of the current study showed the opposite of this prediction. The occurrences of LREs on form were higher in +PK group than –PK group indicating that the interactive simple task promoted more negotiation or interactional modifications as reflected in the high occurrences of LREs. This suggests that, for interactive tasks in text chat, greater attention to language forms may be more likely when task complexity is lowered. It could also be that prior knowledge as operationalized in the current study best represents the current level of learners' subject-matter knowledge. Learners in the +PK condition were well versed in the content allowing them to focus on the forms. On the other hand, those in the –PK condition relied heavily on the description of the task provided to them. Relying solely on the content provided may have directed the learners in –PK condition to do the minimum required. This has reduced the possibility of discussing about their language expression or use. Data from the interview supports this presumption. According to one of the learners in –PK condition (Ayin):

> Although I don't have the knowledge of the software, I still can perform the task because I have the information about it. Well, the instruction to perform the task is to argue for or against each other and finally choose the best one. So, we were only required to do that, nothing more!

The finding in the current study, therefore, differed from Hardy and Moore's (2004) in that they found partial support for Robinson's (2001a, 2001b) as described earlier on. Such mixed findings lead to the inconclusive argument that CH may not be applicable to task-based text chat (Nik, 2010). Instead, more research should be carried out to investigate this.

The above finding may be attributed to the nature of text chat itself. As text chat discourse is characterized by interrupted turns and overlaps, these features make managing the flow of communication particularly difficult (Smith, 2003b). This means learner prior knowledge on the given task simplifies the process of managing the performance in the text chat setting and may be particularly effective in reducing the cognitive load of the task. As a result, learners could attend to their language expressions and use. The feedback in the form of a forum posting from one of the learners in the +PK condition (Rayyan) supports this claim:

> We have learnt about the software in the previous semester. So, I can provide more information to promote my software. We even compete among our team members to provide extra information as much as possible. No doubt that the extra information were sometimes slip off our memory. Luckily we still remember most of them ☺

Although support for Robinson's CH (2001a, 2001b) was not found in the current study, positive feedback on the use of text chat for second language practice and learning was acknowledged by the learners in both conditions. One of the learners (Eija) commented that:

> I enjoyed the discussion in text chat. In face-to-face class discussions, I feel less confident to share my opinions although I know my opinions are sometimes better than my classmates' ;). Because when I talk, everybody will look at me as if I am a criminal! In text chat my friends cannot see my face and sometimes we don't know who our team members are- it is so much fun!

Pedagogical implications

The current study provides further insights into the pedagogic use of tasks via text chat in L2 learning and teaching. These findings show that, in the absence of paralinguistic features of face-to-face communication, providing learners with cognitively simple tasks may help decrease their cognitive burden and hence, their attention may focus more on their language expression and use. This may be useful if lessons are designed to address grammatical forms. On the other hand, the use of text chat may be beneficial for fluency practice rather than learning a new form. Using a cognitively simple task may mean promoting fluency as it allows learners to practise the language familiar to them. This notion is illustrated in a study by Blake (2009). In the study, Blake compared the development of oral fluency by thirty-four English as a Second Language learners in three settings: face-to-face, SCMC, and control groups. He found that students who engaged in text chat achieved significantly greater gains in multiple measures of fluency than did the control group or the face-to-face group. Similarly, Sequeira (2009) investigated the use of SCMC vs face-to-face communication in order to promote oral fluency in 56 ninth- and tenth-grade Spanish learners. The finding showed that the SCMC group performed better than the other group in terms of increased means of language production. Taken together, the studies reported the benefits of text chat in promoting oral fluency.

Although the overall occurrences of LREs in general is rather low, the fact that LREs were evident in the interaction via text chat suggests that the medium may be beneficial for promoting focus on form. As suggested by Sauro and Smith (2010), composing and editing of text messages may contribute to a more nuanced examination of language production during text chat. As such, text chat provides the opportunity for learners to reflect on their language use because they could view and edit messages before posting, and review them visually following posts. Therefore, this visual factor itself may have pushed the learners to engage in their language expressions and use.

Previous studies in text chat have established the notion that it is a positive platform for promoting learner participation, particularly because of lowered anxiety (Satar & Özdener, 2008). The current study also provides evidence that engagement in task-based text chat may lower the learners' anxiety level which ultimately increases learner participation as manifested in the feedback received in the forum posting. In this sense, learners who feel inhibited may gradually gain more confidence to embark on communication in the target language if they are given more time to practise the language using text chat. Abrams (2008) suggested that 'computer-mediated learner-to-learner interaction offers L2 learners unique opportunities for active control of topic selection and management and provides rich opportunities for learners to recognize and adapt to diverse interactional patterns through collaboration among the interactants' (p. 1). This suggests that interaction via text chat may help learners to develop their communicative competence.

Conclusion and suggestions for further research direction

The current study evaluated Robinson's (2001a, 2001b) prediction based on the CH for one *resource-dispersing* variable, prior knowledge, on the language expression and use during task-based text chat by the engineering learners doing an English course in Malaysia. The finding of the current study did not show support for the applicability of the Cognition Hypothesis in text chat. However, conclusive claims arising from this study still cannot be made because there are studies that provide contradictory findings. Several limitations of the current study may have influenced the findings. Future studies may need to consider the following suggestions to increase the chance of significant findings. First, the number of participants should be increased for the statistical data to enhance external validity. The small sample size ($n = 48$) means the results of the study cannot be considered as definitive as they would be if more students had participated in the study. Second, future studies may look into *resource-directing* variables as the variable under study. Or, future studies may also evaluate other variables categorized by Robinson (2007b) as *resource-dispersing* variables. Finally, similar to previous TBLT studies that investigated monologic and interactive tasks in light of the CH framework, future studies may also consider employing this task complexity approach in the comparison between tasks performed via asynchronous CMC (ACMC- monologic) and synchronous CMC (SCMC- interactive) modes.

The current study has also demonstrated the possibility of employing the TBLT approach in the language courses of the engineering degree programs at higher learning institutions at one of the universities in Malaysia. This means integrating tasks at the tertiary education level is a worthwhile effort to be explored by language practitioners at the higher institutions in Asia. In addition to the shift in teaching styles required by TBLT which is the reduction of the teacher role from instructor to facilitator, engaging the learners in performing the tasks via text chat may offer effective language learning practice in a non-traditional teaching and learning medium which will ultimately enrich the learners' communication skills in various modes of communication.

Notes

1 Other engineering degree accreditation bodies are, but not limited to, ABET, Sydney Accord and Dublin Accord.
2 All names found in this paper are pseudonyms.

References

Abrams, Z. I. (2008). Sociopragmatic features of learner-to-learner computer-mediated communication. *CALICO Journal*, 26(1), 1–27.

AbuSeileek, A. F., & Qatawneh, K. (2013). Effects of synchronous and asynchronous computer-mediated communication (CMC) oral conversations on English language learners' discourse functions. *Computers & Education*, 62, 181–190.

Adams, R. (2007). Do second language learners benefit from interacting with each other? In A. Mackey (Ed.), *Conversational interaction in second language acquisition: A collection of empirical studies* (pp. 29–51). Oxford: Oxford University Press.

BEM. (2007). *Engineering program accreditation manual*, Kuala Lumpur, Malaysia: Engineering Accreditation Council.

Blake, C. (2009). Potential of text-based internet chats for improving oral fluency in a second language. *The Modern Language Journal*, 93(2), 227–240.

Brophy, S., Klein, S., Portsmore, M., & Rogers, C. (2008). Advancing engineering education in P-12 classrooms. *Journal of Engineering Education*, 97(3), 369–387.

Chapelle, C. A. (2009). The relationship between second language acquisition theory and computer-assisted language learning. *The Modern Language Journal*, 93, 741–753.

Ellis, R. (2003). *Task-based language teaching and learning*. Oxford: Oxford University Press.

Ellis, R. (2009). The differential effects of three types of task planning on the fluency, complexity, and accuracy in L2 oral production. *Applied Linguistics*, 30(4), 474–509.

Endean, M., Weidmann, G., Armstrong, D., Moffatt, J., Nixon, T., & Reuben, B. (2008). Team project work for distance learners in engineering challenges and benefits. In: Engineering Education 2008 conference proceedings, 12–14 July 2008, Loughborough, UK.

Fouger, X., Almgren, R., Gopalakrishnan, K., & Mailhot, P. (2008). Perspective from industry. *Journal of Engineering Education*, 97(3), 241–244.

Gass, S., & Varonis, E. (1985). Task variation and nonnative/nonnative negotiation of meaning. In S. M. Gass & C. Madden (Eds), *Input in second language acquisition* (pp. 149–161). Rowley, MA: Newbury House.

Gass, S., Mackey, A., & Ross-Feldman, L. (2005). Task-based interactions in classroom and laboratory settings. *Language Learning, 55*(4), 575–611.

Gilabert, R. (2007). Effects of manipulating task complexity on self-repairs during L2 oral production. *International Review of Applied Linguistics, 45*, 215–240.

Givón, T. (1985). Function, structure, and language acquisition. In D. Slibin (Ed.), *The cross linguistic study of language acquisition* (pp. 1008–1025). Hillsdale, NJ: Lawrence Erlbaum Associates.

Hampel, R. (2010). Task design for a virtual learning environment in a distance language course. In M. Thomas & H. Reinders (Eds) *Task-based language learning and teaching with technology* (pp. 131–153). London: Continuum.

Hardy, I. M., & Moore, J. L. (2004). Foreign language students' conversational negotiations in different task environments. *Applied Linguistics, 25*, 340–370.

Hsu, H-C. (2012). Investigating the effects of planning on L2 text-chat performance. *CALICO Journal, 29*(4), 619–638.

Kessler, G. (2013). Collaborative language learning in co-constructed participatory culture. *CALICO Journal, 30*(3), 307–322.

Kim, Y. (2009). The effects of task complexity on learner-learner interaction. *System, 37*(2), 254–268.

Lee, L. (2008). Focus on form through collaborative scaffolding in expert-to-novice online interaction. *Language Learning & Technology, 12*(3), 53–72.

Lee, F.T., & Yeap, B. H. (2005). *Application of effective teaching and learning methods in engineering education*. Paper presented at the 3rd International Conference on Multimedia and Information & Communication Technologies in Education. New Zealand, 7–10 June 2005.

Levelt, W. (1989). *Speaking: From intention to articulation*. Cambridge, MA: MIT.

Levelt, W. (1993). Language use in normal speakers and its order. In G. Blanken, H. Dittman, H. Grimm, J. Marshal, & C. Wallesch (Eds), *Linguistic disorders and pathologies* (pp. 1–15). Berlin: de Gruyter.

Lin, W. -C., Huang, H. -T., & Liou, H. -C. (2013). The effects of text-based SCMC on SLA: A meta analysis. *Language Learning & Technology, 17*(2), 123–142.

Mackey, A., & Gass, S. (2006). Introduction. *Studies in second language acquisition, 28*, 169–178.

Meskill, C. (2005). Triadic scaffolds: Tools for teaching English language learners with computers. *Language Learning & Technology, 9*(1), 46–59.

Morris, F. (2005). Child-to-child interaction and corrective feedback in a computer mediated L2 class. *Language Learning & Technology, 9*(1), 29–45.

Nik, N. (2010). Examining the language learning potential of a task-based approach to synchronous computer-mediated communication. PhD Dissertation, Victoria University of Wellington, New Zealand.

Nik, N., & Adams, R. (2009). TBLT and SCMC: How do students use communication strategies? *Asian Journal of English Language Teaching, 19*, 135–158.

Nik, N., Adams, R., & Newton, J. (2012). Writing to learn via text-chat: Task implementation and focus on form. *Journal of Second Language Writing, 21*(1), 23–39.

Nunan, D. (2004). *Designing tasks for the communicative classroom*. Cambridge: Cambridge University Press.

Ortega, L. (2009). Interaction and attention to form in L2 text-based computer-mediated communication. In A. Mackey & C. Polio (Eds). *Multiple perspectives on interaction in second language acquisition: Second language research in honor of Susan M. Gass*. New York: Taylor & Francis.

Payne, J. S., & Whitney, P. J. (2002). Developing L2 oral proficiency through synchronous CMC: Output, working memory, and interlanguage development. *CALICO Journal, 20*(1), 7–32.

Perdue, C. (1993). *Adult language acquisition: Crosslinguistic perspectives Vol. 1: Field Methods.* Cambridge: Cambridge University Press.

Peterson, M. (2010). Task-based language teaching in network-based CALL: An analysis of research on learner interaction in synchronous CMC. In M. Thomas & H. Reinders (Eds) *Task-based language learning and teaching with technology* (pp. 41–62). London: Continuum.

Pica, T., & Doughty, C. (1988). Variations in classroom interaction as a function of participant pattern and task. In J. Fine (Ed.), *Second language discourse* (pp. 41–55). Norwood, New Jersey: Ablex.

Platt, E., & Brooks, F. (2002). Task engagement: A turning point in foreign language development. *Language Learning, 52*(2), 365–400.

Poole, A. (2005). The kinds of forms learners attend to during focus on form instruction: A description of an advanced ESL writing class. *Asian EFL Journal, 7*(3), article 7. Retrieved http://www.asian-efl-journal.com/sept_05_ap.pdf

Redish, E., & Smith, K. (2008). Looking beyond content: Skill development for engineers. *Journal of Engineering Education, 97*(3), 295–307.

Richards, C. (2004). From old to new learning: Global imperatives, exemplary Asian dilemmas and ICT as a key to cultural change in education. *Globalisation, Societies and Education, 2*(3), 337–353.

Robinson, P. (2001a). Task complexity, cognitive resources, and syllabus design: A triadic framework for examining task influences on SLA. In P. Robinson (Ed.), *Cognition and second language instruction* (pp. 287–318). Cambridge: Cambridge University Press.

Robinson, P. (2001b). Task complexity, task difficulty, and task production: Exploring interactions in a componential framework. *Applied Linguistics, 22*(1), 27–57.

Robinson, P. (2003a). Attention and memory during SLA. In C. Doughty & M. Long (Eds), *Handbook of second language acquisition* (pp. 631–678). Oxford: Blackwell.

Robinson, P. (2003b). The Cognition Hypothesis of adult, task-based language learning. *Second Language Studies, 21*(2), 45–107.

Robinson, P. (2005). Cognitive complexity and task sequencing: Studies in a Componential Framework for second language task design. *IRAL, 43*(1), 1–33.

Robinson, P. (2007a). Task complexity, theory of mind, and intentional reasoning: Effects on L2 speech production, interaction, uptake and perceptions of task difficulty. *IRAL, 45*(3), 193–213.

Robinson, P. (2007b). Criteria for grading and sequencing pedagogic tasks. In M. P. García Mayo (Ed.). *Investigating tasks in formal language learning* (pp. 7–27). Clevedon: Multilingual Matters.

Samuda, V., & Bygate, M. (2008). *Tasks in second language learning.* New York: Palgrave Macmillan.

Sanders, R. (2006). A comparison of a chat room productivity: In-class versus out-of-class. *CALICO Journal, 24*(1), 59–76.

Satar, H. M., & Özdener, N. (2008). The effects of synchronous CMC on speaking proficiency and anxiety: text versus voice chat. *The Modern Language Journal, 92*(4), 595–613.

Sauro, S. (2009). Computer-mediated corrective feedback and the development of L2 grammar. *Language Learning & Technology, 13*(1), 96–120.

Sauro, S. (2011). SCMC for SLA: A research synthesis. *CALICO Journal 28*(2), 369–391.

Sauro, S., & Smith, B. (2010). Investigating L2 performance in text-chat. *Applied Linguistics, 31*(4), 554–577.

Scarborough, J. D. (2011). *Performance tasks*, Workshop on Teaching and Learning Methods in Engineering Program with Northern Illinois University, University of Malaysia Pahang, August 8–19, 2011.

Sequeira, C. A. (2009). *Synchronous computer mediated communication and second language proficiency.* (Unpublished doctoral dissertation). University of Oregon, USA.

Shekary, M., & Tahririan, M. H. (2006). Negotiation of meaning and noticing in text-based online chat. *The Modern Language Journal, 90*(4), 557–573.

Smith, B. (2003a). Computer-mediated negotiated interaction: An expanded model. *The Modern Language Journal, 87*(1), 38–57.

Smith, B. (2003b). The use of communication strategies in computer-mediated communication. *System, 31*, 29–53.

Smith, B. (2004). Computer-mediated negotiated interaction and lexical acquisition. *Studies in Second Language Acquisition, 26*, 365–398.

Smith, B. (2008). Methodological hurdles in captures CMC data: The case of the missing self-repair. *Language Learning & Technology, 12*(1), 85–103.

Smith, B., & Sauro, S. (2009). Interruptions in chat. *Computer Assisted Language Learning, 22*, 229–247.

Skehan, P. (1998). *A cognitive approach to language learning.* Oxford: Oxford University Press.

Skehan, P. (2009). Modelling second language performance: Integrating complexity, accuracy, fluency, and lexis. *Applied Linguistics, 30*(4), 510–532.

Skehan, P., & Foster, P. (2001). Cognition and tasks. In P. Robinson (Ed.). *Cognition and second language instruction* (pp.183–205), Cambridge: Cambridge University Press.

Stockwell, G. (2010). Effects of multimodality in computer-mediated communication tasks. In M. Thomas & H. Reinders (Eds) *Task-based language learning and teaching with technology* (pp. 83–104). London: Continuum.

Storch, N. (2007). Investigating the merits of pair work on a text editing task in ESL classes. *Language Teaching Research, 11*(2), 143–159.

Swain, M., & Lapkin, S. (2001). Focus on form through collaborative dialogue: exploring task effects. In M. Bygate, P. Skehan, and M. Swain (Eds), *Researching pedagogic tasks: Second language learning, teaching, and testing* (pp.99–118), New York: Longman.

Tavakoli, P., & Foster, P. (2008). Task design and second language performance: The effect of narrative type on learner output. *Language Learning, 58*(2), 439–473.

Van den Branden, K. (Ed.). (2006). *Task-based language education*, Cambridge: Cambridge University Press.

Vetter, A., & Chanier, T. (2006). Supporting oral production for professional purposes in synchronous communication with heterogenous learners, *ReCALL, 18*(1), 5–23.

Watanabe, Y., & Swain, M. (2007). Effects of proficiency differences and patterns of pair interaction on second language learning: collaborative dialogue between adult ESL learners, *Language Teaching Research, 11*(2), 121–142.

Yuan, F., & Ellis, R. (2003). The effects of pretask planning and on-line planning on fluency, complexity and accuracy in L2 monologic oral production. *Applied Linguistics, 24*(1), 1–27.

13

Employing Online Chat to Resolve Task-Based Activities:

Using Online Chat to Promote Cultural Language Exchange between Japanese and Taiwanese Learners

Mark R. Freiermuth
Hsin-chou Huang

Summary

In this chapter, we discuss student descriptions of a task-based English language learning activity that was resolved using online chat. Chinese-speaking university students in Taiwan and Japanese-speaking university students in Japan were mixed together in nine small groups and chatted online in English to address the provided task. Data obtained from a post-task questionnaire indicated that the students enjoyed chat because they could communicate and learn about their overseas counterparts whose language and culture were different from their own. The task proved to be highly motivating to them, and although they recognized differences across cultures, it actually sparked their communication. The implication for teachers is that well-developed online chat tasks have the potential to open doors for realistic and motivating interaction in the target language (TL) as well as to encourage positive cultural exchanges.

Introduction

When we consider task-based lessons in concert with computer technology, there are great possibilities for a natural union. Language-learning tasks can be developed which utilize any number of computer applications, and the fact that classrooms are no longer bound by the four walls of the language lab has served to expand the variety of ways in which students can interact. Thus, it is fruitful to consider the effectiveness of internet chat tasks that provide opportunities for participants from different countries to chat in English. Students' perceptions and attitudes concerning such activities are often vital towards gaining a better understanding of their motivation to participate and has the potential to open wide the doors of another culture (Lai, 2013).

Task designs

Analytical language activities, which are inclined to focus on improvement of a particular skill, are generally markedly different from well-designed tasks as defined by Samuda and Bygate (2008). 'Tasks' tend to be more holistic in nature with an overriding goal that language should be viewed as a function of communication. Collaboration tends to be a hallmark of well-designed tasks because such tasks present learners with opportunities to negotiate with other learners in processes that include planning, organizing, monitoring, sharing, identifying, evaluating, countering, hypothesizing, agreeing, disagreeing, solving, asking and drawing conclusions. On the other hand, analytical exercises tend to limit the choices students have by focusing on specific patterns or words (Samuda & Bygate, 2008).

Throughout Japan and Taiwan (as well as many other places where English as a Foreign Language (EFL) has a long history) analytical approaches are still commonly practiced (Call, 1998; Chen, 1999; Harvey, 1985; Jones, 1995; Masuhara, 2003; Rao, 2002a, 2002b; Su, 2007). Analytical tasks may help students gain knowledge about discrete points of grammar or understanding translated vocabulary, but because they lack meaningful, realistic dialogues and conversations, devoid of cultural contextual sensitivities, students may become less willing to interact with others in the TL (Clément, 1986; Freiermuth & Jarrell, 2006; MacIntyre et al., 2001; MacIntyre et al., 2002; MacIntyre et al., 2003; Yashima, 2002; Yashima et al., 2004). Long (1991) and Skehan (1998) argue that communicative tasks that have real-world and relatable problems as a central goal can help learners restructure their own internal linguistic systems. The process of negotiating meaning to resolve such tasks encourages learners to use the TL in a practical manner, just as they would in their native language.

Moreover, well-designed tasks should lead students to a meaningful outcome – as specific as learning a particular structure or as general as negotiating in the TL to resolve it (Samuda & Bygate, 2008). In this study with Japanese and Taiwanese learners, we focus on a problem-solving activity aimed at facilitating a negotiated outcome between two culturally different groups. The 'advantage' to this type of task is that learners determine the outcome via the choices they make during the task resolution process. Essentially, the problem-solving process is critical to any learning that occurs (Ellis, 2000, 2003; Ellis & Siegler, 1994).

Value of reflective activities

To gain a deeper understanding of the influence of the task used in this study, we examined the texts that students produced while negotiating and asked them to describe their experiences by completing a questionnaire. Reflective activities help students focus on what value they may have gained by working through a task, help teachers understand what students actually learn and help them determine whether the task should be used again (Anderson, 2005, 2008; Cohen & Scott, 1996)

Computer technology in a task-based world

That computers are increasingly being used to resolve task-based activities is certainly no surprise. However, the choice of software used by a teacher should be based upon the likelihood that an effective and appropriate task can be developed (Doughty & Long, 2003). In our case, online chat was the most rational choice because we have a high interest in the joint-resolution of problem-based activities that are comprised of students with distinctive backgrounds, and chat seemed to be the best way to get students conversing (Blake, 2000; Collentine, 2009; Freiermuth, 1998, 2001; Freiermuth & Jarrell, 2006; Smith, 2003, 2005; Vandergriff, 2006; Warner, 2004).

Nevertheless, having and using computers in class does not necessarily equate with better tasks. Computers need to be at the heart of task development rather than simply an afterthought. The task designer must imagine how the computer can best help students resolve the task. It would be wise to consider these three questions prior to the mixing of computers and tasks.

- Is the task a good match for computer learning? Teachers still need to create tasks that engage learners in meaningful interaction and that take advantage of what computer technology has to offer (McDonough & Mackey, 2000).
- Does computer use foster communication or hinder it? There are many tasks that if given to students in a regular classroom would be shortened, less cumbersome and frankly, more enjoyable. Certainly not all tasks have an interactive element, and it is not the case that collaboration will automatically benefit learners. Computer use ought to facilitate acquisition due to connections learners are able to make between useable input and productive output (Long, 1991).
- Is the task motivating on its own merits? Simply using a computer is no guarantee that students will be motivated. Good tasks should be designed to be intrinsically motivating (Dörnyei, 2002; Dörnyei & Kormos, 2000; Noel, Pelletier Clément & Vallerand, 2000). Essentially, this means that the various components of the task should be attractive enough to motivate students from start to finish (Crookes & Schmidt, 1991; Dörnyei, 2002).

The answers to these questions ought to shed light on whether or not a computer-based task promotes learning.

Cultural and intercultural dimensions of computer-mediated tasks

The existence of cultural differences in societies can be directly tied to how individuals identify themselves within the society. The public image that each individual hopes to portray – one's *face* – plays a major role in how people behave in specific situations (Brown & Levinson, 1987). Generally, individuals hope to maintain or even enhance their own *face*. In collectivist societies, such as Taiwan and Japan, *face* is maintained through the harmonization of everyone's ideas, whereas in individualistic societies such as the US and Western Europe, individual success is beneficial to one's *face* (Ting-Toomey, 2005; Ting-Toomey & Kurogi, 1998). These elements associated with *face* are undoubtedly important to how students define their role in the classroom and how they interact with the teacher and their classmates. Interestingly, computer interconnectivity has altered the channels of interaction in the classroom and subsequently the way *face* is managed. This has been particularly valuable to language teachers, who have used online chat as a way of reducing pressures on *face*. As an example, by incorporating online chat in the classroom, learners can communicate synchronously but at a more moderated pace than in face-to-face spoken conversation (Freiermuth, 2011). Regarding Asian English language learners, Warschauer (1996) found that in spoken face-to-face conversations Philippine students tended to dominate their Japanese counterparts but this effect was negated in online chat discussions. In Freiermuth's (2001) study, American students so dominated the talk in face-to-face discussions (decision-making and turn-taking) with international students that in two cases the international students were shut out of the discussion process entirely (interestingly a Chinese student and a Japanese student). The discussions using online chat were markedly different. All students contributed to the discussions and turn-taking was significantly more equitable.

In this chapter, we have been discussing students from two Asian cultures that are both collectivist in nature; however, that does not mean they share identical values. Such dissimilarities can result in differing ways of communicating ideas (Chang, 2006). Additionally, cultural similarities and differences must be weighed in light of another factor – group status. Students who are cognizant of the language skills of the group members may consider language proficiency as being quite important and accordingly, assign any member with higher language proficiency a higher level of group status (Woken & Swales, 1989; Zuengler, 1989). Freiermuth and Jarrell (2006) found that Japanese university students placed in groups for discussion in English would cede the decision-making process and consequently, the turn-taking opportunities to the most proficient English speaker. When the same students were placed in online chat groups for a discussion, however, the 'status' effect was nullified. As for our study, the Japanese learners had significantly higher Test of English for International Communication (TOEIC) scores and the students from Taiwan were aware of this.

Aims of the research

In our study, we wanted to find out whether or not the task developed for this text chat would encourage interaction in the TL and due to a rare opportunity to interact in English with culturally different peers, motivate the students from both camps.

Hence, it is our purpose here to investigate the possible value of an online computer chat task by categorizing and discussing students' post-test comments as they relate to the following queries:

- What did participating students express about each of the following?
    a. internet chat as a tool of communication
    b. their experience of interacting with others whose first language was different from their own
    c. their own motivation.
- How were cultural identities and statuses manifest, and were students aware of any similarities and differences?

Methodology

This task was part of a joint project between two universities in Taiwan and Japan. As such, all participants spoke either Chinese or Japanese as a native language. A total of thirty-nine students participated in the project; twenty female Japanese students worked with nineteen students – sixteen females and three males – from Taiwan. English language proficiency was determined with reference to TOEIC scores; the Japanese students averaged 732 on the TOEIC (approximately 550 on Test of English as a Foreign Language (TOEFL)) and the Taiwanese students averaged 552 (approximately 488 on TOEFL).

The researchers synchronized the class periods so that the Japanese and Taiwanese students would be in the computer labs simultaneously. All of the participants did some pre-tasks using internet chat with their in-country classmates. Following this, they were divided into nine groups of four or five members each.

Students chatted using Language Educational Chat System (LECS) chat software, which is freely available software designed specifically for language teachers. Since software plays a vital part when task and technology are intertwined, it is important to select software that meets the needs of the students and can handle the task.

Because the researchers had previously registered for LECS, a new chat was created called 'Cultural Exchange'. A separate chat room was created for each small group. During the intercultural exchange, students typed their entries into a dialogue box and produced their text chats. Students choose an alias and a text colour to distinguish their messages from others in the group and produced text chats as shown in this example:

tvxq_micky:	^v^/~~
sharon:	next time~~i'll visit mount Fuji~~see you~~^^
Dale:	I enjoyed. Thanks. See you!
sharon:	yes~~it's a great experience~~thanks~~
Mary:	yeah, have a nice day!
tvxq_micky:	ok. I'll try it! thanks u guys! C ya!
Christine:	It's a good opportunity to exchange views with all guys
sharon:	such as ~~my favourite crispy chicken~~
Mary:	Taiwanes snack? what kinds of? Sharnon?
Mary:	It was sooooooooooooo fun!! how about you??

Dale:	me too!! thank you.
sharon:	next time when you come to Taiwan~~don't forget to try Taiwanese snacks~~^^nice to talk to you, too~~
Mary:	i really enjoyed chatting with u guys.
Mary:	nice to talk to you, guys
tvxq_micky:	well done!
sharon:	I think so~~^^

Content from the chat sessions was downloaded for analysis and the chat scripts were then compiled in word processing software.

This task consisted of four language processing phases (Samuda & Bygate, 2008). First, the students in each computer lab warmed up with a sample task designed to familiarize them with the software. In the second phase, they were given a prompt (see Figure 13.1) and told to read it. After a brief comprehension check of their understanding, students entered the task resolution phase with their overseas peers. Following the completed chat, students completed the reflection phase, in our case a questionnaire.

The task prompt asked students to develop an idea for a joint business to be operated in either Japan or Taiwan. This task was based on an adaptation of a previously used and successfully applied classroom activity (Freiermuth, 2001). Students were given the prompt (Figure 13.1) to aid them in their decision.

Task Prompt

This is a group exercise in problem solving. Today, you will discuss an issue with a group of students in Taiwan/Japan. Relax and try to do your best to help the group come to a good decision. Please read the prompt carefully. Begin when your teacher tells you. Good luck!

PROMPT

You are part of a group of investors. Representatives from your group are planning to open a company in one of the cities listed in the table below. Because each person in your group is planning on investing a lot of money, you must discuss and decide the following:

- *What type of business would you like to start?*
- *Will the business be international or local?*
- *Why did you decide on that business?*
- *Based upon the characteristics of each city, what city is the best place to start your business?*
- *Why did you choose that city?*
- *Each city has strengths and weaknesses. If you don't know about a particular city, please ask someone in your group for more information about it. The table will help you but might not answer all of your questions.*
- *Why did you decide to start a business in the city that you chose?*

Rating Scale	Cities	Housing Availability	Climate	Safety	Availability of trained workers
5-Excellent	Taipei, TW	4	2	4	5
4-Very Good	Tokyo, JP	2	4	3	5
3-Not Bad	Kaohsiung, TW	3	4	3	4
2-Fair	Sapporo, JP	5	1	5	3
1-Poor					

FIGURE 13.1 *Task prompt.*

Although the prompt provided participants with city characteristics, it was also hoped that students would use their own cultural knowledge and insights to complement the provided attributes.

Students chatted with one another for about an hour – a few groups finished in slightly less than an hour and continued chatting about other topics. Once the chat session had been completed, students were given the questionnaire to fill out.

Results and discussion

In this section we examine students' reflections regarding their experiences during the interactive online chat session. Students' opinions will be discussed as they relate to the task, internet chat, interaction with others outside their immediate peer group and their overall attitude toward the task.

Discussing the task

One of the dilemmas for teachers in homogeneous EFL classes is that language learners can still rely on their native tongue (Freiermuth & Jarrell, 2006). In this project, to effectively address the task, it was essential for students to communicate in English. If participants opted for their native tongue, their overseas counterparts would be excluded from the discussion.

As for the conjoining of technology with a task-based approach, the task and the chat technology dovetailed nicely. In a sense, this kind of classroom immediately projected a unique image to teachers and students. The computer lab and the chat task represented something different from the usual classroom – to communicate in English was suddenly compelling.

Well-designed tasks should be enjoyable, so if students did not enjoy the task, they would likely have little motivation to work vigorously to resolve it. In our study, of the thirty-seven students who filled out the questionnaire, thirty-one *liked the task* or *liked the task very much*, five *liked the task a little* and only one *disliked the task a little*. Here are a few comments from students to support this.

T1: ..I think this activity is meaningful. Everyone can enjoy their chatting. And everyone does not have pressure. Everyone really enjoy class and learn.
T2: I think this activity is meaningful and it's a special experience. After this class, I would like to practice my English speaking skill in order to make some friends from other country.
T3: It's more interesting 10-time better than original course. We had lots of English classes, there are not many classes which let us have chances to chat like this. It's interaction with real people, not just the teacher's speaking the textbook.

J1: ..this course is 'Advanced' inter personal communication and this activity gave us an opportunity to try yourself to communicate with foreigners practically.
J2: Because we usually do activities with people who have known each other, communicating others who I don't know was good and effective way of learning...
J3: I think this activity is really meaningful. We usually communicate with people face-to-face, but the activity gave us good opportunity to have conversation without voice and other's face. It makes me more sensitive about other's opinion (thinking).

Students judged the task to be meaningful because it allowed them to use English as a tool of communication, gave them a chance to make friends using English and provided them with information about another culture. Simultaneously they were learning how to navigate interaction in English electronically.

The chat logs concurred with the student comments and their enjoyment clearly lasted throughout the task as indicated by this sample of a closing chat script:

Zhong_Sha:	Thank you guys for chatting with me^^
Emily:	thank you so much^^
Cynthia:	It's wonderful chance to communicate with you ^_^
Nemo:	Thank you~ nice to meet you
Zhong_Sha:	Hope we can see each other some day...
Nemo:	haha~~i hope so! Welcome to Taiwan
Zhong_Sha:	Awwww I wanna go to Taiwan as soon as I can!!!
Cynthia:	welcome!!

All of the chat conversations ended on similarly positive notes, and although students perceived some cultural differences with their overseas peers (at least at the start), it did little to hinder their enjoyment. Holistic tasks, such as this one, provide students with real opportunities to communicate, and there is a palpable sense that students felt they achieved something through the process of negotiation and ultimately, by arriving at a conclusion together (Samuda & Bygate, 2008). Well-designed decision-making tasks such as the one used in this study are ideal for intercultural online chats because such tasks tend to invigorate discussion as students feel free to infuse the discussion with cultural knowledge about themselves.

Discussing internet chat

Internet chat software was chosen for this activity primarily because of its interactive nature. Students discovered chat interaction to be a unique and refreshing way to communicate. Here are some comments from students who participated in the chat task.

T1: Chatting is a different way to learn English. We always talk about the four skills- reading, writing, listening and speaking to learn English. I think chatting is the most interesting way to learn English. When I am speaking, I have to correct my grammar. Reading can improve my English use, but I can not speak out. I like to use chatting skills to learn English.

T2: The biggest benefit for me is to improve my language skills by chatting with Japanese students in English. Even though we have teachers who are native speakers at school, during the classes and after the classes, we don't get many chances to speak English. (Translated from Chinese.)

T3: It is very helpful using online chat. While chatting, we had to think how we should express ourselves clearly, so we check the sentence grammar, vocabulary, and fluency again and again. After we did this a few times we improved our ability to used vocabulary, and when we examined others' English sentences, we found that they used different structures and usages, which is good for us to understand so we can make changes to our own English sentences. Online chatting has a relaxed style that is derived from having enough time to think about how we should express ourselves. Also, there are no fixed styles, no limitations, no requirements and no rules about how we should chat. When we consider speaking, if our speaking ability is poor, we will be afraid to speak. We may even stutter as we will be fearful of making mistakes. When we consider writing, there is usually a formal format, so we cannot use oral language – we have to follow the writing style. Hence, I think online chat can cause students to have more motivation to learn language. (Translated from Chinese.)

J1: It was like real talking. So, though we don't know each other, I could chat with them peacefully. Chatting is like real speaking. It is easy and quick to communicate with other countrie's people because if we speak with them, we have to meet them or call them, and if writing, It is slow.

J2: It helps me type English words fast, and to do that, my mind has no time to translate Japanese into English, so, eventually, online chatting in English helps me use English and think about something in English at the same time.

J3: I could announce my ideas better than face to face talking. I usually feel ashamed of my English skill but I could have confidence in case of chatting. Chatting is real time so I felt I'm speaking but more comfortable than face to face speaking. And we can see the reply soon unlike writing. I really enjoyed chatting with Taiwanese. I want to chat with overseas students again! I had a great experience.

From these student comments three very important aspects of chat can be pointed to:

1 Students recognized that chat allowed them more time to construct their thoughts. They seemed to feel less pressured and consequently relaxed (Freiermuth & Jarrell, 2006; Warschauer, Turbee & Roberts, 1996).
2 Students recognized that chat provided them with access to a communication device that opened a door of rare opportunity to use the TL in a meaningful way (Halliwell & Jones, 1991).
3 Students were able to analyse other students' grammatical usages and learn from them (Gass & Varonis, 1985).

That students generally feel less pressured while using chat is well documented. Electronic chatting has the effect of equalizing the playing field for all participants (Beauvois, 1999; Warschauer, 1996, 1997; Warschauer et al., 1996; Freiermuth 1998, 2001, 2002; Freiermuth & Jarrell, 2006). Despite any differences in proficiency as well as perceived and real cultural differences between the Taiwanese and Japanese students, they freely communicated with everyone participating. If the groups had been wrangling with issues in a face-to-face discussion, other factors like group status and cultural differences would have likely come into play with the potential to stifle interaction or to open the door for a dominant individual to take over the discussion. Samuda & Bygate (2008) provide this commentary about what can occur during face-to-face tasks:

> Beneficial effects do not follow automatically from working with others, but depend on the nature of the interaction. Studies of the way in which collaborative interactions actually occur suggest that the desired types of collaborative interaction are exceptional. If partners work in parallel, or one partner dominates the interaction, collaborations are no more productive than one person working alone.
>
> (p. 74)

In the present study, Japanese students felt the Taiwanese students were, on the whole, much more assertive as this comment illustrates:

J1: Totally, I think Taiwanese students are good at insisting on their opinions. They were really aggressive during the discussion.

This was a perceived cultural difference that Japanese students held about their counterparts. Despite this, Japanese students were not dissuaded to participate actively. In face-to-face tasks, Freiermuth and Jarrell (2006) found that dominant group members took complete control of discussions even though the groups consisted of Japanese students who were also classmates. We can say with assurance that results from this study would have been markedly different in a face-to-face discussion. In groups, as *face* pressures increases, the group dynamics alter the outcomes. In this study, chat acted as a facilitator towards accomplishing the task as a unit with everyone contributing and feeling free to do so.

Discussing the interaction

Because one of the primary aims of this task was to encourage students to solve the presented problem in English, less attention was given to grammatical accuracy. Generally speaking, Japanese and Taiwanese students at the university level have had ample opportunities to improve their grammatical skills but few opportunities to use English to actively communicate. 'Meaning' was of greater importance than identifying any grammatical shortcomings. When there was confusion about 'meaning,' students primarily wrestled with the interpretation on their own rather than relying on their native language or nearby teachers to help them. Here is an example from the text:

Rose:	i just wanted to make sure what's in your mind..
ada:	gym for twenty four hour, and there are some spa, dancing calss, or yoga class including.
Ruth:	your idea is also sounds nice
ada:	or maybe we can choose one kind of business
Rose:	what do you think about the gym Katie?
Katie:	gym will be fine :)
Katie:	and the main idea will be 'gym' ??
Rose:	ok. . . . how do you think it would work?? i mean spas and dancing classes are not special these days.. i think we should make some diffreence from other gyms..
Rose:	um.. not sure yet
Ruth:	or how about make these ideas altogether. . .like resort hotel?
ada:	sounds good.
Rose:	including gym maybe?
Katie:	yeah

This type of exchange between *Katie*, *Rose* and *ada* is typical of the online chatting texts. 'Misspellings', punctuation and longer propositions are sacrificed because meaningful interaction and communicative fluency is paramount. Discussion elements (aimed at task resolution) – an adaptation of the features of *negotiation of meaning* – are evident in greater than 25 per cent of propositions for every group (developed based upon the research of Gass & Varonis, 1985; Long, 1981; Pica & Doughty, 1985).

Students were also cognizant of the importance of this kind of interaction and contributed the following opinions:

T1:	I thought this session which is good chance to enhance cultural exchanges, you could know a lot about their social. I found many interesting things from chatting with students from Japan. First I know a lot interesting ideas from others. And I get more information about Japan.
T2:	I learned from chatting with foreigner with enjoyable. I am afraid of talking with foreigner before. But when I experience it, I find maybe I can talk to them boldly. And be strong in conversation.

T3: We always learn something from each other. Just because everyone knows and thinks differently. It means everyone can offer and share different ideas, thoughts and knowledge.

J1: In my opinion, the experience was really good opportunity for me to talk to people who has other views, values and so on.
J2: They gave lots of their opinion quickly whether it is good or no. Discussion doesn't mean if there is no opinion, so they stimulated me very much.
J3: I felt Taiwanese students are positive. They often gave suggestion, and lead conversation decide things. Although they had good ideas, they always asked how we were thinking about a topic we were discussing.

From these comments, it is clear that students understood this to be real interaction and saw this as a way to build relationships with their counterparts whose language, backgrounds and experiences were quite different from their own. The comments reveal that students were aware of culturally different approaches to the task. However, rather than widening the gap between them, the opportunities for real communication brought the groups closer together.

Mackey (1999) suggests that as students negotiate meaning via interactive tasks, internal factors within the learners aid their language development. Thus, as students worked to forge a joint-decision, the communicative activities were simultaneously moulding and sharpening their uses of the TL, and the value of this was not missed by the students.

Discussing the motivation

The majority of the student comments have suggested that students were indeed motivated, but they also provided some very specific comments to allay any doubts.

T1: When I talk to foreigner, they understand what I am talking about, this thing makes me happy and feel more confident. The motivation for learning increased comes from the confidence increased when using language.
T2: My motivation increased in some ways. Because their culture is different from ours, it made we want to try harder to explain my culture to the Japanese partners in English. I even had to check the dictionary to me to explain to them.
T3: I think the motivation for learning English can increase, after this chatting opportunity. If my English ability could be better, I will have more different friends in the world. I also can learn many things from them.

J1: My motivation has increased. I felt that not only English, but also Taiwanee culture is interesting.
J2: My motivation for learning (especially about Taiwan and learning English typing skills) has definately increased after having a chat with my partners

since I could know that not only I but also a lot of other students are working hard to improve English skills

J3: . . talking with them was very excited. So, I want to work with foreigners in my future. So, now my motivation for learning is increasing.

Dörnyei (2002) mentions two critical factors that are useful in 'protecting' motivation that are relevant to the present study. First, activities should be promoted that allow students to have control – at least in part – of the learning process. As such, they can learn to make decisions and come to conclusions on their own. With that said, it is also true that if students let other factors such as cultural differences or perceived status differences interfere with this process, it can undermine motivation and consequently active participation. This often occurs in face-to-face tasks, but online chat levels the playing field for all participants irrespective of cultural attributes, language skills and aggressiveness (Freiermuth, 2001; Freiermuth & Jarrell, 2006; Warschauer, 1996). Second, students should be given projects that allow them autonomy without constant teacher interference. In this way, they will navigate, negotiate and communicate as they see fit and, ultimately (hopefully) arrive at a goal – their own goal – not a teacher-decided outcome. Clearly, during this online chat task students took control of the activity, used the TL to negotiate and came to a conclusion that was worthwhile to them because they determined what was meaningful.

Conclusion

In this study, the internet chat software used allowed students to work in small groups; however, the real advantage of this software is that it provided the researchers the chance to make these groups international, immediately elevating the importance of English as a tool of communication. The task complemented the software nicely, and the activity achieved our overall aims. Observation and the chat scripts demonstrated that students were engaged in real discussion and were intent on achieving consensus among members. Ellis and Siegler (1994), as well as Samuda & Bygate (2008), point to the value of tasks that contextualize language learning. Because students were cognizant that the task was supposed to be a joint-effort to come to a conclusion, the students remained motivated and communicative throughout the task and completed it as a unit. Upon reflection, students expressed their satisfaction while communicating with their overseas partners and recognized that online chat was an invaluable tool that allowed them to do this. Additionally, the task was highly motivating to the participating students because they had the opportunity to communicate with others outside their usual circles – making English a necessity rather than just another academic subject. In addition, as various comments indicate, they understood there were differences pertaining to the language skills and culture of their international partners but rather than dissuade them, it fuelled their desire to communicate despite the differences. As a result, they managed the communication quite well. Nevertheless, if the groups had been asked to solve such a task in small groups in a regular classroom, it is likely that language capability, culture, or even fears would have hindered the discussion.

There are some limitations that should be considered in a study such as this. The task was completed with Asian speakers in two separate EFL settings, each with a different first language. Combinations of learners with other first languages would likely yield different results. Both groups of students in the present study come from collectivist societies and perhaps this helped them to achieve a common goal in resolving the task. Nevertheless, both groups of students also recognized differences, namely that Taiwanese students were more aggressive and Japanese students were more proficient in English. Neither of these recognized differences seemed to impede the discussion. On the contrary, from the student comments, we conclude that any perceived and real differences stimulated their discussions. It should also be mentioned that the results would likely be different in English as a Second Language (ESL) settings where students are likely to have significantly more opportunities to speak in the TL, particularly with native speakers. However, there is a caveat attached to such a suggestion as well. Conflicting culturally-based norms of interaction mean that some learners in ESL settings may rarely take chances to express themselves while others (including native speakers) snap up the opportunities, potentially causing group imbalance, discomfort and ultimately, demotivation. On the other hand, tasks developed for chat can open the door to all 'voices' in a group to be heard and considered.

Besides text chat, there are other software programs that allow for voice chat and visual plus voice chat. Such chat systems would likely yield significantly different results compared to text only chat. A caveat must be mentioned here as well; text chat provides the students additional time to manage their thoughts, and although it is necessary to stay abreast of the ever changing chat conversation, chatters are allowed a little breathing space to manage the communication. As for voice chat, it is reasonable to assume that the speed of the interaction would necessarily increase. Without adequate preparation this has potential to relegate students with lower ability and confidence to the status of mere observers or even outsiders. Moreover, voice chats would naturally increase *face* pressures that are common to face-to-face interaction but minimized in text chat.

That *face* pressures are reduced is one of the underlying benefits, which makes internet chat so attractive to use as a communication tool. Before students engaged one another using the chat software, many students had indicated that they lacked confidence to communicate in the TL, so it is vital to understand their perceptions after chatting as well. Here is a brief synopsis of some of the advantages they mentioned.

- Online chat can help students gain confidence using the TL.
- Online chat can lead students to a stronger willingness to communicate in the TL and consequently, increasing motivation.
- Online chat, by the very nature of its application (it is different from the regular class), can help encourage interaction in the TL, effectively contributing to language learning.
- Online chat tends to minimize language status differences between group members.
- Online chat facilitates cultural camaraderie by negating cultural differences while embracing mutual understanding and goals.

As previously mentioned, computer technology cannot save poorly designed tasks; however, the carefully designed chat activity used in this study effectively increased the motivation of Taiwanese and Japanese students to resolve the task, to use the TL, and to use English to communicate while cultivating their relationship at the same time. That students arrived at these conclusions is tantamount to an endorsement of well-designed chat tasks. Finally, online chat was the window through which a real cultural exchange could take place and in such a way that both groups of learners relished the experience. Students' desire to understand the 'other' encouraged them to use English to resolve a task as a team and so they could learn more about what their partners were really thinking about.

References

Anderson, N. (2005). Learning strategies. In E. Hinkel (Ed.). *Handbook of research in second language teaching and learning* (pp. 757–772). Mahwah, NJ: Lawrence Erlbaum.

Anderson, N. (2008). Metacognition and good language learners. In C. Griffiths (Ed.), *Lessons from good language learners* (pp. 99–109). Cambridge: Cambridge University Press.

Beauvois, M. (1999). Computer-mediated communication: Reducing anxiety and building community. In D. Young (Ed.), *Affect in foreign language and second language learning: A practical guide to creating a low-anxiety classroom atmosphere* (pp. 144–165). Boston: McGraw Hill.

Blake, R. (2000). Computer-mediated communication: A window on L2 Spanish interlanguage. *Language Learning & Technology, 4*, 120–136.

Brown, P., & Levinson, S. (1978). *Politeness: Some universals in language use.* Cambridge: Cambridge University Press.

Call, J. (1998). Expanding the learning styles of Japanese analytic learners. In J. M. Reid (Ed.), *Understanding learning styles in the second language classroom* (pp. 136–146). Upper Saddle River, NJ: Prentice Hall Regents.

Chang L. (2006). Subcultural influence on Chinese negotiation styles. *Journal of Global Business Management, 2*, 189–195.

Chen, Q. L. (1999). The whole language approach and EFL Teaching. In Q. L. Chen & M. L. Liao (Eds), *EFL teaching: Teachers' teaching guides at elementary and secondary school levels* (pp. 60–75). Taipei: Caves Books Ltd.

Clément, R. (1986). Second language proficiency and acculturation: An investigation of the effects of second language status and characteristics. *Journal of Language and Social Psychology, 5*, 271–290.

Cohen, A., & Scott, K. (1996). A synthesis of approaches to assessing language learning strategies. In R. L. Oxford (Ed.), *Language learning strategies around the world: Cross-cultural perspectives* (pp. 89–106). National Foreign Language Resource Center, Manoa: University of Hawaii Press.

Collentine, K. (2009). Learner use of holistic language units in multimodal, task-based synchronous computer-mediated communication. *Language Learning & Technology, 13*, 68–87. Retrieved http://llt.msu.edu/vol13num2/collentine.pdf

Crookes, G., & Schmidt, R. (1991). Motivation: Reopening the research agenda. *Language Learning, 41*, 469–512.

Dörnyei, Z. (2002). The motivational basis of language learning tasks. In P. Robinson (Ed.), *Individual differences in second language acquisition* (pp. 137–158). Amsterdam: John Benjamins.

Dörnyei, Z., & Kormos, J. (2000). The role of the individual and social variables in oral task performance. *Language Teaching Research*, 4, 275–300.

Doughty, C., & Long, M. (2003). Optimal psycholinguistic environments for distance foreign language learning. *Language Learning & Technology*, 7, 50–80. Retrieved http://llt.msu.edu/vol7num3/doughty/default.html

Ellis, R. (2000). Task-based research and language pedagogy. *Language Teaching Research*, 4, 193–220.

Ellis, R. (2003). *Task-based language learning and teaching*. Oxford: Oxford University Press.

Ellis, R., & Siegler, R. (1994). Development of problem solving. In R. Sternberg (Ed.), *Thinking and problem-solving* (pp. 334–368). San Diego: Academic Press.

Freiermuth, M. (1998). Using a chat program to promote group equity. *CAELL Journal*, 8, 16–24.

Freiermuth, M. (2001). Native speakers or non-native speakers: Who has the floor? Online and face-to-face interaction in culturally mixed small groups. *Computer Assisted Language Learning*, 14, 169–199.

Freiermuth, M. (2002). Internet chat: Collaborating and learning via e-conversations. *TESOL Journal*, 11, 36–40.

Freiermuth, M., (2011). Debating in an online world: A comparative analysis of speaking, writing and online chat. *Text & Talk*, 31, 127–151.

Freiermuth, M. & Jarrell, D. (2006). Willingness to communicate: Can online chat help? *International Journal of Applied Linguistics*, 16, 189–212.

Gass, S., & Varonis, E. (1985). Task variation and non-native/non-native negotiation of meaning. In S. Gass & C. Madden (Eds), *Input in second language acquisition* (pp. 149–161). Rowley, MA: Newbury House.

Halliwell, S., & Jones, B. (1991). *On target: Teaching in the target language*. Reading, UK: CILT.

Harvey, P. (1985). A lesson to be learned: Chinese approaches to language learning. *ELT Journal*, 39, 183–186.

Jones, N. B. (1995). Business writing, Chinese students, and communicative language teaching. *TESOL Journal*, 4, 12–15.

Lai, C. (2013). A framework for developing self-directed technology use for language learning. *Language Learning & Technology*, 17, 100–122. Retrieved from http://llt.msu.edu/issues/june2013/lai.pdf

Long, M. (1981). Input, interaction and second language acquisition. *Annals of New York Academy of Sciences*, 379, 259–278.

Long, M. (1991). Focus on form: A design feature in language teaching methodology. In K. de Bot, D. Coste, R. Ginsberg & C. Kramsch (Eds), *Foreign language research in cross-cultural perspective* (pp. 9–52). Amsterdam: John Benjamins.

MacIntyre, P., Baker, S., Clément, R., & Conrod, S. (2001). Willingness to communicate, social support and language learning orientations of immersion students. *Studies in Second Language Acquisition*, 23, 369–388.

MacIntyre, P., Baker, S., Clément R., & Donovan, L. (2002). Sex and age effects on willingness to communicate, anxiety, perceived competence and L2 motivation among junior high school French immersion students. *Language Learning*, 53, 537–564.

MacIntyre, P., Baker, S., Clément R., & Donovan, L. (2003). Talking in order to learn: Willingness to communicate and intensive language programs. *Canadian Modern Language Review*, 59, 589–607.

Mackey, A. (1999). Input, interaction and second language development: An empirical study of question formation in ESL. *Studies in second language acquisition*, 21, 557–589.

Masuhara, H. (2003). Materials for developing reading skills. In B. Tomlinson (Ed.), *Developing materials for language teaching* (pp. 340–363). Cambridge: Cambridge University Press.

McDonough, K., & Mackey, A. (2000). Communicative tasks, conversational interaction and linguistic form: An empirical study of Thai. *Foreign Language Annals, 33*, 82–92.

Noel, K., Pelletier, L. Clément, R., & Vallerand R. (2000). Why are you learning a second language? Motivational orientations and self-determination theory. *Language Learning, 50*, 57–85.

Pica, T., & Doughty, C. (1985). Input and interaction in the communicative language classroom: A comparison of teacher-fronted and group activities. In S. Gass & C. Madden (Eds), *Input in second language acquisition* (pp. 115–132). Rowley, MA: Newbury House.

Rao, Z. (2002a). Bridging the gap between teaching and learning styles in East Asian context. *TESOL Journal, 11*, 5–11.

Rao, Z. (2002b). Chinese students' perceptions of communicative and non-communicative activities in the EFL classroom. *System, 30*, 85–105.

Samuda, V., & Bygate, M. (2008). *Tasks in second language learning*. Houndsmills, Basingstoke, Hampshire: Palgrave Macmillan.

Skehan, P. (1998). *A cognitive approach to language learning*. Oxford: Oxford University Press.

Smith, B. (2003). Computer-mediated negotiated interaction: An expanded model. *The Modern Language Journal, 87*, 38–57.

Smith, B. (2005). The relationship between negotiated interaction, learner uptake, and lexical acquisition in task-based computer-mediated communication. *TESOL Quarterly, 39*, 33–58.

Su, Y. (2007). Students' changing views and the integrated-skills approach in Taiwan's EFL college classes. *Asia Pacific Education Review, 8*, 27–40.

Ting-Toomey, S. (2005). The matrix of face: An updated face-negotiation theory. In W. B. Gudykunst (Ed.), *Theorizing about intercultural communication* (pp. 71–92). Thousand Oaks, CA: Sage.

Ting-Toomey, S., & Kurogi, A. (1998). Facework competence in intercultural conflict: An updated face-negotiation theory. *International Journal of Intercultural Relations, 22*, 187–225

Vandergriff, I. (2006). Negotiating common ground in computer-mediated versus face-to-face discussions. *Language Learning & Technology, 10*, 110–138. Retrieved September 11, 2009 from http://llt.msu.edu/vol10num1/vandergriff/default.html

Warner, C. (2004). It's just a game, right? Types of play in foreign language CMC. *Language Learning & Technology, 8*, 69–87.

Warschauer, M. (1996). Comparing face-to-face and electronic discussion in the second language classroom. *Calico Journal, 13*, 7–26.

Warschauer, M., Turbee, L., & Roberts, B. (1996). Computer learning networks and student empowerment. *System, 24*, 1–14.

Woken, M., & Swales, J. (1989). Expertise and authority in native–non-native conversations: The need for a variable account. In S. Gass, C. Madden, D. Preston & L. Selinker (Eds), *Variation in second language acquisition: Discourse and pragmatics* (pp. 211–227). Clevedon, England: Multilingual Matters.

Yashima, T. (2002). Willingness to communicate in a second language: The Japanese EFL context, *Modern Language Journal, 86*, 54–66.

Yashima, T., Zenuk-Nishide, L., & Shimizu, K. (2004). The influence of attitudes and affect on willingness to communicate and second language communication. *Language Learning, 54*, 119–152.

Zuengler, J. (1989). Performance variation in NS–NSS interactions: Ethnolinguistic difference or discourse domain? In S. Gass, C. Madden, D. Preston & L. Selinker (Eds), *Variation in second language acquisition: Discourse and pragmatics* (pp. 228–244). Clevedon, England: Multilingual Matters.

14

A Digital Shift is Not Enough:

Cultural, Pedagogical and Institutional Challenges to Technology-Mediated Task-Based Learning in Japan

Michael Thomas

Summary

Regardless of numerous government policies over the last two decades, Japan continues to rank low among Asian economies in international English language proficiency tests. Recent policy initiatives from the government indicate the need to internationalize the higher education system, start pupils learning English in elementary school and re-evaluate the current model emphasizing teaching rather than testing. These initiatives underline the importance of English language proficiency for maintaining Japan's place in the global economy. This chapter examines the potential for a technology-mediated task-based approach to English language teaching. Establishing a sociocultural context by evaluating key pedagogical and technological policies in Japan, the chapter argues that a fundamental shift in the culture and vision of learning needs to go hand-in-hand with reforms in the way learning technologies are perceived and used in the higher education sector. Moreover, research on foreign language learning in Japan will have little impact and remain peripheral if it is not allied to a fundamental shift in the status of the language teaching profession and the recruitment, career development and role of foreign language educators within it. The quantitative approach used to measure language teaching effectiveness needs to be replaced by a vision of process oriented and lifelong learning.

Introduction

In the context of research on task-based language teaching (TBLT), the publication of Van den Branden, Bygate and Norris' (2009) landmark 512 page reader on TBLT was notable for one significant omission. In a volume incorporating research spanning three decades of scholarship from the early 1980s, none of the chapters discussed the relationship with learning technologies. This is a notable omission for a number of reasons, not least because language education has been at the forefront of innovations in learning technologies over the last decade, but also because technology now mediates almost every aspect of language learners' access to information, be it in the form of social networks, e-books, Wikipedia and Google searches or mobile phones, tablets and other digital devices (Warschauer & Grimes, 2008). Moreover, digital technologies and social media play a similar role for teachers engaged in task-based instruction, as they routinely access lesson plans, share digital resources, communicate with students, or use learning management systems in online environments (Lai & Li, 2011).

Indeed, to further make the point, a year prior to the publication of the *TBLT Reader*, the first book-length collection on TBLT and computer-assisted language learning (CALL) appeared (Thomas & Reinders, 2010). The collection firmly identified the significance of a body of work in CALL that had been using both strong and weak forms of task-based learning for over a decade (Levy & Stockwell, 2006). The interest in technology-mediated task-based learning has developed further with the publication of two special editions of peer-reviewed journals in the last two years (Hamel, 2014; Thomas & Lai, 2013), as well as a new edited book (Gonzalez-Lloret & Ortega, 2014) on the subject.

Notably, in the 'Afterword' to the latter collection, Chapelle argues that the controversy about integrating technology in language education is finally over:

> ... the administrators, who were once portrayed as worrying about the financial cost of technology, are now enthusiastically attempting to get their courses offered online with the desire to reach a wider audience and preside over a program that is up-to-date. For better or worse, the controversy is over ...

According to Chapelle, technology has been accepted in the language classroom because of a societal shift in which technology has become integral to many peoples' everyday social lives:

> Indeed, times have changed. Technology is so routinely used for obtaining information, providing support, and creating opportunities for communication that it has overtaken any hope for a lingering controversy about whether or not technology should be used in language teaching.
> (Chapelle, in Gonzalez-Lloret & Ortega, 2014, p. 221)

While language learning technologies have made significant strides over the last decade as broadband has improved around the work, it is nevertheless clear from the current volume that neither TBLT nor digital technologies currently occupy anything approaching what might be called a hegemonic or normalized position in language education. This is true of the West but is especially relevant in the Asian context, the general subject of this collection, as well as in Japan, the specific context of this chapter.

The acceptance Chapelle alludes to is based rather flimsily on a combination of factors that has led to the use of portable digital devices to enable the creation and, more importantly, *sharing* of information (Kukulska-Hulme, 2009; Kukulska-Hulme & Shield, 2008). They are not however based on the acceptance of pedagogical principles. Without this, challenges are likely to remain, as any educational technologist with a grasp of the history of the discipline will readily confirm, all the way from talking movies to educational radio and iPads (Cuban, 1986, 2001). Although there are reasons to be optimistic, Chapelle's 'end of technology opposition thesis' appears rather premature. In many parts of the world, the widespread acceptance of educational technology, as well as how it can be used productively, still requires a shift in pedagogy, institutional support and understanding to accompany the digital shift in social technologies (Beetham & Sharpe, 2007). This shift needs to be underpinned by a strong pedagogical rationale, relevant continuing professional development and training, mentoring and guidance, a policy of informed educational technology use in place of an *ad hoc* reaction to the latest gadgets on the market, and most importantly, change from the bottom up which gives educators at all levels a voice in how curricula are designed, implemented and evaluated. From the management and policy perspective, clear and realistic career paths as well as incentives and rewards have to be factored into the equation to sustain and drive innovation and to confront one of the biggest challenges faced by language educators and managers throughout the world, namely, the relatively high turnover of language teachers who rarely stay in one location for a sustained period of time. This is a challenge which is of course generally apposite to foreign language educators working abroad and in particular to those working in Japan, who are unlikely to stay for a significant period of time or in significant numbers to produce institutional or curricula change. A more finegrained understanding of the problems facing the use of technology in language education and the types of learners who use digital technologies (one that rejects out of hand any notion of a generation of digital natives) is also required (Bennet, Maton & Kervin, 2008)).

As we have seen in other contributions to this collection, a task-based approach in which learners engage in meaningful activities involving the target language sounds appealing, but also involves a significant shift in attitudes, perceptions and day-to-day practice if it too is be successful in Japan or Asia more widely (Mima, 2003). Experimental research involving small-scale studies of technology-mediated TBLT is likely to have little impact in making the case for change an overwhelmingly convincing one in a national context as complex as Japan (Vallance, 2009). As a contribution to this debate, the following chapter explores the variables shaping English language education and Information Communication Technology (ICT) policy in Japan through a sociocultural lens. In so doing it outlines the challenges educational reformers who seek to utilize more authentic task-based approaches using digital technologies still face. It concludes with the call to: a) produce more qualitative and naturalistic research from a sociocultural and ecological perspective involving a range of native Japanese as well as foreign educator stakeholders on the institutional and policy factors that determine English language policy in Japan; and b) in order to advance the case for technology-mediated language learning involving authentic tasks, to provide a rationale embedded within the wider context of project-based learning, one that is precisely relevant to Japan's socio-economic need to produce graduates capable of dealing effectively with the linguistic, intercultural and digital skills required for the global economy (Belz, 2002; Hashimoto, 2000, 2009).

English language education in Japan

Since the year 2000 policymakers in Japan have sought to establish English as Japan's official second language (MEXT, 2001, 2003). This important shift acknowledges the challenges associated with the current English language education system and its seeming inability to produce university students with similar levels of English proficiency to neighbouring Asian economies and competitors such as China, Singapore and South Korea (Latchem, Jung, Aoki & Ozkul, 2007). Though Japanese university students currently study English in junior high and high school, their productive abilities remain low by comparison (Hood, Elwood & Falout, 2009). While more attention is being paid by policymakers to the number of contact hours in which Japanese students study English, instructors' reliance upon traditional behaviourist approaches in the language classroom provide few opportunities for authentic communicative practice. Print-based commercial textbooks tend to marginalize communicative, interactive and collaborative learning. It is common for instructions in commercial textbooks to be written in Japanese and this is also seen as a contributing factor in approaches which focus on standardized testing rather than encouraging learners to use the target language productively in meaningful situations that correspond to real-life situations (Vallance, 2009).

The origins of this approach stem from the rigorous system of school and university level entrance examinations that place a significant emphasis on knowledge gathering and assimilation rather than language learners' productive or higher-order critical thinking skills (Hood, Elwood & Falout, 2009) and is reproduced across a number of disciplines rather than being specific to language education as Mima (2003) suggests. Widely recognized, various government reforms have been established to target and correct these deficiencies. During the 1990s an effort was made to replace the grammar translation and rote learning methods with communicative language teaching (CLT) (Kikuchi & Sakai, 2009; Nunan, 2004). Such attempts, however, have proved difficult to integrate in traditional face-to-face classroom environments where teaching English as a Foreign Language (EFL) remains focused on formal grammar teaching, particularly by Japanese native speaking instructors who may feel they do not possess the level of English fluency appropriate for communicative approaches (Hood, Elwood & Falout, 2009).

In addition to these policy level factors, researchers have also addressed these challenges via a cultural analysis of Asian learners. Vallance (2009), for example, argues that collectivism and group harmony may affect learner behaviour to the extent that Japanese students are often reticent about taking the initiative, asking teachers questions if they do not understand, or appearing 'different' in front of members of their peer group. The unwillingness to 'lose face' is an important factor that is often identified when attempting to understand Japanese learners' unwillingness to communicate in English in front of their typically large classroom peer groups. According to Tsui and Tollefson (2007) it is not unusual for advanced students to conceal their answers to questions from their teacher or knowingly answer incorrectly, rather than stand out from the crowd.

This unwillingness to demonstrate individual achievement is also related to the position of the instructor, who may occupy an honoured and often unquestioned position of authority that stands in stark contrast to the notion of a facilitator of knowledge typically found in constructivist theory (Carless, 2007). Indeed, when confronted with situations or questions that they do not understand, Vallance (2009) found that Japanese students may be more prone to ask fellow students rather than their language instructors, even when the instructor happens to be Japanese, but especially if the instructor happens to be a foreign educator or native speaker of English.

According to Tsui and Tollefson (2007) Japanese language learners adopt a generally more passive attitude to language learning in large group contexts and it is not uncommon for students to be found sleeping or exhibiting other forms of non-engagement which would be frowned upon in a Western university context. Language learners may have a tendency to display a 'survival' rather than 'academic' orientation to their studies, thus demonstrating lower levels of intrinsic motivation and engagement with each other and the learning environment in general (Littlewood, 2007). Research on language learners in the private university sector where entrance standards are typically less rigorous and less achievement oriented, suggests learners may be more prone to this type of behaviour than those in the national universities.

Since the turn of the new millennium a panel set up to advise former Prime Minister Keizo Obuchi has focused on reforming English language education and led to a series of published reports examining Japan's goals for the twenty-first century. One of the earliest reports entitled, 'The Frontier Within: Individual Empowerment and Better Governance in the New Millennium' (Prime Minister's Commission, 2000) recommended the need to reform the Japanese education system and to encourage greater social diversity in order to enhance Japan's future economic prosperity. According to this vision, language education was given a major role in reshaping and preparing Japan's workforce for the challenges of globalization and technological change driving the twenty-first century.

The report entitled, 'Regarding the Establishment of an Action Plan to Cultivate "Japanese with English Abilities" ' (MEXT, 2003) is symptomatic of this conflation of language skills, internationalization and digital skills. It outlined a five-year plan for the period 2003–2008 based on the importance of language education to globalization. The limitations of the current policies and the importance of reform of English language education are a central concern of the report. In response there have been a number of recurring themes in the proposed reforms. These include examining ways to improve English lessons and teaching methods and to bring them more in line with broadly communicative approaches by giving students more opportunities to listen to and speak English; more focus on the importance of continuing professional development; the requirement to establish professional standards for hiring appropriately qualified academic and teaching staff; and improving high school and university entrance examinations.

The government reports identify recommendations that show the shifting socio-economic significance of English language learning in a globalized economy. This is apparent in documents which make a direct link between language learning skills and those required by employees in the ICT sector, where English is perceived as the primary language of the internet and the gateway to business, science, technology and economic success.

Most significantly, from 2012 English became a compulsory subject for elementary school children. Concomitant with these changes, there has been a consistent growth in the English language industry in Japan, with the development of many language schools and programmes covering the whole gamut of the educational spectrum, from small private schools to the formal school system, as well as the higher education sector, which includes over 700 institutions of higher learning.

In recent years there has been an increasing emphasis on pre-school English and the subject is now studied in more formal contexts from junior high level onwards. The total investment in English Language Teaching (ELT) resources and education in Japan amounts to a highly significant investment that is indicative of the interest in acquiring English language skills shown across Japanese culture as a whole. A measure of English skills, usually exemplified by a score on the Test of English for the International Communication (TOEIC), remains highly beneficial for students graduating from the university sector (Hashimoto, 2009). Like those university entrance examinations, however, the TOEIC is usually a paper-based test with little or no opportunity for learners' English communicative skills to be tested. Nevertheless, TOEIC scores remain extremely influential during graduates' job-hunting programmes and access to management training schemes in multinational corporations such as Toyota is often based on relevant scores in the test.

These areas confirm that English is of great importance to the Japanese within Japan but they may also explain their demotivation to improve English beyond a basic level. While other exposure to English may occur in numerous other points across the culture, through access to English language films, DVD rentals, and increasingly via the internet in the form of social networking sites, sustaining motivation in activities outside of formal study remains challenging in a highly homogenous culture. Japan's unique investment and interest in English language education, then, belies a concomitant characteristic of many of its learners, namely, a reticence to advance to levels of English language competence in communication, seen in other industrialized Asian economies (Hashimoto, 2009, 2011). For the most part, this ambivalence has its roots in an English language education system which still relies on the recruitment of thousands of unqualified Assistant Language Teachers (ALT), typically young international graduates from any discipline each year, or through the reliance on a grammar-translation methodology, often taught by native Japanese teachers, who may lack English language oral proficiency themselves and have no formal English language teaching qualification.

Beyond these failings of the educational system and the policies of successive governments in Japan, is the pervasive influence of cultural characteristics, whether in or outside formal learning environments, the most important being the inherited cultural traditions of a conservative Asian culture that is deeply rooted in collectivism and group harmony. In an educational setting, this cultural behaviour translates into a pedagogical framework in which the teacher occupies an honoured and often unquestioned position and learners are expected to listen rather than engage in critical thinking.

In this respect Japanese language students may exhibit behaviour which is highly unlike that of Western students of languages. Japanese learners of English typically emphasize group harmony over individualism and rarely question their teachers or wish to disturb the established balance of power within a classroom learning environment. Following the process of rigorous entrance examinations, which often determine the broad paths to be followed by students for the rest of their lives, university education is often perceived as a period of relaxation in which students are encouraged to cultivate their social relationships rather than pursue academic excellence and achievement. Although in general Japanese students may work hard to pass high school and university entrance examinations, for which there is an obvious sense of competition between students, university education is typically associated with a decrease in learner motivation related to the development of academic skills. Employers may place a higher emphasis on students' ability to participate and develop social and leadership skills as evidenced by their extra-curricular activities, circles and associations, rather than as a result of the classroom activities they engage in during their university years (Hashimoto, 2000, 2009, 2011).

A typical refrain emphasizing the secondary role of individualism and individual achievement is indicated by the phrase: 'the nail that stands out ought to be hammered down'. In terms of Hofstede's (2004) model of culture, Japan registers a high score for 'uncertainty avoidance', 'power distance', 'collectivism', 'masculinity', and 'long-term orientation'. Learners may be less willing to takes risks in learning for fear of losing face within a group and showing their vulnerability. Being aware of the pervasive influence of such cultural traits and behaviour in classroom environments is highly important when dealing with questions of student interaction and collaboration in task-based language learning environments. In many aspects such behaviour stems from the Japanese moral code, which is Confucian in emphasis, tradition and history, as well as the complex ethical dimensions of this system of thought and behaviour. As opposed to Western society, harmony within and between groups is highly important in classroom learning environments, as is the realization that self-fulfilment through engaging successfully with teachers' questions is not a major concern in terms of learner motivation (Hashimoto, 2011).

Given this context, there are few studies that examine collaboration in second language learning classrooms in Japan. The majority of studies focus on Western contexts, and those that do examine Japan, do so with the aid of Western assumptions and theoretical lenses. Whereas in the West, students' concept of collaboration in learning environments focuses on an individualistic orientation, in Japan collaboration in classroom environments has to be contextualized by a series of cultural factors (Adams & Newton, 2009). Regardless of the overarching influence of collectivism, the Japanese education system, from junior high to universities, is focused on passing a series of discrete examinations, rather than on process-oriented approaches to in-class learning. Project-based work is rather uncommon and students are expected to memorize significant amounts of information prior to undertaking a series of examinations, the results of which may determine their place in the educational hierarchy for decades of their lives. This focus on written examinations inculcates a rather individualistic attitude toward studying second languages that privileges receptive over productive skills and passivity over interactivity and collaboration (Hood, Elwood & Falout, 2009).

In the Japanese context English is a foreign rather than a second language, the difference being that second language status is attributed to languages that are used as the central medium of communication for most of the population in any given country. Moreover, in Japan an often referred to hybrid form of Japanese and English (or 'Japlish'), is cited to refer to the mix of styles that have evolved, mixing katakana pronunciation of English words, English loan words and Japanese. Research suggests that students of EFL face many more obstacles than are normally encountered by learners while living in a culture in which the target language is spoken every day. There are therefore key distinctions between learners of EFL and those learning English as a Second Language. These differences primarily focus on a clear inability to practice in the target language in the sociocultural context in which foreign language learners find themselves (Hashimoto, 2009).

Indeed, research studies investigating Japanese learners on study abroad programmes generally confirm the sharp differences in learner motivation, interactivity in English and achievement when native Japanese reside in an English-speaking country. Participation in these programmes is not limited to focusing on gains in linguistic competence, but also involves a general process of widening horizons, developing cultural competence and the social development of the learners. The need to communicate and the easy access to a context in which English is spoken as the first language have a tremendous affect on altering the mindsets of Japanese learners, so often accustomed to studying English by placing a marginal role on productive communication skills (Hashimoto, 2000, 2009).

The marginalization of productive skills is particularly evident in cultural differences between Japan and English-speaking countries. Being members of a group which perceives itself to be a minority may also lead to attempts to preserve the unique status of the first language in a particular culture. Such trends are in evidence in Japan, where fears continually arose during the 1990s of the widespread use of new katakana or foreign loan words in Japanese, with which many elderly people were unaccustomed. This resistance to acculturation may have contributed to images of Japanese learners held by native English speakers, as well as the perception Japanese speakers have of themselves and their own identity. Resistance to English language proficiency may also be explained by the resistance to the dominant image of Western culture and the sense that Japanese people are a uniquely homogenous culture and race. Just as Japanese people perceive their own language and culture as uniquely difficult for native Japanese to master, so too they understand that they can never truly understand the foreign culture or language whose language they are trying to learn.

Other types of resistance stem from the way English may be perceived as being forced on Japanese learners from a relatively early age, unlike in Western cultures where advanced study is a matter of choice (Kikuchi & Sakai, 2009). Unusually, English study has low dropout rates regardless of the apparent lack of success encountered by the students. This is partly explained by the Japanese students' respect for educational curricula once they have started and the understanding that they may proceed with English by passing written examinations rather than as a result of becoming effective speakers of the language.

Though many of the policies mentioned above have been initiated over the last decade, rankings from Educational Testing Service (ETS) in 2011 continued to locate

Japan third lowest from thirty-three Asian countries in the TOEFL test, with only Cambodia and Laos scoring lower (Japan Times, 2013). While more attention is being paid by policymakers to practical issues, such as the number of hours Japanese students study English, students' reliance upon traditional classroom methodologies provide little room for communicative practice. The Japanese context of language education remains an extremely unique amalgamation of forces and resistances, including geographical, historical and linguistic factors. Although instructors and researchers must be wary of essentialist modes of thinking, this network of factors makes it challenging for native Japanese instructors, as well as foreign language educators in particular, to produce a significant impact in the institutions in which they work vis-à-vis the direction of language education policy and curriculum change (Latchem, Jung, Aoki & Ozkul, 2007).

TBLT in Japan

Over the last decade TBLT has been adopted in a number Asian countries, often led by top-down initiatives following government or education policy (Adams & Newton, 2009). Task-based approaches have been identified as potential solutions to the need to maintain the competitiveness of Asian university graduates globally and improve international mobility. When led by top-down policy and curriculum initiatives there has often been resistance and problems associated with professional development (Mochizuki & Ortega, 2008).

On the other hand, bottom-up approaches are developing and these demonstrate how the concept is being culturally mediated. National curricula in English language education are switching towards a TBLT approach in China, Taiwan, Hong Kong (Adamson & Davison, 2003). In Japan a largely communicative approach is in evidence though this is an amorphous and eclectic term that integrates a wide range of different styles. Though typically associated with a different methodological approach, a number of recent educational policy initiatives are promoting the skills normally associated with TBLT as we have seen above. These include an emphasis on cross-cultural interaction and a greater concern for individual learner development through increased learner autonomy. The attempt to implement large-scale top-down approaches is fraught with difficulties and resistance in a context with varying degrees of professional standards, high turnover of foreign instructors, and where the grammar-translation method is still popular with non-native speaking teachers in particular who may not wish to be pushed out of their existing comfort zone.

National policy directives in Japan over the last ten years have attempted to specify general standards for institutions to follow but have had limited success (Aspinall, 2011; MEXT, 2003). This often results in a process of local adaptation rather than strict compliance. A number of factors have impeded the integration of TBLT in a Japanese language education context. These include, for example, professional development as instructors may be asked (or forced) to use methods they do not understand. Likewise, instructors may not be comfortable with the fundamental change of pedagogical style required by task-based approaches. Instructors may resist the amount of time required to prepare and assess tasks, or prefer a more flexible mix of eclectic approaches. There may be scepticism in adopting TBLT from Japanese instructors of English due to research on its lack of effectiveness for promoting learners' interlanguage development (Ellis, 2003). They may also lack confidence in terms of the range and sophistication of English required in order to develop a TBLT approach. Research suggests that there may be institutional resistance in that language schools are used to norm-referenced examinations focusing on grammar and vocabulary, and thus instructors are familiar and comfortable with 'teaching to the tests' within a culture of high stakes examinations.

Moving away from the macro context, a number of classroom factors may also be significant in this respect. These include the layout of classrooms with fixed seating which may not be conducive to the requirements of the communicative approach adopted in TBLT. Interactive pair work needs a particular type of classroom environment in which both instructors and learners can freely circulate. Other considerations also relate to the mix of students with different language proficiencies.

Most of these factors affect the instructors. There are also factors which impact on the learners and their ability to transition to a TBLT classroom (Ellis, 2003). Learners need to adapt to the change from fluency to accuracy in terms of their language production skills. There is a heightened awareness of the need to speak English, while learners in Japan may prefer to use their first language to scaffold their learning. TBLT approaches require learners to be willing to take risks in speaking aimed at stretching their knowledge of the target language. Research suggests that Japanese learners may be more reluctant to engage with the increased levels of interactivity and focus on productive skills required of TBLT (Doughty & Long, 2003; Ellis, 2003). Studies of digital technologies and task-based learning suggest that it can present learners with more opportunities to engage in meaning-based interaction with native and non-native speakers, but not if students resist the transition from language focused skills. Research does suggest, however, that overcoming these barriers may not be beyond learners in the sense that sustained exposure to TBLT may improve students' willingness to engage in more meaning-based approaches in general (Robinson, 2001).

In order to understand the challenges involved in a specifically technology-mediated approach, it is worthwhile to explore the context of digital technology policy in Japan (Schrooten, 2006) where similar contributing factors are also evident.

ICT policies in Japan

Although Japan is often identified as a high technology nation through the success of its electronics industry and perceived fondness for consumer gadgets, ICT has not been a strategic priority in the field of formal education where administrative rigidity and the lack of Japanese teachers with high-level skills has been identified (Morris-Suzuki & Rimmer, 2003). Centralization has meant that curricula cannot be adapted by local institutions due the priority accorded to established frameworks of reference (Latchem, Jung, Aoki & Ozkul, 2007).

In order to address this situation Japan's Ministry of Education, Culture, Sports, Science and Technology (MEXT) has developed a number of policy documents to make Japan a leading ICT nation. The 1999 ICT strategy entitled, 'Information Technology in Education Project' (ITEP) set out a five-year plan aimed at elementary and secondary school, based on three main ICT targets in relation to professional development, content creation and hardware and software knowledge. These specific targets include improved teaching training and professional development in basic educational ICT as well as the use of ICT in teachers' specific disciplines; production of content to help teach basic ICT; and the goal of integrating internet access into all classrooms. In 2001 MEXT developed these plans further in documents related to the Education Reform Plan for the twenty-first century entitled, 'The Rainbow Plan' (MEXT, 2001), a policy which outlined seven distinct strategies. Significant progress was not made with these plans and Japanese class sizes remain large thus challenging the idea of producing new types of learning environments for a digital age. Japanese students favour portable devices such as mobile phones over laptop computers and this makes them less familiar with using computing devices for formal learning. The Japanese government's strategic policy initiatives in ICT focus more broadly on goals for the hardware infrastructure than on specifying targets for ICT in education and considering the pedagogical and methodological implications of such technologies.

Other Asian nations influenced more by the United States, such as Singapore, have developed different ICT master plans which while focusing on the integration of improved ICT infrastructure, also link this with the development of more social constructivist and project-based learning. As Vallance (2009) points out, policymakers and officials in Singapore may benefit from having participated in foreign education as they are more open to Western styles of teaching and learning based on dialogue, analysis and enquiry; this is not the case in Japan where the education system lacks personalization. While technology is often important for science subjects throughout the school system, humanities education and English language education in particular, has not been identified with an important role for ICTs.

Reform of the English language education system on the other hand has been subject to much debate in Japan as we have seen above, but important policy documents such as the government report, 'Regarding the Establishment of an Action Plan to Cultivate "Japanese with English Abilities" ' (MEXT, 2003), made little reference to the specific or general use of ICT. The prevailing methodology is therefore strongly rooted in cultural attitudes toward existing pedagogy. In a similar vein to some of the research on English language education, Walker (2003) read the reticence to integrate ICT in terms of a series of widely accepted cultural stereotypes. Japanese instructors may resist ICT integration because they do not want to appear to be different to their colleagues and they may have a heightened sense of anxiety about using equipment about which they have little expertise.

As previously mentioned, Japanese students' focus on passing written examinations may present obstacles to dealing with new modes of learning based on collaboration using digital technologies. These cultural factors, allied to the lack of structured continuing professional development (CPD) for language instructors, and an attitude towards technology integration based on how to use it, rather than how to develop appropriate forms of pedagogy, are also significant factors. While there may be lots of 'new technology' on display in universities, it is often used for marketing purposes and to attract students rather than as part of a coherent long-term pedagogical strategy. Foreign English language instructors in Japan may also use technology for their own career purposes and while they have developed innovative practices, they rarely have the influence to design an institution-wide approach that can stand the test of time or affect established assessment procedures.

Indeed, Vallance (2009) argued that ICT integration in Japan highlights the disconnect between government policies and how they are implemented, arguing that innovation often leads to lengthy discussion and inertia rather than action. This point of view is based on cultural attitudes to Japanese management styles in which group decision-making may impede innovation and the speed of change within the already bureaucratic state education system. This impasse has been contributed to by MEXT, which like other government agencies, typically relies on research that is heavily quantitative (e.g., focused on statistics related to access and student-computer ratios), rather than qualitative research in which learners' and instructors' perceptions of teaching strategies are elicited.

The goals of Japan's ambitious ICT policy – access to a high-speed internet connection in educational institutions and across the country as a whole – have by and large been met. Digital divides between home and educational use of the internet are among some of the lowest in the industrialized world. Increased access however has brought with it problems associated with integration and the question of how best to take advantage of ICT through the development of new classroom pedagogies. Fujitani, Bhattacharya and Akahori (2003) argue that the integration of ICT in Japan has been inhibited due to the persistence of established paradigms of teaching and learning. Japan's geography, the dispersal of its population among literally hundreds of islands, has also contributed to the slow pace of educational reform. The reforms that have been developed have been based on a piecemeal approach. Consequently, ICT has been used to bolster information based on behaviourist principles of memorisation rather than the idea that learners are partners in the learning process.

Existing surveys of the use of ICT in Japanese schools support this view, where ICT is viewed as either a tool for communication among geographically dispersed institutions or as a search tool for information. The first is based on putting the technical and hardware infrastructure in place. Secondly, there is a need for the greater availability of information in multimedia formats. Teachers need to transform their teaching practices by using the new technology to involve students in new forms of knowledge discovery. ICT should not therefore be seen as a separate subject but as an element that can be integrated into every subject area, including language learning. This model would be based on a process-oriented approach to curriculum design involving a cycle of activities, reflection on learning and active problem-solving. The role of the language instructor would be that of a reflective practitioner and active researcher. Task-based approaches need to have powerful advocates to dispel the attractions of an instructivist methodology based on the influence of the textbook that mediates and controls social relationships within classroom spaces and to overturn the assumption that students who are not 'on task' may be perceived as disruptive or even disengaged from the learning process (Hampel, 2006; Lankshear & Knobel, 2008). Similarly, in Web 2.0 classrooms in which a variety of media may be used, learners may simply be confused at the open-ended nature of unfocused tasks that do not lead to a predictable outcome. Blending both textbook and digital media without sufficient preparation, may radically alter the expectations and practices found in the classroom environment, juxtaposing different styles and expectations of teaching and social relationships in the classroom. The new social mindset inherent in these technologies underlines the importance of pursuing relationships *between* learners in order to extend and develop their knowledge base.

The challenges identified above indicate the need to develop forms of English language education that enable teachers and learners in Japan to exploit the affordances of digital technologies while drawing on the existing tendency to maintain consensual styles of learning. One solution to this is to develop project-based learning utilizing technology-mediated tasks in the context of a classroom environment based on mutual dependence among learners (Ayas & Zeniuk, 2001). This is a vision of collaborative as opposed to cooperative tasks in that the former focuses on learners who share a holistic understanding of the global task to be completed. In cooperative tasks by contrast, learners concentrate more on their individual tasks without connecting them to the overall task. This leads to a different theoretical approach in that research on cooperation may examine the cognitive aspects of the individual learner as the unit of analysis, whereas collaboration is often investigated with the aid of a sociocultural lens. Mastering these forms of collaborative, digitally-mediated communication are essential precisely for the skills required by students seeking employment in the knowledge economy and this style of pedagogy can be meaningfully aligned with Japan's economic goals for an international workforce (Hashimoto, 2000). A number of challenges need to be thought through however, including learners' ownership of their contributions and how individual and group collaboration is evaluated and assessed.

Research on the field of collaborative learning has developed over the last ten to twenty years and a number of key themes have emerged. These include the importance of carefully designing and sequencing project tasks; developing relationships between learners and instructors that are akin to coaching rather than instructing; and not being restrained by the uncompromising administrative and assessment structures and requirements that may not have been established to accommodate the type of creative learning expected by project-based learning utilizing authentic tasks (Hampel, 2006). In restricted EFL contexts such as Japan, it is important to energise learners around communities of practice (CoP), both inside and outside of formal educational contexts where social technologies are playing an increasingly important role in engaging young people in *learning* (Butler, 2011). Such a vision of technology-mediated task-based learning springs from an acknowledgement of the agency of learners (learners need to be active in the learning process rather than merely acted on); that research understands the complex sociocultural context of learning, moving beyond the micro level to examine the social, cultural and institutional contexts in which activities take place; in place of cognitivist approaches, it is necessary to promote and understand the supportive role of more capable others in the process; and to understand learning as a continuous lifelong process rather than one based on an input-output or cause-and-effect model (Lai & Li, 2011; Levy & Stockwell, 2006).

Conclusion

This chapter has discussed the contextual challenges faced by implementing technology-mediated task-based learning in Japan, examining the barriers posed by culture and pedagogy, as well as institutional and ICT policy. Faced with this complex nexus of factors, small-scale research studies do little to advance the cause of more authentic forms of language pedagogy such as task-based learning. While research suggests significant opportunities exist to take advantage of Web 2.0 collaborative learning with tasks, these stand little chance of success in Japan unless a long-term and integrated national policy of reform emerges. Such a policy would provide support for more effective language teacher training at all levels of the system and, in the context of Japan's mass system of higher education, hire appropriately qualified foreign language educators, offering them partnership and mutual respect with opportunities to invest in the contributions they make. Above all, this kind of learning requires not just a digital shift, but also a fundamental shift in policy and approach in order to stimulate the agency of language learners and grasp the rewards of experiential learning. As Seymour Papert (1980) has argued more broadly in the context of task-based education, instructors are tasked with preparing the opportunities for *learner creativity* rather than merely reproducing existing knowledge.

References

Adams, R., & Newton, J. (2009). TBLT in Asia: Constraints and opportunities. *Asian Journal of English Language Teaching*, 19, 1–17.

Adamson, B., & Davison, C. (2003). Innovation in English language teaching in Hong Kong primary schools: One step forward, two steps sideways? *Prospect*, 18(1), 27–41.

Aspinall, R. W. (2011). Globalization and English language education policy in Japan. In D. B. Willis & I. Rappleye (Eds), *Reimainging Japanese education: Border, transfers, circulation, and the comparative* (pp. 127–146). Oxford: Symposium Books.

Ayas, K., & Zeniuk, N. (2001). Project-based learning: Building communities of reflective practitioners, *Management Learning*, 32(1), 61–76.

Beetham, H., & Sharpe, R., (Eds) (2007). *Rethinking pedagogy for a digital age: Designing and delivering e-learning*. London & New York: Routledge.

Bennett, S. Maton, K., & Kervin, L. (2008). The digital natives debate: A critical review of the evidence, *British Journal of Educational Technology*, 39(5), 775–786.

Belz, J. A. (2002). Social dimensions of telecollaborative foreign language study. *Language Learning and Technology*, 6(1), 60–81.

Butler, Y. G. (2011). The implementation of communicative and task-based language teaching in the Asia-Pacific region. *Annual Review of Applied Linguistics*, 31, 36–57.

Carless, D. (2007). The suitability of task-based approaches for secondary schools: Perspectives from Hong Kong. *System*, 35, 595–608.

Cuban, L. (1986). *Teachers and machines: The classroom use of technology since 1920*. Teachers College, Columbia University: New York and London.

Cuban, L. (2001). *Oversold and underused: Computers in the classroom*. Cambridge Mass. & London: Harvard University Press.

Doughty, C. J., & Long, M. H. (2003). Optimal psycholinguistic environments for distance foreign language learning. *Language, Learning & Technology*, 7(3), 50–80.

Ellis, R. (2003). *Task-based language learning and Teaching*. Oxford: Oxford University Press.

Fujitani, S., Bhattacharya, M., & Akahori, K. (2003). ICT implementation and online learning in Japan, *Educational Technology*, 43(3), 33–37.

González-Lloret, M., & Ortega, L. (2014). *Technology-mediated TBLT: Researching technology and tasks*. Amsterdam: John Benjamins.

Hamel, M-J. (Ed.) (2014). ICT-mediated language tasks in CALL. *Canadian Journal of Learning and Technology*, 40(1).

Hampel, R. (2006). Rethinking task design for the digital age: A framework for language teaching and learning in a synchronous online environment. *ReCALL, 18*(1), 105–121.

Hashimoto, K. (2000). Internationalisation is a Japanisation: Japan's foreign language education in government policy. *Journal of Intercultural Studies, 21,* 39–51.

Hashimoto, K. (2009). Cultivating 'Japanese who can use English': Problems and contradictions in government policy. *Asian Studies Review, 33,* 21–43.

Hashimoto, K. (2011). Compulsory 'foreign language activities' in Japanese primary schools. *Current Issues in Language Planning, 12*(2), 167–184.

Hofstede, G. (2004). *Cultures and organisations: Software of the mind.* New York: McGraw Hill.

Hood, M., Elwood, J., & Falout, J. (2009). Student attitudes toward task-based language teaching at Japanese universities. *Asian Journal of English Language Teaching, 19,* 49–66.

Japan Times (2013). Editorial: Testing English versus teaching it. *The Japan Times,* 31st March. Retrieved from http://www.japantimes.co.jp/opinion/2013/03/31/editorials/testing-english-versus-teaching-it/

Kikuchi, K., & Sakai, H. (2009). Japanese learners' demotivation to study English: A survey study. *JALT Journal, 31*(2), 183–204.

Kukulska-Hulme, Agnes. (2009). *Will mobile learning change language learning, ReCALL, 21*(2), 157–165.

Kukulska-Hulme, A., & Shield, L (2008). An overview of mobile assisted language learning: From content delivery to supported collaboration and interaction, *ReCALL, 20*(3), 271–289.

Lai, C., & Li, G. (2011). Technology and task-based teaching: A critical review. *CALICO, 28*(2), 498–521.

Lankshear, C., & Knobel, M. (2008). *New literacies: Everyday practices and classroom learning.* Maidenhead: Open University Press.

Latchem, C., Jung, I., Aoki, K. & Ozkul, A. E. (2007). The tortoise and the hare enigma in transformation in Japanese and Korean higher education. *British Journal of Educational Technology, 39*(4), 610–630.

Levy, M., & Stockwell, G. (2006). *CALL dimensions: Options and issues in computer-assisted language learning.* Mahwah, New Jersey & London: Lawrence Erlbaum Associates.

Littlewood, W. (2007). Communicative and task-based language teaching in East Asian classrooms, *Language Teaching, 40,* 243–249.

Nunan, D. (2004). *Designing tasks for the communicative classroom.* Cambridge: Cambridge University Press.

MEXT (2001). The education reform plan for the 21st century – The Rainbow Plan –, The seven priority strategies, Tokyo: Ministry of Education, Science, Sports and Culture.

MEXT (2003). Regarding the establishment of an action plan to cultivate 'Japanese with English abilities'. Retrieved http://www.mext.go.jp/b_menu/hakusho/html/hpac200201/hpac200201_2_015.html

Mima, N. (2003). Online technology is not enough: Transforming the teacher-student learning process. In J. M. Bachnik (Ed.), *Roadblocks on the information highway.* Oxford: Lexington.

Mochizuki, N., & Ortega, L. (2008). Balancing communication and grammar in beginning-level foreign language classrooms: A study of guided planning and relativization, *Language Teaching Research, 12*(1), 11–37.

Morris-Suzuki, T., & Rimmer, P (2003). Cyberstructure, society, and education in Japan. In J. M. Bachnik (Ed.), *Roadblocks on the information highway: The IT revolution in Japanese education* (pp. 157–170). Lexington Books, USA.

Papert, S., 1980. *Mindstorms: Children, computers, and powerful ideas.* New York: Basic Books.

Prime Minister's Commission (2000). The frontier within: Individual empowerment and better governance in the new millennium. Retrieved http://www.kantei.go.jp/jp/21century/report/pdfs/

Robinson, P. (2001). Task complexity, task difficulty, and task production: Exploring interactions in a componential framework, *Applied Linguistics*, 22(1), 27–57.

Schrooten, W. (2006). Task-based language teaching and ICT: Developing and assessing interactive multimedia for task-based language teaching. In K. Van den Branden (Ed.), *Task-based language education: From theory to practice* (pp. 129–150). Cambridge: Cambridge University Press.

Thomas, M., & Lai, C. (Eds) (2013). Special Edition on TBLT and Technology. *International Journal of Computer-Assisted Language Learning and Teaching*, 3(1).

Thomas, M., & Reinders, H. (Eds) (2010). *Task-based language learning and teaching with technology.* London & New York: Continuum.

Tsui, A. B. M., & Tollefson, J. W. (Eds) (2007). *Language policy, culture and identity in Asian contexts.* Mahwah, NJ: Lawrence Erlbaum Associates.

Vallance, M. (2009). Beyond policy: Strategic actions to support ICT integration in Japanese schools. *Australasian Journal of Educational Technology*, 24(3), 275–293.

Van den Branden, K., Bygate, M., & Norris, J. M. (Eds) (2009). *Task-based language teaching: A reader.* Amsterdam/Philadelphia: Benjamins.

Walker, N. N. (2003). Technology and Japanese high schools: Why technology integration will take time. *Techlearning*, 1 August. Retrieved http://www.techlearning.com/story/showArticle.php?articleID=12803459

Warschauer, M., & Grimes, D. (2008). Audience, authorship, and artifact: The emergent semiotics of web 2.0, *Annual Review of Applied Linguistics*, 27, 1–23.

15

A Trade-off in Learning:

Mobile Augmented Reality for Language Learning

Hayo Reinders
Onuma Lakarnchua
Mark Pegrum

Summary

In recent years there has been considerable interest in the potential of mobile devices, and of rapidly emerging technologies like mobile augmented reality (AR), to promote situated language learning. This chapter reports on a preliminary action research project carried out to determine the benefits of the kind of situated language learning facilitated by a mobile AR task, in a format accessible to everyday language teachers. One group of English learners at a Thai university followed prompts to create orientation tours by walking around campus to key locations and writing descriptions of those locations, before then taking a tour created by classmates. A control group created orientation tours without leaving the classroom, based on their pre-existing knowledge of the campus, and did not take a tour. A comparison of pre- and post-tests on discourse markers revealed no significant improvement for either the experimental group or the control group. A comparison of the discourse features in the tours created by the two groups revealed slightly more use of detailed descriptive language among the experimental group, but slightly more use of discourse markers, and consequently slightly more syntactically complex language overall, among the control group. These findings suggest that the use of mobile AR tasks may involve a trade-off in language learning, potentially emphasizing some aspects of language at the expense of others. It may therefore be advisable to balance the use of mobile AR with more traditional classroom instruction. The paper concludes with recommendations for teachers considering the use of mobile AR tasks, and a call for more research to inform our understanding of this area.

Introduction

With the spread of mobile devices, new possibilities for promoting situated language learning have opened up. One area currently attracting considerable attention is AR, a rapidly developing technology which has only recently become available in user-friendly formats which lend themselves to use in everyday educational contexts. AR refers to the dynamic overlaying of contextually relevant digital information onto a real-world environment (Pegrum, 2014); it thus 'offer[s] users the ability to access placed-based information in ways that are compellingly intuitive' (Johnson et al., 2011). A broad conceptual definition of this kind is arguably more valuable than a more technocentric definition linked to the annotated viewfinder displays often associated with AR, because it highlights the entire range of tools which produce similar effects (FitzGerald et al., 2012; Wu et al., 2013).

For a number of years, the annual *NMC Horizon Reports* have signalled that AR is an important emerging educational technology. The 2010 *Horizon Report* selected 'simple augmented reality' as one of six key technologies to watch, with a time-to-adoption horizon of two to three years; the 2011 report dropped the adjective 'simple' and included 'augmented reality' as one of its six technologies, with a time-to-adoption horizon of four to five years. The integration of AR with other tools became evident when the 2012 Higher Education *Horizon Report* mentioned AR in an example included under the category of mobile apps (with a time-to-adoption horizon of one year or less), while the 2013 edition mentioned it under the category of wearable technology (with a time-to-adoption horizon of four to five years). While not all kinds of AR depend on mobile devices, the linking of AR with mobile and wearable technologies in the *Horizon Reports* suggests the possible value of mobile AR for education. Mobile AR is likely to be of great relevance to language learning in particular, given the potential to scaffold and prompt language use as students move through real-world contexts. With the recent proliferation of user-friendly mobile AR applications, or 'apps', both for viewing AR overlays and for contributing to them, it is time to investigate more closely the promise of mobile AR tasks for language learning.

Literature review

The educational advantages of mobile AR derive from the fact that today's location-aware smart devices foster the integration of the real (for example, a real-world language learning context) and the virtual (for example, supporting digital information or communication channels) (Pegrum, 2014). Mobile AR, as the 2011 *Horizon Report* points out, 'is appealing because it aligns with situated learning. Students find connections between their lives and their education through the addition of a contextual layer' (Johnson et al., 2012, p. 29). More broadly, mobile AR promotes the return of embodiment to the learning process (Driver, 2012; FitzGerald et al., 2012;

Potter, 2011). It has been used in tasks involving guided tours of campuses or towns, treasure hunts, and geocaching (essentially GPS-enabled treasure hunts). AR tours and games have been created by researchers and teachers for students, but students have also learned to take a more active role and create AR activities for their peers.

A number of cutting-edge projects have foregrounded the learning of language or literacy through mobile AR tasks. In the 'Alien Contact!' game which formed part of the Handheld Augmented Reality Project (HARP) at Harvard University, students encountered digital content, characters, and literacy and maths tasks on their GPS-enabled mobile devices as they moved around their school grounds, working in teams to discover why aliens had landed on earth (HARP, n.d.; Potter, 2011). In the Mentira game at the University of New Mexico, students of Spanish use iPhones or iPod Touches to seek clues in a historical murder mystery, a process which eventually requires them to navigate a real local Spanish-speaking neighbourhood as they collaborate with peers to identify the murderer (Holden & Sykes, 2011; Pegrum, 2014). In the Visitas de la Colonia game, more advanced students at the same university create guided campus tours for historical colonial characters. On the AR Heritage Trails created by LDR for the Ministry of Education in Singapore, students explore their national heritage with the aid of mobile devices which provide contextually relevant information and require them to complete tasks *in situ*, many of them involving language and literacy skills (Pegrum, 2014). In the MASELTOV project in Europe, users of an integrated Android app will be provided with contextually relevant language support and prompted to practise appropriate language, as well as recording and submitting it for evaluation, as they score gaming points (Pegrum, 2014).

There is considerable evidence of the advantages of situated learning, as established by Lave and Wenger (1991) and others (e.g., Driver, 2012; Naismith, Lonsdale, Vavoula & Sharples, 2006). Situated learning provides a good context for social constructivism and other contemporary progressive pedagogical approaches, as observed by Comas-Quinn, Mardomingo and Valentine (2009):

> Social constructivism sits well within a situative perspective of learning, which concentrates on the influence of the social and cultural context where the learning takes place. Moreover, the particular circumstances in which the learning occurs make it more unique and meaningful to the learner and thus more likely to be absorbed into the learner's acquired knowledge (as is the case for apprentices who learn on the job, for example).
>
> (p. 101)

While it is arguably the case that the ideal situated learning experience for language students would be a country or context where the target language is spoken on a regular basis (Comas-Quinn, Mardomingo and Valentine, 2009), it might be surmised that any target language use with a real-world purpose in a real-world context would lead to better embedding of the language being learned.

Moreover, some evidence has begun to emerge that a real-world context can inspire greater and more detailed target language use than a classroom environment which is at a distance from the context being described. For instance, in a situated writing task involving primary school learners of English in Taiwan, students used mobile devices to write texts on topics stimulated by real-world environments, with their writing scaffolded through suggested words and phrases (Hwang et al., 2011). They could also upload pictures. Finally, they were able to read and comment on their classmates' writing. The combination of a real-world setting with linguistic scaffolding appeared to help students write detailed descriptions. Furthermore, it was found that students in the experimental group significantly outperformed peers in a post-test which involved making sentences about objects in context.

Such activities sit well within a task-based framework, in which the emphasis is on activities that involve a degree of real-world relevance and a genuine communicative outcome (Ellis, 2003). AR facilitates such activities, although of course this depends on its implementation. By linking language learning with the broader environment outside the classroom, and with information in the target language about that environment, teachers can scaffold learners' linguistic interactions in or around that environment, as they access, respond to and even add to this information based on their own experiences. This type of active involvement is a common affordance of social technologies like AR (Thomas & Reinders, 2010).

To date, however, there has been very limited empirical research into the ways in which technology-enhanced situated learning – and specifically mobile AR tasks – might improve the learning and retention of language. The current paper reports on a pilot study investigating key elements of the situated learning enabled by mobile AR.

Methodology

While the cutting-edge AR projects outlined in the previous section hold considerable promise, they are at present out of reach of the average language teacher, who requires a simpler approach which can be implemented using a range of widely available and inexpensive tools. However, there is as yet little evidence of whether, and how, technologically-enhanced situated learning improves some, or any, aspects of students' language learning. Consequently, the present study focused on the underlying principles of mobile AR tasks, which can be realized using a range of common tools, and sought to answer the following questions:

- What are the possible benefits of mobile AR tasks for the learning of descriptive language?
- What are the possible benefits of mobile AR tasks for the learning of discourse markers?

Because of the focus on everyday teaching contexts, it was considered appropriate to adopt an action research approach. Such an approach allows teachers to move beyond individual intuitions about what works in their own classrooms and engage in systematic enquiry whose results can be shared widely (Baumfield, Hall & Wall, 2008). Although it has many variations, action research always involves an action-reflection cycle, and typically includes the following steps: developing a question relating to teaching or learning; gathering ideas relevant to the question; implementing an action to improve the teaching or learning; evaluating the results of the action, for example through observations, surveys or assessments; and disseminating the results, while perhaps starting a new action research cycle (Dudeney et al., 2013).

This study involved English learners creating an orientation tour for English-speaking visitors (specifically, visiting faculty members) to their university's campus. In so doing, students followed the steps which would typically be involved in a mobile AR task, without taking the final step of building the tour using the AR interface of a relevant app. This allowed us to examine the principles underpinning mobile AR without the complication of considering the AR interface itself, and will help ensure that our understanding of the potential and limitations of mobile AR will not become outdated as the AR interfaces themselves change.

In order to make our investigation as specific as possible, we chose to focus on two areas of language whose development we anticipated might benefit from an appropriately constructed mobile AR task. The first of these was the number of detailed descriptions which, in light of the work of Hwang et al. (2011), we expected might increase. The second was the number of uses of discourse markers, or connectors, which we took to include both conjunctive adverbs and conjunctions; we expected these might increase in number as they would be important in constructing commentary for the campus tours.

The participants were two whole classes of first-year students studying at a large university in Bangkok, Thailand. One class was designated as an experimental group and the other as a control group. The experimental group had thirty-four participants, while the control group had thirty-one participants, all aged from nineteen to twenty years. All participants were native speakers of Thai and had been studying English for a minimum of ten years. Both groups took a pre-test on conjunctive adverbs (e.g., nonetheless, otherwise, consequently). The test did not particularly focus on descriptive language because of the enormous range of possible vocabulary which this could encompass, whereas conjunctive adverbs constitute a smaller and more easily identifiable set of target language items. A week after the tour creation and tour-taking activities, both groups took a post-test that was exactly parallel to the pre-test. The test comprised thirty multiple-choice items, half of which were distractors, as seen in the examples below.

- Test item: When you're making this soup, you'll have to keep stirring it. [XXX], it will burn.
  - Likewise
  - Otherwise
- Distractor: Because he always works very [XXX], he is popular with his colleagues.
  - Efficient
  - Efficiently

After the pre-test was completed, students in the experimental group created tours, writing their commentary on handouts using one of two sets of prompts supplied by their teachers as they walked around campus to various preselected sites. Two sets of prompts were created for two reasons. First, it was to help with management of the students; having an entire class of more than thirty students at any one site might have created some disturbance. Secondly, since the experimental group had to not only create a tour, but also take one, a different set of sites was required for the latter activity.

It was noted, on a practical level, that time management became a consideration once students moved outside the classroom, an issue that did not occur with the control group. The students in the control group created tours using the same prompts, but without leaving the classroom; they thus based their commentary on what they already knew or could infer about the various sites.

As mentioned, those in the experimental group also took a tour which had been written by their classmates, but where the language had been corrected by teachers. The handout they used provided some information on the various sites they had to visit (different from the ones they had visited initially) and required them to answer questions on a separate sheet of paper in order to engage them at each site.

The data were analysed as follows. First, the tests were scored, and the scores were analysed statistically, to examine changes in students' use of discourse markers from the pre- to the post-test. Second, a sample of the language produced by students in their tours was subjected to a discourse analysis to reveal patterns in the use of descriptive language and in the use of discourse markers.

Findings and discussion

Statistical analysis of pre- and post-tests

In order to determine whether leaving the physical classroom to create the tours had any discernible effects on the language produced by the students, a number of statistical analyses were run. As some of the data were not normally distributed (the experimental pre-test and post-test and the control group post-test had Shapiro Wilk p-values of .019, 0.001 and 0.001 respectively), we used non-parametric tests[1].

We first established whether there was a significant difference between the experimental pre-test and post-test scores by running a Mann-Whitney U-test. The results are shown in Tables 15.1 and 15.2.

The Mann-Whitney U-test showed that there is no statistically significant difference between the experimental group pre-test and post-test scores ($U = 401$, $p = 0.065$). Secondly, we investigated whether there was a difference between the scores on the control group pre-test and post-test. The results are shown in tables 15.3 and 15.4.

As can be seen from Tables 15.3 and 15.4, there was no significant difference between the control group pre-test and post-test scores ($U = 401$, $p = 0.065$). Next, we looked to see whether there was a significant difference between the experimental and control group pre-test scores. The results are shown in Tables 15.5 and 15.6.

TABLE 15.1 *Experimental group pre-test and post-test mean scores*

Group	N	Mean Rank	Sum of Ranks
Experimental pre-test	31	28.95	897.50
Experimental post-test	35	37.53	1313.50
Total	66		

TABLE 15.2 *Mann-Whitney U-test for experimental group pre-test and post-test scores*

	Experimental pre-test and Experimental post-test scores
Mann-Whitney U	401.500
Wilcoxon W	897.500
Z	−1.846
Asymp. Sig. (2-tailed)	.065

TABLE 15.3 *Control group pre-test and post-test mean scores*

Group	N	Mean Rank	Sum of Ranks
Control pre-test	28	25.36	710.00
Control post-test	31	34.19	1060.00
Total	59		

TABLE 15.4 *Mann-Whitney U-test for control group pre-test and post-test scores*

	Experimental pre-test and Experimental post-test scores
Mann-Whitney U	304.000
Wilcoxon W	710.000
Z	−2.008
Asymp. Sig. (2-tailed)	0.045

TABLE 15.5 *Experimental and control group pre-test mean scores*

Group	N	Mean	Std. Deviation	Std. Error Mean
Experimental pre-test	31	12.9677	1.66301	.29868
Control pre-test	28	12.0357	1.97169	.37261

The t-test shows that there is no statistically significant difference between the experimental and control group pre-test scores, t (57) = 1.97, p = 0.054. However, the p-value is close to the significant level, which indicates that the difference between these two groups approaches significance. Analysis of the post-test scores shows there is no significant difference between the experimental and control group post-test scores (t (64) = −0.747, p = 0.458). These results are show in Tables 15.7 and 15.8.

TABLE 15.6 *Independent t-test scores for experimental and control group pre-test scores*
t-test for Equality of Means

T	df	Sig. (2-tailed)	Mean Difference	Std. Error Difference	95% Confidence Interval of the Difference	
					Lower	Upper
1.969	57	0.054	0.93203	0.47340	−0.01594	1.88000

TABLE 15.7 *Experimental and control group post-test mean scores*

Group	N	Mean	Std. Deviation	Std. Error Mean
Experimental post-test	35	13.6000	1.94331	0.32848
Control post-test	31	13.9355	1.67203	0.30031

TABLE 15.8 *Independent t-test scores for experimental and control group post-test scores*
t-test for Equality of Means

T	df	Sig. (2-tailed)	Mean Difference	Std. Error Difference	95% Confidence Interval of the Difference	
					Lower	Upper
−0.747	64	0.458	−0.33548	0.44917	−1.23281	0.56184

In conclusion, no effects were found for completing the tour, either in terms of improvement for the experimental group from pre-test to post-test, or when comparing scores between the experimental and the control group.

Discourse analysis of tours

An analysis of the discourse patterns demonstrated by students in the experimental group as compared to students in the control group revealed minor differences. The discourse produced in response to three location prompts – the first and last, and one from the middle of each tour – was examined across all groups.

In each case, the text was analysed for the number of occurrences of descriptive language, which took the form of the naming of specific activities (generally verbal phrases) or the giving of specific descriptions (such as descriptions of objects or places). It was then further analysed for the presence of discourse markers, or connectors, beyond those provided in the prompts, which were generally adverbs or prepositions used to link sentences or clauses, or introduce phrases.

Two typical samples of experimental and control group commentary are presented in Figures 15.1 and 15.2 respectively. In each case, the first column contains students' text, reproduced verbatim. Descriptive language is signalled by underlining in the first column and described in the second column. Discourse markers are signalled by bold font in the first column and described in the second column. The third column contains total numbers of descriptive language and discourse markers.

As can be seen, the descriptive language mainly consists of descriptions of activities, e.g., 'contact staff' or 'inquire about your educational information', sometimes as summary activities, or examples of summary activities. Much less frequently, it consists of descriptions of objects, e.g., 'student cards' or 'request form

Experimental Group1

Student text	Key elements of student text	Summary of key elements
contact staff and inquire about your educational information for instance courses register, withdrawing courses, registered problems, filing complaints. For filing complaints, it contains postponing test, dropping your semester and resigning. Furthermore, you can find your lost things here and pronounce student's activities.	specific activity; specific activity (as summary) connector 4 x specific activity specific activity repeated (as summary) 3 x specific activity connector specific activity specific activity	12 x descriptive language (12 activities) 2 x connectors

Experimental Group 2

Student text	Key elements of student text	Summary of key elements
– you can request class schedules and maintains class lists – checking out your grade records and mark – check the result of registration – changes in step of withdrawal – paying for semester fees – asking for general request forms including Transcript, request form for Graduation, request form of resignation and request form for sick or business leave	2 x specific activity specific activity specific activity specific activity specific activity specific activity (as summary) connector 4 x specific description	11 x descriptive language (7 activities & 4 descriptions) 1 x connector

FIGURE 15.1 *Excerpts from sample experimental group tours in response to the first prompt, 'This is our first site. This is the "Registrar Office". If you are a student, here you can . . .'.*

Control Group 1

Student text	Key elements of student text	Summary of key elements
You can register your class and you can move or manage your class schedule like withdrawing. Moreover you can add subject and you can ask for class's receipt. In easy word, you can manage your study schedule everything in here. Also, you can do it in website called "regchula".	specific activity specific activity (as summary) connector specific activity; connector specific activity specific activity connector specific activity (as summary) connector; specific activity	7 x descriptive language (7 activities) 4 connectors

Control Group 2

Student text	Key elements of student text	Summary of key elements
get student's information. If you have problems such as study plane, study register, withdraw etc. you can go there and ask officer for help. In addition you can find or ask for missing things like student cards or whatever you lost there. There's also a registar office's website that you can follow to update information.	specific activity connector connector; 3 x specific activity (as needs) specifc activity (as summary); connector specific activity connector 2 x specific description connector; specific description specific activity	10 x descriptive language (7 activities & 3 descriptions) 5 x connectors

FIGURE 15.2 *Excerpts from sample control group tours in response to the first prompt, 'This is our first site. This is the "Registrar Office". If you are a student, here you can . . .'.*

for sick or Business leave' or, occasionally, places. While a number of sophisticated discourse markers were found, e.g., 'furthermore' or 'in addition', there were also many simpler connectors, e.g., 'like' or 'also'. This was true of both the experimental group and control group tours. Naturally, very simple coordinating conjunctions like 'and', 'but' and 'or' also occurred, but were not counted.

These sample texts illustrate a slight trend towards the inclusion of a greater number of instances of descriptive language – in the form of descriptions of activities or objects and places – by participants in the experimental group. Moreover, experimental group texts were on average a little over 10 per cent longer than control group texts, at 283 versus 255 words respectively. This greater level of description is in line with the aforementioned Taiwanese study (Hwang et al., 2011) which suggested that combining a real-world setting with appropriate linguistic prompts may lead to more detailed descriptive writing.

Conversely, there was a slight but noticeable trend towards the inclusion of more discourse markers by the control group. This might be because, not having specific locational detail to rely on, these students opted for slightly more complex general language. In that sense, it is possible to say that, notwithstanding their less detailed descriptions, the control group exhibited more syntactically complex language use overall. These differences, while small, were apparent across the vast majority of tours.

Recommendations and conclusion

The findings of this research, while preliminary because they are based on a pilot study, yield certain insights into the potential for mobile AR in language learning. In fact, they suggest that some caution is necessary in the implementation of technologically-enhanced situated language learning, specifically in the form of mobile AR tasks. Firstly, the experimental group did not improve its knowledge of discourse markers from pre-test to post-test. Similarly, there was no statistically significant difference on the post-tests between the experimental and the control groups. It would appear, therefore, that the AR task did not help participants in regard to the linguistic items chosen for investigation. Secondly, the discourse analysis of the language produced by the students showed that the principles underpinning mobile AR tasks may privilege the use of certain kinds of language, such as descriptive language, while a traditional classroom setting may privilege other kinds of language, such as discourse markers. This suggests that any use of mobile AR should be balanced with more traditional classroom-based forms of language learning, at least until further research is conducted to more clearly elucidate the potential and the limitations of mobile AR for language learning.

Mobile AR is an increasingly viable approach to technology-enhanced situated learning. With the requisite hardware, software and connectivity becoming more widely and cheaply available, it is worthy of teachers' consideration. However, it is important to determine what kinds of language learning might be enhanced by mobile AR tasks, and considerably more research is needed in this area. Teachers should consider adopting an action research approach to mobile AR, ensuring that they disseminate their results to help build understanding in this field. Teachers can apply the principles of mobile AR – essentially, the principles of technologically-enhanced situated learning – before needing to apply, or even consider, the appropriate AR technologies. Doing so will ensure that our understanding of the potential and limitations of mobile AR will not become outdated even as the specific hardware (devices) and software (apps) continue to develop and improve. If teachers wish to take the final step and use mobile AR technologies, however, they should consider using widely available, inexpensive, user-friendly tools, and disseminate their findings about particular combinations of hardware and software. In our own follow-up research based on our pilot project, we intend to work with a larger cohort of learners, investigating the effects of the mobile AR task on the development of their descriptive language and discourse markers, but taking the task to its logical conclusion with the use of an AR app.

Limitations

A number of limitations to our study must be acknowledged. The study employed intact groups as participants, which limits the generalizability of the data. The data were collected over a relatively brief span of time, so longitudinal effects cannot be determined. Due to logistical difficulties, the participants could only visit a limited number of sites, and were not able to leave the relatively familiar confines of their university. Nor was it feasible, in the limited time available, to take the final step of having students create actual AR tours. Future studies, including our own continuing research, should attempt to overcome some of the limitations inherent in the current study, for example by investigating larger cohorts of students across institutions and locations, tracking students over longer periods, encouraging them to move around wider areas beyond institutional campuses, and engaging with the use of AR interfaces.

Notes

1. We did carry out all analyses using both parametric and non-parametric tests and found the results to be almost identical. Here we report the non-parametric test results.

References

Baumfield, V., Hall, E., & Wall, K. (2008). *Action research in the classroom.* London: Sage.

Comas-Quinn, A., Mardomingo, R., & Valentine, C. (2009). Mobile blogs in language learning: Making the most of informal and situated learning opportunities. *ReCALL*, 21(1), 96–112.

Driver, P. (2012). Pervasive games and mobile technologies for embodied language learning. *International Journal of Computer-Assisted Language Learning and Teaching*, 2(4), 50–63.

Dudeney, G., Hockly, N., & Pegrum, M. (2013). *Digital literacies.* Harlow, Essex: Pearson.

Ellis, R. (2003). *Task-based language learning and teaching.* Oxford: Oxford University Press.

FitzGerald, E., Adams, A., Ferguson, R., Gaved, M., Mor, Y., & Thomas, R. (2012). Augmented reality and mobile learning: The state of the art. In M. Specht, M. Sharples & J. Multisilta (Eds), *mLearn 2012: Proceedings of the 11th International Conference on Mobile and Contextual Learning 2012*, Helsinki, Finland, October 16–18 (pp.62–69).

HARP (Handheld Augmented Reality Project) (n.d.). *Handheld Augmented Reality Project (HARP) & Alien Contact! Unit overview.*

Holden, C., & Sykes, J. (2011). Mentira: Prototyping language-based locative gameplay. In S. Dikkers, J. Martin & B. Coulter (Eds), *Mobile media learning: Amazing uses of mobile devices for learning.* Pittsburgh, PA: ETC Press.

Hwang, W.-Y., Chen, C.-Y., & Chen, H. S. L. (2011). Facilitating EFL writing of elementary school students in familiar situated contexts with mobile devices. In *10th World Conference on Mobile and Contextual Learning: mLearn2011 Conference Proceedings*, Beijing, China, October 18–21 (pp.15–23). Beijing: Beijing Normal University.

Johnson, L., Smith, R., Willis, H., Levine, A., & Haywood, K., (2011). *The 2011 Horizon Report.* Austin, TX: The New Media Consortium.

Lave, J., & Wenger, E. (1991). *Situated learning: Legitimate peripheral participation.* Cambridge, MA: Cambridge University Press.

Naismith, L., Lonsdale, P., Vavoula, G., & Sharples, M. (2006). *Report 11: Literature review in mobile technologies and learning.* Bristol: Futurelab.

Pegrum, M. (2014). *Mobile learning: Languages, literacies and cultures.* London: Palgrave Macmillan.

Potter, G. (2011). Augmented reality and mobile technologies. In A. Kitchenham (Ed.), *Models for interdisciplinary mobile learning: Delivering information to students* (pp.212–230). Hershey, PA: Information Science Reference.

Thomas, M., & Reinders, H. (Eds) (2010). *Task-based language teaching and technology.* New York: Continuum.

Wu, H.-K., Lee, S.W.-Y., Chang, H.-Y., & Liang, J.-C. (2013). Current status, opportunities and challenges of augmented reality in education. *Computers & Education, 62*, 41–49.

PART FIVE

Materials and curriculum design

Introduction

Nigel Harwood

The chapters in this part take various approaches to task-based language teaching (TBLT) and its implementation. In the literature we can find different ideas about what TBLT is and what forms TBLT materials can and should take (e.g., Willis & Willis, 2007), but at some stage the effects of TBLT materials on their consumers need to be measured. Peacock (1997, 1998) has explored the effect of various authentic and inauthentic task types on learners with regard to their usefulness and enjoyableness. Also Hadley (2014) has measured the gains in language proficiency resulting from using the *New Interchange* textbook in a Japanese university context. In this tradition, then, Suzuki and Itagaki compare the relative effectiveness of different types of tasks in terms of acquisition. Second Language Acquisition (SLA) research of this kind should help to reduce the perennial lack of fit between what the research tells us are the activities and approaches to be preferred and the activities and approaches many materials contain (cf. Harwood, 2005).

Park's chapter focuses on the cultural appropriacy of a TBLT curriculum reform in a Korean context. It is clearly important to research the effect of different tasks on users in different settings and to determine how comfortably tasks sit with the local culture. It is noticeable that many of the teachers' and students' views in Park's chapter are at odds with those which would normally be associated with TBLT users (for instance, the strong preference of Park's subjects for teacher-centred classrooms), and that the influence of a high-stakes national test appears to have impacted upon the respondents' views. This strand of research can be seen as following in the footsteps of Holliday (1994), inasmuch as it examines the local appropriacy of (imported) innovative tasks and methodologies. Like studies by Kern (1995), Nunan (1988), Peacock (1998), and Willing (1988), it also usefully compares and contrasts teachers' and students' beliefs regarding most and least preferred activities and tasks; and, as in these earlier studies, mismatches between teacher and learner preferences are found.

Darasawang describes the implementation of and changes to a TBLT syllabus over fourteen years in a Thai university context. Providing us with sample activities and data from teacher and student course evaluations, Darasawang explains how and why the syllabus evolved over time to address the concerns of both parties, moving from a task-based to a 'weaker' task-oriented form of TBLT. It is clear from this account that some of the aims of the programme which are often associated with TBLT, such as learner training and reflection, were not straightforward to implement.

Widodo's chapter is a longitudinal study of how TBLT was implemented in an English for Occupational Purposes classroom in Indonesia over the course of a year. The class focused on hotel hospitality, and interview data describes students' reactions to and evaluation of the materials, while excerpts from students' dialogues as they attempted the tasks reveals the rhetorical aims that were fulfilled. Like Darasawang,

Widodo also usefully itemises some of the difficulties encountered when attempting to introduce this TBLT approach.

To close this section, Tomlinson raises key questions for teachers and materials writers wishing to use or produce TBLT materials. For instance, what are the pros and cons of 'strong' and 'weak' versions of TBLT? Should the language to be used in the tasks be predetermined or be allowed to emerge as the materials are being used? What should the aims of TBLT materials be, what kind of tasks should be used, and how should they be sequenced? Tomlinson also speaks of potential resistance from teachers, learners' parents, and publishers to 'strong' TBLT lessons, these parties being worried about the perceived lack of focus on language/grammar. He also notes some of the compromises he has had to make to get textbook publishers to accept his own TBLT materials, bringing to mind other accounts which show how textbook writers must satisfy many publishing requirements, sometimes requirements they disagree with (e.g., Bell & Gower, 2011; Feak & Swales, 2014; Mares, 2003; Singapore Wala, 2003).

In sum then, while all the authors in this section retain their faith in TBLT and its potential efficacy, they encourage us to consider the various types of TBLT which are at the teacher's and materials writer's disposal, and to carefully calibrate the type of TBLT chosen to best meet the needs of the local context.

References

Bell, J., & Gower, R. (2011). Writing course materials for the world: A great compromise. In B. Tomlinson (Ed.), *Materials development in language teaching* (2nd ed., pp.135–150). Cambridge: Cambridge University Press.

Feak, C. B., & Swales, J. M. (2014). Tensions between the old and the new in EAP textbook revision: A tale of two projects. In N. Harwood (Ed.), *English language teaching textbooks: Content, consumption, production* (pp. 299–319). Basingstoke: Palgrave Macmillan.

Hadley, G. (2014). Global textbooks in local contexts: an empirical investigation of effectiveness. In N. Harwood (Ed.), *English language teaching textbooks: Content, consumption, production* (pp.205–238). Basingstoke: Palgrave Macmillan.

Harwood, N. (2005). What do we want EAP teaching materials for? *Journal of English for Academic Purposes, 4*, 149–161.

Holliday, A. (1994). *Appropriate methodology and social context*. Cambridge: Cambridge University Press.

Kern, R. G. (1995). Students' and teachers' beliefs about language learning. *Foreign Language Annals, 28*, 71–92.

Mares, C. (2003). Writing a coursebook. In B. Tomlinson (Ed.), *Developing materials for language teaching* (pp.130–140). London: Continuum.

Nunan, D. (1988). *The learner-centred curriculum*. Cambridge: Cambridge University Press.

Peacock, M. (1997). The effect of authentic materials on the motivation of EFL learners. *ELT Journal, 51*, 144–156.

Peacock, M. (1998). Exploring the gap between teachers' and learners' beliefs about 'useful' activities for EFL. *International Journal of Applied Linguistics, 8*, 233–250.

Singapore Wala, D. A. (2003). Publishing a coursebook: Completing the materials development circle. In B. Tomlinson (Ed.), *Developing materials for language teaching* (pp.141–161). London: Continuum.

Willing, K. (1988). *Learning styles in adult migrant education*. Adelaide: National Curriculum Resource Centre.

Willis, D., & Willis, J. (2007). *Doing task-based teaching*. Oxford: Oxford University Press.

16

A Needs Analysis for a Korean Middle School EFL General English Curriculum

Moonyoung Park

Summary

Since the early 2000s, task-based language teaching (TBLT) has made a considerable impact on English education policy, curriculum design, materials development, and classroom teaching in Korean English as a Foreign Language (EFL) contexts. Although the TBLT approach seems to be applicable, the feasibility of TBLT needs to be examined in Korean contexts in which different cultural and educational backgrounds exist. This curriculum evaluation study was motivated by an emerging need from school administrators, English teachers, and students for the improvement of an English curriculum at a Korean middle school. A needs analysis survey was conducted with 185 secondary EFL learners and twelve full-time English teachers in Korea. The results were triangulated with Korean national curriculum guidelines and local institutional contexts. Needs discrepancies and consistencies between the two groups were identified and suggestions focusing on the potential of computer-assisted TBLT in the Korean secondary EFL context are offered. After triangulating the needs of students, teachers, the institution, and the national curriculum, it can be concluded that students and teachers pursue fluency by enhancing English communication skills as well as accuracy by practising English grammar and reading comprehension. Through well-developed tasks, students may best acquire the target language by engaging in various communicative activities (e.g., productive or receptive, and oral and written tasks) that they are likely to encounter in real-world contexts. Additionally, integrating technology in the implementation of TBLT makes language learning and teaching more effective by offering a variety of language input, and by expanding students' learning experiences in real contexts.

Introduction

TBLT has become one of the most commonly discussed language teaching approaches in the field of instructed second language acquisition since the 1980s with influences reaching English education policy, curriculum design, materials development, and classroom teaching. Due to researchers', syllabus designers', and educators' substantial interest in TBLT, many studies have been conducted which propose a variety of instructional ideas for using tasks for language teaching (Lee, J. F., 2000; Willis & Willis, 2007). Most recently, Norris (2009) defined TBLT as an approach to second or foreign language education that integrated theoretical and empirical foundations for good pedagogy with a focus on tangible learning outcomes in the form of 'tasks' – that is, what learners are able to do with the language. Researchers' perspectives differ to a certain degree in regard to what characterizes a task and how it is applied in the classroom; however, they all seem to agree that learners can best acquire the target language by engaging in activities that they will likely encounter in real-world communicative contexts.

In recognition of the importance of communicative-oriented teaching, the Ministry of Education (MOE) encouraged Korean EFL teachers to develop students' communicative competence by incorporating student-oriented TBLT (Ministry of Education and Human Resources, 2007). However, actual practice in English classes in public education settings in Korea does not yet correspond to the needs and expectations of the national curriculum for several reasons, which agree with the findings on studies evaluating the feasibility of TBLT in Asian contexts (McDonough & Chaikitmongkol, 2007; Yoon, 2004). Accordingly, understanding the local context is the most important step before implementing any new teaching approaches or methods.

The research study discussed in this chapter describes the use of a student and teacher needs analysis as a primary source of information to understand the local implementation of the national English curriculum in the Korean EFL context as well as to collect evidence for how to make innovations to the existing English curriculum. Given the intended uses stated above, the following research questions were posed:

1 What English needs do secondary EFL learners perceive in Korea?
2 What are secondary EFL learners' classroom participation preferences in Korea?
3 What are secondary EFL learners' preferred learning strategies in Korea?
4 What are secondary EFL learners' preferred lesson topics in Korea?
5 What are secondary EFL learners' perceptions about the use of computers and the internet in English classes in Korea?

Review of needs analysis literature

Prior to engaging in a needs analysis, it is important to understand motivations and parameters guiding the process for needs analysis. According to Long (2005), a needs analysis can identify language learners' needs and related tasks in context-specific language programmes. Long and Norris (2000) also emphasize the role of a needs analysis for the successful establishment and evolution of a TBLT language programme. The findings from needs analyses enable the development of courses and teaching materials that are tailored to the specific requirements of stakeholders in specific contexts. Such efforts will lead to an efficient, effective, and successful language programme.

Needs analyses are used not only for the development of language programmes, but also for programme evaluation and curriculum improvement (Alderson & Scott, 1992). Many researchers have implemented needs analyses in curriculum design for language programmes focusing on learner and instructor needs of ESL learners' communication skills (Ferris & Tagg, 1996; Watanabe, 2006). However, few studies have been conducted on needs analysis in EFL contexts (Seedhouse, 1995). Three studies by Choi (2006), Park (1997), and Park and Son (2009) integrated needs analysis methods in evaluating English language programmes. However, these studies relied heavily on questionnaires which contained items that were insufficiently specific and/ or inclusive for gathering enough information to fully understand stakeholder needs and evaluating the programmes. Another limitation of these studies was, arguably, the usefulness of the findings for improving programmes. Furthermore, little research has been done in EFL secondary public school settings at large, presumably due to the heavy focus on college entrance exams, rigid English curricula, textbooks, and lack of recognition of stakeholders, especially the learners. The limitations of previous studies motivated me to focus on secondary learners in public school settings, and to frame my study through an explanation of how the findings of the needs analysis and evaluation were used to improve the current English course.

The study: Korean EFL classroom needs analysis

This curriculum evaluation study was conducted at a Korean middle school, and its intended users included students, English teachers, school administrators, and the evaluator. The intended uses of the project were: (a) to understand the students' and English teachers' needs for English teaching and learning; and (b) to plan revisions to the current language curriculum on the basis of the needs analysis findings.

The evaluation was conducted at Middle School A located in a large metropolitan city in Korea. The study adopts a needs analysis survey focusing on identifying learners' needs, preferences about learning strategies, style, tasks and topics, and perceptions about the use of computers and the use of the internet. First, to understand societal needs, the goals and content of the national English curriculum were explored through a document analysis. Second, the institutional context of the middle school was investigated from the school webpage and personal communication with the English teachers of the school. Third, the perceptions of students and teachers were investigated through two surveys. In Korean EFL school settings, English language instruction is required to be in accordance with the national curriculum, which also mandates which English textbooks are used in the school. To better understand the current English curriculum of the school, information from multiple sources was gathered, including from: (a) the text of the national curriculum for English education; (b) the English language textbook used in conjunction with the national curriculum; (c) the school's website; (d) the school's documents on English programme innovation; and (e) student and teacher testimonies about perceived language education needs.

The study targeted two groups of informants: students and teachers at Middle School A. One survey was administered to 204 first-year middle school students. All students were male and their ages ranged between thirteen and fourteen years. The return rate for the survey was 100 per cent; however, 19 out of 204 students' responses were excluded from the analysis as they were incomplete. A total of 185 students' responses were selected for data analysis. For the teachers' survey, twelve full-time English teachers from the school responded to the survey. Nine were male, three were female, and their teaching experience ranged from four to seventeen years.

The needs analysis questionnaires were based on Watanabe's (2006) utilization-focused needs analysis survey for curriculum improvement in Japanese EFL high school contexts, which was developed from Naganuma and Yoshida's (2003) 'can-do' survey and van Ek's (1975) list of language functions. The student survey was administered at the end of the second semester, a time when students can be assumed to have settled in and adjusted sufficiently to public English education under the national English curriculum. Students completed their online survey in the school computer lab during the English class time and under the supervision of the English teacher. The teacher survey was administered at the same time, and teachers used their personal computers at school to complete it.

The online survey was composed of open-ended and closed-response items. Open-ended responses aimed to obtain insights into students' and teachers' general needs regarding the use of English by the end of middle school. The closed-response survey items sought to obtain information from respondents in six subsections: (a) target tasks based on the four language skills; (b) language use contexts; (c) classroom participation style; (d) topics; (e) learning strategies; and (f) computer-assisted activities.

Student and teacher perceptions: the need for both accuracy and fluency

Data from open-ended questions on respondent needs for the use of English and computers were translated into English and categorized. Descriptive statistics were used to show how students and teachers perceive the degree of importance of the six subsections. As the number of teacher participants was small, both teachers' and students' responses were compared only in a descriptive way. The survey results showed a variety of needs from the students and the teachers. In this section, their perceptions of English needs are triangulated with societal needs and institutional needs.

The social context: English education in general

After realizing the shortcomings of previous grammar-oriented English curricula, the Korean government introduced communicative language teaching (CLT) as an ideal approach to achieve learner communicative competence (Yoon, 2004). However, such changes were generally regarded as being too fluency-oriented and have led to a lack of learners' grammatical accuracy. To correct previous shortcomings, the 7th national curriculum for English education was created as a grammatical-functional syllabus including both communicative functions and grammatical structures. However, the new curriculum still emphasizes communicative competence over grammatical knowledge shifting English teaching methodology to more communicative approaches, such as CLT and TBLT. Though official syllabuses have not been explicitly labelled task-based, the concept of 'English learning through tasks' has become an intrinsic part of professional discourse, and local TBLT-based innovations are frequently introduced (Ministry of Education and Human Resources, 2007).

Along with the national English curriculum, a more pressing issue appears to be the college entrance examination, or the Korean version of the Scholastic Aptitude Test (KSAT). The English section of the KSAT has a washback effect on English education. In reality, most English exams developed by English teachers at middle and high schools employ test methods and formats similar to the KSAT. The most serious problem seems to be that the KSAT does not include speaking and writing components, thus leading to very little, if any, teaching of speaking and writing in secondary school settings. This listening and reading orientation of the KSAT seriously violates the national English curriculum, which mandates a communicative, integrated skills approach. The following section discusses the institutional context of the middle school where this study was conducted in order to gain insights into the English needs of the institution.

The institutional context of the English program

School A is a private middle school with a good reputation among parents and students due to graduated students' high scores on the annual nationwide achievement test. Students are assigned to the middle school by a lottery within the school district. Most students enter the school at age thirteen and finish at age fifteen and the school grades, 1–3, correspond roughly to grades 7–9 in the North American system. Each grade has ten classes with thirty-five to thirty-eight students per class. In spring 2010, there were 1,090 students enrolled in the middle school taking general English education courses taught by ten full-time Korean English teachers and one native English-speaking teacher. Among 1,090 students, 350 were enrolled in the 1st grade, 360 were enrolled in the 2nd grade, and 380 were enrolled in the 3rd grade. After 3rd grade, students are supposed to choose between general education and vocational high schools. As the national high school entrance exam was discontinued in 1998, midterm and final English exams, the only bases of students' grades become high-stakes tests. To prepare for these high-stakes tests, more than 70 per cent of the students receive private education, potentially attending private language institutes and paying for private tutoring and home-school materials.

Survey data

Tables 16.1 to 16.5 summarize the descriptive statistics and open-ended responses of teachers' and students' English needs by the end of middle school (reading, listening/speaking, writing, and foreign language use) (Table 16.1), preferred student participation

TABLE 16.1 Teachers' and students' perception of middle school English needs

Item	Description	Teachers (N = 12)			Students (N = 185)		
		M	SD	Rank	M	SD	Rank
R 1	Read a text from English textbook with correct pronunciation.	3.58	0.9	18	3.26	0.99	5
R 2	Understand words, expressions, & grammar rules in the textbook.	4.17	0.58	2	3.3	0.99	4
R 3	Understand a text equivalent to the level of the textbook.	3.92	0.79	5	3.35	0.98	3
R 4	Understand the main idea of easy stories or novels in English.	3.92	0.52	6	3.08	1.09	11
R 5	Choose & read an interesting article from newspapers/magazines.	3.25	0.97	26	2.75	1.05	24
R 6	Extract necessary info in English from internet website.	3.25	1.14	27	2.79	1.06	20
R 7	Answer the reading section of college entrance English exam.	3.92	0.79	7	3.06	1.09	12
LS1	Engage in a simple daily conversation with foreigners living in Korea.	4	0.74	3	3.49	1.04	1
LS2	Introduce oneself in English.	4.5	0.67	1	3.37	1.01	2
LS3	Talk with a foreigner about what their interest is.	3.67	0.99	13	2.98	1.07	14
LS4	Explain direction when asked by a foreigner on the street.	4	0.95	4	3.22	1.01	6
LS5	Introduce Korean culture and custom in English to a foreign student.	3.17	1.34	30	2.66	1.09	29
LS6	Exchange opinions on personal stories/familiar topics with a friend.	3.5	1.24	21	2.7	1.11	27
LS7	Exchange opinions on social problems with one's friend.	2.92	1	37	2.49	1.16	39
LS8	Understand the main message/ideas of the English pop songs.	3.42	0.9	23	2.87	1.08	16
LS9	Sing one's favourite English song.	3.75	0.97	11	3.11	1.15	10
LS10	Understand the main idea of the favourite TV shows and movies.	3.5	0.91	22	2.78	1.10	21
LS11	Tell the summary of the favourite TV shows and movies to a friend.	3.08	1.24	34	2.53	1.13	37
LS12	Exchange feelings and opinions about TV shows & movies.	3	1.04	36	2.63	1.15	31
LS13	Deliver a speech or give a presentation in English.	2.92	1.38	38	2.85	1.12	17
LS14	Speak English with careful attention to rhythm, intonation, and pronunciation.	2.5	1.45	39	2.69	1.10	28
LS15	Answer the questions in the listening section of entrance exams.	3.83	0.94	10	3.15	1.15	8
LS16	Pass the English interview in the college entrance exam.	3.58	0.67	19	2.62	1.16	32
W 1	Keep a diary in English.	3.42	0.9	24	2.91	1.06	15
W 2	Write English essay.	3.25	1.14	28	2.6	1.07	33

Code	Description				
W 3	Communicate with foreigners by online chatting, or e-mail.	3.67	0.78	14	2.81	1.12	18
W 4	Write a summary of a story, novel, or other people's opinions.	3.17	1.03	31	2.59	1.09	34
W 5	Write opinions about a story, novel, or other people's opinions.	3.08	1.08	35	2.59	1.08	35
W 6	Write thoughts & feelings about one's favourite songs, movies, and TV.	3.17	1.12	32	2.71	1.07	26
W 7	Request/fill in an application form from an institution abroad.	3.17	1.34	33	2.57	1.11	36
W 8	Answer composition questions in the college entrance exams.	3.25	1.06	29	2.81	1.13	19
W 9	Answer grammar & vocabulary questions in the school exams.	3.75	0.87	12	2.76	1.10	23
F 1	Get minimal things done in English when travelling abroad.	3.67	0.99	15	3.15	1.02	9
F 2	Communicate with the local people while travelling/study abroad.	3.67	1.07	16	3.17	1.04	7
F 3	Communicate with a host family during a study programme.	3.92	0.9	8	3.03	1.06	13
F 4	Read course descriptions and choose a course when studying abroad.	3.58	0.67	20	2.77	1.09	22
F 5	Complete the necessary task in a foreign country.	3.92	0.79	9	2.64	1.10	30
F 6	Communicate with students in the university/language school abroad.	3.67	0.65	17	2.75	1.17	25
F 7	Go abroad to work or do volunteer work.	3.42	0.67	25	2.5	1.13	38

styles and learning strategies (Table 16.2), preferred topics (Table 16.3), and open-ended responses of teacher and student preferences of overall in-class activities (Table 16.4) and preferred computer-assisted activities (Table 16.5). Students and teachers were asked to indicate the degree of agreement with various skills-based needs on a five-point Likert scale (1, strongly disagree to 5, strongly agree). A five-point scale was chosen in order not to force participants to either 'agree' or 'disagree', so that the findings would not reduce the reliability of the scale. To analyse the distribution of the teacher and student responses, the means, standard deviations, and ranks are presented.

Results of the teacher and student survey

Teachers' and students' perception of middle school English needs

Teachers Despite the small number of teacher participants, the teachers' survey results indicated somewhat consistent patterns throughout the subsections. Most teachers acknowledged that reading tasks are necessary with items R2, R3, R4, and R7 ranked in the top ten out of thirty-nine items. Among reading tasks, teachers perceived that students should deal with vocabulary, grammar, and the main idea from the English textbook (R2–R4). In addition, R7 (*Answer the questions in the reading section of college entrance exam*) was also regarded as highly necessary. However, using authentic materials from the newspaper and magazine (R5 and R6) were considered the least necessary among the reading tasks.

Introduce oneself in English (LS2) was perceived as the most important task for middle school students. Students' overall ability to communicate with foreigners on daily topics (LS1–LS4) was marked as very important. On the contrary, teacher perceptions of tasks that need complex functions and accuracy, such as exchanging opinions on social problems (LS7), delivering speeches, and speaking English with careful attention to rhythm, intonation, and pronunciation (LS13, LS14), were considered the least important tasks. This may be due to the teachers' concern about task difficulty compared to the students' proficiency level.

Teachers considered writing tasks less important than any other skills. All of the writing tasks were ranked lower than 24 in the overall ranking except two tasks: W3 (*Writing an e-mail and online chatting*) and W9 (*Answering writing sections in the English tests*) which were ranked 14 and 12 respectively. This suggests that teachers acknowledge the importance of practising daily communication as well as preparing for high-stakes tests.

The ability to use English abroad was the second most strongly agreed upon set of tasks teachers believed students needed by the end of middle school. As the school provides students with opportunities such as travelling abroad and exchange student programmes, *communicate with host family* (F3) and *complete necessary tasks at the bank, post office, school office* (F5) were ranked the 8th and 9th most important tasks overall.

Students Students perceived a stronger need for reading than any other skills: listening and speaking, writing, and foreign use. Among reading tasks, English textbook-related tasks such as reading a textbook with the correct pronunciation, understanding vocabulary, grammar, and main ideas from the English textbook (R1–R4), were viewed as highly important by the students. It is understandable that most questions in the high-stakes tests, such as midterm and final exams, are taken from the textbook.

Overall, student needs for listening and speaking tasks are very similar to teacher perceptions. *Engage in a simple daily conversation* (LS1) and *introduce oneself in English* (LS2) were ranked 1st and 2nd among the thirty-nine tasks in the four skills. Tasks involving explaining directions to foreigners (LS4), singing English pop songs (LS9), and answering questions in listening tests (LS15) were also perceived as highly necessary by the students. Contrary to the teacher perceptions, the students found a strong necessity for *delivering a speech or giving a presentation in English* (LS13).

Similar to the results of the teachers, the students viewed the writing tasks as less relevant, except for keeping a diary in English (W1), writing e-mails, online chatting in English (W3), and answering composition questions in college entrance exams (W8). All of the writing tasks were ranked lower than 15. These results indicate that students paid attention to practising personal communication as well as preparing for high-stakes tests.

Students appeared to have high expectations in regard to communicating with local people (F2) and achieving communicative tasks (F1) while travelling abroad or during a home-stay programme abroad. It can be assumed that travelling abroad opportunities provided by the school may have aroused students' interest. In addition, several listening and speaking questions in high-stakes tests ask about situational conversations similar to F1 and F2, so these examination question trends may also influence student needs.

Teachers' and students' perception of participation style and learning strategy

Teachers The most preferred classroom participation style was teacher-centred, followed by pair work, individual work, and group work. These findings indicate that there seem to be few opportunities for students to be involved in communication activities. The findings for learning strategies showed that teachers regard strategies for communicative competence and effective input as the most important, prioritizing *simulating conversational situations* (St9), and '*to listen and read many English sentences and understand them without paying too much attention to grammar*' (St8). However, teachers also believe in the effectiveness of paying attention to accuracy through memorization: '*to memorize many words and idioms*' (St1), '*to memorize many English sentences from the textbook*' (St3), and '*to understand and memorize grammar*' (St2).

Students Students' most preferred classroom participation style was teacher-centred, followed by individual work, pair work, and group work. These findings indicate that the students seem to be more familiar with teacher-centred and individual styles, both of which are more suitable for receptive tasks, rather than communicative tasks. The findings for students' learning strategies suggested that they perceived memorizing vocabulary and idioms (St1) and grammar (St2) as the 1st and 3rd most effective way to learn English. They also believe in the effectiveness of solving comprehension questions (St5). Also worthy of note is that this result

TABLE 16.2 *Teachers' and students' perception of participation style and learning strategy*

Item	Description	Teacher (N = 12)			Students (N = 185)		
		M	SD	Rank	M	SD	Rank
Part1	Teacher centred	4.08	0.67	1	3.3	1.12	1
Part2	Individual	3.42	0.90	3	3.15	1.11	2
Part3	Pair work	3.67	0.78	2	2.61	1.06	3
Part4	Group work	3.42	0.90	4	2.59	1.08	4
St1	Memorize many words and idioms.	4.33	0.65	3	3.55	1.06	1
St2	Understand and memorize grammar.	4.08	0.67	5	3.28	0.98	3
St3	Memorize many English sentences from the textbook.	4.17	0.39	4	3.04	1.04	9
St4	Solve many grammar exercises.	3.92	0.67	7	3.14	1.03	7
St5	Solve many reading comprehension questions.	3.92	0.67	8	3.44	1.02	2
St6	Accurately translate English into Korean.	3	1.04	9	3.05	1.01	8
St7	Verbalize or write correct sentences using words, idioms, and grammar rules one memorized.	4.08	0.90	6	3.19	0.97	4
St8	Listen & read English sentences & understand them without paying too much attention to grammar.	4.5	0.67	2	3.16	0.97	5
St9	Simulate real conversational situations and use English.	4.58	0.52	1	3.16	0.95	6

Note: Part# = Participation style; St# = Learning strategy.

seems to be consistent with current English teaching practice in the classroom when they prepare for midterm and final exams.

Teachers' and students' topic preferences

Teacher The teachers rated student-preferred topics they have introduced in English class. The teachers perceived that students were highly interested in foreign culture, followed by hobbies, travelling, food and cooking, and music. These results indicate that those daily topics have been frequently introduced in the school's English textbooks. It is surprising that school-related topics, such as club activities and school festivals, were rarely introduced to students by most teachers.

TABLE 16.3 *Teachers' and students' topic preferences*

Item	Description	Teacher (N = 12)			Student (N = 185)		
		M	SD	Rank	M	SD	Rank
T1	Language in the world	2.83	0.72	24	2.47	0.74	24
T2	Foreign culture, people	4	0.60	1	2.79	0.68	4
T3	World history	3	1.21	20	2.66	0.71	8
T4	Famous historical sites	2.83	0.94	25	2.86	0.61	3
T5	Current world events	3.08	1.24	18	2.66	0.71	9
T6	Korean around the world	3.42	0.79	10	2.88	0.68	2
T7	Korean culture	3.33	0.78	13	2.9	0.69	1
T8	Domestic news	2.75	1.14	30	2.48	0.73	22
T9	Narrative stories	3.5	1.00	8	2.78	0.79	5
T10	Literature	3	1.04	21	2.63	0.77	14
T11	Drama (play)	3.33	0.78	14	2.46	0.78	26
T12	Art	2.83	0.72	26	2.58	0.71	18
T13	Music	3.75	0.75	5	2.69	0.71	6
T14	Movies	3.58	0.67	6	2.69	0.75	7
T15	Fashion	3.25	1.14	15	2.46	0.77	27
T16	TV drama	3.5	0.91	9	2.37	0.80	30
T17	Animation	3	1.13	22	2.42	0.80	29
T18	People in show biz	2.83	1.19	27	2.47	0.76	25
T19	Education	3	1.13	23	2.62	0.80	15
T20	Psychology	2.75	1.36	31	2.21	0.78	34
T21	Science	2.58	1.17	33	2.6	0.85	17
T22	Nature/environment	2.83	0.84	28	2.66	0.87	10
T23	Computer	2.83	0.72	29	2.62	0.83	16
T24	Animal	3.25	0.97	16	2.64	0.76	12
T25	Sports	3.42	1.00	11	2.64	0.75	13
T26	Travelling	3.83	1.03	3	2.52	0.76	21
T27	Food, cooking	3.83	0.84	4	2.55	0.73	20
T28	Homeroom	3.08	0.90	19	2.17	0.80	35
T29	Club activity	2.67	1.07	32	2.45	0.79	28
T30	School festivals	2.58	0.79	34	2.37	0.79	31
T31	School work (study)	3.42	1.08	12	2.56	0.86	19
T32	Future course	3.25	1.22	17	2.22	0.83	33
T33	Friendship	3.58	1.00	7	2.48	0.80	23
T34	Hobby	3.92	0.67	2	2.65	0.79	11
T35	Religion	2.25	1.29	35	2.37	0.79	32

Students The students' favourite topics were ranked as follows: Korean culture (T7), Koreans around the world (T6), famous historical sites (T4), and foreign culture and people (T2). The popular topics among students were related to their nationality, culture, and history. The least popular topics were homeroom (T28), psychology (T20), future courses (T32), and religion (T35).

Teachers' and students' preferences for overall class activities

TABLE 16.4 *Teachers' and students' preferences for overall class activities*

Teachers	N	Students	N
Authentic & interesting online materials	4	Online materials	34
Reward system, like token, sticker & candies	2	Games (classroom activities)	15
Gestures, changing voice tone	1	PPT Presentation	11
Kinaesthetic warm-ups	1	CD-ROM	5
Games (board game, Jeopardy, bingo, etc.)	1	Cramming for a quiz	5
		English pop songs	4
		Discussion in English	3

Teachers More than 30 per cent of the teachers considered online materials as their preferred teaching realia. They also mentioned reward systems, kinaesthetic warm-ups, and games. However, what is noteworthy is that teachers seem to use a limited number of classroom activities in spite of teaching young language learners.

Students About 38 per cent of students considered computer-assisted tools with online materials, power point presentation, and CD-ROMs as their preferred teaching realia. They also mentioned in-class games, cramming for quizzes, singing songs, and discussions in English as their preferred learning methods.

Teachers' and students' preferences for computer-assisted activities

Teachers The results for teachers' preferred computer-assisted activities revealed that the teachers primarily use computer software in class. This is understandable

TABLE 16.5 *Teachers' and students' preferences of computer-assisted activities*

Teachers	N	Students	N
Computer software	5	Playing computer games	17
Review last session	1	Watching a video clip	15
Quiz show	1	Chatting in English	11
Practising target phrase	1	Listening to English pop songs	9
Games (board game, Jeopardy, bingo, etc.)	1	Writing with E-pals	9
		Internet surfing	9

since English textbook publishing companies provide CD-ROMs containing textbook texts and audio-recorded data.

Students The results for student-preferred computer-assisted activities revealed that they seem to be interested in playing computer games, watching video clips, listening to English pop songs, chatting, and writing e-mails to E-pals. Such results are to be expected given young learners' experience with computers and the internet.

Discussion

Q1. Comparison of English needs

Overall, both students and teachers acknowledged a strong need for reading skills, with these items having the highest mean ratings. There was also agreement between teachers and students that writing is the least important skill. Nevertheless, when it comes to their specific needs throughout the four skills, conversation skills appear to be the most important skills that middle school students should acquire by the end of middle school English education. This finding is also consistent with the government's goal of improving communicative skills, like daily small talk. However, whereas the national curriculum emphasizes writing skills as a way of improving communicative competence, students and teachers did not view them as necessary talk. This is a clear inconsistency among the perceptions of the students, teachers, and the national curriculum.

The highest mean ratings for all seven reading tasks by both students and teachers indicate the necessity of reading ability. Students and teachers both recognized the importance of English textbook-related reading tasks, such as understanding vocabulary, grammar rules, and main ideas. Yet, compared to students' perceptions, teachers wanted to prepare for reading sections in the high-stakes exams. Students' perceptions about the necessity of reading textbooks with correct pronunciation differed from teachers' perceptions. Introducing authentic spoken English through online resources and increased use of the English textbook embedded CD-ROM may be useful for students.

The responses from students and teachers indicated a great deal of similarity. Students and teachers strongly acknowledged the significance of daily conversation, including introducing oneself and explaining directions. Additionally, both groups also placed strong emphasis on singing one's favourite English songs and preparing for the listening section of high-stakes exams. However, contrary to students' and teachers' negative attitudes, the national curriculum placed a greater emphasis on the importance of expressing one's opinion in English, introducing Korean culture, and giving presentations. This gap between achieving goals in the national English curriculum and students' and teachers' perceptions of speaking needs may demonstrate the limitations of a top-down implementation of national curriculum in local school settings.

Both students and teachers did not feel a strong need for writing, which received the lowest mean ratings among the four skills. However, both groups still acknowledged the necessity of writing e-mails and online chatting. In terms of the writing section in high-stakes exams, teachers recognized the importance of grammar and vocabulary, whereas students preferred composition itself. In contrast to teacher perceptions, students placed greater emphasis on keeping a diary. The national curriculum emphasizes the importance of informal writing activities, such as diary writing, essay composition about oneself and family, and personal letters written to friends about school life. These goals in the national curriculum are also consistent with student and teacher preferences for informal writing over formal writing. However, considering the fact that English writing begins from 7th grade in the national English curriculum, it may be more beneficial and motivating to introduce a variety of real-world writing opportunities to students based on their needs and interests. Teachers may need to encourage students to engage in different genres of writing, including formal writing, by allowing them opportunities to be involved in authentic writing tasks.

Students acknowledged the necessity of using English for travelling abroad (conversations at the airport and on a plane, and communicating with local people), whereas teachers wanted students to complete necessary tasks at the bank, post office, and school offices. Though the school used to provide a short-term travelling abroad opportunity for volunteering students, students and teachers expressed a strong need for achieving communicative tasks in specific contexts. To better meet those needs, incorporating such target tasks into the English curriculum may be effective.

Q2. Comparison of participation styles; and
Q3. Learning strategies

Overall, there was strong agreement between the students and teachers that teacher-centred English classes are the most preferred participation style. There seems to be a clear discrepancy between their most highly regarded English needs (engaging in daily conversation and introducing oneself) and preferred or self-reported class participation style. Considering the findings from the data analysis of the national English curriculum and the institutional context of the English programme, this was not surprising. On average, there are thirty-one students in one class, therefore, it may be challenging for the English teacher to give individual feedback and pay attention to all students. Besides, high-stakes exams such as national college entrance exams and midterm and final exams have washback effects on English education, especially on the class participation style. Skewed emphasis on the listening, reading and grammar-oriented high-stakes exams may have an influence on class participation style as well. To better meet both groups' English needs, it may be beneficial to implement well-organized pair and group interaction activities.

In the case of learning strategies, there was a clear gap between students and teachers. Students believed that memorizing words and idioms, and solving comprehension questions were the most effective ways of learning English; on the other hand, teachers believed simulating real conversational situations, using English, and listening to and reading English sentences without paying too much attention to grammar, were the most useful strategies. Contrary to teacher perceptions, students expressed strong needs for understanding and memorizing English grammar. These contradictions in learning strategies may suggest that students were far more willing to focus on accuracy, while teachers aimed to enhance students' fluency and communicative competence. Improving fluency as well as accuracy is also greatly stressed by the national English curriculum. In response to these needs, innovation in current language teaching and learning approaches may be required so that students can still enhance their language fluency without sacrificing accuracy.

Q4. Comparison of topic preference

There was a gap between what students like to talk about versus what is presented in actual English class. Topics related to nationality, culture or history, such as Korean culture, Korean people around the world, famous historical sites, and foreign culture and people, were highly preferred by most students. On the other hand, teachers actually introduced topics, such as foreign culture and people, hobbies, travelling, cooking, and music, which often appear in the English textbooks and English workbooks for reading comprehension. Based on these findings, depending entirely on the topics in the English textbook may be an inadequate way to increase students' motivation and interest. It may be useful to introduce students' preferred topics through online audio-visual teaching materials to better serve their needs.

Q5. Comparison of class activity preference

The open-ended responses from students and teachers revealed similar tendencies in preferred class activities. Students and teachers noticeably acknowledged the value of online materials and the use of computers. As for preferred computer-assisted activities, students expressed strong needs for online materials, such as online games, video clips, and web surfing. Computer-assisted communication activities, such as writing with E-pals and online chatting, are also highly noted by students. Students' preferences and needs are consistent with the national English curriculum in which computer-assisted language learning (CALL) and multimedia-assisted language learning (MALL) are highlighted. Contrary to students' diversified preferences and needs regarding the use of computers, teachers appeared to utilize English textbooks' CD-ROMs for their computer-assisted class activities. To satisfy the needs of students and the requirements of the national curriculum, teachers may need continuing opportunities to learn and practise CALL and MALL through in-service training or teacher research groups.

Conclusion

The compared needs analysis suggests that both students and teachers recognized the importance of preparing for high-stakes exams as well as acquiring communication skills in Korean EFL contexts. In other words, both groups strongly expressed the need for accuracy and fluency at the same time. By the same token, among the four language skills, reading skills and listening and speaking skills were highly emphasized, while writing skills were perceived as the least necessary by both groups of respondents. Their strong needs and preferences are in agreement with the features of college entrance English tests administered by the Korean government and midterm and final exams administered by local secondary schools in Korea, both of which focus heavily on listening and reading. In addition to their English needs, teacher-centred English classes were viewed as the most preferred participation style in Korean EFL contexts by teachers and students. Skewed emphasis on the listening-, reading- and grammar-oriented high-stakes exams, and large class sizes may influence the class participation styles and strategies as well.

Despite this serious washback effect, students and teachers acknowledged a strong need for conversation skills (introducing oneself, engaging in simple talk, etc.), which is also in agreement with the national curriculum. Both students and teachers also acknowledged the necessity of writing an e-mail and chatting online, and achieving communicative tasks in specific contexts. A slight difference in the topics for practising communication skills was observed in that, contrary to students' and teachers' negative attitudes, the Korean national curriculum stressed expressing one's opinion in English and giving formal presentations. This discrepancy may be due to a top-down application of national curriculum to local schools in Korea.

Triangulating the needs of students, teachers, the institution, and the national curriculum in Korean secondary EFL contexts, it can be concluded that students and teachers pursue fluency by enhancing English communication skills as well as accuracy by practising English grammar and reading comprehension. Through well-developed tasks, students may best acquire the target language by engaging in various communicative activities that they likely encounter in real-world contexts. Additionally, integrating technology in the implementation of TBLT makes language learning and teaching more effective by offering a variety of language input, and by expanding students' learning experiences in real and authentic contexts.

An inconsistency was observed between students' preferred topic and those topics introduced by teachers. This result indicates that the English textbook is a primary content source. Though students and teachers have no control once it is selected, it is encouraging to know that most of the topics in newly selected English textbooks are consistent with students' needs. However, topics related to Koreans around the world, famous historical sites, and foreigners may need to be presented via worksheets or tasks. As the student participants are from 7th grade, it would be more informative to consider the needs of 8th and 9th graders for overviews and comparisons of topic preferences according to grade level.

Communicative tasks require students to process language pragmatically to achieve an outcome that can be evaluated in terms of whether the appropriate propositional content has been conveyed. To this end, it is important to give primary attention to meaning and to make use of available linguistic resources. It would be effective for students to identify target tasks and language forms in the pre-task, and to actually accomplish the given tasks in the during-task phase. For a more legitimate analysis of students' task-based learning, I would suggest task-based assessment focusing on some preferred target tasks identified from the survey: conversing with native English speakers (NES), sending an e-mail to E-pals, travelling in English-speaking countries, keeping a diary, ordering food, giving directions to a NES in Korea, playing online games with NES, introducing oneself to NES, volunteering for community service in English-speaking countries, watching English animation and movies.

To better implement TBLT in the given EFL middle school context in Korea, it seems necessary to inform students about how to achieve learning goals. As indicated by their preferred class participation style (teacher-centred), it seems necessary to introduce the task-based approach, assessment, and sequence to students so that they can be more familiar with a new approach, possibly at the beginning of 7th grade. More attention needs to be paid to the progressive change from teacher-centred class activities to peer- or group-centred class activities.

Developing tasks is challenging work. English teachers are usually allotted the most number of teaching hours, and overworked with administration work and homeroom teacher duties. One possible solution may be English teacher collaboration in creating tasks. Additionally, it will also be beneficial if a head English teacher could compile all the created tasks and other teaching materials and share these with new teachers. As for the CALL infrastructure, the school is equipped with two computer labs. However, only one lab has enough computers for one class. As the student and teacher needs analyses revealed, students are highly interested in and capable of using computer technology in English learning, though teachers are rather reluctant to use the computer lab for several reasons (e.g., lack of computer skills and time). It may be necessary for teachers to enhance their computer literacy and confidence.

Overall, the impact of this language programme evaluation may be the school administrators' and English teachers' realization of the importance of reflecting students' needs in the language programme. The findings in this chapter may help to form the basis of course-embedded TBLT lesson plans, syllabus, and curriculum throughout primary school and secondary school in Korean EFL contexts. Studies should continue to expand the empirical basis of TBLT by including more diverse Korean EFL contexts and learners. Finally, in order to examine the feasibility of TBLT in the Korean EFL context, more longitudinal studies need to be conducted at the governmental level so that accumulated findings from these further studies may build a valuable basis for implementing TBLT at national curriculum levels in the Korean context.

References

Alderson, J. C., & Scott, M. (1992). Insiders, outsiders and participatory evaluation. In J. C. Alderson & A. Beretta (Eds), *Evaluating second language education* (pp. 25–58). Cambridge, UK: Cambridge University Press.

Choi, Kyung-Hee. (2006). A needs analysis for the improvement of a tourism English curriculum. *English Language & Literature Teaching, 12*(3), 243–266.

Ferris, D., & Tagg, T. (1996). Academic listening/speaking tasks for ESL students: Problem, suggestions, and implications. *TESOL Quarterly 30*(2), 297–320.

Lee, J. F. (2000). English teachers' barriers to the use of computer-assisted language learning. *The Internet TESL Journal, 6*(12). Retrieved from http://iteslj.org/Articles/Lee-CALLbarriers.html

Long, M. H. (2005). Methodological issues in learner needs analysis. In M. H. Long (Ed.), *Second language needs analysis* (pp. 19–76). Cambridge: Cambridge University Press.

Long, M. H., & Norris, J. M. (2000). Task-based teaching and assessment. In M. Byram (Ed.), *Routledge encyclopedia of language teaching and learning* (pp. 597–603). London: Routledge.

McDonough, K., & Chaikitmongkol, W. (2007). Teachers' and learners' reactions to a task-based EFL course in Thailand. *TESOL Quarterly, 41*(1), 107–132.

Ministry of Education and Human Resources. (2007). *The revised 7th national curriculum for English education.* Retrieved from http://www.moe.go.kr

Naganuma, K., & Yoshida, K. (2003). Eigo can-do anketo chousabunnseki houkokusho: Bassuibann. [English can-do survey report: A summary.] Retrieved from http://benesse.jp/berd/center/open/kokusai/report/2003/07/rep0716.html

Norris, J. M. (2009). Task-based teaching and testing. In M. Long & C. Doughty (Eds.), *Handbook of language teaching.* Cambridge: Blackwell.

Park, C., & Son, J. (2009). Implementing computer-assisted language learning in the EFL classroom: Teachers' perceptions and perspectives. *International Journal of Pedagogies and Learning, 5*(2), 80–101.

Park, J. -E. (1997). Communicative freshman English teaching program by native speaker teachers. *English teaching. 52*(1), 161–187.

Seedhouse, P. (1995). Needs analysis in the general English classroom. *ELT Journal, 49,* 59–65.

van Ek, J. (1975). *Systems development in adult language learning: The threshold level in a European unit credit system for modern language learning by adults.* Strasbourg: Council of Europe.

Watanabe, Y. (2006). A needs analysis for a Japanese high school EFL general education curriculum. *University of Hawaii Working Papers in Second Language Studies, 25*(1). Retrieved from http://www.hawaii.edu/sls/uhwpesl/25(1)/Watanabe.pdf

Willis, D., & Willis, J. (2007). *Doing task-based teaching.* Oxford: Oxford University Press.

Yoon, K. (2004). CLT theories and practices in EFL curricula. A case study of Korea. *Asian EFL Journal.* Retrieved from http://www.asian-efl-journal.com/september_04_yke.php

17

Materials Design for TBLT in Thailand:

Balancing Process and Content

Pornapit Darasawang

Summary

This chapter describes the process of implementing task-based language teaching (TBLT) in a university in Thailand, starting with its initial wholesale adoption fourteen years ago through its gradual revision and adaptation to suit the local context. One of the primary challenges identified was the need to provide considerable attention to language, especially with lower-level learners. This attention has not always been possible because our English as a Foreign Language (EFL) context has a primary focus on process. We describe different attempts to integrate tasks into our curriculum during the development of its current task-oriented (as opposed to task-based) format and identify implications for practitioners in other, similar EFL contexts.

Introduction

The undergraduate students at King Mongkut's University of Technology Thonburi (KMUTT), a university specializing in science and technology, are required to take nine credits of Foundation English. The focus of the curriculum has changed over the years, changing from English for Specific Purposes (ESP) courses to skill-based courses with an integration of learning strategies, and finally to task-based courses. These changes to the curriculum have catered to the changing needs and characteristics of our students (Watson Todd, 2001). A task-based curriculum has been adopted over the last fourteen years to enable students to acquire language while engaging in tasks. This curriculum has been modified continuously to match students' proficiencies, needs, and readiness for the requirements of the curriculum.

Why a task-based curriculum?

Watson Todd (2001) initiated the task-based curriculum at KMUTT because he felt that the curriculum should respond to KMUTT students' characteristics. Despite having at least six years of English instruction using a grammar-focused structural syllabus, they still had little confidence in using English, and could not produce significant English output due to low communicative competence. However, students' real-life uses for English are obvious. Therefore, the new task-based curriculum aimed to change student attitudes towards English by helping them become more confident in using English, and tailoring the English courses to students' real-world needs. From the perspectives of the teachers and students who taught and learned from the skill-based curriculum respectively, students were dissatisfied with the materials because they were dry, unattractive and irrelevant to students' needs. Each course focused on only one skill, for example, study skills, reading or writing, and the students could choose two out of three courses; thus, they had not developed an entire set of skills after finishing the compulsory courses (Pichaipattanasopon, 2001a).

How were tasks used in the task-based curriculum at KMUTT?

A task can be defined in various ways, but it is generally a classroom work or activity that provides an opportunity for students to use a target language to attain an objective (Bygate et al., 2001; Nunan, 2004; Willis, 1996). Krahnke (1987) suggests that the purpose of task-based learning is to provide learning experiences using the real-life needs and activities of the learners. Therefore, when this approach was adopted in the task-based curriculum at KMUTT, the following characteristics were incorporated into the tasks designed by teachers: meaning; solving communication problems; fostering a close relationship with the real world; enabling experiential learning; requiring no specified language points; and involving high quality exposure to English (Skehan, 1998; Watson Todd, 2001).

After implementation, the tasks were modified continuously to suit students' needs and preferences and respond to feedback from teachers. The task-based curriculum has undergone both minimal and substantial adjustments. A course evaluation has been completed every academic year to ensure the effectiveness of the curriculum by taking the views from both students and teachers into consideration. Beginning with the initial implementation of the task-based curriculum in 2000, we can partition the major changes in the curriculum from a task-based format to the current task-oriented format into three phases.

The first phase of the curriculum

The first phase of the curriculum had a task-based format. The implementation of the task-based curriculum was perceived as an innovative method to develop teachers; therefore, teachers were required to be involved in this implementation. They were required to read the literature related to the task-based approach, discuss it in groups to develop their understanding, design tasks, and present these tasks to their colleagues to obtain feedback. Some teachers conducted research on the new curriculum during and after its implementation by evaluating students' and teacher's reactions to the new curriculum. The tasks were designed to cater to students' real-world needs and prepare them for their future academic studies and professional lives (Watson Todd, 2001). Task examples include a library task, a problem-solving task, a survey task and a technological design task. The library task aimed to enhance students' reference and study skills and change their negative attitudes towards reading academic materials. The problem-solving task aimed to develop students' oral communication skills by having them play a decision-making game. The survey task aimed to enable students to write a report and give an oral presentation. The technological design task focused on students using creative thinking to design a technological innovation. This task involved searching for information on the internet, using the target language to describe their design and how it worked, and completing an oral presentation. The tasks ranged from small problem-solving and library tasks to bigger projects such as survey and technological design tasks, which lasted two weeks to one month in duration.

The content of the courses focused on providing the processing steps to finish tasks or other content, which were not necessarily related to language. For example, the survey task taught students how to come up with a topic, survey and analyse data, and make an oral presentation. The library task, which aimed at familiarising the students with the services provided at the library, required the students to visit the library, find a book of interest and give an oral presentation on what they found. They were also required to record in a worksheet all of the different sections/services the library has to offer. It can be said that these learning materials focused more on process than the language.

Sample questions in the Library Task which the students had to complete in the worksheet

Find 2 English journals you like. What are their names and their call numbers?
What can you do if the material that we really need has already been borrowed?
Where do they arrange for interlibrary loans?
Guided reflection of the Library Task
Why did you choose this book? Give reasons.
Explain the process of finding this book.
Point out at least one problem you faced in finding this book. Please give details.
Explain how you solved the problem.
(Pichaipattanasopon, 2001b, pp. 16–21)

However, because they were language courses, the target language learned was used to list the language functions that could be used to finish a task; for example, presenting the target language functions used in giving an agreeing and disagreeing opinion to the students before engaging in the problem-solving task or teaching the students the target language directly relevant to a task, such as the parts of a machine and how they work. The target language was also learned indirectly through a self-editing exercise using concordance as a tool for the students to induce grammar rules when they had to finish a task requiring a written product at the end, such as the survey task. Other activities that helped the learners develop attributes as reflective independent learners and provided other meaningful language inputs were also included in the curriculum as adjunct projects, for example, self-access projects, portfolio projects, and e-mail projects. The adjunct projects were conducted outside of the classroom.

Example of an exercise in the concordance and dictionary unit

Inducing rules and sentence correction

When you read a text, you should observe how words appear in sentences. That will be very useful when you have to make your own sentences. Also, when you get your written work back from your teacher and you find that some words have been circled, you may create a concordance for those words (i.e., find examples of how they appear in sentences). After that, you can make some rules showing how to use them and implement the rules to correct your own work.

The concordance for 'spend'

1	Worker works six days a week and	spends	her weeknights in a school classroom.
2	Experience in food service management and	spends	about 30 hours each week running the business.
3	Appointed consultant to the South London Hospital and	spent	the war years there treating wounded soldiers.
4	Development course would be if he	spent	time in Chicago learning the new offense.
5	They've been	spending	a lot of money on Reel.com and they . . .
6	Nassar adds that Ford is	spending	about 5% of its budget . . .
7	Some people would come to Mali and	spend	three weeks looking for them.

Rules of 'spend'

1   Look at lines 1, 2, 3, 4, 7, and complete Rule 1
    Rule 1 = It can be followed by a noun phrase telling about . . .
2   Look at lines 5 and 6 and complete Rule 2
    Rule 2 = It can be followed by a noun phrase telling about . . .
3   Look at lines 2, 3, 4, 7 and complete Rule 3
    Rule 3 = When there is a verb coming after 'spend' in the same sentence, that verb usually ends in . . .

Now correct the following sentence.
'I usually review my lessons two hours in the evening.'
Correction: ....
(Maneekhao, 2001, p. 49)

Feedback on the task-based curriculum was obtained through teachers' research. For example, Wiriyakarun (2001) conducted a study to discover student attitudes towards task-based learning by having the students write about the new curriculum in post-course guided journals, comparing their experiences of language learning at the secondary school level with those from the task-based curriculum. Most of the students preferred the task-based approach because it was self-directed and self-centred, which was different from the spoon-fed handout-based approach they were given in secondary schools. However, some students expressed negative attitudes regarding the difficulty of the lessons, number of assignments, 'strange' teaching methods and inadequate resources. In the task-based curriculum, the students were involved in selecting activities, writing reports and making oral presentations. This was in contrast to the types of study completed in their high schools, which focused on preparing students to pass the University Entrance Examinations. Therefore, teachers paid more attention to teaching grammatical rules because they were tested. The teaching method, which changed from teacher-centred to learner-centred, caused some students to report that they worked very hard because they were unaccustomed to self-study (Wiriyakarun, 2001). The lack of resources complaint might stem from a requirement for the students to use the Self-Access Learning Centre (SALC) for the self-access adjunct project. The SALC could accommodate only 250 students at a time, therefore, it was inconvenient to use when many of the students had to finish their projects at the same time towards the end of the semester.

Students using the task-based curriculum had positive attitudes about it compared with their experiences studying English in high school; however, there were problems with the management of the curriculum because it was offered to a large group of students. For example, the real-world task, which required the students to post their complaints or opinions on websites, was problematic because some students could not find the websites. In addition, the complaints were not authentic because they were not based on the students' own feelings but on the target language functions in the unit. Many students copied complaints from other sources to fulfil the task requirement. For group work tasks that occurred both inside and outside the classroom, the students did not use the target language (whose language functions were presented to the students before the tasks were performed) because they focused on the output, not the process; therefore, they held group discussions in Thai. The negotiation of meaning, which was supposed to be the outcome of the task-based learning process, did not occur. Some teachers felt that the students were not exposed to new language inputs because they chose to translate their ideas from Thai into English rather than use sources in English. This translation of ideas was a direct translation without the students being aware of the nuances of the English language system.

Another problem was that many students were able to pass the courses because the scores were based on group performance. The last concern for the teachers was how to mark the tasks fairly using the same criteria given that the tasks were offered to 3,000 students studying with different teachers. Task modification was applied continuously to solve management problems; for example, rather than posting their complaints on websites, the department set up a web-board for students to post their opinions on certain topics. However, the topics were teacher-imposed, and some of the topics were not of interest to the students. Although concrete criteria of how to mark the tasks were discussed and presented to the teachers, the marking process was still subjective.

The biggest concern for the teachers was language input and language learning. Most of the students at KMUTT were not proficient in English, thus, they did not actually learn from the target language they were exposed to because they could not identify the language patterns or self-edit their own language. Although consultation was given to the students individually or in groups when they participated in large tasks such as the survey or technological design tasks, the teachers could not attend to all of their errors because the consultation encouraged students to produce spoken output. Thus, students would choose one area of problematic language to discuss with their teachers and frequently memorized what they wanted to discuss, knowing that their speaking skills would be marked. The above-mentioned problems brought about the second phase of the curriculum, which was also centred on tasks, but can be regarded as task-oriented rather than task-based.

The second phase of the curriculum

The second phase of the curriculum was implemented in 2004. Three English foundation courses were designed to solve the problems encountered in the first phase by providing tasks with more language preparation. Because the first phase had proven that most of the students enjoyed completing the tasks, the task remained the learning focus and task performance was a desirable output of what had been learned in each unit. Because the tasks in the first phase were too open-ended and lacked adequate language preparation, students did not acquire the target language as expected. Thus, the second phase aimed to link inputs to tasks at the end of a unit. Inputs were used as models for both the genre and content of the tasks that the students were required to complete at the end of units. Inputs were introduced in listening and/or reading. The objective of the curriculum and task design remained the same: to prepare students for their academic studies and professional lives. Explicit strategy training and encouragement of independent learning in the SALC were integrated. Biography and brochure tasks required students to use the target language learned from the inputs given and to use various language activities to communicate. The task designers tried to make the tasks relevant to the students' interests; for example, inputs on biography were stories about a Korean movie star and a university alumnus singer. At the end of the unit, students interviewed their friends to write their biographies.

After the courses were implemented, an evaluation of the materials was conducted. The results presented in this section are based on an evaluation of LNG 102, one of the compulsory courses. The evaluation was conducted with twenty teachers who had used the materials and were asked to fill out a questionnaire on the content of each unit and their suggestions about what should be added and/or deleted. The focus of the evaluation was on the content and exercises as well as the time provided for each unit. The learning materials linked the inputs and language presented in each unit with the task so the students could master the form, function, and meaning of the target language before fulfilling the tasks. Teachers reported that in general, although the content was presented systematically, additional grammar points and exercises to give greater language exposure should be provided to help students fulfil the tasks successfully (Kritprayote & Yamkate, 2004). According to teachers, grammar points remained an important factor for task completion.

The third phase of the curriculum

To solve the problem of the in-house materials not providing enough language input because the inputs were too short and simplistic in some units, the Department of Language Studies turned to commercial course books and integrated the tasks in the course as a way for students to demonstrate their language output. The new curriculum started in 2012 after the second phase of the curriculum had been in use for nine years. Like its predecessor, it is regarded as a task-oriented-system.

Headway Academic Skills Level 1 (Reading, Writing and Study Skills) (Harrison, 2011) is used in the first English compulsory course, *Headway Academic Skills Level 2* (Listening, Speaking and Study Skills) (Philpot & Curnick, 2011a) is used in the second English compulsory course, and *Headway Academic Skills Level 3* (Reading, Writing and Study Skills) (Philpot & Curnick, 2011b) is used in the third English compulsory course. Different courses use different levels and the focus is on different skills depending on the level of student proficiency and the focus of the course. The *Headway Academic Skills* series was chosen because the content aims at developing academic skills, which have been identified as an important area of student need since the task-based curriculum was adopted. In the *Headway Academic Skills* course books, strategies are presented explicitly, vocabulary, reading and listening inputs are varied and the content can be self-studied.

Tasks still remained integrated into the courses and focused on the learning process such as developing resource skills to obtain more information for task completion. When the curriculum was first implemented in 2012, the tasks 'Natural Disaster' and 'Modern Devices' were used. These tasks were extensions of the 'People and Environment' and 'Technology' units. The output of the 'Natural Disaster' task was a video presentation of a chosen natural disaster. The 'Natural Disaster' unit was completed in pairs. Students were expected to search for information from various sources and synthesize the information to complete the task in the form of an oral presentation. The aim of the second task, the group work task 'Modern Devices' was to enable students to practise their research and note-taking skills and apply the target language learned in various units to finish the task. Examples of the genre and relevant language to describe the devices were provided. The process of how to complete the task, such as reports of the chosen sources, notes taken from the chosen sources, drafts and draft revisions, were marked. Because the unit on 'Technology' did not provide adequate relevant language to complete the task, teachers reported that they had to teach the target language to fulfil the task, which was time-consuming. In addition, the task was not linked closely to the content.

When LNG 101 was taught for the second time, only one task, 'Architecture', was added. To complete the task, the students worked in groups to brainstorm and choose their favourite buildings. They then visited the buildings to take photographs or video-recordings of the buildings and uploaded their presentations, which included 200–250 word explanations in subtitles, to YouTube. They were allowed to apply the target language learned in the unit to their description. Consultation was provided for script preparation. The teachers who taught the course expressed their satisfaction with the fact that the students were able to immediately apply the target language learned in the unit. The students also gave informal feedback on the task indicating that they enjoyed completing it.

Implications for tasks used

The curriculum development at KMUTT shows how tasks have been adopted and adjusted over time. Teachers are aware that tasks are motivational factors in English learning. Therefore, regardless of which modifications were made to the curriculum, tasks were chosen as one of the key aspects of the curriculum, in addition to strategy training and independent learning. The implications for the tasks used will be discussed in the next section.

The importance of language exposure

Task completion involves cognitive processes such as selecting, reasoning, classifying, sequencing information and transforming information from one form of representation to another (Ellis, 2003). A concern for language is a part of the definition of a task. For example, a task is a classroom activity that involves students producing or interacting with the target language with a focus on meaning, not form (Nunan, 2004). Willis (1996) defines a task as an activity which provides an opportunity for students to use the target language communicatively to reach an outcome. Bygate et al. (2001) also define a task as an activity that requires learners to use language by emphasizing meaning to attain an objective. Ellis (2003, p. 7) suggests that the level of cognitive processing required and the structuring and restructuring of language that tasks are designed to bring about are related.

Over time, the task description and curriculum modifications indicate that teachers were concerned that KMUTT students were failing to acquire grammatical competence even though they were involved in reading and/or listening as part of the resource processing to complete tasks. This concern corresponds to previous findings from second language acquisition studies that learners can be exposed to content-based instructions for years and still not acquire grammatical and sociolinguistic competence (Swain, 1985 cited in Ellis, 2003). In the first phase of the curriculum, teachers expected students to identify forms from exposure to contents in resources used to complete the tasks, but they could not. Schmidt (1990) stresses the importance of conscious 'noticing' of forms in inputs. Thus, inadequate language input does not enable students to notice forms. Although form focus can also be achieved by other means such as teacher response to learner errors (Lyster & Ranta, 1997 cited in Ellis, 2003), these types of consultation sessions were unsuccessful because students were memorizing material to perform spoken output rather than engaging in real discussions of language errors with their teachers.

The explicit introduction of language forms into the inputs in the second phase of the curriculum was intended to show students how the target language was used. However, the target language inputs remained inadequate according to feedback from teachers indicating that students required additional exercises. The use of course books in the third phase was another attempt to give more language exposure to students because the course book vocabulary, especially with respect to collocations and grammatical points, is taught explicitly. In addition, students can perform self-study and have more guidelines to finish tasks. This approach is perceived as a move from reproduction to creation (Nunan, 2004). However, other learning aspects must also be provided to ensure that the students 'acquire' the target language and can use it pragmatically, for example, self-editing processes, consultations with teachers on task development, and teacher feedback after task submission. Although the students learned more vocabulary in this phase of the curriculum, the acquisition of language via exposure to inputs and other exercises to enhance noticing provided by the course books requires further investigation.

Providing learner training through the use of task-based learning

In language pedagogy, task-based teaching provides an opportunity to address the roles of meaning-based activity, learner-centredness, affective factors, learner training, and focus-on-form in language learning (Ellis, 2003). At KMUTT, learner training has been integrated into the task-based and task-oriented curricula through students' reflections of their learning and use of metacognitive strategies while performing tasks wherein the students plan how to finish a task, monitor their performance and evaluate their performance. In the first phase, the adjunct projects, which included a self-access and a portfolio project, were deliberately used to encourage students to plan their learning, talk about the strategies they used and reflect on their learning. Peer correction and evaluation were used when the tasks were presented orally in class. The learner training feature was also promoted in the second and third phases of the curriculum. This learner training is regarded as a focus on the process of the task, not the content, and must be assessed. The students were required to present their progress in performing the tasks by justifying what they planned to do, submitting their first drafts, editing their first drafts based on teacher feedback using signals to indicate grammatical errors, and resubmitting their final drafts.

Learner training, particularly with respect to the use of metacognitive strategies, attempts to help learners to learn more systematically and complete tasks on time. Therefore, to help the students perform a task successfully, learner training should be incorporated into the process of task performance and should not be evaluated. Based on our experiences with integrating metacognitive strategies into the curriculum and evaluating how well the students used them, the training made teachers compare the students' planning or evaluating processes rather than help the students become aware of their use of the strategies. Rather than being an interactive process between teachers and students, reflections were required and evaluated. Many students were only recording what they had done versus reflecting on what they had learned to fulfil the requirements of the courses. Nunan (2004) indicates that reflection is one of the principles for TBLT because it can help students see the rationale of their learning. Thus, we should focus on process to make learning more meaningful and effective.

Factors taken into consideration when designing the task

There were many factors that influenced the decisions made by the Department of Language Studies as the curriculum changed from a task-based to task-oriented system. Learner factors of concern to teachers were the same as those that Brindley suggested: confidence of the students in performing the task; how motivating the task is; prior learning experiences; the learning pace; language skill abilities; cultural knowledge and/or awareness; and linguistic knowledge (Brindley, 1987 cited in Nunan, 2004). Indeed, teachers modified tasks based on an evaluation of these factors.

Procedural factors should also be taken into consideration. These factors involve operations that learners must perform on inputs, including the relevance of the task, the complexity of the task, including the cognitive demands of the task, the amount of context provided prior to the task, the processability of the task language or whether the language expected to be produced matches the learner's process capability, the amount of help available to the learner, the degree of grammatical complexity, the time available to the learner or how long the learner has to perform the task, and follow-up such as feedback (Nunan, 2004).

Both personal and procedural factors should be taken into consideration when designing a curriculum centred on tasks because they help task designers choose inputs that are relevant to students' needs, interests, and levels of language proficiency. Both of these factors emphasize the preparation of language. However, completing a task successfully also involves student knowledge of the task. Therefore, task designers must balance their focus on both the process of completing the task and the content, i.e., the language.

Conclusion

This chapter demonstrates how tasks that motivate students to learn English have been used in the curriculum at KMUTT. Modification of the curriculum from a task-based to task-oriented format was performed to respond to the concerns of teachers regarding how well the students could acquire the target language while performing tasks. The type and amount of language exposure to be provided were addressed each time the curriculum was changed. A balance between process and content was also addressed during the process of task modification because the use of tasks in language learning focuses not only on learning a target language, but also on training the learners to be aware of their learning to become effective learners.

References

Bygate, K., Skehan, P., & Swain, M. (2001). Introduction. In M. Bygate, P. Skehan & M. Swain (Eds), *Researching pedagogic tasks, second language learning, teaching and testing* (pp.1–20). Harlow: Longman.

Ellis, R. (2003). *Task-based language learning and teaching.* Oxford: Oxford University Press.

Harrison, R. (2011). *Headway academic skills: Reading, writing and study skills, Level 1.* Oxford: Oxford University Press.

Krahnke, K. (1987). *Approaches to syllabus design for foreign language teaching.* Englewood Cliffs, NJ: Prentice Hall.

Kritprayote, W., & Yamkate, K. (2004). *Survey on the lecturers' opinions of the LNG 101 Materials.* (Unpublished Document). Department of Language Studies, King Mongkut's University of Technology Thonburi, Bangkok.

Maneekhao, K. (2001). Concordances and dictionaries. In R. Watson Todd (Ed.), *Task-based learning and curriculum innovation seminar* (pp.41–50). King Mongkut's University of Technology Thonburi: Department of Languages, School of Liberal Arts.

Nunan, D. (2004). *Task-based language teaching.* Cambridge: Cambridge University Press.

Philpot, S., & Curnick, L. (2011a). *Headway academic skills: Listening, speaking and study skills, Level 2.* Oxford: Oxford University Press.

Philpot, S., & Curnick, L. (2011b). *Headway academic skills: Reading, writing and study skills, Level 3.* Oxford: Oxford University Press.

Pichaipattanasopon, N. (2001a). The new English curriculum at KMUTT. In R. Watson Todd (Ed.), *Task-based learning and curriculum innovation seminar* (pp.13–15). King Mongkut's University of Technology Thonburi: Department of Languages, School of Liberal Arts.

Pichaipattanasopon, N. (2001b). Basic Library Task. In R. Watson Todd (Ed.), *Task-based learning and curriculum innovation seminar* (pp.16–21). King Mongkut's University of Technology Thonburi: Department of Languages, School of Liberal Arts.

Schmidt, R. (1990). The role of consciousness in second language learning. *Applied Linguistics, 11,* 129–158.

Skehan, P. (1998). *A cognitive approach to language learning.* Oxford: Oxford University Press

Watson Todd, R. (2001). Designing a task-based curriculum. In R. Watson Todd (Ed.), *Task-based learning and curriculum innovation seminar* (pp.3–9). King Mongkut's University of Technology Thonburi: Department of Languages, School of Liberal Arts.

Willis, J. (1996). *A framework for task-based learning*. London: Longman.
Wiriyakarun, P. 2001. Student-centred evaluation of the curriculum. In R. Watson Todd (Ed.), *Task-based learning and curriculum innovation seminar* (pp.58–62). King Mongkut's University of Technology Thonburi: Department of Languages, School of Liberal Arts.

18

Designing and Implementing Task-Based Vocational English Materials:

Text, Language, Task, and Context in Indonesia

Handoyo Puji Widodo

Summary

While task-based language teaching (TBLT) has been pervasive in research on first and second language classroom materials and English for Specific Purposes (ESP), few studies have focused on the design and implementation of task-based Vocational English (VE) materials in the secondary education sector. In response to this gap, this chapter reports on the creation and enactment of these materials at a secondary school in Indonesia. In particular it examines to what extent these materials may promote active engagement in language learning. Using an ethnographic classroom design, the present study highlights four main findings: (1) the importance of navigating authentic texts digitally; (2) how learners make and negotiate meaning through dialogic interaction; and (3) the need to explore registers and genres, language appraisal, and lexico-grammatical resources. In addition, challenges and opportunities confronted by students are highlighted. Drawing on these findings, the students learned not only text and task, but also language and context where both text and task operate within a particular sociocultural domain. The findings suggest that task design plays a pivotal role in language use, text creation, and contextual positioning. The main contributions of the chapter are to demonstrate the design of VE materials using a task-based framework and to provide empirical evidence concerning the implementation of the materials in the classroom using an ethnographic approach.

Introduction

Task-based approaches (TBA) are well-established in the area of English language teaching and learning. They have acquired popularity in that the primary goal is to 'engage language learners in meaningful, goal-oriented communication to solve problems, complete projects, and reach decisions' (Pica, 2008, p. 71). Tasks have been designed for a myriad curricular and pedagogical purposes. Among others, tasks serve as a starting point for doing needs analysis, designing course syllabi and lesson plans, materials, and assessments to achieve pedagogical goals and outcomes that reflect real-life experiences. In line with this argument, Doughty and Long (2003, p. 50) point out that '[TBLT] . . . constitutes a coherent, theoretically motivated approach to all six components of the design, implementation, and evaluation of a genuinely task-based teaching programme: (a) needs and means analysis, (b) syllabus design, (c) material design, (d) methodology and pedagogy, (e) testing and (f) evaluation.' This accentuates the importance of TBA in an educational domain, including English language education.

Socioculturally speaking, the implementation of a task-based framework in the vocational high school context is not without challenges, primarily as a result of pedagogical practices that underline the importance of cognitively-laden exercises. From the viewpoint of language policy, TBA is mistakenly perceived to be incompatible with the current curriculum, which relies on a combination of scientific inquiry, a competency-based framework, and a genre-based approach. In fact, there is potential to interweave these approaches. In this post-method era, English teachers are supposed to explore what works best in their own pedagogical contexts. From a teacher perspective, English instructors have become accustomed to asking students language- and comprehension-oriented exercises, which hinder them from using English as a means of making sense of the world around them. The teachers still view English as a school subject, rather than as a means for students to develop their communicative competence in English (Griffiths, 2001).

In terms of factors relating to students, their perceived poor language ability means they are often deemed incapable of doing tasks in English. This problem can be solved by providing students with pre-task activities, which prioritize language as a means for communicating, rather than simply reinforcing form-based instruction (Kathleen Graves, Personal Communication). Thus, a task can be viewed as a means for accomplishing something. On an institutional level, schools do not encourage English teachers to experiment with pedagogical approaches that are not prescribed by the current curriculum. Prescribed textbooks contain test-based or cognitively demanding exercises, discouraging English teachers from exploring new methods. In terms of time constraints, both teachers and students are reluctant to engage in TBLT and learning in that their classes typically meet once a week for only two hours. Operating within these constraints, teachers are more likely to prioritize exercises included in high-stakes examinations (e.g., *Ujian Nasional* or the National Examination) rather than communication. While there are many other sociocultural factors that influence the adoption of TBA in the Indonesian vocational sector, there are also opportunities for adopting such an approach.

Even though the adoption of TBA in ESP materials is not a new enterprise in the Second Language (L2) context around the globe, including Indonesia, a handful of research studies touch upon the creation and enactment of VE materials on a secondary education level. For this reason, this chapter addresses to what extent such materials enhance students' engagement in teacher–student and student–student interactions. The aim of the chapter is to demonstrate how task-based VE materials enhance the meaningfulness of language use through communicative interaction. In addition, the chapter highlights some challenges and opportunities confronted by student participants within the current study.

Vocational English

There are a variety of ESP programmes that commonly start with needs analysis or assessment. This analysis attempts to capture types of texts, tasks or activities, knowledge, and discourse in a particular area of ESP. In doing so, learners are expected to learn and develop their content knowledge, disciplinary language, and specialist task discourse while contextually situated.

It is important to list the three main types of ESP adapted from Basturkmen's (2010) classification as shown in Figure 18.1. Based on this classification of ESP, one unexplored ESP domain is VE or English for Vocational Purposes (EVP). Within the English as a Second Language (ESL) context, VE has had a long history since it started in the 1970s (Gage & Prince, 1982). Since its inception, this programme has been designed for language minority/immigrant learners in adult education programmes and in secondary and post-secondary education to prepare them for possible study and employment opportunities (Platt, 1993). In vocationally oriented language education, VE pertains to a programme 'enabling learners to communicate not only in the (future) workplace but also provides a more general competence that integrates vocational, linguistic, and social skills' (Egloff, as cited in Vogt & Kantelinen, 2013, p. 64), and it involves 'the vocational aspects of the learner's life but is not limited to the immediate occupational demands of work' (Vogt & Kantelinen, 2013, p. 65). Historically speaking, VE has long been pervasive in the educational sphere, such as secondary vocational education.

The term VE is here referred to as one of the ESP programmes that is socio-institutionally situated in secondary school education. I contend that VE is a springboard for developing EAP, EPP, or EOP competencies as students further their studies into higher education programmes. Following Basturkmen's (2010) classification of ESP, VE can be designed from wide-angled (English for General Vocational Purposes) and narrow-angled (English for Specific Vocational Purposes) perspectives, depending on how specific the focus of the programme is. Examples of VE include English for the Hospitality Industry and English for the Hotel Hospitality Industry (Widodo, 2014). This classification also depends upon vocations that schools offer to students in the context of secondary education.

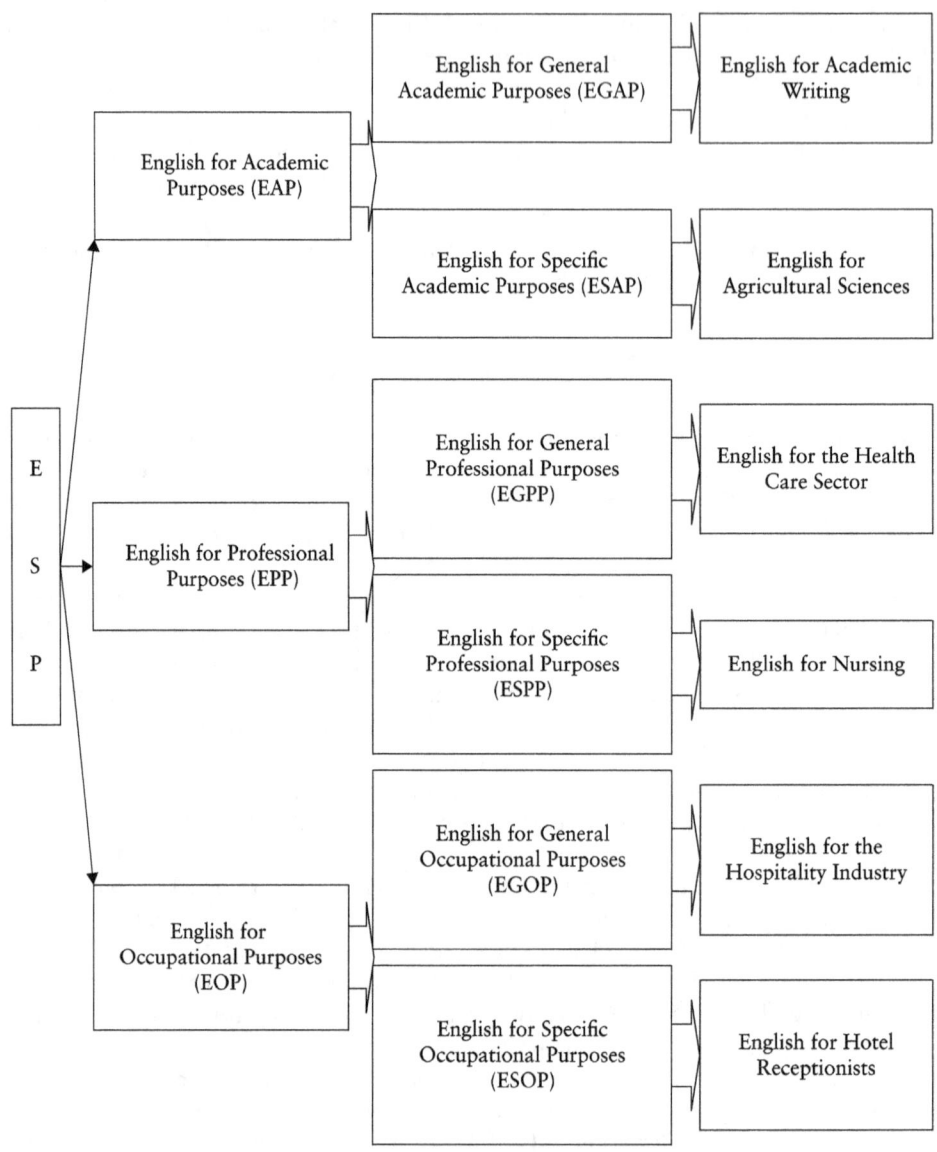

FIGURE 18.1 *Classification of English for Specific Purposes (ESP).*

Definitions of Text and Language and Task and Context

Text and Language

Learning any language has a lot to do with understanding texts. Texts can be defined as social, historical, and cultural reproductions of experience or social activity (e.g., events, places, people, cultural artifacts, emotions, and symbols). This experience is historically situated within sociocultural contexts. Bloor and Bloor (2004) define a 'text' as 'any stretch of language, regardless of length, that is spoken or written for the purposes of communication by real people in actual circumstances' (p. 5). Texts are the realization of social interaction in which language mediates the process of interaction. This definition suggests that any text has an intended readership because it conveys a particular message either overtly or covertly so that social interaction may occur. This social interaction involves both understanding and constructing (or producing) text. This process deploys a variety of language features or resources. In short, texts are the social realization of language in use.

Widodo (2012) contends that texts are manifested through different modes (e.g., visual and verbal), genres (e.g., traffic lights), registers (e.g., traffic communication), and forms (e.g., traffic signs). This argument implies that texts are presented multimodally and convey social meaning and function in a certain situation. Particularly in VE, texts are social and cultural reproductions of a myriad of vocational domains (e.g., accounting, hotel hospitality, software engineering, tour guide, travel management). These vocational domains have unique texts manifested through social semiotic resources (e.g., vocabulary and grammar). As previously pointed out, VE texts can mainly be grouped into: English for general vocational purposes (e.g., English for the Hospitality Industry); and English for specific vocational purposes (e.g., English for the Hotel Hospitality Industry). These two types of text have sub-texts, including food and beverage management and operation, hotel planning and development, convention and exhibition management, hotel marketing strategy, hospitality marketing, food service management, hotel reception, housekeeping, and hotel marketing. These texts contain particular communicative purposes (e.g., informative, instructive, persuasive, procedural), linguistic features (e.g., the use of tense, modality, and discourse markers), organizational features (e.g., deductive positioning and inductive positioning), rhetorical moves (e.g., introduction, body, and conclusion), attitudinal stances (e.g., optimistic, promising, promotional), and genres (e.g., biographies or short stories). These texts are distinguished by their unique use of language, and this language varies from one text to another. Thus, both text and language are mutually complementary.

Task and Context

Vocational texts are seen as social practice or discourse (Feighery, 2006) in a vocational area. VE text varies by its very nature, depending upon communicative purposes, sub-texts of vocational areas, readership, content, genres, modes, and sociocultural contexts of vocation. This variability determines the nature of tasks in a vocational domain. I argue that authentic or real-world texts in a vocational domain are couched in real-life tasks in vocational environments in that tasks themselves are mediated by authentic language use. Generally, tasks can be operationalized within two domains of language learning: understanding text and constructing it.

There have been a myriad of task definitions over the last three decades (Thomas & Reinders, 2010). Tasks are defined differently, depending on particular theoretical stances, e.g., the interaction hypothesis, the output hypothesis, or through a variety of theoretical lenses, e.g., cognitivism or sociocultural approaches (see Shehadeh, 2005). This chapter does not review these stances, but shows the nature of tasks and how these serve as the foundation for creating pedagogical activities, which reflect real-life social practices and authentic language use. Klapper (2003, p. 35) defines tasks as:

> ... meaning-based activities closely related to learners' actual communicative needs and with some real-world relationship, in which learners have to achieve a genuine outcome (solve a problem, reach a consensus, complete a puzzle, play a game, etc.) and in which effective completion of the task is accorded priority.

This definition suggests that tasks involve situational authenticity, authentic language use, goal-oriented activity, and the completion of the real-life activity. Skehan (1998) adds that the primary focus of tasks is on meaning making, not on 'practicing pre-specified language forms or functions and displaying their ability to "produce" these patterns' (pp. 95–96).

Nunan (1989), for example, categorizes tasks into real-world tasks (such as using the telephone) and pedagogic or classroom tasks (such as information gap activities). He defines a classroom task as 'a piece of classroom work which involves learners in comprehending, manipulating, producing, or interacting in the target language while their attention is principally focused on meaning rather than form' (Nunan, 1989, p. 10). Additionally, classroom tasks reflect real-life tasks, which involve real-world contexts of language use and language need (Kiernan, 2005). Though tasks are designed for pedagogical purposes, they should resemble real-life tasks and activities. These tasks are mediated by authentic language use. Willis (1996) classifies tasks into listing tasks, ordering and sorting tasks, comparing tasks, problem solving tasks, sharing personal experiences, and creative tasks. Pica, Kanagy and Falodun (1993) suggest five task types: jigsaw tasks, information gaps, problem solving, decision-making, and opinion exchange. Lee (2005) also suggests a task for completing missing information, which involves such negotiation devices as confirmation checks, comprehension checks, clarification requests, repetition requests, and repetition. These devices are found to be effective in engaging young learners in meaning negotiation. Tasks are therefore not confined to the definitions of TBA scholars, as there is a myriad of tasks that students can perform mediated by authentic language use. To consider activities as tasks, it is important to identify the nature of tasks.

Firstly, Candlin (as cited in Robinson, 2011, p. 7) lists key features of tasks, including:

- *Input.* This is the written, visual, or aural information that learners performing a task work on to achieve the goal of the task.

- *Roles*. These are the roles that learners have in performing a task, such as information-giver and information-receiver.
- *Settings*. These are the grouping arrangements in and outside of classrooms for which pedagogy prepares learners to communicate.
- *Actions*. These are the procedures to follow in performing the task or the various steps that learners must take along the road to task completion.
- *Monitoring*. This is the supervisory process of ensuring that the task performance remains on track.
- *Outcomes*. These are the oral, written, and/or behavioural outcomes in which the task is intended to result.
- *Feedback*. This includes evaluation of the whole or parts of a task performance by the teacher or other learners, including corrective feedback on language use as well as other helpful feedback.

In addition to these features, tasks embrace five main variables: accuracy, fluency, complexity, difficulty, and condition. In any process of language learning, accuracy is a key factor that facilitates the flow of communication. In this chapter, the term, accuracy, is replaced with appropriateness in that the latter pertains to the ability to appropriate and adjust linguistic resources to a communicative context. Thus, any utterances or expressions should be appropriate at a linguistic level. This accuracy plays a crucial role in fluency. Fluency focuses on the meaning or message. Thus, both accuracy and fluency complement one another. Concerning complexity, tasks can be guided (closed) or unguided (open). The more complex a task is, the more complicated the use of language is. The complexity of tasks should suit the current level of students' language and experience. Another factor is task difficulty. The term 'difficulty' here refers to language difficulty. Whether students perform a task appropriately and fluently and whether they are able to carry out a complex or easy task using complex or simple language depends entirely upon a particular situation (context). Thus, the task context provides an appropriate social environment.

Tasks in a vocational domain are varied. They should be work that practitioners perform in routine vocationally-situated interactions. For example, in the hotel hospitality industry, there are major tasks that hotel receptionists perform, such as making a reservation, handling a reservation, picking up the telephone and making telephone reservations, responding to reservation emails, etc. These tasks are real-world activities at a hotel reception desk. This social environment is also called a context. Thus, the term, context, is defined as a socially fluid environment where tasks are performed and mediated through language use.

Factors impacting the implementation of TBA in the Vocational Education landscape

Though as previously mentioned, there are some factors that affect the adoption and implementation of TBA, particularly in senior high schools, I would like to address some factors in relation to text, language, task, and context from a sociocultural perspective. There are, indeed, many other factors affecting the enactment of TBA in an educational context (see the chapter by Chun Lai in Part One of this volume).

In TBA, texts play a crucial role in providing students with appropriate exposure to the target language. Therefore, it is important to choose vocational texts, which can serve as a starting point for the selection of tasks related to students' needs and a situational context where the students use English as a means for getting things done. English teachers also need to examine how tasks are practiced in a particular vocational domain, such as hotel hospitality and management. In other words, texts should be appropriate from a sociocultural perspective and relevant so that students can exploit texts as useful resources for performing tasks. More importantly, texts can serve as a means for mediating socioculturally appropriate and relevant task-based VE pedagogy.

The second factor is language. There is no point in asking students with limited language ability to perform a particular task in English, particularly where students do not use this language on a daily basis. To help students do tasks in English, English teachers should provide students with sufficient language resources through pre-task activities, for instance. In this respect, TBA accommodates the language needs of the students in which exposure to the language is mediated through texts. Students can be told to notice and examine language features, which are useful for doing certain tasks. Within the task-based framework, language should be viewed as a tool for meaning making (see Willis & Willis, 2007).

How instructors perceive and define tasks are crucial factors that impact the implementation of TBA as a whole. Willis and Willis (2007, pp. 12–14) highlight six criteria for selecting tasks, including:

1   Will the activity engage learners' interest?
2   Is there a primary focus on meaning?
3   Is there a goal or an outcome?
4   Is success judged in terms of outcome?
5   Is completion a priority?
6   Does the activity relate to real-world activities?

In the context of a vocationally oriented language education domain, I would like to add two important questions: (1) Is the activity socioculturally practiced in a particular vocational domain? and (2) Does the activity reflect a vocational task that is socioculturally relevant to students' learning needs and situational context?

In addition, in the Javanese context where collaboration or *Gotong Royong* is highly valued, students would rather work collaboratively. The Javanese culture can be considered as a high culture in that it values collectivism. Through this collectivistic lens, students prioritize 'the needs of the family or group, such as social relationships, group success, group consensus, respect, and shared property' (Rothstein-Fisch, Trumbull & Garcia, 2009, p. 475). Anchored in this cultural setting, collaborative tasks can be engineered appropriately to cater to the cultural values students hold.

Last but not least, context is a social environment where tasks are performed. In this environment, a myriad of culturally laden activities exists. In this respect, two contexts that English teachers take into account include the situational context and the cultural context. Thus, text, language, and task should be relevant to these contexts. In particular, cultural norms are not strictly bounded, but contextually fluid in terms of values, expectations, and practices (Strauss & Quinn, 1997). Therefore, student, teacher, institutional, and sociocultural factors leave an imprint on what types of text, language, and task are culturally appropriate to students.

Research method

Research context

The present research study was conducted in one of the vocational secondary schools located in East Java. This school was purposefully chosen for three reasons. First, the school offers a hotel hospitality major that puts more emphasis on English competency. Students are expected to attend on-the-job training and work in an international five-star hotel. Second, the author gained entry access to this school because the project was relevant to its vision and mission. This focus allowed for relatively easy access to this school to undertake ethnographic fieldwork. Third, the school has institutional collaborations with companies or institutions where English is used at work.

The school is ISO-certified and offers areas of vocation such as office administration, accounting, multimedia, marketing, hotel hospitality, software engineering, and computer network engineering. Students are grouped into these majors, which they choose in their first year. Each of the classes comprises between twenty-five and thirty-five students. The nature of instruction involves both theory and practice. For example, students, majoring in hotel hospitality attend formal classroom instruction, and they also practice hotel reception-related work in a mini hotel laboratory. All the students also undergo on-the-job training in a relevant company or institution. This training aims to complement students' vocational competencies gained in school and immerse them in a real-life work environment. Students are also expected to have sufficient command of both written and spoken English. Therefore, the design and implementation of VE materials attempted to cater to the needs of vocational students.

Research design

The research design was based on an ethnographic classroom study for four main reasons. The first reason is that the fieldwork attempted to look at naturally occurring phenomena in the classroom or in-class interactions between teachers and students, students and their peers, and students and lesson units as classroom materials. Secondly, as the teacher-researcher I immersed myself in a school community. This process of self-immersion enabled me to closely examine classroom phenomena, and helped me understand the context of the classroom, both socially and psychologically. This self-immersion also attempted to build personal and professional trust through daily social encounters and negotiated participation (Wang, 2012). The third reason is that the ethnographic classroom research was longitudinal in that it lasted over a period of twelve months. During this period I engaged in routine classroom interactions and played different roles as a researcher, materials co-designer, teacher, and teacher instructor. These roles enabled me to better understand different social encounters both inside and outside the classroom. Thus, the ethnographic fieldwork was contextually situated in classrooms as a social-psychological site enabling me to investigate students' and teachers' learning and teaching journeys.

Ethical consideration and participants

Before the ethnographic fieldwork commenced, I convened three informal meetings with six English teachers and thirty students majoring in hotel hospitality to provide them with information on the project along with an informed consent form. All of them were asked to read the research information (e.g., the benefits and risks of the project) and agree to the consent form. Three English teachers and thirty hotel and hospitality students volunteered to participate in the research project.

The English teachers had received formal and informal training in English education and English language curriculum respectively. Two English teachers had taught in a vocational high school for more than ten years, and one English teacher had taught English for two years in a junior high school. None of the English teachers had attended training in ESP materials design, so for this reason the project assisted them with ESP materials design, which suited the context of vocational education. It afforded the English teachers an opportunity to learn something new from the project as part of their professional learning.

Regarding the student participants, they had received formal English instruction for eleven years, and their language ability ranged from elementary to intermediate based on the Test of English for International Communication (TOEIC) paper-based placement test. These students were in the second year when the present research study commenced. All of the students were competent in two languages: Bahasa Indonesia (national lingua franca) and one of the local languages (e.g., Javanese, Madurese, Balinese). Some of the students were competent in Javanese, Madurese, and Bahasa Indonesia. They had been brought up in families with different socio-economic backgrounds (e.g., government employees, merchants, farmers, teachers, entrepreneurs, and casual workers).

The two groups of participants engaged in the project via routine class meetings in that the project was integrated in the school curriculum. No separate class sessions were arranged to enable the English teachers or the researcher to trial VE lesson units and the students to learn these materials.

Materials and procedure

The twelve-month research project emphasized the importance of the design and implementation of VE lesson units. These units were created based on a needs analysis. At the analysis stage, data were collected from textbook analysis, classroom observations, focus group discussions, and interviews. These instruments were deployed to capture a closer picture of students' previous experience in English learning and of teachers' teaching experience. The needs analysis also looked at available learning resources and constraints. Some key points from the needs analysis data are given below:

- Both the teachers and students did not work on VE texts. They have engaged in EGP.
- The teachers traditionally teach EGP because the national examination does not include ESP test items.
- The teachers focus on the official textbook and curriculum that do not cater to the VE needs of students.
- Students need to learn both EGP and VE as these are required for their on-the-job training and further employment and/or study.
- Many high quality vocational textbooks are written in English.
- Vocational teachers argue that VE materials should include tasks required in a vocational domain and language resources commonly used to perform these tasks.
- Students expect to work on task-based projects, which familiarizes them with vocational tasks in the hotel hospitality domain.

Based on the needs analysis data, the English teachers and the researcher designed lesson units. Each of the lesson units consisted of some vocational tasks. In this chapter, I focus on one lesson unit, which included four major tasks: (1) Text Navigation, (2) Information or Content Identification, (3) Meaning Making, and (4) Text Comparison (see Appendix 18.1. Sample teaching materials). The tasks were implemented in four class periods, each of which lasted for approximately 120 minutes. The goals of the tasks were to introduce students to how information in English is organized and realized through website texts; to familiarize them with different international hotel webpages; to build and develop their lexico-grammatical resources in relation to hotel hospitality; and to familiarize the students with how these resources operate within the digital genre.

Data collection methods and analysis

All the data were collected from participant observations, focus group discussions, and interviews. The participant observation and focus group discussion data were video recorded, while interview data were digitally recorded. The participant observation data were used to examine important episodes in the classroom. The digital recording was necessary as the author played a role as a teacher along with the full-time English teacher. Moreover, the zoom lens of the video recorder was able to capture students' interactions while they completed the assigned tasks. The zoom lens was thus both unobtrusive and effective in capturing classroom activities in the required level of detail (Aralas, 2007). More importantly, digital recordings generated rich data and enabled a careful process of moment-by-moment data analysis and interpretation as they could be replayed in an iterative process.

All the empirical data are constructions of social experiences; thus, the research participants' subjective standpoints both explicitly and implicitly become a catalyst for data analysis and interpretation. From a sociological perspective, 'subjective interpretations are not a source of bias, instead they are considered a piece of the empirical puzzle that helps us understand how people "accomplish" social reality' (Garfinkel, as cited in Marvasti, 2004, p. 5). All the digital data were transcribed, tabulated, and categorized and key findings were identified in the qualitative analysis. Where large amounts of data exist, Yan and He (2012) suggest the use of data reduction techniques to examine only those episodes that are relevant to the research questions. The data analysis therefore focused primarily on four major themes: (1) navigating authentic texts online or digitally; (2) making and negotiating meanings through dialogic interaction; (3) exploring registers and genres, language appraisal, and lexico-grammatical resources; and (4) challenges and opportunities vis-à-vis appropriating task-based VE materials.

Findings and discussion

Navigating authentic texts online or digitally

One of the ways to engage students in any instructional task is to ask them to find and work on real-life texts, which take the form of spoken, written, and visual artifacts. These texts represent social experiences. At the outset, the teachers provided students with a sample real-life text, which was relevant to their major, a hotel website text. This text assisted the students in recognizing the nature of the hotel website text. The teachers explained why the text warranted closer reading in order to help the students recognize the importance of texts. This approach suggested that a text is a starting point for doing assigned tasks. Texts are social products of the performed tasks, so both texts and tasks are mutually complimentary.

The task of navigating texts digitally does not simply find a target text, but involves 'browsing, searching, navigating, hyperlinking, decoding, responding, interpreting, and analyzing' (Walsh, 2010, p. 222). In line with this, the students were asked to browse, navigate, weigh, and select an appropriate text, which catered to their needs of VE. Nina (a female student participant) reported that 'nowadays, we live with digital texts because we can browse such texts anytime as long as we get connected with the internet. Thanks to technology, we can access a myriad of digital texts. We can use these texts for language learning' (Interview # 1, April 2012). This evidence shows that the students completed tasks in a multimodal way in that one major tasks built on the use of smaller, sub-tasks. The main task thus incorporated such sub-tasks as browsing, exploring, and evaluating content-rich knowledge and information. Serafini (2012, p. 28) argues that in today's digital era, students play a role as 'text navigators' who are capable of selecting a text that suits their need for knowledge acquisition or learning. In this respect, Herman (a male student participant) remarked that:

> We can easily access a wide array of online resources, including hotel hospitality related texts as far as there is the internet connection. I feel that an internet-

connected laptop or mobile phone is the window of text resources. So, because of this technology, I can access a variety of digital texts through my mobile phone and tablet everywhere. I can see mobile phones and tablets as part of today's classroom. I think that texts are not confined to in-print documents, but are seen as digital ones.

(Interview # 2, April 2012)

Drawing on these two students' accounts, students see themselves as members of a digital community of practice. They are literate in mobile and digital technologies. They emphasize the crucial role of technology in an information-finding task. In short, technology gives easy access to the language through texts. Asking the students to navigate authentic texts online is part of a student's daily social encounter and this task could motivate students to explore texts they find.

In addition, all the students said that the task of navigating real-life texts enables them to play a role as text navigators. The role of teachers as text providers is minimized. This does not necessarily mean that teachers should refuse to scaffold the students in finding, navigating, and weighing the relevance of texts, as teachers still have a role in demonstrating how to complete multimodal tasks. Nevertheless, the student participants also maintained that the task afforded them an opportunity to democratize what to navigate and select what interests them. Andi (a male student participant) noted that:

I have never experienced self-selecting texts. My former teachers always gave me texts and asked me to answer questions based on the text. I never did follow-up tasks as a result of reading activities. I felt that there was no learning autonomy and engagement. They just spoon-fed me with texts that they thought useful for me.

(Interview # 3, April 2012)

This finding shows the importance of building motivation and engagement enabling the learners to self-select texts. For this reason, teacher support or modelling plays a crucial role in igniting students' interest and motivation to browse, navigate, and read authentic texts (Hastie & Sharplin, 2012). It is also important to note that teachers should allow students to voice what kind of text they are interested in reading.

Most of the students suggested that the text navigation task allowed them to search for or navigate a particular hotel website, which suited their needs and in turn empowered them to become autonomous learners. Wati (a female student participant) argued that 'the task gives me autonomy to better understand my learning needs. I felt motivated to read the text I found. I also felt that navigating texts digitally always encourages me to read more texts' (Interview # 4, April 2012). This testimony indicates that the Text Navigation Task recognized student learning ownership, and it personalized the type of text students needed to read.

To summarize, through teacher scaffolding, the task of navigating texts digitally builds student motivation, raises a sense of learning autonomy and ownership, and allows for active engagement.

Making and negotiating meaning through dialogic interaction

The nature of task completion is strongly connected with meaning making. Texts mediate meaning making processes. International hotel website texts were chosen because their homepages offer a virtual space for exploring social service practices and social language. This digital genre provides a wide range of interactive multimodal texts in which verbal and visual (semiotic) artifacts enrich such texts and articulate a myriad of meanings that students could explore.

In Task 2, the students were asked to identify website content or information. This task also aimed to identify the social and vocational tasks that hotel receptionists perform. Hotel homepages serve as the virtual window of information on such tasks, and provide the students with rich content knowledge of social tasks in that different hotels practice unique tasks. For instance, on the homepage, there is a content area called *Make a Reservation*, indicating that guests should make an online reservation. Widi (a female student participant) indicated that:

> This is the first time that I have learned to explore hotel hospitality related activities online. I never thought that we not only learned language, but also recognized such activities. From the homepage, I learned many things, and I recognized the nature of tasks that I would prepare if I attended on-the-job training in a hotel.
>
> (Interview # 5, May 2012)

Siti (a female student participant) noted that:

> Exploring hotel website content provides me with contextual topics, related to vocational tasks in the hotel hospitality industry. These topics inform me of services and facilities that hotels offer to guests. From this, I have learned what competencies I have to master so that I would be able to work in an international five-star hotel in the future.
>
> (Interview # 6, May 2012)

The findings suggest that the students focused not only on language, but also on content information. As closely observed in student-student interaction, the students were concerned with the meaning of the text. For example, questions such as 'What epitomizes Sheraton Towers Singapore as a hotel of excellence?' and 'What is the tone of the text?' encouraged the students to negotiate meaning. The following dialogue shows how two students negotiated an appropriate response to Task 3.1, Question 2 'What epitomizes Sheraton Towers Singapore as a hotel of excellence?' (See Appendix 18.1).

> **Budi** (a male student participant): I think . . . we need to define what a hotel of excellence is.
>
> **Lilis** (a female student participant): I agree. For me, errr a hotel of excellence refers to excellent services and facilities. What do you think?

Budi: I think so... because we have to serve our guests with these services and facilities. Well, let's have a look at the text.
Lilis: Based on our definition, I noticed some words such as *hotel of timeless style and grace, outstanding quality standards and personalised butler service, the detailed elegant furnishings, delicate presentation of culinary experience,* and *warm, discreet service.* These words show a hotel of excellence.
Budi: That's terrific!
Lilis: Look at the phrase, *the detailed elegant furnishings*, which answers Question 6.
Budi: Spot on! So, this visual reinforces what a hotel of excellence means.
(Classroom Observation # 1, November 2011)

Based on the dialogue, the students started defining the idea of 'a hotel of excellence'. They drew on some prior knowledge and experience and attempted to reach agreement on the idea. Through dialogic interaction, the two students arrived at the same perception of 'a hotel of excellence' based on the importance of services and facilities as two common standards in the hotel hospitality industry. The two students tried to relate one question to another, and one participant showed evidence of the interpretation of a hotel of excellence visually which demonstrates the importance of visuals in a meaning making process.

In Task 4, the students were told to explore more hotel website texts. Similar to other vocational texts, hotel websites provide students with rich semiotic resources for meaning making that the students could explore. The students were asked to search and navigate another hotel website and negotiate and decide whether both hotels were similar in terms of hotel rating, geographic location, and website content. Drawing on sample questions of Tasks 3.1 and 3.2, the students were asked to list similarities and differences between the two texts. This comparison task enriched student's content knowledge, knowledge of genre and discourse, and lexico-grammatical knowledge. Also, they were afforded an opportunity to explore more social practices on two different hotel websites. Comparing and contrasting tasks such as these offer learners the potential to enrich their content knowledge. Thus, a meaning making task not only allows the students to make connections across texts in order to gain complex and interconnected understandings of what constitutes hotel websites, but also enables them to recognize which social practices are integral to the websites.

Exploring registers and genres, language appraisal, and lexico-grammatical resources

While working on the assigned tasks, the students also noticed a variety of registers and genres, language appraisal (tone of text), and lexico-grammatical resources. Genres operate in any instance of language use in that they have particular social purposes. These social purposes are shaped by a field of register (e.g., field-social action, tenor-relationships among people using language, and mode-channel of communication). Genres and tasks share the same principle, that is, any given instantiation of language use is goal-oriented and used to get things done. Using Halliday's systemic functional theory (Halliday, 1985), language use occurs within contexts. Hotel websites, for instance, provide a variety of contexts where language is functionally used and both registers and genres operate within the context (Feez, 2002). All the students felt that working on different texts allowed them to experience a myriad of registers and genres. In this respect, Garid (a male student participant) reported that:

> [R]eading hotel website texts provided me with rich situations and types of text such as descriptive or information report and argumentative. The tones of the text, particularly in the hotel overview are mostly informative and promotional. I think the hotel wants to attract more guests to stay in the hotel.
> (Interview # 7, May 2012)

Yanti (a female student participant) added that:

> Navigating different texts helps better understand a variety of themes and contexts such as types of rooms and how to make a reservation. I see a close relationship between the hotel as a service provider and guests. I think most of the texts in hotel websites are informative and persuasive because the nature of the texts is promotional.
> (Interview # 8, May 2012)

As seen in the two narratives, the students could identify registers and genres by reading more texts. They independently read and made sense of the texts. This argument implies that a text survey task allows students to familiarize themselves with different registers and genres couched in different texts. Therefore, teachers can scaffold the students to do a textual survey to build and raise textual and contextual awareness of different texts. Building and raising this awareness helps students identify different voices in the texts.

In addition to noticing registers and genres, the students paid attention to a multitude of language appraisals. This appraisal embraces the recognition of attitudinal stances (e.g., affect, judgement, and appreciation) in Martin and White's (2005) term. These stances show different evaluative words that hotels use to attract more customers and promote an ethic of hotel excellence. This task was used to build and enhance student's informed awareness of evaluative discourse inherent in hotel website texts. Yula (a female student participant) remarked that, 'very often, I found numerous evaluative words like *charm, elegant, comfortable, generous, grace, luxury, world-renowned*, and other similar words. I realize that promotional text like a hotel website contains evaluative words' (Interview # 9, May 2012). Adam (a male student participant) also noted that 'because a hotel needs to attract more guests to stay in the hotel, they would rather use more convincing language. From this point, I conclude that a hotel website always has a promotional tone' (Interview # 10, May 2012).

By working on a variety of texts, the students also learned technical or vocational terms. These terms are not only a representation of specialized or specific vocabulary, but also key concepts, which describe social practices (Widodo, 2014). For example, reservation information can be associated with the following terms: *room rates, online/real time/call/email reservations, view or cancel a reservation, check-in and check-out time*, and *payment options*. This suggests that one concept can contain sub-concepts. The students also noticed particular specialized words that they might be familiar or unfamiliar with. As I observed, the students deployed online dictionaries as listed below to aid them in this task:

- Cambridge Dictionary: http://dictionary.cambridge.org/
- Macmillan Dictionary: http://www.macmillandictionary.com/

As the students reported, these online dictionaries gave them quick access to the meanings of unfamiliar words. Budi (a male student participant) argued that the 'suggested online dictionaries give rich access to updated words and provide me with thesaurus along with definitions of related words. For me, online dictionaries are language resources that show appropriate use of vocabulary along with how words are jointly connected' (Interview # 11, May 2012). Rohima (a female student participant) added that 'I could explore more related words by navigating online dictionaries. These resources help me increase my vocabulary' (Interview # 12, May 2012). Empirical studies (Nergis, 2013) show that both breadth and depth of vocabulary facilitate a meaning making process. Thus, it appears that e-dictionaries can serve as useful resources for pre-task and in-task activities.

Challenges and opportunities: Appropriating task-based VE materials

The implementation of task-based VE materials was not without a series of challenges and many students encountered difficulties. The three main challenges were: text, language, and task. The first challenge is that many students had difficulty in selecting and evaluating appropriate texts over the first two weeks. Rudi (a male student participant) remarked that:

> [A]t the outset, I did not know how to select texts, which are relevant to my area of interest because there are a lot of texts online. I wish that I had training in picking and assessing vocational texts written in English.
>
> (Interview # 13, May 2012)

Another student participant argued that 'selecting good vocational texts is a tough task. So, the role of a teacher in explaining some criteria for selecting these texts and in showing some good texts are important' (Interview # 14, May 2012). These two students emphasize the importance of teacher scaffolding in order to help them in selecting and evaluating texts. This empirical evidence shows the significance of the pre-task activity, which familiarizes students with important features of texts. These activities also help students prepare for actual tasks. Thus, English teachers need to give students materials, which include pre-task activities (both language-oriented and content-based activities) so that students can make sense of the language they experience and build motivation for them to use the language (Willis & Willis, 2007).

In meaning making and negotiating tasks, many students still used Bahasa Indonesia. Laila (a female student participant) indicated that:

> I got a lot of ideas to express, but I still have difficulty articulating such ideas in English in that I needed to search for appropriate vocation-specific words in English. My English teachers in the first year never introduced me English for specific purposes.
>
> (Interview # 15, May 2012)

Some students argued that they wanted to discuss texts with their peers in English, but their peers refused to do so. They kept on speaking English, but their peers responded in Bahasa Indonesia. Working on tasks, which put more emphasis on meaning, allows them to practise their English. These students expressed different concerns. For less capable students, engaging in meaning making and negotiation in English was a difficult task, but for more able students, they viewed such tasks as an opportunity to use their English as a means for meaning making. This language difficulty can be overcome by providing students with numerous language resources before asking them to do assigned tasks. In addition, pairing less capable students and more capable peers is one of the ways in which instructors can make peer scaffolding possible.

The third challenge that many students faced was that the tasks required the students to work beyond the remit of language-oriented tasks. For example, while working on Navigating Authentic Texts Online or Digitally, the students had to negotiate the task collaboratively and wisely. Many students commented that such a task required a lot of time, energy, and knowledge of the process of negotiation. They were challenged to play different roles as the chooser of the text, assessor, and negotiator. Hamdam (a male student participant) argued that 'I get used to read texts provided by my teachers. Now, I play three important roles: selecting, assessing, and negotiating texts with my peers' (Interview # 16, May 2012). Another example is that many students had difficulty identifying registers, genres, and language appraisal. For a few students, they did enjoy exploring these aspects as they had never experienced them previously. They argued that they learned that texts are never neutral and contain attitudinal stances. Though it was difficult for many students to work on the assigned tasks, they found such tasks useful, particularly for language development and exposure to vocational tasks in a real-life setting.

Conclusion

This chapter has examined how the design and implementation of VE materials was informed by a task-based framework. Though the designed tasks benefited student participants, the adaptation of the sample tasks is encouraged to meet diverse students' needs. Moreover, VE materials should be locally designed based on a needs analysis that examines text, language, task, and context. Equally important, the design of task-based VE materials should take into account cultural appropriateness in relation to text, language, task, and context. Students and teachers should share the same vision and mission so that sociocultural values underpin the selection of language materials. Understanding this point will help researchers, teachers and materials designers to produce more innovative ways to optimize the use of TBA, particularly in the Indonesian secondary school context, and provide practically and empirically informed decisions on the implementation of TBA in general.

Appendix 18.1. Sample teaching materials

Task 1: Hotel Website Navigation
Search for an international five-star hotel website that you would like to learn. Work in pairs.

Goal of Task 1: Familiarize students with authentic texts, which are relevant to hotel hospitality.

Task 2: Website Content Identification
List information that the international five-star hotel provides on the website.

Goal of Task 2: Find out and list key information, which makes up hotel hospitality related texts.

Task 3.1: Meaning Making of Specific Information Listed
Overview Text: Sub-Text 1
Look at this text, and respond to the questions following the text.

> Sheraton Towers Singapore is a hotel of timeless style and grace. Voted by Conde Nast Traveller Gold List as one of the best places to stay in the world, Sheraton Towers Singapore sets the benchmark in the hospitality industry with its outstanding quality standards and personalised butler service. From the detailed elegant furnishings, delicate presentation of culinary experience to warm, discreet service, the hotel believes in pampering its guests with the comfort, luxury and conveniences that they are accustomed to at home.

1. What is the main point of the text?
2. What epitomizes Sheraton Towers Singapore as a hotel of excellence?
3. What is the tone of the text?
4. What is the nature of the text?
5. List some specialized words commonly used in the hotel hospitality industry.

Goal of Task 3.1: Understand hotel website texts in terms of main points, tones, attitudes, visuals, and specialized vocabulary.

Task 3.2: Meaning Making of Specific Information Listed
Take a closer look at the following text, and respond to the questions below.
Guest Rooms Text: Reservations
Reservations Text: http://www.sheratonsingapore.com/rooms

1. How do potential guests make a reservation?
2. What should potential guests do before making the reservation?
3. What kinds of reservation does the hotel offer to potential guests?
4. List some evaluative words which demonstrate specific hotel hospitality or code of services.

Goal of Task 3.2: Understand hotel website sub-texts in terms of social practices/tasks and attitudes.

Task 4: Hotel Website Text Comparison
Find another hotel website that contains the same information as the hotel website you found. Focus on a hotel overview or a hotel web page and guest room texts. Identify some similarities and differences between the two texts. Bear in mind that the hotel should be located in the same geographic area.

Goal of Task 4: Compare and contrast two hotel website texts in terms of a hotel overview and guest room texts so that students are fully aware that each of the hotels share similarities, but have differences in terms of service tasks and other characteristics.

(Taken from Widodo, 2014, 160–162)

References

Aralas, D. (2007). Extending video ethnographic approaches. *Studies in Educational Ethnography, 12,* 169–184.

Basturkmen, H. (2010). *Developing courses in English for specific purposes.* New York: Palgrave Macmillan.

Bloor, T., & Bloor, M. (2004). *The functional analysis of English: A Hallidayan approach* (2nd edn). London: Arnold.

Doughty, C. J., & Long, M. H. (2003). Optimal psycholinguistic environments for distance language learning. *Language Learning & Technology, 7*(3), 50–80.

Feez, S. (2002). Heritage and innovation in second language education. In A. M. J. Johns (Ed.), *Genre in the classroom: Multiple perspectives* (pp. 43–69). Mahwah, NJ: Lawrence Erlbaum.

Feighery, W. (2006). Reading tourism texts in context: A critical discourse analysis. *Tourism Analysis, 11,* 1–11.

Gage, J., & Prince, D. (1982). Vocational English: Preparing for a first job. *TESOL Quarterly, 16,* 349–358.

Griffiths, A. (2001). Implementing task-based instruction to facilitate language learning: Moving away from theory. *TEFLIN Journal, 12*(1). Retrieved from http://journal.teflin.org/index.php/teflin/article/view/37/132

Halliday, M. A. K. (1985). Part A. In M. A. K. Halliday & R. Hasan (Eds), *Language, context, and text: Aspects of language in a social-semiotic perspective* (pp. 1–49). Geelong, Victoria: Deakin University Press.

Hastie, M., & Sharplin, E. (2012). Why did you choose that text? Influences on English teachers' choices of reading materials for students? *English in Australia, 47*(2), 36–44.

Kiernan, P. (2005). Storytelling with low-level learners. Developing narrative tasks. In C. Edwards & J. Willis (Eds) (2005), *Teachers exploring tasks in English language teaching* (pp. 58–68). New York: Palgrave Macmillan.

Klapper, J. (2003). Taking communication to task? A critical review of recent trends in language teaching. *Language Learning Journal, 27,* 33–42.

Lee, S-M. (2005). Training young learners in meaning negotiation skills: Does it help? In C. Edwards & J. Willis (Eds), *Teachers exploring tasks in English language teaching* (pp. 103–112). New York: Palgrave Macmillan.

Martin, J. R., & White, P. (2005). *The language of evaluation: Appraisal in English*. New York: Palgrave Macmillan.

Marvasti, A. B. (2004). *Qualitative research in sociology: An introduction*. London: Sage.

Nergis, A. (2013). Exploring the factors that affect reading comprehension of EAP learners. *Journal of English for Academic Purposes, 12*, 1–9.

Nunan, D. (1989). *Understanding language classrooms: A guide for teacher-initiated action*. Hemel Hempstead: Prentice Hall.

Pica, T. (2008). Task-based instruction. In N. Van Deusen-Scholl & N. H. Hornberger (Eds), *Encyclopedia of language and education* (2nd edn) (pp. 71–82). New York: Springer.

Pica, T., Kanagy, R., & Falodun, J. (1993). Choosing and using communicative tasks for second language instruction. In G. Crookes & S. Gass (Eds), *Tasks and language learning: Integrating theory and practice* (pp. 9–54). Clevedon, England: Multilingual Matters.

Platt, E. (1993). Vocational ESL teacher collaboration: Some substantive issues. *English for Specific Purposes, 12*, 139–157.

Robinson, P. (2011). Task-based language learning: A review of issues. *Language Learning, 61*(Suppl. 1), 1–36.

Rothstein-Fisch, C., Trumbull, E., & Garcia, S. G. (2009). Making the implicit explicit: Supporting teachers to bridge cultures. *Early Childhood Research Quarterly, 24*, 474–486.

Serafini, F. (2012). Reading multimodal texts in the 21st century. *Research in the Schools, 19*(1), 26–32.

Shehadeh, A. (2005). Task-based language learning and teaching: Theories and applications. In C. Edwards & J. Willis (Eds), *Teachers exploring tasks in English language teaching* (pp. 13–30). New York: Palgrave Macmillan.

Skehan, P. (1998). *A cognitive approach to language learning*. Oxford: Oxford University Press.

Strauss, C., & Quinn, N. (1997). *A cognitive theory of cultural meaning*. Cambridge: Cambridge University Press.

Thomas, M., & Reinders, H. (Eds). (2010). *Task-based language learning and teaching with technology*. New York: Continuum.

Vogt, K., & Kantelinen, R. (2013). Vocationally oriented language learning revisited. *ELT Journal, 67*(1), 62–69.

Walsh, M. (2010). Multimodal literacy: What does it mean for classroom practice? *Australian Journal of Language and Literacy, 33*, 211–239.

Wang, J. (2012). The use of e-dictionary to read e-text by intermediate and advanced learners of Chinese. *Computer Assisted Language Learning, 25*, 475–487.

Widodo, H. P. (2012). The use of complaint letters as an authentic source of input for an interactive task in second language learning. *Electronic Journal of Foreign Language Teaching, 9*(2), 245–258.

Widodo, H. P. (2014). Contextually framing the design of ESP materials: Vocational English reading tasks. In H. Emery & N. Moore (Eds), *Teaching, learning and researching reading in EFL*. Dubai, UAE: TESOL Arabia, 140–163.

Willis, J. (1996). *A framework for task-based learning*. Harlow: Longman Addison-Wesley.

Willis, D., & Willis, J. (2007). *Doing task-based teaching*. Oxford: Oxford University Press.

Yan, C., & He, C. (2012). Bridging the implementation gap: An ethnographic study of English teachers' implementation of the curriculum reform in China. *Ethnography and Education, 7*(1), 1–19.

19

The Effects of an Output-based Task on Subsequent Aural Input in a Japanese University Setting

Wataru Suzuki
Nobuya Itagaki

Summary

The effects of output-based tasks on noticing and acquisition of second language (L2) forms have been demonstrated in recent second language acquisition (SLA) research (e.g., Izumi, 2002; Leeser, 2008; Uggen, 2012). One of the fundamental assumptions among SLA researchers is that language output draws learners' attention to lexis and grammar in the subsequent input (Swain, 1985, 2005). In this study, we extend this line of research by exploring what types of subsequent input effectively draw learners' attention to linguistic forms. The participants were sixty-seven Japanese university students studying English as a foreign language (EFL) at a low-intermediate level. These participants were divided into three groups: (a) listening, (b) parallel reading, and (c) shadowing. All three groups first listened to a passage and engaged in a text reconstruction task. Then, these three groups listened to the same passage again but in different ways: (a) the listening group listened to the same passage, (b) the parallel reading group listened to the same passage with its written script, and (c) the shadowing group orally repeated what the speaker said in English, either verbatim or in close paraphrase. Finally, all three groups were asked to reproduce the passage. Analyses of the reconstruction tasks revealed that the parallel reading group reproduced more than the shadowing and listening groups. These findings are discussed with reference to Swain's (1985, 1995, 2005) Output

Hypothesis and the relevant SLA research. Implications for pedagogical practice are also briefly considered.

Introduction

In recent years, task-based language teaching (TBLT) has received considerable attention among L2 theoreticians, researchers, and practitioners in East Asian countries such as China, Korea, Japan, and Thailand. According to Ellis (2008), TBLT is defined as 'an approach to the teaching of second/foreign languages based on a syllabus consisting of communicative tasks and utilizing a methodology that makes meaningful communication rather than linguistic accuracy primary' (p. 980). Simply put, TBLT is language pedagogy that centres on language as a tool for communication. One of the reasons why TBLT might merit further exploration in the Asian context is that many students and teachers seem to be disappointed and frustrated with the general failure of more traditional instructional approaches, such as presentation-practice-production (PPP) to promote communicative competence in the L2. As this general idea is associated with the term communicative language teaching (CLT), TBLT has been welcomed by most researchers and practitioners in many Asian countries.

There are many versions of TBLT in terms of the degree to which they focus on linguistic forms such as grammatical, phonological, lexical, and pragmatic ones. A strong version of TBLT supposes that L2 learners acquire linguistic forms through communicative activities which exclusively focus on meaning (i.e., without focus on linguistic forms). A typical example of school programmes based on such a strong version of TBLT is the French immersion programmes in Canada where students learn school subjects such as mathematics and science in their L2 French (Lapkin, Hart & Swain, 1991; Lyster, 2007). On the other hand, a weaker version of TBLT may be associated with a focus on linguistic forms and integrated into meaningful communication in L2 classrooms (i.e., with focus on forms). Willis's (1996) *three-cycle model* fits into this category (see also Willis & Willis, 2007). In her model, learners are first engaged in vocabulary learning or brainstorming (pre-task cycle). Then, learners carry out spontaneous communicative tasks (task cycle), followed by various language-based activities such as sentence completion and matching exercises (language focus cycle). A number of SLA researchers have produced empirical evidence to support a weak version of TBLT (see Keck, Iberri-Shea, Tracy-Ventura & Wa-Mbaleka, 2006; Li, 2011; Lyster & Saito, 2011; Mackey & Goo, 2007; Spada, 2011 for meta-analyses and research syntheses). Current views among many TBLT advocates thus support a weak version of TBLT, arguing for the inclusion of focus on linguistic forms during communicative activities (e.g., Ellis, 2003; Skehan, 1996; Samuda & Bygate, 2008; Willis & Willis, 2007).

One of the ways in which a weak version of TBLT can be implemented is with an *output-based* approach: *dictogloss* (e.g., Kowal & Swain, 1997; Swain & Lapkin, 1998, 2000, 2001), jigsaw task (e.g., Swain & Lapkin, 2002; Pica, Kang & Sauro, 2006), picture-cued production (e.g., Izumi & Izumi, 2004; Uggen, 2012; Song & Suh, 2008; Suzuki, Itagaki, Takagi & Watanabe, 2009), text reconstruction (e.g., Izumi, 2002; Izumi & Bigelow, 2000; Izumi, Bigelow, Fujiwara & Fearnow, 1999; Leeser, 2008; Song & Suh, 2008), text-editing (e.g., Nassaji & Tian, 2010) and three-stage-writing task (e.g., Hanaoka, 2007; Iwanaka & Takatsukasa, 2007; Sachs & Polio, 2007, Storch & Wigglesworth, 2010). In this chapter, we report findings from an empirical study aimed to test the effectiveness of a text reconstruction task on L2 learning with EFL learners in an East Asian context (i.e., Japan). Before describing our study in detail, we will first briefly review previous SLA research that demonstrates that text reconstruction as an output task promotes L2 learning.

Text reconstruction tasks in SLA research

Text reconstruction tasks are often selected for research due to the fact that they are popular classroom tasks, and that they force the participants to attend to form as they attempt to reconstruct the text from memory. One common design for a research study in this area is to compare an output group engaged in a text reconstruction task with a non-output group engaged in a text comprehension task in terms of noticing and acquisition of L2 linguistic forms (e.g., Izumi, 2002; Izumi & Bigelow, 2000; Izumi et al., 1999; Leeser, 2008; Song & Suh, 2008). In these studies, the grammatical targets and task modalities vary. The targeted forms include English relativization (Izumi, 2002), English past hypothetical conditional (Izumi & Bigelow, 2000; Izumi et al., 1999; Uggen, 2012), English past counterfactual conditional (Uggen, 2012; Song & Suh, 2008), and Spanish past tense (Leeser, 2008). In terms of modalities, most studies have examined the effects of text reconstruction on subsequent processing of *written* input (Izumi, 2002; Izumi & Bigelow, 2000; Izumi et al., 1999; Uggen, 2012; Song & Suh, 2008), while limited studies (e.g., Leeser, 2008) have examined these effects on *oral* input. More studies investigating the effects of a text reconstruction task on subsequent aural input are needed, because L2 learners are likely to process written and oral input differently due to the extra cognitive load placed on their processing capabilities by oral (i.e., real time) input (see Leow, 1995; Sanz, 1997). Of all studies in this area, the study most similar in terms of research design and having the most direct relevance to the present study is Leeser's (2008) work, which we will describe in detail below.

Leeser attempted to ascertain whether producing output would promote the noticing and learning of Spanish past tense morphology. He asked two groups of adult L2 learners learning Spanish in a university setting, output and non-output groups, to listen to a short story containing many examples of Spanish past tense morphology (i.e., input 1). While listening to the story, both the output and non-output groups were asked to take note of any words or phrases (note-taking 1). After listening to the story, the output group performed a text reconstruction task (output task 1), and the non-output group performed a text comprehension task (non-output task 1). Then, both groups were asked to listen to the same story (input 2) and take notes (note-taking 2). Next, the output group performed a second text reconstruction task (output task 2), and the non-output group performed the same text comprehension task again (non-output task 2). For one of the measures of noticing, Leeser counted the amount of note-takings 1 and 2 (i.e., nouns, inflected verbs such as present, preterite, and imperfect, and other including adjectives, adverbs, pronouns, conjunctions, and prepositions) and compared the means between the output and non-output groups. It was predicted that participants in the text reconstruction condition (output task 1) would take more notes of words or phrases (especially Spanish past tense morphology) important for their subsequent text reconstruction task than the non-output group participants. That is, Leeser theorized that cognitive processes which output triggers (i.e., noticing) would facilitate subsequent input processing (i.e., intake). However, no difference was found in the amount of noticing of the target forms between the output and non-output groups. As predicted, the output group outperformed the non-output group on their learning of Spanish past tense morphology as measured by a post-test (i.e., new writing). Like Leeser's work, the study we discuss in this chapter aims to further our understanding about the effects of a text reconstruction on subsequent oral input.

An important consideration, which has not been adequately researched in SLA, is that attention to forms during subsequent input can be enhanced in various ways. Instead of listening to the same passage twice (i.e., Leeser, 2008), students could read a passage aloud while they listen to taped speech (i.e., parallel reading). Or they could repeat what the native speaker in the speech has said in English, either verbatim or by paraphrase without having access to a written script of the speech (i.e., shadowing). Because parallel reading and shadowing have been extensively used in English language classrooms in Japan (see Hamada, 2009, 2011; Kadota, 2007; Murphey, 2001; Tamai, 2005), it is ecologically valid to test the effects of parallel reading and shadowing in this study. Thus, this study builds on Leeser's (2008) methodology from his study in the USA using a TBLT approach that is compatible with current instructional approaches already used in Japan.

Our study

This text reconstruction study was conducted in a university setting with young adult students who were randomly assigned to one of three groups, in order to compare the relative efficacy of the input tasks of listening, parallel reading, and shadowing on their final output (i.e., their final attempt to reconstruct the target passage). The total time for all groups to complete their tasks was identical: 14 minutes. While this time for the tasks may seem quite short, it is important to note that the focus of the study was not to prove that output leads to L2 language acquisition, but to demonstrate the effect of an output task on subsequent input processing (i.e., intake).

The listening material was adopted from a college-level text called *Reading tasks for college students* published in 2007 (see Appendix 19.1). It consists of 101 words with ten sentences and seven items of two target structures (i.e., present perfect and infinitives). The rationale for selecting the two target structures was not theoretical but pedagogical and practical. Prior to the current study, we had selected several target structures for the model essay which we wanted students to pick up or at the very least to obtain receptive knowledge about. Then, we chose the present perfect and infinitives as the target linguistic forms in the passage. Through this study, we wanted our students to internalize these two target structures.

The text reconstruction task used in this study was a variation of a dictogloss (Swain & Lapkin, 1998, 2000; Wajnryb, 1990). In a typical dictogloss task, students jot down any words or phrases contained in a short story the teachers read at a normal pace. Students then work in pairs or small groups to reproduce the text as closely as possible to the original text. We modified this task procedure in three ways. First, we used an audio-recoded tape instead of a teacher reading the passage aloud (also see Leeser, 2008). Second, we did not ask students to take notes of words or phrases in the passage (also see Leeser, 2008). Third, we asked our participants to reconstruct the passage individually rather than in pairs (also see Izumi, 2002; Leeser, 2008).

The participants in the study were sixty-seven Japanese university students of English aged between eighteen and twenty years old. They were enrolled in a general English course with a specific focus on developing Test of English for International Communication (TOEIC) listening skills at a public university in Japan during the fall semester from October 2009 to February 2010. All of them had a high school diploma in Japan. The majority of the participants had started learning EFL at or after the age of twelve within the framework of the Japanese curriculum. None had studied in English-speaking countries. We judged participants to have achieved a low-intermediate proficiency level of English, because they followed the same curriculum prescribed by the Ministry of Education, Culture, Sports, Science and Technology (MEXT) during their years of education. They had also passed two standardized national university entrance examinations with exclusive focus on grammar and reading administered by the National Center for University Entrance Examination in Japan. We randomly divided the participants into three groups, with eighteen assigned to the listening group (six males and twelve females), nineteen to the parallel reading group (nine males and ten females), and thirty to the shadowing group (twenty-one males and nine females), described below.

For the three groups, the task cycle was conducted during a total of 14 minutes of regularly scheduled university English lessons (i.e., 90 minutes). The study consisted of four phases described in Table 19.1. First, participants in all the three groups listened to a passage in two minutes. Then, they reconstructed the passage as accurately as possible with reference to the original text on a sheet of paper in five minutes (i.e., output 1). To ease the reconstruction task, the initial words or phrases of every sentence were provided (see Appendix 19.2). We refer to the first text reconstruction as the pre-test. Then, participants listened to the same passage again for two minutes, but this differed according to the groups. The listening group listened to the same passage again (i.e., task repetition). The parallel reading group listened to the same passage while following along with the written script. The shadowing group orally repeated what the speaker has said in English, either verbatim or in close paraphrase. Finally, participants in the three groups were asked to reproduce the passage again as closely as possible to the original passage in five minutes (i.e., output 2). We refer to the second text reconstruction as the post-test.

TABLE 19.1 *Experimental procedures*

	Group		
	Listening	Parallel reading	Shadowing
1	Listen to a story (2 min)		
2	Reconstruct (5 min) (pre-test)		
3	Listen to the story (2 min)	Listen with script (2 min)	Repeat (2 min)
4	Reconstruct (5 min) (post-test)		

We used two categories (lexis and grammar) to analyse how much of the model story participants accurately recalled in both pre- and post-tests (output 1 and output 2). Note that spelling errors were permitted for this analysis. In the lexis-level analysis, we counted the total number of words per sentence participants accurately recalled from the model story. We scored one point for each word and calculated the average of the scores for the three groups. As we provided the beginning words and phrases (twenty-three out of 101) in the reconstruction task, the maximum score was seventy-eight for the lexis-level analysis. In the grammar-level analysis, we focused on only seven items of the two pre-determined grammatical structures (i.e., present perfect, infinitives). We scored one point for each correctly recalled structure. Spelling errors were also permitted for this grammar-level analysis. The maximum score was seven for the grammar-level analysis.

Because coding data such as these can be subjective and impact on a study's validity, we adopted a very strict criterion for recall accuracy. We defined recall accuracy as the exact usage of the same words and grammatical expressions as the model passage. We did not score points for any different words and grammatical expressions participants used in the text reconstruction task, even when their meanings were similar to those of the original words and expressions in the model essay. Our strict criterion about recall accuracy will later be identified as one of the limitations of this study. Because the coding categories were transparent in the data, we felt that a second coding was not necessary.

For statistical analyses, we conducted analyses of variances (ANOVA) on each dependent variable (lexis and grammar). The procedure of using a Bonferoni-adjustment on alpha to protect against an inflated familywise (or experimentwise) Type I error rate is recommended when performing multiple univariate ANOVAs (Huberty & Morris, 1989). We thus set p-value at 0.025 (i.e., 0.05 divided by two dependent variables). A statistical package for the social sciences (SPSS) 17.00 was used to conduct the statistical analyses.

Findings

First, we conducted paired sample t-tests to evaluate improvement from pre- to post-tests for both lexis and grammar scores in the three groups. The results were significant, $t(64) = 9.12$, $p < 0.01$ for lexis and $t(64) = 6.81$, $p < 0.01$ for grammar, meaning that our participants reproduced more lexis and more grammar in the first compared to the second reconstruction tasks.

Table 19.2 shows the mean and standard deviations of the pre-recall score of lexis and grammar analyses for the three experimental conditions. We conducted one-way ANOVA to examine the differences in the lexis and grammar pre-test scores among the three groups. Statistical differences were not found in terms of pre-test lexis scores among the three groups, $F(2, 62) = 0.02$, $p = 0.98$. One-way ANOVA did not also produce significant differences in the pre-test grammar scores among the three groups, $F(2, 62) = 0.32$, $p = 0.72$. These results indicate that all the three groups were similar in terms of the ability to reproduce a text in L2.

Table 19.3 presented the mean and standard deviations of the post-recall scores of lexis and grammar analyses for the three experimental conditions. One-way ANOVA

TABLE 19.2 *Means and standard deviations of the pre-recall scores of word and grammar for three experimental groups*

Groups	Lexis		Grammar	
	mean	SD	mean	SD
Listening	8.56	5.80	0.28	0.46
Parallel reading	8.50	6.25	0.33	0.59
Shadowing	8.21	6.27	0.41	0.63
Total	8.47	6.06	0.35	0.57

Note: Maximum scores are 78 and 7 for lexis and grammar, respectively.

TABLE 19.3 *Means and standard deviations of the post-recall scores of word and grammar for three experimental groups*

Groups	Lexis		Grammar	
	mean	SD	mean	SD
Listening	14.56	7.78	0.78	0.94
Parallel reading	24.83	12.25	1.78	1.44
Shadowing	17.31	11.08	1.41	1.38
Total	18.86	11.15	1.34	1.33

Note: Maximum scores are 78 and 7 for lexis and grammar, respectively.

TABLE 19.4 *Multiple comparisons among three groups using Bonferoni tests*

(I) G	(J) G	Difference (I − J)	p
Listening	Parallel reading	−10.28*	0.016
	Shadowing	−2.76	1.00
Parallel reading	Listening	10.28*	0.016
	Shadowing	7.52	0.065
Shadowing	Listening	2.76	1.00
	Parallel reading	−7.52	0.065

produced statistically significant differences in the lexis post-test among the three groups, $F(2, 62) = 4.61$, $p < 0.01$. Then, we conducted multiple comparisons among the three groups using Bonferoni tests. Table 19.4 presents a significant difference found only between the listening group (M = 14.56) and the parallel reading group (M = 24.83). These results show that the parallel reading group reproduced more words in the second reconstruction task than the listening group did. Finally, one-way ANOVA did not produce any significant differences in the post-test grammar scores among the three groups, $F(2, 62) = 2.79$, $p = 0.07$, meaning that the three groups equally reconstructed the grammatical forms in the second reconstruction task.

To summarize, the following two major findings emerged from our analysis. First, the text reconstruction task promoted subsequent processing of aural input for all groups. Second, the parallel reading group processed subsequent aural input at the lexical level more efficiently than the listening group (and the shadowing group with approaching significance).

Discussion

A text reconstruction task and learner output

Our first interest in this study was whether a text reconstruction task promotes learner noticing of lexis and grammar during subsequent aural input. According to tables 19.2 and 19.3, participants' recall performance for lexis- and grammar-levels was significantly better in the post-test (M = 18.86 and 1.34) than in the pre-test (M = 8.47 and 0.35). That is, the text reconstruction task likely encouraged participants to notice lexis and grammar during subsequent input. These findings are consistent with recent SLA studies showing that learners who engaged in a text reconstruction task (i.e., output groups) noticed more linguistic forms in subsequent input than did non-output groups (e.g., Leeser, 2008; Uggen, 2012). For example, Leeser (2008) found that his output participants reported more noticing of nouns and of total passage words, not of the target structure (i.e., Spanish past tense), than his non-output participants did. Similarly, Uggen (2012) reported that the participants who reproduced a passage looked for more words during subsequent input to use in their production than non-output participants did.

The findings of the current study, along with those of previous SLA studies, can be explained by the Output Hypothesis. As Swain (1985, 1995, 2005) argues, producing language, under some circumstances, facilitates cognitive processes which may be conducive to L2 acquisition (see Izumi, 2003; Muranoi, 2007 for reviews). In reproducing a text, L2 learners likely noticed the gaps between what they wanted to write and what they could actually write. Text reconstruction might also encourage L2 learners to notice what they have not learned yet (i.e., noticing the hole). Furthermore, when reproducing a passage, L2 learners may have engaged in hypothesis-testing and metalinguistic reflections on their use and knowledge of the target language (Swain, 1998). By doing so, it is plausible that they engaged in cognitive processes in which they could consolidate existing knowledge (Swain & Lapkin, 1995). Thus, the cognitive processes that output had promoted may have facilitated the learner's attention to relevant linguistic information in the subsequent input (Izumi, 2002; Schmidt, 2001; Swain, 2000). As de Bot (1996) argues, 'actively making [a] particular trace in memory is more effective than merely perceiving it. The explanation probably lies in the amount of attention invested' (p. 549). In other words, the cognitive processes that output had triggered may have allowed learners to engage in a cognitive comparison to notice the gap between their interlanguage and the target language contained in the subsequent input (Doughty, 2001; Swain, 2005). When L2 learners experience difficulty in producing the target language during text reconstruction and relevant input is immediately available, they may notice the difference between what they wrote and what a target language speaker would write to convey the same intention (also see Izumi, 2002). Put differently, production of specific linguistic forms during the output task may prime the comprehension of these structures during the subsequent input task (Gass, 1997).

Differences among the three task groups

We were also interested in this study in how subsequent input type (listening, parallel reading, and shadowing) mediates the effects of text reconstruction on learner noticing. As can be seen in Table 19.3, the parallel reading group recalled significantly more lexis in the post-test (M = 24.83) than the listening (M = 14.56) and shadowing groups (M = 17.31). The latter two did not significantly differ. As Table 19.3 shows, all the three groups did not differ significantly in terms of the grammar recall in the post-test (M = 0.78 for Listening, 1.78 for Parallel reading, and 1.41 for shadowing). These results are discussed in more detail below.

Parallel reading was found to be more effective than listening at lexis level. The listening activity used in this study (i.e., listening to a short text without scripts) might be cognitively demanding to the low-intermediate proficiency level participants whose phonological processing is not automatized. It would be reasonable to assume that those students used cognitive resources to pay more attention to lower-level processing such as phonological encoding than higher-level processing (e.g., semantic processing). Due to overloaded cognitive capacities, students in the listening group could not hold the information for a long enough time, which was shown by the inferior performance of the post-test (M = 14.56) compared to those engaged in parallel reading (M = 24.83). A similar explanation can be applied to the results of the parallel reading group, in which, unlike the listening group, written scripts were provided during subsequent input processing. This might have helped the participants to use their resources to pay more attention to semantic processing than phonological and orthographical processing of words, leading to better memory in the post-test.

Interestingly enough, significant differences among the three groups were found to be at the lexical level, not the grammar level. This can be explained by previous SLA research (e.g., Hanaoka, 2007; Leeser, 2008; Qi & Lapkin, 2001; Uggen, 2012; Storch & Wigglesworth, 2010). That is, L2 learners may need more explicit/direct feedback to focus their attention to grammatical problems in their interlanguage output. For example, Hanaoka found that his Japanese university students of English concentrated exclusively on words, not grammar, while receiving written input (90 per cent). Similarly, a participant in Qi and Lapkin paid attention to more lexical issues (about 60 per cent) than grammatical ones (about 30 per cent) in comparing his/her essay with the reformulated version (i.e., a native speaker rewrites learners' sentences keeping their original intention identical). A similarity between the present study and previous SLA studies is that students are not asked to process explicit/direct feedback on their interlangauge output. Instead, L2 learners must have spontaneously focused on forms while receiving implicit/indirect kinds of feedback such as a native speaker's model (the present study, Hanaoka, Leeser, Uggen) and reformulation (Qi & Lapkin, Storch & Wigglesworth) on their interlangauge output. In other words, it is the learners who are responsible for paying attention to linguistic forms. Implicit/indirect feedback may not be sufficient to draw learners' attention to grammatical problems, as limited processing capacity forces L2 learners to comprehend the meanings of the input passage. A potential drawback for this implicit type of input tasks following output activities is that students tend to focus on lexical issues without paying much attention to grammatical problems. Therefore, input task types did not significantly play an important role in determining participants' grammatical processing. Future research needs to be conducted to examine different types of input tasks, particularly more explicit ones. For example, we might need to use input enhancement techniques such as <u>underling</u>, **bold**, and *italics* to highlight targeted grammatical forms in the script for the parallel reading group to improve learner noticing.

Finally, we would like to discuss why shadowing was not found to be as effective as parallel reading. One possible reason, among others, is that we did not ask students to practise shadowing before the experiment. Shiki, Mori, Kadota and Yoshida (2010) showed that effectiveness of shadowing improves when students were provided with sufficient practice (also see Hamada, 2009, 2011). The second reason is that shadowing in this study may have been cognitively more demanding than expected. As shadowing is a cognitively demanding task in that it asks for dual processing (i.e., listening and speaking at the same time), we carefully chose the passage that we believed was relatively easy for our students (i.e., i-1 in Krashen's sense). However, the passage chosen in this study may have been too difficult for students to perform shadowing. Kadota (2007) speculates that an i-10 passage might be most suitable for shadowing. Also, the passage was new to the participants. Some students might not have known the meanings of some words and how targeted grammatical forms work. It is important to note that in a dictogloss task, teachers often debrief target forms before the task. This debriefing encourages L2 learners to focus on grammatical forms.

Limitations and future research

Before concluding this chapter, we would like to mention several limitations inherent to this study. The first limitation is the generalizability of our findings. We used only one type of output task (i.e., text reconstruction). Different results might have been generated by using different output-based tasks such as dictogloss, jigsaw, picture-cued production, text reconstruction, text-editing, and three-stage-writing task. Further investigation into task types with Japanese learners is important, as Song and Suh (2008) showed that task types mediated the effect of output-based tasks on noticing and L2 acquisition (also see Izumi & Bigelow, 2000; Izumi et al., 1999). Borgjin, Suzuki and Itagaki (2013) also argue that the degree of attention (i.e., noticing) may depend on the complexity of output tasks L2 learners are asked to perform. Furthermore, the type of modality (i.e., oral vs written) may play an important role in determining the effect of output on subsequent input tasks (see Leow, 1995; Sanz, 1997). Clearly, future research should explore different effects of various output-based tasks on noticing and L2 learning.

Second, we did not control for participants' prior knowledge of the target lexis and grammar contained in the listening passage. This makes it difficult to differentiate the extent to which the findings were affected by output-generated cognitive processes or the amount of prior knowledge that participants possessed before this experiment. However, it is worth remembering that producing language helped our participants process the model passage more effectively or deeply enough to remember it for the post-test (i.e., the second text reconstruction). Therefore, we believe that lack of pre-testing did not entirely diminish the effects of output-generated cognitive processes on subsequent input. However, future inquiries should include a pre-test about the targeted lexical and grammatical forms.

Third, we defined recall accuracy as usage of the same lexical and grammatical forms as the input passage. It is reasonable to assume that forms that were noticed and encoded in memory during subsequent input tasks would be recalled more often in participants' post-test. However, it is also true that people tend to store information in meaning form, not in exact wording (Anderson, 2005). Therefore, when participants used different lexical and grammatical forms, it may have indicated that the information was actually better understood and internalized into interlangauge. In addition, the text reconstruction task was open-ended and tended to deviate from the original passage, compared with other more guided text reconstruction task with cues provided (Nassaji & Tian, 2010; Suzuki & Itagaki, 2012). Therefore, it is debatable if the recall accuracy defined in this study is a valid measure.

Finally, we did not measure L2 development using delayed post-tests (e.g., one week later, one month later). However, it is almost impossible to include delayed post-tests in this research design paradigm. If we had incorporated delayed post-tests, we would not have been able to distinguish the extent to which delayed post-test performance was affected by the output-generated cognitive processes that participants engaged in during or after the experiment. The aim of this study is not to claim that output leads to L2 acquisition, but to demonstrate the effect of an output task on subsequent input processing (i.e., intake).

Despite these limitations, we hope that this study, along with previous SLA studies, encourages more L2 practitioners to use output-based activities such as text reconstruction in their classrooms. Our study also shows that after text reconstruction, subsequent oral input tasks can be manipulated in various ways. One option is to provide learners with written scripts that they can follow during subsequent oral input tasks. As this study indicates, listening with written scripts (parallel reading) helps these Japanese learners of English to process subsequent input and internalize it more effectively into long-term memory, compared to simply listening to the passage again (and probably shadowing). As we stated in our Introduction, parallel reading and shadowing are popular pedagogical approaches in English language classrooms in Japan (see Kadota, 2007; Murphey, 2001; Tamai, 2005). While the results of our research do find parallel reading to benefit immediate recall by participants, more studies are needed to investigate the effects of these techniques on L2 acquisition (see Hamada, 2009, 2011).

We hope this chapter will be useful for many language researchers and encourage practitioners in Asian countries to make output-based tasks proposed in SLA research ecologically valid in their own contexts, and test their effectiveness in their own classrooms.[1]

Appendices

Appendix 19.1

In recent years, more and more women <u>have been</u> working. They may earn money <u>to help</u> their husbands. In some cases, they earn all of the money for the family. In this way, the woman and the man reverse their traditional roles. The woman earns all of the money. And the man stays at home <u>to take care</u> of the children and the house. More women recently <u>have decided</u> not <u>to have</u> children at all. Some women have children and <u>continue to</u> work. They do not leave their jobs just because they have children. These are some of the ways that women's roles <u>have changed</u>. (Tsuyuki, 2007: 24).

Appendix 19.2

Instruction: Please reconstruct the passage you have just listened to. The beginning words or phrases of every sentence were provided. You have five minutes to perform this task.

1. In recent years, _____
2. They may _____
3. In some cases, _____
4. In this way, _____
5. The woman _____
6. And the man _____
7. More women _____
8. Some women _____
9. They _____
10. These are _____

Note

1 This work was supported by *Grant-in-Aid for Scientific Research* (C) (21520561). Earlier versions of this paper were presented (a) at the annual conference of the Japan Society of English Language Education (JSELE) held at Kansai University, Osaka, 7–8 August 2010, and (b) at Second Language Research Forum (SLRF) 2010 held at University of Maryland, College Park, Maryland, 14–17 October 2010.

References

Anderson, R. (2005). *Cognitive psychology and its implications* (6th edition). New York: Worth Pub.

Borgjin, S., Suzuki, W., & Itagaki, N. (2013). The effect of an output task on L2 acquisition: Does task difficulty make a difference? *The Tohoku English Language Education Society Bulletin, 33*, 59–71.

de Bot, K. (1996). The psycholinguistics of the output hypothesis. *Language Learning, 46*, 529–555.

Doughty, C. (2001). Cognitive underpinning of focus on form. In P. Robinson (Ed.), *Cognition and second language instruction* (pp. 206–257). Cambridge: Cambridge University Press.

Ellis, R. (2003). *Task-based language learning and teaching*. Oxford: Oxford University Press.

Ellis, R. (2008). *The handbook of second language acquisition* (2nd edition). Oxford: Oxford University Press.

Gass, S. M. (1997). *Input, interaction, and the second language learner*. Mahwah, NJ: Lawrence Erlbaum.

Hamada, Y. (2009). The effects of shadowing with two different difficulties of texts on listening comprehension and metacognitive strategies. *Second Language, 8*, 27–49.

Hamada, Y. (2011). Shadowing training with difficult materials. *Journal of Asia TEFL, 8*, 137–162.

Hanaoka, O. (2007). Output, noticing, and learning: An investigation into the role of spontaneous attention to form in a four-stage writing task. *Language Teaching Research, 11*, 459–479.

Huberty, C. J., & Morris, J. D. (1989). Multivariate analysis versus multiple univariate analyses. *Psychological Bulletin, 105*, 302–308.

Iwanaka, T., & Takatsukasa, S. (2007). Roles of output and noticing in SLA: Does exposure to relevant input immediately after output promote vocabulary learning? *Annual Review of English Language Education (ARELE), 18*, 121–130.

Izumi, S. (2002). Output, input enhancement, and the noticing hypothesis: An experimental study on ESL relativization. *Studies in Second Language Acquisition, 24*, 541–577.

Izumi, S. (2003). Comprehension and production processes in second language learning: In search of the psycholinguistic rationale of the output hypothesis. *Applied Linguistics, 24*, 168–196.

Izumi, S., & Bigelow, M. (2000). Does output promote noticing and second language acquisition? *TESOL Quarterly, 34*, 239–278.

Izumi, S., Bigelow, M., Fujiwara, M., & Fearnow, S. (1999). Testing the output hypothesis: Effects of output on noticing and second language acquisition. *Studies in Second Language Acquisition, 21*, 421–452.

Izumi, Y., & Izumi, S. (2004). Investigating the effects of oral output on the learning of relative clauses in English: Issues in the psycholinguistic requirements for effective output tasks. *Canadian Modern Language Review, 60*, 587–609.

Kadota, S. (2007). *Science of shadowing and oral reading*. Tokyo: Cosmoier.

Keck, C. M., Iberri-Shea, G., Tracy-Ventura, N., & Wa-Mbaleka, S. (2006). Investigating the empirical link between task-based interaction and acquisition: A meta-analysis. In J. M. Norris & L. Ortega (Eds), *Synthesizing research on language learning and teaching* (pp. 91–131). Philadelphia: John Benjamins.

Kowal, M., & Swain, M. (1997). From semantic to syntactic processing: How can we promote it in the immersion classroom? In R. K. Johnson & M. Swain (Eds), *Immersion education: International perspectives* (pp. 284–309). Cambridge: Cambridge University Press.

Lapkin, S., Hart, D., & Swain, M. (1991). Early and middle French immersion programs: French-language outcomes. *Canadian Modern Language Review, 48*, 11–40.

Leeser, M. J. (2008). Pushed output, noticing, and development of past tense morphology in content-based instruction. *Canadian Modern Language Review, 65*, 195–220.

Leow, R. (1995). Modality and intake in second language acquisition. *Studies in Second Language Acquisition, 17*, 79–89.

Li, S. (2010). The effectiveness of corrective feedback in SLA: A meta-analysis. *Language Learning, 60*, 309–365.

Lyster, R. (2007). *Learning and teaching language through content: A counter-balanced approach*. Amsterdam: John Benjamins.

Lyster, R., & Saito, K. (2010). Oral feedback in classroom SLA: A meta-analysis. *Studies in Second Language Acquisition, 32*, 265–302.

Mackey, A., & Goo, J. (2007). Interaction research in SLA: A meta-analysis and research synthesis. In A. Mackey (Ed.), *Conversational interaction in second language acquisition: A collection of empirical studies* (pp. 407–451). New York: Oxford University Press.

Muranoi, H. (2007). Output practice in the L2 classroom. In R. DeKeyser (Ed.), *Practice in second language learning: Perspectives from applied linguistics and cognitive psychology* (p. 51–84). Cambridge University Press.

Murphey, T. (2001). Exploring conversational shadowing. *Language Teaching Research, 5*, 128–155.

Nassaji, H., & Tian, J. (2010). Collaborative and individual output tasks and their effects on learning English phrasal verbs. *Language Teaching Research, 14*, 397–419.

Pica, T., Kang, H., & Sauro, S. (2006). Information gap tasks: Their multiple roles and contributions to interaction research methodology. *Studies in Second Language Acquisition, 28*, 301–338.

Qi, D. S., & Lapkin, S. (2001). Exploring the role of noticing in a three-stage second language writing task. *Journal of Second Language Writing, 10*, 277–303.

Sachs, R., & Polio, C. (2007). Learners' uses of two types of written corrective feedback on an L2 writing revision task. *Studies in Second Language Acquisition, 29*, 67–100.

Samuda, V., & Bygate, M. (2008). *Tasks in second language learning*. London: Palgrave.

Sanz, C. (1997). Experimental tasks in SLA research: Amount of production, modality, memory, and production process. In W. Glass, & A. Perez-Leroux (Eds), *Contemporary perspectives on the acquisition of Spanish* (pp. 41–56). Somerville, MA: Cascadilla.

Schmidt, R. (2001). Attention. In P. Robinson (Ed.), *Cognition and second language instruction* (pp. 3–32). Cambridge: Cambridge University Press.

Shiki, O., Mori, Y., Kadota, S., & Yoshida, S. (2010). Exploring differences between shadowing and repeating practices: An analysis of reproduction rate and types of reproduced words. *Annual Review of English Language Education in Japan (ARELE), 21*, 81–90.

Skehan, P. (1996). A framework for the implementation of task-based instruction. *Applied Linguistics, 17*, 38–62.

Spada, N. (2011). Beyond form-focused instruction: Reflections on past, present and future research. *Language Teaching, 44*, 225–236.

Song, M.-J., & Suh, B. R. (2008). The effects of output task types on noticing and learning of the English past counterfactual conditional. *System, 36*, 295–312.

Storch, N., & Wigglesworth, G. (2010). Learners' processing, uptake, and retention of corrective feedback on writing. *Studies in Second Language Acquisition, 32*, 303–334.

Suzuki, W., & Itagaki, N. (2012). *Differential effects of input-based and output-based instructions: A trade-off between form and meaning*. Paper presented at an annual conference of the American Association of Applied Linguistics held in Boston, USA, March 24–27, 2012.

Suzuki, W., Itagaki, N., Takagi, T., & Watanabe, T. (2009). The effect of output processing on subsequent input processing: a free recall study. *Teachers College, Columbia University Working Papers in TESOL & Applied Linguistics*, 9, 1–17.

Swain, M. (1985). Communicative competence: Some roles of comprehensible input and comprehensible output in its development. In S. Gass & C. Madden (Eds), *Input in second language acquisition* (pp. 235–253). Rowley, MA: Newbury House.

Swain, M. (1995). Three functions of output in second language learning. In G. Cook & B. Seidlhofer (Eds), *Principles and practice in the study of language: Studies in honour of H. G. Widdowson* (pp. 129–144) Oxford: Oxford University Press.

Swain, M. (1998). Focus on form through conscious reflection. In J. Doughty, & J. Williams (Eds), *Focus on form in classroom second language acquisition* (pp. 64–81). Cambridge, UK: Cambridge University Press.

Swain, M. (2000). The output hypothesis and beyond: Mediating acquisition through collaborative dialogue. In P. Lantolf. (Ed.) *Sociocultural theory and second language learning* (pp. 97–114). Oxford: Oxford University Press.

Swain, M. (2005). The output hypothesis: Theory and research. In E. Hinkel (Ed.), *The handbook of research in second language teaching and learning* (pp. 471–483). Mahwah, NJ: Lawrence Erlbaum.

Swain, M., & Lapkin, S. (1995). Problems in output and the cognitive processes they generate: A step towards second language learning. *Applied Linguistics*, 16, 371–391.

Swain, M., and Lapkin, S. (1998). Interaction and second language learning: Two adolescent French immersion students working together. *The Modern Language Journal*, 82, 320–337.

Swain, M., and Lapkin, S. (2000). Task-based second language learning: The uses of the first language. *Language Teaching Research*, 4, 251–274.

Swain, M., & Lapkin, S. (2001). Focus on form through collaborative dialogue: Exploring task effects. In M. Bygate, P. Skehan, & M. Swain (Eds), *Researching pedagogic tasks: Second language learning, teaching and testing* (pp. 99–118). Harlow, England: Longman.

Swain, M., & Lapkin, S. (2002). Talking it through: Two French immersion learners' response to reformulation. *International Journal of Educational Research*, 37, 285–304.

Tamai, K. (2005). *Research on the effect of shadowing as a listening instruction method*. Tokyo: Kazama Publishing.

Tsuyuki, Y. (2007). *Reading tasks for college students*. Tokyo: Nanundo.

Uggen, M. S. (2012). Reinvestigation the noticing function of output. *Language Learning*, 62, 506–540.

Wajnryb, R. (1990). *Grammar dictation*. Oxford: Oxford University Press.

Willis, J. (1996). A flexible framework for task-based learning. In J. Willis. & D. Willis (Eds), *Challenges and change in language teaching* (pp. 52–62). Oxford: Heinemann.

Willis, D., & Willis, J. (2007). *Doing task-based teaching*. Oxford: Oxford University Press.

20

TBLT Materials and Curricula:

From Theory to Practice

Brian Tomlinson

Summary

This chapter provides a personal and critical review of the issues involved in designing and using curricula and learning materials for task-based language teaching (TBLT). It focuses on controversial issues (such as 'Should the materials encourage students to focus on language before, during or after the task, or not at all?'), summarizes the arguments for the different positions and then puts forward a personal view based on my extensive experience of applying theory to practice in classrooms and in materials projects around the world. In providing this review the chapter articulates theories and exemplifies them in practice. In addition it specifies those principles and procedures of task-based learning which are likely to facilitate language acquisition, it lists procedures which are unlikely to facilitate language acquisition and it relates the approach advocated in the chapter to the approaches put forward in other chapters in Part Five. In doing the latter it recognizes the importance of accommodating approaches to their context of learning whilst warning that contextual constraints should not dictate an approach.

Materials design

There is literature outlining the principles and procedures of TBLT (e.g., Ellis, 2010, 2011; Mishan, 2005; Samuda & Bygate, 2008; Van den Branden, Bygate & Norris, 2009; Willis & Willis, 2007), there is some literature reporting research findings in relation to the effectiveness of TBLT (e.g., Ellis, 2010, 2011; Van den Branden, 2006), there is some literature reporting TBLT projects (e.g., Prabhu, 1987; Van den Branden, 2006) but there is hardly any literature focusing on materials and curriculum design for TBLT. So, instead of reviewing the literature I am going to give my own views about some important questions in relation to materials and curriculum design for TBLT and then relate them to the English as a Foreign Language (EFL) teaching context in South East and East Asia and to the other chapters in this part of this book. My views are based on my experience of using TBLT and observing it used in many different countries around the world, of being involved in the development of TBLT materials and on my critical reading of the literature.

Should the materials address the teacher, the students or both?

If the materials address the students there is a danger that some tasks might be linguistically, culturally or topically unsuitable for certain classes which the materials are used with. If the tasks are delivered in a teacher's book with a suggested script the teacher can select appropriate tasks, can modify the scripts in relation to the actual level of the students in class, can change the sequence of the tasks and can make changes to the objectives and intended outcomes of the tasks. The teacher also has the option of copying and distributing the original or modified written task instructions and then reading them aloud as the students follow the script (a practice endorsed by research into what facilitates comprehension), or of giving the original or modified instructions orally. If the learners are of a very basic language level, giving the learners photos of equivalent learners performing the task (as we once did on a primary project in China) could help the teacher to make her instructions clear. However, if the materials have been developed for sale, then selling forty student books is much more profitable than selling one teacher's book. That is probably why all the commercially published TBLT materials I have seen in use in Asia address the student (including materials I have authored for China, Japan and Singapore). The only TBLT book I know which is addressed to the teacher is Tomlinson (1981), a book of tasks developed by a large group of primary teachers at a workshop in Vanuatu and published by the Ministry of Education for use in primary schools throughout the country. This book is addressed to the teacher but does also provide cue cards and instructions for the teacher to give to the students (possibly after class-specific modification).

Should the materials encourage students to focus on language before, during or after the task, or not at all?

I favour the strong form of TBLT in which achieving the task, rather than learning the language, is given prominence. Weak forms often encourage pre-teaching of language which could be useful when doing the task and in doing so risks changing the task into a practice activity. Most students are already predisposed to focus on language items and starting the lesson by satisfying this predisposition is likely to mean that the students and their teacher treat the task as an opportunity to strengthen the students' knowledge of the pre-selected language items rather than as an opportunity to develop their ability to communicate effectively. However, if the lesson starts with a readiness activity which activates their minds in relation to the task (Tomlinson 2013b), the students are more likely to focus on communicating meaning and achieving intent whilst performing the task.

This does not mean though that there should never be any attention to language during a task-based lesson. I am in favour of a form of responsive teaching in which the teacher provides language to the students when they need and ask for it whilst attempting informal communication. After all, the best time to learn something is when you really need it. I am also in favour of returning to the task performance after its completion in order to help the students to make discoveries about language features which turned out to be salient for the successful performance of the task. I would only do this though if the task has engaged the learners and if they have achieved at least partial success in achieving their task objectives. I would also give the learners an opportunity to make use of their discoveries either in a revision of their first task performance or in a subsequent and similar task (Tomlinson, 2013b). We used this approach on the PKG English Programme in Indonesia with twelve-year-old beginners (Tomlinson, 1990). We started using TPR Plus activities (Tomlinson, 1994b) in which the task was to mime a story whilst it was being narrated by the teacher, or to paint a picture dictated by the teacher, or to cook food from oral instructions or to play a game from oral instructions. There was no pre-teaching of language at all. But a few weeks later the 'text' was used for language discovery activities. Later in the course the students took part in locally developed scenarios (di Pietro, 1987) in which the task was to use English to achieve your intent (e.g., getting a taxi to take you the way you wanted to go; persuading your mother to let you stay up to watch a badminton tournament on television; getting the birthday present you wanted). In each scenario there were two roles. Half the class in groups prepared for one role and half prepared for the other. The students knew who the other role represented but not what they were going to say and do. After the preparation of strategies representatives from the two halves played out the scenario and tried to achieve their intent. At any time a 'time out' could be called and advice given or a substitution made. Afterwards the teacher led a post-mortem in which the strategies and language used were reviewed and suggestions were made for what might have been more effective. Then another similar scenario was prepared for and acted out. The TPR Plus and scenario tasks were very popular with the students in the experimental classes (i.e., one class in each secondary school) but at first Principals, Inspectors and parents were worried that the students would not learn enough language. However they changed their mind when it was revealed that not only was attendance much higher in the experimental classes but that the students from them were outperforming equivalent students from the traditional classes on the grammar-based end of year examinations.

I have been using a strong version of the task-based approach for thirty-five years now and I am convinced of its value in engaging learners, in stimulating them to use English for communication and in helping them to achieve communicative effectiveness (though I do not have much empirical evidence to prove this). I started promoting meaning focused communicative activities at a teacher training college in Zambia in the early 1970s and then used them as part of my course at a language college in the UK in the late 1970s. In the early 1980s I moved towards a more task-based approach and since them have used it in my teaching and promoted it in my teacher training in Vanuatu, Indonesia, Japan, Singapore, Oman and the UK. I have also published a number of TBLT textbooks. Tomlinson (1981) is a collection of tasks for use in Class

4 in primary schools in Vanuatu. Some of the tasks have no language focus at all, some have a language discovery activity after a first task and before a similar second task, and many of them involve problem solving. Tomlinson (1994a) is a book first published in 1986 which offers teachers forty-five extracts from contemporary world literature accompanied by suggestions for using them in task-based units. Tomlinson and Masuhara (1994) is a collection of text-driven, task-based units for use in Japanese universities. As in Tomlinson (1994a) the tasks have no language focus at all. I used both these books in Japan and in Singapore and they were very popular with both the students and with my teacher trainees. However, I must admit neither book sold very well, probably because they did not satisfy the teachers' apparent need for books which help them to teach language. Tomlinson et al. (2000) is a book of text-driven, task-based units for use in secondary schools in Singapore. This book did eventually sell quite well, probably because it does contain language discovery activities after the tasks and because there are also many follow-up activities in addition to the tasks (most of them encouraging critical thinking). Another text-driven textbook is Tomlinson (2004), a course for the language improvement of primary teachers in Ethiopia. Many (but not all) of the units were task-based with a language focus activity following the task. This book was published and distributed by the Ministry of Education and received very positive feedback from the teachers and their trainers.

Hitomi Masuhara and I tried to use a strong TBLT approach on a task-based book we were invited to write in China but the publishers rejected our draft unit because it did not include the language drills which they were convinced that the students needed (especially those from rural areas). We did however manage to publish a course for primary schools in China which included tasks (Tomlinson et al., 2002) – but the tasks were language driven so as to conform to the Ministry syllabus. The feeling that TBLT approaches will not work without discrete language teaching and language practice seems to be currently prevalent in my experience in such countries as China, Japan, Malaysia, Singapore, South Korea and Vietnam (see the other chapters in this part of the book). However I know of Process Drama TBLT materials being successfully used in a South Korean high school (Park, 2010) and I have seen the strong TBLT materials produced by trainee teachers from Universiti Putra Malaysia and used very successfully in local high schools to stimulate language use through video-recorded performance.

Should the materials pre-determine a language focus or encourage the teacher (and the students) to decide on this after the initial task has been completed?

Very definitely I am in favour of deciding on the language focus after the task has been completed. If the language focus is pre-determined it will probably be given priority by the teacher and there will be a danger of the task being turned into a language practice activity (especially if the students know what the language focus will be). Ideally the language focus should be decided after task completion by the teacher, because of an observed problem, or by the students, because of a perceived difficulty, or because they have become curious about a salient language feature. This is another reason for the materials being addressed to the teacher and unavailable to the students. If only the teacher sees the materials, the materials writer can suggest potential language features for post-task exploration and even provide sample discovery activities. The teacher can then decide which, if any, of the suggested features to focus on as well as which, if any, of the activities to make use of.

It is very rare for published TBLT materials to risk this approach and almost unheard of in South and South East Asia where teachers are judged on the ability of their students to learn the language structures and items prescribed in the syllabus. Such materials are reported in Van den Branden (2006) as being successful in promoting communicative competence in Belgium; I did devise and use such materials at Kobe University in Japan (e.g., the students in groups had to devise and then present to a 'company' a cheaply produced device for saving water) and I have co-authored books in Japan (Tomlinson & Masuhara, 1994) and in Singapore (Tomlinson et al., 2000) which contained texts and tasks devised for their potential for engagement rather than their focus on items from the syllabus. However it would be unthinkable for a commercial publisher to publish a global TBLT coursebook in which the tasks were not at least overtly influenced by pre-selected language items.

What should the learners be asked to do?

My experience with TBLT as a teacher and a materials writer tells me that tasks are most effective in facilitating eventual language skills acquisition in a target language if the learners are asked to:

1. understand input in the target language (whether it be in the form of a text, a cue card or just instructions for performing the task);
2. use the target language to achieve a non-linguistic goal (e.g., solve a problem; cook a meal; repair a machine; play a musical instrument; tell a joke to make people laugh);
3. do something which either replicates a real-life task (e.g., compiling an agenda for a meeting) or is a pedagogic task which requires the use of language skills which would be useful in real-life tasks (seeking clarification from a 'runner' who is dictating a hidden picture for her group to reproduce);
4. do something which engages the learners both affectively and cognitively (e.g., competing to be the first group to solve a complex problem; devising a bizarre other planet world to locate a story in; writing a response to a newspaper article which proposes controversial action in relation to a complex and emotive local issue);
5. do something which is either perceived to be relevant to their world or alternatively which is bizarrely different from any previous experience;
6. reflect on the effectiveness of their language use during the task, make discoveries about a language feature and ideally perform another similar task with the benefit of their discoveries (e.g., making a paper aeroplane from faulty oral instructions, realising they had not sought clarification and then

making a paper boat from instructions whilst seeking clarification of any confusing instructions).

As Van den Branden (2006, p. 1) points out the term TBLT 'was coined, and the concept developed, by SLA researchers and language educators'. Many of the early publications on TBLT were research-based and gave examples of tasks which were used in experiments. Most of these tasks were chosen because they were easy to control in experiments as they did not involve the multiplicity of variables which many of the communication activities used in the 1970s and 1980s did. I am referring to such tasks as spotting the difference between two pictures, telling a story from a picture prompt, following directions to find a location on a map and putting a mixed-up text into the correct sequence. Because these type of tasks have been frequently cited in the literature they have tended to dominate TBLT teaching and materials. This is unfortunate in my view because many such tasks do not meet my criteria 3, 4, 5 and 6. In particular, many of them are trivial and unengaging.

Van den Branden (2006) does contain many multi-faceted tasks which were used successfully in Belgium and which meet most of my criteria (e.g., working out how a fakir performs a gruesome trick) but not many of the tasks exemplified in the literature do meet my demanding criteria. Many of the tasks in the collection of those developed by primary teachers in Vanuatu (Tomlinson, 1981) did meet my criteria. For example, the pupils were asked in groups to take a role card as a member of a family. Each member needed a certain amount of money urgently that morning but the only one with any money was the father, who only had a 500 Vatu note. This was not enough to meet the urgent needs of the others and, in any case, could not be divided up. The members of the family had to share their need with each other and then come up with a solution to the problem. When they found a solution they then looked for another group who had succeeded too and then shared their solution with them. The teacher joined in the discussions and mentally noted a focus for a language follow-up. There are other such examples in the books I have been involved in which were referred to in item 2 above. Most of them have taken a text-driven task-based approach in which meaning focused listening to and/or reading of a potentially engaging text drives a follow-up task. The sequence of activities (described in detail in Tomlinson 2013b) usually goes:

1 A **readiness activity** to activate the learners' minds in relation to the location, topic or theme of the core text (e.g., 'Think back to your first day at school. Try to see pictures in your mind of you getting ready to go to school, of you on your way to school and of you in the classroom for the first time.').

2 An **initial response activity** to help the learners to respond to the text holistically rather than to follow their inclination to study it (e.g., 'Read the poem, "First Day at School" and as you read it try to see pictures in your mind of what happens to the boy in the poem.').

3 An **intake response activity** to help the learners to express and deepen their understanding of the text (e.g., 'Draw pictures of anything you can remember in the poem. Show your pictures to your group and tell them what you have drawn.').

4 A **development task** in which the learners use the target language to produce a written or spoken text developed from or in response to the core text (e.g., 'Write a poem about yourself called, "First Day at University". Read your poem to the other members of your group, listen to their poems and then discuss how your poems are similar and how they are different.').

5 An **input response** activity in which the learners return to the core text to make discoveries about a salient language feature (e.g., 'In the poem the boy seems to ask a lot of questions. In your group find these questions in the poem. Who is he talking to? Is he really asking questions? What is he using these "questions" for?').

6 A **research task** in which the learners investigate other instances of the salient feature they focused on in 5 above (e.g., 'In the readers in our class library find other examples of "questions" which are not really asking questions. For each one decide what the "question" is being used for.').

7 Another **development task** in which the learners either produce another similar 'text' or revise their original text (e.g., 'In your group choose one of your poems and then together write an improved version of it. You can insert some "questions" if you like.').

At Sultan Qaboos University in Oman I used tasks which matched my criteria, in particular text-driven tasks which I developed by using a text from the coursebook and adding a task (e.g., reading a text about horse racing in Sienna was followed by group drawings of photos they 'took' at a local camel race and at the horse race in Sienna, which they then sent with a letter to someone they had 'met' in Sienna). I also often ended a lesson with a five minute mini-task. These usually involved pair or group solving of a bizarre riddle (e.g., 'Where do fish keep their money?') or a bizarre problem (e.g., 'Why did the customer on the next table to me suddenly burst into flames?'). These mini-tasks were very popular as the students soon realized that there were no right answers and they could be as creative and silly in English as they liked in their responses.

Which features of materials for TBLT are likely to promote language acquisition?

From my experience as a teacher, materials writer and researcher I would say that TBLT materials can facilitate both language acquisition and language development (Tomlinson, 2007, 2013a) if they:

- expose the learners to language in use;
- engage the learners cognitively (i.e., the learners are involved in thinking before, during and after the task);
- engage the learners affectively (i.e., the learners are positive about doing the task and experience such emotions and feelings as enjoyment, achievement, excitement, satisfaction, etc., whilst doing the task);
- ensure that the learners use the target language in order to achieve non-linguistic outcomes;

- replicate real-life tasks or involve the learners in pedagogic tasks which require the use of real-life skills and/or strategies;
- set the learners an achievable challenge;
- focus on communication but also provide opportunities for the learners to make outcome-related discoveries about language use.

Which features of materials for TBLT are unlikely to promote language acquisition?

TBLT materials are unlikely to facilitate language acquisition and development if they:

- only expose the learners to language which has been contrived to illustrate language points;
- provide overt teaching of language points prior to doing the task;
- provide so much preparation help and time that task performance is easy or even automatic;
- make it possible for the learners to achieve task completion without effective communication in English;
- do not engage the learners cognitively and affectively;
- focus on content, objectives and/or actions which are perceived as irrelevant.

Unfortunately many of the materials I have seen which claim to be task-based (and sometimes even text-driven) do many of the things which are listed above as preventers of language acquisition and development. They do so not because of any applied linguistics or any evidence of effectiveness but because it is considered to be what teachers and their students want.

Issues of materials design

Many of the chapters in this volume move away from my favoured strong version of TBLT towards a much weaker version which their authors consider more appropriate for their Asian context. They do so after considering such factors as the perceived needs and wants of the learners and their teachers, the demands of external examinations and what appears to be a common belief that the language needed to perform a task needs to be 'acquired' by the learners before that task can usefully be attempted. For example, in Suzuki and Itagaki the conclusion which seems to be reached from their research is that in Japan the main concern is with the eventual accuracy of output and that this favours a weak version of TBLT in which texts and tasks are chosen for their potential for facilitating acquisition of language rather than their ability to promote communicative effectiveness. Park comes to a similar conclusion for learners in South Korea so that the required language accuracy can be achieved for college entrance examinations. Darasawang reports how a task-based curriculum in Thailand was revised over time into a task-oriented curriculum as a result of concerns about the learners' lack of accuracy and to satisfy a perception that in order to acquire language accuracy the learners need to focus primarily on language. This approach did retain task performance as one of its components and was still concerned with fluency. But the linguistic accuracy thought to be attainable through a weak version of TBLT was given primacy, as it is in the other countries reported on in Part Five. My own experience of using TBLT in these countries is that the students, whether they be young learners, teenagers or adults, are easily persuaded to use and appreciate task-based approaches if teachers who they respect are committed to them. However many local teachers are hesitant to use them because they contradict their training and previous experience, because they are not confident in their ability to 'teach' such approaches and because they are afraid that using such approaches will result in their students using inaccurate English and failing their examinations. I commented on this problem with pedagogical innovation in Tomlinson (2005) and have found that it can only be overcome through in-service training which informs the teachers of the principles of the new approach, gives them experience of it as learners, gives them opportunities to question and maybe modify it and gives them a lot of monitored experience of implementing it. This was the case on the PKG Programme in Indonesia reported above.

Of course, I am not saying that strong versions of TBLT should be imposed on teachers and students in South East and East Asia. I agree with the other authors in Part Five that all the influencing factors in the context of learning need to be taken into account and that no approach will be successful without the willing and enthusiastic support of the teachers and the students. What I am saying though is that for over thirty years I have used a strong version of TBLT in many different countries and I have never had any negative reactions from students or teacher trainees. It could be, of course, that my obvious investment of belief and enthusiasm in the materials has been an important factor in their acceptance and it could also be that it is easier for an outsider to introduce an innovation as this does not confound expectation in the same way that innovation by insiders might.

Curriculum design

Again, instead of reviewing the literature, I am going to give my views about some important questions in relation to curriculum design for TBLT and then to relate them to my experience in South East and East Asia as well as the chapters in this volume. For discussions in the literature of task-based syllabuses see Prabhu (1987), Long and Crookes (1992), Mishan (2005), Van den Branden (2006) and Nation and Macalister (2010).

Should the curriculum pre-determine the tasks to be used on a course?

If the curriculum is based on a TBLT approach then I think that many of the tasks (or at least the task types) should be pre-determined so that they cover the situations, the objectives, the outcomes, the skills and the strategies which are relevant to the learners' post-course performance in the target language. It would be important though to list more tasks than the learners actually have to do so that the teacher (or the learners) can select those within each group which are most likely to match interests and achieve engagement.

If only a part of the curriculum is devoted to TBLT then pre-determining the actual tasks is less important and might be considered to be an imposition by teachers who know their learners better than the curriculum developers do. If the teachers are given the opportunity to select the tasks from a menu or even find or develop tasks themselves there is a greater likelihood of perceived relevance and of engagement. If teachers are given this freedom it is important that they are encouraged to ensure variety of task types and content.

If a curriculum does pre-determine tasks should they be specified according to situations, to topics, to task types, to task skills or to language features?

I would specify and categorize group tasks according to task types but I would also make it easy for the teachers to find where specific situations, topics and skills will be involved. I would definitely not specify (or even cross-refer to) language features as you cannot always predict which language features will be salient in a task and trying to do so can encourage the teacher to teach and the learner to practise. This is a phenomenon I have observed in hundreds of classrooms all over the world when the syllabus has linked a suggested task or task type to a prescribed language point. So, for example, instead of facilitating scenarios in which one student is asking another student to turn his music volume down the teacher pre-teaches expressions like, 'Could you please . . .', 'I'd be grateful if . . .' and 'I'd appreciate it if . . .'. Then the students in pairs practise these expressions in totally unrealistic dialogues.

Should pre-determined tasks be sequenced in a curriculum?

I cannot see any advantage in sequencing tasks in a curriculum as progression from simple to complex or from one learning point to another related one. These considerations might be important in a language-based curriculum but are much less important in a TBLT curriculum. What I would do is to group tasks according to their task type and then let the teachers (or better still the learners) decide which group to start with.

I might however have a starter group of facilitating tasks which help to develop skills which will be useful when performing tasks in all the groups (e.g., seeking clarification; giving instructions; expressing opinions; achieving consensus).

Issues of curriculum design

The chapters in this volume seem to conclude that, given the characteristics of their Asian contexts of learning, the only feasible approach in their situation is for the curriculum to specify the tasks and for the tasks to be designed to focus on language features. This is not what I have done in South East and East Asia but it might be a reasonable conclusion in the contexts which the authors are reporting on. I was fortunate in that I had the great advantage of deciding on my own syllabus at Kobe University in Japan and, as Programme Leader, influencing what happened on the PKG English Programme in Indonesia (even though we were ultimately constrained by the Ministry syllabus).

Conclusion

What seems to emerge from my comments is that I am in favour of TBLT materials which:

- provide the learners with any necessary texts, illustrations, encouragement etc.;
- provide the teacher with the above plus suggested (but modifiable) task objectives, instructions, outcomes and follow-up activities;
- are based on a principled strong approach to TBLT which provides exposure to language in use and opportunities to use language to achieve non-linguistic purposes, as well as engaging the learners both cognitively and affectively and helping them to make discoveries about language use;
- follow a principled sequence of: 1) Readiness activity; 2) Task preparation; 3) Task performance; and 4) Task follow-up;
- provide a menu of tasks for the teacher (and ideally the students) to select from.

I would really welcome materials, either commercially published or institutionally provided, which attempt to follow the recommendations above. Whilst doing so I would also accept that when implementing TBLT approaches in a specific context there is a need, as the chapters in Part Five do, to consider the constraints that appear to be made by the context of learning and to make appropriate accommodations to the approach.

References

di Pietro, R. (1987). *Strategic interaction: Learning languages through scenarios*. Cambridge: Cambridge University Press.
Ellis, R. (2010). Second language acquisition research and language-teaching materials. In N. Harwood (Ed.), *English language teaching materials: Theory and practice* (pp. 33–56). Cambridge: Cambridge University Press.
Ellis, R. (2011). Macro- and micro-evaluations of task-based teaching. In B. Tomlinson (Ed.), *Materials development in language teaching* (pp. 212–235). Cambridge: Cambridge University Press.
Long, M. H., & Crookes, G. (1992). Three approaches to task-based syllabus design. *TESOL Quarterly*, 26(1), 27–56.
Mishan, F. (2005). *Designing authenticity into language learning materials*. Bristol: Intellect.
Nation, I. S. P., & Macalister, J. (2010). *Language and curriculum design*. New York: Routledge.

Park, H. (2010). Process drama in the Korean EFL secondary school classroom: A case study of Korean middle school classrooms. In B. Tomlinson & H. Masuhara (Eds), *Research for materials development in language learning: Evidence for best practice* (pp. 155–171). London: Continuum.

Prabhu, N. S. (1987). *Second language pedagogy*. Oxford: Oxford University Press.

Samuda, V., & Bygate, M. (2008). *Tasks in second language learning*. Basingstoke: Palgrave Macmillan.

Tomlinson, B. (1981). *Talking to learn*. Port Vila: Vanuatu Ministry of Education.

Tomlinson, B. (1990). Managing change in Indonesian high schools. *ELT Journal, 44*(1), 25–37.

Tomlinson, B. (1994a). *Openings*. London: Penguin.

Tomlinson, B. (1994b). Materials for TPR. *Folio, 1*(2), 8–10.

Tomlinson, B. (Ed.) (2004). *Improve your English*. Addis Ababa: Ministry of Education.

Tomlinson, B. (2005). Suiting EFL methodologies to social contexts. In E. Hinkel (Ed.), *Handbook of research in second language teaching and learning* (pp. 137–153). Hillsdale, NJ: Lawrence Erlbaum.

Tomlinson, B. (2007). Introduction: Some similarities and differences between L1 and L2 acquisition and development. In B. Tomlinson (Ed.) *Language acquisition and development: Studies of learners of first and other languages* London: Continuum, pp. 1–12.

Tomlinson, B. (2013a). Second language acquisition and materials development. In B. Tomlinson (Ed.) *Applied linguistics and materials development* (pp. 11–30). London: Bloomsbury.

Tomlinson, B. (2013b). Developing principled frameworks for materials development. In B. Tomlinson (Ed.), *Developing materials for language teaching* (pp. 95–118) (2nd edition). London: Bloomsbury.

Tomlinson, B., & Masuhara, H. (1994). *Use your English*. Tokyo: Asahi Press.

Tomlinson, B., Hill, D. A., & Masuhara, H. (2000). *English for life*. Singapore: Marshall Cavendish.

Tomlinson, B., Buchanan, H., Islam, C., Masuhara, H., & Timmis, I. (2002). *Success with English for primary schools*. Guangzhou: Guangzhou Education Bureau.

Van den Branden, K. (2006). *Task-based language education: From theory to practice*. Cambridge: Cambridge University Press.

Van den Branden, K., Bygate, M., & Norris, J. (2009). *Task-based language teaching: A reader*. Amsterdam: John Benjamins.

Willis, D., & Willis, J. (2007). *Doing task-based teaching*. Oxford: Oxford University Press.

PART SIX

Assessment and evaluation

Introduction

Ali Shehadeh

Task-based language assessment (TBLA) is an approach for language testing that takes the task as the fundamental unit for assessment and testing. It is based on the same underlying principles of task-based language teaching (TBLT), but extends them from the learning-and-teaching domain to the testing domain. Specifically, as in TBLT methodology, assessment in TBLA is also organized around tasks. For instance, Long and Norris (2000, p. 600) state that 'genuinely task-based language assessment takes the task itself as the fundamental unit of analysis, motivating item selection, test instrument construction and the rating of task performance.' Similarly, Weaver (2012, p. 287) posits that '[a]t its core, task-based language assessment (TBLA) involves evaluating the degree to which language learners can use their L2 to accomplish given tasks.'

The main goal and validity of TBLA is measured against the extent to which it can successfully achieve a close link between the testee's performance during the test and his/her performance in the real world. For instance, Ellis (2003, p. 279) states that 'task-based testing is seen as a way of achieving a close correlation between the test performance, i.e., what the testee does during the test, and the criterion of performance, i.e., what the testee has to do in the real world.' Assessment tasks are thus viewed as 'devices for eliciting and evaluating communicative performances from learners in the context of language use that is meaning-focused and directed towards some specific goal' (Ellis, 2003, p. 279).

Four main features characterize TBLA. *First*, it is a formative assessment; that is, it is an assessment undertaken as part of an instructional programme for the purpose of improving learning and teaching. *Second*, it is performance-referenced assessment; that is, it is an assessment that seeks to provide information about learners' abilities to use the language in specific contexts, that is directed at assessing a particular performance of learners, and that seeks to ascertain whether learners can use the second language (L2) to accomplish real target tasks. *Third*, it is direct assessment; that is, it is an assessment that involves a measurement of language abilities using tasks where the measure of the testee's performance is incorporated into the task itself. *Fourth*, it is an authentic assessment; that is, it is an assessment that involves either real-world language use (or as close as possible to this), or the kinds of language processing found in real-world language use (Ellis, 2003, p. 285; Shehadeh, 2012a, for reviews).

The implementation of TBLT and assessment in Asia has received considerable attention in the literature. In many instances, researchers have identified the factors that hinder the adoption of TBLT and assessment in Asian educational settings like administrative constraints, exam pressures, cultural pressures and expectations, time pressures, available materials, and the top-down process of decision-making (e.g., Adams & Newton, 2009; Carless, 2012, this volume; Ellis, this volume; Shehadeh, 2012b). The cultural context (including cultural pressures and expectations) and the nature of high-stakes examinations that students have to take are commonly viewed as the main factors that hinder the implementation of TBLT and assessment in Asian countries. With respect to the cultural context, Cortazzi and Jin (1996), for instance, point out that many TBLT principles are incompatible with the Confucian heritage for language education in China that advocates the authoritative role of the teacher, memorization, and rote learning. Many teachers in these settings consider TBLT an alien concept not applicable to their specific teaching situation or educational setting because it is incompatible with their own experiences of language learning and teaching. These teachers feel more secure and in control in the traditional, teacher-fronted, teacher-centred instruction. They feel uncomfortable with the shifts in teaching styles and classroom dynamics required by TBLT and assessment because they feel that these reduce their 'authority' from the role of instructor to that of a facilitator or counsellor (e.g., Carless, 2012; Iwashita & Li, 2012).

Turning to high-stakes examinations, studies in several Asian countries including China (Zhang, 2007), Hong Kong (Chow & Mok-Cheung, 2004), Korea (Shim & Baik, 2000), and Japan (Gorush, 2000) have shown that the measurement of success in L2 teaching and learning is frequently sought through norm-referenced, summative, knowledge-based, vocabulary- and grammar-focused exams. These likely hinder successful adoption of TBLT and assessment in the classroom. For instance, Zhang (2007) shows that grammar and vocabulary knowledge-based high-stakes national examinations are the main barriers preventing the adoption of TBLT and assessment in China because they do not take into account or reflect communicative curricular objectives.

Similarly, Carless (2012, p. 352) argues that the use of School-Based Assessment (SBA) or teacher assessment in traditionally examination-oriented systems is a challenge because these systems have a long history of public assessment. In such systems, the uniform test, which emphasizes grammar, vocabulary and reading comprehension, can be an obstacle to the implementation of alternative modes of assessment like SBA, teacher assessment or TBLA (Ng & Tang, 1997). Language tests in these systems play a key part in success in the pursuit of personal well-being and future employment opportunities. According to Cheng (2008), for example, the high status of English tests in China does not support teaching but drives it. Carless (2012, p. 352) cites an example a TBLA test from a study by Luk (2010) which reveals that 'a careful analysis of the discourse of test interaction ... shows how students colluded in producing utterances aimed at creating the impression of being effective interlocutors for the purpose of scoring marks rather than for authentic communication' (see also Yu, 2010, below).

The two chapters that focus on assessment and evaluation in this volume are those by Butler (Chapter 21) and Carless (Chapter 22). The former is based on an experimental study that focuses on implementing TBLA with young language learners in China, and the latter is an overview and discussion of the challenges and opportunities for implementing TBLT and assessment in Hong Kong.

Investigating the possibility of utilizing assessment *for* learning (rather than assessment *of* learning), Butler examines how TBLA is implemented with young foreign language learners in an elementary school setting in China, a context which can be largely characterized as having an exam culture, where assessment is primarily concerned with measuring the learners' accurate production. Butler examined the role of teachers as both providers of assistance as well as evaluators during TBLA as implemented in authentic classroom situations with these elementary school pupils. Based on the constructivist perspective (Vygotsky, 1978) that learning takes place through collaborative interaction with more capable individuals, the investigator describes and examines the way in which individual teachers interacted with their students during a TBLA oral test administered in two separate formats: a paired-assessment format (PA, child–child dyads) and an individual-assessment format (IA, child–teacher dyads). She examined data from three teachers and twenty-four, eleven- to twelve-year-old students using a range of decision-making tasks that were administered as a classroom-based oral assessment for their study. Butler found that the IA format (child–teacher dyads) almost exclusively yielded novice/expert interactional patterns irrespective of the students' general proficiency levels, whereas the PA format showed more successful collaboration, allowing the researcher to conclude that the latter format, rather than the former, may potentially be used as a successful *assessment for learning* condition for this age group.

Carless (Chapter 22) discusses TBLA as part of his overview and discussion of the challenges and opportunities for implementing TBLT and assessment in Hong Kong during the last two decades. He frames his discussion of TBLA in light of the findings of a recent study by Yu (2010). Yu investigated SBA within the general framework of TBLA using a peer group discussion task as an oral assessment format. Findings of the study show that although SBA has the potential of providing students with opportunities to produce 'real-life' spoken interactional abilities, a detailed analysis of the students' discourse shows that in many instances students had actually produced utterances aimed at creating the impression of being effective interlocutors for the purpose of scoring marks rather than for authentic communication as was the case with Luk's study (2010) in mainland China mentioned above. Carless concludes that a tension continues to exist between SBA and the requirements of high-stakes assessment in Hong Kong because tests and examinations are often seen as a barrier to the implementation of communicative approaches. He relates this to the local sociocultural setting; that is, the Hong Kong community expects competitive examinations to be standardized and objective, whereas assessment of student performance in context is seen less standardized and less objective because it requires individual focus and a certain degree of subjectivity.

In spite of the challenges facing TBLA in Asia mentioned above, there is potential for successfully utilizing TBLA in Asian countries. For example, Carless (2012, p. 352) argues that traditionally examination-oriented systems can be an impetus, not just a challenge as mentioned above, for changing teachers' mindsets because these systems fail to equip students with the interactional competence needed for communication in the real world. Indeed, Carless confirms, high-stakes examinations in several Asian countries have over the last twenty years increased the weighting awarded to oral performance and that examinations have become increasingly task-based. Carless (this volume) also suggests that successful utilization of TBLA necessitates mutual adaptations between the needs of TBLA and the local context, whereby the needs of the local culture and society, the needs of SBA as well as the interplay between formative and summative assessment are all catered for. On the other hand,

Ellis (this volume) advocates a hybrid or mixed-approach in which high-stake tests include tasks that assess communicative ability alongside grammatical correctness.

The two chapters in this section are a step forward in this direction, but more work and more research need to be done to address the challenges in the design and implementation of TBLA in Asian countries, as well as other similar educational settings.

References

Adams, R., & Newton, J. (2009). TBLT in Asia: Constraints and opportunities. *Asian Journal of English Language Teaching, 19*, 1–17.

Carless, D. (2012). TBLT in EFL settings: Looking back and moving forward. In A. Shehadeh & C. Coombe (Eds), *Task-based language teaching in foreign language contexts: Research and implementation* (pp. 345–358). Amsterdam: John Benjamins.

Cheng, L. (2008). The key to success: English language testing in China. *Language Testing 25*(1), 15–37.

Chow, A. K. W., & Mok-Cheung, A. H. M. (2004). English language teaching in Hong Kong SAR: Tradition, transition, and transformation. In H. W. Kam & R. Y. L. Wong (Eds), *Language policies and language education: The impact in East Asian countries in the next decade* (pp. 150–177). Singapore: Times Academic Press.

Cortazzi, M., & Jin, L. (1996). English teaching and learning in China. *Language Teaching 29*, 61–80.

Ellis, R. (2003). *Task-based language learning and teaching*. Oxford: Oxford University Press.

Gorush, G. J. (2000). EFL educational policies and educational cultures: Influences on teachers' approval of communicative activities. *TESOL Quarterly, 34*, 675–710.

Iwashita, N., & Li, H. (2012). Patterns of corrective feedback in a task-based adult EFL classroom setting in China. In A. Shehadeh & C. Coombe (Eds), *task-based language teaching in foreign language contexts: research and implementation* (pp. 137–161). Amsterdam: John Benjamins.

Long, M. H., & Norris, J. M. (2000). Task-based language teaching and assessment. In M. Byram (Ed.), *Encyclopedia of language teaching* (pp.597–603). London: Routledge.

Luk, J. (2010). Talking to score: Impression management in L2 Oral Assessment and the Co-construction of a Test Discourse Genre. *Language Assessment Quarterly, 7*(1), 25–53.

Ng, C., & Tang, E. (1997). Teachers' needs in the process of EFL reform in China: A report from Shanghai. *Perspective 9*, 63–85.

Shehadeh, A. (2012a). Task-based language assessment: Components, development, and implementation. In C. Coombe, P. Davidson, B. O'Sullivan, & S. Stoynoff (Eds), *The Cambridge guide to second language assessment*, (pp. 156–163). Cambridge: Cambridge University Press.

Shehadeh, A. (2012b). Broadening the perspective of task-based language teaching scholarship: The contribution of research in foreign language contexts. In A. Shehadeh & C. Coombe (Eds), *Task-Based Language Teaching in Foreign Language Contexts: Research and Implementation* (pp. 1–20). Amsterdam: John Benjamins.

Shim, R., & Baik, M. (2000). South and North Korea. In H. W. Kam & R. Y. L. Wong (Eds), *Language policies and language education: The impact in East Asian countries in the next decade* (pp. 246–261). Singapore: Times Academic Press.

Vygotsky, L. S. (1978). *Mind and society*. Cambridge, MA: Harvard University Press.

Weaver, C. (2012). Incorporating a formative assessment cycle into task-based language teaching in a university setting in Japan. In A. Shehadeh & C. Coombe (Eds), *task-based language teaching in foreign language contexts: research and implementation* (pp. 287–312). Amsterdam: John Benjamins.

Yu, Y. (2010). *The washback effects of school-based assessment on teaching and learning: A case study*. Unpublished PhD thesis, University of Hong Kong.

Zhang, E. Y. (2007). TBLT innovation in primary school English language teaching in mainland China. In K. Van den Branden, K. Van Gorp, & M. Verhelst (Eds), *Tasks in action: Task-based language education from a classroom-based perspective* (pp. 68–91). Newcastle: Cambridge Scholars Press.

21

Task-Based Assessment for Young Learners:

The Role of Teachers in Changing Cultures

Yuko Goto Butler

Summary

Tasks have become increasingly popular in the teaching of foreign language to young learners in Asia. However, we still have limited knowledge about how best to introduce task-based language assessments (TBLA) among young learners. In addition, while the notion of *assessment for learning* is widely suggested for young learners, such a notion does not seem to fit well in practice in an *exam culture*. The present chapter focuses on how teachers interact with young learners during TBLA from a constructivist point of view. Drawing upon examples from a case study at the sixth grade level in China, we examine the roles of teachers as providers of assistance as well as evaluators in a TBLA in two formats: a paired-assessment format (PA, child–child dyads) and an individual-assessment format (IA, child–teacher dyads). A holistic analysis of the interactional patterns of dyads indicated that the IA format almost exclusively showed novice/expert interactional patterns and tended to yield a relatively limited range of language use from students. On the other hand, the PA format mostly yielded collaborative patterns and potentially could better elicit a greater variety of language use from the students. While such general patterns were observed, a more detailed analysis showed that the ways in which individual teachers interacted with the students and offered assistance differed greatly, perhaps reflecting their orientations towards assessment.

Introduction

The teaching of a foreign language at elementary school (FLES) has gained substantial attention worldwide. East Asia is particularly illustrative of this trend. Many FLES programs place a strong emphasis on developing oral communicative abilities and enhancing students' motivation to communicate with others in the target language as their major goals. In recent years, task-based language teaching (TBLT) has been promoted as a leading means of achieving these goals. The implementation of TBLT, however, has been a challenge for teachers, especially in contexts where form-focused instruction has widely prevailed for a long time, as we often see in different parts of East Asia (Butler, 2011).

Teachers in FLES programs also face challenges with respect to assessment. While they are increasingly held accountable for their students' foreign language development, we still have relatively limited knowledge regarding how best to assess young learners' communicative abilities in a foreign language. It has been suggested that assessments for young learners should be designed to facilitate their language use through tasks and activities. Cognitive and social developmental factors should be carefully considered when deciding the types of tasks, their formats (e.g., group/pair or individual assessments), and interpreting the results of assessments. It is also important to note that there are substantial individual differences among young learners with respect to their cognitive and social development (Bailey, 2008).

In addition, the notion of *assessment for learning* embedded in the classroom has gained increased attention among researchers and educators worldwide (Black et al., 2003). Despite the call for *assessment for learning*, however, its implementation is often reported as being a challenge for teachers, especially in the context of an *exam culture*. The underlying assumptions for implementing *assessment for learning*, namely 'a new understanding of the interactive nature of learning and the role of assessment and assessors in the instructional-learning cycle' (Inbar-Lourie, 2008, p. 287), require a conceptual shift among teachers who are used to focusing on measuring student performance and ensuring fairness in test administration.

Taking a constructivist point of view, the present chapter discusses the role of teachers as providers of assistance for learning as well as evaluators in a TBLA. In particular, we are interested in examining the case of TBLA when it is implemented as a classroom-based assessment for young foreign language learners in a context which can be largely characterized as having an exam culture. Drawing upon examples from a case study that we conducted in an elementary school in China where TBLT was mandated by the curriculum, we describe and examine the way in which individual teachers interacted with their students during a TBLA administered in two separate formats: a paired-assessment format (PA, child–child dyads) and an individual-assessment format (IA, child–teacher dyads). By uncovering how individual teachers deal with TBLA, the study described herein aimed to address the possibilities and limitations for implementing TBLA by teachers who are in the midst of adapting new teaching and assessment approaches.

Cultures of Pedagogy: Form-focused to meaning-focused approaches

As a partial response to repeated criticisms towards traditional approaches for not being effective in helping learners develop communicative competence, communicative language teaching (CLT) and more recently TBLT have been widely promoted among teachers in many parts of East Asia. In spite of the promotion of CLT/TBLT at the policy and curriculum levels, however, a number of studies have claimed that it is challenging to implement CLT and TBLT in East Asian classrooms. Butler (2011) reviewed such studies and classified the reported constraints in implementing CLT/TBLT into three types: (1) conceptual constraints (e.g., teachers misunderstanding CLT/TBLT and having to resolve ideological conflicts between CLT/TBLT and local traditional values); (2) classroom-level constraints (e.g., large class sizes, limited instructional hours, and issues related to classroom-management); (3) social-institutional constraints (e.g., exam pressures and limited opportunities to use the target language). However, not all of these 'constraints' were empirically validated; some are more speculative in nature.

Regardless of the types of 'constraints' that teachers face, observational studies have indicated that 'communicative activities' or 'tasks' which were implemented in East Asian classrooms are not fully communicative. Such studies include various observations conducted at the elementary school level (e.g., Deng & Carless, 2009). While tasks can generally be considered as 'activities that call for primarily meaning-focused language use' (Ellis, 2003, p. 3), the interpretation of tasks and communicativeness appear to vary substantially among individual teachers in East Asia.

Littlewood (2007) proposed *a model of communicativeness in activities* in which activities are categorized according to the degree of communicativeness along a continuum ranging from activities which are almost exclusively focused on forms to activities which focus on meaning. The continuum Littlewood proposed included 'non-communicative learning, pre-communicative language practice, communicative language practice, structured communication, and authentic communication' (p. 247). Littlewood suggested that teachers who become accustomed to the traditional approaches 'can maintain their base in activities represented in the first and second categories, but gradually expand their repertoire into the other three' (p. 247). It appears that the implementation of CLT/TBLT in classrooms requires localized *adaptation* processes (Butler, 2011), and that as the main actors in these processes, teachers often struggle with figuring out how best to do so, particularly in contexts where form-focused traditional practices are still generally well-accepted and subscribed to by a wide segment of the population.

Cultures of assessment: From assessment *of* learning to assessment *for* learning

In addition to instructional practices, assessment practices are also undergoing changes in many parts in East Asia. Assessment cultures have been largely characterized as *exam-cultures* and *learning-cultures*. In exam-cultures, assessment is primarily concerned with measuring one's output accurately and fairly, and focuses on one's language proficiency in relation to the performance of other learners. The learning culture values individual learners' learning experiences, and is concerned with learners' achievement and progress towards defined goals (Hamp-Lyons, 2007). While such a dichotomy can easily oversimplify reality, and while assessment cultures must be regarded as a continual construct, this classification is still useful to understand how assessment is generally conceptualized and used in a given context.

In East Asia, it has often been noted that the historical exam culture has had a tremendous influence over educational practices as well as society in general. In recent years, however, classroom-based assessment has gained substantial attention among educators and policymakers. Classroom-based assessment, which can be defined as 'nonstandardized local assessment carried out by teachers in the classroom' (Leung, 2005, p. 871), is rooted in the learning culture. It is embedded in the classroom, is intrinsically tied to instruction, and has formative as well as summative functions. In the classroom-assessment paradigm, the assessment itself can be considered as part of learning, and its measurement is embedded in a greater context that includes the instruction itself as well as teachers' beliefs and knowledge about the instructional content and their learners (Brookhart, 2003). If one takes a constructivist perspective (e.g., Vygotsky, 1978), providing assistance during assessment can even be encouraged because this process of *assisted performance* (also referred to as *scaffolding*) by teachers and capable peers is exactly where learning takes place.

Classroom-based assessment is not a foreign practice in East Asia. However, as Hamp-Lyons (2007) has indicated, if classroom-based assessments are employed in an exam culture, it is often treated 'as simply preparation for an externally set and assessed examination' (p. 488), instead of as a source of formative information (formative-assessment) and a learning opportunity. Carless (2011) introduced the concept of different degrees of 'formativeness' in assessment. He developed the notion that a theoretically-desirable type of formative assessment (which he referred to as *extended formative-assessment*) may be perceived as less feasible by teachers in certain contexts. He suggested that a more pragmatically oriented and teacher-directed type of formative assessment (which he referred to as *restricted formative-assessment*) may be perceived as more practical and realistic for some teachers, students, and schools, especially in those contexts where the exam culture is predominant and teachers are generally not sufficiently trained to conduct extended forms of formative assessment in the classroom. Davison and Leung (2009) also proposed various types of formative assessments that teachers can employ including ones originally prescribed for the end-of-course assessment. Therefore, the implementation of classroom-based assessment also appears to require localized adaptation processes for figuring out how best to implement *assessment for learning* in their own teaching contexts.

Formats of task-based pair-assessment in the classroom: IA and PA

Considering the close ties between instruction and assessment, one can surmise that assessment using tasks (TBLA) will be an option for FLES programs in which TBLT is implemented as part of their curriculum. Ellis (2003) stated that using TBLA is different from TBLT in that TBLA requires greater consideration of task choices (including the format) and that TBLA has more focus on measuring task performance. As has been discussed already, if TBLA is used as a classroom-based assessment, the process of TBLA itself is expected to shed light on student learning as well.

One can suggest that the paired-assessment format (PA, child–child dyads) can be an attractive option for teachers because tasks in FLES classrooms are typically conducted in pairs and/or groups. The PA format is also found to evoke less anxiety among learners (Csépes, 2009). Moreover, the PA format can be a more practical option than the individual-assessment format (IA, child–teacher dyads) for teachers who have large class sizes.

PA has gained substantial attention in oral performance assessment in recent years. The popularity of the PA format is in part a response towards one of the criticisms of the IA format. IA is often characterized by its asymmetrical relationship between the examiner and the examinee, as reported typically in one-to-one interviews. In IA, the examiner predominantly tends to ask questions and control the flow of the conversation and topic development. As a result, the IA format often elicits relatively unauthentic and limited types of language use from the examinee (e.g., Johnson, 2001; van Lier, 1989).

Compared with IA, PA generally yields a more symmetric relationship between the participants. Thus, it has been reported that a greater variety of language use and strategies can be elicited, at least among older/adult learners (e.g., Brooks, 2009; May, 2009). Despite such potential merits, a number of interlocutor effects have been noted in PA when it is analysed from a psychometric point of view, such as stemming from the co-participants' proficiency levels (e.g., Davis, 2009), gender (e.g., O'Sullivan, 2000), and acquaintanceship (e.g., O'Sullivan, 2002) each of which have been cited as potentially giving rise to validity concerns.

If the PA format is employed in classroom-based assessments for young learners, other concerns may arise. According to Carpenter, Fujii and Kataoka (1995), their trial of implementing PA among five to ten year-olds was 'extremely problematic' (p. 168) since one of the children in the dyads often dominated the tasks. Their study also found that the children tended to use their first language more extensively in PA than in IA. From an *assessment for learning* perspective, one also has to wonder if the PA format can provide young learners with learning opportunities and allow them to engage in meaningful communication. As we have discussed already, in the constructivist paradigm, collaboration is considered to be critical for making *learning* possible. However, young children may not be ready to work on tasks collaboratively.

In sum, teachers in East Asia have been asked to play a major role in implementing a more 'communicative-based approach' in teaching as well as in implementing 'assessment for learning.' These implementations require localized adaptation processes, and one can hypothesize that teachers may encounter challenges during such processes, especially if their teaching contexts still largely value more traditional approaches to both teaching and assessment.

In the following, therefore, we describe a case study in which we examine the role of teachers in assessment in classrooms in which they are adapting new teaching and assessment practice. More specifically, the study explores the ways in which individual teachers interact with their young learners during a TBLA, which itself was administered using the two paring formats described above (i.e., IA and PA formats).

A case study on the role of teachers in TBLA

Context

The participants of the study were three Chinese teachers of English and their sixth grade students at an elementary school located in Southern China (twenty-four students in total). Based on the results from Carpenter et al. (1995) mentioned above, we targeted slightly older children for participation in this study than the students in their study (namely, we chose sixth graders who were eleven to twelve years old). In China, the National English Curriculum Standards for Compulsory and Senior High Schools (NECS) issued by the Ministry of Education in 2001 adopted a constructivist approach to language education where student-centred and interactive learning are promoted and individual students' personal growth and discovery are celebrated. Following the NECS, curricula in China began mandating tasks in English FLES. As an experimental school in the region, the participating elementary school was expected to take a leading role in implementing innovative approaches to education. The school was offering English instruction to their first to fourth grade students for four hours per week, and to their fifth and sixth grade students for five hours per week.

The three participating teachers (Ms Chen, Ms Wu, and Ms Lee[1]) were all experienced teachers. They had more than fifteen years of English-teaching experience and were all in their late thirties. All of them had received awards for excellence in teaching from the provincial educational bureau. One of the teachers (Ms Chen) was sent to England for a three-month professional training programme which was built on constructivist principles, where she received a series of classes on English-teaching methodologies, material development, and assessment. The other two teachers also had participated in workshops and teacher training programs offered by the local educational bureau, and seemed to be generally positive towards the constructivist approaches to education, judging from our unstructured interviews with them.

Despite the school's promotion of TBLT, when it came to assessment, the school still mainly relied upon teacher-made paper-and-pencil examinations administered in the middle and at the end of each semester. Based on the paper-and-pencil examination results, eighteen students out of the twenty-four participants were considered to be students with relatively high general proficiency (referred to as H-students) and the rest were considered to be relatively lower-proficiency students (referred to as L-students)[2]. For the PA format of the assessment, the students were paired with a classmate while controlling for gender, resulted in six H–H dyads and six H–L dyads.

Tasks and procedures

A set of decision-making tasks were administered as a classroom-based oral assessment for this study. The specific tasks used were the creation of a plan for a school trip and a Safari trip by the students. Similar tasks had been used in previous classroom activities and so the students were generally familiar with the task procedure. The students completed the tasks once with their teacher (in the individual format, IA) and once with a peer (in the paired format, PA). The students were given a sheet of paper with picture items, and they were asked to discuss what activities they wished to do during the trip and to choose up to ten items to bring with them, while considering price or weight limitations that were specified as part of the tasks (i.e., the students were asked to circle their chosen items on a sheet of paper). According to Pica, Kanagy and Falodun (1993), a decision-making task is characterized as follows: it does not necessarily required contribution from all of the participants (i.e., one person can complete the task without interacting with his/her partner); it has one convergent goal; and it has multiple possible outcomes. The tasks employed in this study were also meant to fit the higher end of Littlewood's model of communicativeness in activities; namely, the focus was on meaning in communicative exchanges rather than forms. On average, it took 15–20 minutes for a student to complete both task formats.

Following the constructivist principles, the teachers were encouraged to assist their students during the assessment in both the IA and PA formats. The present TBLA can be considered as a restricted formative assessment in Carless' (2011) model in the sense that the teachers would be the primary users of the assessment results in order to provide the students with feedback and other assistance. All of the interactions were videotaped and transcribed[3]. After completing each task, the teachers evaluated the performance of individual students and the students self-evaluated their own performance. In addition, unstructured interviews with the teachers were conducted. The present chapter, however, focuses on the results of the analysis of participants' interactions during the assessment.

Interactions during the TBLA found in the study

The interactions during the TBLA were analysed in two steps. First, the overall interactional patterns were classified based on Storch (2002) and the results were compared between the IA and PA formats. Second, the individual teachers' interactional behaviours with their students were examined in detail.

Overall interactional patterns

Storch (2002) proposed a model of dyadic interaction in which interactional patterns are classified into four types based on binary features (i.e., *equality* and *mutuality*). Equality here refers to 'the degree of control or authority over the direction of the task' whereas mutuality refers to 'the level of engagement with each other's contribution' (p. 127). Based on these two features, interactions were characterized as *collaborative* (relatively high in both equality and mutuality); *expert/novice* (relatively low in equality but high in mutuality); *dominant/passive* (relatively low in both equality and mutuality); and *dominant/dominant* (relatively high in equality but low in mutuality). While dyads' interactional patterns can change moment by moment, Storch's model is useful to capture such interactions holistically. In the present study, two researchers independently classified thirty-six interactions (twenty-four IAs and twelve PAs); the inter-rater reliability was 0.94.

Out of twelve interactions in the PA format, all six H–H dyads (two higher-proficiency student dyads) showed the collaborative interaction pattern. Among the six H–L dyads, two pairs showed the collaborative pattern, three pairs showed the expert/novice pattern, and one pair showed the dominant/passive pattern. In contrast to what was seen with the younger (five to ten years old) students in Carpenter et al. (1995), our eleven to twelve year-olds appeared to be developmentally more ready to work collaboratively and/or assist peers during the TBLA. In stark contrast to what was seen with the PA format, all twenty-four student–teacher dyads in the IA format (except for two dyads) showed the expert/novice pattern regardless of the students' general proficiency levels. The two exceptional cases did not fit well with any of the four types in Storch's model and thus were unable to be classified.

Individual teachers' interactions with their students

While we found the general patterns of interaction mentioned above, when we analysed how the individual teachers interacted with their students (including how they offered assistance during the TBLA), we found striking individual differences both in terms of the frequencies and types of assistance that they offered to their students.

Ms Chen's case

As mentioned already, Ms Chen joined a professional training programme in the UK for three months and received a series of courses on English teaching which were built on constructivist principles of learning and education. As the head English teacher at the school, she played a major role in advocating innovative approaches to English teaching including CLT/TBLT in their classes. Interestingly, however, when it came to assessment, she seemed to have a stronger faith in the notion of *assessment of learning* (rather than *assessment for learning*) and believed that the teachers' involvement should remain minimal during the assessment, as one can see from some of her statements during the interview:

> Since this is assessment, I try to be involved with the students as little as possible. They are the ones who should talk as much as possible in order to display their language abilities and to be assessed. I'm more like a solicitor, only to use a little prompting to get the students started.

During the TBLA in this study, Ms Chen offered procedural directions to her students and carefully monitored them so that they could complete the tasks following the necessary requirements. However, in line with her previous statement, she provided the students with minimum direct feedback and modelling. She hardly presented her own opinions, which in turn contributed little towards mutual topic development in the discourse.

In the IA format, Ms Chen completely controlled the management of the conversational floor and frequently gave her students directions for the next step by offering directions such as 'Tell me what you want' and 'Tell me why.' As a result, as one can see in Excerpt 1, the interaction typically exhibited an interview-like discourse. Ms Chen's responses to the student's answers were usually very brief such as 'OK' and 'Good'. One may associate this type of interaction with a widely-observed classroom interaction pattern, namely, Initiation-Response-Evaluation (IRE).

Excerpt 1 (IA, S1(H))

1	S1(H)	I think we'll play (. . .) football.
2	Ms Chen	Football. Circle it.
3	S1(H)	And paint some picture. ((Circling the clip art)) Ah (:::) And also fly some . . . fly the kites.
5	Ms Chen	Tell me the reason why?
6	S1(H)	Oh, first, you can see (:::) this (. .) picture, it's very beautiful, so. I . . . so I . . . I want our . . . our students to draw the pictures, so I wanted to, so I circle the (. .) the painting activity.
7	Ms Chen	OK.
8	S1(H)	And next it's the football, becau(⊠)se spring is a very good season to play sports, and I also like football, so . . . so . . . so I would like our second activity to be the football . . . to play the football.
9	Ms Chen	OK.

In the PA format, Ms Chen's minimum-involvement policy in the assessment seemed to work well when the students were both relatively high in proficiency and collaborative because the PA format provided the students with opportunities to use language with various functions (e.g., questioning, giving orders, suggesting, etc.) and strategies (e.g., requesting confirmation, asking for help, repairing, etc.). These rarely emerged during the interaction with Ms Chen in the IA format.

However, when the equality in the interaction between the students was lower, more direct assistance from the teacher appeared to be indispensable, especially for lower proficiency and/or passive students. In Excerpt 2, in an H–L dyad, the L-student (S3) was struggling with conducing the task and the H-student (S2) started using Chinese to assist S3 (Lines 15 and 17). Ms Chen encouraged S2 to start working on the task in English by saying 'You can choose, you can decide' (Lines 19 and 21). That led S2 to completely monopolize the task.

Excerpt 2 (PA, H–L dyad, S2(H) and S3(L))

10	Ms Chen	((explaining the task procedure in English))
11	S2(H)	What kind of clothes do we take?
12	S3(L)	((Looking at the task sheet))
13	S2(H)	What kind of clothes do we take?
14	S3(L)	((Murmuring something to S2, use one hand to cover his mouth))
15	S2(H)	(In Chinese) Do you understand what it means specifically? ((smiling))
16	S3(L)	((smiling))
17	S2(H)	(In Chinese) It means what clothes we should choose.

18	S2+S3	((looking at the task sheet together))
19	Ms Chen	((Looking at S2)) You can choose, you can decide.
20	S2(H)	Because it says 'hot during the day' . . .
21	Ms Chen	You can choose, you can decide.
22	S2(H)	So (..) so (.) so we must take some shorts, and sweaters and coat. (..) We can wear sweaters during (.) at night and (..) wear (.) shorts (..) wear T-shirts during the day. ((Pointing at the sheet.))
23	S3(L)	((Deep breath. Looking at the sheet. Both arms on the table with one on the other.))
24	S2(H)	I think we also can wear sandals during the daylight.

After the interaction above, S2 continued to state what he wanted to bring on the trip while Ms Chen had minimum involvement (e.g., she occasionally gave S2 very brief evaluative remarks such as 'yes' and 'great,' which was a very similar pattern to what we have seen in the IA format in Excerpt 1). S3 was completely left out of the task in the process. A couple of minutes later (shown in Excerpt 3 below), Ms Chen suddenly suggested to S2 that he should ask his partner for his opinion (Line 25). In Line 27, Ms Chen asked S3 'Do you agree?' which was repeated by S2 (Line 29). In fact, Line 27 was the only time when Ms Chen directly addressed S3 during the entire task and she continued trying to invite S3 to the task indirectly by ordering S2 to ask 'Do you agree with me?' to S3 (Line 33). This can be considered as her effort to encourage the students to use English as much as possible, without using Chinese by herself, while keeping her position limited to being what she referred to as 'a solicitor'. In Line 34, S2 followed Ms Chen's order and asked S3 if he agreed with him. After finding that S3 did not know how to respond in English, S2 offered S3 a model response (Line 36), which was immediately used by S3 (Line 37).

Excerpt 3 (PA, H–L dyad, S2(H) and S3(L))

25	Ms Chen	You ask what about your partner's opinion.
26	S2(H)	What's your opinion?
27	Ms Chen	Do you agree? ((looking at S3))
28	S3(L)	((smiling))
29	S2(H)	Do you agree?
30	S3(L)	What's 'agree'? ((Looking at S2))
31	S2(H)	*(In Chinese) 'Agree' means consent.*
32	S3(L)	((Looking at the task sheet.))
33	Ms Chen	You ask him, do you agree with me?
34	S2(H)	Do you agree with me? *(In Chinese) Do you agree?*
35	S3(L)	*(In Chinese) I don't know how to say.*
36	S2(H)	Yes, I agree with you.
37	S3(L)	Yes, I agree with you.

Ms Wu's case

Compared with Ms Chen, Ms Wu had more direct involvement in the interactions during the TBLA in general. In the IA format, as with Ms Chen, Ms Wu initiated the majority of the topics and controlled the floor-management most of the times, as Excerpt 4 exemplifies. While Ms Wu provided the students with much more modelling and feedback when they were stuck, such assistance was frequently on areas such as lexical choice, grammar, sentence structure and expression. In other words, she tended to pay close attention to accuracy and the proper use of words and expressions. She also frequently commented on her students' statements, but such comments did not necessarily contribute very much to the mutual development of topics.

In Excerpt 4, as one example from the IA format, Ms Wu advised S4 not to use deixis (i.e., 'this') (Line 42) and offered a model for the collocational phrase 'flying a kite' (the picture showed a boy flying a kite, not a kite) (Line 44). She offered a similar model in Line 48 for 'catching' and it was taken up by S4 (Line 49). She also made comments on the students' choices much more frequently and in a more extended fashion compared to Ms Chen. However, given the inherent power relationship in teacher–student dyads, her comments often resulted in the closing of a given topic, as one can see in the case of Line 50 below.

Excerpt 4 (IA, S4(L))

38	Ms Wu		Yes. OK. Now let's decide what activities we can choose. What activity do you think is the best for us?
39	S4(L)		uh(. .)
40	Ms Wu		Or is popular between us?
41	S4(L)		This. ((pointing at the 'kite' clip art.))
42	Ms Wu		This? What? You can speak English.
43	S4(L)		Kite. This kite.
44	Ms Wu		Kite? Or flying a kite?
45	S4(L)		Flying a kite.
46	Ms Wu		You can circle it. Flying a kite or . . . Yes, maybe. The girls like it very much. It is suitable or not . . . it is suitable for either boys or girls. OK, anymore?
47	S4(L)		This. ((pointing at another clip art image))
48	Ms Wu		Flying (. .) oh no, catching?
49	S4(L)		Catching the butterfly.
50	Ms Wu		Catching the butterflies. Hmm, but I think it's not good for us to do so because I think butterfly (. .) is very important for our environment. Do you think so?
51	S4(L)		Yes.

In the PA format, her close monitoring of her students' language use and frequent modelling of their lexical choices and expressions occasionally resulted in preventing the students from either focusing on the meaning of the tasks and/or having a natural flow in the interactions. In Excerpt 5 below, one can see that Ms Wu was trying hard to maximize the students' use of English. However, in turn, her rather excessive modelling made it difficult for the students to interact with each other.

Excerpt 5 (PA, H–H dyad, S5(H) and S6(H))

52 S6(H)   ((Circling an item.))

53	Ms Wu	You can by asking. OK? Don't just take it by yourself. You should (. . .) think about (.) negotiation.
54	S5(H)	This one?
55	S6(H)	OK.
56	Ms Wu	Maybe you can say 'shall we take this one?' Don't say . . . just say 'this one,' 'that one.'
57	S5(H)	This?
58	Ms Wu	This? What's this?
59	S5(H)	Um, water (. . .)
60	Ms Wu	You can say water (. .) bottle, the blue one, or the red one?
61	S5(H)	Blue one?
62	Ms Wu	Just take one?
63	S5(H)	Uh (::) two
64	Ms Wu	Two, yes, one for each.
65	S6(H)	We also need some (.) clothes.
66	S5(H)	Yes
67	S6(H)	Which one?
68	S5(H)	[. . .do you like]((completing S6's utterance for S6))
69	Ms Wu	[No, which one do you like?]((overlapping with S5))
70	S5 + S6	((Negotiating with their pen pointing at the items and shaking their pen for disagreement))

Ms Lee's case

As with the two teachers above, Ms Lee also paid close attention to see if the students followed the task procedures properly and completed the task. She also had more involvement in the interaction in general compared with Ms Chen. Notably, however, she focused primarily on meanings rather than forms. She offered lexical assistance, but typically only upon request from her students, and she offered such assistance much less frequently by way of direct form-focused support.

In IA, Ms Lee mostly controlled the floor-management and topics, similar to what we've seen with the other two teachers, but she also invited her students to be more mutually engaged in the tasks by using expressions such as 'how about . . .?' and 'shall we . . .?', as one can see in both Excerpts 6 and 7 below.

Excerpt 6 (IA, S7(L))

71	Ms Lee	How about painting?
72	S7(L)	Yes.
73	Ms Lee	Are you good at painting?
74	S7(L)	Sometimes.
75	Ms Lee	I think you do it very well.
76	S7(L)	Thanks. ((Smiling))
77	Ms Lee	And what activities will boys have? Do you think they will like football or uh (. .)
78	S7(L)	Football.
79	Ms Lee	So, shall we take it for them?

80	S7(L)	((Nodding))
81	Ms Lee	What are other activities?
82	S7(L)	Hmm (::), fly a kite.
83	Ms Lee	Oh, fly kite. Do you think it's good to fly kite in spring?
84	S7(L)	Yes.
85	Ms Lee	There's square so we can fly a kite.

Excerpt 7 (IA, S8(H))

86	Ms Lee	Do you like skateboard?
87	S8(H)	I don't like skateboard. It's very (. . .) dangerous.
88	Ms Lee	How about painting? Do you like painting?
89	S8(H)	No, I don't think so. It isn't funny.
90	Ms Lee	What about, uh, what about catching butterflies?
91	S8(H)	It sounds good.
92	Ms Lee	OK.
93	S8(H)	((Writing))
94	Ms Lee	Catch insects.
95	S8(H)	((Writing))
96	Ms Lee	Can you play football?
97	S8(H)	I can't play football, but I like football.
98	Ms Lee	So, do you bring football for the boys?
99	S8(H)	No, for the girls.
100	Ms Lee	For the girls. ((Both are laughing))

In Excerpt 7, when Ms Lee was interacting with an H-student (S8), one could observe a fair amount of negotiation between them. Ms Lee also made comments on the students' statements or built-on questions in order to develop topics further, as once can see, for example, in Lines 83 and 85 in Excerpt 6. In terms of the affective aspects of her interaction, Ms Lee managed to create a relatively encouraging and relaxing atmosphere during the assessment. In Line 75 in Excerpt 6, Ms Lee's positive comment about S7's painting ability made her feel good about herself. Ms Lee's interaction with her students often invited laugher during the assessment.

In the PA format, Ms Lee's involvement mostly concentrated on overseeing the procedures for completing the tasks and managing the interactions between the students. In Excerpt 8, when the two girls disagreed over coats, Ms Lee offered the suggestion that 'So maybe a thick coat is better.' (Line 107) and suggested that each of the girls could bring a coat. Except for a few modellings of lexical items, which she usually provided upon requests from her students, Ms Lee hardly provided the students with direct modelling of forms, in contrast to the case of Ms Wu.

Excerpt 8 (PA, H–L dyad, S9(H) and S10(L))

101	Ms Lee	You two start. Circle the things you want to bring. Speak English as much as possible.
102	S9(H)	Maybe we (:) we should have a bag. This one or this one? ((Pointing at the different bags on the sheet))
103	S10(L)	This one. ((Pointing at the second bag))

104	S9(H)	((Circling the selected bag)) And should we have a (::) should we take a T-shirt? Or a coat?
105	S10(L)	Coat? Is very warm. Coat is very warm.
106	S9(H)	But it's chilly at the night. ((Pointing at the weather indication on the sheet)) ((Touching her nose. Smiling))
107	Ms Lee	So maybe a thick coat is better. Two. Two thick coats. ((Pointing at the weather indication on the sheet.))
108	S9(H)	Which coat?
109	Ms Lee	You can decide yours and you can decide yours.
110	S9(H)	I think I'd like this one. ((Circles a pink jacket in the second row)) How about you?
111	S10(L)	I like this one. ((Circles a black jacket in the first row))
112	S9(H)	We (. .) we will have a (:) two . . . [two pair of shoes].
113	S10(L)	[two pair of shoes]. ((Looking at each other. Nodding))
114	S9(H)	((Smiling at S10)) And we maybe . . . uh . . . we maybe we will take a (:) two T-shirts.

Discussion

This study examined the role of teachers as both providers of assistance as well as evaluators in a classroom-based TBLA in a FLES programme in China. A holistic analysis of the interactional patterns of dyads, based on Storch (2002), indicated that the IA format (child–teacher dyads) almost exclusively yielded novice/expert interactional patterns irrespective of the students' general proficiency levels. While one can expect that the IA format potentially makes it easier for teachers to provide individualized assistance to students in TBLA, it tended to yield a relatively limited range of language use from the students in this study. Largely due to the teachers' strong control over floor-management, turn-taking, and topic development, the students primarily answered the teachers' questions and rarely initiated a topic or challenged the teachers' opinions. This could pose a challenge to using tasks in the IA format for assessment.

It is unclear, however, if such interactional patterns in the teacher–child dyads were largely rooted in the current study's particular socio-historical context of teaching or can be more generally observable in teacher–child dyads at the elementary school level. Chinese teachers' interpersonal behaviour is typically characterized as tolerant-authoritative or authoritative styles (e.g., Wei, den Brok & Zhou, 2009). On the one hand, one may be inclined to think that teachers' strong control over the interactions found in the present study may be due to the particular cultural and educational expectations and the environment in which the study was conducted. On the other hand, it may be a common phenomenon found in wider contexts at the elementary school level. Oliver (2000) examined interactions in native English speaking (NS) teacher and non-native English speaking (NNS) child dyads in Australia and compared the results with that in NS-teacher and NNS-adult learner dyads. She found that NS teachers had much stronger control over topic selection and learners' production when interacting with children, which was in fact consistent with our results.

In the PA format, unlike younger students (five to ten year-olds) in Carpenter et al. (1995), the majority of the students (eleven to twelve year-olds) in this study showed the collaborative pattern, followed by the novice/expert pattern. Accordingly, one can argue that the PA format also may potentially be used as an *assessment for learning* among this age group, based on the constructivist premise that learning takes place through collaborative interaction with more capable individuals. Moreover, the PA format potentially allows teachers to elicit from students a wider variety of language use and interactional strategies. However, when the student dyads did not show collaborative or novice/expert patterns, the ways in which the teachers were involved in the interactions appeared to be critically important in order to make the best use of such potential strengths of the PA format.

A closer look at individual teachers' ways of interacting with students showed significant variations among them. The teachers in the current study were asked to implement more communicative-oriented teaching and a constructivist-principled assessment in an educational context that traditionally has been characterized as an exam culture. The variability that we observed among teachers' interactions with their students during the TBLA indicates the challenges that they face in conducting assessment in a FLES programme in the midst of adapting new cultures of teaching and assessment. It also raises a number of issues that we need to consider when promoting TBLA in classrooms in general. We identify three separate issues in particular below.

The first issue to be considered when promoting TBLA is the identification of the goals of assessment, namely, what needs to be captured and what goals are to be achieved through the assessment. Most FLES programs have a strong emphasis on developing young learners' oral communicative skills and strategies as their main instructional goals, along with enhancing the students' motivation or willingness to communicate, while celebrating their learning process. The Chinese government is no exception to this trend and the promotion of TBLT is part of their broader efforts to achieve these goals. However, when it comes to assessment, most FLES programs rarely specify clear assessment criteria, and external exams largely remain form-focused and are usually conducted in a paper-and-pencil format in mainland China. Under such circumstances, it is not surprising to see some teachers mainly taking either form-focused or measurement-oriented approaches to TBLA in their classrooms. What are the potential components of language learning (e.g., linguistics, interactions, pragmatics, motivational components, etc.) that teachers should be dealing with in TBLA in their classrooms? How should non-verbal components such as motivation be treated? The lack of specification of assessment criteria in FLES programs is in part due to our limited understanding of what accounts for young learners' foreign language communicative competence at the theoretical level (Johnstone, 2000). Theory-building in this area is an urgent matter. At the practical level, the lack of specification also relates to the unclear role and status of classroom-based assessment in the entire teaching and accountability system. How does TBLA in the classroom relate to external exams and the accountability system at the secondary school level and beyond, or in the entire educational system? These issues need to be defined within a specific educational context.

A second issue is how to conceptualize the role of teachers (i.e., teachers' assistance) when theorizing the validity and reliability of TBLA in the classroom and how to operationalize it in practice. The present study shows that depending on the teachers' beliefs and the ways in which they provide assistance, the interactions that emerge during TBLA can be very different. It also shows that in some cases, the teachers' involvement appears to be inevitable for this age group. The question then becomes on what basis can individual teachers decide what types of assistance should be incorporated in assessment criteria? As we have mentioned already, if the measurement context includes teachers' beliefs, then assistance and scaffolding during the interaction are all validity-relevant concerns in classroom-based assessment (Brookhart, 2003). As Davison and Leung (2009) rightly suggest, we need to build an explicit theory which links the following three components: teachers' assistance, students' interactions as a result of such assistance, and students' learning. Without having such a theory, one can easily imagine that it is hard for classroom-based TBLA to gain acceptance in an educational context where the exam culture is still dominant and fairness is considered to be crucial in assessment.

Finally, a third issue that needs to be considered when promoting TBLA is a call for more attention to the affective components of TBLA. Given the fact that enhancing young learners' motivation to communicate in the target language is one of the major objectives of many FLES programs and that TBLT is largely promoted to serve this purpose at this age level, it is reasonable to expect that TBLA should incorporate affective components in its processes and in the assessment criteria. The research on TBLT as well as TBLA to-date has paid substantial attention to the cognitive components of tasks and their relation to learning. However, little has been considered with respect to the various affective factors in task design such as fun, enjoyment, feelings of achievement, feelings of challenges, motivation, willingness to communicate, anxiety and so forth. What kind of tasks and TBLA can make young learners feel excited and want to engage even more in learning and using the target language? While it has been claimed that tasks should reflect language use in real life, Butler (2005) found that 'unexpected' consequences and/or 'imaginary' settings in task design often made young learners excited and motivated to complete a given task. The present data indicated that some teachers could foster their students' affective components through interactions more than the others. How do teachers assist young learners to be motivated to participate in TBLA? How can or should teachers incorporate young learners' motivations in assessment criteria? Are there any particular formats or task types that enhance students' motivation or reduce anxiety in TBLA? In the process of socializing in an exam culture such as China, many young learners experience substantial pressure and quickly lose their motivation to learn English. Thus, assessment for young learners needs to be designed not only to enhance student learning but also to maintain their interest and motivation, in addition to its traditional purpose of measuring attainment.

Conclusion

In conclusion, the present study examined the role of teachers as providers of assistance as well as evaluators during TBLA as implemented using two approaches in classrooms in a FLES programme in China. This study revealed that different interaction patterns emerged in the two formats. Individual differences across the teachers were also notable. Such variability in interactions may be a reflection of the challenges they face in adapting communicative-based teaching and constructivist-principled assessment practices in an exam culture where exams are strongly expected to serve only as a fair measurement device. Perhaps teacher training programs should focus on raising teachers' awareness of the various functions that assessment can have in their daily practice. There is no doubt that a series of theoretical and practical considerations must be factored in when implementing TBLA in FLES programs. In order to make TBLA work in Asia, flexibility and close attention to local instructional needs and goals are indispensable. We must not forget that teachers play a central role in this adaptation process.

Notes

1 Pseudonyms were used for the participants mentioned in this chapter.
2 Since this classification was not based on the students' oral proficiency, it should be taken as a gross measure.
3 For the transcription convention, we adapted the transcription convention used by Richards (2003) and Brooks (2009).

References

Bailey, A. L. (2008). Assessing the language of young learners. In E. Shohamy & N. H. Hornberger (Eds), *Encyclopedia of language and education: Vol. 7. Language testing and assessment* (pp. 379–398). Dordrecht: Springer.

Black, P., Harrison, C., Lee, C., Marshall, B., & Wiliam, D. (2003). *Assessment for learning: Putting it into practice*. Berkshire, UK: Open University Press.

Brookhart, S. M. (2003). Developing measurement theory for classroom assessment purposes and uses. *Educational Measurement: Issues and Practice, 22*(4), 5–12.

Brooks, L. (2009). Interacting in pairs in a test of oral proficiency: Co-constructing a better performance. *Language Testing, 26*(3), 341–366.

Butler, Y. G. (2005). *Nihon-no shogakko eigo-o kangaeru: Ajia-no shiten-karano kensho-to teigenn* [English language education in Japanese elementary schools: Analyses and suggestions based on East Asian perspectives]. Tokyo: Sansedo.

Butler, Y. G. (2011). The implementation of communicative and task-based language teaching in the Asia-Pacific region. *Annual Review of Applied Linguistics, 31*, 36–57.

Carless, D. (2011). *Form testing to productive student learning: Implementing formative assessment in Confucian-Heritage settings*. New York: Routledge.

Carpenter, K., Fujii, N., & Kataoka, H. (1995). An oral interview procedure for assessing second language abilities in children. *Language Testing, 12*(2), 158–181.

Csépes, I. (2009). *Measuring oral proficiency through paired-task performance*. Frankfurt: Peter Lang.

Davis, L. (2009). The influence of interlocutor proficiency in a paired oral assessment. *Language Testing, 26*(3), 367–396.

Davison, C., & Leung, C. (2009). Current issues in English language teacher-based assessment. *TESOL Quarterly, 43*(3), 393–415.

Deng, C., & Carless, D. (2009). The communicativeness of activities in a task-based innovation in Guangdong, China. *Asian Journal of English Language Teaching, 19*, 113–134.

Ellis, R. (2003). *Task-based language learning and teaching.* Oxford: Oxford University Press.

Hamp-Lyons, L. (2007). The impact of testing practices on teaching: Ideologies and alternatives. In J. Cummins, & C. Davison (Eds), *The international handbook of English language teaching, Vol. 1.* (pp. 487–504). Norwell, MA: Springer.

Inbar-Lourie, O. (2008). Language assessment culture. In E. Shohamy & N. H. Hornberger (Eds), *Encyclopedia of language and education: Vol. 7. Language testing and assessment* (pp. 285–299). Dordrecht: Springer.

Johnson, M. (2001). *The art of non-conversation: A reexamination of the validity of the Oral Proficiency Interview.* New Haven: Yale University Press.

Johnstone, R. (2000). Context-sensitive assessment of modern language in primary (elementary) and early secondary education: Scotland and the European experience. *Language Testing, 17*(2), 123–143.

Leung, C. (2005). Classroom teacher assessment of second language development: Construct as practice. In E. Hinkel (Ed.), *Handbook of research in second language teaching and learning* (pp. 869–888). Mahwah, NJ: Lawrence Erlbaum.

Littlewood, W. (2007). Communicative and task-based language teaching in East Asian classrooms. *Language Teaching, 40,* 243–249.

May, L. (2009). Co-constructed interaction in a paired speaking test: The rater's perspective. *Language Testing, 26*(3), 397–421.

Oliver, R. (2000). Age differences in negotiation and feedback in classroom and pairwork. *Language Learning, 50*(1), 119–151.

O'Sullivan, B. (2000). Exploring gender and oral proficiency interview performance. *System, 28,* 373–386.

O'Sullivan, B. (2002). Learner acquaintanceship and oral proficiency test pair-task performance. *Language Testing, 19*(3), 277–295.

Pica, T., Kanagy, R., & Falodun, J. (1993). Choosing and using communicative tasks for second language research and instruction. In S. Gass & G. Crookes (Eds), *Task-based learning in a second language* (pp. 9–34). Clevedon: Multilingual Matters.

Richards, K. (2003). *Qualitative inquiry in TESOL.* New York: Palgrave Macmillan.

Storch, N. (2002). Patterns of interaction in ESL pair work. *Language Learning, 52*(1), 119–158.

Wei, M., den Brok, P., & Zhou, Y. (2009). Teacher interpersonal behavior and student achievement in English as a foreign language classrooms in China. *Learning Environments Research, 12,* 157–174.

van Lier, L. (1989). Reeling, writhing, drawling, stretching, and fainting in coils: Oral proficiency interviews as conversation. *TESOL Quarterly, 23,* 489–508.

Vygotsky, L. S. (1978). *Mind and society.* Cambridge, MA: Harvard University Press.

22

Teachers' Adaptations of TBLT: The Hong Kong Story

David R. Carless

Summary

The Hong Kong school setting is the first within the Asia-Pacific region to adopt Task-Based Language Teaching (TBLT) as a core part of its English language curriculum. TBLT has manifested itself in various forms since the early 1990s, including the current 'New Senior Secondary' (NSS) curriculum where school-based assessment plays a major part. Framing the analysis through a mutual adaptation lens, I show how teachers have mainly adapted task-based principles in line with their existing practices, emphasizing grammatical input and contextualized language practice. Local implementation has only partially followed what might be regarded as international guidelines on TBLT. The extent to which the resulting hybrid is a dilution of TBLT or a healthy contextual adaptation is discussed. In order to probe the classroom implementation of TBLT in Hong Kong, I describe and analyse four selected tasks from research carried out in primary and secondary school settings. I bring out some key issues from these studies and relate them to other relevant research. The main implications are threefold: tensions between conventional modes of presenting grammatical knowledge and more flexible and inductive modes in TBLT; the potential for contextual adaptations to TBLT suitable for the host culture; and the relationship between TBLT and high-stakes assessment.

Introduction

How teachers interpret and engage with TBLT in the Asia-Pacific region is a central theme of this volume. In this chapter, I explore how teachers in the compulsory school sector in a specific context respond to the introduction of task-based curricula.

I do this through analysing different manifestations of TBLT in Hong Kong over the period 1993–2013. The Hong Kong Government is the first within the Asia-Pacific region to introduce TBLT as a core part of its English language curriculum. The aim of the chapter is to use the Hong Kong experience to analyse how teachers adapt or re-interpret TBLT in a context where ongoing and frequent educational reforms co-exist with a predominantly conventional Confucian-influenced teaching culture.

TBLT is generally seen as sharing many of the principles of communicative language teaching (CLT) and a communicative syllabus was introduced in Hong Kong in the early 1980s but not widely implemented in classrooms. A task-based curriculum was adopted in primary schools from the mid-1990s onwards and in secondary schools from the turn of the millennium. Currently in the NSS curriculum, TBLT retains a key role in the syllabus and tasks are also a part of school-based assessment (SBA), which counts towards the high-stakes examination result at the culmination of secondary schooling. In sum, this represents a long-term attempt to introduce TBLT into a school system, so is particularly worthy of analysis in that it may generate insights relevant to other jurisdictions, particularly those within the region.

The analysis principally carries implications in three interlinked areas: tensions between teacher presentation of grammatical knowledge and more flexible, inductive modes recommended in TBLT; contextual adaptations to TBLT to mesh them with the host culture; and the relationship between TBLT and high-stakes assessment. The remainder of the paper is organized in the following way. First, I set out a framework discussing the interplay between the teacher and the implementation context. The development of TBLT in Hong Kong follows. Then I analyse four tasks carried out in primary and secondary schools and relate them to issues in other relevant literature. Finally, I draw out some conclusions and implications.

Framework: Mutual adaptation perspectives on change

TBLT represents an innovation so its implementation needs to be informed by literature on the management of educational change. The framework for the paper is developed in two interlinked stages. The first strand of the framework reaffirms the centrality of teachers in educational change. The second element emphasizes the role of context in shaping reform as a process of mutual adaptation. The argument is that the process of implementing TBLT involves a mutual adaptation between the principles of the innovation and how it is interpreted in school contexts by teachers. The discussion builds principally on educational literature about the management of change. In my view, applied linguistics is well-served when it draws on its parent discipline of education.

Educational reform and the teacher

The teacher has long been recognized as being central to attempts at curriculum reform. Whilst policymakers and educational ministries may set directions and form proposals, it is what teachers do in classrooms that directly affects the success of any reform agenda. Teachers' response to reforms involves primarily a cognitive process of sense-making (Spillane, Reiser & Reimer, 2002). In their review, Spillane et al. suggest various aspects of teacher response to change relevant to this chapter: affective costs to self-image can work against adopting reforms; the historical context affects sense-making in implementation; and teachers are biased towards interpretations consistent with their prior beliefs and values. Teachers' belief systems form an essential part of what they do in the classroom, for example, a teacher's conception of pedagogy impacts on their orientation towards TBLT. The more constructivist their orientation, the more likely they are to sympathize with learner-centred, process-oriented principles of TBLT.

If teachers are to implement an innovation such as TBLT successfully, it is essential that they have a thorough understanding of its principles and practice. For the purpose of this chapter, understanding is defined as the ability to engage with the principles of TBLT and an awareness of classroom applications of these principles. Understandings are central to reform agendas, as Fullan (2001) puts it: 'change will always fail unless we find some way of developing infrastructures and processes that engage teachers in developing new understandings' (p. 37).

Teacher response to an imposed innovation is highly complex and may vary from side-stepping and ignoring a reform to engaging with it positively and pro-actively so as to develop ownership. Adapting an innovation, explored further below, represents some interface between prior teacher beliefs and those of the proposed change. This often entails some compromises to make the innovation manageable in a particular context.

Context and mutual adaptation

Innovations are implemented within micro-level school contexts and also within wider national settings and cultures. The role of context in affecting methodological choices is influenced by ecological perspectives on language education. Ecological perspectives focus on the subjective reality which various aspects of pedagogy assume for participants in a particular sociocultural setting (Tudor, 2003). From an ecological viewpoint, context is not just something that needs to be taken into account, but is at the heart of the matter (van Lier, 2004). A methodology is only effective to the extent that teachers and students are willing to accept and implement it with good faith, and this depends largely on the set of values and beliefs that these teachers and students have been socialized into (Hu, 2005).

Implementation of an innovation is a process of mutual adaptation between innovation principles and local realities (McLaughlin, 2004). Mutual adaptation is a process of adjustments made by proponents of an innovation and those who actually use it in a school context (Snyder, Bolin & Zumwalt, 1992), taking into account existing practices and local conditions. Mutual adaptation is the most effective way to ensure that change efforts are not superficial, trivial or transitory (McLaughlin, 2004). Sometimes this mutual adaptation leads to dilution or derailment of innovation objectives, but at other times it shapes implementation in ways best suited to local resources, traditions and personnel (McLaughlin, 2004). A diluted version of TBLT risks losing its pedagogical essence, particularly if the principles underlying relevant teaching processes are only partially understood.

Datnow, Hubbard and Mehan (2002) extend the mutual adaptation perspective by emphasizing the co-constructed nature of the implementation process, as innovations involve interaction between schools and the wider social sphere, including political and cultural elements. They argue that 'all change is local' (p.39) and conditions in local contexts prompt teachers to modify reforms in ways that make sense to them within their existing body of professional knowledge and beliefs. Adaptations occur through a process in which teachers and schools creatively recombine strengths of an innovation and components already existing within the system to create a new manifestation (Hargreaves, 2007).

Local development of TBLT

The CLT syllabus of the 1980s failed to take root fully because of the failure of policymakers to take into account features of the Hong Kong context which would clearly militate against the implementation of a learner-centred, process-oriented teaching approach (Evans, 1996). Education in Hong Kong is largely about gaining credentials: examination grades, certificates, degrees and qualifications (Carless, 2011). As examinations were not communicative and almost exclusively emphasized accuracy of language production, CLT did not appear relevant to teachers' and students' most pressing needs (Evans, 1996).

A repercussion of the focus on accuracy is that Hong Kong teachers generally present grammar deductively through explicit explanation and controlled practice with an emphasis on form rather than meaning (Andrews, 2007). This is often attempted through methods that are loosely within a framework of presentation-practice-production (PPP) approaches. This represents some conflict with more flexible or inductive approaches to grammar instruction congruent with TBLT.

The first manifestation of TBLT in Hong Kong took place during the early 1990s under the so-called Target-Oriented Curriculum (TOC) which was a high-profile reform initiative attracting funding, resources and an international profile (see, for example, Candlin, 2001). After a period of trialling and experimentation commencing in 1993, the TOC was fully introduced in primary schools in 1995 in the three main subjects of the school curriculum: Chinese, English and Mathematics. The main aim was for students to progress towards clearly defined learning targets through carrying out learning tasks. The cross-curricular definition of task adopted in the TOC included five elements (Clark, Scarino & Brownell, 1994):

- a *purpose* or underlying reason for doing the task, involving more than the display of knowledge or practice of skills;
- a *context* in which the task takes place, which may be simulated, real or imaginary;
- a *process* of thinking and doing required in carrying out the task;
- a *product* or the result of thinking and doing, which may be tangible or intangible;
- a *framework of knowledge, strategy and skill* used in carrying out the task based on 'five fundamental ways of learning': communicating, inquiring, conceptualizing, reasoning and problem-solving.

This definition of task was an attempt to synthesize previous definitions of task and add to them perspectives of the TOC project team. In terms of critiques of this definition, one might comment that many types of learning have a process and a product, and this would not necessarily be a defining feature of task. The TOC definition also fails to address the issue of communication of new information which is implicit or explicit in most applied linguistic interpretations of task (e.g. Littlewood, 2011). The fifth component of the framework addressed this, to some extent, by including communicating within its five ways of learning. The cross-curricular nature of the reform precluded some of the elements of standard definitions of task found in the applied linguistics literature and a repercussion was that second language acquisition aspects of TBLT were not highlighted to a great extent. The main focus was on purposefulness, contextualization and the 'five fundamental ways of learning'.

During the 1990s, the Hong Kong Government provided considerable training and support for the development of TBLT. This consisted of both large-scale one-off seminars and more focused school-based curriculum development, both carrying mixed successes and challenges. In 1999, TBLT was introduced into secondary schools in an incremental way as students who had learnt through TOC proceeded through the school system. In the current NSS curriculum, the syllabus focuses on English for interpersonal communication; for developing and applying knowledge; and for responding and giving expression to real and imaginative experience (Curriculum Development Council, 2007). This third language arts strand involves various elements, such as poems and songs, and electives, such as debating or sports communication. They are focused on authentic materials; the use of English language in context; and developing productive skills, orally or in writing through task-based activities (Carless & Harfitt, 2013).

The current documentation (Curriculum Development Council, 2007) describes tasks as 'activities in which learners are required to draw together and further develop their knowledge and skills. They are characterized by an emphasis on activity, participation and communication among participants through a variety of modes and media (p.75)'. The same five features as those in the cross-curricular TOC definition from the early 1990s are also re-stated. Whilst one might argue that this represents admirable consistency, it could also be seen as failing to adapt the definition in the light of experience and local research. One would also have expected a purely English Language Teaching (ELT) syllabus (rather than the cross-curricular TOC) to shift conceptualization towards exclusively applied linguistics concerns, e.g. a focus on meaning or the communication of new information.

The same document also contains a detailed description of the relationship between TBLT and grammar in a section entitled *Learning grammar in context*. The main emphasis is on providing grammar instruction in the form of exercises in the pre-task stage, with the post-task stage being mainly focused on remediation. This differs significantly from the well-known Willis and Willis (2007) form of TBLT in which the pre-task stage is mainly to introduce the topic and identify topic language; the task involves students using their existing linguistic resources to transact the task; and language focus and explicit language instruction occurs in the post-task stage.

A major barrier to the implementation of CLT or TBLT in the region has been the role of examinations (Littlewood, 2007). In Hong Kong, this issue has been tackled over the last twenty years by increasing the weighting awarded to oral performance, and the examinations have become increasingly task-based. Accordingly, a major feature of the NSS curriculum is SBA oral tasks, either group interactions or oral presentations, involving responses to a print or non-print 'text', such as a book or movie which counts for 15 per cent of the grade in the public examination procedure at the end of secondary schooling (Davison & Hamp-Lyons, 2010). In comparison with the earlier manifestations of CLT or TBLT which could be downplayed or even ignored by some teachers, SBA demands attention because it counts towards high-stakes assessment. These SBA tasks represent a link between TBLT and assessment, but this is not referred to explicitly in the documentation, instead being inferred by teacher educators and university researchers. Another notable aspect is that under SBA the source of input preceding the task is either the reading of a text or the listening skills of watching a movie. This represents a different pre-task input to the kind of grammar input described in the syllabus.

Examples of the implementation of tasks

In order to illustrate how teachers in Hong Kong have interpreted and implemented TBLT in their classrooms, I now examine four tasks drawn from doctoral theses using classroom data from primary schools (Carless, 2001; Chan, 2006) and secondary schools (Tong, 2005; Yu, 2010). These examples are selected to provide a flavour of the typical kind of tasks being implemented and draw out issues arising. It is worth pointing out that teacher participants in these studies were obviously those who were engaging with and adapting the innovation, not those who saw it as irrelevant or unworkable.

Example Task 1

My doctoral study (Carless, 2001) focused on the classroom implementation of TBLT in the classes of three teachers in three different primary schools. I carried out seventeen lesson observations of each of the three teachers over the course of the academic year 1996/7 in the early stage of the implementation of the TOC. Below I introduce one of the case study teachers, Alice, and discuss a task she enacted with a Year 1 (students aged six to seven years old) class of higher than average ability.

Alice has eight years of teaching experience and has been trained in and is positively disposed towards communicative approaches. She describes one of the aims of TBLT under the TOC as 'To make learning more like real-life not very class constrained, to let pupils learn happily, creatively to involve them in learning by doing' (Carless, 2001, p. 158). She goes on to describe 'task' as follows: 'Task is an activity. In the task, pupils should have the chance to use the language meaningfully not just read after the teachers or repeat something' (Carless, 2001, p. 158). In my judgement, this is quite a good personal interpretation of TBLT.

One of the observed lessons was focused on describing a clown which the teacher drew on the blackboard. A subsequent writing task was for students to give a name to and describe their own clown in a short text of four or five sentences. The language focus was on using previously taught vocabulary on parts of the body and colours e.g. What colour is the mouth? What shape is the face? The latter question involved creative answers, including circle, triangle or square.

In the pre-task stage, Alice and her students constructed together a text to describe the clown which the teacher had drawn on the blackboard: 'This is Ping. He is a clown. His eyes are ... etc.' Students were then given a worksheet with a clown on it; they were asked to colour the clown as they wished and then write appropriate sentences about it. Within the framework provided, this gave them some opportunity to create their own four- or five-line text. This task is roughly congruent with the TOC definition of task in that there was a purpose, a process and a product with students creating a text at their own level. There was not much relationship with daily life and the task was not particularly well-contextualized in providing a rationale for drawing the clown.

In a post-lesson interview, Alice reflected on this teaching sequence:

> When I feel that the pupils enjoy the lesson and I can see their response, then I feel satisfied. When I was doing the process writing with them, asking them to suggest the colour and the shape of the clown they seemed to enjoy it, so I think that part is quite good. In the process writing they have to create their own clown and they also enjoy this. And to some extent they are involved in reasoning and problem-solving.
>
> (Carless, 2001, p. 207)

This quotation exemplifies some features of Alice's implementation of TBLT. She likes to involve the pupils actively in lessons, in this case contributing their ideas to the appearance and colour of the clown. Her belief in motivation, enjoyment and students learning happily is also exemplified through the design of an activity which pupils seemed to find interesting, for example, the appearance and colouring of the clown. The final sentence of the quotation invokes two of the 'five fundamental ways of learning' in TOC: reasoning and problem-solving.

During the pre-task stage the teacher orchestrated a description of the clown by drawing on student suggestions. In the task stage, students could decide for themselves the extent to which they would like to follow the teacher guidance or add their own independently produced sentences. In that particular case, more than half of the class mainly followed the suggested model; around a quarter followed the teacher guidance with one or two sentences of variation; and a small number of adventurous students attempted to create their own text more independently (Carless, 2001). One of the positive aspects of this teacher approach was that it provided scaffolding for all the students, whilst they had a certain amount of freedom to decide how much of that support they would use.

Example Task 2

The focus of Chan (2006, 2012) was on qualitative differences in four teachers' enactments of TBLT in the teaching of tasks on the topic of weather in year 2 and 3 classes. The database for the study was twenty videotaped lesson observations and semi-structured interviews with teachers and students. The reporting of the study was mainly based on the researcher's interpretation of a sequence of five observed lessons for each teacher. Relatively little teacher data is reported, and Chan acknowledges that it was difficult to elicit views on the lessons from learners aged eight years old.

One of the case study teachers in this study was Linda, a teacher with five years of experience. She conducted a series of activities with her Year 3 class on a unit entitled, 'Weather and activities they do'. Activities included a weather chart: using symbols to record weather conditions for a week; and guessing the activity that a character in a story likes doing in different weather conditions. The task which concluded the unit of five lessons required students to write four sentences about their preferred activities in different weather conditions. It was a mini-booklet entitled, 'My favorite activities in different weather'. The language focus was on adjectives to describe weather, such as sunny, cloudy or windy; activities like playing basketball or having a barbeque; and asking for information, for example, what do you like doing on sunny days?

Linda introduced the unit as follows (Chan, 2006, p. 84), 'I will use a big book to tell a story about a boy doing different things in different weather conditions. I'll ask the students some questions about the weather and the concepts of indoor and outdoor activities.' In her commentary, Chan points out that Linda's notion of 'story' was predominantly a way of contextualizing a specific target structure rather than what one would normally expect a children's story to be. The main focus of the teaching unit was on the sentences using the following structure:

On rainy days, I like singing songs.

On cloudy days, I like drawing pictures.

In her analysis, Chan indicates that there was sometimes a meaning relationship between the weather and the activity, and often there was not. She perceives that this may act as a barrier to student understanding and language development.

For the task about favourite activities in different weather, there was a set of pictures as a stimulus with two options; in other words, students had some, but limited, freedom to express their own meanings. Chan notes that the teacher was mainly focusing on accuracy of production rather than genuine communication and there was little interactional requirement or negotiation of meaning in the task. She suggests that although students have some freedom to choose the activities they mention, it is predominantly a contextualized exercise to practise the target structure. Students' attention is directed towards reproducing the target structure by slotting in some personal information related to an activity (Chan, 2006). The students tended to follow the suggested structure and produced sentences such as 'On rainy days, I like sleeping'.

Overall, Chan (2006) judges that Linda attached primary importance to language practice and the main emphasis of her instruction was on form rather than meaning. Task 2 was basically a contextualized exercise designed to practise a pre-taught language structure. In terms of selected aspects of the TOC definition of task, its purposefulness is relatively weak and its development of any of 'the five fundamental ways of learning' is also modest. Chan judges example task 2 as lacking the negotiation of meaning and genuine communication which would create the conditions for the development of student interlanguage.

Example Task 3

The focus of Tong (2005) was on what forms TBLT took in the intended and implemented curriculum and what factors shaped these forms at the classroom level. Case studies were conducted in three different secondary schools involving multiple teachers in each school. The database for the study included 110 lesson observations and fifty-four semi-structured interviews with twenty-three school personnel (Adamson & Tong, 2008).

Tong describes a series of tasks related to the theme of Healthy Eating in a unit of teaching conducted by Florence who was teaching a Year 9 class. Tong (2005) characterizes the approach in Florence's school as involving a mixture of the long-standing PPP approach with some concessions to TBLT in that student participation and input were encouraged within teacher-controlled work. Florence was a relatively inexperienced teacher judged by the researcher as having quite a good understanding of TBLT in comparison with other teachers taking part in the research. She viewed tasks as activities that involved practising individual language items in an interesting way, e.g. through games, but she felt it was not easy to integrate language input or grammar instruction into tasks. She was reported as stating that it was important for students to learn grammar so that they have something tangible to grasp. The following quotation illustrates Florence's views of TBLT:

> Task-based learning is a series of tasks that help students connect different aspects of knowledge. We need ... to integrate various topical, linguistic and skill aspects systematically into the activities ... Students may not feel that they have learnt something if ... the activities and the teaching content are not related.
>
> (Tong, 2005, p. 163)

The first two sentences of the quotation illustrate some of the connectedness implicit in TBLT, whilst the rather unclear final sentence seems to hint at concerns about the kind of learning emanating from activities.

Sub-tasks within the unit of teaching revolved around food and eating habits. An interview with a partner was carried out regarding eating habits using pre-set questions on a worksheet, e.g. 'how often do you go to fast food shops?' Students also designed menus, such as a breakfast menu for a trip to a camp. A further task was to write a report to the school principal related to the food in the school tuck shop. Language functions included types of food, describing foods and categorizing foods. The language focus included asking questions and making statements about food preferences using present and simple past tenses, and adjectives to describe foods, such as oily or delicious.

Tasks were mainly focused on writing or producing a written product. Florence made some related comments, as follows:

Every time my students finish a task, I ask them to keep their product together with the grammar exercises I have given them so that when they do the revision for the exams or tests, they can also refer to the grammar items.

(Tong, 2005, pp. 163–4)

Although student response was not a major focus of the study, Tong did collect some views from learners who expressed some preference for activity-based learning over conventional teacher-fronted teaching in that it was perceived as less boring. Students also stated that they derived some satisfaction from completing tasks and it helped to reinforce some of the language that they had learnt.

Example Task 4

The focus of Yu (2010) was on the washback of SBA on teachers and students. She carried out a case study in one secondary school, involving seventy lesson observations, questionnaire data and semi-structured interviews with teachers and students. The study involved two teachers, Rachel (a non-Chinese native speaking expatriate English teacher) and Chloe, a local teacher with five years of teaching experience. In view of the focus of the chapter on how local Hong Kong teachers interpret TBLT, I draw here solely on Chloe's perspectives and teaching of her Year 11 class. Her views of SBA were that it is a good way to learn English through exposure to reading and watching movies. In particular, she viewed it as having positive potential to prompt students to read more widely. Her main stated concerns were about the fairness of grades awarded by different teachers in different schools; and the heavy load of administrative work in relation to the conduct and moderation of SBA tasks (Yu, 2010).

Given that the study was focused on SBA rather than TBLT, it is not surprising that the tasks conducted are somewhat less clearly defined in Yu's thesis than in the three previous examples. I discuss here a group interaction task, one of the two SBA task types, focused on the plots of three movies students had watched: *National Treasure*, *High School Musical* and *Harry Potter*. In the teaching input stage, Chloe introduced some terminology related to movies, such as plot, setting and scene. She then presented a worksheet analysing the plot of a movie. A focus question for student discussion was, 'Among the three movies, which movie has the most exciting plot?' In addition to this input, Chloe also provided guidance to the students on how they should prepare for and conduct oral interaction. She was reported as emphasizing that students should interact spontaneously and should avoid rehearsed or unnatural interactions (Yu, 2010).

In the task, the focus of interaction in the groups was on issues such as interesting characters from the movies and discussion of the plots. In accordance with the recommendations of the SBA guidelines, students were involved in peer assessment of the group discussions, with each student providing verbal and written peer feedback to one member of the group. Chloe also provided feedback on different aspects of the students' performance. Her comments included advising students to use more eye contact; not to refer too frequently to their notes; and use stronger voice projection. She also recommended students to make more contrastive comments amongst the three movies rather than just talking about one of them. Some students were appreciative of the feedback comments, whilst others felt that the feedback was not sufficiently individualized and that, for example, comments on eye contact are invariably made by teachers. Others experienced some anxiety from SBA processes and reported that they tended to forget teacher feedback because of this (Yu, 2010).

Some benefits of SBA tasks and processes were reported by the students in terms of encouraging them to increase their exposure to English through reading books and watching movies which helped, for example, to enlarge their vocabulary. Some of them expressed concerns about fairness of grading in SBA, whilst others felt that the process of SBA was too time-consuming and gave them less time to prepare for other English papers and other examination subjects (Yu, 2010).

Discussion

The previous section has described four tasks at the micro level of the classroom. Now I relate insights from these tasks to other relevant research studies at the primary and secondary school levels in Hong Kong.

Task 1 above shows the interplay between teacher input and student activities: the teacher directed the construction of a text describing a clown by involving students actively and creatively in producing English language as preparation for writing their own short text. This is a more teacher orchestrated form of pedagogy in comparison with asking students to complete a task using pre-existing linguistic knowledge as recommended by Willis and Willis (2007). From the wider evidence of the study (Carless, 2004), it was seen that teachers generally interpreted TBLT along the lines of contextualized language practice activities; working as they were with young learners of relatively modest language proficiency, they believed reasonably enough that it was appropriate to pre-teach the language required by a task.

Contextualized language practice was also evident in task 2 on the theme of activities done during certain types of weather. In her analysis, Chan (2006, 2012) notes that language acquisition possibilities were not fully exploited in relation to creating conditions for noticing salient features of form; and facilitating language restructuring to occur. Task 2 also failed to demonstrate a convincing linkage between form and meaning in that some of the stated activities, such as drawing or sleeping, could take place during any weather. One of the problems in task 2 related to the design of the task. Challenges in the conceptualization and design of tasks also emerged from an evaluation study of the implementation of TBLT within TOC, where Tong, Adamson and Che (2000) found that 'tasks' in the English language lessons they observed only partially met the criteria for purposefulness and contextualization in the TOC definition.

Task 3 illustrated that products of tasks in secondary schools often took the form of written work as teachers did not feel secure for learning to be in an oral mode without tangible written record (Tong, 2005). A study, based on interview data from secondary school teachers and tertiary-based teacher educators in Hong Kong, further elaborated a rationale for a local focus on reading and writing tasks: they are generally more manageable; better tuned to the realities of the need to maintain discipline and order in the secondary school classroom; and congruent with the perceived needs of school and external examinations (Carless, 2007).

Implicit in these three example tasks and also in the wider literature (Adamson & Tong, 2008; Carless, 2009) is that teachers tended to see their main role as to present grammar and vocabulary to students. Accordingly, TBLT in Hong Kong was often subsumed under the PPP approach which was a core aspect of the practice of many teachers. PPP was seen to carry a number of advantages over TBLT: it provides a clearer instructional role based on providing grammatical input; it can be more easily integrated with the use of textbooks; and it appears less 'risky' to teachers (Carless, 2009).

Task 4 exemplifies the latest generation of tasks within SBA. These seem useful in stimulating extensive reading and encouraging communication around content rather than the practice of grammatical structures. SBA processes also encourage students to engage with criteria through peer assessment. A repercussion of SBA's dual role in TBLT and assessment contributes to its emergence as a research trend (Carless, 2012). Analysis of the discourse derived from a task based on choosing a gift for the main character in the movie *Forrest Gump*, found that peer group discussion as an oral assessment format has the potential to provide opportunities for students to demonstrate 'real-life' spoken interactional abilities (Gan, Davison & Hamp-Lyons, 2009). Conversely, a detailed analysis of a different discourse interaction shows students colluding in producing utterances aimed at creating the impression of being effective interlocutors for the purpose of scoring marks rather than for authentic communication (Luk, 2010). These studies produced contrasting findings, not surprisingly as Gan et al., purposefully selected an extract from a larger database in order to exemplify good practice, whilst Luk's study was more naturalistic based on data from a single school.

Conclusions and implications

Hong Kong has experienced twenty years of research and development related to TBLT. The general picture emerging reaffirms the centrality of teacher agency in appropriating or side-stepping aspects of pedagogic reform. A process of mutual adaptation between the intended curriculum and the implemented curriculum is evident with a hybrid emerging, comprising conventional practices and aspects of the reform which could easily be assimilated, rather than changed practices to accommodate TBLT (Adamson & Tong, 2008). This reinforces findings from other contexts (Spillane, Reiser & Reimer, 2002) which indicate that implementing teachers may rely excessively on superficial similarities between their current practice and the reform ideas; and may lose important aspects of a reform in the desire to assimilate it into existing repertoires.

Some positive trends also emerge. There has been more progress towards implementation of CLT than during the 1990s and teachers have assimilated some relevant features within their pedagogical repertoire: contextualization of language practice; attempts to increase student participation in motivating language learning experiences; and relating language learning to real-life uses of English. At the same time, they have maintained core aspects of their own prior pedagogy, such as forms of PPP which involve grammatical input at the pre-task stage or as an end in itself.

Features of TBLT which have been downplayed include those that relate to second language acquisition theory, and the acquisition of grammatical form. In the diluted version of TBLT implemented in Hong Kong, there appears to be less negotiation of meaning, students are often not communicating new information and grammar is taught deductively rather than acquired inductively. Evidence from the 1990s indicated that the pre-task stage was mainly used for the presentation and practice of language needed for the task, rather than an opportunity for input through different modes, such as reading and listening. The advent of SBA has led to more use of reading materials and movies as a source of pre-task input. Turning to the post-task stage of the task cycle, this has mainly been interpreted by Hong Kong teachers as focusing on remediation (Carless, 2007) rather than the more varied strategies envisaged in the literature, such as focus on form, language analysis or task repetition (Ellis, 2003; Willis & Willis, 2007).

A way forward may lie in developing contextually grounded sources of good practice or what Tudor (2003) calls a 'local' approach to pedagogical decision-making. A strand of a localized form of TBLT for schooling may involve identifying a suitable balance between different modes of interaction. CLT and TBLT do seem to privilege, to some extent, the oral mode of communication, and in respect to schooling at the secondary level this may not be the most feasible, especially within the region where student reticence in speaking English is often a challenge. We have seen from Tong (2005) that teachers wished to ensure that written products from tasks were generated, to provide a sense of completion and as a record for subsequent revision for school tests. As suggested in Carless (2007), due emphasis on reading and writing tasks and an appropriate balance between the four modes may fit the Hong Kong secondary school learning context and may merit consideration for other comparable settings.

A further important aspect of a local approach relates to catering for the needs of assessment. Tests and examinations are often seen as a barrier to the implementation of communicative approaches and this was indeed the case in Hong Kong during the 1980s and 1990s. Since then high-stakes examinations have been designed to encourage the adoption of TBLT and SBA extends this trend. Any school system serious about implementing TBLT clearly needs to align the curriculum with its high-stakes examinations. This provides an incentive for teachers to engage with communicative or task-based teaching. The extent to which they will enact it productively, however, is likely to depend on three key issues: their understandings; values and beliefs; and the training and support provided (Deng & Carless, 2010). The assessment of English Language in the NSS also gives rise to tensions between SBA and the requirements of high-stakes assessment. The Hong Kong community expects competitive examinations to be standardized and objective, whereas assessment of student performance in context requires some individual focus and a certain degree of subjectivity (Tong, 2011). Assessment in the curriculum, SBA and the challenge of developing productive interplay between formative and summative assessment are ongoing challenges requiring further research and development (Carless, 2011).

Finally, educational reform is so often characterized by the search for the new and compelling. Now that TBLT has been a part of the Hong Kong educational scene for twenty years, it is no longer a fresh concept with resources and attention devoted to it. Task is a recognized term as part of local educational discourse, yet remaining elusive to deep teacher understanding. Unlike many reforms which preceded it, TBLT has not been abandoned and it retains its place in the curriculum documentation but its era in the limelight has clearly passed. SBA and the NSS are now central features, and the notion of task remains as an aspect of their implementation.

References

Adamson, B., & Tong, S.Y.A. (2008). Leadership and collaboration in implementing curriculum change in Hong Kong secondary schools. *Asia Pacific Education Review*, 9(2), 180–189.
Andrews, S. (2007). *Teacher language awareness*. Cambridge: Cambridge University Press.
Candlin, C. (2001). Afterword: Taking the curriculum to task. In M. Bygate, P. Skehan & M. Swain (Eds), *Researching pedagogic tasks: Second language learning, teaching and testing* (pp. 229–243). Harlow: Longman.
Carless, D. (2001). Curriculum innovation in the primary EFL classroom: Case studies of three teachers implementing Hong Kong's target-oriented curriculum. Unpublished PhD thesis, University of Warwick.
Carless, D. (2004). Issues in teachers' re-interpretation of a task-based innovation in primary schools. *TESOL Quarterly*, 38(4), 639–662.
Carless, D. (2007). The suitability of task-based approaches for secondary schools: Perspectives from Hong Kong. *System*, 35(4), 595–608.
Carless, D. (2009). Revisiting the TBLT versus PPP debate: Voices from Hong Kong. *Asian Journal of English Language Teaching*, 19, 49–66.
Carless, D. (2011). *From testing to productive student learning: Implementing formative assessment in Confucian-heritage settings*. New York: Routledge.
Carless, D. (2012). TBLT in EFL settings: Looking back and moving forward. In A. Shehadeh & C. Coombe (Eds), *Task-based language teaching in foreign language contexts: research and implementation* (pp. 345–358). Amsterdam: John Benjamins.
Carless, D., & Harfitt, G. (2013). Innovation in secondary education: A case of curriculum reform in Hong Kong. In K. Hyland & L. Wong (Eds), *Innovation and change in English language education* (pp. 172–185). London: Routledge.
Chan, S. P. (2006). Qualitative differences in teachers' enactment of task-based language teaching in the ESL primary classroom. Unpublished PhD thesis, University of Hong Kong.
Chan, S. P. (2012). Qualitative differences in novice teachers' enactment of task-based language teaching in Hong Kong primary classrooms. In A. Shehadeh & C. Coombe (Eds), *Task-based language teaching in foreign language contexts: Research and implementation* (pp. 187–213). Amsterdam: John Benjamins.
Clark, J., Scarino, A., & Brownell, J. (1994). *Improving the quality of learning: A framework for target-oriented curriculum renewal*. Hong Kong: Institute of Language in Education.
Curriculum Development Council (2007). *English language curriculum and assessment guide (Secondary 4–6)*. Hong Kong: Hong Kong Government Printer.
Datnow, A., Hubbard, L., & Mehan, H. (2002). *Extending educational reform: From one school to many*. London: Routledge Falmer.
Davison, C., & Hamp-Lyons, L. (2010). The Hong Kong certificate of education: School-based assessment reform in Hong Kong English language education. In L. Y. Cheng, & A. Curtis (Eds), *English language assessment and the Chinese learner* (pp.248–266). New York: Routledge.

Deng, C. R., & Carless, D. (2010). Examination preparation or effective teaching: Conflicting priorities in the implementation of a pedagogic innovation. *Language Assessment Quarterly*, 7(4), 285–302.

Ellis, R. (2003). *Task-based language learning and teaching*. Oxford: Oxford University Press.

Evans, S. (1996). The context of English language education: The case of Hong Kong. *RELC Journal*, 27(2), 30–55.

Fullan, M. (2001). *The new meaning of educational change* (3rd edition). New York: Teachers College Press.

Gan, Z., Davison, C., & Hamp-Lyons, L. (2009). Topic negotiation in peer group oral assessment situations: A conversation analytic approach. *Applied Linguistics*, 30(3), 315–334.

Hargreaves, A. (2007). Sustainable leadership and development in education: Creating the future, conserving the past. *European Journal of Education*, 42(2), 223–233.

Hu, G. W. (2005). Contextual influences on instructional practices: A Chinese case for an ecological approach to ELT. *TESOL Quarterly*, 39(4), 635–660.

Littlewood, W. (2007). Communicative and task-based language teaching in East Asian classrooms. *Language Teaching 40*, 241–249.

Littlewood, W. (2011). Communicative language teaching: An expanding concept for a changing world. In E. Hinkel (Ed.), *Handbook of research in second language teaching and learning* (pp. 541–557). New York: Routledge.

Luk, J. (2010). Talking to score: Impression management in L2 Oral Assessment and the Co-construction of a Test Discourse Genre. *Language Assessment Quarterly*, 7(1), 25–53.

McLaughlin, M. (2004). Implementation as mutual adaptation: Change in classroom organization. In D. Flinders, & S. Thornton (Eds), *The curriculum studies reader* (2nd edition) (pp.171–182). New York: Routledge.

Snyder, J., Bolin, F., & Zumwalt, K. (1992). Curriculum implementation. In P. Jackson (Ed.), *Handbook of research on curriculum* (pp. 402–435). New York: Macmillan.

Spillane, J., Reiser, B., & Reimer, T. (2002). Policy implementation and cognition: Reframing and refocusing policy implementation research. *Review of Educational Research*, 72(3), 387–431.

Tong, S. Y. A. (2005). Task-based learning in English language in Hong Kong secondary schools. Unpublished Ph.D. thesis, University of Hong Kong.

Tong, S. Y. A. (2011). Assessing English language arts in Hong Kong secondary schools. *The Asia-Pacific Education Researcher*, 20(2), 387–394.

Tong, S. Y. A., Adamson, B., & Che, M. M. W. (2000). Tasks in English language and Chinese language. In B. Adamson, T. Kwan, & K. K. Chan (Eds), *Changing the curriculum: The impact of reform on Hong Kong's primary schools* (pp. 145–174). Hong Kong: Hong Kong University Press.

Tudor, I. (2003). Learning to live with complexity: Towards an ecological perspective on language teaching. *System*, 31(1), 1–12.

van Lier, L. (2004). *The ecology and semiotics of language learning: A sociocultural perspective*. Boston: Kluwer.

Willis, D. & Willis, J. (2007). *Doing task-based teaching*. Harlow: Longman.

Yu, Y. (2010). The washback effects of school-based assessment on teaching and learning: A case study. Unpublished Ph.D. thesis, University of Hong Kong.

Epilogue

Rod Ellis

Swan (2005), in a provocative article critiquing task-based language teaching (TBLT), argued that:

> [TBLT[1]] is of obvious use to learners who do not need much new input from their language classes (either because they receive substantial out-of-class exposure, or because they have already been taught more language than they can use), and whose main concern is to improve accuracy, fluency and complexity of their output. It is, however, not clear how [TBLT] can fully meet the requirements of those learners – the vast majority – who fall outside these categories.
>
> (p. 392)

In effect, Swan is arguing that TBLT might serve as a valid form of language pedagogy for learners in a *second* language context and for those who have already achieved substantial proficiency in the second language but it is not suitable to learners in a *foreign* language context and for beginner-level learners. The reason he offers for this opinion is that 'it remains true that TBLT provides learners with substantially less new language than "traditional approaches" ' (p. 392) but he offers not one shred of evidence in support of this.

The chapters in this book document attempts to introduce TBLT in exactly the kinds of contexts that Swan considers it inappropriate for – for example, in Cambodia, China, Japan, Myanmar, Thailand, and Vietnam – all essentially foreign language settings. Other chapters describe TBLT in contexts such as Hong Kong and Singapore that are closer to the kind of context Swan considers TBLT suited to. Many of the chapters also document the use of TBLT with learners of limited second language (L2) proficiency. These chapters provide clear evidence that TBLT is implementable in these contexts and with this kind of learner and also that it is capable of providing learners with 'substantial new language'.

These chapters, however, also describe the problems that the teachers faced in introducing TBLT in their classrooms. In many Asian countries, the introduction of TBLT has been a top-down process, warranted by Ministries of Education, and, as Carless points out in his chapter, 'while policymakers and educational ministries may set directions and form proposals, it is what teachers do in classrooms which directly affect the success of any reform agenda' (this volume). And what teachers do is influenced by their local context and their own beliefs about language pedagogy. Some of the chapters, however, describe the implementation of TBLT through the personal choice of the teachers involved. Readers of this book might like to examine to what extent differences emerge when TBLT is implemented as a result of a top-down mandate as opposed to teachers' own decisions.

I would like to comment briefly on some of the problems of implementation that authors of these chapters have identified. These can be classified into three categories:

1. Problems associated with teachers' understanding of TBLT and teacher's belief systems.
2. Problems associated with students' understanding of what it means to learn a language (i.e., learners' belief systems).
3. Problems associated with the external context (e.g., the nature of the high-stakes examinations that students have to take).

In many ways, it is not surprising that teachers have difficulty in developing a clear understanding of TBLT. There is no agreed definition of 'task' in either the SLA or the educational literature on TBLT. In Ellis (2003) I proposed four basic criteria for deciding what a task is: (1) a primary focus on meaning (and by this I mean pragmatic meaning when comprehending or producing messages for some communicative purpose); (2) a gap that motivates the exchange of information or opinions or the use of reasoning to solve some problem; (3) the students are required to use their own linguistic (and non-linguistic resources) when performing the task; and (4) an outcome other than simply the display of language. While I think that these criteria do provide a basis for evaluating whether a particular instructional activity is a 'task' and thus serve as a basis for helping teachers develop a clear understanding of a 'task', I acknowledge that many activities will satisfy some of the criteria but not all. In other words, there will be activities that are 'task-like' rather than 'pure tasks' and these will still have instructional value. Readers might like to look back at the tasks described in the chapters of this book and decide for themselves to what extent they are 'pure tasks' and, if they conclude they are not, whether it matters. Perhaps the key criterion is the third one. Do learners have to use their own linguistic resources or are they given the language they need to perform the task?

However, the problem of helping teachers develop a clear understanding of TBLT goes beyond defining 'task'. TBLT is an approach, not a method, and has a number of manifestations as the chapters in this book illustrate so clearly. TBLT is generally viewed as 'learner-centred', involving students working in small groups to perform oral production tasks – a perception of TBLT that derives in large part from how tasks have been researched in second language acquisition (SLA). But this is an overly narrow view of TBLT. TBLT can, in fact, be teacher-centred, when the teacher performs a task with the whole class, taking on the role of a participant in the task. TBLT can also involve tasks that involve any one of the four language skills or any combination of them. Thus TBLT can be comprehension-based as well as production-based and can focus on facilitating learning through input as well as output. I have argued that, for teachers and students new to TBLT, a teacher-centred approach involving input-based tasks, which gives the teacher more control over the conduct of the task, is the way to start. Input-based tasks, too, are surely needed with learners who have not yet developed the linguistic resources needed for production. What is perhaps central to all versions of TBLT is that language is treated as a 'tool' for achieving the outcome of the task rather than as a set of 'objects' to be studied, practised and mastered. This is what teachers and students need to understand along with the fact that learning a language does not necessitate always treating it as an 'object'.

There is a further problem relating to teachers' understanding of TBLT. TBLT is frequently seen as an alternative to 'traditional approaches'. Indeed, this is how Swan approached it. But it is not necessary to view TBLT in this way. Again, I have argued that in teaching contexts where teachers and students are used to traditional approaches it would be unwise to make a sudden and total switch to TBLT. Rather teachers would do better to introduce TBLT in some lessons while continuing with familiar traditional approaches in others. However, I have never been convinced with the argument that teachers should *adapt* TBLT to the local context by opting for task-supported rather than task-based instruction as Littlewood (2005) has proposed. Carless pointed out that when this happens, the end result is a version of presentation-practice-production (PPP). In other words, the task loses its 'taskness' and ends up as a situational grammar exercise. So, instead, I have argued that teachers should *adopt* TBLT but use it alongside PPP in a kind of modular syllabus (Ellis, 2012). There is plenty of evidence to show that PPP, when executed skilfully, is effective but if students are to develop the interactional competence needed for communication in the real world, they also need to experience language used as a tool (i.e., TBLT). This mixed approach would seem well-suited to many of the Asian contexts addressed in this book.

Learners have their own beliefs about how to learn a language. These have been shaped by their previous experiences of learning in classrooms – both in language classrooms and other-subject classrooms – and also by their own preferred learning styles. It is likely that in Asia (and indeed in other parts of the world as well) analytical beliefs that centre on seeing language as an object-for-study predominate. But there will always be some learners who orientate naturally to a more experiential approach of the kind TBLT affords. In line with the argument of the previous paragraph, this suggests the need for a hybrid approach. Students also need to be encouraged to inspect and reflect on their own beliefs to help them understand the importance of both a focus on forms and a focus on meaning/form. Learner training should be an important component of any language programme to help students understand what it means to treat language as an object and as a tool and why successful language learning involves both.

The problems associated with the external context of teaching are the hardest to overcome as teachers often lack the means to address them. For example, teachers generally have little influence on the content of high-stakes examinations. If these examinations emphasize grammatical correctness, it will be hard to convince teachers that they should not also focus on grammatical correctness. Again, though, the kind of hybrid approach I have advocated may be feasible as students are likely to want to learn to communicate as well as to be prepared for tests. It will obviously help, however, if the high-stake tests include tasks that assess communicative ability and this book indicates that in some educational contexts in Asia this is happening.

Other external factors that are beyond teachers' control are nevertheless manageable. In Asia, large classes are common, and this is sometimes given as a reason for not adopting TBLT. But the problem of large classes is really only evident if TBLT is seen exclusively as learner-centred and focused on oral production in small group work. Input-based tasks and written tasks performed individually by students can be quite easily carried out in large classes. Let us not forget that one of the first TBLT projects to be reported (Prabhu, 1987) was carried out in India with large classes of students and eschewed the use of small group work. Also, if needed, there are ways of conducting small group work in large classes.

There are, of course many other implementation problems I have not addressed. Some problems that are often cited, however, are not really problems at all. For example, teachers' lack of (or lack of confidence in) their own English proficiency will be problematic in any approach except perhaps grammar-translation. Similarly, the so-called passive nature of Asian students is not a reason for rejecting TBLT. Asian students are not inherently passive but may only appear to be so because they have been socialized into passivity in the classroom. TBLT provides a means of re-socializing them. But what is needed as part of teacher training – pre-service and in-service – is the identification of real and putative problems so that they can be addressed in a systematic way, for example in terms of the three categories of problems mentioned above. The chapters in this book serve as an excellent source for drawing up such a list.

I am an advocate of TBLT but not as an alternative to traditional approaches, rather as an adjunct to them. My own experience of Asian students is that all too often they end up with no, or very little, ability to use English for communicative purposes even after spending years in an English classroom. This is sometimes because they lack the motivation to learn English. But there is plenty of evidence that many Asian students do aspire to develop communicative skills and have failed because they did not experience the conditions inside the classroom that foster these skills. TBLT provides a means of creating these conditions. It is encouraging to see in the chapters of this book that there are now attempts to introduce TBLT throughout Asia.

Note

1 The original quotation uses 'TBI' (task-based instruction) in place of TBLT in this passage.

References

Ellis, R. (2003). *Task-based language learning and teaching.* Oxford: Oxford University Press.
Ellis, R. (2012). Task-based language teaching in Asian primary schools: Policy, problems and opportunities. In H. Pillay (Ed.), *Teaching language to learners of different age groups, RELC Anthology Series 53* (pp. 74–91). Singapore: SEAMEO Regional Language Centre.
Littlewood, W. (2007). Communicative and task-based language teaching in East Asian classrooms. *Language Teaching, 40,* 243–249.
Prabhu, N. (1987). *Second language pedagogy.* Oxford: Oxford University Press.
Swan, M. (2005). Legislation by hypothesis: The case of task-based instruction. *Applied Linguistics, 26,* 376–401.

INDEX

analytical approach, 14, 212, 383
Association of Southeast Asian Nations (ASEAN), 47
Augmented Reality (AR), 244–55
authentic texts, 291, 302–3, 309

Bangalore Project, 12, 13, 24
Bloom's taxonomy, 42

Cambodian Secondary English Teaching Project (CAMSET), 48
Chinese Ministry of Education, 140
Chinese National English Curriculum Standards, 30, 37
classroom research, 81, 170, 185, 299
code switching, 160, 162
codemeshing, 162
Cognition Hypothesis (CH), 197, 206
cognitive burden, 205–6
collectivist societies, 214, 224, 298
Communication-Oriented Language Teaching (COLT), 11
communicative competence, 137, 140, 173, 206, 264, 265, 266, 273, 275, 280, 292, 314
Communicative Language Teaching (CLT), 4, 9–11, 31, 34, 112, 137, 140, 157, 231, 264, 314, 350, 367
Confucian-Heritage culture, 12, 16, 17, 18, 56, 96, 184, 234, 344, 367
Content-based Instruction (CBI), 30, 34, 25, 287, 307
Continuing Professional Development (CPD), 230, 232, 238
creative thinking, 42, 93, 172, 183, 281
cross-cultural awareness, 33, 40
cultural language exchange, 211–25

deep learning, 106
dialogic interaction, 120, 291, 302, 304
digital natives, 230

E-pals, 272, 275, 276
Educational Testing Service (ETS), 235
English as a Foreign Language (EFL), 41, 125, 140, 147, 182, 231, 261
English as an International Language (EIL), 32
English for Specific Purposes (ESP), 125, 279, 291, 293–4, 300, 301, 312
English Language Teaching (ELT), 31, 233, 292, 370
English as a Second Language (ESL), 41, 161, 172
experiential learning, 17, 18, 65, 163, 168, 280, 383

Fink's taxonomy, 110–11
form-focused instruction, xvii, 17, 21, 73, 88, 92, 94, 157, 170, 349, 359, 363

genres, 274, 291, 395, 302, 305–6
Global Positioning System (GPS), 246
globalization, 1, 4, 9, 32, 87, 94, 232, 241, 302

Headway Academic Skills, 285

in-service teacher training, 37, 48, 49, 93, 123–33, 137, 157, 164, 336, 384
Information Communication Technology (ICT), 230
interactionist approach, 194, 302, 344
intercultural communication, 32, 41, 106, 112, 120, 141, 214, 231
interlanguage development, 199

Korean Scholastic Aptitude Test (KSAT), 265

Language Educational Chat System (LECS), 215
Language-related Episodes (LRE), 172, 194

INDEX

learner autonomy, 39, 65, 123, 223, 236, 303
learner collaboration, 159, 195, 206, 212, 213, 288, 345, 352
learner motivation, 222, 303, 307, 349, 362, 384
learner-centred, 65–7
lifelong learning, 106, 201, 228, 240
Limited Attentional Capacity Model, 197
linguistic imperialism, 33
loop input approach, 163, 164
loss of face, 214, 220, 231

Malaysian Education Blueprint, 159
Malaysian School of English Language Project, 158
materials design, 279–89, 328–38
Meaning making 296, 298, 301, 304, 305, 307–8, 310
Ministry of Education Korea, 262
Ministry of Education, Culture and Sport (MEXT), 237–8
Mobile-assisted Language Learning (MALL), 244–55, 275
multi-culturalism, 33
multimedia assisted language learning, 275
multimodal, 103, 295, 302

native speakerism, 30–1, 41
needs analysis, 42, 139, 157, 159, 262, 292, 301
negotiation of meaning, 221, 284, 304
NMC Horizon Report, 245
Non-Governmental Organisation (NGO), 48

online chat 211–25
orientalism, 20
Output Hypothesis (OH), 313–14

pedagogic tasks, 194
peer correction, 111, 287
plurilingual classrooms, 156, 165
Presentation, Practice, Production (PPP), 15, 21, 69, 80, 175
Primacy Theory, 158
professional communication, 109
psycholinguistic model, 107
Public English Test System (PETS), 38

reflective practice, 124
rote learning 163

Second Language Acquisition (SLA), 184, 313
Self-Access Learning Centre (SALC), 283, 284
Sociocultural Theory, 107, 298
sociolinguistic competence, 148, 167
South-East Asian context, 9–11
stimulated recall, 174
surface learning, 106
survival orientation, 232
Synchronous Computer-Mediated Communication (SCMC), 193
synthetic approach, 14
systemic functional linguistics, 306

task complexity, 198
Task-Based Assessment (TBA), 43
TBLT
  Belgian learners, 23
  Cambodia, 4, 10, 28, 46–61, 381
  China, 30–45, 66, 87–100, 139–55
  constraints, 146
  definition, 68, 88, 107, 124, 141, 156, 196, 280, 286, 296–7
  design, 146
  education reform, 368
  ethnography, 291, 299
  exercises, 15, 71, 88
  form-focused, 68
  framework, 291, 292, 298, 308
  grammar teaching, 14
  Hong Kong, 17, 366–80
  hybrid approach, 21
  implementation studies, 13, 70
  India, 13
  Indonesia, 23, 291–312
  institution challenges, 15
  Japan, 221–7, 228–43, 313–27
  Korea, 261–78
  large-class sizes, 16
  learner-centredness, 14
  local adaptation, 22
  localisation, 150–1, 369, 383
  lower-level learners, 279–89
  Malaysia, 156–69
  problem-solving tasks, 13, 212
  psychological burden, 15
  scaffolding, 79, 166, 247, 303, 351

Singapore, 103–22
socio-cultural challenges, 16
strong, 68, 88, 185, 329
Taiwan, 17
Task-Based Assessment (TBA), 348–64
task-specific training, 22
teacher challenges, 14–15
teacher training, 2, 15, 46, 51, 92, 228–41, 330, 353, 364, 384
technology, 22
Thailand, 279–90
the role of the teacher, 148
top-down implementation, 16, 80
Vietnam, 170–88
Vocational English (VE), 291–311
weak version, 68, 88, 185, 329
task-oriented curriculum, 284

Task-Supported Language Teaching (TSLT), 20, 80, 171
tertiary teaching, 124
TESOL, 51, 59, 165
text chat, 191, 194, 198, 201, 204
text reconstruction tasks, 315
The Rainbow Plan, 238
TOEIC test, 214
top-down implementation, 16, 142, 230, 276, 343, 381

Vocational education, 293, 297, 300
vocational English materials, 291–311
Voluntary Service Overseas (VSO), 48

washback effect, 274
Wikipedia, 229

www.ingramcontent.com/pod-product-compliance
Lightning Source LLC
Chambersburg PA
CBHW082025300426
44117CB00015B/2355